4.95

The Process of American History

VOLUME II

MODERN AMERICA

THE PROCESS OF

EDITED BY

PAUL GLAD, *University of Wisconsin*
ALLEN WEINSTEIN, *Smith College*
JOSEPH BRENT III, *Federal City University*
R. JACKSON WILSON, *Smith College*

AMERICAN HISTORY

FROM COLONIAL BEGINNINGS

TO THE PRESENT

Volume II

MODERN AMERICA

Prentice-Hall, Inc., Englewood Cliffs, New Jersey

Glad, Weinstein, Brent, and Wilson

THE PROCESS OF AMERICAN HISTORY:
FROM COLONIAL BEGINNINGS TO THE PRESENT

Volume II: *Modern America*

© 1969 BY PRENTICE-HALL, INC., *Englewood Cliffs, New Jersey*

13–723247–0

Library of Congress Catalog Card Number 72–76311
Printed in the United States of America

Current printing (last digit):
10 9 8 7 6 5 4 3 2 1

Prentice-Hall International, Inc., *London*
Prentice-Hall of Australia, Pty. Ltd., *Sydney*
Prentice-Hall of Canada, Ltd., *Toronto*
Prentice-Hall of India Private Ltd., *New Delhi*
Prentice-Hall of Japan, Inc., *Tokyo*

Acknowledgments

The editors are grateful to the following publishers and individuals for permission to reprint selections in this volume:

THE AMERICAN MERCURY, Torrance, California, for Henry Steele Commager, "Twelve Years of Roosevelt," *The American Mercury,* LX (April, 1945), 391–397, 400–401.

WILLIAM BEARD and MIRIAM BEARD VOGTS for Charles A. Beard, "National Politics and War," *Scribner's Magazine,* XCVII (February, 1935), 69–70.

BUSINESS HISTORY REVIEW for Robert Lively, "The American System: A Review Article," *Business History Review,* XXIX (March, 1955), 81–96.

COLUMBIA UNIVERSITY PRESS for Andrew Hacker, *The Triumph of American Capitalism* (New York: Columbia University Press, 1940), pp. 339–345.

THE JOHN DAY COMPANY, INC., for Rexford Guy Tugwell, *Mr. Hoover's Economic Policy* (New York: The John Day Company, Inc., © 1932 by Rexford Guy Tugwell), pp. 5–7, 10, 11, 13–14, 18–19.

DELACORTE PRESS for A. M. Rosenthal, "Hiroshima Today," in *Hiroshima Plus 20,* prepared by *The New York Times* (New York: Delacorte Press, 1965; copyright © 1945, 1951, 1963, 1964, 1965 by The New York Times Company), pp. 49–51.

FOREIGN AFFAIRS for George F. Kennan, "The Sources of Soviet Conduct," *Foreign Affairs,* XXV (July, 1947; copyright by the Council on Foreign Relations, Inc., New York), 580–582; and Arthur Schlesinger, Jr., "Origins of the Cold War," *Foreign Affairs,* XLVI (October, 1967; copyright 1967 by the Council on Foreign Relations, Inc., New York), 22–52.

FORTUNE for Gilbert Burck and Charles E. Silberman, "Why the Depression Lasted So Long," *Fortune,* LI (March, 1955), 192–200.

HARCOURT, BRACE & WORLD, INC., for Vernon Louis Parrington, *Main Currents in American Thought,* Volume III, *The Beginnings of Critical Realism in America* (New York: Harcourt, Brace & World, Inc., 1927–1930), pp. 401–413.

HARVARD UNIVERSITY PRESS for Norman Pollack, *The Populist Response to Industrial America* (Cambridge, Mass.: Harvard University Press, copyright 1962 by the President and Fellows of Harvard College), pp. 68–72, 82–83.

HOUGHTON MIFFLIN COMPANY for Claude G. Bowers, *The Tragic Era* (Boston: Houghton Mifflin Company, 1929), pp. v–vi, 60–64, 90–96.

KENNIKAT PRESS for Louis D. Brandeis, *The Curse of Bigness* (Port Washington, N.Y.: Kennikat Press, 1965), pp. 104–107, 109–110.

ALFRED A. KNOPF, INC., for Richard Hofstadter, *The Age of Reform: From Bryan to F.D.R.* (New York: Alfred A. Knopf, Inc., copyright © 1955 by Richard Hofstadter), pp. 62–96; Christopher Lasch, *The New Radicalism in America* (New York: Alfred A. Knopf, Inc., 1965), pp. ix–xvii; and Hans J. Morgenthau, *In Defense of the National Interest: A Critical Examination of American Foreign*

C. VANN WOODWARD for his article, "The Age of Reinterpretation," *American Historical Review,* LXVI (October, 1960), 1–19.

YALE UNIVERSITY PRESS for Thurman Arnold, *The Folklore of Capitalism* (New Haven, Conn.: Yale University Press, 1937), pp. 33–39, 48–51.

Preface

A Dutch scholar, Johan Huizinga, has argued that history is "the intellectual form in which a generation renders account to itself of its past." Inevitably, the way any historian approaches his subject is to some degree determined by the needs and problems of his own time. Not only do students of history differ in their perspective from one generation to another, but they differ within a given generation in comprehension and analysis. This book explores the interpretive and chronological variance within American historiography and examines some of the central issues under scholarly debate. It is based on a belief in the value of historical dialogue, dialogue arising from different perceptions of historical change. To view history as a process by which succeeding generations have assessed their past requires continuous and critical reworking of current interpretation.

To portray the process of American history, we have divided each chapter into five parts. The first is an introduction to a particular topic such as Reconstruction, Progressivism, or the New Deal. The second part offers interpretations from one or more historians of an earlier generation. The third section of each chapter contains documents from the period in question. The fourth presents a sampling of recent historians' interpretations. Finally, each chapter concludes with a short historiographical note.

At this point a caveat is in order. We do not intend to suggest that those who wrote first on any given subject were either naïve or less perceptive than those who followed. In every era, one of the historian's chief functions is to pose meaningful questions about the past. The earlier historians whose work is represented in this collection performed this function admirably. In many cases they established the terms of subsequent historical debate. Often, the nature of that debate helped to shape the present, for people tend to act according to how they perceive the past.

Men are never completely the prisoners of any interpretation, of course, and changing conditions invariably make younger historians aware of problems that older ones never recognized. New awareness may lead to investigation of unused material, to a re-examination of already known documents, and to adoption of new methods of analysis. Thus, we are not arguing that later scholars necessarily are better than their predecessors; we are saying only that recent historical writing is generally more relevant to today's problems, if only because it is written by men influenced by these problems.

In time many of the "recent" interpretations in this collection will seem dated. No matter how inadequate or inaccurate they may appear to future historians, however, they will always reveal important characteristics of the mid-twentieth-century American mind. Histories written by some of the students who use this book will one day replace those written by the historians whose work is included in these pages.

THE EDITORS

Contents

9. THE AFTERMATH: PROBLEMS OF A RECONSTRUCTED NATION

INTRODUCTION   1

I. *EARLY INTERPRETATIONS*   3

    CLAUDE G. BOWERS   *4*
    JAMES FORD RHODES   *12*
    LOUIS M. HACKER   *15*

II. *DOCUMENTS*   19

    1. *The Politics of Reconstruction*   19
    GIDEON WELLES   *19*
    CHARLES SUMNER   *20*
    SHELBY CULLOM   *23*

    2. *Southern Reconstruction*   25
    EDWARD A. POLLARD   *25*
    CARL SCHURZ   *27*
    ROBERT SOMERS   *33*

    3. *Northern Businessmen and Southern Policy*   39
    JOHN SHERMAN   *39*
    THE MERCHANTS' MAGAZINE   *40*

III. *RECENT INTERPRETATIONS*   48

    W. R. BROCK   *49*
    JOHN HOPE FRANKLIN   *57*
    IRWIN UNGER   *62*

HISTORIOGRAPHICAL NOTE   68

10. THE FOUNDATIONS OF AN INDUSTRIAL SOCIETY

INTRODUCTION   71

I. *EARLY INTERPRETATIONS*   73

    IDA TARBELL   *73*
    ARTHUR SCHLESINGER, SR.   *78*

II. *DOCUMENTS* 83

    1. *Industrialization* 83

        JOHN D. ROCKEFELLER *83*

        CHAUNCEY M. DEPEW *86*

        JAMES BRYCE *91*

    2. *Immigration and Urban Growth* 100

        HUTCHINS HAPGOOD *101*

        JAMES BRYCE *102*

III. *RECENT INTERPRETATIONS* 105

        STEPHAN THERNSTROM *105*

        ROBERT A. LIVELY *116*

        ROBERT WIEBE *125*

HISTORIOGRAPHICAL NOTE 129

11. THE AGRARIAN RESPONSE TO INDUSTRIAL SOCIETY

INTRODUCTION 131

  I. *EARLY INTERPRETATION* 132

        JOHN D. HICKS *133*

II. *DOCUMENTS* 138

    1. *A Proclamation and a Platform* 138

        LORENZO D. LEWELLING'S "TRAMP CIRCULAR" *139*

        THE OMAHA PLATFORM *140*

    2. *The Campaign of 1892* 143

        THOMAS E. WATSON *143*

        JAMES B. WEAVER *145*

    3. *Silver* 146

        WILLIAM JENNINGS BRYAN *147*

    4. *An Echo from '76* 148

        "THE POPS ARE MARCHING" *148*

III. *RECENT INTERPRETATIONS* 149

        RICHARD HOFSTADTER *150*

        NORMAN POLLACK *153*

HISTORIOGRAPHICAL NOTE 158

12. EXPANSIONISM AND THE EXERCISE OF WORLD POWER

INTRODUCTION 160

I. *EARLY INTERPRETATION* 162
 ARCHIBALD CARY COOLIDGE *162*

II. *DOCUMENTS* 167
 1. *Rationales for Expansion* 167
 "MCKINLEY TO THE MANUFACTURERS" *168*
 THEODORE ROOSEVELT *172*
 JAMES L. EWELL *176*
 2. *Anti-Imperialism* 178
 WILLIAM GRAHAM SUMNER *178*

III. *RECENT INTERPRETATION* 180
 WILLIAM A. WILLIAMS *181*

 HISTORIOGRAPHICAL NOTE 186

13. PROGRESSIVISM: NEW NATIONALISM, NEW FREEDOM, AND NEW ERA

INTRODUCTION 188

I. *EARLY INTERPRETATIONS* 189
 BENJAMIN PARKE DE WITT *190*
 CHARLES A. BEARD *197*

II. *DOCUMENTS* 200
 1. *Progressive Ideologies* 200
 LOUIS D. BRANDEIS *200*
 HERBERT CROLY *203*
 WALTER LIPPMANN *209*
 2. *The Persistence of Progressivism* 214
 E. DANA DURAND *214*

III. *RECENT INTERPRETATION* 219
 SAMUEL HABER *220*

 HISTORIOGRAPHICAL NOTE 236

14. DARWINISM, PRAGMATISM, SCIENCE, AND POWER

INTRODUCTION 238

I. *EARLY INTERPRETATION* 241
   VERNON LOUIS PARRINGTON *241*

II. *DOCUMENTS* 250

   1. *Pragmatism: A Definition* 250
      WILLIAM JAMES *251*

   2. *The Influence of Darwinism* 257
      JOHN DEWEY *258*
      THORSTEIN VEBLEN *262*

   3. *The Science of Society* 265
      WILLIAM GRAHAM SUMNER *265*
      EDWARD ALSWORTH ROSS *269*

   4. *The Mastery of Politics* 273
      HERBERT CROLY *273*

III. *RECENT INTERPRETATION* 278
   CHRISTOPHER LASCH *278*

   HISTORIOGRAPHICAL NOTE 282

15. THE DEPRESSION AND THE NEW DEAL

INTRODUCTION 285

I. *EARLY INTERPRETATION* 287
   HENRY STEELE COMMAGER *287*

II. *DOCUMENTS* 293
   1. *The New Deal* 293
      REXFORD GUY TUGWELL *294*
      GILBERT BURCK and CHARLES E. SILBERMAN *297*
      CHARLES A. BEARD *301*

   2. *A Troubled Society* 304
      THURMAN ARNOLD *304*
      HADLEY CANTRIL *309*

III. *RECENT INTERPRETATIONS* 313

      RICHARD HOFSTADTER *314*

      ARTHUR M. SCHLESINGER, JR. *321*

HISTORIOGRAPHICAL NOTE 325

16. THE COLD WAR

INTRODUCTION 328

I. *EARLY INTERPRETATION* 330

      HANS J. MORGENTHAU *330*

II. *DOCUMENTS* 337

    1. *"Hiroshima Today"* 337

      A. M. ROSENTHAL *337*

    2. *The Cold War* 339

      LEONARD C. COTTRELL, JR., and SYLVIA EBERHART *340*

      GEORGE F. KENNAN *342*

      GEORGE C. MARSHALL *343*

      JAMES RESTON *345*

    3. *Disarmament and Disengagement* 348

      EDMUND WILSON *348*

      JOHN F. KENNEDY *351*

III. *RECENT INTERPRETATIONS* 355

      ARTHUR SCHLESINGER, JR. *356*

      CHRISTOPHER LASCH *369*

      C. VANN WOODWARD *374*

HISTORIOGRAPHICAL NOTE 388

The Process of American History

VOLUME II

MODERN AMERICA

9. The Aftermath:
Problems of a
Reconstructed Nation

INTRODUCTION

Arriving in Boston in 1868 after spending the Civil War years in England, Henry Adams noted in the *Education* that had he and his family "been Tyrian traders of the year B.C. 1000, landing from a galley fresh from Gibraltar, they could hardly have been stranger on the shore of a world, so changed [was the country] from what it had been ten years earlier." Adams credited the changes around him primarily to the accelerating process of industrial growth that had touched most aspects of American life during the previous decade: "The last ten years had given to the great mechanical energies—coal, iron, steam—a distinct superiority in power over the older industrial elements—agriculture, handiwork, and learning." Adams considered the America he left behind in 1860 "dead" and claimed to have felt in 1868 like "the Indians or the buffalo who had been ejected from their heritage by his own people."

If the rapid transformation of *Northern* society seemed so complete to this returning post-bellum expatriate, what might Adams have found had he debarked in the South? Slavery had ended, the rebellion been crushed, Negro freedmen and sympathetic white allies administered the state governments below the Mason-Dixon line, and hostile masses of ex-Confederates counted impatiently the remaining days of "reconstruction" while waiting for "redemption." "The duration will last longer than the war," announced a character in Paul Goodman's novel, *The Empire City*, and these words—although used in connection with post-World War II America—seem applicable to the reconstruction experience in the South. The nation had emerged after four years of war with its unity preserved only to embark on twelve years of political conflict for control of the former Confederacy. For both North and South, therefore, the period immediately following the Civil War represented a pivotal link between past and future patterns of economic, social, and political development. Not only the South but the whole United States underwent an era of reconstruction in the aftermath of Appomatox.

For a politician absorbed in the drama of Southern reconstruction, either

1

at the national or local level, the basic dilemma of the episode remained the absence of precedents in American history to guide response to this revolutionary postwar situation. Twentieth-century students have at their disposal abundant comparative evidence on the treatment meted out by the victors in civil wars to their conquered brethren, whether in Spain, Russia, Cuba, China, or Vietnam. Americans could draw on no similar fund of experiences concerning "reconstruction" in 1865 when, for the South at least, the future seemed to hold, in Matthew Arnold's words, "neither . . . light, nor certitude, nor peace, nor help for pain." Similarly, Northern business leaders, concerned with assuring the continuation of protective tariffs, government subsidies, and plentiful issues of currency, which had all flowed from the war, had little in the way of an older tradition of political lobbying to fall back upon.

As the fighting drew to a close, the elaborate governmental skeleton in the United States had little administrative coherence. There existed a ruling coalition—the "Union Party" of Republicans and War Democrats—but no stable national party system, a vast collection of new industries, railroads, and businesses but only the vaguest outlines of a self-conscious industrial system. The events of the reconstruction decade can be viewed in this context as efforts in a haphazard and anguished nationwide struggle to create an institutional structure capable of both encouraging and containing the political and economic forces freed during the Civil War from most previous ante-bellum restraints.

The political storm broke first in Washington with the battle between Andrew Johnson and his Republican Congressional associates in the Union Party. Basically, the dispute between the President and the Radicals (later joined by most moderate Republicans as well) involved the fundamentally unanswered question of which governmental branch and which political forces within the Union Party would dominate the post-Civil War national political structure. Would the high degree of centralized executive authority necessitated by the imperatives of waging successful civil war be allowed to maintain its authority in peacetime? Or would Congress regain its traditional governing role in postwar America? Furthermore, would the reconstructed nation be ruled by a revived Jacksonian coalition of prewar Democrats—Southern secessionists, Northern Copperheads, and Johnson Unionists reunited in the aftermath of sectional conflict? Or would the prewar Republicans prove capable of maintaining their minority party in national power, thus preserving wartime economic policies, providing patronage for the party faithful, and fulfilling the solemn pledges of protection of freed slaves sworn to the Union dead? These profoundly divisive issues of power crystallized in the abrasive struggle between Johnson and the Radicals, which led to imposition of Congressional reconstruction upon the defeated and unregenerate South.

While Johnson struggled to uphold the prestige of his presidential office,

Northern businessmen waged a series of disorganized campaigns in Congress itself to maintain and increase the high duties of the 1862 Morrill Tariff, to strengthen the value of the hundreds of millions worth of greenbacks issued during the Civil War, and to squeeze even larger sums from the government in the form of expanded railroad subsidies. The business community succeeded in these efforts to a remarkable extent, setting the stage for later Gilded Age cooperation between the national government and American industry. Historians continue to dispute, however, the precise relationship between these business efforts on behalf of economic legislation and Northern business response to Republican reconstruction policy.

In the South itself, *un*reconstructed ex-Confederates fought against the novel presence of a mobile freed Negro population and substantial numbers of white collaborators who dominated Radical state governments. The freedmen, in turn, looked for assistance and leadership to Republican politicians in Washington and to the Radicals, home-grown or recent emigrants, who controlled the Southern states for varying lengths of time following enactment of the Congressional program of reconstruction. In return for their loyalty at the polls, the emancipated slaves received a mixed bag: a small degree of protection from Southern terrorist groups such as the Ku Klux Klan; an insufficient measure of economic and legal assistance from agencies such as the Freedmen's Bureau; a tiny share of actual political power and of the profits derived from office-holding; and, finally, an increasing measure of indifference or hostility from the white community, both North and South. By 1877, the former states of the Confederacy had completed the "redemption" process, and local governments returned entirely to white control. The freedmen, untutored in the arts of political self-defense, lacking economic power, surrounded by armed white irregulars, and abandoned by their Republican patrons in Washington, now lost even that subordinate role in Southern politics and government, which they acquired in the years following approval of the Fourteenth Amendment. Thousands of Negroes, unwilling to accept the "Compromise of 1877," which sealed their return to political bondage, trekked North or West, but the great majority began tempering hope and adjusting expectations as a hostile white master caste regained control of the South.

I. EARLY INTERPRETATIONS

The three selections that follow illustrate the state of historical understanding of the reconstruction question before World War II. Claude G. Bowers offers a traditional view of the national political story, with dictatorial Radical Republicans in Congress cruelly besmirching the name and authority of a conciliatory Andrew Johnson. Bower's discussion summarizes the perspectives of Americans before and during the 1930's on the genesis of

Radical reconstruction. James Ford Rhodes, a Northerner, proved more virulent in his racist reaction to the freedmen than even most Southern narrators of the reconstruction story. Rhodes' popular *History of the United States Since the Compromise of 1850* nurtured several generations of Americans on the traditional fantasies of an oppressive "Black Reconstruction." Finally, Louis Hacker, in *The Triumph of American Capitalism,* draws the Beardian connections between Radical policies on controlling the South and the Republican party's economic program. Hacker, Beard, and such recent analysts as Barrington Moore have all found a close affinity between Radical support for industrial development and the Radicals' Southern policy, arguing that opponents of conciliation received strong support from influential segments of the American business community.

CLAUDE G. BOWERS

PREFACE

If Hilaire Belloc is right in his opinion that 'readable history is melodrama,' the true story of the twelve tragic years that followed the death of Lincoln should be entertaining. They were years of revolutionary turmoil, with the elemental passions predominant, and with broken bones and bloody noses among the fighting factionalists. The prevailing note was one of tragedy, though, as we shall see, there was an abundance of comedy, and not a little of farce. Never have American public men in responsible positions, directing the destiny of the Nation, been so brutal, hypocritical, and corrupt. The Constitution was treated as a doormat on which politicians and army officers wiped their feet after wading in the muck. Never has the Supreme Court been treated with such ineffable contempt, and never has that tribunal so often cringed before the clamor of the mob.

Reprinted from Claude G. Bowers, THE TRAGIC ERA *(Boston: Houghton Mifflin Company, 1929), pp. v–vi, 60–64, 90–96, by permission of the publisher.*

So appalling is the picture of these revolutionary years that even historians have preferred to overlook many essential things. Thus, Andrew Johnson, who fought the bravest battle for constitutional liberty and for the preservation of our institutions ever waged by an Executive, until recently was left in the pillory to which unscrupulous gamblers for power consigned him, because the unvarnished truth that vindicates him makes so many statues in public squares and parks seem a bit grotesque. That Johnson was maligned by his enemies because he was seeking honestly to carry out the conciliatory and wise policy of Lincoln is now generally understood, but even now few realize how intensely Lincoln was hated by the Radicals at the time of his death.

A complete understanding of this period calls for a reappraisal of many public men. Some statesmen we have been taught to reverence will appear in these pages in sorry rôles. Others, who played conspicuous parts, but have been denied the historical recognition due them, are introduced and shown in action. Thus the able leaders of the minority in Congress are given fuller treatment than has been fashionable, since they represented more Americans, North and South, than the leaders of the Radical majority, and were nearer right on the issues of reconstruction. Thus, too, the brilliant and colorful leaders and spokesmen of the South are given their proper place in the dramatic struggle for the preservation of Southern civilization and the redemption of their people. I have sought to re-create the black and bloody drama of these years, to show the leaders of the fighting factions at close range, to picture the moving masses, both whites and blacks, in North and South, surging crazily under the influence of the poisonous propaganda on which they were fed.

That the Southern people literally were put to the torture is vaguely understood, but even historians have shrunk from the unhappy task of showing us the torture chambers. It is impossible to grasp the real significance of the revolutionary proceedings of the rugged conspirators working out the policies of Thaddeus Stevens without making many journeys among the Southern people, and seeing with our own eyes the indignities to which they were subjected. Through many unpublished contemporary family letters and diaries, I have tried to show the psychological effect upon them of the despotic policies of which they were the victims. Brutal men, inspired by personal ambition or party motives, assumed the pose of philanthropists and patriots, and thus deceived and misguided vast numbers of well-meaning people in the North.

In the effort to re-create the atmosphere and temper of the times, I have made free use of the newspapers of those times. Invaluable for this purpose has been my access to the unpublished diary of George W. Julian, which covers the entire period. Through him we are able to sit in at important conferences that hitherto have been closed to the historians.

Much attention has been given to the amusements and the social background because of the unprecedented prominence of women throughout these struggles. Gay ribbons and furbelows and flirting fans were not far distant from the fighting. The women ranged in culture and character from the incomparable Kate Chase Sprague to the dusky sisters of the mixed salon in Columbia, South Carolina. Never had women lobbyists used their sex in securing legislative favors for selfish groups so brazenly—or so cleverly. The tragedy of Mrs. Belknap is as significant of the spirit of the times as the impeachment proceedings against Johnson.

The story of this Revolution is one of desperate enterprises, by daring and unscrupulous men, some of whom had genius of a high order. In these no Americans can take pride. The evil that they did lives after them. They changed the course of history, and whether for ultimate good or bad is still on the lap of the gods. The story carries lessons that are well worth pondering.

· · ·

Meanwhile the Southern people were fighting for the preservation of their civilization. The negroes would not work, the plantations could not produce. The freedmen clung to the illusion planted in their minds by demagogues that the economic status of the races was to be reversed through the distribution of the land among them. This cruelly false hope was being fed by private soldiers, Bureau agents, and low Northern whites circulating among the negroes on terms of social equality in the cultivation of their prospective votes. 'Nothing but want will bring them to their senses,' wrote one Carolinian to another. At the time, however, the negroes were warding off want by prowling the highways and byways in the night for purposes of pillage. In one week, in one town in Georgia, one hundred and fifty were arrested for theft.

More serious than this annoying petty stealing was the wholesale pillaging by Treasury agents, who swarmed over the land like the locusts of Egypt following the order confiscating all cotton that had been contracted to the fallen Confederacy. It mattered not whether the cotton had been contracted for or not; these petty officials rumbled over the roads day and night in Government wagons with soldiers, taking whatever they could find. One agent in Alabama stole eighty thousand dollars' worth of cotton in a month. The burden of proof was put upon the owner, and the agent in Arkansas enforced rules of evidence no planter could circumvent. When, in Texas, agents caught redhanded were indicted, the army released them. When, as in Alabama, the stealing was so flagrant that prosecutions were forced, proceedings were suddenly stopped as the trail of crime led toward politicians of importance.

This, then, was the combination against the peace of a fallen people—the soldiers inciting the blacks against their former masters, the Bureau agents preaching political and social equality, the white scum of the North fraternizing with the blacks in their shacks, and the thieves of the Treasury stealing cotton under the protection of Federal bayonets. And in the North, demagogic politicians and fanatics were demanding immediate negro suffrage and clamoring for the blood of Southern leaders. Why was not Jeff Davis hanged; and why was not Lee shot?

The gallant figure of the latter had ridden quietly out of the public view. No word of bitterness escaped his lips, and he sought to 'promote harmony and good feeling.' His own future was dark enough, the fine old mansion at Arlington gone, and he had no home. Sometimes, astride old Traveller, he cantered along country roads looking for a small farm. 'Some quiet little home in the woods,' he wrote, declining the offer of an estate in England. June found him settled in a four-room house in a grove of oaks near Cartersville, with his wife and daughters. Then came the offer of the presidency of Washington College. Should he accept? Was he competent? Would it injure the institution? He would like to 'set the young an example of submission to authority.' One September day, his decision made, found him mounted on old Traveller riding toward Lexington. The ladies of the town helped furnish his little office, and admirers sent articles of furniture for his house and the family took possession. In old letters we have a vision of Lee, the sinister conspirator pictured in the Northern papers, proudly displaying to his wife and daughters the pickles, preserves, and brandied peaches the neighbors had sent in, and the bags of walnuts, potatoes, and game the mountaineers had given. But the patriots of the North were not to be deceived by appearances. 'We protest,' said 'The Nation,' 'against the notion that he is fit to be put at the head of a college in a country situated as Virginia is.' And Wendell Phillips was exclaiming to a cheering crowd at Cooper Union that 'if Lee is fit to be president of a college, then for Heaven's sake pardon Wirtz, and make him professor of what the Scots call "the humanities." '

Such was the spirit of the North when the Southern Conventions and Legislatures began to meet. Mississippi led off with a hundred delegates, all but two of whom were able to qualify, since ninety-eight had opposed secession. Seven had been members of the Secession Convention and six had voted against the ordinance. Having nothing to conceal, it was decided to report the debates in full to satisfy the North that the results of the war had been accepted in good faith. But when a few, discussing abolition, proposed some form of compensation, the skeptics above the Ohio cried 'Aha!' The proposal was thereupon abandoned. Moving with the utmost circumspection, the action of the Convention was a challenge to the fairness of the foe, but Charles Sumner denounced it as 'a rebel conspiracy to obtain political power.'

Then came the election, with the legislative candidates called upon in the canvass to define their position on negro testimony in the courts. 'Aha!' exclaimed the Radicals, their eyes glued upon the scene. 'Negroes as a class must be excluded from the witness stand,' declared the 'Jackson News.' 'If the privilege is ever granted, it will lead to greater demands, and at last end in the admission of the negro to the jury box and ballot box.' 'Aha!' screamed the Radicals, advocating suffrage. True, the 'Jackson Clarion' favored negro testimony, but it was only the adverse attitude that interested Thad Stevens and Sumner. And when a Confederate Brigadier who had voted against secession was elected Governor, and the opponents of negro testimony carried the Legislature, a howl of derision came down on the winds from the North.

Came then the Legislature, and the attempt to find laws to meet the new conditions born of emancipation. Negroes were forbidden the use of cars set apart for the whites, and the Stevenses and the Sumners ground their teeth.

When the races intermarried, they could be imprisoned for life. It was made a crime to give or lend deadly weapons, ammunition, or intoxicating liquors to the freedmen, and this was denounced as discrimination. Negro orphans could be apprenticed, under rigid court regulations, and the abolitionists pricked up their ears and heard the rattle of chains. If the apprentice ran away, could he not be apprehended and restored—just like a slave? More: when a freedman broke a contract to labor, could he not be arrested and taken back? If he could no longer wander whistling at noonday from the field, and leave his work to witness an immersion, what a mockery would be his freedom! Laws against vagrancy, against adultery, the latter bearing harder on the whites than on the blacks, 'tis true, but still aimed at freedom—all bad.

Instantly the Northern politicians, bent on the exclusion of the Southern States until negro suffrage could fortify their power, were up in arms. 'The men of the North will convert . . . Mississippi into a frog pond before they will allow any such laws to disgrace one foot of soil,' thundered the 'Chicago Tribune.'

During the fall and winter, the Southern Legislatures proceeded with similar enactments to meet a similar social and economic crisis. The vagrancy laws, so desperately needed and so bitterly denounced, were little different from those of Northern States. Nor were they so severe as those enforced by the military authorities seeking the same end—the ending of idleness and crime and the return of the freedmen to the fields. A Southern writer has described these military orders as 'tyrannical as ukases of a czar.' These provided severe punishment for negroes using disrespectful language to a former master, forbade them going from one plantation to another without a pass, and ordered daily inspections of negro cabins to discourage stealing. At Milledgeville, all who could, and would not, work were set to compulsory labor in the street without pay. At Atlanta, a curfew law was put into operation. In Texas the negroes were told that unless they returned to work on the old plantation, they would be forced to work without wages, and they were denied the right to travel the highways without the permission of their employers. Thus the higher army officers on the ground, familiar with conditions, sought to serve both races through the rehabilitation of industry. This, too, was the intent of the Black Codes of the South. An eminent historian has pronounced these laws for the most part 'a conscientious and straightforward attempt to bring some sort of order out of the social and economic chaos,' and in principle and detail 'faithful on the whole to the actual conditions with which they had to deal.'

But there was nothing judicious in the attitude of the Radical politicians. Sitting in his little office in Lancaster, grim Thad Stevens, meditating a plan of reconstruction of his own, and girding his loins for a death struggle with Johnson, chortled in sardonic glee. These hated men of the South were stocking his arsenal. And he was whetting his knife.

. . .

The gavel falls. The clerk, born in Gettysburg, where Stevens began the practice of the law, editor for a while of a paper in Lancaster where Stevens lived, had his orders from the caucus through Stevens himself, and began to call the roll. When Tennessee was passed, Maynard sprang to his feet, waving his certificate of election. 'The clerk cannot be interrupted while ascertaining whether a quorum is present,' said the clerk severely, and Maynard resumed his seat. At the conclusion, Brooks rose to protest and to demand the authority for ignoring Tennessee.

'I can give my reason if necessary,' said the clerk.

And then, from the seat halfway back, the contemptuous tones of Stevens: 'It is not necessary. We know all.'

Yes, retorted Brooks, the resolution of a party caucus. And could the gentleman from Pennsylvania inform him when he intended to press this resolution?

Stevens seemed bored. 'I propose to present it at the proper time,' he drawled. The galleries chuckled loudly and clapped hands. The revolution had begun.

Proceeding to the election of officers, Stevens rose to nominate for chaplain a minister described as 'the most eloquent man in the United States since the fall of Henry Ward Beecher.' Again the galleries chortled at this thrust at the clergyman who had espoused the cause of Johnson. It was the beginning of Beecher's troubles, from which he was to extricate himself by crying 'mea culpa, mea culpa,' to the revolutionists.

That day, after Sumner in the Senate had introduced a series of impossibly extreme resolutions on reconstruction, the two Houses adjourned without the customary naming of a committee to inform the President that they were ready for his communication. 'I am most thoroughly convinced that there was design in this . . . to let the President know that he must wait the motion of Congress,' wrote Gideon Welles. For henceforth, through the revolution, Congress was to assume supremacy in the affairs of government.

The Committee of Fifteen, the Committee of Public Safety of this revolution, was named on the motion of Stevens. The Message of Johnson, a powerful, dignified, and sound State paper, which Welles thought Seward had touched up, but which was in fact written by Bancroft, the historian, was read. The reaction of the country to this forceful Message chilled the hearts of the extremists. 'Full of wisdom,' said the 'New York Times.' 'Force and dignity' was noted by 'The Nation,' which thought it 'certainly clearer' than Lincoln's, and assuredly 'the style of an honest man who knows what he means and means what he says.' Sumner was hysterical. 'The greatest and most criminal error ever committed by a government,' he declared. What is a republican government? he demanded of Welles. Sumner knew, for he 'had read everything on the subject from Plato to the last French pamphlet.' And here negroes were being excluded from the State Governments—outrageous! Had not a general officer from Georgia just informed him that 'the negroes . . . were better qualified to establish and maintain a republican government than the whites?' And how could Welles, a New England man, support the President? Had he read Sumner's Worcester speech? 'Yes,' the Connecticut Yankee replied, but 'I did not endorse it.' 'Stanton does,' said Sumner. He had thought it 'none too strong' and 'approved every sentiment, every opinion and word of it.' Thus Stanton's treachery unfolds.

Meanwhile Stevens, infinitely stronger and more practical than Sumner, was planning to force the issue. In the interval, one bitterly cold day, Grant stood before Johnson reporting on his observations in the South. Sumner had been deluged with letters from strangers in that section, charging butchery and outrages against the blacks; and Grant reported conditions satisfactory, the people loyal, and was asked to make a written report. This intensified Sumner's annoyance, and he fumed and fretted.

In the White House, Johnson, calm, busy with conferences, not unmindful of the treachery about him, moved with caution and awaited events. He had begun to suspect Stanton, but when that official returned after an absence to speak sneeringly of Sumner, the mystery deepened. 'Some one is cheated,' wrote the Cabinet diarist.

But there was nothing cowardly or underhand about Thad Stevens. The old man, shut up in his house, was forging his thunderbolt, and on December 18, with galleries packed, with a sprinkling of negroes, the floor crowded, he rose to challenge the Administration. An historical moment. Here spoke a man who was determining the immediate destiny of a people, and he spoke with the decision and force of an absolute monarch laying the law down to a cringing parliament.

Who could reconstruct? he demanded. Not the President, he said, for Congress alone had power. 'The future condition of the conquered power depends on the will of the conqueror,' he continued. 'They must come in as new States or come in as conquered provinces.' Thereafter he referred to them as provinces—'provinces that would not be prepared to participate in constitutional government for some years.' Then what? 'No arrangement so proper for them as territorial governments,' where they 'can learn the principles of freedom and eat the fruit of foul rebellion.' And when consider their restoration? Only when the Constitution had been so amended 'as to secure perpetual ascendancy to the party of the Union,—meaning the Republican Party.

That was the persuasive feature of Stevens's amazing programme that was intended to overcome the momentary scruples of the more conservative of his fellow partisans. Negro domination —before it the conservatives drew back shocked. But such domination in the South, or the loss of the loaves and fishes—that was different. The old man was a good psychologist. He was really thinking primarily of the negroes, for whom most of his party associates cared not a tinker's dam; but they were interested in power, and how so certainly perpetuate that power as by denying these States a vote in the Electoral College until they agreed to grant suffrage to the freedman.

Yes, negro domination in the South or the loss of power. 'They [Southerners and Democrats] will at the very first election take possession of the White House and of the halls of Congress.' And then, ruin! But there were no pious poses in the bitter old man now speaking. Make the South enfranchise the negroes, and 'I think there would always be Union men enough in the South, aided by the blacks, to divide the representation and thus continue Republican ascendancy.' This a white man's government? 'Sir, this doctrine of a white man's government is as atrocious as the infamous sentiment that damned the late Chief Justice [Taney] to everlasting fame and I fear everlasting fire.'

When Stevens sank wearily into his seat, he had planted the most attractive of ideas in the minds of his fellow partisans who had held back. He had conducted them to the mountain-top and offered them the indefinite power they sought. 'The Nation' found his reference to Taney in hell something 'we can hardly trust ourselves to commend,' and concluded that 'many people will be ready to believe that a person who uses such language in debate is hardly in a fit state of mind to legislate for . . . any State or Territory.' But the politicians in the cloak-rooms, the hotels, and bar-rooms were deeply interested in the suggestion.

Three days later the galleries again were packed when the elegant Raymond replied in defense of the President's policies. To a conservative audience of judicious men the speech of Raymond, finely phrased, sanely tempered, and logical, would have appealed, but not to the crowd in the galleries. Restating the theory on which the war was fought, that the Southern States had not been out of the Union and certainly not a separate power, he said: 'They were once States of the Union—that every one concedes—bound to the Union and made members of the Union by the Constitution of the United States. . . . They did not secede. They failed to maintain their ground by force of arms—in other words, they failed to secede.'

And talk of 'loyal men in the South'? Loyal to what? 'Loyal to a foreign independent power, as the United States would become under those circumstances?' Certainly not. Simply disloyal to their own government and 'deserters from that to which they owe allegiance.' More: if an independent power, they had the authority to contract debts, 'and we would become the successors and inheritors of its debts and assets, and we must pay them.' And why, having fought for the Union, now forbid reunion? 'I am here,' he concluded, 'to act with those who seek to complete the restoration of the Union. . . . I shall say no word and do no act and give no vote to recognize its division, or to postpone or disturb its rapidly approaching harmony and power.'

Raymond had courageously and handsomely discharged a patriotic duty, but he had signed his political death-warrant. He had joined the Gironde when the Mountain, backed by the mob, was in the ascendant.

There was a third party to this debate whom it is the fashion to ignore, albeit he spoke for more white men in the country than either, though representing a party with a meager representation in the House. He spoke for the 1,835,985 men who had voted the Democratic ticket in the election of 1864, and for all the whites of the South, and these men are entitled to their word in this debate. Daniel W. Voorhees spoke on the proposition embodied in resolutions he had previously offered in behalf of the Democracy that 'no State or number of States . . . can in any manner sunder their connection with the Federal Union except by a total subversion of our present system of government.'

When Voorhees, a favorite orator, rose, the galleries were crowded. The little group of Democrats gathered about him. Thad Stevens had business outside, but Raymond found a seat close by. If he was embarrassed by the support of the brilliant orator, he made no sign. This was easily the oratorical masterpiece of the three; and, read to-day, seems as the voice of prophecy. Beginning with a reference to the Radical pose of friendship for Johnson during the summer, he described it as 'the conspiracy to assail him with the masked face of friendship and the treacherous sword of Joab.' He analyzed the purpose of the Colfax speech as intended to pave the way for the select committee 'created by the magic wand of the conscience-keeper of the majority [Stevens] . . . that potent wand which has evoked from the vasty deep more spirits of evil and malignant mischief than generations will be able to exorcise and put down.' Seizing on

Stevens's reference to the States as dead carcasses, he continued: 'He knows that dead carcasses are more easily carved to pieces, torn limb from limb and devoured by the hungry maw of confiscation, than living States.' Yes, 'it is safer and less troublesome to rob a corpse than to pick the pockets of the living.' Hurrying on to the painting of a picture of the carpetbaggers in the offing, he paid tribute to the Provisional Governors, and said: 'But then what a military governor of South Carolina, for instance, that idol of the Radicals, Ben Butler, would have made! Aye, there is the rub. What fat, unctuous, juicy pickings have been lost to the faithful by this cruel policy of the President. . . . All the wolves and jackals that wait till the battle is over to mangle the dead and wounded snarled their disappointment and rage at the President, but will now open in full chorus over the delightful vision which arises before them from the formation of the committee of fifteen.' Rebel debt? 'Every one knows, of course, that it will never be paid. All history tells us that the debt of a defeated revolution is always lost.' And what did Stevens's theory mean? 'It is a notice that the war to restore the Union was an utter failure—that the war is over and yet the Union is rent in twain.'

Pleading for a speedy restoration of the Union, he passed on to the wrongs of Government thriving unnoticed behind the smoke screen of sectional prejudice and hate. 'How long,' he asked, 'can the inequalities of our revenue system be borne? . . . We have two great interests in this country, one of which has prostrated the other. . . . The agricultural labor of the land is driven to the counters of the most gigantic monopoly ever before sanctioned by the law.' Then on he hurried, to favors to the bondholders, through their immunity from taxation. 'The Nation's gratitude takes a strange turn,' he said. 'It lavishes its gifts, its garlands, and its favors on the money-changers of the temple, and causes the defenders of the Government at the cannon's mouth to pay tribute to their monstrous greed.'

This speech foreshadowed the policies and effects of the next ten years with marvelous prescience. The merciless lashing so picturesquely given the extremists goaded them to fury, and Bingham of Ohio replied with personal abuse. 'One of the most brilliant and polished efforts ever delivered by the gentleman . . . a masterly effort,' said the 'New York World' of Voorhees's speech. Many years later, Blaine recalled it as a 'powerful speech.' The Republican press was unanimous in abuse, the Radical papers because they had been stung, the conservatives because they had been embarrassed at the outset of their contest with the Radicals by the approval of the Democrats. The Voorhees resolutions were voted down by a strict party vote, but the Democrats had defined their position and taken their stand. And the Radical group had served notice on the conservatives in the Republican Party that no quarter would be given. The war was on.

JAMES FORD RHODES

The operation of negro suffrage had consolidated nearly all decent white men into the Democratic or conservative party; and the passage by the United States Senate of a Civil Rights

Reprinted from James Ford Rhodes, THE HISTORY OF THE UNITED STATES . . . *(New York: Kennikat Press, 1893), VII, 79, 91–92, 95, 104–105, 168–171.*

bill, which was substantially Sumner's measure, had intensified the race issue. The Republican or Radical party was composed of about nine-tenths negroes and one-tenth whites. Of these the negroes as a body were ignorant and their moral standard was low; the whites were "chiefly professional politicians and their hangers-on, who live by office, and a few worthy people who have been induced heretofore to act with the Republican party."

•   •   •

In accordance with my plan I shall now take up the story of Mississippi. This State remained under Republican rule, the basis of which was negro suffrage, from 1870 to 1875 inclusive. The first Republican governor, James L. Alcorn, was inaugurated March 10, 1870; he had lived in Mississippi twenty-six years, had been an old-line Whig, but in convention had voted for the ordinance of secession; he had been a slaveholder and was now a planter, having saved some of his property from the wreckage of the war which he deplored. In his inaugural address, he professed his unaltered sympathy with his fellow-Southerners and disclaimed any affection for their conquerors; nevertheless he accepted reconstruction and negro suffrage and believed in the right of coloured men to hold office although recognizing that against the laws which secured these rights were arrayed for the most part "the wealth, intelligence and social influence of the State."

On the inauguration of Alcorn, the troops with the exception of some small detachments in the larger towns were withdrawn and civil government held sway. Alcorn was an honest man, of considerable ability and of some political experience, and the other administrative officers who had been elected on his ticket, one of whom was a mulatto, were reputable men. The judges were appointed by the governor and, so far as he could find competent men, he named Southern Republicans but owing to the paucity of such material he was obliged to have recourse to Northerners and even Democrats. Integrity, and on the whole respectable ability, might be predicated of the judiciary. The Justices of the Supreme Court were jurists of high repute: two were old citizens of the State, one a Democrat, the other a Republican, and the third an ex-Union soldier from New York, who had come to Mississippi at the close of the war. While the executive and judicial branches of the government were not equal in character to the average at the North yet, had they been backed by an equally intelligent constituency, good government was not only possible but certain. But an examination of the legislature reveals the common blight. Thirty-six negroes were members, most of whom had been slaves. A number could neither read nor write and, when they drew their pay, acknowledged its receipt by making their mark. From out this massive ignorance there rose, indeed, the occasional shape of enlightenment: a coloured minister such as Revels the quadroon; also John R. Lynch layman and mulatto who was a credit to his race and in 1872 made an impartial and dignified speaker of the House. But the aspirations of most of the negroes were as low as their life experience had been narrow.

· · ·

The new governor sincerely endeavoured to carry out the Reconstruction Acts in the letter and the spirit. He believed that, since the negroes were in the majority, theirs was the right to rule; and he constituted himself their champion, convinced as he was that the white people when in power would override them and de-prive them of the right to vote. Nevertheless he overrated their mental capacity and moral caliber. Like the men who had enacted Congressional reconstruction, he did not appreciate the great fact of race, that between none of the important races of mankind was there a difference so wide as between the Caucasian and the Negro.

· · ·

The story of Louisiana under carpet-bag-negro rule from 1868 on is a sickening tale of extravagance, waste, corruption and fraud. The Republican party was composed of negroes, carpet-baggers and a small number of native whites, but, as, the coloured population exceeded the white by 2000 and the negroes were almost wholly Republicans, they were the real basis of the party at the ballot-box. When it came to the division of the offices they got at the outset by no means a proportionate share: their cleverer white allies took most of the fat places, but in the composition of the legislature the constituencies could not be ignored and there the negroes had a large representation. Ignorant beyond any previous conception of legislators, except in their sister Southern States, they were not at first as corrupt as their white colleagues, but this was due not to virtue but to inexperience. As time went on they proved apt pupils.

Corruption was unblushing. Legislation was openly bought and sold. "What was the price of a senator?" asked a member of a Congressional committee. "I think, six hundred dollars" was the reply. In the rotunda of the St. Charles Hotel, New Orleans, among railroad lobbyists who were corrupting the legislature, a more frequent inquiry than "What's cotton?" was "How are negro votes selling to-day?"

Nordhoff saw coloured members of the legislature, who ten years before were slaves, "driving magnificent horses, seated in stylish equipages and wearing diamond breastpins." The grotesqueness and horror of negro rule struck honest observers no matter what were their predilections. . . .

. . . A contrast of 1868–1875 with the years succeeding will show how unpractical and unjust was the endeavour to found a State on universal negro suffrage in a community where the blacks exceeded the whites. It is noteworthy that the remembrance of the misery of carpet-bag-negro rule has tended to obliterate the memory of war's distress. "Those pitiless years of reconstruction!" said Bishop Galloway in 1903. "Worse than the calamities of war were the 'desolating furies of peace.' No proud people ever suffered such indignities or endured such humiliation and degradation."

Universal negro suffrage had a fair trial in Mississippi. Two coloured men of ability, Revels and Lynch, rose to the top as leaders. The three Republican governors were honest and capable. Ames's career was indeed a tragedy. His courage and devotion to the coloured people would have won him distinction had not the plan he set himself to work out been inherently bad. His government could not go on without concessions and rewards to the ignorant constituency whose brutish instincts prevented their developing political capacity and honesty. But the fault was neither his nor the negroes. The wrong had been committed by Congress. . . .

No large policy in our country has ever been so conspicuous a failure as that of forcing universal negro suffrage upon the South. The negroes who simply acted out their nature were not to blame. How indeed could they have acquired political honesty? What idea could barbarism thrust into slavery obtain of the rights of property? Even among the Aryans of education and intelligence public integrity has been a plant of slow growth. From the days of the Grecian and Roman republics to our own, men have stolen from the State who would defraud no individual. With his crude ideas of honesty between man and man, what could have been expected of the negro when he got his hand in the public till? The scheme of Reconstruction pandered to the ignorant negroes, the knavish white natives and the vulturous adventurers who flocked from the North; and these neutralized the work of honest Republicans who were officers of State. Intelligence and property stood bound and helpless under negro-carpet-bag rule. And the fact that such governments continued to exist, were supported by Federal authority and defended by prominent Republicans had a share in the demoralization of politics at the North. . . .

From the Republican policy came no real good to the negroes. Most of them developed no political capacity, and the few who raised themselves above the mass did not reach a high order of intelligence. At different periods two served in the United States Senate, thirteen in the House; they left no mark on the legislation of their time; none of them, in comparison with their white associates, attained the least distinction. When the Southern States recovered home rule, negroes were of course no longer sent to Congress from the South but they have had a fair chance at the North were they obtained the suffrage in every State within a few years after the Civil War. Politically very active and numerous enough in some of the Northen States to form a political force, that has to be reckoned with, no one of them (I believe) has ever been sent to Congress; few get into legislature or city council. Very few if any are elected to administrative offices of responsibility. The negro's political activity is rarely of a nature to identify him with any movement on a high plane. He takes no part in civil service or tariff reform; he was not a factor in the contest for honest money; he is seldom, if ever, heard in advocacy of pure municipal government and for him Good Government Associations have no attraction. He is greedy for office and emolument; it is for this reason that he arrogantly asserts his right to recognition; and he has had remarkable success in securing offices under the Federal government. In a word he has been politically a failure and he could not have been otherwise. In spite of all the warnings of science and political experience, he was started at the top and, as is the fate of most such unfortunates, he fell to the bottom.

Truly the negro's fate has been hard. Torn from his native land he was made a slave to satisfy the white man's greed. At last, owing to a great moral movement, he gained the long-wished-for boon of freedom; and then when in intellect still a child, instead of being treated as a child, taught gradually the use of his liberty and given rights in the order of his development, he, without any demand of his own, was raised at once to the white man's political estate, partly for the partisan designs of those who had freed him. His old masters, who understood him best and who, chastened by defeat and by adversity, were really his best friends, were alienated. He fell into the hands of rascals who through his vote fattened on the spoils of office. He had a brief period of mastery and indulgence during which his mental and moral education was deplorable and his worst passions were catered to. Finally by force, by craft and by law his old masters have deprived him of the ballot and, after a number

of years of political power, he has been set back to the point, where he should have started directly after emancipation. He is trying to learn the lesson of life with the work made doubly hard by the Saturnalia he has passed through.

LOUIS M. HACKER

1. THE HISTORIC ROLE OF THE CIVIL WAR AND RECONSTRUCTION PERIODS

The argument presented in my analysis may now be recapitulated. By 1860, a critical situation had arisen in American affairs. Because the southern planter capitalists were in control of the instrumentalities of the national state and, as a result, were thwarting the advance of the (too slowly) growing northern industrial capitalism, their claims to power had to be challenged. This the newly formed Republican party did. The partial success of the Republican party at the polls in 1860 drove the southern leaders—pushed on by extremists in their midst who were under heavy economic pressures—into secession. The Civil War broke out. The Union government, after the departure of the southern legislators, was now wholly possessed by the Republican party.

But what was to be the program of the Civil War—of this "Second American Revolution," as it has been correctly described by Charles A. and Mary R. Beard? Like all revolutionary hosts, the Republican party had a Radical and a Conservative wing. William H. Seward, the Secretary of State, was the leader of the Conservative wing. (Abra-

Reprinted from Louis M. Hacker, THE TRIUMPH OF AMERICAN CAPITALISM *(New York: Columbia University Press, 1940), pp. 339–345, by permission of the publisher.*

ham Lincoln was associated with it and became, as the head of the government, its spokesman. One must say, however, that he was not consciously aware of the significance of the whole economic program of industrial capitalism. But without having personal or indeed emotional associations with that class, as did Seward, he accepted its position. The Mexican Rivera's portrait of him as a bemused man is an apt characterization.) Thaddeus Stevens in the House, Charles Sumner in the Senate, Horace Greeley in the press, and Wendell Phillips in the pulpit were the leaders of the Radical wing. The Republican Conservatives wanted to end the war as quickly as possible without deranging the essential *political* and *social* patterns of the nation. They were neither Abolitionists nor egalitarians: the unequal status of Negroes and poor southern whites was of no interest to them. But, as spokesmen for industrial capitalism, the war furnished them the opportunity to round out the *economic* program of the class which they represented. Industrial capitalism was now in control of the state and they used it for the following purposes: 1. A vast extension of the credit base of the nation took place (as a result of bond flotations and greenback issues) and these resources were used to build up industrial capitalism via the route of war contracts. 2. The tax scheme was heavily weighted against the small consumers through a ramified program of indirect taxation, again aiding accumulation. 3. A protective tariff was written. 4. A national banking system was devised. 5. A Pacific railway was chartered which was not only given generous grants from the public domain but also lent federal funds. 6. A homestead law was passed. 7. Appropriations for internal improvements—river and harbor legislation—were made. 8. The admission of immigrant contract labor was authorized. 9. The military was employed to put down strikes.

The Republican Radicals—the so-called Radical Republicans—did not oppose this economic program in the interests of industrial capitalism. (To this extent, it is a mistake to assume that, like the Jacobins in the French Revolution, the Radical Republicans spoke for the petty bourgeois only. Thus, Stevens and Greeley were high protectionists; and Stevens was as eager as any mercenary despoiler of the public domain to lay his hands on mineral lands for his own aggrandizement. Nevertheless, while the Radical Republicans were not Jacobins in a class sense, they were akin to the Jacobins in their uncompromising and determined use of political power.) What, then, differentiated the leaders of the Radicals from the leaders of the Conservatives? We must understand that among the Radical Republicans there were two factions, which, however, did not part company until the Civil War itself was over. These we may call the Old Radicals and the New Radicals. Both were in agreement on this basic point: the war could be won only by the freeing and arming of the Negroes and the smashing of the economic and political power, once and for all, of southern planter capitalism. The Old Radicals were committed to this program for emotional reasons; the New Radicals from the point of view of expediency only.

Energetic, resourceful, embittered men (they had gone through the cruel fires of the Abolitionist controversy before the Civil War broke out), the Old Radicals pressed every advantage the revolutionary situation of the war afforded them: they voted to enthrone the industrial-capitalist class, for it was their class; but they also labored heroically in the interests of the establishment of Negro rights. Lincoln was opposed to the sudden and whole emancipation of the Negroes because he was not an egalitarian and because he feared to lose the support of the important Border States which had not seceded; and to this end he looked forward to compensating the slave-owners for the loss of their human chattels. But the Old Radicals (supported by the New Radicals) were ruthless. Over Lincoln's protests they passed through Congress the Confiscation Acts of 1861 and 1862. They drove Lincoln into issuing the Emancipation Proclamation. They established their own so-called Committee on the Conduct of the War (in Congress) and hounded the President until he got rid of weak generals and was ready to prosecute the struggle relentlessly. They clamored, until they were successful, for the arming of the Negroes and their use in the Union's armed forces. Indeed, in 1864, just when the Radical Republicans were on the point of dropping Lincoln, only military triumphs in the field made his renomination inevitable.

Thus the Old Radicals were revolutionists, in their use of political weapons, and egalitarians, for emotional reasons, as far as the Negroes were concerned. The New Radicals were revolutionists, too, but only in the political and economic senses. Wholeheartedly, these younger men in Congress—Conkling of New York, Blaine of Maine, Sherman and Garfield of Ohio—believed in the rising star of industrial capitalism; they completely accepted the tactic that the war had to be waged uncompromisingly. But they were too young themselves to have suffered in the Abolitionist struggle; and Negro emancipation, for them, was not a burning faith but a weapon. While the war raged, the New Radicals

accepted the leadership of the Old Radicals. When it was over, they took over control of the Republican party.

Whatever the individual personal motives, then, we may say that the Radical Republicans, as a group, were deeply hostile to Lincoln and his tactic of conciliation. They were numerous on the floors of Congress, they had powerful support among the generals, some of them in fact served in both capacities, so that it was their prodding that compelled Lincoln slowly to move farther to the left. . . .

Lincoln's successor, Johnson, had neither his political talents nor his detachment as far as the South was concerned: for Johnson came from Tennessee. Johnson was prepared to adopt the position of the Radical Republicans in 1864, but this was no longer enough. The Radicals did not want the readmission of the South—the South was to be treated as a "conquered province"—until their *political* and *social* program was now fully implemented. For three whole years (1867–70), therefore, we have the seizure of political power by Congress, controlled by the Radical Republicans.

The first phase of Reconstruction, then, had as its intention the debasement of the South, through a military rule under the guidance of Congress. For what purpose? *To grant and protect the civil rights of the now emancipated Negroes as citizens and voters so that these could assure the permanent victory of Republicanism in the South and therefore in the nation.* We must have in mind that the political program of industrial capitalism had been written during the Civil War years by a minority party operating in a series of rump Congresses. Power over the state had been seized by a *coup d'état*, in effect. With the war over, if the southern states were permitted to return to the Union unreconstructed, there was nothing to prevent southern and western agrarianism from joining once more, on the floors of Congress and in presidential elections; and thus wiping out the victory by making a successful attack on protectionism, the national banking system, and the rest. This then, was the grand scheme of Reconstruction, as it was devised by the Old Radicals: the South was to be captured for Republicanism through the instrument of the Negroes. And in this way the seizure of political power by industrial capitalism in the national arena would be made permanent.

. . . As early as 1871, it was already becoming evident, Reconstruction in the southern states was doomed to failure.

What had happened? Had the victors become more merciful? Had the high idealism of the war years become spent as men returned to more mundane pursuits? Not at all. The New Radical faction had taken control away from the Old Radicals in the Republican party. They were not Abolitionists, as has already been pointed out. They wanted to maintain the South in vassalage, too, but not in a *political,* only in an *economic* dependent relationship. In short, as conscious and clear-eyed spokesmen for the triumphant industrial-capitalist class, they saw that the South was an important element in establishing a vast domestic market and a functioning capitalist economy. Southern products—cotton, tobacco, sugar, turpentine, lumber, hemp—were needed at home and to help balance international payments abroad. Southern raw materials—iron, coal—could be exploited by the investment of northern capital surpluses. Southern railroads could be built, factories erected, cities furnished with public utilities—always provided the section was prepared to

co-operate with northern capital. To achieve this grand intention, political peace was imperative. The South was permitted to redeem itself, with the tacit consent of the New Radicals. It is significant to note that many of the redeemers, the so-called Bourbons, were not the old planter capitalists. A large company of them were the allies or agents of northern capitalism—railroad concessionaires, factory owners, mineral-land promoters. *But these redeemers were compelled to take over the southern states in the interests of the Democratic party.*

What, then, assured the triumph of Republicanism in the national political arena? The answer is plain. From 1870 on, after the Old Radicals were no longer in power, Reconstruction was continued until 1877 in a dwindling number of southern states: but not in the interests of the Negro. From 1870 to 1877, it may be said, the military was maintained in a number of southern states, purely as a temporary device, until the New Radicals could find allies for the support of industrial capitalism's program in the West. This they succeeded in doing. By admitting new states; by extending the benefits of protective-tariff legislation to western woolgrowers; by lavish grants of land to western railroads; by turning capitalists loose on the nation's rich timber and mineral resources; by pork-barrel river and harbor legislation: a large enough portion of the West was won away from its old agrarian and Democratic allegiances. When the Old Northwest and a goodly part of the new Far West began to vote Republican tickets in congressional and presidential elections, as they did after 1876, then the political design had been achieved.

Political control over the national state in the interests of industrial capitalism was now assured: the New Radicals could withdraw their military and judicial support from the Negroes in the South. At this point, that is to say, in 1877, when the final withdrawal took place, the Reconstruction era was formally ended. And industrial capital-ism itself took up where the Freedmen's Bureau and the Union League clubs left off; so that there now began the peaceful penetration, industrially and financially, of the South with the as-sistance of the southern Bourbons.

II. DOCUMENTS

1. The Politics of Reconstruction

Following Lincoln's assassination, three political attitudes emerged among the Republicans in Washington: some supported the new Johnson ad-ministration; more radical Republicans determined to supervise the de-feated South stringently and to control reconstruction policy from Congress; and an even larger swing group of moderate Republicans wished primarily to maintain party unity in the face of deepening divisions between their intransigent Radical colleagues and an accidental but equally obstinate President. The following three selections illustrate the cleavages among these groups over the formulation of reconstruction policy. Gideon Welles, Secretary of the Navy under Lincoln and Johnson, kept a running account of the battle between the Radicals and the new President in his valuable diary, while Charles Sumner spoke for the Radicals in letters to English friends. Finally, Shelby Cullom, an Illinois Republican legislator, described the dilemma of the moderates in his autobiography. Study particularly the explanations of Radical political behavior given by Bowers, Hacker and Rhodes in the light of Sumner's letters. Do these earlier writers adequately explain the motives behind the political actions of men such as Sumner?

GIDEON WELLES

Tuesday, June 27. The President still ill, and the visit to the Pawnee further postponed. No Cabinet meeting. The President is feeling the effects of in-tense application to his duties, and over-pressure from the crowd.

A great party demonstration is being made for negro suffrage. It is claimed

Reprinted from Howard K. Beale, ed., THE DIARY OF GIDEON WELLES, *II (New York: W. W. Norton & Company, Inc., 1960), June 26–27, 1865, pp. 324–326, by permission of the pub-lisher.*

the negro is not liberated unless he is also a voter, and, to make him a voter, they who urge this doctrine would sub-vert the Constitution, and usurp or assume authority not granted to the Federal government. While I am not inclined to throw impediments in the way of the universal, intelligent en-franchisement of all men, I cannot break down constitutional barriers, or violate the undoubted rights of the States. In the discussion of this ques-tion, it is evident that intense partisan-ship instead of philanthropy is the root of the movement. When pressed by arguments which they cannot refute, they turn and say if the negro is not allowed to vote, the Democrats will get control in each of the seceding or rebellious States, and in conjunction with the Democrats of the Free States they may get the ascendency in our political affairs. As there must and will be parties, they may as well form on this question, perhaps, as any other. It is curious to witness the bitterness and intolerance of the philanthropists in this matter. In their zeal for the negro they lose sight of all constitutional rights and safeguards, and the civil regulations and organization of the government.

Friday, June 30. The weather for several days has been exceedingly warm. For some time there have been complaints of mismanagement of affairs in the storekeeper's department at Boston, and on Monday last I made a change, appointing an officer who lost a leg in the service. Mr. Gooch comes to me with an outcry from the Boston delegation wanting action to be deferred. Told G. if there was any reason for it I would give it consideration. He wished to know the cause of the change. I told him the welfare of the service. It is not my purpose in this and similar cases to be placed on the defensive. I do not care to make or prefer charges, yet I feel it a most unpleasant task to remove even objectionable men.

The President is still indisposed, and I am unable to perfect some important business that I wished to complete with the close of the fiscal year. There are several Radical Members here, and have been for some days apparently anxious to see the President. Have met Senator Wade two or three times at the White House. Complains that the Executive has the control of the government, that Congress and the Judiciary are subordinate, and mere instruments in his hands—said the form of government was on the whole a failure—that there are not three distinct and independent departments but one great controlling one with two others as assistants. Mentions that the late President called out 75,000 men without authority. Congress when it came together approved it. He then asked for 400,000 men and four hundred millions of money. Congress gave him five of each instead of four. I asked him if he supposed or meant to say that these measures were proposed without consulting, informally, the leading members of each house. He replied that he did not, and admitted that the condition of the country required the action which was taken, and that it was in conformity with public expectation.

Thad Stevens called on me on business and takes occasion to express ultra views, and had a sarcastic hit or two but without much sting. He is not satisfied, nor is Wade, yet I think the latter is mollified and disinclined to disagree with the President. Yet his friend Winter Davis it is understood is intending to improve the opportunity of delivering a Fourth-of-July oration, to take ground distinctly antagonistic to the Administration on the question of negro suffrage.

CHARLES SUMNER

TO THE DUCHESS OF ARGYLL, APRIL 3, 1866

These are trying days for us. I am more anxious now than during the war. . . . Believe me, the people are

Reprinted from Edward L. Pierce, ed., MEMOIR AND LETTERS OF CHARLES SUMNER, *Vol. IV (Boston, 1894).*

with Congress. When it is considered that the President has such an amazing power, it is extraordinary to see how the conscience of the masses has stood firm. Congress is misrepresented in England. I speak of the lower House now. In my opinion it is the best that has ever been since the beginning of our government. It is full of talent, and is governed by patriotic purpose. There is no personal or party ambition which prompts its course. It is to save the country that it takes its present responsibilities.

You say, "Why not urge the abolition of the black codes?" This I have done from the beginning. There are several speeches of mine which you have never seen, three years ago, against any exclusion of witnesses on account of color; also an elaborate report. A partial measure I carried. Since the cessation of hostilities this subject has occupied me constantly. In my speech at Worcester I dwelt on the black codes; then again in a speech early this session. At last we passed a bill, known as the Civil Rights bill; it went through both houses by unprecedented majorities. The President refuses to sign it. By our Constitution it requires a vote of two thirds to pass it over his veto. It is still uncertain if we can command this large vote; the division will be very close. The loss of this bill will be a terrible calamity. It leaves the new crop of black laws in full force, and gives to the old masters a new letter of license to do anything with the freedman short of making him a chattel. A new serfdom may be substituted, and this is their cruel purpose. But after most careful consideration I see no substantial protection for the freedman except in the franchise. He must have this—(1) For his own protection; (2) For the protection of the white Unionist; and (3) For the peace of the coun-

try. We put the musket in his hands because it was necessary; for the same reason we must give him the franchise. Unionists from the South tell me that unless this is done they will be defenceless. And here is the necessity for the universality of the suffrage: every vote is needed to counterbalance the rebels.

It is very sad that we should be tried in this way. For our country it is an incalculable calamity. Nobody can yet see the end. Congress will not yield. The President is angry and brutal. Seward is the marplot. In the Cabinet, on the question of the last veto, there were four against it to three for it; so even there, among his immediate advisers, the President is left in a minority. Stanton reviewed at length the bill, section by section, in the Cabinet, and pronounced it an excellent and safe bill every way from beginning to end. But the veto message was already prepared, and an hour later was sent to Congress.

You hear that I do not bear contradiction. Perhaps not. I try to bear everything. But my conscience and feelings are sometimes moved, so that I may show impatience. It is hard to meet all these exigencies with calmness. I hope not to fail.

I despair of the President. He is no Moses, but a Pharaoh to the colored race, and they now regard him so. He has all the narrowness and ignorance of a certain class of whites, who have always looked upon the colored race as out of the pale of humanity.

TO JOHN BRIGHT, MAY 27, 1867

. . . For a long time I was perplexed by the subtlety so often presented that the suffrage was a "privilege" and not a "right," and being a "privilege" it was subject to such limitations as the policy or good-will of the legislature chose to impose. The more I think of it, the more it seems to me an essential right, which government can only regulate and guard, but cannot abridge. All just government stands on "the consent of the governed." Starting with this principle from our Declaration of Independence, I see no other conclusion than that every citizen having a proper residence must be a voter. If it be said that, then, the ignorant man has the same electoral weight as the intelligent, I reply: "No; each has the same vote; but the other exercises an influence over the result,—in other words, over other votes,—in proportion to his intelligence." In the vote itself all are equal. This is another instance of equality before the law. I cannot but think that you will be driven in England to discuss the question on higher grounds; parties will then arrange themselves anew. Until then there will be no response; nothing short of this will be hard pan. As our discussion has proceeded here, the hard pan has prevailed. In Massachusetts we have what is equivalent to a small rating; every voter, before his name can be registered, must pay a poll-tax, which is usually $1.50, or about six shillings. Thus far, our great change at the South promises well. Without the colored vote the white Unionists would have been left in the hands of the rebels; loyal governments could not be organized. The colored vote was a necessity; this I saw at the beginning, and insisted pertinaciously that it should be secured. It was on this ground, rather than principle, that I relied most; but the argument of principle was like a reinforcement. I do not know that I have mentioned to you how the requirements of universal suffrage in the new constitutions came to be readjusted in our reconstruction bill. The bill, as it came from the House, was simply a military bill. In the Senate several amendments were moved in the nature of conditions of restoration. I did not take much interest in them, as I preferred delay, and therefore was content with anything that secured this, believing that Congress must ultimately come to the true ground. In the confusion which ensued, a caucus of Republican senators was called. Then Mr. Sherman moved that all the pending propositions be referred to a committee of seven. Of this committee he was chairman: I was a member. In the committee I insisted that the existing governments should be declared invalid: adopted. Then that the States in question be designated simply 'rebel States': adopted. Then that in the new constitutions there should be no exclusion from suffrage on account of color. This was voted down: only one other member of the committee sustaining me, Mr. Sherman being strongly averse. When the committee reported their bill to the caucus, I stated my objections and moved my amendment in an enlarged form, to the effect that in the new constitutions all citizens with a proper residence should be voters. In moving it, I simply said that it was in our power to decide this question, and to supersede its discussion in the Southern States: that if we did not decide it, every State and village between here and the Rio Grande would be agitated by it. It was dinner-time, and there was impatience for a vote, which was by the ayes standing and being counted, and then the noes. There were two counts, seventeen ayes to fifteen noes: so this important requirement was adopted. Mr. Sherman, as chairman of the committee, was directed to move the amended bill as a substitute for the pending measure, and it was passed by the usual Republican majorities. That evening in a caucus some few saw the magnitude of the act, and there was corresponding exultation. Wilson wished to dance with somebody. I have given you this narrative because it concerns an important event, and will show you how business with us is sometimes conducted. Could my way have prevailed, I would have provided provisional governments of a civil character, which should have shaped the rebel States into their new political forms and superintended the transition. I am entirely satisfied now that this would have been the better course; but we were obliged to sacrifice to the impatience of politicians, who thought that the President could be met only by the promptest reconstruction. It is in politics as in life,—we rarely obtain precisely what we desire. . . .

SHELBY CULLOM

. . . Congress was not in session when Johnson came to the Presidency in April, 1865. To do him no more than simple justice, I firmly believe that he wanted to follow out, in reconstruction, what he thought was the policy of Mr. Lincoln, and in this he was guided largely by the advice of Mr. Seward.

But there was this difference. Johnson was, probably in good faith, pursuing the Lincoln policy of reconstruction; but when the Legislatures and Executives of the Southern States began openly passing laws and executing them so that the negro was substantially placed back into slavery, practically nullifying the results of the awful struggle, the untold loss of life and treasure, Mr. Lincoln certainly would have receded

Reprinted from Shelby Cullom, FIFTY YEARS OF PUBLIC SERVICE *(Chicago, 1911), pp. 145–146, 149–150, 152–153.*

and would have dealt with the South with an iron hand, as Congress had determined to do, and as General Grant was compelled to do when he assumed the Presidency.

From April to the reassembling of Congress in December, Johnson had a free hand in dealing with the seceding States, and he was not slow to take advantage of it. He seemed disposed to recognize the old State Governments; to restrict the suffrage to the whites; to exercise freely the pardoning power in the way of extending executive clemency not only to almost all classes, but to every individual who would apply for it. The result was, it seemed to be certain that if the Johnson policy were carried out to the fullest extent, the supremacy of the Republican party in the councils of the Nation would be at stake.

To express it in a word, the motive of the opposition to the Johnson plan of reconstruction was the firm conviction that its success would wreck the Republican party, and by restoring the Democrats to power bring back Southern supremacy and Northern vassalage. The impeachment, in a word, was a culmination of the struggle between the legislative and the executive departments of the Government over the problem of reconstruction. The legislative department claimed exclusive jurisdiction over reconstruction; the executive claimed that it alone was competent to deal with the subject.

. . .

What determined Johnson in his course, I do not know. It was thought that he would be a radical of radicals. Being of the "poor white" class, he may have been flattered by the attentions showered on him by the old Southern aristocrats. Writers of this period have frequently given that as a reason. My own belief has been that he was far too strong a man to be governed in so vital a matter by so trivial a cause. My conviction is that the radical Republican leaders in the House were right; that he believed in the old Democratic party, aside from his loyalty to the Union; and was a Democrat determined to turn the Government over to the Democratic party, reconstructed on a Union basis.

I cannot undertake to go into all the long details of that memorable struggle. As I look back over the history of it now, it seems to me to bear a close resemblance to the beginning of the French Revolution, to the struggle between the States General of France and Louis XVI. Might we not, if things had turned differently, drifted into chaos and revolution? If Johnson had been impeached and refused to submit, adopting the same tactics as did Stanton in retaining the War Department; had Ben Wade taken the oath of office and demanded possession, Heaven only knows what might have been the result.

. . .

But to return to the struggle between the President and Congress. Trumbull, Sumner, Wade, and the leaders were bound in one way or another to get the necessary two-thirds. The vote was taken in the Senate: "Shall the Civil Rights bill pass the veto of the President to the contrary notwithstanding?" It was well understood that the vote would be very close, and the result uncertain.

The excitement was intense. The galleries were crowded; members of the House were on the Senate floor. The result seemed to depend entirely on the vote of Senator Morgan, of New York, and he seemed to be irresolute, uncertain in his own mind which way he would vote. The call of the roll proceeded. When his name was reached there was profound silence. He first

voted nay, and then immediately changed to yea. A wonderful demonstration burst forth, as it was then known that the bill would pass over the veto of the President, and that the Republican party in Congress at last had complete control. Senator Trumbull made a remarkable speech on that occasion, and I was never prouder of any living man.

So the struggle went on from day to day and year to year, growing all the time more intense. I have always been disposed to be conservative; I was then . . .

I disliked to follow the extreme radical element, and when the row was at its height, Judge Orth, a colleague in the House from Indiana, and I concluded to go and see the President and advise with him, in an attempt to smooth over the differences. I will never forget that interview. It was at night. He received us politely enough, and without mincing any words he gave us to understand that we were on a fool's errand and that he would not yield. We went away, and naturally joined the extreme radicals in the House, always voting with them afterwards.

The row continued in the Fortieth Congress. Bills were passed, promptly vetoed, and the bills immediately passed over the President's veto. Many of the bills were not only unwise legislation but were unconstitutional as well. We passed the Tenure of Office bill; we attempted to restrict the President's pardoning power; and as I look back over the history of the period, it seems to me that we did not have the slightest regard for the Constitution. Some of President Johnson's veto messages were admirable. He had the advice and assistance of one of the ablest lawyers of his day, Jeremiah Black.

To make the feeling more intense, just about this time Johnson made his famous "swing around the circle," as it was termed. His speeches published in the opposition press were intemperate and extreme. He denounced Congress. He threatened to "kick people out of office," in violation of the Tenure of Office act. He was undignified in his actions and language, and many people thought he was intoxicated most of the time, although I do not believe this.

2. Southern Reconstruction

Southern reconstruction was both a national trauma and an individual experience for the entire Civil War generation. To document the great variety of reactions to the period of Radical rule in the South would be both fruitless and bewildering within a chapter of this limited scope. The perspectives which follow reflect the view of the author that no attempt to understand the tragedy of our First Reconstruction, as C. Vann Woodward has called it, can omit the three central actors in the story: the intransigent Southern white, the compassionate but increasingly impatient Northern liberal, and, most important, the ambitious freedman himself. Edward Pollard's denunciation of Radical rule reflected the opinions of a large majority of Southern whites toward the liberties given their ex-slaves under Radical rule. In the space of a decade, Carl Schurz—like other Northern reformers—changed his mind almost completely on the question of how best to treat the South and to protect the freedmen, as his comments of 1865 and 1872 reveal. Finally, the English traveler, Robert Somers, offered some acute observations on the problems, condition, and behavior of Negro freedmen during the brief period of Southern reconstruction.

EDWARD A. POLLARD

The author of the present work wrote a history of the recent war under the title of "The Lost Cause." The fitness of the title was singularly complimented, and the words have since been permanently incorporated in the common language of the people. The author now proposes a title yet more fit and happy for the continuation of his historical work: "The Lost Cause Regained." He does not hesitate to confess that a prolonged and mature reflection has given him larger and perhaps better views of the true nature of

Reprinted from Edward A. Pollard, THE LOST CAUSE REGAINED *(New York, 1868), pp. 13–15.*

the recent war, and especially of its consequences; and he has risen from that reflection profoundly convinced that the true cause fought for in the late war has not been "lost" immeasurably or irrevocably, but is yet in a condition to be "regained" by the South on ultimate issues of the political contest.

It is scarcely possible in any introduction to recite the whole design of a literary work. But the meaning of a title, which perhaps piques curiosity, may be fixed at once in the mind of the reader by the following brief summary of propositions:

That the late war was much misunderstood in the South, and its true inspiration thereby lost or diminished, through the fallacy that Slavery was defended as a property tenure, or as a peculiar institution of labour; when the true ground of defence was as of a barrier against a contention and war of races.

That the greatest value of Slavery was as such a barrier.

That the war has done nothing more than destroy this barrier, and liberate and throw upon the country the ultimate question of the Negro.

That the question of the Negro practically couples or associates a revolutionary design upon the Constitution; and that the true question which the war involved, and which it merely liberated for greater breadth of controversy was the supremacy of the white race, and along with it the preservation of the political traditions of the country.

That in contesting this cause the South is far stronger than in any former contest, and is supplied with new aids and inspirations.

That if she succeeds to the extent of securing the supremacy of the white man, and the traditional liberties of the country—in short, to the extent of defeating the Radical party—she really triumphs in the true cause of the war, with respect to all its fundamental and vital issues.

That this triumph is at the loss only of so many dollars and cents in the property tenure of Slavery—the South still retaining the Negro as a labourer, and keeping him in a condition where his *political* influence is as indifferent as when he was a slave;—and that the pecuniary loss is utterly insignificant, as the price of "the lost cause regained."

These propositions, we believe, sum a novel, and even sublime philosophy on the political questions of the day. They contain the true hope of the South; they suggest a new animation of a contest which lingers too much on mere partial and contracted issues. The great difficulty of the Southern mind is, and always has been, its extreme narrowness on the Negro question. This intellectual defect, in a concern so important and peculiar, is especially remarkable, when we consider what renown the South has obtained for her schools of statesmanship, that she has contributed the largest and best part of the political literature of the country; nevertheless it is a fact. We shall see further on in these pages that the best of Southern statesmen had no clear ideas, either of the nature or the object of the defence of Negro Slavery; that they were incapable of conveying distinct inspirations to the people in the past war, which failed on the side of the South for this reason as well as from material causes; and that in the political controversy which has followed, they have exhibited a pitiful want of due conception of the nature and magnitude of the contest. It is indeed mortifying to witness the present superficiality of the Southern mind, and to read the commentaries of its statesmanship on the political situation. The reigning Radicalism at Washington is lightly treated as a wanton and ephemeral display of party, or, in the most serious mood of the Southern "statesman," is described after the words of Emerson: "the spirit of our American radicalism is destructive and aimless—it is not loving—it has no ultimate ends—but is destructive only out of hatred and selfishness." The common mistake is in regarding as a wanton and aimless excitement, without "ultimate ends," as an extravagant episode of party, what has really the depth and significance of a great revolution—a revolution of unbroken tenour and resolution, proceeding by distinct and firm steps from the time the Anti-Slavery party erected its first starting-post in the theory of Consolidation, and made its first movement upon the Constitution of the United States.

We are living not in the excitement of party, but in the solemnity of a Revolution. We are aware that it has often happened that a people has shown but little contemporary realization of the events of a Revolution; history is full of pictures of men buying and selling, and perplexed with the paltry cares of every-day life in the midst of great political changes; and it seems indeed to be an unvarying law of the progress of human opinion, that the true proportions of the crisis through which it passes become visible only on retrospect. But in the case we are considering, this popular dullness, especially in the South, is unusually remarkable and excessively curious. The imperfect appreciation of current events, and the degraded estimate of them are so extreme as to claim a particular notice and merit a signal rebuke.

It is to develop the significance of the present revolution in the political affairs of America; to pass in brief review its history; to show its coherent and dramatic design on the twin subjects of Reconstruction and Negrophilism; to deduce from all a new and animating hope for the South, and to point the path to the victory of the Constitution, that we have designed this work.

CARL SCHURZ

TO MRS. SCHURZ

JACKSON, MISS., AUG. 27, 1865.

About my experiences in the South, I can tell you only a few generalities.

Reprinted from Frederic Bancroft, ed., SPEECHES, CORRESPONDENCE AND POLITICAL PA- PERS OF CARL SCHURZ *(New York, 1913), I, 268– 269, 279–281, 372–373; II, 321–328, 331.*

I have found all of my preconceived opinions verified most fully, no, more than that. The real state of affairs leaves my expectations far behind. This is the most shiftless, most demoralized people I have ever seen. The influence of slavery has confused their moral conceptions, their childish, morbid self-complacency has not allowed them to approach, even in the slightest degree, a correct realization of their situation. At the present moment, society is in a state of complete dissolution and can only be held in check by iron force. All respect for the rights of personal property seems to have disappeared entirely. Everybody takes what he wants and seems completely to forget that this is what is called stealing. Since the negro is no longer a slave and no longer costs a thousand dollars, his life is not deemed worth a wisp of straw. I have a list of the murders committed by Southern "gentlemen" upon negroes, which would enrage the people of the North, if I were to submit it to a mass-meeting there. If we were to remove our troops today, the Southern States would swim in blood tomorrow. I am expressing convictions based on experience, when I say, that the only highlight in his dark picture is the conduct of the negro. Not only has the colored population passed from slavery to freedom without making a single attempt to take vengeance for past sufferings, but they are at this very moment engaged with laudable zeal in the effort to found for themselves a substantial future. Wherever a negro school is opened, it is full of children. It is delightful to see the little woolly-headed pickaninnies studying their spelling-books in the streets. The negroes are unjustly accused of not wishing to work. They are the only people here who do work. I have not seen one white man in the fields. Strangely enough, only the negroes have money; they are the only persons that do not shrink from any sort of remunerative labor.

If I can only make my main report, I shall open the eyes of the people of the North.

REPORT ON THE CONDITION OF THE SOUTH [1]

Sir: When you did me the honor of selecting me for a mission to the States lately in rebellion, for the purpose of inquiring into the existing condition of things, of laying before you whatever information of importance I might gather, and of suggesting to you such measures as my observations would lead me to believe advisable, I accepted the trust with a profound sense of the responsibility connected with the performance of the task. . . . I would not have accepted the mission, had I not felt that whatever preconceived opinions I might carry with me to the South, I should be ready to abandon or modify, as my perception of facts and circumstances might command their abandonment or modification. . . .

These instructions confined my mission to the States of South Carolina, Georgia, Alabama, Mississippi, and the department of the Gulf. . . .

Before laying the results of my observations before you, it is proper that I should state the *modus operandi* by which I obtained information and formed my conclusions. Wherever I went I sought interviews with persons who might be presumed to represent the opinions, or to have influence upon the conduct, of their neighbors; I had thus frequent meetings with individuals belonging to the different classes of society from the highest to the

[1] This report accompanied President Johnson's message of Dec. 18, 1865, and is a part of Executive Document No. 11, House of Representatives, 39th Congress, 1st Session.

lowest; in the cities as well as on the roads and steamboats I had many opportunities to converse not only with inhabitants of the adjacent country, but with persons coming from districts which I was not able to visit; and finally I compared the impressions thus received with the experience of the military and civil officers of the government stationed in that country, as well as of other reliable Union men to whom a longer residence on the spot and a more varied intercourse with the people had given better facilities of local observation than my circumstances permitted me to enjoy. When practicable I procured statements of their views and experience in writing as well as of copies of official or private reports they had received from their subordinates or other persons. . . .

I may sum up all I have said in a few words. If nothing were necessary but to restore the machinery of government in the States lately in rebellion in point of form, the movements made to that end by the people of the South might be considered satisfactory. But if it is required that the Southern people should also accommodate themselves to the results of the war in point of spirit, those movements fall far short of what must be insisted upon.

The loyalty of the masses and of most of the leaders of the Southern people consists in submission to necessity. There is, except in individual instances, an entire absence of that national spirit which forms the basis of true loyalty and patriotism.

The emancipation of the slaves is submitted to only in so far as chattel slavery in the old form could not be kept up. But although the freedman is no longer considered the property of the individual master, he is considered the slave of society, and all independent State legislation will share the tendency to make him such. The ordinances abolishing slavery, passed by the conventions under the pressure of circumstances, will not be looked upon as barring the establishment of a new form of servitude.

Practical attempts on the part of the Southern people to deprive the negro of his rights as a freedman may result in bloody collisions, and will certainly plunge Southern society into restless fluctuations and anarchical confusion. Such evils can be prevented only by continuing the control of the National Government in the States lately in rebellion until free labor is fully developed and firmly established, and the advantages and blessings of the new order of things have disclosed themselves. This desirable result will be hastened by a firm declaration on the part of the Government, that National control in the South will not cease until such results are secured. Only in this way can that security be established in the South which will render numerous immigration possible, and such immigration would materially aid a favorable development of things.

The solution of the problem would be very much facilitated by enabling all the loyal and free-labor elements in the South to exercise a healthy influence upon legislation. It will hardly be possible to secure the freedman against oppressive class legislation and private persecution, unless he be endowed with a certain measure of political power.

As to the future peace and harmony of the Union, it is of the highest importance that the people lately in rebellion be not permitted to build up another "peculiar institution" whose spirit is in conflict with the fundamental principles of our political system; for as long as they cherish interests peculiar to them in preference to those

they have in common with the rest of the American people, their loyalty to the Union will always be uncertain.

I desire not to be understood as saying that there are no well-meaning men among those who were compromised in the rebellion. There are many, but neither their number nor their influence is strong enough to control the manifest tendency of the popular spirit. There are great reasons for hope that a determined policy on the part of the National Government will produce innumerable and valuable conversions. This consideration counsels lenity as to persons, such as is demanded by the humane and enlightened spirit of our times, and vigor and firmness in the carrying out of principles, such as is demanded by the national sense of justice and the exigencies of our situation.

GENERAL AMNESTY [1]

I beg leave to say that I am in favor of general, or as this word is considered more expressive, universal amnesty, believing as I do that the reasons which make it desirable that there should be amnesty granted at all, make it also desirable that the amnesty should be universal. . . .

In the course of this debate we have listened to some Senators, as they conjured up before our eyes once more all the horrors of the rebellion, the wickedness of its conception, how terrible its incidents were and how harrowing its consequences. Sir, I admit it all; I will not combat the correctness of the picture; and yet, if I differ with the gentlemen who drew it, it is because, had the conception of the rebellion been still more wicked, had its incidents been still more terrible, its con-

[1] From a speech in the Senate, January 30, 1872.

sequences still more harrowing, I could not permit myself to forget that in dealing with the question now before us we have to deal not alone with the past, but with the present and future interests of this Republic.

What do we want to accomplish as good citizens and patriots? Do we mean only to inflict upon late rebels pain, degradation, mortification, annoyance, for its own sake, to torture their feelings without any ulterior purpose? Certainly such a spirit could not by any possibility animate high-minded men. I presume, therefore, that those who still favor the continuance of some of the disabilities imposed by the fourteenth amendment, do so because they have some higher object of public usefulness in view, an object of public usefulness sufficient to justify, in their minds at least, the denial of rights to others which we ourselves enjoy.

What can those objects of public usefulness be? Let me assume that, if we differ as to the means to be employed, we are agreed as to the supreme end and aim to be reached. That end and aim of our endeavors can be no other than to secure to all the States the blessings of good and free government and the highest degree of prosperity and well-being they can attain, and to revive in all citizens of this Republic that love for the Union and its institutions, and that inspiring consciousness of a common nationality, which, after all, must bind all Americans together.

What are the best means for the attainment of that end? This, sir, as I conceive it, is the only legitimate question we have to decide. Certainly all will agree that this end is far from having been attained so far. Look at the Southern States as they stand before us today. Some are in a condition bordering upon anarchy, not only on account of the social disorders which are occurring there, or the inefficiency of their local governments in securing the enforcement of the laws; but you will find in many of them fearful corruption pervading the whole political organization; a combination of rascality and ignorance wielding official power; their finances deranged by profligate practices; their credit ruined; bankruptcy staring them in the face; their industries staggering under a fearful load of taxation; their property-holders and capitalists paralyzed by a feeling of insecurity and distrust almost amounting to despair. Sir, let us not try to disguise these facts, for the world knows them to be so, and knows it but too well.

What are the causes that have contributed to bring about this distressing condition? I admit that great civil wars resulting in such vast social transformations as the sudden abolition of slavery are calculated to produce similar results; but it might be presumed that a recuperative power such as this country possesses might during the time which has elapsed since the close of the war at least have very materially alleviated many of the consequences of that revulsion, had a wise policy been followed.

Was the policy we followed wise? Was it calculated to promote the great purposes we are endeavoring to serve? Let us see. At the close of the war we had to establish and secure free labor and the rights of the emancipated class. To that end we had to disarm those who could have prevented this, and we had to give the power of self-protection to those who needed it. For this reason temporary restrictions were imposed upon the late rebels, and we gave the right of suffrage to the colored people. Until the latter were enabled to protect themselves, political disabilities even more extensive than those which now exist, rested upon the plea of eminent political necessity. I would be the last man to conceal that I thought so then, and I think now there was very good reason for it.

But, sir, when the enfranchisement of the colored people was secured, when they had obtained the political means to protect themselves, then another problem began to loom up. It was not only to find new guaranties for the rights of the colored people, but it was to secure good and honest government for all. Let us not underestimate the importance of that problem, for in a great measure it includes the solution of the other. Certainly, nothing could have been better calculated to remove the prevailing discontent concerning the changes that had taken place, and to reconcile men's minds to the new order of things, than the tangible proof that that new order of things was practically working well; that it could produce a wise and economical administration of public affairs, and that it would promote general prosperity, thus healing the wounds of the past and opening to all the prospect of a future of material well-being and contentment. And, on the other hand, nothing could have been more calculated to impede a general, hearty and honest acceptance of the new order of things by the late rebel population than just those failures of public administration which involve the people in material embarrassments and so seriously disturb their comfort. In fact, good, honest and successful government in the Southern States would in its moral effects, in the long run, have exerted a far more beneficial influence than all your penal legislation, while your penal legislation will fail in its desired effects if we fail in establishing in the Southern States an honest and success-

ful administration of the public business.

Now, what happened in the South? It is a well-known fact that the more intelligent classes of Southern society almost uniformly identified themselves with the rebellion; and by our system of political disabilities just those classes were excluded from the management of political affairs. That they could not be trusted with the business of introducing into living practice the results of the war, to establish true free labor and to protect the rights of the emancipated slaves, is true; I willingly admit it. But when those results and rights were constitutionally secured there were other things to be done. Just at that period when the Southern States lay prostrated and exhausted at our feet, when the destructive besom of war had swept over them and left nothing but desolation and ruin in its track, when their material interests were to be built up again with care and foresight—just then the public business demanded, more than ordinarily, the coöperation of all the intelligence and all the political experience that could be mustered in the Southern States. But just then a large portion of that intelligence and experience was excluded from the management of public affairs by political disabilities, and the controlling power in those States rested in a great measure in the hands of those who had but recently been slaves and just emerged from that condition, and in the hands of others who had sometimes honestly, sometimes by crooked means and for sinister purposes, found a way to their confidence.

This was the state of things as it then existed. Nothing could be farther from my intention than to cast a slur upon the character of the colored people of the South. In fact, their conduct immediately after that great event which struck the shackles of slavery from their limbs was above praise. Look into the history of the world, and you will find that almost every similar act of emancipation, the abolition of serfdom, for instance, was uniformly accompanied by atrocious outbreaks of a revengeful spirit; by the slaughter of nobles and their families, illumined by the glare of their burning castles. Not so here. While all the horrors of San Domingo had been predicted as certain to follow upon emancipation, scarcely a single act of revenge for injuries suffered or for misery endured has darkened the record of the emancipated bondmen of America. And thus their example stands unrivalled in history, and they, as well as the whole American people, may well be proud of it. Certainly, the Southern people should never cease to remember and appreciate it.

But while the colored people of the South thus earned our admiration and gratitude, I ask you in all candor, could they be reasonably expected, when, just after having emerged from a condition of slavery, they were invested with political rights and privileges, to step into the political arena as men armed with the intelligence and experience necessary for the management of public affairs and for the solution of problems made doubly intricate by the disasters which had desolated the Southern country? Could they reasonably be expected to manage the business of public administration, involving to so great an extent the financial interests and the material well-being of the people, and surrounded by difficulties of such fearful perplexity, with the wisdom and skill required by the exigencies of the situation? That as a class they were ignorant and inexperienced and lacked a just conception of public interests, was certainly not their fault; for those who have studied the history of the world know but too well that slavery and oppression are very bad political schools. But the stubborn fact remains that they *were* ignorant and inexperienced; that the public business *was* an unknown world to them, and that in spite of the best intentions they *were* easily misled, not infrequently by the most reckless rascality which had found a way to their confidence. Thus their political rights and privileges were undoubtedly well calculated, and even necessary, to protect their rights as free laborers and citizens; but they were not well calculated to secure a successful administration of other public interests.

I do not blame the colored people for it; still less do I say that for this reason their political rights and privileges should have been denied them. Nay, sir, I deemed it necessary then, and I now reaffirm that opinion, that they should possess those rights and privileges for the permanent establishment of the logical and legitimate results of the war and the protection of their new position in society. But, while never losing sight of this necessity, I do say that the inevitable consequence of the admission of so large an uneducated and inexperienced class to political power, as to the probable mismanagement of the material interests of the social body, should at least have been mitigated by a counterbalancing policy. When ignorance and inexperience were admitted to so large an influence upon public affairs, intelligence ought no longer to so large an extent to have been excluded. In other words, when universal suffrage was granted to secure the equal rights of all, universal amnesty ought to have been granted to make all the resources of political intelligence and experience available for the promotion of the welfare of all.

But what did we do? To the un-educated and inexperienced classes—uneducated and inexperienced, I re-peat, entirely without their fault—we opened the road to power; and, at the same time, we condemned a large pro-portion of the intelligence of those States, of the property-holding, the in-dustrial, the professional, the tax-pay-ing interest, to a worse than passive attitude. We made it, as it were, easy for rascals who had gone South in quest of profitable adventure to gain the control of masses so easily misled, by permitting them to appear as the ex-ponents and representatives of the Na-tional power and of our policy; and at the same time we branded a large num-ber of men of intelligence, and many of them of personal integrity, whose material interests were so largely in-volved in honest government, and many of whom would have coöperated in managing the public business with care and foresight—we branded them, I say, as outcasts, telling them that they ought not to be suffered to exercise any influence upon the management of the public business, and that it would be unwarrantable presumption in them to attempt it.

I ask you, sir, could such things fail to contribute to the results we read to-day in the political corruption and demoralization, and in the financial ruin of some of the Southern States? These results are now before us. The mistaken policy may have been pardon-able when these consequences were still a matter of conjecture and speculation; but what excuse have we now for con-tinuing it when those results are clear before our eyes, beyond the reach of contradiction?

. . .

Well, then, what policy does com-mon-sense suggest to us now? If we sincerely desire to give to the Southern States good and honest government,

material prosperity and measurable contentment, as far at least as we can contribute to that end; if we really desire to weaken and disarm those prejudices and resentments which still disturb the harmony of society, will it not be wise, will it not be necessary, will it not be our duty to show that we are in no sense the allies and abet-tors of those who use their political power to plunder their fellow-citizens, and that we do not mean to keep one class of people in unnecessary degrada-tion by withholding from them rights and privileges which all others enjoy? Seeing the mischief which the system of disabilities is accomplishing, is it not time that there should be at least an end of it? Or is there any good it can possibly do to make up for the harm it has already wrought and is still work-ing?

ROBERT SOMERS

The testimony generally borne of the negroes is that they work readily when regularly paid. Wherever I have con-sulted an affected employer, whether in the manufacturing works of Richmond or on the farms and plantations, such is the opinion, with little variation, that has been given. In the country, negroes get from eight to ten dollars a month, with house and provisions. In Rich-mond, for common and ordinary labour, they are paid fifteen dollars a month with provisions, or thirty dollars and find themselves in the necessaries of life. In various branches of more or less skilled labour of which negroes are capable the wages are much higher, and approach the standard of remuneration to white men in the same occupations. A dollar a day for common labour will

Reprinted from Robert Somers, THE SOUTHERN STATES SINCE THE WAR *(London and New York, 1871), pp. 17–18, 41–43, 50–51, 54–55, 280–281.*

appear high to the best labourers in England or Scotland, but there is a necessary qualification to be made in any comparison of the relative rates of wages in the two countries. The dollar does not go so far as its exchange-worth in British money would imply. The price of nearly everything bought in the shops is very high; the labourer cannot command the same comfort as the labourer of other countries, save at a much higher monetary rate of wages, which necessarily augments the cost of American products, and impairs the commercial and competitive power of American industry. This state of things, arising from artificial causes operating over the whole United States, and inflating the monetary rate, not of wages alone, but of every form of profit, without making the working or any other class richer (what is gained nominally in wages and profits passing away in expenditure), has already all but destroyed various branches of American trade, and enhances materially the productive cost even of such staples as wheat, tobacco, and cotton, in which the United States have a natural pre-eminence. This will probably be more apparent now every year, until it forces itself on the public mind, and brings about a wholesome rectification.

· · ·

Charleston, like Boston—for a good comparison there is nothing like the antipodes—has an English look about it. The old city has not fallen so mathematically into the parallelogram formation as the cities of the United States in general. The inhabitants still cast many a fond look towards the old country, and contrast the present misrule with the time when the laws of England were the laws of South Carolina. Such is the deep sense of change and revolution produced by the downfall of State Rights and the inroad of

Federal power and innovation, that they profess not to know what the laws of South Carolina now are, or whether she has any laws at all. Ask what the system of rule is, and the reply will uniformly be that it is "nigger rule," which is in one sense true. The negroes are more numerous than the whites in South Carolina. Being all citizens of the United States, they have all the right of voting, while many of the whites are not naturalized; and the War Radicals who came in to take the lead in political affairs, and to hold offices for which the prominent men of the States were disqualified by the test oath, have succeeded in controlling the negro vote, and casting it almost *en masse* in their favour at the polls. There not being "carpet-baggers" or "scalawags" enough in the State to fill all the seats in the Legislature, the negroes have largely returned men of their own race to watch over "laws and learning," and "ships, colonies, and commerce," at the Capitol. The House of Representatives consists of 80 coloured men and 44 whites, and the Senate of 11 coloured men and 20 whites—there being one seat vacant just now. The white people of South Carolina are thus practically disfranchised, and a proletariat Parliament has been constituted, the like of which could not be produced under the widest suffrage in any part of the world save in some of these Southern States. The outcry of misgovernment, extravagant expenditure, jobbery, and corruption is both loud and general. The negroes are declared to be the dupes of designing men, comparative strangers to the State, whose object is simply to fill their pockets out of the public spoil. Political charges are not minced in South Carolina. There is room, indeed, to hope for a good deal of exaggeration. The exclusion of the superior part of the population from all influence in public affairs must of itself tend to magnify the enormity of everything enormous, and to distort everything not quite square that is done. The members and dependents of the State are said, after having depreciated the South Carolina bonds to 40 and 35 cents, and bought in largely at such prices, to have then offered gold interest in New York, which at once advanced the price to 95 cents, and enabled them to pocket millions. Possible and condemnatory enough, but it was a good thing in itself to restore the financial credit of the State; and in North Carolina, for example, the businessmen and the proprietor have since the war urged upon the Legislature to place the public credit of the State on the best footing, and will not desist till they succeed; under the conviction that honesty to the public creditor is the best policy, and the cornerstone of all progress and improvement. State Commissions are said to be issued on roads, lands, and other departments, the members of which do little but job and make profit to themselves and their friends. The State Government buys the lands on which to settle and give homes to negroes. This is commissioned, and land is said to undergo sale and resale before it becomes the property of the State. It is not believed that the negroes will in any considerable number make homes of these properties, and the only advantage I have incidentally discovered from such settlements is in one instance where the negroes, not having crops enough of their own to occupy their labour, formed a reserve force from which a neighboring planter has drawn extra hands to gather in his cotton. Railway contracts and railway bonds, in which the State has its finger, are also suspected of offering opportunities not exactly consistent with the

public good. The phosphate deposits in the bay and rivers have been leased at a royalty of a dollar per ton to a single company, not, I am to believe, without heavy sums distributed in the House of Representatives; but the principle of this transaction is discussed freely by all parties, and it is thought by some that the law of the United States will not sanction a commercial monopoly of what is public estate. A State census was taken last year, which is thought to have been a superfluous labour, seeing that the decennial census ordered by Congress fell to be taken this year, and the Governor is supposed to have sought in this way to give employment to partisans, and to secure votes. Everything thus moves in an atmosphere of political suspicion. One of the most favourable signs, indeed, is the keenness with which the acts of the State Government and Legislature are scrutinized, and the activity with which the native white population endeavour to recover influence and authority both in the State and in Congress. Prior to the recent elections, they organized a Reform Union on the basis of the political and civil equality of the negroes, turned out in large numbers to the ballot-boxes, protected the negroes who were voting on their side, and in Charleston succeeded. But, throughout the State, the movement so far has failed to divide the negro vote with the Radical party, who remain in a large majority. The principles of the Reform Union seem to be consistently maintained in practice. Many of the white electors in the city voted for Delarge, a negro tailor, as representative of their district in Congress, because they believed him to be more trustworthy than his white opponents.

I allude at this length to political affairs in South Carolina, because it is

very obvious that a system of government resting almost wholly on the votes
of the negroes is not a desirable state
of affairs as regards either the State
itself or the general interests of the
Union. It destroys confidence in the
integrity and stability of the Administration, prevents the investment of
money, and renders impossible that
hearty co-operation of the public
authorities with the substantial people
of the State which is so essential to the
interests of all classes of the community.

Apart from the passing excitement
of the elections just over, and the disappointment of the white population
at the voting of the negroes *en masse*
for the Republican or Radical party,
the general tone of social life in
Charleston is kindly and temperate,
and all classes of society are working
together with considerable harmony
for mutual good. The negro is beset
at present by two parties who claim to
be his "best friends." The Republicans,
who came in with the close of the
war, appeal to him as his best if not
only friends; and, looking at the political issues of the war, and the decree
of emancipation, with its elaborate
guarantees of reconstruction, the negroes could not but regard the Republican party politically as their
friends. Nor can it be denied that the
organs of the Federal Government have
laboured to introduce institutions for
the moral and social benefit of the
negroes, and, as far as their limited
means would allow, have befriended
that large portion of the population. I
have not found any one on the other
side who is prepared to blame the
negroes for voting almost universally
as they did in the elections which raised
General Grant to the Presidentship,
or who appears to have expected that
they would or should have been other

than fast adherents of their emanci-
pators. But the political agitators and
hungry spoil-and-office hunters of the
party are accused of appealing to the
ignorance and passions of the negro
population—of telling them that the
white people of the State are eagerly
seeking an opportunity of restoring
slavery, which they have certainly no
wish to do, and which they could not
do even if they would; and now, after
five years of this, it is considered hard
that the negroes—when there are great
public objects of economy, protection
from jobbery and corruption, and a
sound and healthy administration of
the affairs of the State to promote, in
which the blacks are as closely interested as others—should cast their votes in
a body against the great majority of the
white population, and terrorise such of
their own colour as are disposed to act
differently. This feeling breaks out violently just now in bar-rooms and at
street corners, and is often expressed
more quietly and reasonably, yet firmly,
in private circles. Many seem ready to
despair of the negro as a politician,
while others talk of a "war of races"
and other disorders sure to arise. The
feeling is no doubt all the stronger
since the evils of "carpet-bagging" and
negro demagoguery are apparent to respectable men of both parties, and,
while violently denounced on one side,
are not denied, but sometimes admitted
and deplored, on the other. Though
politics in South Carolina thus wear
a somewhat sinister complexion, yet
there is a healthy action and a sober
practical opinion underneath the surface that promise beneficial results. The
issues left by the war are being rapidly
closed; the *Reform Union*, which has
figured prominently in the late elections as the organ of the native white
people of the State, recognizes fully the
civil and political equality of the ne-

groes not only as an election platform, but as the fundamental law of the United States; this position is likely to be maintained, and may be expected soon to bring about in this, as in other Southern States, a better balance of parties. Meanwhile social bonds are being knit together, and many ameliorative influences are quietly at work. The ladies, who had a long apprenticeship of self-devotion during the war, are exerting themselves to give work, and to sell the work of poor needlewomen of both races. Nearly all the old charities of Charleston remain in operation, and schools and missions are doing much to improve the population.

. . .

That the negroes are improving, and many of them rising under freedom into a very comfortable and civilized condition, is not only admitted in all the upper circles of society, but would strike even a transient wayfarer like myself in the great number of decent coloured men of the labouring class and of happy coloured families that one meets. There is an institution in Charleston which early attracted my attention. In Broad Street one sees the office of the National Freedmen's Savings and Trust Company. I believe this form of National Savings Bank for the negroes was founded by the Freedmen's Bureau in the first years after the war. It has spread over all the chief towns of the South, and has already in deposit upwards of two millions of dollars, almost entirely the savings of the negro population. The deposits in the Charleston branch were 165,000 dollars at the end of October, and are monthly on the increase. Go in any forenoon, and the office is found full of negroes depositing little sums of money, drawing little sums, or remitting to distant parts of the country where they have relatives to support

or debts to discharge. The Freedmen's Savings Bank transacts a general exchange business betwixt the various points at which it has branches. Perhaps "branches" is not the exactly proper designation, for each bank is an independent corporation in itself, has a subscribed capital, is governed by its stockholders, and is altogether probably too like an ordinary commercial bank for the humble functions it has to discharge. Yet there is a certain degree of national concentration and control. The banks are under the patronage and protection of the Federal Government, and from the centre at Washington a monthly Circular is published, which reports the progress of all the various offices, and contains an amount of general matter very suitable to the negroes, and very desirable for them to read. The funds are for the most part invested in the Federal Debt, the high interest of which enables from 5 to 6 per cent to be paid to the depositors. But the Federal Government does not appear to be bound to make good to the depositors any loss accruing from the failure of a bank through embezzlement or any other cause. The responsibility in such a case would fall on the subscribed capital of the stockholders so far as it was sufficient to make good the deficiency. There is an opening in this state of affairs for partial and local disasters, which is happily closed in the National Security Savings Banks of the United Kingdom. But practically the Freedmen's Savings and Trust Companies do for the negroes what our National Savings Banks do for the working classes of England, Scotland, and Ireland; and it is gratifying to find that the negroes have in five years accumulated nearly half a million sterling of deposits. This result is the more significant since it is confined almost wholly to what were formerly the Slave States, and is but very feebly developed in New York and other Northern towns where it has been tried. The number of depositors in Charleston is 2,790, of whom nine-tenths are negroes. The average amount at the credit of individual depositors is about 60 dollars. The negro begins to deposit usually with some special object in view. He wishes to buy a mule and cart, or a house, or a piece of land, or a shop, or simply to provide a fund against death, sickness, or accident, and pursues his object frequently until it has been accomplished.

While some portion of the former slaves are probably sinking into an even worse condition than the first, there are others who are clearly rising, both morally and socially. The system of free labour, as was to be expected, will thus, in its own rough but salutary way, sift the chaff from the wheat; and but for the electoral antagonism of the moment, and the parading more than enough of negroes as senators, as policemen, as militia, as the armed force and the dominant power of the State, the relations of the two races on both sides would here be more kindly and cordial, and the prospects of the negroes themselves more hopeful than could well have been anticipated.

The system of free labour has been attended with a degree of success to which the planters themselves are the most forward of all in the Southern community to bear testimony. Complaints are rife enough of negro legislators, negro lieutenant-governors and office-bearers, and of the undue political elevation given to the coloured people by the transitional state of government through which the country has been passing since the war; and even on this effervescing subject I have found it necessary to distinguish, on

the one hand, betwixt the outcries of the bar-rooms and the street-corners—the echoes too often, it may be feared, of undone slave-traders and overseers—and, on the other, the true public opinion of the white population; but apart from this vexed question of politics, on which there are substantial grounds of grievance, I can scarcely recall an instance in which any planter or other employer of negro labour has not said that the result of emancipation, in its industrial bearings, has been much more favourable than could have been anticipated, or who has not added an expression of satisfaction that slavery, however roughly, has been finally effaced. Yet now proceeding on my own observation, the introduction of free labour in the Southern States has been bound up with such novel relations betwixt employer and employed, in particular the payment of the field-labourers by one-half the produce of the land that I confess I have had the greatest difficulty in attempting to reconcile them with any sound principle. One may understand how an agricultural communism among a group of people on a farm might be carried out; but the project would require an economy and mutuality of arrangement betwixt the members of the group to which there is no resemblance in the existing conditions of a Southern cotton plantation. While payment by share of the crops affords the careful and hard-working labourer an opportunity of doing well, in which his employer participates, it tends to introduce a confusion of sense as regards right and duty, and an uncertainty and fluctuation of reward for labour, that are more likely to be adverse than favourable to the formation of steady industrious habits among a race so lately freed from the most absolute dependence. The few negroes who are wise enough to thrive under this system take advantage of the abundance of land to rent and crop for themselves, while the planter is left to struggle with the mass who abuse the opportunities and privileges they possess; so that the worst results of the system are apt to be reproduced, if not aggravated, from year to year on the great majority of the farms. The share system is so stoutly defended by many persons of practical experience that it requires some hardihood of conviction to avow an opposite opinion; but the judgment I have formed must be given,

however deferentially. I cannot think that the payment of field-hands by shares of the crop, however liberal, is consistent either with the well-being of the negroes or with the agricultural development of the South. It is more like a half-way slavery than any relation of capital and labour of an advanced type; and its incompatibility with progress will be seen more and more clearly as the Southern farmers proceed to keep live stock, to introduce deep or steam ploughing, to diversify their crops, or to carry out any improvement on their lands.

3. Northern Businessmen and Southern Policy

That by 1865 politicians in Washington were aware of the immense changes which the war had wrought on American industry becomes clear from reading the letter which follows, written by Senator John Sherman to his brother, General William Tecumseh Sherman. Does it follow, however, that the business community or its spokesmen found particular virtue in the policies pursued by Radical Republicans toward the South, or that American businessmen felt it imperative that a harsh reconstruction policy be established in order to preserve and extend their wartime economic gains? The selections from a major New York business publication, representative of comments from similar periodicals expressing opposition to Radical Southern policy, indicate that the story is more complex than Beard, Hacker, and other believers in a Radical Republican–business community alignment imagined.

JOHN SHERMAN

UNITED STATES SENATE CHAMBER, WASHINGTON, NOV. 10, 1865

Dear Brother: Your note of the 4th is received. I am glad to hear you are settled, and from all accounts delight-

Reprinted from Rachel Sherman Thorndike, ed., THE SHERMAN LETTERS *(New York, 1894), from John Sherman to William Tecumseh Sherman, November 10, 1865, pp. 258–259.*

fully. You deserve quiet and repose after five years of change and labor. When in New York the other day, I found that party of English capitalists were delighted with their visit with you, and seemed especially polite to me on that account. I got for two of them Bowman and Nichols' works,[1] which they wanted to take home. But for my

1 Lives of General Sherman.

political employment I could have received from them very lucrative employment in the prosecution of their vast railroad schemes. Even as it is, if they, within six months, show their ability to execute their plans, I will identify myself much more with them. The truth is, the close of the war with our resources unimpaired gives an elevation, a scope to the ideas of leading capitalists, far higher than anything ever undertaken in this country before. They talk of millions as confidently as formerly of thousands. No doubt the contraction that must soon come will explode merely visionary schemes, but many vast undertakings will be executed. Among them will be the Pacific R. R. and extensive iron works, like some in England. Our manufactures are yet in their infancy, but soon I expect to see, under the stimulus of a great demand and the protection of our tariff, locomotive and machine shops worthy of the name. I do not fear, whatever may be the result of the senatorial election, but I can find enough to do, and without lowering the position I have occupied. As for the chances, from all the information I can gather, there is but little doubt a majority of the Legislature is for me. Still I know enough of the shifts and dangers in a new body of men like a Legislature not to be over sanguine. Since I am in the contest I will do all I can for success, and hope my friends will do likewise, but if defeated will bear it patiently. In a short time I will send you a list of the members who are from the military service, in the hope that you may know some of them well enough to influence them. You can feel perfectly easy in doing this, as my opponents use to the uttermost against me any prejudice or feeling against you. This election over, I think I shall be very willing to say good-by to politics, and will then seek to settle myself comfortably in some part of Ohio where I can engage in railroads, banking, or manufacturing. The law in this country is now only useful as the pathway to other pursuits.

I have seen Johnson several times. He seems kind and patient with all his terrible responsibility. I think he feels what every one must have observed, that the people will not trust the party or men who, during the war, sided with the rebels. The Democratic party is doomed forever as a disloyal organization, and no promises, or pledges, or platform they can make will redeem them from the odium they justly gained.

Yours affectionately,
John Sherman

THE MERCHANTS' MAGAZINE

COMMERCIAL CHRONICLE AND REVIEW

Of those events, either directly or remotely, affecting the supply and demand of capital which we are called upon to chronicle and review this month, the principal ones are the appointment of a provisional Governor to the last of the insurgent States, the reports of Mexican complications, the exodus of negroes from some parts of the South, the recent tax laws enacted in New Hampshire and proposed in Connecticut, and the introduction of greenback currency into the South.

Of those which mediately or immediately affect the supply and demand of commodities, the most noteworthy are the state of the growing crops, the opening of railroad communication throughout the South, the proceedings of the Detroit Convention, and the ravages of the privateer Shenandoah.

Reprinted from THE MERCHANTS' MAGAZINE AND COMMERCIAL REVIEW *(New York), LIII (August 1865), 133–135; LIV (March 1866), 169–174.*

Judge Marvin has been appointed Provisional Governor of Florida, with the same power and duties as were attached by the President to the previous appointments in other States. This completes the whole series of appointments to the late insurgent States, and places them all in a condition to reestablish civil government within their respective boundaries.

Reports of Mexican complications have from time to time created brief sensations in financial circles. These reports mainly emanate from New Orleans, and are probably the offspring of the fertile imagination of some ingenious agitator, whose role is played to suit the operations of a clique of operators in New York. At one time a peremptory demand by the United States for some rebel arms is reported, coupled with threats of immediate war. At another an army of observation is on the Rio Grande composed of 100,000 United States troops. Then Maximilian is about to abdicate, or he dare not leave the capital without a strong guard, so incensed are the population against him. Again, thirty thousand Americans are reported in Sonora or California, ready to pounce upon Mexico and wipe out the Imperialists as soon as the United States Government gives them the signal. In short, every conceivable *canard* is circulated. The latest one came by way of Cairo, and had the effect of temporarily putting up the price of gold from 143⅜ to 146⅞. It was couched in the following language:

Cincinnati, July 27, 1865

A despatch from Cairo, dated the 26th inst., conveys the following warlike intelligence:

The Galveston correspondent of the Houston *News* writes under date of July 1 as follows—

Orders have been issued to the officials of Matamoros to prepare accoutrements for thirty-five thousand troops of the Empire, the troops to consist of French, Austrians, and Algerians.

The reason given for this collection of troops is because the United States has a similar number at Brownsville and adjacent points.

French officers assert that there is no reason why the United States should send an army of eighty or a hundred thousand men to Texas unless it was designed to make aggressive movements upon Mexico.

The spirit of the two armies is described as being exceedingly hostile, and there is no affiliation between our officers and those of the Empire.

The vexed question of Negro status seems likely, if left alone, to settle itself in a way most satisfactory to all concerned. The slave population of Kentucky are rapidly escaping into Southern Ohio and Indiana, from whence it is ridiculous to expect they ever will be returned. The result is, that labor is becoming scarce in Kentucky, and plentiful in Ohio and Indiana; and though the laboring population of the latter States are not over pleased with the fact, since they erroneously look at this increased and unlooked for supply of laboring element as detrimental to their own interests, yet in the end it cannot but prove beneficial to them. For if the immigrant negroes become industrious, they must add largely to the general welfare by cultivating the wild lands of those States; while, if they are idle, the consequences will scarcely injure anybody but themselves.

Now, if the individual States in the South are left free to determine for themselves the status of the freed negroes, they will legislate so as to keep them within their borders if they are desirable inhabitants; and if they are not, their legislation will tend to drive them to sections of the country where their value is better appreciated. Assuming that the negroes will from necessity become industrious wherever they are, it is evident that as capital always accompanies and co-operates with labor, then wherever the negro population is seen to flow there will capital flow also, unless a corresponding movement of white emigration occurs to maintain those industrial pursuits which the blacks will have deserted. Of this, there is as yet but little indication. Many laboring whites have undoubtedly of late removed to the Southern States, but this movement bears no comparison with the exodus of the blacks.

The Legislature of New Hampshire lately enacted a law taxing income derived from Government securities, and the Legislature of Connecticut now have a similar law under consideration. As such incomes are not taxed in the other States, these laws will probably have the effect of discouraging such investments within those States, and as long as such investments are declared superior to others by reason of their exemption from taxation, capital will tend to flow away from those States and seek investment at other places.

The apprehensions expressed in our June number that Northern capital would not be likely to find its way very readily into the re-opened South, pending the settlement of the reconstruction and negro status questions are being fulfilled. The twenty thousand dollar exemption clause in the President's proclamation of amnesty not only keeps Southern capital tied up, but from the insecurity it engenders also frightens away Northern capital; while the constitutional limit to the term of confiscation (confining it to the lifetime of the attainted owners) makes persons chary of investing capital in

such property. As to the increased field expected to be opened for the circulation of greenback currency, accounts from various parts of the South would tend to show that such is not the fact. In many parts of the South, United States currency is either wholly refused or passed at a heavy discount as compared to specie or local shinplasters; while in still more numerous places it has not been introduced, and consequently is not used at all.

Accounts of the crops from various parts of the country are still very conflicting. The local papers express grave apprehensions as to the effect of the late rains and thunder storms, and these fears appear to be seriously entertained among dealers on the Corn Exchange, the prices of flour and grain having steadily gone up during the month. The journals located at the interior grain shipping centres report otherwise though, and more than an average crop is predicted.

The reopening of rail roads throughout the South has been actively progressing. The following table [page 43] exhibits their present condition.

THE REHABILITATION OF THE SOUTH

The question of the admission of the Southern delegations to Congress appears to be still the only subject discussed in our Legislative Halls at Washington. President Johnson also has, during the month, been visited by numerous delegations, and his opinions, with regard to the reorganization of the South, have been fully made known. Among others a Committee from the Senate and House of Delegates of Virginia, presented to the President a series of resolutions adopted by the General Assembly of that State on this subject. In reply, Mr. Johnson reiterated the principles which have actuated his

From	To	Miles	Remarks
Augusta	Millen	53	Part destroyed; remainder of road destroyed.
Atlanta	West Point	82	Four miles yet unbuilt.
Goldsboro	Morehead City	95	In running order throughout.
Montgomery	Pollard	71	Trains run through every other day.
Columbian	Charlotte	109	No repairs in progress.
Charleston	Savannah	104	No trains running, but repairs in progress.
Florence	Cheraw	40	Repairs will be completed in August.
Macon	Savannah	191	Badly destroyed; repairs in progress.
Dalton	Knoxville	110	Trains running through.
Knoxville	Bristol	130	Do do.
Pollard	Pensacola	50	Repairs in progress.
Augusta	Atlanta	171	Road and branches in good order and running.
Chester	Yorkville	24	Badly damaged.
West Point	Montgomery	88	Running 47 miles; repairs in progress.
Columbus	Union Springs	40	In good order and trains running.
Mobile	Columbus, Ky.	233	In running order to Corinth, Miss.
Atlanta	Macon	101	Running through.
Memphis	Stevenson, Ala.	272	Running to a point near Corinth.
Columbus	Butler, Ga.	50	Nearly repaired.
Canton	Jackson	237	Running to Oxford; further repairs progressing.
Memphis	Granada	97	Thirty-eight miles running; further repairs progressing.
New Orleans	Canton	206	Running from Summit; repairing north from New Orleans.
Nashville	Chattanooga	153	In operation.
Charlotte	Goldsboro, N. C.	223	Do.
Charleston	Florence	102	Repairs in progress.
Raleigh	Weldon	97	In operation.
Kingston	Rome, Ga.	97	Not in operation.
Macon	Albany	106	Trains running.

course, and gave further reasons for the policy adopted. After setting forth the position which he had taken during the recent civil war, he said:

I am gratified to meet you to-day, expressing the principles and enunciating the sentiments to which you have given utterance. I have no doubt that your intention is to carry out and comply with every principle laid down in the resolutions which you have submitted. I know that some of you are distrustful; but I am of those who have confidence in the judgment, in the integrity, in the intelligence, and in the virtue of the great mass of the American people, and having such confidence, I am willing to trust them; and I thank God that we have not yet reached that point where we have lost all confidence in each other. The spirit of the Government can only be preserved, we can only become prosperous and great as a people by mutual forbearance and confidence. Upon that faith and confidence alone can the Government be successfully carried on.

In these words of Mr. Johnson is embraced the single idea upon which depends the great issue now before the nation—Shall we or shall we not, trust the South? The President holds to the doctrine so emphatically expressed in his letter to General Slocum that "the people must be trusted with their Government." He is a Southern man, born and bred among that people, and has shown his devotion to his government by the readiness with which he sided against the majority in his own State at a time when patriotism in Tennessee cost something. We should be inclined, therefore, to place great confidence in the President's views, and especially in this instance when they are supported by the opinions of the leading military men who have had opportunities for judging. But aside from the views of the President and others, we believe that every consideration of national interest and of national pride, require the prosecution of the more generous policy.

We do not impugn the motives of those who think differently. It is natural that men who have given their best exertions, their lives, and the lives of those dear to them, to maintain the integrity of the Republic, should require ample security against a repetition of the controversy. They apprehend the revival, under some form, of the doctrine of secession, and the continuance of laws oppressive to the race that the war has enfranchised. We are convinced, however, that such fears are groundless. The South staked their all on the issue of the war. They lost; and now the heresies which gave rise to it, no power on earth could vitalize. The Constitutional Amendment has also denationalized slavery, and the people and the States are showing, through their legislatures, and through private contracts with the freedmen, the good faith with which they accept the situation.

This frank avowal of Mr. Johnson will, therefore, we are persuaded, be accepted in the same spirit in which it was made. It is not by the holding of the conquered party to extravagant and humiliating conditions that the Union is to be established anew, that civil law is to be maintained in the Southern commonwealths, and their prosperity restored to its former condition. Enough that the majesty of the nation has been asserted, and the problem of secession has been determined by the arbitrament of war, that the social system of the South, which many regarded as the original source of the mischief, has been overturned. The time for peace has come, and the duty of the

hour is restoration. The basis of this restoration must be mutual confidence, as the President has so clearly indicated. The Southern States must invite this by assuming a political attitude before the nation; the North, by cordial acceptance of their assurances.

The most important considerations of public interest demand this. When the war began, every one felt that the breaking up of the Union would involve the general disintegration of society, and endanger our national existence. The same feeling, rightly applied, must lead to the universal conviction that territorial dependence and military subjection of the Southern States, expose us to similar peril. We cannot safely permit a colonial system to grow up among us, tending as it does to concentrate power in the hands of the Executive, and to enlarge it even to the dimensions of imperialism. This was the real issue upon which our fathers fought in the revolution; and it is tangibly expressed in their watchword, the reason why John Hampden refused to pay ship-money,—"No taxation without representation." Till our Southern States are permitted to have their Senators and Representatives in Congress, they are but colonies of their sister commonwealths, and can have no joint interest in our great national system.

This disorganized condition is liable at any moment to operate unfavorably upon our foreign relations. We cannot press so boldly upon the British Government the settlement of the questions of international law arising out of the spoliations upon our commerce by privateers fitted out, manned and chartered in British ports; nor venture with proper assurance to demand the evacuation of Mexico. The general lawlessness existing in that Republic, and the weakness of the acknowledged Government, afford to Maximilian and his

COTTON EXPORTED FROM THE UNITED STATES.
[*Expressed in Thousands of Pounds.*]

	1858–59.	'59–60.	'60–61.	'61–62.	'62–63.	'63–64.	'64–65.
Sea Island lbs	13,713	15,599	6,170	66	528	133	330
Other Cottons	1,372,755	1,752,087	301,306	4,998	10,857	11,861	8,564
Total lbs	1,386,468	1,767,686	307,516*	6,064	11,385	11,994	8,894
From Boston, Mass.	2,752	3,103	12,850	178	174	101	9
New York, N.Y.	70,323	103,341	110,769	4,827	9,168	9,648	5,956
Philadelphia, Pa.	677	146	1,608	2	31	—	—
Baltimore, Md.	10	111	1,700	—	—	—	—
Charleston, S.C.	136,793	157,348	39,652	—	—	—	—
Savannah, Ga.	123,183	153,865	1,111	—	—	—	—
Mobile, Ala.	250,220	351,541	87,202	—	—	—	—
Key West, Fla.	656	3,319	1,169	—	—	—	—
Apalachicola, Fla.	22,292	2,427	913	—	—	—	—
New Orleans	743,596	922,748	31,539	—	1,862	2,192	†2,838
Texas (Galv'n &c)	35,636	56,255	11,472	—	—	—	—
Saluria, Tex.	155	808	741	—	—	—	—
Other Ports	181	2,619	615	57	149	53	92
To Russia	43,619	21,698	4,251	—	—	—	—
Sweden & Norway	11,033	11,663	583,851	—	—	—	—
Hamburg	9,556	12,081	3,305 ⎫	⎱ 8	—	⎱ 23	⎱ 49
Bremen	56,125	53,639	8,585 ⎰				92
Holland	16,156	12,757	2,659	—	13	—	—
Belgium	14,328	14,800	5,682	—	—	—	—
England ⎫	900,572	1,204,028	198,931 ⎫				
Scotland ⎬ United Kingdom	8,195	17,096	2,331 ⎬	3,545	9,840	9,651	7,289
Ireland ⎭	25,919	31,013	2,598 ⎭				
France	186,490	280,384	51,717	23	1,267	1,777	1,276
Spain	60,523	44,022	11,155	583	—	—	—
Italy	21,488	27,018	11,686	844	—	59	—
Austria	16,556	7,471	—	—	—	—	—
Mexico	5,994	9,043	1,411	—	—	417	—
Other countries	913	5,388	556	61	265	65	188

* As recorded without correction for the omission of actual exports for nearly three quarters at the leading Southern ports. Including these the Treasury Department estimates the total export at 1,750,000,000 pounds, valued at $185,000,000.

† No returns from New Orleans for the quarter ending June 30, 1865.

Gallican sponsor a pretext for their armed occupation almost as good as our own for military subjection of two-thirds of our own territory. So long as this state of affairs remains, the possession of that territory is a source of relative national weakness. Every foreign statesman knows this, and the diplomatic correspondence of Messrs. Seward and Adams cannot disprove so palpable a fact. It has been the great difficulty in our foreign intercourse; and we appreciate the feelings of the President when he declares that—

The moment it can be announced that the Union of the States is again complete, that we have resumed our career of prosperity and greatness, at that very instant almost all our foreign difficulties will be settled. For there is no power on earth which will care to have a controversy or a rupture with the Government of the United States, under such circumstances.

We wish most earnestly that Congress could take as broad and just a view of this question.

But most of all it is necessary to the prosperity of the country that this policy should be speedily put into operation. The vast region lately overrun by war was the garden of the Republic, and furnished to our export trade the staples which gave us our commercial preponderance in the markets of the world. In this connection the table [on page 45] will be of interest, showing the exports of cotton from the United States during the last seven fiscal years, distinguishing the ports from which it was shipped, and the countries of its destination. The figures for the year ending June 30, 1856, we have obtained from the Treasury Department at Washington through the politeness of the Register; the figures for the other years were also compiled from the records of that office.

In the year before the war, besides the production of manufacturers to the value of over $200,000,000, and the supply of raw material to New England and the North, the South sent to Europe cotton, tobacco, rice, &c., to the value of about $210,000,000. Now that the incubus of slavery has been removed, there is every reason to expect the speedy restoration of that commerce and home production. Freedmen having an interest in the products of their industry, take the place of slaves, while mechanical ingenuity is set free to make agriculture more productive, and immigration is afforded a new and more attractive field. Mr. Johnson is amply warranted in his sanguine declaration that if all the States were restored, all the industrial pursuits and avocations of peace again resumed, the day could not be far distant when the United States would put into the commerce of the world cotton and tobacco to the value of $250,000,000 to $300,-000,000. With such a result we would not long be compelled to see our bonds quoted in Europe at only about two-thirds their par value. Our men of business would not, as at present, be holding back from investment and active operations, for fear that they would be suddenly arrested in their progress by financial revolution. The population of the Southern States, inured by the experience of war to greater familiarity with practical life and activity, and possessing in their soil, their mines and climate, the elements of incalculable wealth, would soon divide with us the national burdens and aid us in increasing manifold the resources of our common country.

But, in order that we may develope the wealth of the South, all political questions must be settled, so that peace and security may become universal. The South has lost its capital, and has not of itself the ability to resume, on a large scale, the cultivation of cotton. At the same time, the means of transportation are greatly crippled, while the plantations have been devastated, so that gin-houses, machinery, agricultural implements, fences, &c., will have to be provided anew. How is the capital to be attracted that is to supply these necessary wants? Alone by ensuring large profits; and this can only be by encouraging, in every possible way, those attempting the cultivation of cotton in the South, and, above all, by giving to capital the security of a civil government. We have again the opportunity, and it brings with it the duty, to occupy the first place in the markets of the world. The same natural advantages we have always possessed remain to us, the same laboring population are there ready to engage in the culture, and with an interest in the result which must add largely to the profit of both the laborer and the employer. Besides, machinery can be used instead of old negro hoes to prepare the soil, and emigration from Europe will add largely to the volume of industry. If, therefore, we can encourage the production now, capital will be attracted to the South, the waste of the war will be supplied, and the future condition of our country cannot be doubtful.

It must be remembered too that this country has not the monopoly in cotton production which previous to the war many supposed it had. High prices have led to its cultivation elsewhere, and to-day the Egyptian staple commands a higher price than the American. Brazil and India have also furnished large supplies. It depends upon ourselves whether this will be continued until increased facilities in those new countries for producing and bringing to market this much needed staple, shall enable them to compete with us. The following tables furnish at a glance the history of cotton the past few years. The first gives the imports, &c., from the United States separately, and the total from other sources during the last four years.

The following shows the amount (in thousands of bales reduced to an uniform weight of 400 pounds) supplied from the several producing countries, and the amount delivered for consumption in the years 1860, 1863, '64, and '65.

These figures demonstrate the fact,

IMPORTS, STOCK AND CONSUMPTION OF COTTON IN EUROPE, 1862–65.
[Expressed in thousands of bales.]

	1862 U.S.	1862 Total.	1863 U.S.	1863 Total.	1864 U.S.	1864 Total.	1865 U.S.	1865 Total.
STOCK, January 1	434,	883,	88,	507,	42,	364,	24,	648,
IMPORT—G. Britain	72,	1,445,	132,	1,932,	198,	2,587,	462,	2,755,
France	24,	225,	8,	315,	15,	429,	36,	560,
Holland	11,	74,	10,	136,	9,	119,	7,	101,
Belgium	1,	17,	—	37,	1,	22,	6,	75,
Germany	5,	98,	11,	158,	6,	181,	12,	258,
Trieste	—	32,	—	26,	—	28,	1,	56,
Genoa	1,	10,	1,	23,	—	18,	—	27,
Spain	18,	73,	6,	106,	12,	92,	6,	93,
	132,	1,974,	168,	2,733,	241,	3,476,	530,	3,925,
Deduct intermediate shipments	38,	388,	19,	514,	21,	468,	37,	659,
NEW SUPPLY	94,	1,586,	149,	2,219,	220,	3,008,	493,	3,266,
Add stock from above	434,	883,	88,	507,	42,	364,	24,	648,
TOTAL SUPPLY	528,	2,469,	227,	2,726,	262,	3,372,	517,	3,914,
Deduct stock Dec. 31,	88,	507,	42,	364,	24,	648,	155,	466,
TOTAL DELIVERIES	440,	1,962,	195,	2,362,	238,	2,724,	362,	3,448

SUPPLIES AND CONSUMPTION OF COTTON IN EUROPE 1860 AND 1863–65.
[Expressed in thousands of bales of 400 pounds.]

	1860. Imp.	1860. Con.	1863. Imp.	1863. Con.	1864. Imp.	1864. Con.	1865. Imp.	1865. Con.
United States	3,551,	3,384,	164,	214,	281,	261,	522,	386,
Brazil	106,	125,	67,	80,	117,	113,	149,	140,
West Indies	47,	46,	36,	34,	40,	37,	84,	80,
East Indies	573,	524,	1,258,	1,317,	1,607,	1,372,	1,320,	1,626,
Mediterranean	158,	145,	472,	477,	650,	638,	837,	834,
Total	4,435,)	4,224,	1,997,)	2,122,	2,655,)	2,421,	2,912,)	3,066,
OLD STOCK	571,)		451,)		326,)		560,)	

that with cotton at the present high prices the sources of supply can be greatly multiplied; yet with lower prices there is no prospect that any of the countries which have of late years become the dependence for European consumption will be able to keep up their unusual supply. In fact even now India, fearing the resumption of the cotton supply from America, has begun to turn its attention to the cultivation of other staples. In the Presidency of Madras there was on the 31st of October only 931,727 acres of cotton under cultivation, whereas in the previous year there had been 1,663,300 acres, showing a decrease of 131,670 acres in one year. All that is necessary for us to do is to encourage the flow of capital south by taking away as soon as possible military rule and stimulating the production so that lower prices may drive out all competition.

Hence, we see that every consideration of national interest and public policy, requires the early rehabilitation of the Southern States and their restoration to the family of Union; and the President's eagerness to lay aside the extraordinary powers which the exigencies of the war had conferred upon him, affords the highest proof of his sincerity and patriotism. We want the aid of Southern statesmen to solve the problem of necessary legislation for the South, and it is damaging to the best interests of the country to dispense with it any longer; we want the moral influence of a united country in adjusting our foreign relations; and, perhaps more than all, we want capital attracted to the South, and its industry and wealth free to develope itself, and this cannot be, so long as the States are under semi-military rule.

III. RECENT INTERPRETATIONS

The following three selections could serve as a modern counterpoint to the earlier historians already presented in the chapter. Brock, for example, takes recurrent issue with the traditional version (embodied in Bower's argument) of the Washington political crisis over reconstruction policy in 1865–1866. His sympathies are with the Radicals and their aspirations, yet Brock manages to clarify the major political and constitutional factors which operated against the success of Radical Southern policy. John Hope Franklin takes aim at the standard account of Negro "atrocities" and "barbarities" during "Black Reconstruction" and, himself a Negro, presents a balanced account of the freedmen's achievements, failures, and unresolved problems. Finally, Irwin Unger's recent study of reconstruction finance revises and deepens our understanding of the relationship between group interest and economic policy-making in the post-Civil War era. Unger demonstrates the impossibility of treating the business community during this period as if it held a single set of perspectives on any political or economic question, and he criticizes severely the reigning Beardian analysis of business response to problems of reconstruction politics and finance.

W. R. BROCK

THE NATURE OF THE CRISIS

Reconstruction presented the United States with a probing challenge to their institutions and political beliefs, and it cannot be understood at the superficial level of recrimination and apologetics. It followed upon the greatest failure in American history, and it is intimately bound up with the subsequent failure to solve the problems of a bi-racial society or to produce real harmony between the North and the South. It has been tempting to find scapegoats to bear the responsibility for failure and there has been a tendency to blame individuals and groups rather than to appreciate the character of the Reconstruction crisis. Books have been written upon the assumption that a little good-will and a little good sense could have combined reconciliation with justice to all, while ignoring the fact that after April 1861 nothing could ever be the same again. When war broke out the argument over constitutional obligations, the rights of States or the extension of slavery, ceased; thereafter the question was simply which side would gather enough force and show sufficient pertinacity to win. When the South surrendered the Northern forces remained in command of the situation, and with the power to act went the necessity of decision. Whatever happened in the South—whether it were a resumption of the old life or a revolutionary departure—must be the result of Northern decision. Responsibility

Reprinted from W. R. Brock, AN AMERICAN CRISIS: CONGRESS AND RECONSTRUCTION, 1865–1867 (New York: St. Martin's Press, Inc., 1963), pp. 1–9, 13–14, 284–285, 300–304, by permission of the publisher.

lay with the power which had won the military victory, and it could not be avoided by pretending that the page could be turned back to 1861. It is the purpose of this book to examine the nature of that responsibility, the interpretations placed upon it by those who had to act, and the arguments which produced the decision reached by the Northern people through their elected representatives.

It is a great error to suppose that the ideals enunciated by people during war are insincere and that their force evaporates when the fighting ends. The catastrophe of war had cut deeply into the emotions and forced men to decide for themselves why, how, and with what objectives it was necessary to fight. Ideas which had been dimly perceived before the war emerged as clear-cut propositions, and views which had been held by small minorities suddenly became great national convictions. It was a war to preserve the Union, and a good many men hoped that it need be no more than that; but the political and material ascendancy of the Union was too cold a cause to sustain the will and enthusiasm of a people trained in idealistic modes of thought. Two years after the end of the war a sober Northern journal, catering for educated opinion, could assert editorially that 'if there be anything which the press, the pulpit, the prayers, the hymns, the conversations of the North have been emphatic in affirming during the last six years, it is that the late war was not merely a contest for empire, as Earl Russell called it, not merely a struggle to settle a political difference, but a struggle between moral right and moral wrong. . . . We took a far higher than political ground. We said that the rebellion was an immoral enterprise, conceived and carried out not by mistaken men, but by bad and unscrupulous men, animated by corrupt and selfish motives, and determined to gain their ends at whatever cost or suffering to others'. It is impossible to understand the crisis of Reconstruction unless one also understands the depth, extent and sincerity of feelings such as these; and whether they were justified or unjustified it is an idle hypothesis to suppose that people who had fought through a soul-searing war would calmly abandon ideals which had been so loudly proclaimed. The war had been started to preserve the Union, but for the majority in the victorious North it had become a war to create a more perfect Union.

In July 1861 Lincoln had described the war as 'essentially a people's contest' to preserve that form of government 'whose aim was the betterment of mankind'. The idea of defending a form of government was easily translated into the need to eradicate those elements in American society which had threatened American government with failure. At the end of the war there might be malice towards none, but in the meantime Northern propaganda had sown deep in the Northern mind a picture of all the evils propagated and preserved by the leaders of the South. It was not only a political clique but a whole system of society which fell under the axe of condemnation; the South had to be fought not only because it had broken the Union but because 'aristocracy' and forced labour were incompatible with American aims. It was not only necessary to defeat the South but also to democratize it, and of all needs the first was the abolition of slavery. In a famous letter Lincoln told Horace Greeley that his sole object was to save the Union, and that if he could save it without touching slavery he would do so; but when

this letter was written Lincoln had already drafted the Emancipation Proclamation and was waiting only for an expedient opportunity to issue it. The process by which the character of the war was changed was described in oversimplified but illuminating terms by Senator Stewart of Nevada: 'We commenced to force the Southern people to obey the Constitution. We said they had no right to secede. That was the first proposition. In the progress of the war it was ascertained that the negro had become an element of strength to the South . . . and President Lincoln, patriotically and properly, thank God, had the boldness to issue his proclamation and strike a blow at the war power. We then declared, and the nation's honour was pledged, that we would maintain for the negro his freedom. Then the issue became the Union and the freedom of the negro.' Indeed the end of slavery came to assume ever greater significance in Northern eyes; if the passions of war looked less happy as enthusiasm cooled, if the 'democratization' of the South was too elusive and too much in conflict with treasured notions of local self-government, the abolition of slavery stood forth as a single, simple and essential contribution to the betterment of mankind. But was the achievement a simple one? If the negro was not a slave, what was he? And who would decide?

. . . In fact negro status stood at the heart of the whole Reconstruction problem and presented a devastating challenge to American civilization. In October 1867 *The Nation* summed it up by saying that 'We boast of having gone beyond others in social and political science, but we have at last come to a place where the claim is to be most solemnly tested. This question of race is put before us as stone of stumbling, or a rock of exaltation. It is for the rising or falling of our Israel. . . . Over and over again, in every form but one, have we set forth the principle of human equality before the law. We have boasted of our land as the free home of all races. We have insulted other nations with the vehemence of our declamation. And now we are brought face to face with a question that will test it all. . . . Is the negro a man? Say what we will, this is the real issue in the controversy respecting him'.

If one preoccupation of Reconstruction was with the poorest in the land, the other was with the men who were to fill the highest offices and provide government for the people. The Confederate leaders were the avowed enemies of the Union and countless Northerners held them personally responsible for the war and all its losses. It was a perfectly proper question to ask whether these men could be allowed to continue to rule in their States and to resume their old power in the national government. Yet side by side with this problem was the indubitable fact that the war had been fought to force the Southern States to remain as States in the Union and, if States in the Union were to be denied the right to place in office those whom their people chose, a traditional bastion of American Federal government would have fallen. Many Northern Americans believed that State rights had been the cause of the war, but few emerged from the war with any clear idea of the way in which the rights of States could or ought to be modified. Were the States to be denied the right to do wrong, to elect the wrong people, or to commit whatever folly the local majority might sanction? Again it was idle to suppose that these questions could be ignored, or answered by reference back to the Constitution as it was in 1861. The words

of the precious document might remain unaltered but the people for whom it was provided had changed.

To Charles Sumner 'the problem of reconstruction did not appear perplexing at all'. He believed that the Declaration of Independence was the charter document incorporating the American nation and that the Constitution must be interpreted in the light of its assertion of self-evident equality and inalienable rights. On the other side Democrats became frantic when confronted with the suggestion that the work of their great Founding Father could be invoked to justify an attack upon the rights of States. The right to amend was, of course, a part of the Constitution, and the principles of the Declaration could well be added in this way, but it might be argued that the Constitution could not be amended without the participation of all the States. Many Republicans were inclined to agree that there was no power in the Declaration to control interpretation of the Constitution, and were troubled by the thought that an amendment made only by the loyal States might be legally invalid. Yet everyone knew that any proposed amendments must affect adversely the Southern States and that once in Congress they would have power to block them for ever. It might have been simplest to do what Thaddeus Stevens wished: to regard the Constitution as suspended, to alter it as might be necessary to guarantee the results of the war, and to present the amended document as the Constitution to which 'rebels' must swear allegiance. But in a world governed by lawyers the idea of suspending the Constitution seemed to offer far more difficulties than remedies, and the majority of Republicans preferred to get the illogical best of both worlds by excluding the Southern States from participating in the making of amendments, but by asking them to ratify, and then making ratification an explicit or implicit condition for re-admission to Congress. This constitutional tangle, and the other means by which the Republican majority sought to keep within the Constitution while breaking it, has been made a standing reproach by those who wish to discredit congressional Reconstruction. It might be fairer to ask whether the Constitution itself was not responsible for many of the difficulties and whether an instrument of government which had failed deserved the veneration which a subsequent generation bestowed upon it.

Within the national government the problems of Reconstruction imposed a severe strain upon the system of checks and balances. The outstanding political novelty of the crisis was the solidarity of the Republican party. At no other period did an American party stand together with such consistency. The Fourteenth and Fifteenth Amendments both obtained the necessary two-thirds in both Houses of Congress. Of President Johnson's seven vetoes of major Reconstruction bills only the first failed —by one vote in the Senate—to win re-passage by the requisite two-thirds. In addition the Republicans won a resounding electoral victory in 1866 half-way through the Reconstruction controversy. It has sometimes been customary to dismiss this record with a sneering reference to 'strict party votes' though it is never explained how the party whip was applied or why party loyalty should be regarded as discreditable. In fact the Republicans could hardly fail to be conscious of the weight of opinion behind them, and it was not unexpected that they should have spoken of themselves as national representatives of the national will, and regarded a President who had been re-

pudiated and a Supreme Court which represented no one and still contained members who had concurred in the notorious Dred Scott decision as their inferiors in the scales of popular government. Legislative supremacy looked more logical, more desirable and more just than executive encroachments or judicial usurpations. . . .

The political controversies over Reconstruction took place at a significant moment in American economic history. The war had distorted and in some cases retarded the development of the Northern economy and it had ruined the economy of the South but, as it ended, the United States were on the threshold of a great age of expansion. The first benefits of growth were enjoyed by the economy of the Northeast, the middle Atlantic and the Midwestern States; the less-developed regions of the South and West were certain to feel the impact of this vigorous society mesmerized by the benefits to be gained from entrepreneurial activity. In a sense political Reconstruction reflected the economic tension between developed and under-developed societies, but it would be an error to oversimplify the relationship between economic and political aims. The great political upheaval which lay behind congressional Reconstruction is not to be explained by the aims of comparatively small business groups. The Republican party was predominantly the party of the small entrepreneur—both in farming and in manufacturing—and of the small towns. Its heartland was the Midwestern rural region where everyone was interested in economic betterment and small towns were established with amazing rapidity as commercial, marketing and manufacturing centres. On specific economic issues there was, however, little agreement within the party. Leading Radicals professed currency heresies which were equally shocking to old Jacksonian hard money men and to banker adherents of the gold standard. The tariff tended to divide Eastern from Western Republicans, and among the Easterners there was often a sharp difference of opinion upon what should be protected. Many Republicans carried on the old anti-monopoly theme which was most unpleasing to railway promoters and operators, and some Radicals were beginning to interest themselves in labour causes such as the eight hour day. Disagreement upon these economic questions was muted because men felt that the political questions of Reconstruction were more urgent and more important. It was the crisis of Reconstruction which gave solidarity to the Republican party not the economic aspirations of business.

At a more profound level it is possible to seek a reconciliation between political and economic aims of the Northern and Midwestern society. If men differed about the incidence of economic policy, they agreed upon the great benefits to be expected from economic enterprise, and the South had a long record of obstruction to railway land grants, homestead laws, internal improvements and tariffs. The Northern and Midwestern society was not united in its opposition to the Southern economic policy, but almost every part of it had reason to regard the former policy of the South as having been, at some point, harmful and obstructive. The picture of the South as the enemy of economic progress completed the picture of the South as opposed to that government whose object was the betterment of mankind. Like their English contemporaries, the Gladstonian Liberals, the Republicans saw moral and material progress as two aspects of the same great movement, and the crisis of Reconstruction was a part of the world-wide crisis of the nineteenth-century liberal tradition.

. . .

At the heart of the Reconstruction crisis was a momentous question about the character of national existence. It was framed most often with reference to the vexed question of loyalty. What did it mean to be a loyal American? Was it enough to give formal allegiance to the Constitution, or did it mean acceptance of a once despised but now triumphant political doctrine? In February 1865 a respected Republican senator, Jacob Collamer of Vermont, asked when Congress ought to admit the Southern States back into full membership of the Union, and answered that 'It is not enough that they should stop their hostility and are repentant. They should present fruits meet for repentance. They should furnish us by their actions some evidence that the condition of loyalty and obedience is their true condition again'. This typical Republican comment confused the loyalty of individuals with the loyalty of States, substituted a vague concept of a change of heart for precise and legal tests, and left unspecified the conditions of real loyalty. But if there was no such 'loyalty', how could the nation ever be reunited and safe from its enemies? If the Southerners of 1865 had been ready, like the Germans of 1945, to repudiate their leaders and their past, it might have been possible to solve the problem in political terms; as they were not, all that could be done was to ask for 'guarantees' of Southern good behaviour and to treat their formal professions of loyalty as insufficient.

A new concept of national existence demanded a new construction of the Union. Once it had been defended as an expedient; then it had gathered symbolical power; now it must have an ideological core. It must be dedicated to a belief in equal rights, and the faithless could not be considered as true Americans. It seemed self-evident that anything less would be a betrayal of those who had died, and this was not the mere rhetoric of politicians but the profound reaction of millions who had been touched by the agonies of war. The restoration of the Southern States was not enough without a reconstruction of Southern minds. On the one hand was an unshakable confidence in the justice and morality of the Northern cause, and on the other a deep-seated and popular conservatism sustained by traditional modes of life. Reconstruction was an ideological struggle, and the crisis must be understood in emotional terms and not merely as a record of personal rivalries, conflicting interests and political manoeuvre. This was the true crisis of Reconstruction.

. . .

It is comparatively easy to explain the waning of Radicalism in terms of personal failure, evaporating enthusiasm, the urgent demands of business, and the tendency of all political organizations to fall into the hands of professionals. It is easy also to see how the challenge of the new age, with its manifest problems of the relationship between private business and public authority, had a divisive effect upon the Radicals—turning Kelley into a fanatical protectionist, Schurz into a free trader, Butler into a Greenbacker, and Donnelly into an agrarian radical—while drawing together the main body of Republicans around the citadel of American capitalism. But the break-up of Radicalism may also reflect more profound weaknesses in the position which it maintained.

It has been argued that much of the Radical success was explained by the pressures from below which drove cautious politicians even further than they had intended, and that this pressure must be explained in ideological terms and not as the product of mere interest groups. The ideology had expressed in abstract but attractive terms certain propositions about man in society which, for a moment in time, seemed to epitomise the aspirations of the Northern people. Racial equality, equal rights and the use of national authority to secure both were living ideas in the Reconstruction era as they have since become, in some quarters, in the mid-twentieth century. For the first time these concepts were cast in the form of a political programme which could be achieved; but their success depended upon the response which they aroused from the Northern people. After Reconstruction the ideas persisted but failed to rouse the same enthusiasm; their formal acceptance was a very different thing from the popular emotion which could push them forward despite the usual obstacles to policies which disturb complacency and refuse to let men rest in peace. The question remains whether the slackening of the pressure behind the Radical ideology should be explained by rival distractions and changing interests or by a weakness in the ideology itself. Examination will show that the generalities of the Radical ideology—so attractive at first sight—could not stand pressure. The weapons bent and broke in the hands of those who used them.

. . .

In their presentation of the case for national power the Radicals were inhibited by conventional American and nineteenth-century political thought. While the old Whigs, whose ideas they inherited, had believed in more positive action by the national government than their Democratic opponents, they had never thought of writing a blank cheque for government intervention. What they wanted was Federal responsibility for the performance of certain economic functions defined by the economic interests concerned, and since that time the concepts of *laissez-faire* had tended to narrow the sphere of action which business interests were likely to prescribe for government. Northern intellectuals who were attracted by the political aims of Reconstruction were precisely those who were equally attracted by the utopian elements in *laissez-faire,* by the theory of natural harmony, and by the faith in betterment through individual enterprise. The government was therefore being asked to 'secure the blessings of liberty' at the very time when it was being asked to contract its responsibility for 'promoting the general welfare', and the hope of securing civil justice for the Southern negro was not coupled with the expectation of securing social justice for the Northern farmer and worker. Thus the Radicals' concept of national power was too wide to satisfy conservative men but not wide enough to gather support from the nineteenth-century movements of protest.

Even if the concept of national power had not suffered from these inherent weaknesses it would still have had a precarious hold upon the nation. Radical Reconstruction declared certain principles of national responsibility but it did nothing to create the institutions of government which could give these principles a permanent place on the national stage. The Freedmen's Bureau was such an institution but even its friends recognized that its life must be limited. The Fourteenth Amendment left the door open for Congress to make laws which would enforce the civil rights clause, but it did not make it mandatory for Con-

gress to do so and the assumption was that the law would be self-enforcing through the existing machinery of government and courts. The initiative remained with the traditional instruments of government—with the President, with the judges and with the States themselves—and no new instruments of government were brought into being. One can contrast this with the experience of the New Deal with its proliferation of governmental agencies; when enthusiasm receded the administrative achievement remained, and many Americans (ranging from highly paid government servants to the very poor) had acquired a vested interest in these new institutions. When Radical enthusiasm withered away it left behind it no such institutional bulwarks, and when the Freedmen's Bureau expired there remained no new government departments, no new government agencies, and no administrative doctrine to carry out those obligations to citizens of the United States of which so much had been heard.

The arguments which have been presented in the preceding pages have attempted to show why the ideology of Radical Republicanism, which appeared so powerful during the crisis of Reconstruction, failed to gather that momentum which could have carried it forward in the years which followed. It is of course exceedingly improbable that the Radicals of the Reconstruction period could have conceived their problems in any other way or that they could have gone on to produce the ideas and institutions which would have corrected the weaknesses in their edifice. Radicalism shared the weaknesses of all liberal bourgeois movements of the nineteenth century, and it would have required a far more profound revolution in thought and action to make them view their situation through the eyes of twentieth-century liberals. In their equalitarian sentiments, in their realization that individual rights might be incompatible with local self-government, and in their attitude towards national power they were prophets of the future; yet they remained children of their age and were bound by its assumptions and inhibitions. And even if their vision occasionally transcended these limitations they were unlikely to persuade the majority of their countrymen that the revolution which they had initiated ought to proceed to further innovation. The failure of Radicalism is thus a part of the wider failure of bourgeois liberalism to solve the problems of the new age which was dawning; but having said this it is important to remember that if the Radicals shared in the weaknesses of their age they also had some achievements which were exceptional.

First among civilized nations the United States had met the problems of a bi-racial society, and first among civilized nations they had committed themselves to the proposition that in such a society human beings must have equal rights. If the definition of 'rights' was confused the idea that they must be recognized was clear. The civil rights clause of the Fourteenth Amendment was in many ways unsatisfactory, but it contained explosive material which could shatter the lines of racial discrimination. The United States had committed themselves to the statement that suffrage should be colour-blind, and if the phrasing of the Fifteenth Amendment invited evasion the principle which it enunciated would outlive attempts to defeat it. Americans may well differ upon the wisdom of these equalitarian ideas, but it is impossible to deny their importance for the future. The Fourteenth and Fifteenth Amendments could have been enacted only during the period of Reconstruction, and without them the subsequent history of the United States would have been very different. Not least important has been their effect upon the negro race in America, for the knowledge that the goals of negro aspiration are already written into the Constitution has had the powerful consequence of turning American negroes aside from thoughts of revolution. In his quest for equality the negro appeals to established national law and not against it, and one of the most striking developments of twentieth-century history has been the failure of Communists amongst a people who had many reasons for dissatisfaction. The constitutional amendments had an equally powerful effect upon Northern thought. If Northern opinion, in the later years of the nineteenth century, was not prepared to implement the principles of the amendments, they were not removed from the Constitution and were to become the basis for further thought about the problem of race in America and in the world at large. It is possible to attribute the modern American hostility to 'colonialism' —which so often embarrasses the European allies of the United States—to memories of the Revolution, to ingrained suspicion of Great Britain and to mere calculation about the changing balance of power in the world; but it is equally significant that during Reconstruction Americans rejected the idea that law should recognize the 'inferiority' of non-European races. These are not unimportant consequences and may serve to lighten the gloom with which Americans have been accustomed to regard the crisis of Reconstruction.

The great failure of Radical Reconstruction lay in its attempt to remould Southern Society. Hypothetical arguments may be produced to show that the attempt should never have been made, or that it was not made thoroughly enough, that too much or too little pressure was applied to the white people of the South; all that the historian can do is to record that the attempt as made did not produce the immediate results for which Radicals hoped. If it is believed that nothing should have been done the responsibility of the Radicals for having done something is clear; if it is believed that not enough was done it has been argued that moderate pressure nor Radical initiative laid the ground for a Southern counter-revolution. Radicals argued at the outset that compromise and conservatism were not the principles with which to meet an unprecedented situation, and though one may blame them for their determination to have a revolution it is a little unfair to blame them for being forced to stop half-way. On the other hand if the revolution was going to stop half-way it is fair to blame the Radicals for insisting upon the alienation of the Southern ruling class whose support was vital for any compromise solution. It can be shown—and it is likely that the evidence will gather weight—that the Reconstruction governments in the South were not so bad as they have been painted in the Southern picture, but no amount of argument is likely to convince anyone that they were successful governments. This book has been concerned with the ideas and motives of Northern Reconstruction policy and not with the consequences of that policy in the South. It is true that the policy cannot be divorced from its consequences but motives cannot be judged from results. The authors of Reconstruction policy did not intend that it should perpetuate racial antagonism in Southern society, discredit colour-blind democracy, and provide further ammunition for Southern attacks upon the North. They were not disunionists, as

Andrew Johnson called them, but they believed that the old Union, containing elements which could not combine, must be reconstructed. They hoped that the preamble to the Declaration of Independence should become the new formula for national existence, and they hoped to endow the national government with the power to ensure this result. These ideas were not negligible, absurd or unworthy. Their presentation was marred by a bitterness which was the legacy of war but was sometimes redeemed by the idealistic impulses which war had released. They left a record of failure in the South and permanent alterations in the law of a great nation. They faced intractable problems which still vex the modern world and they anticipated many of the assumptions with which men now tackle these problems. There was tragedy in the crisis of Reconstruction, but the tragic element transcends the particular circumstances of the post-war era and belongs to the whole condition of modern man.

JOHN HOPE FRANKLIN

It would, of course, be folly to suggest that we now have an adequate picture of the Negro during Reconstruction. We still know *all too little* about the relationship between Negroes, Carpetbaggers, and Scalawags. The picture of the Negro in Congress is far from complete. What kind of party men were they; were they race men or merely the representatives of their congressional districts? No one has yet given us a full account of the Negro in the early

Reprinted from John Hope Franklin, "Reconstruction and the Negro," in NEW FRONTIERS OF THE AMERICAN RECONSTRUCTION, *ed. Harold Hyman (Urbana, Ill.: University of Illinois Press, 1967), pp. 64–76, by permission of the publisher.*

days of peace: what the role was of the Negro conventions in 1865 and 1866, how many actually were in a position to assume leadership roles, and what they wanted from the state and federal governments. We need to know a great deal more than we know about Negro *office-holders* at the *state and local* levels and the reactions of Negroes to the growing indifference of the federal government to their needs and their plights as well as their aspirations. In other words, we have *just begun* to see the results of the extensive reexamination of the role of the Negro during Reconstruction, and it would not be too much to say that at least some of the recent works could themselves bear critical examination.

Despite the fact that the student of Reconstruction can hardly be satisfied with what is now known about the Negro's role, he already has sufficient knowledge to conclude that some modification of the old view is fully justified. It would be well, therefore, to take notice of some of the new ways of looking at the problem and to examine their implications for the study of the general problem of Reconstruction.

. . .

As historians have viewed the early weeks and months following the close of the Civil War, they have had a good deal to say about the desperate plight of the freedmen. It is, of course, difficult to exaggerate this situation, and there has been much emphasis on the freedman's lack of competence to care for himself in a condition of freedom. Indeed, there has been much emphasis on the freedman who, in consequence of his ignorance and inexperience, was the ready prey of any and all who might seek to exploit him. There was more than a semblance of truth in this as it applied to the vast majority of Negroes. This view does not, however, give sufficient consideration to the not inconsiderable

number of Negroes who, by training and experience, were quite prepared in 1865 to take care of themselves and even to assume some leadership roles.

In 1860 there were some 488,000 free Negroes in the United States, of whom 261,000—slightly more than one-half—lived in the slave states. Although the teaching of slaves and free Negroes to read and write was strictly forbidden by law in the slave states, thousands of slaves and free Negroes actually became literate. There were clandestine schools for Negroes in many communities in the South. In 1850, according to the census returns, there were 68 free Negroes attending school in Charleston, 53 in Mobile, 1,008 in New Orleans, and 1,453 in Baltimore. In numerous instances slaveholders taught their human chattel to read and write. Laws forbidding the teaching of slaves were for people on the other plantations; masters did whatever they pleased regarding their own slaves. And if they saw fit, they taught their slaves to read and write. Frederick Douglass received his first instruction from his mistress. Isaiah T. Montgomery of Mississippi received sufficient training to become the confidential accountant for his master, the brother of Jefferson Davis.

Meanwhile, Negroes were attending schools in many parts of the North. In 1850 there were more than 2,000 Negroes in Philadelphia; New York and Boston reported more than 1,400 each, while cities such as Providence, Brooklyn, New Haven, and Cincinnati each had several hundred Negroes in school. In some communities, such as Boston after 1855, they attended desegregated schools, while in other communities segregated education was the rule. In any case, the number of literate Negroes was steadily increasing.

It might actually be possible to compile some rather impressive figures on

Negro literacy, especially when one recalls that many Negroes were educated abroad and when one adds to this number those who began their education in schools established by religious and philanthropic agencies during the war years. The point, however, is not to emphasize the general increase in literacy among Negroes—important as that may be—but to underscore the fact that by the end of the Civil War thousands of Negroes in the North and South were able to read and write. A further point is that in their various organizations—religious and benevolent—Negroes had opportunities to use their education and acquire experience in the management of their affairs.

One of the best proofs we have of the level of literacy and education of a considerable group of Negroes by 1865 is in their organizational activities. Within the first year following the close of the war Negroes in the North and South met in conventions to consider their common problems. These are the months that many historians have described as months of wandering and drifting on the part of the freedmen. Many of them did drift—from place to place—to "test" their freedom. Others, however, did not drift. Instead, they met in convention at Alexandria, Norfolk, Raleigh, Savannah, Charleston, Vicksburg, Nashville, and Cleveland to give attention to the problems they faced. The deliberations were orderly and dignified, and they were carefully recorded.

It is not too much to say that some of the representations made by these all-Negro conventions in 1865 are eloquent, and they give evidence not only of ample training but of a degree of understanding of the function of government that must have surprised many observers. For example, in their letter to President Andrew Johnson in May,

1865, a group of North Carolina Negroes said:

> Some of us are soldiers and have had the privilege of fighting for our country in this war. Since we have become Freemen, and been permitted the honor of being soldiers, we begin to feel that we are men, and are anxious to show our countrymen that we can and will fit ourselves for the creditable discharge of the duties of citizenship. We want the privilege of voting. It seems to us that men who are willing on the field of danger to carry the muskets of Republics in the days of peace ought to be permitted to carry its ballots; and certainly we cannot understand the justice of denying the elective franchise to men who have been fighting for the country, while it is freely given to men who have just returned from four years fighting against it.

These are the words of literate people, perfectly capable of thinking through their problems and perfectly aware of their betrayal by their own government.

During these years, thanks to the increasing educational opportunities provided by the Freedmen's Bureau and other agencies and thanks to their own organizational activities, many Negroes were rapidly assimilating the training and experience they needed to become participants in the affairs of their government. . . .

The absence of protection for the former slaves in the crucial first years following the end of the Civil War is one of the very remarkable phenomena of the early Reconstruction era. Even if one should argue—unsuccessfully, I believe—that the former masters continued to have the best interests of their former slaves in mind, there were the millions of whites, indeed the vast majority of southern whites, who had not been slaveholders. Many of them had much antipathy not only for the institution of slavery but for slaves as well. Whatever the attitude of former slaveholders or of nonslaveholders, the freedmen were left exposed to them and at their mercy. This was, of course, because of the rapid demobilization of the Union Army and the preoccupation of the military leaders with that process.

From the time that the Secretary of War issued the demobilization order on April 28, 1865, the troops were to be mustered out at the staggering rate of 300,000 per month. It was simply impossible to process that many men with the machinery in existence, but a vigorous effort was made to comply with the order. Within six months after the war's end more than 800,000 of the 1,034,064 officers and men in the United States Army had been demobilized. By the end of 1865 the government had 150,000 troops for all purposes, including garrisoning frontier posts and fighting the Indians, as well as supervising postwar operations in the South. Thus, by the end of December, 1865, North and South Carolina had 352 officers and 7,056 enlisted men. In the entire Division of the Gulf the number of white troops had been reduced to 10,000 men. There were vast stretches of territory in the former Confederacy where no Union soldier appeared after the late spring of 1865.

By the close of the Civil War some 186,000 Negroes had seen service in the Army of the United States. They were not demobilized at quite the rate of white soldiers. They had no businesses and professions and jobs to which to return. There was no reason for them to make an immediate return to civilian life. If anyone could be spared from civilian life, it was the Negro serviceman. Some former Confederates would claim, of course, that the Negro troops were being detained for the specific purpose of humiliating the prostrate South. There is not a shred of evidence to support this claim. . . . The point

here is that in 1865 and 1866 there was not a sufficient number of United States troops, white or black, to provide even a semblance of protection for the 4,000,000 freedmen. The only protection they had was at the hands of the former Confederates, who hardly recognized any rights of Negroes that they were bound to respect.

When Congress took over the program of Reconstruction in 1867, the military supervision that had been reinstituted as the new governments were established was not only of short duration, but was, on the whole, ineffective. As soon as the new governments showed signs of stability the troops were withdrawn. In November, 1869, there were only 1,112 federal soldiers in Virginia, including those at Fortress Monroe. In Mississippi, at the same time, there were 716 officers and men scattered over the state. Since state militias could not be established without the permission of the federal government, the Reconstruction governments—and the Negroes—were with little or no protection from the antigovernment Ku Klux Klan and other guerrillas that sprang up all over the South. The situation became so desperate that Congress finally gave permission in 1869 for North Carolina, South Carolina, Florida, Alabama, Louisiana, and Arkansas to organize state militias. Some of the other states proceeded to organize militias without congressional authorization.

It was not always easy to enlist a sufficient number of white men to fill the militia quotas, and under the new dispensation Negroes were eligible anyway. To many white observers, the number of Negro militiamen seemed excessive, and the inference was drawn, as it was drawn in 1865, that the presence of such large numbers of armed Negroes was for the purpose of humiliating the whites. Because of the growing hostility to these armed groups and because of the increasing strength of the enemies of the Reconstruction governments, the state militias contributed, in a sense, to the downfall of the governments they were supposed to protect. It cannot be argued, however, that armed men, whether white or black, or whether federal or state, were of such numbers as to constitute a military occupation of the South. And without such occupation, the Negroes of the former Confederate states became the special targets and the victims of the groups who were determined to overthrow congressional Reconstruction.

. . .

The period of congressional Reconstruction has been described by some as Negro rule, and the new governments in the South have been described as Black and Tan governments. The clear implication is that Negroes dominated the governments of the former Confederacy or that at least their role and their vote were crucial. Today, few, if any, serious students of the period would countenance any such description. It should be added, somewhat hastily, however, that many politicians and laymen who today attack civil rights and voting legislation do so on the ground that it would deliver the South to the Negro, whose role would be reminiscent of the Reconstruction era. While such a claim is both specious and fallacious, there persists the view, even among some serious students, that the Negro's influence during congressional Reconstruction was considerable and even decisive.

The only states in which Negroes were in the government in any considerable number were South Carolina, Mississippi, and Louisiana. In the first South Carolina legislature Negroes outnumbered whites eighty-seven to forty, but they controlled at no time any other branch of the state government. In Louisiana, they numbered forty-two out of eighty-four members of the lower house, although it should be remarked that the number is not precisely known because of the racial admixture of so many of the members. In Mississippi there were forty Negroes out of a total of 115 members in the first Reconstruction legislature. It is not necessary to review here the racial composition of the legislatures of the several states or of the other branches of the governments. One can state categorically that Negroes did not rule anywhere in the South.

This is not to say that there were not any individual Negroes who were without responsibility and influence. Here one must recall that much of the Negro leadership was both literate and experienced. In the several southern states not only were there Negroes who emerged as leaders but also the black Carpetbaggers, so-called, who returned to their southern homes after many years of absence. . . .

. . . Most of the white *and* Negro leaders were self-made men, who, through perseverance, native ability, and sometimes a little bit of luck, made their way up to positions of influence and importance. Obviously also, there were some men in both races who made their way to power through chicanery, duplicity, and fraud. Once in power they used their positions, as one might expect, to advance their own interests, frequently at the expense of the welfare of the larger community.

One principal reason why there was not and could not have been any such thing as Negro rule is not merely because the Negroes had insufficient political power but also because the coalition to which they belonged was both loose and ineffective. One group in the so-called coalition, the Scalawags, belonged to it not because they shared the Negro's ideals or aspirations but because they were qualified under the strict requirements laid down by the Congress. The other group, the Carpetbaggers, contained people whose views differed from each other almost as much as their general view differed from the former Confederates. Some were investors who were politically neutral, some were Union soldiers who just liked the South, some were clever politicians, some were teachers in Negro schools, and indeed some were Negroes. It is inconceivable that these many groups could have agreed on a political or social program, and in the absence of substantial agreement the Negro wielded little influence and received few benefits.

In the constitutional conventions and in the subsequent governments in each of the states, the groups making up the coalition were at odds with each other over such fundamental questions as the nature and amount of power to be vested in the state government, the matter of public education, and what, if anything, should be done to guarantee the rights of Negroes. Many of the native whites went over to the opposition when it appeared that the governments were moving toward equal rights for Negroes. Many northerners became lukewarm when the new governments threatened to impose restrictions on capital investments. Others from the North, the idealists, became disgusted with the manner in which the governments came under the influence of the venal business interests of all groups. Small wonder, under the circumstances, that they were unable to agree on the outlines of programs of welfare, social reform, and public education—conveniently segregated almost everywhere.

The Reconstruction governments in the South have been described by almost all historians as radical. While the description is almost permanently fixed, it does not appear to be very accurate. If some of the governments were corrupt and extravagant—and not all of them were—they were very much like state governments in other parts of the country at the time; indeed the federal government was not without its crooks and knaves. If some of them pressed for welfare legislation and public education, they were seeking to close the gap that had separated them for a generation from the progressive states of the Northeast. If they moved toward universal suffrage, they were following the lead of states in the North and some countries abroad. The only possible radical aspect was that, at the insistence of the federal government, Negroes had to be included in the new concept of universal education. But when one considers the growing number of Negroes who were acquiring education and experience, many of them could meet the standards that had not been required or expected of any other group in the history of American suffrage.

IRWIN UNGER

Since the seventeenth century, financial questions have often been the distinctive form social conflict has taken in America. Periodically, from the earliest colonial difficulties in finding a sufficient circulating medium to the most recent dispute over a balanced budget, differences over currency and the related subject of banking have expressed basic American social and political antagonisms. It is not surprising, then, that the Civil War, initiating sweeping

Reprinted from Irwin Unger, THE GREENBACK ERA *(Princeton: Princeton University Press, 1964), pp. 3–8, 401–405, 407, by permission of the publisher.*

financial change, made the problems of money and banking of extraordinary national concern. In the decade and a half following Appomatox, national finance absorbed more of the country's intellectual and political energy than any other public question except Reconstruction. The debate over paper money, debt repayment, the national banks, and silver remonetization reflected the ambitions, aspirations, and frustrations of the most active and vigorous men of the republic and set the terms of American political conflict for the remainder of the century.

The passion and drama surrounding the post-Civil War money debate are enough to justify its description. Yet more important is the light the conflict sheds on the question of national political power in the momentous postwar era. The pushes and pulls of competing groups, local and national, in the unfolding of federal financial legislation, identify the locus of control in emerging modern America.

The interest in American *Realpolitik* is, of course, not new. For the last half-century, scholars have sought to peel away the opaque surface of post-Civil War political life to reveal its inner workings. In particular, Charles A. Beard, J. Allen Smith, and their disciples, have been concerned with the question: who ran the United States? And their conclusions have long since become part of the accepted historical canon. To the Beardians, the formal politics of the late nineteenth century were an elaborate ritual designed to disguise the blunt truths of domestic power politics. Beneath the day-to-day intrigues for place and perquisite, they argued, one could discern a raw struggle between the older agrarian America and the emerging, assertive, industrial America.

The key to our nineteenth-century history, the Beardians claimed, was the confrontation of farmer and capitalist along a broad front of vital public issues. The Civil War itself was the culmination of eighty years of economic rivalry between the plantation South and the business-dominated Northeast, allied at the end with the grain-producing West. But while the nation's agricultural heartland poured out its blood and its wealth in the common cause, Union victory in the "Second American Revolution" was a triumph of the "investing section" alone. Acting through their servile instrument, the Republican Party, eastern businessmen crammed through Congress a legislative program which subordinated public interest to private profit and ushered in a reign of predatory capitalism. Tariff protection, federal subsidies for railroads, government-sponsored rivers and harbors improvements, and, finally, "sound money," the story goes, all testified to the postwar capture of the national government by the "business interests." Although bemused for a while by appeals to northern solidarity against a resurgent South, the western farmer finally rose against the dominant Northeast. The Granger movement, Greenbackism, the free silver and Populist crusades, were in turn all manifestations of agrarian resistance to capitalist control and exploitation.

The Beardian story is so familiar that we tend to overlook the assumptions that underlie it. As a picture of American history it is fundamentally dualistic. Capitalist versus farmer, debtor versus creditor, East versus West, conservative versus radical, hard money versus soft money—these appear as successive guises of the same inherent division. The nation's story is a battle of two great antagonists who, although their names may vary, always remain essentially the same. As two disciples of

Beard have recently written, "a single basic cleavage can be distinguished as running through most of our history." ". . . the 'two major complexes of interest' which have been arrayed against one another time and again are the agricultural interest on the one hand and the mercantile and financial interests, together with the industrial interest which grows out of them, on the other. Primarily this dualism may be defined as a contest between wealth in the form of land and wealth seeking outlets in commerce and industry."

As the quotation implies, along with the dualism the Beardians also accepted the central role of economic drives in our history. Both contenders in the power struggle are interest groups propelled by the acquisitive instincts appropriate to their role in the economy. It is true that the disciples of Beard and Smith, political liberals to man, displayed far greater tenderness for the agrarian than for the capitalist, but if they were partial to the farmer or the "little man," they had no illusions about his altruism. Like the capitalist, his primary concern was for his livelihood.

This economic emphasis, of course, parallels that of Marx, and it is clear that Beard was aware of the most ambitious and challenging analysis of historical forces that the nineteenth century produced. Nevertheless, Beard was not a Marxist. He owed far more to the very agrarian tradition he so sympathetically described. Beard was a neo-Populist, and his version of post-Civil War America leaned heavily on the interpretation accepted by the contemporary leaders of agrarian dissent. There is little in Beard's "Second American Revolution" thesis that cannot be found in the reform polemics of the Granger era, the Populist revolt, and most immediately, the Progressive move-

ment. The Manichaean view of the basic struggle, the belief in conspiracy, even the economic determinism, all belong to the Jacksonian antimonopoly thread connecting all three movements. It is this native neo-Populism, rather than an exotic European Socialism, that is responsible for both the dualism and the determinism of the Beardian philosophy.

In what follows it is this neo-Populist picture of post-bellum America that I am seeking to evaluate. This is primarily a political, not a financial history. Although fixed to a skeleton of financial events, my story is largely concerned with the decision-making process in American society. I do not wish to compete with the existing excellent surveys of financial history. I shall examine the politics of money between the end of the Civil War and the resumption of specie payments in 1879, but I shall emphasize the events of the 1870's. A recent study of the immediate postwar half-decade by Dr. Robert Sharkey of Johns Hopkins University enables me to limit my work. It has also made my task more challenging. Though we share similar conclusions, we do disagree on several important points. Briefly, Dr. Sharkey remains convinced that the governing forces in America after 1865 were economic; he disputes Beard's implied "monolithic" business, labor, and agricultural interests, but adopts an economic determinism even more complete. I cannot accept this conclusion. The events of our lifetime seemingly have revealed how weak in crisis are social and ethical restraints. Yet we must not in our despair read our own attitudes and experiences into the past. Implanted values and controls were, I believe, tougher then than now. In the matter of post-Civil War finance men indeed marshaled principle to rationalize expediency, but they also rejected perceived interest for conscience' sake. In general, most men tried to strike a balance between their pocket books and their duty. This mixture of ethics and interest, this very human attempt to serve both God and Mammon, must be recognized if we hope to understand the events of these years.

Unfortunately, adding ethics to interest greatly complicates any attempt to analyze the postwar money question. When economic self-interest is made the prime mover of human events, profit or loss will explain any historical happening. This simplification is all the more appealing since it becomes possible to deal with measurable quantities which may be summarized on a balance sheet. We record changing price per bushel, the rise and fall of interest rates, miles of track built, tons of iron produced, annual bankruptcy rates, and perform the appropriate additions and substractions; history loses its human complexities and becomes a form of social accountancy. Moral and ideological considerations not only defy quantifying—how does one count or weigh a man's religious convictions?—but they also raise special new problems. With several determinants instead of a single one, every historical effect becomes a conundrum. It is certain to be the resultant of several forces; but which—and even more puzzling, in what proportions? It is not surprising, therefore, that such a method is unsatisfactory to many social analysts. Nevertheless, it is probably the inevitable limitation of our discipline. Paring down human events for the sake of simple answers not only distorts reality but in the end denies the special quality of historical knowledge itself.

. . .

January 1, 1879, was a bank holiday, a fact that the Republican Forty-third

Congress in its haste to get a financial bill on the books had overlooked, and resumption, already delayed for a decade and a half, was postponed still another day. On the second, New York, the legal place of redemption, wore a festive air in anticipation of the great financial reform. The Customs House and the banks were covered with bunting, and flags flew from many public buildings. The gold room at the Stock Exchange was deserted, and across the great board, on which for seventeen years had been chalked the latest gold quotations, somebody had scrawled in large letters, "PAR." At the Sub-Treasury large bags of coin were piled up at the redemption counter ready so that no delay need occur to set loose rumors of the Treasury's inability to pay. In the vaults lay over $100 million in coin reserves.

The Sub-Treasury doors opened at 10 A.M., accompanied by a salute from the Navy Yard; but the rest of the day was anti-climactic. One person was on hand at opening to demand coin. He was paid $210, and by noon, less than $3000 had been paid out. At the close of business, $132,000 in notes had been redeemed and $400,000 in gold exchanged for the more convenient paper.

At the banks the story was the same. The tellers, well supplied with coin, had paid out virtually nothing. At the First National less than $50 was exchanged for paper; at the Mechanics' Bank Association not one dollar was redeemed the entire day, and by evening the bankers were congratulating Sherman and themselves on the end of the paper era.

During the next few days jubilation reigned among the hard money men. Letters and telegrams poured into Sherman's office offering congratulations on "the magnificent success of the greatest event of modern times." The Honest Money League Executive Committee met and passed resolutions praising Sherman. The conservative press burst into ringing hosannas. To the *Commercial and Financial Chronicle* resumption meant "that the farmer's grain, the planter's cotton, the Chinaman's tea are all interchangeable anywhere on a common basis of value, and as every venture is thus relieved of the element of uncertainty, enterprise becomes less hazardous and therefore freer." *Banker's Magazine* saw it as a great victory for self-discipline over "demagogism," made possible only by a secure banking system. The *Nation* called it the triumph of the "rational, reflective, remembering element in society" over "folly and ignorance." The religious press hailed it as a great moral triumph and a credit to the American people, brought to see the light through the "practical instruction of the American pulpit in the fundamental principles of national honor and honesty." To *Harper's Weekly* it was another great victory of the Republican party, one which could be placed alongside the abolition of slavery and the preservation of the Union.

These responses, full of the exuberance of the moment, are actually capsule statements of historical causation. Sherman, the foreign traders, the bankers, the educated elite, the pulpit, the Republican party, are all given credit, directly or by implication, for the great consummation. Much of this may be put down to rhetoric or self-importance, but taken together it is a remarkable composite description of the forces which actually carried resumption through.

Any analysis of these years which fails to note the crucial role of strategically placed individuals grossly distorts reality. On the soft money side, Alexander Campbell shaped the course of events by implanting an attractive

theoretical abstraction in the fertile soil of working-class and rural discontent. Carey, by making accessible the submerged mercantilist thought of an earlier day, translated the needs of the industrialists into soft money terms. At the opposite end of the spectrum, McCulloch seriously crippled the hard money cause at the outset by identifying resumption with the remorseless burning of the people's money. But above all, it is impossible to exaggerate the role of John Sherman, the supple master of accommodation. Following in the footsteps of his great Whig predecessors, he subordinated the ideal to the workable and succeeded where men more righteous, perhaps, had failed.

The hard money businessmen, the seaboard merchants and bankers, the Yankee textile magnates, all had reason to congratulate themselves on resumption day. Against the great and growing power of a class of businessmen identified with postwar industrial expansion and western development, they had carried their point. Resumption was a victory for A. A. Low, the transplanted Yankee and China Trader, and for A. A. Lawrence, second generation Brahmin Lord of the Loom; it was a defeat for Jay Cooke, the upstart Ohio railroad promoter, and the self-made western industrialist Eber Ward.

The political parties, with their separate traditions, their distinctive textures, their individual inner compulsions and needs, were also movers of events. The Democrats, thrust from leadership into persistent minority status, possessing deep Jeffersonian roots, drawing their strength in the West from the southern-born and the immigrant, were susceptible to Agrarian greenback appeal and coalition with dissident labor and farmer elements. The Republicans, not so much as the instrument of rising industrial capitalism, but as the majority party and the party of the Yankee and the Teuton, the respectable middle class, the erstwhile Whig, the church-goer, the professional man, proved resistant to greenbackism, though not to free banking—the respectable version of soft money.

The intellectual and moral leaders of the community also added considerable weight to the scales. Soft money and hard money were far more than congeries of economic interests, or even economic *cum* political interests. They were also competing intellectual and ethical systems. On the moral plane, Agrarianism confronted Calvinism; on the intellectual, a revived mercantilism confronted the prevailing economic orthodoxy. In both cases the hard money position, reinforced by the prestige of the Protestant Churches and the academy respectively, enjoyed an immense advantage over the soft money ideology so often identified with quacks, visionaries, and charlatans.

The conservative post-mortem reveals, then, an impressive grasp of contemporary reality. In rough outline it identifies the leading actors in the drama of specie payments. They were not the "rising" industrial capitalists. In a strict economic sense, measured by shares of the national income contributed, manufacturing had indeed outstripped, individually, agriculture, construction, transportation, and services by the mid-'80's. But in the previous decade, if their role in the currency fight is any measure, there was a significant gap between the dynamism of American industrial progress and the social power and prestige of American industrialists.

The composite conservative estimate is also a remarkably penetrating general overview of post-Civil War America. It recognizes, in the first place, a society deeply divided internally. There was

not, indeed, the conflict over the political and social fundamentals that often turned nineteenth-century Europe into a battleground of irreconcilable elements ready to resort to bombs and barricades. The American struggle was always tamer, and to this extent, the recent discovery of a continuing American "consensus" is surely valid. Political democracy, an expanding economy, and a relatively fluid social system softened class asperities and narrowed the area of disagreement among Americans. Yet conflict there was, and often it generated frustrations and aggressions just short of the social flash point. Men have a way, in the absence of truly fundamental issues, of turning lesser differences into matters of life and death.

The men who congratulated themselves on January 2 were close enough to events to comprehend also the intricacy of what they observed. If it is hard to see the consensus in post-bellum America, it is also difficult to detect a simple Beardian polarity. On the money question there were not two massive contending interests; there were many small ones. If the financial history of Reconstruction reveals nothing else of consequence, it does disclose a complex, pluralistic society in which issues were resolved—when they were not simply brushed aside—by the interaction of many forces. And yet the ghost of dualism still lingers. It has been impossible to avoid using the terms "hard money" and "soft money," although the intent has always been to tag coalitions rather than the homogeneous entities posited by Beard. This seems to return dualism through the back door after it has been ejected through the front. But it does only in a verbal sense, I think. The need for stylistic shorthand, the demands of rational organization, and the very laws of thought, perhaps, impose a kind of dualism on the historian even when he rejects it as a true picture of reality. Each coalition was not, however, a tug-of-war team, pulling against its opponent along a single axis. Instead, each was a jostling crowd, full of seeming random activity, which nonetheless managed to move in a consistent direction.

. . .

This study, finally, may help us re-evaluate the concept of the Civil War as the great watershed of the nation's history. Does the War in fact divide American history into an older rural-agrarian and a newer urban-industrial phase? Did a new society, transformed in its political, cultural, economic, and social life, emerge from the ashes of fratricidal strife? It has been suggested here that until 1880 continuity was at least as characteristic of the nation's history as cataclysm. To be sure, the flash of Union and Confederate guns signaled a physical and human destruction such as the country had never experienced before. But when quiet returned, much remained of the old America. Many of the old centers of power and social prestige survived. The prewar commercial-financial community remained influential. The power of the South and West as revealed in the silver struggle remained formidable. The clergy, the educated elite, and the professoriate continued to exercise intellectual and moral leadership. Nor had ideas or norms changed drastically. The economic orthodoxy of Ricardo and Mill continued to compete with mercantilistic doctrines, as it had in different terms for a century previously. Calvinism, surprisingly little altered in its general fervor for a moral society from the days of Cotton Mather, continued to battle Agrarianism, virtually unchanged from John Taylor's *Arator* and Jefferson's *Notes On Virginia*. Even the ante-bellum humanitarian impulse, translated into monetary reform, persisted.

This is not to say that America in 1880 was identical with America in 1860. The nation has never stood still for two decades. But if this historical test boring bears true witness, it seems a little less certain, perhaps, that the Civil War was the momentous turning point we have all supposed.

HISTORIOGRAPHICAL NOTE

"The Republican leaders were quite aware in 1865," C. Vann Woodward wrote recently, "that the issue of Negro status and rights was closely connected with the two other great issues of Reconstruction—who should reconstruct the South and who should govern the country." Important to an understanding of the differences between earlier twentieth-century historians of reconstruction and recent interpreters is Woodward's observation of the post-Civil War Republican leaders: The constituencies on which they "relied in the North lived in a race-conscious segregated society devoted to the doctrine of white supremacy and Negro inferiority." Historians such as William A. Dunning, James Ford Rhodes, and Claude G. Bowers were reared in similar environments a generation later, and their writings on the reconstruction period assumed the inferiority of the Negro either on physical or environmental grounds. Similarly, revisionist Charles Beard shared the predominant racism of his Progressive era contemporaries, Dunning and Rhodes. Beard, however, saw the Civil War and reconstruction years as a "Second American Revolution," in which the owners of capital developed the industrial economy itself while Republican politicians utilized their control of the federal government to establish a political and social climate favorable to such industrial growth. In Louis Hacker's Beardian phrases: "The American Civil War turned out to be a revolution indeed. But its striking achievement was the triumph of industrial capitalism." Behind these twin banners of racialism and economic interpretation, Progressive period historians of the reconstruction experience marshalled their major arguments.

Between the racial assumptions of the Dunning school and those of contemporary reconstruction historians lay the pioneering scholarship of men such as anthropologists Franz Boas and Melville Herskovits, sociologist Gunnar Myrdal, and historian W. E. B. DuBois. Acceptance of the Negro's capacity for equal advancement and of his legal and political right to equality had little impact on popular historical treatment of reconstruction during the 1930's and 1940's. America's favorite book and movie, *Gone With the Wind,* along with similar epics of Southern white resistance to black oppression, helped reinforce existing racial stereotypes.

Yet history has begun to overtake mythology during the past two decades, and world events have provided both the opportunity and the setting for an elaborate reassessment of the reconstruction episode. In the aftermath of World War II, the United States itself undertook to reconstruct conquered German and Japanese societies. This role as an occupation power—along with evidence of "reconstructions" which followed modern civil wars in Spain, Russia, China, and elsewhere—provided a fuller context within which to assess the relative intensity and harshness of our own post-Civil War experience. Unfortunately, in the period from 1865 to 1877, Americans lacked similar perspectives and therefore assumed both the unique severity and failure of reconstruction, which they blamed in large measure on the presence of an untutored Negro electorate. Also, the shift toward more sympathetic racial attitudes on the part of recent historians—the decline of scholarly Negrophobia—has led to a much more pronounced attitude of compassion for the freedmen following their abrupt and unprepared manumission. Finally, more sophisticated assessments of the psychology of stress, partly a posthumous reaction to the stark patterns of behavior symbolized by such place names as Coventry, Warsaw, Auschwitz, Dresden, and Hiroshima, have made recent scholars suspicious of earlier moralistic judgments of the tumultuous reconstruction years.

The search for more precise analysis of political behavior caused some historians to re-evaluate the relationship between economic interest groups and Southern reconstruction and has led to fundamental questioning of the

Beard-Hacker "Second American Revolution" thesis.[1] The actions and policies of Andrew Johnson in his struggle with the Radicals have been subjected to keen and often merciless scrutiny by other scholars.[2] One direct
result of these shifts in racial, psychological, and social assumptions has
been a reversal of the traditional heroes and villains of reconstruction.
Johnson, after a century's glorification by conservative and pro-Southern
scholars, has been sharply criticized in modern monographs for his political
ineptness, while the Radicals, formerly viewed either as tools of the great
capitalists or as opportunists, now are studied more seriously as revolutionary politicians. Radical writings and speeches are being read again, perhaps for the first time since reconstruction, and the Radicals' Unionist convictions as well as their concern for the freedmen are being seen once more
as principles governing their political activities.

The new emphasis awarded to the Negro experience in recent studies
of the post-Civil War decade remains perhaps the predominant feature of
the current "reconstruction" of reconstruction history. Major modern interpretive volumes by John Hope Franklin, Kenneth Stampp, and Rembert
Patrick have all distilled findings by recent scholars concerning the high
degree of political, economic, and social advancement made by freedmen
against enormous odds during the aborted moment of full liberation.[3] The
problem of reconstruction in the South clearly centered around the future
place of the Negro in American society, and in this vital sense the dilemma
remains the most troubling social problem still unresolved in American
life. "Reconstruction confronts American writers of history," Bernard Weisberger observed, "with things they prefer, like other Americans, to ignore—
brute power and its manipulation, class conflict, race antagonism." [4] Yet
as Weisberger and other modern students of the period remind us, precisely
"these things made it an essentially modern period" whose failures and
tragedies bear directly on the anguish faced by both Negroes and whites
during our present "Second American Reconstruction."

[1] Stanley Coben, "Northeastern Business and Radical Reconstruction: A Re-examination," *Mississippi Valley Historical Review*, XLVI (June, 1959), 67–90; Robert P. Sharkey,
Money, Class, and Party: An Economic Study of Civil War and Reconstruction (Baltimore,
1959); Irwin F. Unger, *The Greenback Era: A Social and Political History of American
Finance, 1865–1879* (Princeton, 1964); Peter Kolchin, "The Business Press and Reconstruction, 1865–1868," *Journal of Southern History*, XXXIII (May, 1967), 183–196.

[2] Eric L. McKitrick, *Andrew Johnson and Reconstruction* (Chicago, 1960); John H. Cox
and LaWanda Cox, *Politics, Principle, and Prejudice, 1865–1866* (New York, 1963); W. R.
Brock, *An American Crisis: Congress and Reconstruction, 1865–1867* (New York, 1963).

[3] John Hope Franklin, *Reconstruction After the Civil War* (Chicago, 1961); Kenneth M.
Stampp, *The Era of Reconstruction* (New York, 1965); Rembert W. Patrick, *The Reconstruction of the Nation* (New York, 1967).

[4] Bernard Weisberger, "The Dark and Bloody Ground of Reconstruction Historiography," *Journal of Southern History*, XXV (1959), 427–447.

10. The Foundations of an
Industrial Society

INTRODUCTION

Few Americans living in the post-Civil War decades failed to feel the effects of the major transformations of that period. Industrialization, mass immigration, and urbanization during those decades revolutionized the traditional foundations of American society and shaped the structure of a modern nation that was in many essentials dissimilar to the early republic. A political system run as late as the Jacksonian period by representatives of Western farmers, Southern planters, and Eastern workers became, during the Gilded Age, closely aligned with the new industrial leaders and was, in turn, alienated from its older bases of support.

Millions of impoverished Eastern and Southern European peasants flocked to new lives in the manufacturing centers of the United States, co-existing there in uneasy truce with older and somewhat more assimilated migrants from Ireland, Germany, and other Western European countries. This flood of "new immigration," mainly non-English speaking, raised questions among skeptical native-born Americans concerning the newcomers' capacity for absorption into the society. Often forced to live in brutally cramped ghetto sections of large cities or factory towns, this urban proletariat remained unassimilated into American society during the Gilded Age and beyond. More than one nostalgic middle-class citizen of older ethnic and religious stock, viewing the changes around him, might have endorsed Thomas Jefferson's view of an urban industrial culture. "It is better to carry provisions and materials to workmen [in Europe]," Jefferson wrote in his *Notes on Virginia*, "than bring them to the provisions and materials [in this country], and with them their manners and principles. . . . The mobs of great cities add just as much to the support of pure government, as sores do to the strength of the human body." To the agrarian or small-town Americans who did not share in either the high prosperity or the degrading poverty brought by industrial developments, even the jargon of this urban culture must have appeared strange: "trusts" and "tenements," "padrones" and "greenhorns," "sweatshops" and "pools."

A few relevant statistics testify to the intense and revolutionary character of these social and economic changes. Between the end of the Civil War and the end of the century, the United States rose from fourth to first

71

place among the world's manufacturing nations. Along with this vast growth in overall national production went a parallel development of huge industrial and financial consolidations, beginning with the formation of Rockefeller's Standard Oil Trust in 1879. By 1900, 300 such aggregates of corporate wealth represented the merger, over three decades, of more than 5000 separate plants and factories. More strikingly, by 1900 only two per cent of America's plants produced over half the total value of the country's manufactured goods! Historians have asked certain obvious questions concerning this profound transformation in American life. What factors stimulated economic development in the post-Civil War decades? Most especially, what role did business leadership play in the process? Did the new corporations and trusts influence the character of national politics and American social values? Many of the readings and documents in this chapter touch on these questions as part of the central theme in late nineteenth-century American history—the transforming impact of industrial growth.

The new factories found an easily recruited labor force not only among the native born, but among the almost 25,000,000 immigrants who arrived in the United States between 1860 and 1914. Until the 1880's, most immigrants continued to come from the countries of Northern and Western Europe. Southern and Eastern European countries did not become important sources of immigrant labor in the United States until the 1880's, but by the 1890's, these "new" immigrants—from such countries as Austria-Hungary, Italy, Russia, Greece, Romania, Poland, Hungary, and Turkey—had begun to predominate. In 1882, for example, 788,000 immigrants entered the country, 87 per cent from "old" countries and only 13 per cent from "new" ones. By 1907, the percentage had almost been reversed. Of the 1,285,000 immigrants who came that year, only 19 per cent came from Northern and Western Europe while over 80 per cent came from more southerly or eastern nations. Millions of these "new" immigrants clustered in the cities and industrial towns where they provided a regular stream of poorly paid laborers for American factories.

Their presence in such monumental numbers triggered campaigns for immigration restriction from among nativist elements in American society. Yet even those older Americans most sympathetic to the new immigrants and most concerned with improving living conditions in the urban slums often questioned whether this industrial labor force could adapt to American life as readily as those who came prior to the Civil War. "It is a dreary old truth," wrote the New York muckraker Jacob Riis, "that those who would fight for the poor must fight the poor to do it. It must be confessed that there is little enough in their past experience to inspire confidence in the sincerity of the effort to help them." Those who draw overly pessimistic forecasts from current racial upheaval in the cities might reflect that Riis' observation was directed toward that variety of contentious groups then occupying the urban ghetto—the Irish, Italians, Jews, Greeks, Turks, Hungarians, Poles, and other basic ingredients in America's ethnic stew.

I. EARLY INTERPRETATIONS

In the following selections, Ida Tarbell and Arthur Schlesinger, Sr., summarize the pre-World War II interpretations of late nineteenth-century American economic and social changes. Both selections contain strong moralistic underpinnings: Tarbell's with regard to the character of American business leaders, and Schlesinger's on the quality of the "new immigrants."

IDA TARBELL

By 1878 the American people were feeling the full impact of the new forces which had been remaking their economic life since the Civil War. Within the memory of living man a strangely different America had taken form: an America which Lincoln would hardly have recognized and of which indeed he could scarcely have approved. To the generation which now came upon the scene fell the problem of mastering and guiding these mighty forces: The leaders of society, however, were not of one mind as to how this should be accomplished. Some saw only beneficence in a reign of untrammeled individualism with the real prizes going to the few. The major task, as they viewed it, was to press forward economic expansion at an ever swifter pace and without too nice a regard for human costs. Others were appalled at the passing of the older America with its assurance of generous opportunities for the common folk. They bent their energies to curbing concentrated capital and extending the benefits of the nation's wealth to the masses of the people.

This conflict of opinion had its unacknowledged philosophic basis in the challenge which socialism was throwing at the inherited frontier interpretations of individualism. In the twenty years ahead the conflict was to assume many forms and to engage a variety of contending hosts: those who sought special privileges "for the good of business" and those who opposed all forms of privilege as contrary to a realization of the democratic dream; those who fought governmental regulation as an interference with business and those who deemed it necessary for a healthful economic life; the protected manufacturers and the unprotected farmers; organized capital and organized labor. Nor was the outcome conclusive so far as the central issue was concerned. The conflict, nevertheless, had a profound effect upon American economic life. In all fields of endeavor it forced organization on a nation-wide scale and left the country consolidated in vast economic units. Whatever this might portend for the future, the generation accomplished the Herculean task of forging a national economic order.

The wealth over which the contest was waged had grown in the twenty years before 1878 from a little over sixteen billion dollars to nearly forty-four billion.[1] This increase had come in spite of two major calamities: a civil

Reprinted from Ida Tarbell, THE NATIONAL-IZING OF AMERICAN LIFE, *1877–1900 (New York: The Free Press, 1936), pp. 1–9, by permission of the publishers.*

[1] J. G. Blaine, *Twenty Years of Congress* (Norwich, Conn., 1884–1886), I, 617.

war which in 1865 had left prostrate eleven states of the Union; and a depression, beginning with the Panic of 1873, from which the nation was only just beginning to recover.[2] The primary sources of this rapid accumulation of wealth lay in the opening of great areas of grain-growing land in the region west and northwest of the Mississippi and in the discovery of vast mineral deposits—gold, silver, copper, iron and coal. To these world-old wealth producers had been added a new substance, rock-oil or petroleum, unknown to the census of 1860 but which in the year ending May 31, 1880, yielded manufactured products valued at $43,705,218.[3] Quite as significant for the country's economic future was the demonstration that in electricity the world had a new and exhaustless source of light and power awaiting harness. Already it had been applied to the telegraph so effectively that rapid communication between the Atlantic and Pacific coasts and between the United States and Europe was accepted as a matter of course, and in the mid-seventies its uses in telephonic communication were beginning to be explored.[4] The nation's natural dowry was of such great extent that it was generally believed that only the first step in its development had been taken.

The addition to American economic life of these new resources served as a tremendous challenge to the scientist, the engineer and the inventor. Instruction in science and technology had increased until in 1880 there were nearly four hundred and fifty colleges and schools offering courses in chemistry and physics, in metallurgy, mining and mechanical and electrical engineering. They were, for the most part, poorly endowed, the equipment generally homemade and the libraries small.[5] Yet out of the scientific departments of high schools and fresh-water colleges were to come some of the great inventors and engineers of the next twenty years, the men who were to unfold and make practical further possibilities of ore and oil and electricity. Though their initial impulse and primary instruction came from the schools, their future development was to come largely from self-directed and independent efforts.

The geographic distribution of the nation's wealth reflected the varied economic growth of the country. The five wealthiest states in the Union in 1860 were still the five wealthiest states in 1878. In order of their ranking they were New York, Pennsylvania, Ohio, Illinois and Massachusetts. The proportion of increase in each case approximately matched the national increase. Although the South had lost the place it had held in 1860, its recovery, despite its devastating economic and political experiences, was assured. If Virginia had lost to Iowa her position as the six richest state, Virginia was reestablishing herself. And the majority of the Southern states were following her example.[6]

It was in the states west of the Mississippi that the effect of the augmented national wealth was most striking. Kansas, credited with less than $32,000,000 in 1860, now boasted $760,000,000. Nebraska's record was even greater in proportion. Colorado, not even noticed among wealth producers in the census

[2] See Allan Nevins, *The Emergence of Modern America* (*A History of American Life*, VIII), chaps. i, xi, xiii–xiv.

[3] *U. S. Compendium of the Tenth Census* (1880), pt. ii, 1253.

[4] Nevins, *Emergency of Modern America*, 86, 88–89.

[5] Blaine, *Twenty Years of Congress*, I, 642.

[6] Nevins, *Emergence of Modern America*, 1–30, 349–364.

of 1860, now was worth $240,000,000. California had an increase of six hundred per cent. And each of these states and neighboring territories believed, and believed rightly, that hardly a scratch had been made on the surface of its resources.[7]

Population had shifted with wealth —men and families following rumors of new wheat and corn lands, new mines, new industries. The fifty million people in the land stirred restlessly under the bombardment of announcements of discoveries of natural resources, novel inventions, new manufacturing and engineering undertakings. They made a mighty caravan moving westward and northward, to the cities and to the great open spaces, in whatever direction fresh sources of wealth beckoned. In the shifting masses of men and women there were two predominating types. Some went on a chance, hoping to "strike it rich," sell and move on to a new speculation. Others sought an opportunity to establish themselves permanently on farms, in businesses, trades or professions.

The extent of the natural wealth and of the opportunities for business expansion opened the way for consolidations of brains, privilege and money which operated with the largest latitude. In no other manner could the swift development which the ambition and the temperament of the nation demanded be insured. The brains for these consolidations came most frequently from the bottom rank, from men who saw more clearly than their fellows what could be done to meet the impatient demands of communities and nation. These men had not only personal ambition for wealth and power but also a genius for management on a large scale. They based their operations usually on exclusive privileges which competitors in the same field were unable to get. It had long been the practice of the government to make grants of one kind or another to encourage private economic undertakings. To this end tariff protection had been given to industrialists; large concessions of land with the mineral resources which might underlie them had been granted to builders of railroads; perpetual franchises and rights of way to builders of utilities. When the government conferred such privileges, the individuals so favored felt it their right to demand from those with whom they did business discriminatory treatment. Thus the big shipper demanded, and usually received, special rates on the railroads and privileged accommodations in cars, on docks and in markets.

It was not difficult for men armed with these advantages to draw the money they needed from the country by organizing stock companies and marketing their securities. In an earlier time individual savings had gone into the business or into land or farm mortgages near home, but now such forms of investment were giving way rapidly to the buying of stocks in railroads and telegraphs, in mining and industrial promotion. Money, in other words, no longer "stayed at home": it was becoming as mobile as men, nationalizing itself. When the census of 1880 tabulated the location of property owned by inhabitants of different states, it found that citizens of New York had $1,300,-000,000 invested outside of the state; residents of Pennsylvania $450,000,000. Half of the property of Nevada was owned in other states.[8]

The phenomenon of absentee land-

7 Blaine, *Twenty Years of Congress*, I, 616–618.

8 Blaine, *Twenty Years of Congress*, I, 618.

lordism was becoming more and more frequent. The resident manager of a mine or railroad or telegraph company did not necessarily represent local interests. He took orders from the great financial centers—New York, Chicago or even London—and these looked rather to returns on capital than to benefiting the locality. The character of management depended on whether its purpose was speculation or operation. That is, the great organizations which served the communities of the country were of the same two predominating types as the people who settled the communities.

Whatever the motives behind an enterprise, its management regarded it as a private business; and the larger it grew, the greater its wealth and power, the more solidly the owners resisted any attempt of the government to regulate its affairs. Thoughtful people recognized that the law had not kept up with the consolidation of finance and industry, and as the period opened there was a movement to reëstablish the authority of law in the field of business. To shape such tendencies the great corporations were annexing lawyers to their staffs. Where once the lawyer's chief interest outside of his profession had been office holding, now he extended his activities to embrace the strategy of Big Business. The drive behind the demand for regulation came chiefly from two of the essential factors in producing the nation's wealth: the farmer and the laborer. Alarmed by the growing concentration of wealth, they claimed that an equilibrium was necessary between agriculture and industry, between employer and employee, if there was to be a proper national economy.

Increasingly the beneficiaries of consolidation found themselves on the defensive. Few of them, however, were articulate when it came to a philosophic or even an economic defense of their position. The readiest and the most persuasive was one of the greatest of them: Andrew Carnegie. Carnegie belonged to that section of the population called by the census taker "foreign-born white males," of whom there were in the United States in 1880 over three and a half million.[9] Scotch by birth, he had come to the United States at the age of seventeen, settling in Pittsburgh with his family in 1852. Beginning as a bobbin boy at $1.50 a week, he was eleven years later the assistant of Thomas Scott, superintendent of the western division of the Pennsylvania Railroad, at a salary of $2400 a year. More significant were the investments he had made by this time, which were netting him an income of $47,860.[10] His first venture had been ten shares of Adams Express stock which in 1863 paid him $1440; his most successful, an investment in the Columbia Oil Company, from which in 1863 he had received $17,868.

He had already begun, however, to invest his savings in iron making, and in iron-bridge building, the importance of which he had learned while handling men and freight for the army. Carnegie steadily increased his iron holdings, but took no interest in steel until 1872 when he saw a Bessemer converter in blast and awoke to the fact that, as he said, "The day of iron has passed." He at once set about building a steel mill at Braddock's Field on the Monongahela River, calling it the Edgar Thomson Steel Works. Profits soon became phenomenal. In 1877 the company earned forty-two per cent, paid partly in stock, partly in cash; and this

9 *U. S. Compendium of the Tenth Census*, pt. i, 625.

10 B. J. Hendrick, *The Life of Andrew Carnegie* (Garden City, 1932), I, 120–124.

was, as Carnegie himself believed, only the beginning. By 1880 the steel works netted the group $1,625,000; the furnaces and iron mills, $446,600—a total of $2,071,600.[11]

His own astonishing success plus the brilliant showing of the census of 1880 led Carnegie to give the world his considered views of the economic and social progress of the United States. To him it was an attestation of triumphant democracy, and that title he gave to his analysis of the country's achievements. "The old nations of the earth creep on at a snail's pace"; he wrote, "the Republic thunders past with the rush of the express." [12] As a graphic foreword to the volume he printed a table prepared by Edward Atkinson, a statistical authority, demonstrating America's vast superiority in acreage over any and all countries of Europe. He exulted at the growing number of occupations, the multiplication of schools, churches and libraries, the fact that while the United Kingdom had thirty-three paupers to every thousand persons, Italy forty-eight and Prussia fifty, the United States had but five, of whom more than a third were foreigners.[13]

Carnegie waxed most eloquent, however, in chronicling the country's industrial triumphs. There was no contesting the comparisons he drew between the United States and European nations. It was a splendid story of material progress which he unfolded, and in his mind it came from the superiority of democracy over monarchical forms of government. "Never will the British artisan rival the American until from his system are expelled the remains of serfdom and into his veins is instilled the pure blood of exalted manhood." [14] The consolidation of capital in the hands of a few strong men was, he claimed, the price society had to pay for cheap comforts and luxuries. These could only come through competition, and the competition to be effective must be carried on by giants, not pygmies. The results were not only beneficial for the race but essential to its progress. Business on a grand scale required special talent for organization and management, and that talent was rare. He pointed out that business leaders were more concerned about securing the right men for high executive posts than in securing new capital. If the right men were obtained, they soon created capital; otherwise capital soon took wings.[15]

This was the philosophy which guided the efforts of the great captains of industry and finance. Though challenged with increasing frequency and vigor, it continued to be the dominant philosophy throughout the score of years. Some of these men were unscrupulous and corrupt, but most of them were sincere and, according to their lights, upright and patriotic. They regarded themselves as pioneers in a new stage of America's growth, carrying forward more effectively the old work of developing the country's natural resources, finding fresh avenues of power and achievement and enlarging the theater of the nation's activities.

---

11 H. N. Casson, *The Romance of Steel* (N. Y., 1907), 91; J. H. Bridge, *The Inside History of the Carnegie Steel Company* (N. Y., 1903), chap. vi.

12 Andrew Carnegie, *Triumphant Democracy* (N. Y., 1886), 1.

13 Carnegie, *Triumphant Democracy*, 168–169.

14 Carnegie, *Triumphant Democracy*, 238.

15 Andrew Carnegie, "Wealth," *N. Am. Rev.*, CXLVIII (1889), 653–664.

ARTHUR SCHLESINGER, SR.

The extraordinary growth of its bigger cities was one of the marvels of Middle Western life in the eighties. Chicago, which best represented the will power and titanic energy of the section, leaped from a half million in 1880 to more than a million ten years later, establishing its place as the second city of the nation. The Twin Cities trebled in size; places like Detroit, Milwaukee, Columbus and Cleveland increased by from sixty to eighty per cent.[1] Of the fifty principal American cities in 1890 twelve were in the Middle West.

The rapid urbanization was, of course, accelerated by the swarming of foreigners into the section. During the eighties the immigrant population of Middle America increased nearly nine hundred thousand, reaching a total at the close of the decade of three and a half million.[2] Every fifth or sixth person in 1890 was of alien birth. Though the Scandinavians, as we have seen, generally preferred the farm to the city, seventy thousand of them were working in Chicago in 1890, the men as mechanics or factory hands, the daughters usually as domestic servants. Fifty thousand more dwelt in the Twin Cities. The Germans also divided their allegiance. James Bryce heard German commonly spoken on the streets of Milwaukee; the Teutonic element in Chicago, while thrice as numerous, was less conspicuous because of the babel of other tongues. As skilled workers the newcomers from the *Vaterland* were generally found in such trades as photography, tailoring, baking, lock-

Reprinted from Arthur Schlesinger, Sr., THE RISE OF THE CITY, 1878–1898, History of American Life (New York: The Macmillan Company, 1933), X, 64–68, 72–77, by permission of the publisher.

smithing and lithography.[3] The nationalities which most thoroughly identified themselves with city life, however, were the Irish and particularly the increasing stream of Russian and Polish Jews and Italians who constituted the "new immigration."

So great was the influx of all races into Chicago that its foreign-born inhabitants in 1890 numbered nearly as many as its entire population in 1880. A writer in the nineties, analyzing its school census, pointed out that "only two cities in the German Empire, Berlin and Hamburg, have a greater German population than Chicago; only two in Sweden, Stockholm and Göteborg, have more Swedes; and only two in Norway, Christiania and Bergen, more Norwegians."[4] If the "seacoast of Bohemia" was a figment of the poet's imagination, the third largest city of Bohemians in the world could at least boast an extended lake front.

These and other immigrant groups huddled together in dense colonies like islands in a sea of humanity. They jealously maintained their own business institutions, churches, beneficial societies, foreign-language newspapers and often their own parochial schools. In the small district about Hull House on South Halsted Street eighteen nations were represented. As individuals ventured forth from these racial fastnesses into the bewildering world outside, they generally found it their lot to perform the disagreeable or arduous work which Americans of older stock disdained. The sweatshops in the gar-

1 *U. S. Eleventh Census*, I, lxvii.

2 *Ibid.*, lxxxiii, lxxxviif., xc, cxxxviiif.

3 J. F. Willard (Josiah Flynt, *pseud.*), "The German and the German-American," *Atlantic Mo.*, LXXVIII (1896), 655–664.

4 Quoted by Turner, "Dominant Forces in American Life," 438. See also G. W. Steevens, *The Land of the Dollar* (N. Y., 1897), 144, and J. C. Ridpath, "The Mixed Populations of Chicago," *Chautauquan*, XII (1891), 483–493.

ment industry were recruited largely from Bohemians and Russian Jews; the rough unskilled jobs in the building trades fell chiefly to Irish and Italians; while the business of peddling became a specialty of Jews.

Assimilation went on at an uneven pace, being notably slow in the case of the new arrivals from southern Europe and Russia. Timidity and ignorance on the part of the immigrant, suspicion and contempt on the part of the native-born, constantly retarded the process. Even the American-born children, if reared in an Old World atmosphere and taught their school lessons in an alien tongue, were more apt to be second-generation immigrants than first-generation Americans. But sooner or later the influences of the new land began to penetrate. Perhaps unusual business success or the liberalizing effect of membership in a labor union helped break down the barriers. More often, however, the change reflected the influence of the public school carried into the immigrant home by the children. Though a regrettable breach sometimes resulted between the older and younger generations, the democratic school system was a major force for rapid Americanization. The number of American-born immigrant children in Chicago in 1890 nearly equaled that of the total alien-born, thus increasing, though not by that proportion, the foreign character of her population.[5]

As was Chicago, so in a measure were Cleveland, Minneapolis and Detroit. Yet Chicago's four hundred and fifty thousand foreign-born, Cleveland's one hundred thousand, Detroit's eighty thousand and Minneapolis's sixty thousand formed only two fifths of all the people in those cities in 1890. In places like Columbus and Indianapolis

seven eighths of the population continued to be of American nativity. Many of the native-born, however, were of alien parentage and still in the process of learning American ways.

In so far as the swiftly growing urban localities drew population away from the countryside, the effects were severe enough to threaten many rural districts with paralysis. A map of the Middle West, shading the counties which suffered the chief losses between 1880 and 1890, would have been blackest across central Missouri and in the eastern half of Iowa, northern and western Illinois, central and southeastern Indiana, southern Michigan and central and southern Ohio.[6] Though some of the depletion, particularly in Iowa and western Illinois, was connected with the building up of the agricultural country to the west, much of it was due to the cityward flight. In Ohio 755 townships out of 1316 declined in population; in Illinois 800 out of 1424. Yet during the same decade every Middle Western state gained substantially in total number of inhabitants—Ohio about one seventh and Illinois nearly a quarter —an advance only in part to be accounted for by immigrant additions and the natural increase of population.

Such indications of rural decay, however, were mild as compared with conditions in the North Atlantic states. In this great seaboard section stretching from the Potomac to the St. Croix the city had completed its conquest.

---

5 *U. S. Eleventh Census*, I, clxii–clxiii.

6 For this purpose the Census Bureau classifies as urban any compact community of one thousand or more. *U. S. Eleventh Census*, I, lxix–lxxi. See also E. W. Miller, "The Abandoned Farms of Michigan," *Nation* (N. Y.), XLIX (1889), 498; H. J. Fletcher, "The Doom of the Small Town," *Forum*, XLX (1895), 214–223: anon., "The City in Modern Life," *Atlantic Mo.*, LXXV (1895), 552–556.

Already in 1880 about half the people —seven and a half million—lived in towns and cities of four thousand or more inhabitants; within a decade the proportion grew to nearly three fifths or eleven million.[7] In 1890 about two out of every three persons in New York and Connecticut were townsfolk, four out of every five in Massachusetts and nine out of every ten in Rhode Island. Only the states of northern New England preserved their essentially rural character. In the East, too, most of the nation's great cities were to be found. New York City, with already more than a million people in 1880, reached a million and a half in 1890 without the help of Brooklyn which contained eight hundred thousand more. Philadelphia attained a million in 1890, though since the previous census Chicago had supplanted her as the second city of the United States. Boston, Baltimore and Washington had about half a million each, Buffalo and Pittsburgh a quarter million each. Countless smaller places spotted the landscape and gave to the entire region a strongly urban cast.

. . .

Despite the decline of rural population in New England and other parts of the East the attractions of city life were so great that from 1880 to 1890 the section in general gained twenty per cent in number of inhabitants. By the latter year nineteen million, or somewhat less than a third of all the nation, lived there. Urban growth, even more than in Middle America, was nourished by foreign immigration.[8] A larger proportion of the alien arrivals settled in the East and fewer of them took up farming as a livelihood. The census of 1890 disclosed a million more immigrants than a decade earlier. In the section as a whole one out of every five persons was foreign-born.

Nor could one assume, as ten years before, that any immigrant he met was likely to belong to the older racial strains that had fused into the historic American stock. The Eastern commonwealths with their great ports and thriving industries were the first to feel the impact of the new human tide that was setting in from southern and eastern Europe. While in 1890 they contained more Irish and Britons than did any other section—a total of two and a third million—and with nine hundred thousand Germans ranked in that respect next to the Middle West, they also embraced more Italians, Russians and Hungarians than any other section, to the number of a quarter million.

A fourth of the people of Philadelphia and a third of the Bostonians were in 1890 of alien birth. New York-Brooklyn was the greatest center of immigrants in the world, having half as many Italians as Naples, as many Germans as Hamburg, twice as many Irish as Dublin and two and a half times as many Jews as Warsaw.[9] Four out of every five residents of Greater New York were foreigners or of foreign parentage. Different from Boston and Philadelphia, the newer type of immigrant had become a considerable element in the city's population though

---

[7] *U. S. Twelfth Census*, I, lxxxiv–lxxxv. In terms of cities of eight thousand or more inhabitants the urban percentages for the two years were 43.1 and 51.8. *U. S. Eleventh Census*, I, lxviii.

[8] *U. S. Eleventh Census*, I, cxviii–cxix, clv, 606–609.

[9] Compared with Chicago, Greater New York in 1890 possessed more Irish, English, Germans, Russians and Italians, but Chicago had a larger number of Scandinavians, Bohemians, Poles and Canadians. Thirty-nine per cent of the population of New York-Brooklyn was foreign-born in 1890.

the Germans and Irish still greatly predominated.

These latest arrivals, ignorant, clannish, inured to wretched living conditions, gravitated naturally to the poorest quarters of the city toward the tip of Manhattan and gradually pushed the older occupants into the better sections to the north.[10] Lower New York was like a human palimpsest, the writings of earlier peoples being dimmed, though not entirely effaced, by the heavier print of the newest comers. Through the eighties the Italians crowded into the old Irish neighborhoods west of Broadway, while the Russian and Polish Jews took possession of the German districts to the east with the tenth ward as their center.[11] The Hungarians settled thickly east of Avenue B, about Houston Street, and the Bohemians near the river on the upper East Side from about Fiftieth to Seventy-sixth Street. Smaller groups like the Greeks and Syrians also had their special precincts where picturesque Old World customs and trades prevailed; and in the heart of the lower East Side grew up a small replica of San Francisco's Chinatown.

Quite as strange to Americans as the South Europeans were the French Canadians who began their mass invasion of New England shortly after 1878. For over two centuries these descendants of the pioneers of New France had tilled the soil of the province of Quebec where, intensely race-conscious and devoted to Catholicism, they had stubbornly maintained their identity and language apart from the conquering English. Harried, however, by hard times from the 1860's on and tempted by better opportunities elsewhere, many of them sought escape in migration.[12] Some moved westward to set up farm colonies in Ontario and Manitoba. Others, feeling the pull of the busy mill towns across the international border, succumbed to *le mal des États-Unis*. Presently the trickle of population into New England became a flooding stream. About fourteen thousand had removed to Rhode Island by 1875, sixty-four thousand to Massachusetts ten years later. Northern New England made less appeal though occasional settlements of farmers and lumberjacks were to be found. By 1890 the French Canadians, then numbering two hundred thousand, formed approximately a sixth of the entire immigrant population of New England.[13] Nearly half of them were in Massachusetts.

Living in the manufacturing towns, they were eagerly welcomed by employers who found them not only hard workers but also slow to give trouble even when conditions were galling. The opprobrium of being the "Chinese of the Eastern states," however, they scarcely deserved, although their ready acceptance of low living standards naturally roused the ire of organized

---

[10] Kate H. Claghorn, "The Foreign Immigrant in New York City," U. S. Industrial Comn., *Reports*, XV, 465–492. See also J. A. Riis, *How the Other Half Lives* (N. Y., 1890), chap. iii.

[11] The specialized character of Italian clannishness is shown by the fact that Neapolitans and Calabrians clung to the Mulberry Bend district, a colony of Genoese lived in Baxter Street, a Sicilian colony in Elizabeth Street, between Houston and Spring, while north Italians predominated in the eighth and fifteenth wards west of Broadway, and south Italians in "Little Italy" between 110th and 115th streets in Harlem.

[12] D. M. A. Magnan, *Histoire de la Race Française aux États-Unis* (Paris, 1912), 250; Alexandre Beslisle, *Histoire de la Presse Franco-Américaine* (Worcester, 1911), 4–9.

[13] Before 1890, when the federal enumerators (*Eleventh Census*, I, clxxiii–clxxv) first took cognizance of French Canadians as distinguished from Anglo-Canadians, statistics of settlement must be based on state census reports.

labor.[14] Religiously, too, they were viewed askance by the older elements. Added to the already large Irish Catholic contingent, their presence seemed to threaten the traditional Puritan and Protestant character of the section. "Protestant New England will soon have within itself, a Roman Catholic New France, as large as, if not larger than itself," cried one alarmist.[15] As a matter of fact, the language barrier and the desire of the newcomers to import their own priests caused more friction than friendship between them and the resident Irish-American clergy.[16] It was said that French-Canadian support of the Republican party at the polls was due to no reason so good as that the Irish preferred the Democrats.

A race so resistant could hardly be expected to adopt new ways of life overnight. Yet, scattered in a hundred different communities and obliged constantly to rub elbows with people unlike themselves, the chemistry of Americanization worked as quickly with them as with most other alien groups. Intermarriage, while not common, took place most readily with Anglo-Canadians.[17] Less adept politically than the Irish, they nevertheless gradually found their way into local offices and by 1890 thirteen French

Canadians were members of New England legislatures.[18] Different from other immigrant peoples, however, they massed themselves in New England, few of them going into the Middle West or even into other parts of the East.

As a lodestone for both immigrant and native-born the city had decisively placed the East under thrall. Its hand already lay heavily upon the Middle West. Even in the farther West and the South its power and distant allure were strongly felt though society as yet lingered in an agricultural state. Through the nation in general every third American in 1890 was an urban dweller, living in a town of four thousand or more inhabitants.[19] Cities of from twelve to twenty thousand people had since 1880 increased in number from 76 to 107; cities of from twenty to forty thousand from 55 to 91; larger places up to seventy-five thousand inhabitants from 21 to 35; cities of yet greater size from 23 to 39.[20]

Moreover, the concentration of population had been attended by a significant concentration of wealth. This latter circumstance furnished ample basis for the agrarian contention that the rural districts were not sharing proportionately in the advancing national wealth. In 1880, according to the census, the value of farms was equal to that of urban real estate, about ten billion dollars for each. In 1890 the value of farms was returned as thirteen billion while other real estate—mostly urban—was listed at twenty-six billion. Nor did the people on the farms and in the rural hamlets of the East fare

14 Massachusetts Bureau of Labor Statistics, *Twelfth Annual Report* (1881), 469. This document should be read in the light of the record of the public hearings held in 1882. See *Thirteenth Ann. Rep.* (1882), 3–92.

15 C. E. Amaron, *Your Heritage; or New England Threatened* (Springfield, Mass., 1891), 116.

16 Édouard Hamon, *Les Canadiens-Français de la Nouvelle-Angleterre* (Quebec, 1891), 57, 60, 175; Magnan, *Histoire*, 255–261, 266, 273–274, 296–297; Prosper Bender, "A New France in New England," *Mag. of Am. History*, XX (1888), 391.

17 *U. S. Eleventh Census*, I, 698–701; *U. S. Twelfth Census*, I, 850–853; *Mass. Census of 1895*, III, 152–154.

18 Adélard Desrosiers and P. A. Fournet, *La Race Française en Amérique* (Montreal, 1910), 240.

19 *U. S. Twelfth Census*, I, lxxxiv–lxxxv.

20 *U. S. Eleventh Census*, I, lxvii.

better than those of the West and South. On the contrary, the farms in the Eastern states declined in absolute value during the decade.

If personalty were included, the contrast between city and country became even sharper, particularly since the tangible personalty on the farms was in considerable degree offset by mortgages held in the towns and cities. The most careful contemporary student of the subject estimated that in 1890 the average wealth of families in the rural districts did not exceed $3250 while the average wealth of city families was over $9000.[21] The wider implications of urban growth, however, reached far beyond exigent considerations of wealth and income. These, as they affected the character of American civilization for good or ill, remain yet to be examined.

[21] The data for the above discussion are derived from C. B. Spahr, *An Essay on the Present Distribution of Wealth in the United States* (N. Y., 1896), 46–49, which concludes the passage with the observation: "When American political parties shall again divide upon issues vitally affecting the distribution of wealth, the clearly marked line of division will not be between East and West, but between city and country."

II. DOCUMENTS

1. Industrialization

Three perspectives on late nineteenth-century American industrial growth— the views of a leading capitalist, the opinions of a politician associated with the new tycoons, and the observations of a foreign student of American folkways—are presented in this section. John D. Rockefeller explains Standard Oil's business methods and achievements in the selection from his Reminiscences *which defends large-scale monopolistic enterprise. Chauncey Depew describes and tries to justify the process of consolidation among American railroads, while James Bryce discusses the contrast between laissez-faire ideals and actual business practices in the United States. A careful reader might also detect material in both the Depew and Rockefeller selections which supports Bryce's argument that most Gilded Age industrialists lacked true laissez-faire convictions.*

JOHN D. ROCKEFELLER

It would be surprising if in an organization which included a great number of men there should not be an occasional employee here and there who acted, in connection with the

Reprinted from John D. Rockefeller, RANDOM REMINISCENCES OF MEN AND EVENTS *(New York: Doubleday & Company, Inc., 1909 and 1937), pp. 55–63, by permission of the publisher.*

business or perhaps in conducting his own affairs, in a way which might be criticized. Even in a comparatively small organization it is well-nigh impossible to restrain this occasional man who is over-zealous for his own or his company's advancement. To judge the character of all the members of a great organization or the organization itself by the actions of a few individuals would be manifestly unfair.

It has been said that I forced the men who became my partners in the oil business to join with me. I would not have been so shortsighted. If it were true that I followed such tactics, I ask, would it have been possible to make of such men life-long companions? Would they accept, and remain for many years in positions of the greatest trust, and finally, could any one have formed of such men, if they had been so browbeaten, a group which has for all these years worked in loyal harmony, with fair dealing among themselves as well as with others, building up efficiency and acting in entire unity? This powerful organization has not only lasted but its efficiency has increased. For fourteen years I have been out of business, and in eight or ten years went only once to the company's office.

In the summer of 1907 I visited again the room at the top of the Standard Oil Company's building, where the officers of the company and the heads of departments have had their luncheon served for many years. I was surprised to find so many men who had come to the front since my last visit years ago. Afterward I had an opportunity to talk with old associates and many new ones, and it was a source of great gratification to me to find that the same spirit of coöperation and harmony existed unchanged. This practice of lunching together, a hundred or more at long tables in most intimate and friendly association, is another indication of what I contend, slight as it may seem to be at first thought. Would these people seek each other's companionship day after day if they had been forced into this relation? People in such a position do not go on for long in a pleasant and congenial intimacy.

For years the Standard Oil Company has developed step by step, and I am convinced that it has done well its work of supplying to the people the products from petroleum at prices which have decreased as the efficiency of the business has been built up. It gradually extended its services first to the large centres, and then to towns, and now to the smallest places, going to the homes of its customers, delivering the oil to suit the convenience of the actual users. This same system is being followed out in various parts of the world. The company has, for example, three thousand tank wagons supplying American oil to towns and even small hamlets in Europe. Its own depots and employees deliver it in a somewhat similar way in Japan, China, India, and the chief countries of the world. Do you think this trade has been developed by anything but hard work?

This plan of selling our products direct to the consumer and the exceptionally rapid growth of the business bred a certain antagonism which I suppose could not have been avoided, but this same idea of dealing with the consumer directly has been followed by others and in many lines of trade, without creating, so far as I recall, any serious opposition.

This is a very interesting and important point, and I have often wondered if the criticism which centered upon us did not come from the fact that we were among the first, if not the first, to work out the problems of direct selling to the user on a broad scale. This was done in a fair spirit and with due consideration for every one's rights. We did not ruthlessly go after the trade of our competitors and attempt to ruin it by cutting prices or instituting a spy system. We had set ourselves the task of building up as rapidly and as broadly as possible the volume of consumption. Let me try to explain just what happened.

To get the advantage of the facilities we had in manufacture, we sought the utmost market in all lands—we needed volume. To do this we had to create selling methods far in advance of what then existed; we had to dispose of two, or three, or four gallons of oil where one had been sold before, and we could not rely upon the usual trade channels then existing to accomplish this. It was never our purpose to interfere with a dealer who adequately cultivated his field of operations, but when we saw a new opportunity or a new place for extending the sale by further and effective facilities, we made it our business to provide them. In this way we opened many new lines in which others have shared. In this development we had to employ many comparatively new men. The ideal way to supply material for higher positions is, of course, to recruit the men from among the youngest in the company's service, but our expansion was too rapid to permit this in all cases. That some of these employees were overzealous in going after sales it would not be surprising to learn, but they were acting in violation of the expressed and known wishes of the company. But even these instances, I am convinced, occurred so seldom, by comparison with the number of transactions we carried on, that they were really the exceptions that proved the rule.

Every week in the year for many, many years, this concern has brought into this country more than a million dollars gold, all from the products produced by American labour. I am proud of the record, and believe most Americans will be when they understand some things better. These achievements, the development of this great foreign trade, the owning of ships to carry the oil in bulk by the most economical methods, the sending out of men to fight the world's markets, have cost huge sums of money, and the vast capital employed could not be raised nor controlled except by such an organization as the Standard is to-day.

To give a true picture of the early conditions, one must realize that the oil industry was considered a most hazardous undertaking, not altogether unlike the speculative mining undertakings we hear so much of to-day. I well remember my old and distinguished friend, Rev. Thomas W. Armitage, for some forty years pastor of a great New York church, warning me that it was worse than folly to extend our plants and our operations. He was sure we were running unwarranted risks, that our oil supply would probably fail, the demand would decline, and he, with many others, sometimes I thought almost everybody, prophesied ruin.

None of us ever dreamed of the magnitude of what proved to be the later expansion. We did our day's work as we met it, looking forward to what we could see in the distance and keeping well up to our opportunities, but laying our foundations firmly. As I have said, capital was most difficult to secure, and it was not easy to interest conservative men in this adventurous business. Men of property were afraid of it, though in rare cases capitalists were induced to unite with us to a limited extent. If they bought our stock at all, they took a little of it now and then as an experiment, and we were painfully conscious that they often declined to buy new stock with many beautiful expressions of appreciation.

The enterprise being so new and novel, on account of the fearfulness of certain holders in reference to its success, we frequently had to take stock to keep it from going begging, but we had such confidence in the fundamental value of the concern that we were willing to assume this risk. There are always a few men in an undertaking of this kind who would risk all on their judgment of the final result, and if the enterprise had failed, these would have been classed as visionary adventurers, and perhaps with good reason.

The 60,000 men who are at work constantly in the service of the company are kept busy year in and year out. The past year has been a time of great contraction, but the Standard has gone on with its plans unchecked, and the new works and buildings have not been delayed on account of lack of capital or fear of bad times. It pays its workmen well, it cares for them when sick, and pensions them when old. It has never had any important strikes, and if there is any better function of business management than giving profitable work to employees year after year, in good times and bad, I don't know what it is.

Another thing to be remembered about this so-called "octopus" is that there has been no "water" introduced into its capital (perhaps we felt that oil and water would not have mixed); nor in all these years has any one had to wait for money which the Standard owed. It has suffered from great fires and losses, but it has taken care of its affairs in such a way that it has not found it necessary to appeal to the general public to place blocks of bonds or stock; it has used no underwriting syndicates or stock-selling schemes in any form, and it has always managed to finance new oil field operations when called upon.

It is a common thing to hear people say that this company has crushed out its competitors. Only the uninformed could make such an assertion. It has

and always has had, and always will have, hundreds of active competitors; it has lived only because it has managed its affairs well and economically and with great vigour. To speak of competition for a minute: Consider not only the able people who compete in refining oil, but all the competition in the various trades which make and sell by-products—a great variety of different businesses. And perhaps of even more importance is the competition in foreign lands. The Standard is always fighting to sell the American product against the oil produced from the great fields of Russia, which struggles for the trade of Europe, and the Burma oil, which largely affects the market in India. In all these various countries we are met with tariffs which are raised against us, local prejudices, and strange customs. In many countries we had to teach the people—the Chinese, for example—to burn oil by making lamps for them; we packed the oil to be carried by camels or on the backs of runners in the most remote portions of the world; we adapted the trade to the needs of strange folk. Every time we succeeded in a foreign land, it meant dollars brought to this country, and every time we failed, it was a loss to our nation and its workmen.

One of our greatest helpers has been the State Department in Washington. Our ambassadors and ministers and consuls have aided to push our way into new markets to the utmost corners of the world.

CHAUNCEY M. DEPEW

When I entered the service of the railroad on the first of January, 1866,

Reprinted from Chauncey M. Depew, MY MEMORIES OF EIGHTY YEARS *(New York: Charles Scribner's Sons, 1924), pp. 227–35, by permission of the publisher.*

the Vanderbilt system consisted of the Hudson River and Harlem Railroads, the Harlem ending at Chatham, 128 miles, and the Hudson River at Albany, 140 miles long. The Vanderbilt system now covers 20,000 miles. The total railway mileage of the whole United States at that time was 36,000, and now it is 261,000 miles.

My connection with the New York Central Railroad covers practically the whole period of railway construction, expansion, and development in the United States. It is a singular evidence of the rapidity of our country's growth and of the way which that growth has steadily followed the rails, that all this development of States, of villages growing into cities, of scattered communities becoming great manufacturing centres, of an internal commerce reaching proportions where it has greater volume than the foreign interchanges of the whole world, has come about during a period covered by the official career of a railroad man who is still in the service: an attorney in 1866, a vice-president in 1882, president in 1885, chairman of the board of directors in 1899, and still holds that office.

There is no such record in the country for continuous service with one company, which during the whole period has been controlled by one family. This service of more than half a century has been in every way satisfactory. It is a pleasure to see the fourth generation, inheriting the ability of the father, grandfather, and great-grandfather, still active in the management.

I want to say that in thus linking my long relationship with the railroads to this marvellous development, I do not claim to have been better than the railway officers who during this time have performed their duties to the best of their ability. I wish also to pay tribute to the men of original genius, of vision and daring, to whom so much is due in the expansion and improvement of the American railway systems.

Commodore Vanderbilt was one of the most remarkable men our country has produced. He was endowed with wonderful foresight, grasp of difficult situations, ability to see opportunities before others, to solve serious problems, and the courage of his convictions. He had little education or early advantages, but was eminently successful in everything he undertook. As a boy on Staten Island he foresaw that upon transportation depended the settlement, growth, and prosperity of this nation. He began with a small boat running across the harbor from Staten Island to New York. Very early in his career he acquired a steamboat and in a few years was master of Long Island Sound. He then extended his operations to the Hudson River and speedily acquired the dominating ownership in boats competing between New York and Albany.

When gold was discovered in California he started a line on the Atlantic side of the Isthmus of Darien and secured from the government of Nicaragua the privilege of crossing the Isthmus for a transportation system through its territory, and then established a line of steamers on the Pacific to San Francisco. In a short time the old-established lines, both on the Atlantic and the Pacific, were compelled to sell out to him. Then he entered the transatlantic trade, with steamers to Europe.

With that vision which is a gift and cannot be accounted for, he decided that the transportation work of the future was on land and in railroads. He abandoned the sea, and his first enterprise was the purchase of the New York and Harlem Railroad, which was only one hundred and twenty-eight miles long. The road was bankrupt and its road-bed and equipment going from bad to worse. The commodore reconstructed the line, re-equipped it, and by making it serviceable to its territory increased its traffic and turned its business from deficiency into profit. This was in 1864. The commodore became president, and his son, William H. Vanderbilt, vice-president. He saw that the extension of the Harlem was not advisable, and so secured the Hudson River Railroad, running from New York to Albany, and became its president in 1865. It was a few months after this when he and his son invited me to become a member of their staff.

The station of the Harlem Railroad in the city of New York was at that time at Fourth Avenue and Twenty-sixth Street, and that of the Hudson River Railroad at Chambers Street, near the North River.

In a few years William H. Vanderbilt purchased the ground for the Harlem Railroad Company, where is now located the Grand Central Terminal, and by the acquisition by the New York Central and Hudson River Railroad of the Harlem Railroad the trains of the New York Central were brought around into the Grand Central Station.

In 1867, two years after Mr. Vanderbilt had acquired the Hudson River Railroad, he secured the control of the New York Central, which ran from Albany to Buffalo. This control was continued through the Lake Shore on one side of the lakes and the Michigan Central on the other to Chicago. Subsequently the Vanderbilt System was extended to Cincinnati and St. Louis. It was thus in immediate connection with the West and Northwest centering in Chicago, and the Southwest at Cincinnati and St. Louis. By close connection and affiliation with the Chicago and Northwestern Railway Company, the Vanderbilt system was extended beyond to Mississippi. I became director in the New York Central in 1874 and in the Chicago and Northwestern in 1877.

It has been my good fortune to meet with more or less intimacy many of the remarkable men in every department of life, but I think Commodore Vanderbilt was the most original. I had been well acquainted for some years both with the commodore and his son, William H. When I became attorney my relations were more intimate than those usually existing. I was in daily consultation with the commodore during the ten years prior to his death, and with his son from 1866 to 1885, when he died.

The commodore was constantly, because of his wealth and power, importuned by people who wished to interest him in their schemes. Most of the great and progressive enterprises of his time were presented to him. He would listen patiently, ask a few questions, and in a short time grasp the whole subject. Then with wonderful quickness and unerring judgment he would render his decision. No one knew by what process he arrived at these conclusions. They seemed to be the results as much of inspiration as of insight.

The Civil War closed in 1865, and one of its lessons had been the necessity for more railroads. The country had discovered that without transportation its vast and fertile territories could neither be populated nor made productive. Every mile of railroad carried settlers, opened farms and increased the national resources and wealth. The economical and critical conditions of the country, owing to the expansion of the currency and banking conditions, facilitated and encouraged vast schemes of railroad construction. This and a wild speculation resulted in the panic of 1873. Nearly the whole country went bankrupt. The recovery was rapid, and the constructive talent of the Republic saw that the restoration of credit and prosperity must be led by railway solvency. In August, 1874, Commodore Vanderbilt invited the representatives of the other and competitive lines to a conference at Saratoga. Owing, however, to the jealousies and hostilities of the period, only the New York Central, the Pennsylvania, and the Erie railways were represented.

The eastern railway situation was then dominated by Commodore Vanderbilt, Colonel Thomas A. Scott, of the Pennsylvania, and John W. Garrett, of the Baltimore and Ohio. Both Scott and Garrett were original men and empire builders. There was neither governmental nor State regulation. The head of a railway system had practically unlimited power in the operation of his road. The people were so anxious for the construction of railways that they offered every possible inducement to capital. The result was a great deal of unprofitable construction and immense losses to the promoters.

These able men saw that there was no possibility of railway construction, operation, and efficiency, with a continuance of unrestricted competition. It has taken from 1874 until 1920 to educate the railway men, the shippers, and the government to a realization of the fact that transportation facilities required for the public necessities can only be had by the freest operations and the strictest government regulations; that the solution of the problem is a system so automatic that public arbitration shall decide the justice of the demands of labor, and rates be advanced to meet the decision, and that public authority also shall take into consideration the other factors of in-

creased expenses and adequate facilities for the railroads, and that maintenance and the highest efficiency must be preserved and also necessary extensions. To satisfy and attract capital there must be the assurance of a reasonable return upon the investment.

The meeting called by Commodore Vanderbilt in 1874, at Saratoga, was an epoch-making event. We must remember the railway management of the country was in the absolute control of about four men, two of whom were also largest owners of the lines they managed. Fierce competition and cutting of rates brought on utter demoralization among shippers, who could not calculate on the cost of transportation, and great favoritism to localities and individuals by irresponsible freight agents who controlled the rates. Under these influences railway earnings were fluctuating and uncertain. Improvements were delayed and the people on the weaker lines threatened with bankruptcy.

Public opinion, however, believed this wild competition to be the only remedy for admitted railway evils. As an illustration of the change of public opinion and the better understanding of the railway problems, this occurred in the month of October, 1920. A committee of shippers and producers representing the farmers, manufacturers, and business men along a great railway system came to see the manager of the railroad and said to him: "We have been all wrong in the past. Our effort has always been for lower rates, regardless of the necessities of the railways. We have tried to get them by seeking bids from competing lines for our shipments and by appealing to the Interstate Commerce Commission. The expenses of the railroads have been increased by demands of labor, by constantly rising prices and cost of rails, cars, terminals, and facilities, but we have been against allowing the railroads to meet this increased cost of operation by adequate advances in rates. We now see that this course was starving the railroads, and we are suffering for want of cars and locomotives to move our traffic and terminals to care for it. We are also suffering because the old treatment of the railroads has frightened capital so that the roads cannot get money to maintain their lines and make necessary improvements to meet the demands of business. We know now that rates make very little difference, because they can be absorbed in our business. What we must have is facilities to transport our products, and we want to help the railroads to get money and credit, and again we emphasize our whole trouble is want of cars, locomotives, and terminal facilities."

Happily, public opinion was reflected in the last Congress in the passage of the Cummins-Esch bill, which is the most enlightened and adaptable legislation of the last quarter of a century.

To return to the conference at Saratoga, the New York Central, the Pennsylvania, and the Erie came to the conclusion that they must have the co-operation of the Baltimore and Ohio. As Mr. Garrett, president and controlling owner of that road, would not come to the conference, the members decided that the emergency was so great that they must go to him. This was probably the most disagreeable thing Commodore Vanderbilt ever did. The marvellous success of his wonderful life had been won by fighting and defeating competitors. The peril was so great that they went as associates, and the visit interested the whole country and so enlarged Mr. Garrett's opinion of his power that he rejected their offer and said he would act independently.

A railway war immediately followed, and in a short time bankruptcy threatened all lines, and none more than the Baltimore and Ohio.

The trunk lines then got together and entered into an agreement to stabilize rates and carry them into effect. They appointed as commissioner Mr. Albert Fink, one of the ablest railway men of that time. Mr. Fink's administration was successful, but the rivalries and jealousies of the lines and the frequent breaking of agreements were too much for one man.

The presidents and general managers of all the railroads east of Chicago then met and formed an association, and this association was a legislative body without any legal authority to enforce its decrees. It had, however, two effects: the disputes which arose were publicly discussed, and the merits of each side so completely demonstrated that the decision of the association came to be accepted as just and right. Then the verdict of the association had behind it the whole investment and banking community and the press. The weight of this was sufficient to compel obedience to its decisions by the most rebellious member. No executive could continue to hold his position while endeavoring to break up the association.

It is one of the most gratifying events of my life that my associates in this great and powerful association elected me their president, and I continued in office until the Supreme Court in a momentous decision declared that the railroads came under the provision of the Sherman Anti-Trust Law and dissolved these associations in the East, West, and South.

It was a liberal education of the railway problems to meet the men who became members of this association. Most of them left an indelible impression upon the railway conditions of the time and of the railway policies of the future. All were executives of great ability and several rare constructive geniuses.

In our system there was John Newell, president of the Lake Shore and Michigan Southern, a most capable and efficient manager. Henry B. Ledyard, president of the Michigan Central, was admirably trained for the great responsibilities which he administered so well. There was William Bliss, president of the Boston and Albany, who had built up a line to be one of the strongest of the New England group.

Melville E. Ingalls, president of the Cleveland, Cincinnati, Chicago and St. Louis, had combined various weak and bankrupt roads and made them an efficient organization. He had also rehabilitated and put in useful working and paying condition the Chesapeake and Ohio.

JAMES BRYCE

A European friend of a philosophic turn of mind bade me, when he heard that I was writing this book, dedicate at least one chapter to the American Theory of the State. I answered that the Americans had no theory of the State, and felt no need for one, being content, like the English, to base their constitutional ideas upon law and history.

In England and America alike (I pursued) one misses a whole circle and system of ideas and sentiments which have been potent among the nations of the European continent. To those nations the State is a great moral power, the totality of the wisdom and

Reprinted from James Bryce, THE AMERICAN COMMONWEALTH *(New York, 1911), II, 587–99.*

conscience and force of the people, yet greater far than the sum of the individuals who compose the people, because consciously and scientifically, if also by a law of nature, organized for purposes which the people indistinctly apprehend, and because it is the inheritor of a deep-rooted reverence and an almost despotic authority. There is a touch of mysticism in this conception, which has survived the change from arbitrary to representative government, and almost recalls the sacredness that used to surround the mediæval church. In England the traditions of an ancient monarchy and the social influence of the class which till lately governed have enabled the State and its service to retain a measure of influence and respect. No one, however, attributes any special wisdom to the State, no one treats those concerned with administration or legislation as a superior class. Officials are strictly held within the limits of their legal powers, and are obeyed only so far as they can show that they are carrying out the positive directions of the law. Their conduct, and indeed the decisions of the highest State organs, are criticised, perhaps with more courtesy, but otherwise in exactly the same way as those of other persons and bodies. Yet the State is dignified, and men are proud to serve it. From the American mind, that which may be called the mystic aspect of the State, and the theory of its vast range of action, are as conspicuously absent as they are from the English. They are absent, not because America is a democracy, but because the political ideas of the two branches of the race are fundamentally the same, a fact which continental observers of the United States constantly fail to appreciate. In America, however, even the dignity of the State has vanished. It seems actually less than the individuals who live under it. The people, that is to say, the vast multitude of men who inhabit the country, inspire respect or awe, the organism is ignored. The State is nothing but a name for the legislative and administrative machinery whereby certain business of the inhabitants is despatched. It has no more conscience, or moral mission, or title to awe and respect, than a commercial company for working a railroad or a mine; and those who represent it are treated in public and in private with quite as little deference.

Hereupon my friend rejoined that people in America must at least have some general views about the functions of government and its relations to the individual. "We are told," he continued, "that the whole American polity is more coherent, more self-consistent, than that of England; it must therefore have what the Germans call 'ground-ideas.' There is a profusion of legislation. Legislation must proceed upon these ideas, and by examining the current legislation of the Federal government and of the States you will be able to discover and present the beliefs and notions regarding the State which the Americans cherish."

The term "ground-ideas" does not happily describe the doctrines that prevail in the United States, for the people are not prone to form or state their notions in a philosophic way. There are, however, certain dogmas or maxims which are in so far fundamental that they have told widely on political thought, and that one usually strikes upon them when sinking a shaft, so to speak, into an American mind. Among such dogmas are the following:—

Certain rights of the individual, as, for instance, his right to the enjoyment of what he has earned, and to the free expression of his opinions, are primordial and sacred.

All political power springs from the people, and the most completely popular government is the best.

Legislatures, officials, and all other agents of the sovereign people ought to be strictly limited by law, by each other, and by the shortness of the terms of office.

Where any function can be equally well discharged by a central or by a local body, it ought by preference to be entrusted to the local body, for a centralized administration is more likely to be tyrannical, inefficient, and impure than one which, being on a small scale, is more fully within the knowledge of the citizens and more sensitive to their opinion.

Two men are wiser than one, one hundred than ninety-nine, thirty millions than twenty-nine millions. Whether they are wiser or not, the will of the larger number must prevail against the will of the smaller. But the majority is not wiser because it is called the Nation, or because it controls the government, but only because it is more numerous. The nation is nothing *but* so many individuals. The government is nothing but certain representatives and officials, agents who are here to-day and gone to-morrow.

The less of government the better; that is to say, the fewer occasions for interfering with individual citizens are allowed to officials, and the less time citizens have to spend in looking after their officials, so much the more will the citizens and the community prosper. The functions of government must be kept at their minimum.

The first five of these dogmas have been discussed and illustrated in earlier chapters. The last of them needs a little examination, because it suggests points of comparison with the Old World, and because the meaning of it lies in the application. It is all very well to say that the functions of government should be kept at a minimum; but the bureaucrats of Russia might say the same. What is this minimum? Every nation, every government, every philosopher, has his own view as to the functions which it must be taken to include.

The doctrine of *Laissez faire,* or non-interference by government with the citizen, has two foundations, which may be called the sentimental and the rational. The sentimental ground is the desire of the individual to be let alone, to do as he pleases, indulge his impulses, follow out his projects. The rational ground is the principle, gathered from an observation of the phenomena of society, that interference by government more often does harm than good—that is to say, that the desires and impulses of men when left to themselves are more likely by their natural collision and co-operation to work out a happy result for the community and the individuals that compose it than will be attained by the conscious endeavours of the State controlling and directing those desires and impulses. There are laws of nature governing mankind as well as the material world; and man will thrive better under these laws than under those which he makes for himself through the organization we call Government.

Of these two views, the former or sentimental has been extremely strong in America, being rooted in the character and habits of the race, and seeming to issue from that assertion of individual liberty which is proclaimed in such revered documents as the Declaration of Independence and the older State constitutions. The latter view, incessantly canvassed in Europe, has played no great part in the United States; or rather it has appeared in the form not of a philosophic induction from experience, but of a common-sense notion that everybody knows his own business best, that individual enterprise has "made America," and will "run America," better than the best government could do.

The State governments of 1776 and the National government of 1789 started from ideas, mental habits, and administrative practice generally similar to those of contemporary England. Now England in the eighteenth century was that one among European countries in which government had the narrowest sphere. The primitive paternal legislation of the later Middle Ages had been abandoned. The central government had not begun to stretch out its arms to interfere with quarter sessions in the counties, or municipal corporations in the towns, to care for the health, or education, or morals of the people. That strengthening and reorganization of administration which was in progress in many parts of the continent, as in Prussia under Frederick the Great, and in Portugal under Pombal, had not spread to England, and would have been resisted there by men of conservative tendencies for one set of reasons, and men of liberal tendencies for another. Everything tended to make the United States in this respect more English than England, for the circumstances of colonial life, the process of settling the western wilderness, the feelings evoked by the struggle against George III, all went to intensify individualism, the love of enterprise, and the pride in personal freedom. And from that day to this, individualism, the love of enterprise, and the pride in personal freedom, have been deemed by Americans not only their choicest, but their peculiar and exclusive possessions.

The hundred years which have passed since the birth of the Republic have, however, brought many changes with them. Individualism is no longer threatened by arbitrary kings, and the ramparts erected to protect it from their attacks are useless and grass-grown. If any assaults are to be feared they will come from another quarter. New causes are at work in the world tending not only to lengthen the arms of government, but to make its touch quicker and firmer. Do these causes operate in America as well as in Europe? and, if so, does America, in virtue of her stronger historical attachment to individualism, oppose a more effective resistance to them?

I will mention a few among them. Modern civilization, in becoming more complex and refined, has become more exacting. It discerns more benefits which the organized power of government can secure, and grows more anxious to attain them. Men live fast, and are impatient of the slow working of natural laws. The triumphs of physical science have enlarged their desires for comfort, and shown them how many things may be accomplished by the application of collective skill and large funds which are beyond the reach of individual effort. Still greater has been the influence of a quickened moral sensitiveness and philanthropic sympathy. The sight of preventable evil is painful, and is felt as a reproach. He who preaches patience and reliance upon natural progress is thought callous. The sense of sin may, as theologians tell us, be declining; but the dislike to degrading and brutalizing vice is increasing; there is a warmer recognition of the responsibility of each man for his neighbour, and a more earnest zeal in works of moral reform. Some doctrines which, because they had satisfied philosophers, were in the last generation accepted by the bulk of educated men, have now become, if not discredited by experience, yet far from

popular. They are thought to be less universally true, less completely beneficial, than was at first supposed. There are benefits which the laws of demand and supply do not procure. Unlimited competition seems to press too hardly on the weak. The power of groups of men organized by incorporation as joint-stock companies, or of small knots of rich men acting in combination, has developed with unexpected strength in unexpected ways, overshadowing individuals and even communities, and showing that the very freedom of association which men sought to secure by law when they were threatened by the violence of potentates may, under the shelter of the law, ripen into a new form of tyranny. And in some countries, of which Britain may be taken as the type, the transference of political power from the few to the many has made the many less jealous of governmental authority. The government is now their creature, their instrument —why should they fear to use it? They may strip it to-morrow of the power with which they have clothed it to-day. They may rest confident that its power will not be used contrary to the wishes of the majority among themselves. And as it is in this majority that authority has now been vested, they readily assume that the majority will be right.

How potent these influences and arguments have proved in the old countries of Europe, how much support they receive not only from popular sentiment, but from the writings of a vigorous school of philosophical economists, all the world knows. But what of newer communities, where the evils to be combated by state action are fewer, where the spirit of liberty and the sentiment of individualism are more intense? An eminent Englishman expressed the general belief of Englishmen when he said in 1883:—

How is it that while the increasing democracy at home is insisting, with such growing eagerness, on more control by the state, we see so small a corresponding development of the same principle in the United States or in Anglo-Saxon colonies? It is clearly not simply the democratic spirit which demands so much central regulation. Otherwise we should find the same conditions in the Anglo-Saxon democracies across the seas.[1]

That belief of Englishmen was then the general belief of Americans also. Nine men out of ten told the stranger that both the Federal government and the State governments interfered little, and many ascribed the prosperity of the country to this noninterference as well as to the self-reliant spirit of the people. So far as there can be said to be any theory on the subject in a land which gets on without theories, *laissez aller* has been the orthodox and accepted doctrine in the sphere both of Federal and of State legislation.

Nevertheless the belief was mistaken then and has since then become still more evidently groundless. The new democracies of America are as eager for state interference as the democracy of Britain, and try their experiments with even more lighthearted promptitude. No one need be surprised at this when he reflects that the causes which have been mentioned as telling on Europe, tell on the United States with no less force. Men are even more eager than in Europe to hasten on to the ends they desire, even more impatient of the delays which a reliance on natural forces involves, even more sensitive to the wretchedness of their fellows, and to the mischiefs which vice and ignorance breed. Unrestricted competition has shown its dark side: great corporations have been more powerful than in Britain, and more inclined to abuse

their power. Having lived longer under a democratic government, the American masses have realized more perfectly than those of Europe that they are themselves the government. Their absolute command of its organization (except where constitutional checks are interposed) makes them turn more quickly to it for the accomplishment of their purposes. And in the State legislatures they possess bodies with which it is easy to try legislative experiments, since these bodies, though not of themselves disposed to innovation, are mainly composed of men unskilled in economics, inapt to foresee any but the nearest consequences of their measures, prone to gratify any whim of their constituents, and open to the pressure of any section whose self-interest or impatient philanthropy clamours for some departure from the general principles of legislation. For crotchet-mongers as well as for intriguers there is no such paradise as the lobby of a State legislature. No responsible statesman is there to oppose them. No warning voice will be raised by a scientific economist.

Thus it has come to pass that, though the Americans have no theory of the State and take a narrow view of its functions, though they conceive themselves to be devoted to *laissez faire* in principle, and to be in practice the most self-reliant of peoples, they have grown no less accustomed than the English to carry the action of government into ever-widening fields. Economic theory did not stop them, for practical men are proud of getting on without theory.[2] The sentiment of individualism did not stop them, because State intervention has usually taken

1 Mr. Goschen, in an address delivered at Edinburgh.

2 Till recently, there has been little theoretical discussion of these questions in the United States. At present the two tendencies, that of *laissez faire* and that which leans to State interference, are well represented by able writers.

the form of helping or protecting the greater number, while restraining the few; and personal freedom of action, the love of which is strong enough to repel the paternalism of France or Germany, was at first infringed upon only at the bidding of a strong moral sentiment, such as that which condemns intemperance. So gradual was the process of transition to this new habit that for a long time few but lawyers and economists became aware of it, and the lamentations with which old-fashioned English thinkers accompany the march of legislation were in America scarcely heard and wholly unheeded. Now however the complexity of civilization and the desire to have things done which a public authority can most quickly do, and the cost of which is less felt by each man because it comes out of the public revenue, to which he is only one of many contributors—these causes have made the field of governmental action almost as wide as it is in Europe, and men recognize the fact.

As ordinary private law and administration belong to the States, it is chiefly in State legislation that we must look for instances of such intervention. Recent illustrations of the tendency to do by law what men were formerly let to do for themselves, and to prohibit by law acts of omission and commission which used to pass unregarded, might be culled in abundance from the statute-books of nearly every commonwealth.[3] It is in the West, which plumes itself on being pre-eminently the land of freedom, enterprise, and self-help, that this tendency is most active and plays the strangest pranks, because legislators are in the West more impatient and self-confident than elsewhere.

[3] I have collected some instances in a note to this chapter.

The forms which legislative intervention takes may be roughly classified under the following heads:—

Prohibitions to individuals to do acts which are not, in the ordinary sense of the word, criminal (e.g. to sell intoxicating liquors, to employ a labourer for more than so many hours in a day).

Directions to individuals to do things which it is not obviously wrong to omit (e.g. to provide seats for shop-women, to publish the accounts of a railway company).

Interferences with the ordinary course of law in order to protect individuals from the consequences of their own acts (e.g. the annulment of contracts between employer and workmen making the former not liable for accidental injuries to the latter, the exemption of homesteads, or of a certain amount of personal property, from the claims of creditors, the prohibition of more than a certain rate of interest on money).

Directions to a public authority to undertake work which might be left to individual action and the operation of supply and demand (e.g. the providing of schools and dispensaries, the establishment of State analysts, State oil inspectors, the collection and diffusion, at the public expense, of statistics).

Retention, appropriation, or control by the State of certain natural sources of wealth or elements in its production (e.g. the declaration, made by Washington, Wyoming, Montana, and Idaho, that the use of all waters, whether still or flowing, within their respective bounds, is a public use, and forever subject to State control, the prohibition by Indiana of the wasteful use of natural gas).

In every one of these kinds of legislative interference the Americans, or at least the Western States, seem to have gone farther than the English Parliament. The restrictions on the liquor traffic have been more sweeping; while (except in the South) those upon the labour of women and children, and of persons employed by the State, have been not less so. Moral duties are more frequently enforced by legal penalties than in England. Railroads, insurance and banking companies, and other corporations are, in most States, strictly regulated. Efforts to protect individuals coming under the third head are so frequent and indulgent that their policy is beginning to be seriously questioned.[4] Gratuitous elementary and secondary education is provided all over the Union, and in the West there are also State universities provided for women as well as for men at very low charges. And although the State has not gone so far in superseding individual action as to create for itself monopolies, it is apt to spend money on same objects not equally cared for by European governments. It tries to prevent adulteration by putting its stamp on agricultural fertilizers, and prohibit-

ing the sale of oleomargarine; it establishes dairy commissions, bureaus of animal industry, and boards of live-stock commissioners armed with wide powers of inspection, it distributes seed to farmers, provides a State chemist to analyze soils gratuitously and recommend the appropriate fertilizers, subsidizes agricultural fairs, sends round lecturers on agriculture, and encourages by bounties the culture of beetroot and manufacture of sugar therefrom, the making of starch from State-grown potatoes, tree-planting, and the killing of noxious animals,—English sparrows in Massachusetts, panthers and wolves in Wyoming.[5] The farmer of Kansas or Iowa is more palpably the object of the paternal solicitude of his legislature than the farmer of any European country. And in the pursuit of its schemes for blessing the community the State raises a taxation which would be complained of in a less prosperous country.[6]

What has been the result of this legislation? Have the effects which the economists of the physiocratic or *laissez aller* school taught us to expect actually followed? Has the natural course of commerce and industry been disturbed, has the self-helpfulness of the citizen been weakened, has government done its work ill and a new door

---

[4] "A numerous and ever-increasing list of possessions has been entirely exempted from execution for debt, starting with the traditional homestead, and going on through all the necessities of life, implements of trade, and even corner-lots and money, until in some States, as in Texas, almost every conceivable object of desire, from a house and corner-lot to a span of fast horses, may be held and enjoyed by the poor man free from all claims of his creditors. Without going further into details it may be boldly stated that the tendency of democratic legislation on this subject has been to require the repayment of debts only when it can be made out of superfluous accumulated capital."—Mr. F. J. Stimson, in a vigorous and thoughtful article on the "Ethics of Democracy," in *Scribner's Magazine* for June, 1887.

The latest Constitution of Texas provides that where a contractor becomes bankrupt, the labourers employed by him shall have a right of action against the company or person for whose benefit the work on which they were employed was done.

[5] In Kansas the gift of bounties for the heads of coyotes (prairie-wolves) led to the rearing of these animals on a large scale in a new description of stockfarms!

[6] "Speaking broadly, and including indirect taxation, it may be stated that the laws now purport to give the State power to dispose of at least one-third the annual revenues of property. . . . Of course these taxes are largely, by the richest citizens, evaded, but upon land at least they are effectual. It is certainly understating it to say that the general taxation upon land equals one-third the net rents, *i.e.* Ricardo's margin of cultivation less expenses of management."—Stimson, *ut supra*.

to jobbery been opened? It is still too soon to form conclusions on these points. Some few of the experiments have failed, others seem to be succeeding; but the policy of State interferences as a whole has not yet been adequately tested. In making this new departure American legislatures are serving the world, if not their own citizens, for they are providing it with a store of valuable data for its instruction, data which deserve more attention than they have hitherto received, and whose value will increase as time goes on.

It is the privilege of these unconscious philosophers to try experiments with less risk than countries like France or England would have to run, for the bodies on which the experiments are tried are so relatively small and exceptionally vigorous that failures need not inflict permanent injury. Railroads and other large business interests complain, and sometimes not without reason, but no people is shrewder than the American in coming to recognize the results of overbold legislation and modifying it when it is found to tell against the general prosperity.

NOTE

I collect a few instances of legislation illustrating the tendency to extend State intervention and the scope of penal law:—

New York provides that no guest shall be excluded from any hotel on account of race, creed (some had refused to receive Jews), or colour.

Wisconsin requires every hotel above a certain height to be furnished with fireproof staircases; and Michigan punishes the proprietors of any shop or factory in which the health of employees is endangered by improper heating, lighting, ventilation, or sanitarian arrangements.

Michigan compels railroad compa-nies to provide automatic car couplings. Other States direct the use of certain kinds of brakes.

Georgia orders railway companies to put up a bulletin stating how much any train already half an hour late is overdue; Arkansas requires this even if the train is only a few minutes late.

Wyoming requires railroads passing within four miles of any city to provide, at the nearest point, a depot whereat all local trains shall stop; while Arkansas forbids baggage to be tumbled from cars on to the platform at a depot; and Ohio permits no one to be engaged as a train conductor unless he has had two years' previous experience as trainhand.

Massachusetts forbids the employment of colour-blind persons on railways, and provides for the examination of those so employed.

Ohio requires druggists to place on bottles containing poison a red label, naming at least two of the most readily procurable antidotes.

Several States order employers to find seats for women employed in shops, warehouses, or manufactories.

Several States forbid any one to practise dentistry as well as medicine unless licensed by a State Board.

Massachusetts, Rhode Island, and Illinois compel corporations to pay workmen weekly. (Massachusetts forbade employers to deduct fines from the sums payable by them for wages, but the Supreme Court of the State [by a majority] held the statute unconstitutional.)

Maryland institutes a "State Board of Commissioners of Practical Plumbing," and confines the practice of that industry to persons licensed by the same. New York provides Boards of Examiners to supervise plumber's work.

Kansas punishes as a crime the making any misrepresentation to or deceiving any person in the sale of fruit or shade trees, shrubs or bulbs; and New Jersey does the like as regards fruit trees or briars.

Mississippi punishes with fine and imprisonment any legislative, executive, judicial, or ministerial officer, who shall travel on any railroad without paying absolutely, and without any evasion whatever, the same fare as is required of passengers generally.

Many States offer bounties on the raising of various agricultural products or on manufactures, while California appropriates money for the introduction from Australia of parasites and predaceous insects, with a view to the extermination of a moth which injures orange trees.

Texas makes it a punishable misdemeanour to deal in "futures" or "keep any 'bucket shop' or other establishment where future contracts are bought or sold with no intention of an actual delivery of the article so bought or sold," while Massachusetts is content with making such contracts voidable.

Michigan prescribes a system of minority voting at the election of directors of joint-stock corporations; Kentucky prescribes cumulative voting in like cases.

Pennsylvania forbids the consolidation of telegraph companies.

Ohio punishes by fine and imprisonment the offering to sell "options," or exhibiting any quotations of the prices of "margins," "futures," or "options." Georgia imposes on dealers in "futures" a tax of $500 a year.

New York forbids the hiring of barmaids, and Colorado permits no woman to enter a "wine room."

Colorado, Kansas, and North Carolina make the seduction under promise of marriage of any chaste woman a felony.

New York punishes with fine and imprisonment any person "who shall send a letter with intent to cause annoyance to any other person."

Virginia punishes with death the destruction by dynamite or any other explosive of any dwelling, if at night, or endangering human life.

Kentucky makes it a misdemeanour to play with dice any game for money, and a felony to keep, manage, or operate any such game.

Washington punishes any one who permits a minor to play at cards in his house without the written permission of the minor's parent or guardian.

Oregon prohibits secret societies in all public schools; and California also forbids the formation of "secret oath-bound fraternities" in public schools.

Maine requires every public school teacher to devote not less than ten minutes per week to instruction in the principles of kindness to birds and animals, and punishes any nurse who fails at once to report to a physician that the eye of an infant has become reddened or inflamed within five weeks after birth. Rhode Island in a similar statute fixes a fortnight from birth and allows six hours for the report.

Illinois and Arizona forbid marriages between first cousins.

Virginia punishes with a fine of $100 the sale to a minor, not only of pistols, dirks, and bowie-knives, but also of cigarettes. Twenty-four other States have similar laws forbidding minors to smoke or chew tobacco in public. Arizona makes it penal to sell or give liquor to a minor without his parents' consent, or even to admit him to a saloon.

Several States have recently made the smoking of cigarettes a punishable offence.

Kentucky prohibits the sale of any book or periodical, "the chief feature of which is to record the commission of crimes, or display by cuts or illustrations of crimes committed, or the pictures of criminals, desperadoes, or fugitives from justice, or of men or women influenced by stimulants"; and North Dakota punishes the sale or gift to, and even the exhibition within sight of, any minor of any book, magazine, or newspaper "principally made up of criminal news or pictures, stories of deeds of bloodshed, lust, or crime."

Some States permit judges to hear in private cases the evidence in which is of an obscene nature.

Massachusetts compels insurance companies to insure the lives of coloured persons on the same terms with those of whites.

Oregon requires the doors of any building used for public purposes to be so swung as to open outwards.

Minnesota enacts that all labour performed by contract upon a building shall be a first lien thereon; and declares that the fact that the person performing the labour was not enjoined from so doing shall be conclusive evidence of the contract; while Iowa gives to all workers in coal mines a lien for their wages upon all property used in constructing and working the mine.

Alabama makes it penal for a banker to discount at a higher rate than 8 per cent.

Many States have stringent usury laws.

Pennsylvania forbids a mortgagee to contract for the payment by the mortgagor of any taxes over and above the interest payable.

Kentucky and some other States have been making strenuous (but imperfectly successful) efforts to extinguish lotteries. On the other hand, Nevada appears to have authorized one.

Some of the newer states by their constitutions, and many others by statutes, endeavour to destroy the combinations of capitalists called "Trusts," treating them as conspiracies, and threatening severe penalties against those concerned in them.

Laws purporting to limit the hours of adult male labour have been passed by Congress and in many States. None, however, appear to forbid under penalty overtime work, except as respects public servants (under the Federal Government, and in Massachusetts, Maryland, Pennsylvania, Colorado), the limit being 8 or 9 hours, railway servants (Maryland, New Jersey, Michigan), 10 to 12 hours, and coal-miners (Wyoming), 8 hours. These laws, in fact, amount to little more than a declaration that the number of hours mentioned shall (except as aforesaid) constitute a legal day's work in the absence of an agreement for longer service.

Congress and the legislatures of at least fourteen States have by statute created or provided for the creation of Boards of Arbitration in trade disputes, but have conferred very restricted powers for that purpose.

2. Immigration and Urban Growth

Americans in the Gilded Age disagreed profoundly over whether the newer immigrants from Southern and Eastern Europe, most of whom flocked into the cities and factory towns as industrial workers, could be assimilated successfully. The actual drama of Americanization occurred among second generation children of immigrants, whose American education and experi-

ences contrasted starkly with the Old World culture and habits of their families. In writing about a Jewish youth in New York City, Hutchins Hapgood describes the tensions inherent in this assimilation process. The English writer James Bryce then takes issue with the nativism of many contemporary Americans in his spirited defense of the newer immigrants. Bryce's balanced discussion of the problems and possibilities of their assimilation probably appeared utopian to many of his readers at the time.

HUTCHINS HAPGOOD

The shrewd-faced boy with the melancholy eyes that one sees everywhere in the streets of New York's Ghetto, occupies a peculiar position in our society. If we could penetrate into his soul, we should see a mixture of almost unprecedented hope and excitement on the one hand, and of doubt, confusion, and self-distrust on the other hand. Led in many contrary directions, the fact that he does not grow to be an intellectual anarchist is due to his serious racial characteristics.

Three groups of influences are at work on him—the orthodox Jewish, the American, and the Socialist; and he experiences them in this order. He has either been born in America of Russian, Austrian, or Roumanian Jewish parents, or has immigrated with them when a very young child. The first of the three forces at work on his character is religious and moral; the second is practical, diversified, non-religious; and the third is reactionary from the other two and hostile to them.

Whether born in this country or in Russia, the son of orthodox parents passes his earliest years in a family atmosphere where the whole duty of man is to observe the religious law. . . .

In a simple Jewish community in Russia, where the "chaider" is the only

Reprinted from Hutchins Hapgood, THE SPIRIT OF THE GHETTO *(New York, 1909), pp. 18, 22–24, 32–33.*

school, where the government is hostile, and the Jews are therefore thrown back upon their own customs, the boy loves his religion, he loves and honors his parents, his highest ambition is to be a great scholar—to know the Bible in all its glorious meaning, to know the Talmudical comments upon it, and to serve God. Above every one else he respects the aged, the Hebrew scholar, the rabbi, the teacher. Piety and wisdom count more than riches, talent and power. The "law" outweighs all else in value. Abraham and Moses, David and Solomon, the prophet Elijah, are the kind of great men to whom his imagination soars.

But in America, even before he begins to go to our public schools, the little Jewish boy finds himself in contact with a new world which stands in violent contrast with the orthodox environment of his first few years. Insensibly—at the beginning—from his playmates in the streets, from his older brother or sister, he picks up a little English, a little American slang, hears older boys boast of prize-fighter Bernstein, and learns vaguely to feel that there is a strange and fascinating life on the street. At this tender age he may even begin to black boots, gamble in pennies, and be filled with a "wild surmise" about American dollars.

With his entrance into the public school the little fellow runs plump against a system of education and a set of influences which are at total variance with those traditional to his race and with his home life. The religious element is entirely lacking. The educational system of the public schools is heterogeneous and worldly. The boy becomes acquainted in the school reader with fragments of writings on all subjects, with a little mathematics, a little history. His instruction, in the interests of a liberal non-sectarianism, is entirely secular. English becomes his most familiar language. He achieves a growing comprehension and sympathy with the independent, free, rather sceptical spirit of the American boy; he rapidly imbibes ideas about social equality and contempt for *authority,* and tends to prefer Sherlock Holmes to Abraham as a hero.

. . .

If this boy were able entirely to forget his origin, to cast off the ethical and religious influences which are his birthright, there would be no serious struggle in his soul, and he would not represent a peculiar element in our society. He would be like any other practical, ambitious, rather worldly American boy. The struggle is strong because the boy's nature, at once religious and susceptible, is strongly appealed to by both the old and new. At the same time that he is keenly sensitive to the charm of his American environment, with its practical and national opportunities, he has still a deep love for his race and the old things. He is aware, and rather ashamed, of the limitations of his parents. He feels that the trend and weight of things are against them, that they are in a minority; but yet in a real way the old people remain his conscience, the visible representatives of a moral and religious tradition by which the boy may regulate his inner life.

. . .

JAMES BRYCE

In enquiring how far these newest comers are intermingling with the pre-existing population, one must carefully distinguish between the original immigrants and their children born in the United States. The latter attend the common schools,—in places where truancy laws are enforced,—mix with the native inhabitants, grow up speaking English, and mostly forget their own language before they reach manhood. So far from desiring to remember it and to cling to their old nationality, they are eager to cast it away and to become in every sense Americans. Often they treat their parents, because foreign-born, with a sort of contempt. However slight may be their social contact with their native neighbours, they receive the same instruction, they tend to form the same habits of life, they read the same newspapers, they frequent the same public entertainments, and the more capable rise before long into positions where they are not merely units in a herd of workers "bossed" by an American or Irish foreman, but have a chance of forcing their own way upward. Exactly how far they intermarry outside their own race is not easy to say, but we may safely assume that those who have been born in the United States, or, entering very young, have grown up under American influences, find their race no insurmountable obstacle to alliances with those of native stock. There are more men than women among them, and the men try to marry into a social stratum a little above their own, a native American girl, if possible, or an Irish one. In such a land as the United States distinc-

Reprinted from James Bryce, THE AMERICAN COMMONWEALTH *(New York, 1911), II, 477–478, 481–484.*

tions of race, unless marked by distinctions of colour, count for little.

Both as respects social admixture, however, and as respects propensity to crime, one must emphasize the difference between immigrants settling in large cities, or in mining regions, and those who are scattered out into smaller cities or country districts. In the latter they soon tend to mingle with the other residents, and the children grow up under similar and fairly wholesome conditions. But in such places as New York or Chicago they keep to themselves, often in streets inhabited entirely by those of the same race. It is difficult for parents who must themselves toil all day long to retain any control over children who enjoy the license and are exposed to the temptations of a vast city. Accordingly, the percentage of juvenile crime among the children of the foreign-born is more than twice as great as it is among children of native white parents.[1] This is so easily explicable by the conditions under which they live that it need not be taken to indicate moral inferiority. It has often happened that when people of rude and simple habits come into a more civilized environment they lose their best native qualities and acquire the vices of civilization before its virtues. Out of this transitory phase the children of the immigrants may ere long pass.

. . .

There were in the United States only forty-eight millions of white people, when the ten millions from Central and Southern Europe who have arrived since 1885 began to enter, an addition to the nation such as no nation ever received before. These ten millions, whose children are now counted by millions more, have indeed hardly yet begun to blend with the older popula-

[1] Commons, *Races and Immigrants*, p. 170.

tion. But they must ultimately do so. Already they tell on the social and economic life of the country. Long before the end of the century their blood will have been largely mingled with that of the Anglo-American and Irish and German inhabitants. Thus the reflection is forced upon us, What changes in the character and habits of the American people will this influx of new elements make? elements wholly diverse not only in origin but in ideas and traditions, and scarcely less diverse from the Irish and Teutonic immigrants of previous years than from the men of predominantly English stock who inhabited the country before the Irish or the Continental Teutons arrived.

This is the crucial question to which every study of the immigrant problem leads up. It is a matter of grave import for the world, seeing that it is virtually a new phenomenon in world history, because no large movement of the races of mankind from one region of the earth to another has ever occurred under conditions at all resembling these. But it is primarily momentous for the United States, and that all the more so because these new immigrants go to swell the class which already causes some disquietude, the class of unskilled labourers, the poorest, the most ignorant, and the most unsettled part of the population.

In the United States the uneasiness which this invasion excites takes shape in the question so often on men's lips, Will the new immigrants be good Americans? In the most familiar sense of these words the enquiry can be easily answered. If by the words "good Americans" is meant "patriotic Americans," patriotic they will be. They will be proud of America, loyal to the flag, quick to discard their European memories and sentiments, eager to identify themselves with everything distinctive of their new country. Within a few years the Italian or the Magyar, the Pole or the Rouman deems himself an American even if he be not yet a citizen. Much more do his children glory in the flag under which they were born. So far as politics are concerned, the unity and the homogeneity of the nation will not ultimately suffer.

Neither is there ground for apprehending any decline in the intellectual quality or practical alertness of the composite people of the future. Nearly all the instreaming races are equal in intelligence to the present inhabitants. Of the acuteness of Jews and Greeks and Italians it is superfluous to speak. One is told that the children of these stocks are among the brightest in the public schools, and that in New York they use the public libraries more than any others do. So, too, the Poles and Czechs are naturally gifted races, quite as apt to learn as are the Germans, even if less solid and persistent. Than the Armenians there is no abler race in the world. A blending of races has often in past times been followed by an increase in intellectual fertility. It is possible that from among the Jews and Poles with their musical faculty, or the Italians with their artistic faculty, there may arise those who, stimulated by the new opportunities that surround them here, will carry the creative power of the country to a higher level of production in those branches of art than it has yet reached.

Whether the ethical quality of the nation will be affected, it is more difficult to conjecture. Of the races that are now entering, some have suffered in their birthland from economic and political conditions unfavourable to veracity and courage. Others, banded together against authority, have become prone to violence. But there are others, the Piedmontese and Lombards for instance, who come of a manly and industrious stock. The Czechs and the Poles, the Magyars and the Slovenes, do not appear to one who has seen them in their European homes to have less than their Teutonic neighbours of the virtues that belong to simple peasant folk. If the new immigrants or their children are found to sink below the average of conduct in the class they enter and show themselves more disorderly or dishonest than the native American, this will happen, not because the races are naturally more criminal, but rather because the conditions under which they begin life in their new country are unfavourable. The immigrant is cut loose from his old ties and from the influences that restrained him. He is far from his parents and his priest. He has no longer the public opinion of his neighbours to regard, no longer any disapproval of the local magnate to fear. He does not see round him the signs of a vigilant, even if oppressive, public authority which were conspicuous in his native village. In the rough, unsettled, perhaps homeless, life he leads, a tossing atom in a seething crowd who toil for employers with whom they have no healthy human relation, propensities towards evil are apt to spring into activity, and the softer feelings as well as the sense of duty to perish from inanition. The immigrant's child is in one way better placed, for he is influenced by his American school-teachers and school companions, but in another way worse, because the traditions and habits of the simple life of rural Europe have for him faded away altogether, if indeed he ever knew them. He starts in life as an American, but without the fundamental ideas and ingrained traditions of the New Englander or Virginian of the old stock, for these ideas and sentiments do not go with the language and the right to vote. Whether his religion will cling to him remains to be seen. Its power is at any rate likely to be weaker, perhaps least weak among the Jews, whom their faith and their habits hold apart. Though they also are divided into sects some of which render slight or no obedience to the Mosaic law, they show much less tend- ency to blend with the rest of the popu- lation than do the other races. How long the Greeks and the Armenians will be kept distinct by loyalty to their ancient churches I will not venture to predict. Among all the immigrants the grasp of religion seems to loosen; many are lost to their church in the second and even more in the third generation.

III. RECENT INTERPRETATIONS

In the past decade, historians have begun re-evaluating many basic assump- tions concerning late nineteenth-century economic and social changes in the United States. The following selections represent three major strands of historical revision. Stephan Thernstrom examines the entire problem of immigrant mobility and urbanization in late nineteenth-century America, and his analysis challenges many traditional assumptions concerning this entire process. Robert Lively synthesizes recent literature on the crucial role played by government policy in shaping the course and character of indus- trial development. Lively helps dispose of the persistent myth that the American business community felt attracted to laissez-faire beliefs during its great period of corporate growth and consolidation. Finally, Robert Wiebe criticizes the notion that a single consensus of values connected the differ- ent American social classes and thereby modified the intensity of class conflict. Wiebe argues that the reduced level of conflict reflected an almost total absence of communication between rich and poor rather than com- mon agreement on American principles, and this insight remains relevant to today's studies of the behavior patterns of urban ghettoes.

STEPHAN THERNSTROM

The United States, it has been said, was born in the country and has moved to the city. It was during the half-cen- tury between the Civil War and World War I that the move was made. In

Reprinted from Stephan Thernstrom, "Urbani- zation, Migration, and Social Mobility in Late Nineteenth-Century America," in Barton J. Bernstein, ed., TOWARDS A NEW PAST: DISSENTING ESSAYS IN AMERICAN HISTORY *(New York: Pan- theon Books, Inc., 1968), pp. 158–173, by per- mission of the publisher.*

1860, less than a quarter of the Amer- ican population lived in a city or town; by 1890, the figure had reached a third; by 1910, nearly half. By more sophisti- cated measures than the mere count of heads, the center of gravity of the so- ciety had obviously tilted cityward well before the last date.

If to speak of "the rise of the city" in those years is a textbook cliché, the impact of this great social transforma- tion upon the common people of Amer- ica has never been sufficiently explored. This essay is intended as a small contribution toward that task. It sketches the process by which ordinary men and women were drawn to the burgeoning cities of post-Civil War America, assesses what little we know about how they were integrated into the urban class structure, and suggests how these matters affected the viability of the political system.

The urbanization of late nineteenth-century America took place at a dizzying pace. Chicago, for instance, doubled its population every decade but one between 1850 and 1890, growing from 30,000 to over a million in little more than a generation. And it was not merely the conspicuous metropolitan giants but the Akrons, the Duluths, the Tacomas that were bursting at the seams; no less than 101 American communities grew by 100 percent or more in the 1880s.[1]

Why did Americans flock into these all too often unlovely places? There were some who were not pulled to the city but rather pushed out of their previous habitats and dropped there, more or less by accident. But the overriding fact is that the cities could draw on an enormous reservoir of people who were dissatisfied with their present lot and eager to seize the new opportunities offered by the metropolis.

Who were these people? It is conventional to distinguish two broad types of migrants to the American city: the immigrant from another culture, and the farm lad who moved from a rural to an urban setting within the culture. It is also conventional in historical accounts to overlook the latter type and to focus on the more exotic of the migrants, those who had to undergo the arduous process of becoming Americanized.

This is regrettable. To be sure, immigration from abroad was extremely important in the building of America's cities down to World War I. But the most important source of population for the burgeoning cities was not the fields of Ireland and Austria, but those of Vermont and Iowa. The prime cause of population growth in nineteenth-century America, and the main source of urban growth, was simply the high fertility of natives living outside the city.

We tend to neglect internal migration from country to city, partly because the immigrants from abroad seem exotic and thus conspicuous, partly because of the unfortunate legacy left by Frederick Jackson Turner's frontier theory, one element of which was the notion that the open frontier served as a safety valve for urban discontent. When there were hard times in the city, according to Turner, the American workers didn't join a union or vote Socialist; he moved West and grabbed some of that free land. This theory has been subjected to the rather devastating criticism that by 1860 it took something like $1,000 capital to purchase sufficient transportation, seed equipment, livestock, and food (to live on until the first crop) to make a go of it; that it took even more than $1,000 later in the century; and that it was precisely the unemployed workmen who were least likely to have that kind of money at their command. It is estimated that for every industrial worker who became a farmer, twenty farm boys became urban dwellers.[2] There was an urban safety valve for rural discontent, and an extremely important one. The dominant form of population move-

---

[1] C. N. Glaab and A. T. Brown, *A History of Urban America* (New York, 1967), pp. 107–11.

[2] Fred Shannon, "A Post Mortem on the Labor-Safety-Valve Theory," *Agricultural History*, XIX (1954), 31–37.

ment was precisely the opposite of that described by Turner.

Since scholarly attention has been focused upon immigrants from abroad, upon Oscar Handlin's "Uprooted," it will be useful to review what is known about their movement to the American city and then to ask how much the same generalizations might hold for native Americans uprooted from the countryside and plunged into the city.

Immigration is as old as America, but a seismic shift in the character of European immigration to these shores occurred in the nineteenth century, as a consequence of the commercial transformation of traditional European agriculture and the consequent displacement of millions of peasants.[3] Compared to earlier newcomers, these were people who were closer to the land and more tradition-bound, and they generally had fewer resources to bring with them than their predecessors. One shouldn't overwork this; a substantial fraction of the German and Scandinavian immigrants had enough capital to get to the West to pick up land. But some of the Germans and Scandinavians, and most men of other nationalities, had just enough cash to make it to the New World and were stuck for a time at least where they landed—New York, Boston, or wherever. They swelled the population appreciably and the relief rolls dramatically, particularly in the pre-Civil War years, when they entered cities which were basically commercial and had little use for men whose only skill in many cases was that they knew how to dig. Eventually, however, the stimulus of this vast pool of cheap labor and the demands of the growing city itself

[3] For general accounts, see Marcus L. Hansen, *The Atlantic Migration, 1607–1860* (paperback ed.; New York, 1961); Oscar Handlin, *The Uprooted* (Boston, 1951).

opened up a good many unskilled jobs —in the construction of roads, houses, and commercial buildings, and in the manufacturing that began to spring up in the cities.

That they were driven off the land in the Old World, that they arrived without resources, immobilized by their poverty, and that they often suffered a great deal before they secured stable employment is true enough. But these harsh facts may lead us to overlook other aspects which were extremely significant.

One is that immigration was a *selective* process. However powerful the pressures to leave, in no case did everyone in a community pull up stakes. This observation may be uncomfortably reminiscent of the popular opinion on this point: that it was the best of the Old World stock that came to the New—the most intelligent, enterprising, courageous. But this should not lead us to neglect the point altogether. The traits that led some men to leave and allowed them to survive the harrowing journey to the port, the trip itself, and the perils of the New World, could be described in somewhat different terms: substitute cunning for intelligence, for example, or ruthlessness for courage. Still, whatever the emphasis, the fact remains: as weighed in the scales of the marketplace, those who came—however driven by cruel circumstance—were better adapted to American life than those who remained in the village or died on the way.

The other main point about the immigrants, and especially those who suffered the most extreme hardships— the Irish in the 1840s and 1850s, the French Canadians in the 1870s, the Italians and various East Europeans after 1880—is that they appraised their new situations with standards developed in peasant society. Lowell was

terrible, with its cramped stinking tenements, and factory workers labored
from dawn till dark for what seems a
mere pittance. Children were forced to
work at a brutally early age; the factories and dwellings were deathtraps.
But Lowell was a damn sight better
than County Cork, and men who knew
from bitter experience what County
Cork was like could not view their life
in Lowell with quite the same simple
revulsion as the middle-class reformers
who judged Lowell by altogether different standards. It is not so much the
objectively horrible character of a
situation that goads men to action as
it is a nagging discrepancy between
what *is* and what is *expected*. And what
one expects is determined by one's reference group—which can be a class, an
ethnic or religious subculture, or some
other entity which defines people's
horizon of expectation.[4] Immigration
provided an ever renewed stream of
men who entered the American economy to fill its least attractive and least
well rewarded positions, men who
happen to have brought with them
very low horizons of expectation fixed
in peasant Europe.

That those Americans with greatest
reason to feel outrageously exploited
judged their situation against the dismally low standards of the decaying
European village is an important clue
to the stunted growth of the labor
movement and the failure of American

Socialism. Working in the same direction was what might be called the
Tower of Babel factor. A firm sense of
class solidarity was extremely difficult
to develop in communities where people literally didn't speak each other's
language. Even in cases where groups
of immigrant workers had unusually
high expectations and previous familiarity with advanced forms of collective action—such as the English artisans who led the Massachusetts textile
strikes in the 1870s—they found it hard
to keep the other troops in line; a
clever Italian-speaking or Polish-speak-
ing foreman could easily exploit national differences for his own ends, and
if necessary there were always the most
recent immigrants of all (and the Negroes) to serve as scabs to replace the
dissenters en masse.

A somewhat similar analysis applies
to the migrants who left the Kansas
farms for Chicago. They were linguis-
tically and culturally set apart from
many of their fellow workers; they too
had low horizons of expectation fixed
in the countryside and brought to the
city. The latter point is often missed
because of the peculiar American reverence for an idealized agrarian way of
life. As we have become a nation of city
dwellers, we have come more and more
to believe that it is virtuous and beautiful to slave for fourteen hours a day
with manure on your boots. Recently
that sturdy small farmer from Johnson
City, Texas, remarked that "it does not
make sense on this great continent
which God has blessed to have more
than 70 per cent of our people
crammed into one percent of the land."
A national "keep them down on the
farm" campaign is therefore in the
offing.[5] But it is damnably hard to
keep them down on the farm after

---

[4] For discussion of the sociological concepts
of reference groups and the theory of relative
deprivation, see Robert K. Merton, *Social
Theory and Social Structure*, rev. ed. (Glencoe,
Ill., 1957) and the literature cited there. The
problem of assessing the level of expectations
of any particular migratory group in the past
is extremely complicated, and it is obvious
that there have been important differences between and within groups. But the generalizations offered here seem to me the best starting
point for thinking about this issue.

[5] *Boston Globe*, February 5, 1967.

they've seen New York (or even Indianapolis), and it was just as hard a century ago, for the very good reason that the work is brutal, the profits are often miserably low, and the isolation is psychologically murderous. Virtuous this life may be, especially to people who don't have to live it, but enjoyable it is not—not, at least, to a very substantial fraction of our ever shrinking farm population.

This applies particularly to young men and women growing up on a farm. Their parents had a certain stake in staying where they were, even if it was a rut. And the eldest son, who would inherit the place eventually, was sometimes tempted by that. But the others left in droves, to tend machines, to dig and haul and hammer—or in the case of the girls, to sell underwear in Marshall Field's, to mind someone else's kitchen, or in some instances to follow in the footsteps of Sister Carrie.

There were some large differences between native-born migrants to the cities and immigrants from another land, to be sure. But the familiar argument that native workmen "stood on the shoulders" of the immigrant and was subjected to less severe exploitation is somewhat misleading. The advantages enjoyed by many American-born laborers stemmed more from their urban experience than their birth, and they did not generally accrue to freshly arrived native migrants to the city. The latter were little better off than their immigrant counterparts, but then they too were spiritually prepared to endure a great deal of privation and discomfort because even the bottom of the urban heap was a step up from the farms they had left behind. The two groups were one in this respect, and perceptive employers recognized the fact. In 1875, the Superintendent of one of Andrew Carnegie's steel mills summed up his

experience this way: "We must steer clear as far as we can of Englishmen, who are great sticklers for high wages, small production and strikes. My experience has shown that Germans and Irish, Swedes and what I denominate 'Buckwheats'—young American country boys, judiciously mixed, make the most honest and tractable force you can find."[6]

The move to the city, therefore, was an advance of a kind for the typical migrant. Were there further opportunities for advancement there, or did he then find himself crushed by circumstance and reduced to the ranks of the permanent proletariat? Did his children, whose expectations were presumably higher, discover correspondingly greater opportunities open to them? Remarkably little serious research has been devoted to these issues. Historians who see American history as a success story have been content to assume, without benefit of data, that the American dream of mobility was true, apparently on the principle that popular ideology is a sure guide to social reality. Dissenting scholars have been more inclined to the view that class barriers were relatively impassable, an assumption based upon generalized skepticism about American mythology rather than upon careful empirical study. Some recent work, however, provides the basis for a tentative reappraisal of the problem.

We know most about mobility into the most rarified reaches of the social order regarding such elite groups as millionaires, railroad presidents, directors of large corporations, or persons listed in the *Dictionary of American Biography*. What is most impressive about the literature on the American elite is that, in spite of many variations

[6] Quoted in Oscar Handlin, *Immigration as a Factor in American History* (Englewood Cliffs, N.J., 1959), pp. 66–67.

in the way in which the elite is defined, the results of these studies are much the same. It is clear that growing up in rags is not in the least conducive to the attainment of later riches, and that it was no more so a century ago than it is today.[7] There have been spectacular instances of mobility from low down on the social scale to the very top—Andrew Carnegie, for instance. But colorful examples cannot sustain broad generalizations about social phenomena, however often they are impressed into service toward that end. Systematic investigation reveals that even in the days of Andrew Carnegie, there was little room at the top, except for those who started very close to it.

Furthermore, this seems to have been the case throughout most of American history, despite many dramatic alterations in the character of the economy. It seems perfectly plausible to assume, as many historians have on the basis of impressionistic evidence, that the precipitous growth of heavy industry in the latter half of the nineteenth century opened the doors to men with very different talents from the educated merchants who constituted the elite of the preindustrial age, that unlettered, horny-handed types like Thomas Alva Edison and Henry Ford, crude inventors and tinkerers, then came into their own; that the connection between parental wealth and status and the son's career was loosened, so that members of the business elite typically had lower social origins and less education, and were often of immigrant stock. Plausible, yes, but true, no. It helped to go to Harvard in Thomas Jefferson's America, and it seems to have helped just about as much in William McKin-

ley's America. There were the Edisons and Fords, who rose spectacularly from low origins, but there were always a few such. Cases like these were about as exceptional in the late nineteenth century as they were earlier. The image of the great inventor springing from common soil, unspoiled by book-larnin', is a red herring. It is doubtful, to say the least, that the less you know, the more likely you are to build a better mousetrap. And in any event it was not the great inventor who raked in the money, in most cases—Henry Ford never invented anything—but rather the organizer and manipulator, whose talents seem to have been highly valued through all periods of American history.

These conclusions are interesting, but an important caution is in order. It by no means follows that if there was very little room at the top, there was little room anywhere else. It is absurd to judge the openness or lack of openness of an entire social system solely by the extent of recruitment from below into the highest positions of all. One can imagine a society in which all members of the tiny elite are democratically recruited from below, and yet where the social structure as a whole is extremely rigid with that small exception. Conversely, one can imagine a society with a hereditary ruling group at the very top, a group completely closed to aspiring men of talent but lowly birth, and yet with an enormous amount of movement back and forth below that pinnacle. Late nineteenth-century America could have approximated this latter model, with lineage, parental wealth, and education as decisive assets in the race for the very peak, as the business elite studies suggest, and yet with great fluidity at the lower and middle levels of the class structure.

Was this in fact the case? The evidence available today is regrettably

---

[7] For a convenient review of this literature, see Seymour M. Lipset and Reinhard Bendix, *Social Mobility in Industrial Society* (Berkeley, Cal., 1959), Ch. 4.

scanty, but here are the broad outlines of an answer, insofar as we can generalize from a handful of studies.[8] At the lower and middle ranges of the class structure there was impressive mobility, though often of an unexpected and rather ambiguous kind. I will distinguish three types of mobility: geographical, occupational, and property, and say a little about the extent and significance of each.

First is geographical mobility, physical movement from place to place, which is tied up in an interesting way with movement through the social scale. Americans have long been thought a restless, footloose people, and it has been assumed that the man on the move has been the man on the make; he knows that this little town doesn't provide a grand enough stage for him to display his talents, and so he goes off to the big city to win fame and fortune, or to the open frontier to do likewise. When you examine actual behavior instead of popular beliefs, however, you discover that things are more complicated than that.

It proves to be true that Americans are indeed a footloose people. In my work on Newburyport, a small industrial city, I attempted to find out what fraction of the families present in the community in the initial year of my study—1850—were still living there in the closing year, 1880, one short generation. Less than a fifth of them, it turned out—and this not in a community on the moving frontier, like Merle Curti's Trempealeau County, where you would expect a very high turnover. There the true pioneer types, who liked to clear the land, became nervous when there was another family within a half day's ride of them and sold out to the second wave of settlers (often immigrants who knew better than to try to tame the wilderness without previous experience at it). But to find roughly the same volatility in a city forty miles north of Boston suggests that the whole society was in motion.

The statitstics bear out the legend that Americans are a restless people. What of the assertion that movement and success go hand in hand, that physical mobility and upward social mobility are positively correlated? Here the legend seems more questionable. It seems likely that some who pulled up stakes and went elsewhere for a new start did not improve their positions; they found better land, or discovered that they possessed talents which were much more highly valued in the big city than in the place they came from. What ever would have happened to Theodore Dreiser in small-town Indiana had there been no Chicago for him to flee to?

[8] The main sources for the generalizations which follow, unless otherwise indicated, are: Stephan Thernstrom, *Poverty and Progress: Social Mobility in a Nineteenth Century City* (Cambridge, Mass., 1964); Merle E. Curti, *The Making of an American Frontier Community* (Stanford, Cal., 1959); Donald B. Cole, *Immigrant City: Lawrence, Massachusetts, 1845–1921* (Chapel Hill, N.C., 1963)—for my reservations about this work, however, see my review in the *Journal of Economic History,* XXIV (1964), 259–61; Herbert G. Gutman, "Social Status and Social Mobility in 19th Century America: Paterson, N.J., A Case Study," unpublished paper for the 1964 meetings of the American Historical Association; Howard Gitelman, "The Labor Force at Waltham Watch During the Civil War Era," *Journal of Economic History,* XXV (1965), 214–43; David Brody, *Steelworkers in America: The Nonunion Era* (Cambridge, Mass.: 1960); Pauline Gordon, "The Chance to Rise Within Industry" (unpubilshed M.A. thesis, Columbia University); Robert Wheeler, "The Fifth-Ward Irish: Mobility at Mid-Century" (unpublished seminar paper, Brown University, 1967); and the author's research in progress on social mobility in Boston over the past century, in which the career patterns of some 8,000 ordinary residents of the community are traced.

But the point to underline, for it is less commonly understood, is that much of this remarkable population turnover was of quite a different kind. As you trace the flow of immigrants into and then out of the cities, you begin to see that a great many of those who departed did so in circumstances which make it exceedingly hard to believe that they were moving on to bigger and better things elsewhere. There is no way to be certain about this, no feasible method of tracing individuals once they disappear from the universe of the community under consideration. These questions can be explored for contemporary America by administering questionnaires to people and collecting life histories which display migration patterns, but dead men tell no tales and fill out no questionnaires, so that part of the past is irrevocably lost. But some plausible inferences can be drawn about the nature of this turnover from the fact that so many ordinary working people on the move owned no property, had no savings accounts, had acquired no special skills, and were most likely to leave when they were unemployed. They were, in short, people who had made the least successful economic adjustment to the community and who were no longer able to hang on there. At the lower reaches of the social order, getting out of town did not ordinarily mean a step up the ladder somewhere else; there is no reason to assume that in their new destinations migrant laborers found anything but more of the same. When middle-class families, who already had a niche in the world, moved on, it was often in response to greater opportunities elsewhere; for ordinary working people physical movement meant something very different.

That is a less rosy picture than the one usually painted, but I think it is more accurate. And we should notice one very important implication of this argument: namely, that the people who were least successful and who had the greatest grievances are precisely those who never stayed put very long in any one place. Students of labor economics and trade union history have long been aware of the fact that there are certain occupations which are inordinately difficult to organize simply because they have incessant job turnover. When only 5 percent or 1 percent of the men working at a particular job in a given city at the start of the year are still employed twelve months later, as is the case with some occupations in the economic underworld today (short-order cooks or menial hospital workers, for instance), how do you build a stable organization and conduct a successful strike?

An analogous consideration applies not merely to certain selected occupations but to a large fraction of the late nineteenth-century urban working class as a whole. The Marxist model of the conditions which promote proletarian consciousness presumes not only permanency of membership in this class—the absence of upward mobility—but also, I suggest, some continuity of class membership *in one setting* so that workers come to know each other and to develop bonds of solidarity and common opposition to the ruling group above them. This would seem to entail a stable labor force in a single factory; at a minimum it assumes considerable stability in a community. One reason that a permanent proletariat along the lines envisaged by Marx did not develop in the course of American industrialization is perhaps that few Americans have *stayed* in one place, one workplace, or even one city long enough to discover a sense of common identity and common grievance. This may be a vital clue to the divergent political development of American and Western Europe in the industrial age, to the striking weakness of socialism here, as compared to Europe—though we can't be sure because we don't definitely know that the European working-class population was less volatile. I suspect that it was, to some degree, and that America was distinctive in this respect, but this is a question of glaring importance which no one has yet taken the trouble to investigate.

When I first stumbled upon this phenomenon in sifting through manuscript census schedules for nineteenth-century Newburyport, I was very doubtful that the findings could be generalized to apply to the big cities of the period. It seemed reasonable to assume that the laborers who drifted out of Newburyport so quickly after their arrival must have settled down somewhere else, and to think that a great metropolis would have offered a more inviting haven than a small city, where anonymity was impossible and where middle-class institutions of social control intruded into one's daily life with some frequency, as compared to a classic big-city lower-class ghetto, where the down-and-out could perhaps huddle together for protective warmth and be left to their own devices—for instance, those Irish wards of New York where the police made no attempt to enforce law and order until late in the century. Here if anywhere one should be able to find a continuous lower-class population, a permanent proletariat, and I began my Boston research with great curiosity about this point.

If Boston is any example, in no American city was there a sizable lower class with great continuity of membership. You can identify some more or less continuously lower-class areas, but the crucial point is that *the same people do not stay in them.* If you take a sample of unskilled and semi-skilled laborers in Boston in 1880 and look for them in 1890, you are not much more likely to

find them still in the city than was the case in Newburyport.[9]

The bottom layer of the social order in the nineteenth-century American city was thus a group of families who appear to have been permanent transients, buffeted about from place to place, never quite able to sink roots. We know very little about these people, and it is difficult to know how we can learn much about them. Yet get only occasional glimpses into the part of this iceberg that appears above the surface, in the person of the tramp, who first is perceived as a problem for America in the 1870s and reappears in hard times after that—in the 1890s and in the great depression most notably. But what has been said here at least suggests the significance of the phenomenon.

So much for geographical mobility. What can be said about the people who come to the city and remain there under our microscope so that we can discern what happened to them? I have already anticipated my general line of argument here in my discussion of migration out of the city—which amounted to the claim that the city was a kind of Darwinian jungle in which the fittest

9 Recent work suggesting that even the most recent U.S. Census seriously undernumerated the Negro male population may make the critical reader wonder about the accuracy of the census and city directory canvases upon which I base my analysis. Some elaborate checking has persuaded me that these nineteenth-century sources erred primarily in their coverage—their lack of coverage, rather—of the floating working-class population. For a variety of reasons it seems clear that families which had been in the community long enough to be included in one of these canvases—and hence to be included in a sample drawn from them—were rarely left out of later canvases if they were indeed still resident in the same city. A perfect census of every soul in the community on a given day would therefore yield an even higher, not a lower, estimate of population turnover for men at the bottom, which strengthens rather than weakens the argument advanced here.

survived and the others drifted on to try another place. Those who did stay in the city and make their way there did, in general, succeed in advancing themselves economically and socially. There was very impressive mobility, though not always of the kind we might expect.

In approaching this matter, we must make a distinction which is obscured by applying labels like "open" or "fluid" to entire whole social structures. There are, after all, two sets of escalators in any community; one set goes down. To describe a society as enormously fluid implies that there are lots of people moving down while lots of others are moving up to take their place. This would obviously be a socially explosive situation, for all those men descending against their will would arrive at the bottom, not with low horizons of expectation set in some peasant village, but with expectations established when they were at one of the comfortable top floors of the structure.

Downward mobility is by no means an unknown phenomenon in American history. There have been socially displaced groups, especially if you take into account rather subtle shifts in the relative status of such groups as professionals.[10] But the chief generalization to make is that Americans who started their working life in a middle-class job strongly tended to end up in the middle class; sons reared in middle-class families also attained middle-class occupations in the great majority of cases. Relatively few men born into the middle class fell from there; a good many born into the working class either escaped from it altogether or advanced themselves significantly within the class. There is a well-established tradition of writing about the skilled workman, associated with such names as the Hammonds, the Lynds, Lloyd Warner, and Norman Ware, which holds the contrary, to be sure.[11] This tradition still has its defenders, who argue that with industrialization "class lines assumed a new and forbidding rigidity" and that "machines made obsolete many of the skill trades of the antebellum years, drawing the once self-respecting handicraftsmen into the drudgery and monotony of factory life, where they were called upon to perform only one step in the minutely divided and automatic processes of mass production."[12] Rapid technological change doubtless did displace some skilled artisans, doubtless produced some downward mobility into semiskilled positions. But defenders of this view have built their case upon little more than scattered complaints by labor leaders, and have not conducted systematic research to verify these complaints.

Careful statistical analysis provides a very different perspective on the matter. Two points stand out. One is that as certain traditional skilled callings became obsolete, there was an enor-

---

[10] The assumption that discontent stemming from social displacement has been the motive force behind American reform movements has exerted great influence upon American historical writing in recent years. See for instance David Donald, "Toward a Reconsideration of Abolitionists," *Lincoln Reconsidered* (New York, 1956), pp. 19–36; Richard Hofstadter, *The Age of Reform: From Bryan to F.D.R.* (New York, 1955). Donald's essay is easily demolished by anyone with the slightest acquaintance with sociological method. Hofstadter's work, while open to a very serious objection, is at least sufficiently suggestive to indicate the potential utility of the idea.

[11] J. L. and Barbara Hammond, *The Town Labourer (1760–1832)* (London, 1917); Robert S. and Helen M. Lynd, *Middletown* (New York, 1929), and *Middletown in Transition* (New York, 1937); W. Lloyd Warner and J. O. Low, *The Social System of the Modern Factory* (New Haven, Conn., 1947); Norman J. Ware, *The Industrial Worker, 1840–1860* (Boston, 1924).

[12] Leon Litwak, ed., *The American Labor Movement* (Englewood Cliffs, N.J., 1962), p. 3.

mous expansion of *other* skilled trades, and, since many of the craftsmen under pressure from technological change had rather generalized skills, they moved rapidly into these new positions and thus retained their place in the labor aristocracy.[13] Second, it is quite mistaken to assume that the sons of the threatened artisan were commonly driven down into the ranks of the factory operatives; they typically found a place either in the expanding skilled trades or in the even more rapidly expanding white-collar occupations.[14]

As for workers on the lower rungs of the occupational ladder, the unskilled and semiskilled, they had rarely drifted down from a higher beginning point. Characteristically, they were newcomers to the urban world. A substantial minority of them appear to have been able to advance themselves a notch or two occupationally, especially among the second generation; a good many of their sons became clerks, salesmen, and other petty white-collar functionaries. And the first generation, which had less success occupationally, was commonly experiencing mobility of another kind —property mobility. Despite a pathetically low (but generally rising) wage level, despite heavy unemployment rates, many were able to accumulate significant property holdings and to establish themselves as members of the stable working class, as opposed to the drifting lower class.[15]

It may seem paradoxical to suggest that so many Americans were rising in the world and so few falling; where did the room at the top come from? The paradox is readily resolved. For one thing, our attention has been fastened upon individuals who remained physically situated in one place in which their careers could be traced; an indeterminate but substantial fraction of the population was floating and presumably unsuccessful. By no means everyone at the bottom was upwardly mobile; the point is rather that those who were not were largely invisible. Furthermore, the occupational structure itself was changing in a manner that created disproportionately more positions in the middle and upper ranges, despite the common nineteenth-century belief that industrialization was homogenizing the work force and reducing all manual employees to identical robots. The homogenizing and degrading tendencies that caught the eye of Marx and others were more than offset, it appears, by developments which made for both a more differentiated and a more top-heavy occupational structure. Third, there were important sources of social mobility that could be attained without changing one's occupation, most notably the

---

13 This is evident from aggregated census data and from my Boston investigation, but we badly need an American counterpart to Eric Hobsbawm's splendid essay on "The Labour Aristocracy in Nineteenth Century Britain," in *Labouring Men: Studies in the History of Labour* (London, 1964), pp. 272–315.

14 So, at least, the evidence from Boston and Indianapolis indicates; for the latter, see Natlic Rogoff, *Recent Trends in Occupational Mobility* (Glencoe, Ill., 1953).

15 The clearest demonstration of this is in Thernstrom, *Poverty and Progress*, Ch. 5. It

might be thought, however, that the remarkable property mobility disclosed there depended upon the existence of an abundant stock of cheap single-family housing available for purchase. It could be that where real estate was less readily obtainable, laborers would squander the funds that were accumulated with such sacrifice in places where home ownership was an immediate possibility. It appears from Wheeler's unpublished study of nineteenth-century Providence, however, that the working-class passion for property did not require an immediate, concrete source of satisfaction like a home and a plot of land. The Irish workmen of Providence were just as successful at accumulating property holdings as their Newburyport counterparts; the difference was only that they held personal rather than real property.

property mobility that was stimulated by the increases in real wages that occurred in this period. Finally, there was the so-called "demographic vacuum" created by the differential fertility of the social classes, best illustrated in the gloomy late nineteenth-century estimate that in two hundred years 1,000 Harvard graduates would have only 50 living descendants while 1,000 Italians would have 100,000. The calculation is dubious, but the example nicely clarifies the point that high-status groups failed to reproduce themselves, thus opening up vacancies which had necessarily to be filled by new men from below.

For all the brutality and rapacity which marked the American scene in the years in which the new urban industrial order came into being, what stands out most is the relative absence of collective working-class protest aimed at reshaping capitalist society. The foregoing, while hardly a full explanation, should help to make this more comprehensible. The American working class was drawn into the new society by a process that encouraged accommodation and rendered disciplined protest difficult. Within the urban industrial orbit, most of its members found modest but significant opportunities to feel that they and their children were edging their way upwards. Those who did not find such opportunities were tossed helplessly about from city to city, from state to state, alienated but invisible and impotent.

ROBERT A. LIVELY

The role of government in the antebellum American economy has been boldly redefined in a score of books and

Reprinted from Robert Lively, "The American System: A Review Article," BUSINESS HISTORY REVIEW, *XXIX (March, 1955), 81–96, by permission of the publisher.*

articles published during the past decade.[1] Close analysis of state and local sponsorship of enterprise, initiated and supported by the Committee on Research in Economic History,[2] has suggested a thesis that appears to invite a new view of American capitalism in its formative years. Taken together, the works here reviewed form a consistent report of economic endeavor in an almost unfamiliar land. There, the elected public official replaced the individual enterpriser as the key figure in the release of capitalist energy; the public treasury, rather than private saving, became the major source of venture capital; and community purpose outweighed personal ambition in the selection of large goals for local economies. "Mixed" enterprise was the customary organization for important innovations, and government everywhere undertook the role put on it by the people, that of planner, promoter, investor, and regulator.

No scholar has yet attempted a general description of an America so dependent on its public authorities. The several authors who have conducted the recent surveys of little known state and local functions have carefully qualified their findings, and each has confined himself to a specific area or a selected problem in his restatement of the relation of government to enterprise. The most ambitious and inclusive accounts of positive state endeavors may be found in the articles and monographs of Louis Hartz, and Oscar and Mary Handlin. Concerned primarily with what the people wanted from their governments, rather than with what they

[1] [The bibliographical material referred to will be found at the end of this selection.]

[2] Arthur H. Cole, "Committee on Research in Economic History. A Description of Its Purposes, Activities, and Organization," *Journal of Economic History,* XIII (1953), 79–82.

got, Hartz and the Handlins were free to let their speculations carry them to extreme views. More limited but more impelling conclusions are presented in the works of Carter Goodrich and Milton Heath: their restraint lends force to their views of the carefully defined issues they analyze. Harry Pierce, John Cadman, James Neal Primm, Earl Beard, and other avoid bold generalizations, but add essential detail to the Goodrich–Heath story. These authors are united in their belief that the activities of state and local governments were of crucial importance in the stimulation of enterprise in the United States. Their variations on this theme are so numerous that the principal concern to which all return is surprisingly familiar. Their common specific task is the rescue of the internal improvements movement from the political historian, and the inflation of this issue as primary evidence for their new view of America's economic organization. In their report of the struggle of communities and states for control of inland produce or for access to markets, they document the emergence of a sturdy tradition of public responsibility for economic growth. The tradition as they describe it, persistent to the very end of the nineteenth century, was so extensively employed that it seems expanded in no theoretical respect by its modern uses in the Tennessee Valley or in the exploitation of atomic energy.

Recent notice of the age and respectability of this tradition began with attack on what Louis Hartz called the "'laissez faire' cliche" that "has done much to distort the traditional analysis of our early democratic thought" (Hartz, 2, xi). Historians, according to Hartz and others, have compounded this distortion by concentration on national issues, and by excessive concern with limitations put by the Constitu-

tion or by jealous sections on the Federal government. The story obscured, meanwhile, has been that of the broad uses to which the ante-bellum states put the powers reserved to them in a Federal system. In three papers read to the 1943 meeting of the Economic History Association, Oscar Handlin, Hartz, and Milton Heath reported that the states of Massachusetts, Pennsylvania, and Georgia were in no way inhibited by laissez-faire notions. "In the realm of the practical," observed Handlin, "there never was a period in Massachusetts history when this conception was of the slightest consequence. From the very first organization of the Commonwealth in 1780, the state actively and vigorously engaged in all the economic affairs of the area, sometimes as participant, sometimes as regulator" (Handlin, 1, 55). Of Pennsylvania, Hartz later said that, "Far from being limited, the objectives of the state in the economic field were usually so broad that they were beyond its administrative power to achieve" (Hartz, 2, 292). Milton Heath concurred, though with variations, when he concluded that of Georgia "it may be said that during the early decades there developed no definite philosophies defending the exclusive validity of either individual or public action" (Heath, 3, 100).

King Laissez Faire, then, was according to these reports not only dead; the hallowed report of his reign had all been a mistake. The error was one of monumental proportions, a mixture of overlooked data, interested distortion, and persistent preconception. Scholars who tried to set the story right, moreover, found the void before them yawning constantly wider. Authors of the first major books addressed to the issue met with boldness and imagination the problem of guiding readers through a land from which theoretical signposts had been removed. Oscar and Mary Handlin, and Louis Hartz, who published their full-length studies of Massachusetts and Pennsylvania in 1947 and 1948, were engaged by hypotheses that outreached their evidence, but the shock effect of their works was a useful stimulant to fresh and original thought about the role of government in early state history. It now seems evident that the Handlins and Hartz, in their enthusiasm for the demolition of laissez-faire mythology, substituted new theories almost as unsatisfactory as the ones they so adequately undermined. They were victims, in a way, of the assumptions they discovered to be false when employed in description of the antebellum period. Instead of eliminating the laissez-faire theme from analysis of public policy, they merely changed its chronology. Each assumed general adherence to the philosophy *after* the mid-century point at which their studies ended; and with this presupposition they gave to their account of earlier alternative policies a tone more appropriate for description of antique curiosities than for revelation of continuing themes in American economic history. They wrote as though state sponsorship of economic development had been an all or nothing proposition, a point of view that obligated them to demonstrate the total collapse and failure of the schemes and visions they had discovered.

· · ·

As an early American institution, to be sure, the corporation was a public school for enterprise. Its graduates were never very loyal, but they were no less obligated to it for their experience with major engineering projects, their knowledge of managerial problems, and their skill at gathering and handling large capital. Its modern "private" form was a very late achievement:

The attributes of peculiar economic efficiency, of limited liability, and of perpetual freedom from state interference were . . . not present at the birth of the American business corporation. Divested of these characteristics, the form assumes a new significance. At its origin in Massachusetts the corporation was conceived as an agency of the government, endowed with public attributes, exclusive privileges, and political power, and designed to serve a social function for the State. Turnpikes, not trade, banks, not land speculation, were its province because the community, not the enterprising capitalists, marked out its sphere of activity (Handlin, 2, 22).

In Pennsylvania, of 2,333 business corporations chartered by special act, 1790–1860, 64.17 per cent were in the field of transport, 7.2 per cent in banking, 11.4 per cent in insurance, 7.72 per cent for manufacturing, 2.79 per cent for water, 3.21 per cent for gas, and 3.77 per cent in miscellaneous categories—the form, in other words, was predominantly employed for works of public utility (Hartz, 2, 38). Society, in creating agents to perform social services, attempted through the several states to keep a firm hand both on the evolving corporate agents, and on the quality of the services the agents rendered. At the very least cities and states attempted to protect their investments in transportation companies, and at most they attempted to harness and direct growing corporate power. Both the minimum and maximum attempts were on the whole failures. In the end, society sought the measure of its achievement in the intangibles of community growth and prosperity; there were no other measures, for communities lost their money and they lost control of their corporations.

The state struggle to maintain controls, however, left the issue in doubt for a very long time. In the first place the chartering power was maintained until after the Civil War as a means of potential corporate regulation. The Dartmouth College Doctrine did not break legislative power over the state's creations; it only invited more careful charter limitations (Cadman, 426, 429; Hartz, 2, 236–52; Primm, 35–52). Corporate charters included detailed specifications on the size and power of directorates, the liability of stockholders and officers, the nature of capital structures, and on the details of the operations the organizations might attempt. Regulation of corporate services was generally undertaken. Banks were restricted to collection of interest rates specified in charters, and were often required to reserve a certain part of their loans for named classes. Dividends were controlled by law, especially when specie payments had been suspended (Hartz, 2, 258; Primm, 26–28). Public utilities were subjected to rate regulation, to requirements that certain customers get preferential treatment, and to the maintenance of minimum service schedules (Hartz, 2, 258–60). Illustration of the extent of detailed control might be expanded indefinitely for there were almost as many specific regulations as there were charters.

Effective administration of these laws proved possible only when the regulating authority worked toward reasonably defined and sensibly limited ends. Pennsylvania, equipped with the most ambitious regulatory program, failed in almost all her objectives. The reporting system by which the state's auditor-general kept in touch with state investments broke down completely; state officials responsible for public shares in mixed corporations were assigned more duties than they could identify, much less discharge; and legislative investigating committees proved to be clumsy and inadequate instruments of control (Hartz, 2, 96–103, 262–67). In Virginia,

on the other hand, an excellent reporting system was maintained. The Virginia Board of Public Works avoided detailed problems in the administration of mixed corporations, and concentrated on the protection of the state's financial interests, and on the provision of expert engineering services to enterprise. Even when the board controlled a majority interest in a project, it left to private hands the detailed responsibilities of management (Goodrich, 3, 378–83). In Maryland, where the state and the City of Baltimore selected a majority of the B & O directors until 1867, a similarly effective review of financial and engineering detail was maintained. Baltimore treated the road as a public institution as long as the city had a stake in it; the City Council was seeking wage raises for B & O employees as late as 1880 (Goodrich & Segal, 5, 27).

The nature of the alliance between politics and trade cannot be revealed by facts drawn only from the records of public authorities. For one thing, public directors in mixed corporations were often private stockholders in their own right: the Virginia Board, in fact, required such a display of "interest" by its agents after 1847 (Goodrich, 3, 378–9). The distinction between politician and entrepreneur was consistently vague; three mayors of Baltimore, for instance, served as presidents of railroads aided by the city. John W. Garrett, president of the B & O from 1858 to 1884, was not master of his railroad until he was master of the state of Maryland. He continued then to welcome public subscriptions to the road's development, but he preferred control to remain in private hands (Goodrich & Segal, 5, 19–20, 28–32). Harry Pierce's analysis of the battle between capitalists of Albany and Troy, New York, for control of the western trade, reveals the difficulty of judging such public endeavors as Troy's municipally owned road in the narrow context of either "public" or "private" enterprise (Pierce, 60–81).

Analysis of the intimate association of public and private officials has for the most part been avoided by the authors considered; they have tended to concentrate instead on themes demonstrating a sharp division between public and private interests. In particular they have emphasized the persistent anticorporate spirit evident throughout the nation until deep into the nineteenth century. Abundant evidence has been resurrected to demonstrate popular expression of traditional hostility to concentrated power, to the grant of privilege and monopoly, and to the mysterious or dishonest manipulations by which irresponsible corporate managers maintained themselves. Small businessmen and conservative investors feared corporations, and the public often felt misused by them. These sentiments, however, appear not to have controlled state policies; chartering programs were constantly expanded, and the form was made available to every type of business. The most distinct policy change related to the anticorporate spirit was the frequent adoption of general incorporation laws. Studies of the general incorporation movement in Massachusetts, New Jersey, Pennsylvania, and Missouri, however, reveal it to be something other than a Jacksonian extension of privilege to all comers. For enterprisers, general laws in these states were rigid and unwelcome rules written by men who wanted to restrict corporate power and growth. They were not employed by businessmen, who continued to seek and get the special charters given freely until after the Civil War. Even the Democrats, who tended to be authors of the laws, seemed

to be satisfying emotional needs rather than executing serious policy; they passed general laws, and then continued in the same sessions to grant special privileges on request (Handlin, 3, 233–5; Cadman, 431–8; Hartz, 2, 38–42; Primm, 54–62).

While communities indulged their anticorporate emotions, they continued to charter, regulate, and subsidize in their search for necessary social services. The retreat from public investment came only after the railroads had been built, and usually under the pressure of major economic crises. Increasingly, though, the regulatory effort was designed for the protection of public funds, rather than for the direction of corporate behavior. Massachusetts, in fact, demonstrated no other purpose from the start (Kirkland, I, 325). State activity declined sharply in the early 1840's, and then revived for a briefer season in the 1850's. The local aid movement reached its climax after the Civil War, before the substantial reaction of the 1870's (Goodrich, 6, 145–52). The retreat from aid by the cities was accompanied by widespread effort to dishonor municipal bonds; communities were without scruple in their efforts to repudiate debts blamed on dishonest promoters, incapable builders, and venal public officials (Pierce, 84–86; Goodrich, 6, 152–5; Beard, 16).

The retreat was not universal, and the sense of having been cheated was not generally shared. Bangor and Baltimore continued to subsidize, and in the southern states the Civil War only delayed for a season the Reconstruction climax of state aid. The financial record of the southern states had been good, the roads well built, and the hope of public profit reasonable (Heath, 2, 250–2). Communities, moreover, had never staked their hopes on business balance sheets. Only one city in 25 made a profit from railroad investments in New York, but 85 per cent of the cities subsidizing got the improved transport for which they had worked. Public losses were probably no greater than those of early private investors, and the communities had more to show for their effort (Pierce, 127). Massachusetts suffered a $9,500,00 loss on her $28,856,396 Hoosac Tunnel expenditures; profits went to the "tunnel ring" in the northwestern part of the state. But early in the twentieth century 60 per cent of Boston's exports flowed east through the "great bore" of Massachusetts politics, and all New England depended heavily on this gateway to the West (Kirkland, I, 430–2). In Virginia a committee of the Senate, balancing profit and loss on the ante-bellum effort, concluded in 1876 that state investments had been justified by the increased wealth of the whole area served (Goodrich 3, 387). The state-owned and operated Western and Atlantic Railroad of Georgia was not only the first railroad to penetrate the Appalachian Chain; the road won for the state control of western imports into the eastern cotton belt. Georgia, whose public planners share with the builders of the Erie Canal the greatest reputations in the improvements field, has long been recognized as the executor of a "master-stroke in railway policy." [3]

Conclusions invited by summary of the 25 books and articles digested in the preceding pages tend to take the form of questions rather than assertions. The significance of the literature reviewed cannot be established until the themes suggested are tested in a more general synthesis than has been attempted by any of the authors referred to here. At present the works present an extended and more exact analysis of the spirit,

policies, and achievements of the internal improvements era. This much is clear gain. The considerable influence of the newly reported theory and detail is measured by the prominence accorded government as sponsor of enterprise by George Rogers Taylor in the most recent volume of the Rinehart *Economic History of the United States.* But the most basic reappraisal of the internal improvements movement can scarcely be regarded as "new" in any bold sense; the subject is too much a staple of American economic history, and has for too long been a principal retreat for Ph.D. students seeking thesis topics. Also, more than 50 years have passed since Guy S. Callender contributed a brilliant explanation for state accumulation of $200,000,000 in capital for investment in ante-bellum industrial development, and if two more generations pass before the current version of the Callender thesis is further refined, then the recent burst of scholarly energy may not seem very significant.

One can hope for alternative developments. Taken together, the works reviewed now end on a tentative note, and leave unresolved some of the more fundamental questions they raise. Studies of the theory and practice of local aid, for instance, reveal no changes in the public mind that justify continued use of the Civil War as a convenient point to close off the story of government activity. The absence of the Federal government from the new literature is inexplicable, particularly during the 1860's and 1870's, when Washington assumed for the states so many of their services to enterprise. A fresh approach to Federal sponsorship of economic growth, undertaken in knowledge of the traditions that descended to national officers from the era of state aid, might give a new look to

[3] Ulrich Bonnell Phillips, *A History of Transportation in the East Cotton Belt to 1860* (New York, 1913), p. 334.

Radical Republican policy. The decade of monetary reform, tariff revolution, and resource alienation has been so rudely handled in the liberal historical tradition that the postwar era is remembered for corrupt deviations, rather than as a time for logical extension of established public procedures. Yet the story of public risk-taking and private profit-making does not appear to have been altered very much by transfer of the issues to the Federal sphere. The Goodrich–Heath explanations and chronology for government intervention and withdrawal might add as much meaning to Federal policy as they did to the lesser efforts by states and cities. A further test of the thesis certainly seems merited; controversies on the role of government seem almost interchangeable as the decades pass. The same angry words echo out of debates in widely separated eras, whether the subject is the delivery of monopoly powers to the Camden and Amboy, the sale of the Main Line System to the Pennsylvania Railroad, the alienation of the trans-Mississippi West, or, for that matter, the negotiation of the Dixon-Yates Contract. Perhaps historians, in their dismay at certain memories they report, have too long delayed resignation before a persistent theme in the nation's economic development—the incorrigible willingness of American public officials to seek the public good through private negotiations.

The detail of these negotiations should be pursued with infinite care. No one has undertaken extended or precise description of the way public and private obligations were combined by officers and public guardians of antebellum mixed corporations. Their compromise of sometimes contradictory duties, nonetheless, established ruling conventions for postwar economic organization. The mixed railroad corporation was not only parent to "big" business in the United States; its leaders also defined the character of business-government relationships, the duties of corporation to public, and the responsibility of manager to investor. Customary procedures and standards of behavior for managers of the modern corporation were thus conceived in ideological twilight, and had become habitual before the individual entrepreneur achieved a firm grip on the corporate form. Perhaps from the divided loyalties of the public-spirited men who planned so boldly for early community growth there emerged the ethical confusion characteristic of subsequent corporate behavior. Speculation on this point needs support from more abundant and specific fact than is yet available from the era of the mixed corporation.

To studies of the continuing association of government and enterprise should be added the equally unbroken theme of state regulatory efforts. The hiatus between stories of state control policies before and after the war becomes increasingly hard to justify, particularly after recent indictment of the view that "Granger" laws were the product of agrarian discontent.[4] Just as individual enterprisers of the forties and fifties had joined in unsuccessful efforts to reduce corporate power, so, in the sixties and seventies, merchants and shippers maintained and strengthened control mechanisms. The considerable complexity of the postwar laws may possibly reflect long years of uninterrupted experience and concern with protection of the public interest. The only major break in regulatory policy appears to lie in the uneven assumption by the Federal government of earlier state responsibilities. Even at

[4] George H. Miller, "Origins of the Iowa Granger Law," *Mississippi Valley Historical Review*, XL (1954), 657–80.

Washington, state patterns were repeated; controls, whatever the level of government, tended to lag about a generation behind aids.

The substantial energies of government, though, were employed more often for help than for hindrance to enterprise. The broad and well-documented theme reviewed here is that of public support for business development. Official vision and public resources have been associated so regularly with private skill and individual desire that the combination may be said to constitute a principal determinant of American economic growth. Internal improvements dominated the association in ante-bellum years, but opportunities for broader use of the alliance multiplied as controls over the economy became more centralized. Resolute Federal decision was in time revealed to be a key to remarkable productive achievement, most notably during the wars of the twentieth century. States and cities meanwhile transformed their record of debt from millions to billions as they constructed the nation's highways and public buildings, and extended their public services; B. U. Ratchford's analysis of American state debts might serve as an outline for a score of theses on the influence of Keynesian experiments, before Keynes. Rising constantly from the impulse to public-spirited undertakings, moreover, was the neomercantilism of regions and provinces of the American economy which came to replace the earlier and simpler competition of cities and states. Commercial clubs in the cities, industrial commissions in the states, and governors' conferences in the regions all joined in sponsorship of industrial expansion.[5] The story sprawls out to un-

governable proportions, to tax exemptions, police-guaranteed labor discipline, municipal power-plant construction, and on to RFC, TVA, and AEC. Even communities in Mississippi, the very oldest and deepest of the southern states, have in the past 14 years spent $29,206,000 in the construction of free factories for 92 enterprises who have agreed to locate there. From the grass roots putting up shoots before Chamber of Commerce buildings to the Office of the President's Council of Economic Advisors there can be documented the unceasing pressure for public sponsorship of economic growth.

Milton Heath, in the earliest contribution to the literature here considered, described the public aid movement of ante-bellum years as possibly the "last great associative effort on American soil" (Heath, 2, 60). In this judgment he was probably as wrong as other authors who have analyzed the internal improvements effort as something unique in the American experience. The distant historical phenomenon they report proves very close at hand. Instead of the last great associative effort, they have revealed theory and practice for the first of continuing efforts to associate the massive powers of government with the skill of enterprise. Historians have been unaccountably slow in seeking the general themes of this story; they catalogue the plans of a Hamilton, a Gallatin, or a Clay, but they have ignored the rapid translation of these schemes into essential elements of a lasting American System. The notable accomplishment of the authors reviewed lies in the bold step they have taken down the road that leads from Hamiltonian dreams toward the mixed economy of contemporary America. This road is not yet fully marked, but its general direction is now clear. Further studies of government's partnership with enterprise may

---

[5] Robert A. Lively, "The South and Freight Rates: Political Settlement of an Economic Argument," *Journal of Southern History*, XIV (1948), 357–84.

reveal it to be one of the major routes connecting early American hopes with recent material achievements.

The following list of books and articles reviewed is arranged to serve as an index to specific data employed in the text. Review-style citation is utilized, where reference is to material in the subject literature. The several contributions of a single author are numbered to simplify identification of the work cited. E. C. Kirkland's study of New England railroads, G. R. Taylor's general history of the ante-bellum period, and G. S. Callender's seminal article are grouped with the works below so that they can be cited conveniently, but no effort is made to summarize their generally known contributions.

Earl S. Beard, "Local Aid to Railroads in Iowa," *Iowa Journal of History*, L (1952), 1–34.

John W. Cadman, Jr., *The Corporation in New Jersey. Business and Politics 1791–1875* (Cambridge, 1949).

Guy S. Callender, "The Early Transportation and Banking Enterprises of the States in Relation to the Growth of Corporations," *Quarterly Journal of Economics*, XVII (1902–1903), 111–62.

Carter Goodrich
1. "Public Spirit and American Improvements," *Proceedings of the American Philosophical Society*, XCII (1948), 305–9.
2. "National Planning of Internal Improvements," *Political Science Quarterly*, LXIII (1948), 16–44.
3. "The Virginia System of Mixed Enterprise. A Study of State Planning of Internal Improvements," *Political Science Quarterly*, LXIV (1949), 355–87.
4. "Local Planning of Internal Improvements," *Political Science Quarterly*, LXVI (1951), 411–45.
5. with Harvey H. Segal, "Baltimore's Aid to Railroads. A Study in the Municipal Planning of Internal Improvements," *Journal of Economic History*, XIII (1953), 2–35.

6. "The Revulsion Against Internal Improvements," *Journal of Economic History*, X (1950), 145–69.

Bray Hammond
1. "Banking in the Early West: Monopoly, Prohibition and Laissez Faire," *Journal of Economic History*, VIII (1948), 1–25.
2. "Jackson, Biddle, and the Bank of the United States," *Journal of Economic History*, VII (1947), 1–23.
3. "Free Banks and Corporations: The New York Free Banking Act of 1838," *Journal of Political Economy*, XLIV (1936), 184–209.

Oscar Handlin
1. "Laissez-Faire Thought in Massachusetts, 1790–1880," *Journal of Economic History*, III, *Supplement* (1943), 55–65.
2. with Mary Flug Handlin, "Origins of the American Business Corporation," *Journal of Economic History*, V (1945), 1–23.
3. with Mary Flug Handlin, *Commonwealth: A Study of the Role of Government in the American Economy. Massachusetts, 1774–1861* (New York, 1947).

Louis Hartz
1. "Laissez Faire Thought in Pennsylvania, 1776–1860," *Journal of Economic History*, III, *Supplement* (1943), 66–77.
2. *Economic Policy and Democratic Thought: Pennsylvania, 1776–1860* (Cambridge, 1948).

Milton S. Heath
1. "Public Railroad Construction and the Development of Private Enterprise in the South before 1861," *Journal of Economic History*, X, *Supplement* (1950), 40–53.
2. "Public Co-operation in Railroad Construction in the Southern United States to 1861" (Unpublished Ph.D. dissertation, Harvard University, 1937).
3. "Laissez Faire in Georgia, 1732–1860," *Journal of Economic History*, III, *Supplement* (1943), 78–100.

Frederick K. Henrich, "The Development of American Laissez Faire. A General View of the Age of Washington," *Journal of Economic History*, III, Supplement (1943), 51–54.

Edward Chase Kirkland, *Men, Cities, and Transportation. A Study in New England History 1800–1900* (Cambridge, 1948).

Harry H. Pierce, *Railroads of New York. A Study of Government Aid, 1826–1875* (Cambridge, 1953).

James Neal Primm, *Economic Policy in the Development of a Western State, Missouri 1820–1860* (Cambridge, 1954).

George Rogers Taylor, *The Transportation Revolution 1815–1860*, Vol. 4, *The Economic History of the United States* (New York, 1951).

ROBERT WIEBE

Historians distrust the theorizer as a matter of principle only to adopt his theories as a matter of necessity. Seeking a course somewhere between philosophy and antiquarianism, they have borrowed whatever theories happen to be current under the illusion that they can then enjoy the best of both worlds: a study of the particular with general significance. One result has been a remarkably broad agreement on fundamentals. For half a century historians debated Frederick Jackson Turner's frontier thesis within the rules Turner himself had established. Between the mid-twenties and the mid-forties a far larger body of literature disputed the claims of Charles Beard and Vernon Louis Parrington by arguing the consequences of history as Beard and Parrington conceived it. Instead of questioning whether or not great liberal and conservative forces had contended

Reprinted from Robert Wiebe, "The Confinements of Consensus," NORTHWESTERN TRI-QUARTERLY, No. 6 (1966), pp. 155–58, by permission of the publisher.

for control of the nation, historians evaluated results. Were the liberals really that pure or practical? Were the conservatives really that callous or destructive?

When a handful of adventurers finally did re-examine the fundamentals around mid-century, they rocked the profession. Rather than begin by sorting their subjects into liberal and conservative camps, Richard Hofstadter, Daniel Boorstin, David Potter, and Louis Hartz attacked the predicate itself. Had there not been qualities common to Americans generally, qualities that had held them together throughout their history? A set of capitalist assumptions, perhaps; a pragmatic style; a uniquely rich, exploitable land; a peculiarly benign heritage. Moreover, would we not see these characteristics more clearly by setting America's development against that of Western Europe or even against a culture outside Western Civilization? These men went abroad not simply for comparisons but for basic questions about social behavior. Together they provided that most valuable of contributions: a fresh frame of reference.

With the zeal of converts their successors have run back through the American past discovering consensus everywhere; great battles have dissolved into the squabblings of like-minded men. The product of their labors is a new stereotype to compete with the old. Is the nation's past a story of grand contests or of unfolding agreement? *Conflict or Consensus in American History*, asks the title of a recent anthology. Take your pick. Little more than a decade after the pioneers blazed a trail, the spirit of the quest is dead. We have turned prophets into priests, stultifying their message by worship. Is it not possible to extend the search rather than merely hoard answers?

Surely, for example, all of us are now willing to acknowledge that any society requires certain elements of agreement in order to function. In this light consensus in American society is redundant and the argument a tautology. To debate a self-evident proposition only obscures the important inquiries. What realms of behavior has this consensus covered? How many people situated where have had to accept what values, what assumptions, what expectations, before American society could operate? How and why has that pattern varied, and what have been the results, the implications, of those changes?

The most popular method of resolving such problems is to test the American experience by a European gauge. Ideology, politics, and revolt—singly or in combinations—comprise the crucial indices because these, we are told, give meaning to Europe's turmoil during the nineteenth and twentieth centuries. If theorists stand at divergent polls, if groups engage systematically in political subversion, and if rivals shoot instead of shout at each other, society lacks cohesion. By this standard the American story is quite easy to grasp. We have not generated great ideological conflicts; we have not indulged in the politics of sabotage; and we have produced neither revolutionary upheavals nor even a respectable number of little uprisings. Sometimes the Civil War appears as the exception proving the rule, and sometimes as additional evidence, a conflict so reluctantly joined and so quickly regretted that it actually strengthens the case.

This at best is a rather convoluted logic. These European troubles, the argument seems to say, embody the very substance of disunity throughout western culture. By definition, therefore, any part of western culture without them—in this instance, America—

has a cohesive society. The persuasiveness of such negative evidence depends upon a very strict set of conditions, the most significant of which is the essential identity between Europe and America, an identity oddly enough that the argument itself tends to disprove. Viewing America within the context of Western Civilization is one of the important contributions the original historians of consensus made, and certainly no one today cares to reconstruct the insular, national perspective these pioneers so effectively destroyed. Yet an awareness that Europe and America appear twins when contrasted with a China or a Ghana does not mean we must dismiss those differences which do exist.

Everyone has nodding acquaintance with two of these: that vast expanse of land which enthralled Turner; and the ethnic heterogeneity of an immigrant nation. In fact we acknowledge them so readily that they tend to become two-dimensional truths, facts we grant rather than explore, and in that form we usually employ them additively. If America has had *more* rich land, it will consequently have *more* of something else: more space to accommodate more people on larger farms; a more diversified economy; more wealth; and the like. If America has had more ethnic groups, it will therefore have more religious compromise, more contributions to its cultural heritage, more men seeking recognition through politics, and so forth. Or we make simple substitutions in the standard equations: American "imperialism" in the nineteenth century, for instance, involved contiguous rather than distant territory. Yet the truly significant effects have not been quantitative but qualitative ones, effects which have altered the very nature of American society. Two examples may suggest the relevance of these inner differences to the subject of consensus. The first concerns the relative ease and speed with which America industrialized, presumably demonstrating a fundamental harmony of values. The second concerns the peaceful processes of immigrant assimilation, ostensibly illustrating the health of America's stable democratic society.

Modern American industry emerged in an exceptionally decentralized society. The rapid movement of people across a continent during the nineteenth century located most citizens in towns that were linked only by a most tenuous system of communication. Discourse among these islands was severely limited and highly erratic, and the power both to form opinion and to enact public policy was diffused. Men and women with comparable interests who might have joined to act together remained blind to the possibilities of a broader cooperation. The heart of democracy was local autonomy. A century after France had developed a reasonably efficient, centrally directed public bureaucracy, Americans could not even conceive of an administrative government. Local officials construed laws to serve local needs, and informal actions still managed most of a community's affairs. An elaborate procedure for transmitting skills, one that inhibited specialization and discouraged the accumulation of knowledge, grew out of this wholesale dispersal.

American society, in other words, was radically at variance with the impersonal, regulative, hierarchical requirements of industrialization and at the same time peculiarly powerless to halt that alien invasion. Thin, undependable sources of information kept people ignorant of what happened elsewhere: a great deal of industrialization would occur before millions really

comprehended the fact. Indicatively, the first movements of national potential to challenge modern capitalism arrived not toward the beginnings of the process where one might normally have expected them but during the 1880's and 1890's just as the United States was surpassing all other nations as an industrial power. Even at that astonishingly late date the dissenters' parochial illusions led them to anticipate an effortless victory once the "people" were aroused. But what could they do? Their islands still did not communicate with each other. Men's minds still did not comprehend responses suitable to the danger they would meet; Populism bore a far closer relationship to the utopianism of Jackson's time than to the bureaucratic reforms of the New Deal. Industrialization arrived so peacefully not because all Americans secretly shared the same values or implicitly willed its success but because its millions of bitter enemies lacked the mentality and the means to organize an effective counterattack. What mobilized power did exist belonged to the sponsors of industrialization, and they swept the field with remarkable ease.

Despite the warnings of such men as Oscar Handlin, the usual method of interpreting America's ethnic heterogeneity is to measure behavior by an undefined and covert "American" standard. How rapidly and how well have newcomers shed their old ways and adopted new ones? The underlying assumption is that consciously or otherwise each ethnic group is striving to reach the American norm; or, alternatively, that "social forces" are willy-nilly drawing these people toward it. In part this cast of mind derives from a centuries-old, uneasy involvement with national unity and social cohesion. In our time, however, it is a particular response to the racist arguments of the twentieth century. Historians are still trying to disprove the bigoted conclusion that immigrants and Negroes could never assimilate because they were congenitally inferior. If one could only say "Look, see how beautifully they have blended!" he could finally put the lie to this nativist cant. Of course not all the arguments are that elementary. Nevertheless, even those which carefully describe a residue of ethnic peculiarities tend to do so in a way that highlights the assimilative character of the orientation.

Even if we accept a mystical American norm—which on the face of it we certainly should not—we have excellent reason to believe that immigrants and Negroes have not marched a series of paths with a single terminus. They have followed a hundred winding routes of their own, as groups and as individuals; and their pattern is a labyrinthine pluralism rather than so many markers along the way to a simple assimilation. We should not require studies of "the alienated voter," of disintegrative Negro families, of antifluoridation campaigns to remind us that over the centuries countless Americans have lived in ways that bore little relationship to the articulated principles of the comfortable and the educated. Work hard, postpone desires, save money, prepare for your profession, and in time your wants will be fulfilled: generations of substantial citizens have found this a sensible guide. But what relevance did it have in a slum world predicated on poverty and chance, violence and catastrophe? Men living only a few city blocks apart might have nothing they could say to each other. The same types of behavior —voting, for instance—might hold sharply different meanings to the two, or no meaning at all to one of them. They would not argue, in other words, because they could not communicate with each other. And if one had practically no power while the second held a surplus, they could not even fight each other. Sambo masks, subterfuge, and sublimated aggressions would replace the ballot and the rifle, not because they really agreed upon the fundamentals but because they disagreed so basically and enjoyed such radically disparate means of expression that they could not even dispute.

In both examples the immediate implications are the same: the absence of ideological debate, hard political battle, and armed conflict may indicate social distance and power differentials so great that they preclude any direct confrontation. The very evidence which has been used to prove a consensus may actually demonstrate its opposite. By this I certainly do not mean to suggest that A should always read Z, that some new brittle truth should replace the old. The last thing we require now are reinforcements in an arid debate of stereotypes. On the contrary, we need quite simply a little daring, a little of that explorer's sense which the pioneers in consensus history once exemplified, so that we can substitute fresh questions for the stale answers.

HISTORIOGRAPHICAL NOTE

Most historians have written on American industrial and urban development from deep personal feelings of shock, outrage, or dismay. Indignant radical writers such as Matthew Josephson and Gustavus Myers, for example, detailed every malpractice they could discover concerning late nineteenth-century business leaders, men whom they considered dangerous "robber barons." [1]

Following the progressive era's journalistic exposés of the "trusts"—Myers himself began as a muckraker—an entire generation of historians painted the history of post-Civil War industrial consolidation in Manichean hues, forces of light and anti-trust reform battling the forces of darkness and business villainy. Charles Beard, himself, stood aloof from this general liberal condemnation of corporate practices. Instead, he celebrated his democratic heroes but characterized American industrial development—and the patterns it assumed—as natural and inevitable.[2] Ida Tarbell worked both ends of the street on the question of business leadership, portraying the foibles of Standard Oil in harsh terms for readers of *McClure's Magazine*, while maintaining quiet respect for the achievements of Rockefeller, Carnegie, and other post-Civil War magnates. The selection from Tarbell presents a remarkably balanced early treatment of American industrialization. Many more of her historical generation preferred instead merely to document their outrage at the activities of Gilded Age "robber barons," just as a more recent generation of "entrepreneurial" historians has attempted to defend the soiled reputation of that era's "industrial statesmen." Allan Nevins' admiring biography of John D. Rockefeller pioneered in these scholarly efforts to counter earlier critics and to document the achievements of American businessmen.[3] There exists a vast literature on this so-called "robber baron" question which has seemed increasingly a sterile dispute to those recent historians who remain uninvolved in the political issue of business regulation.

In similar fashion events have overtaken earlier trends in historical writing on American immigration and urbanization. The shock, concern, or anxiety over the impact which the new immigration would have on the stability of American life has been effectively dissipated as third and fourth generation descendants of European peasants have moved into every major profession and type of influential position—including the Presidency.

---

[1] Matthew Josephson, *The Robber Barons* (New York, 1934); Gustavus Myers, *History of the Great American Fortunes* (New York, 1907).

[2] Charles A. Beard, *The Rise of American Civilization* (New York, 1927).

[3] Allan Nevins, *John D. Rockefeller: The Heroic Age of American Enterprise* (New York, 1940). On the entire controversy, see Hal Bridges, "The Robber Baron Concept in American History," *Business History Review*, XXXII (Spring, 1958).

Anxiety over racial purity, evident even in the writing of liberal social historians such as Arthur Schlesinger, Sr., has been replaced by more detached, less frenetic studies of immigrant community behavior, writings which lack either the troubled moralism or the ethnic pietism of earlier works. Stephan Thernstrom's examination of the Newburyport, Massachusetts, community, Donald Cole's book on another *Immigrant City* (Lawrence, Massachusetts), and Gilbert Osofsky's recent work on the evolution of a Negro ghetto in Harlem are three such major writings which mark the social historian's emancipation from earlier moralistic reactions to immigrant behavior patterns.[4] All three authors employ new source materials ranging from tax records to census data in order to study as dispassionately as possible the process of immigrant assimilation and urban development.

The portrayal of economic and social processes with only minimal intrusion of the historian's own moral judgments or ideological perspectives on such processes has also become a dominant theme in recent historical literature on industrialization. The events being examined are neither attacked nor defended but instead studied in relative detachment, reflecting the degree to which some modern historians have either absorbed or by-passed the traditional economic and social controversies of the eight decades since the close of the Civil War. Many of these arguments over whether the business leaders of late nineteenth-century America were "good" or "bad" men, whether their industries should be totally regulated or not at all, have come to seem outmoded to many Americans in the post-World War II period. Alfred Chandler's masterful work on the development of our modern corporate structure, for example, almost entirely avoids this earlier "robber baron" debate in favor of a dispassionate account of the methods and processes employed in achieving large-scale corporate development.[5] Robert Lively's article itself represents a model of imaginative historical synthesis, reconstructing the categories traditionally used in examining the relationship between business and government in America while making few judgments on this relationship. Removing the factor of moral judgment from historical writing is no sure-fire guarantee of producing *better* history. In dealing with recent commentators on American industrial society, however, it seems clear that the increased detachment of professional historians has already borne impressive results.

[4] Stephan Thernstrom, *Poverty and Progress: Social Mobility in a Nineteenth Century City* (Cambridge, Mass., 1964); Donald B. Cole, *Immigrant City: Lawrence, Massachusetts, 1845–1921* (Chapel Hill, N.C., 1963); Gilbert Osofsky, *Harlem: The Making of a Ghetto* (New York, 1966).

[5] Alfred Chandler, *Strategy and Structure: Chapters in the History of the Industrial Enterprise* (Garden City, N.Y., 1962).

11. The Agrarian Response to Industrial Society

INTRODUCTION

The nineteenth century was a period of technological innovation, industrial expansion, railroad construction, and urbanization. The productive capabilities of the American economy soared to unprecedented heights, and stories of enormous abundance attracted millions of immigrants to the New World. A predominantly agricultural nation of less than 4,000,000 people when the Constitution was ratified, the United States had become a highly industrialized nation of more than 75,000,000 by 1900. Panegyrists of the Land of Opportunity confidently predicted fulfillment of the "American dream."

Yet the same economic changes that made great expectations seem plausible also produced severe social and political dislocations. The years of change were therefore years of unrest. Farmers and laborers, especially, found themselves beset by economic difficulties, and they sought to form organizations through which they could increase their power and influence. Through labor unions workers hoped to bargain with management on wages, hours, and working conditions. After the Civil War, farmers joined the Patrons of Husbandry and, later, farmers' alliances. Supposedly nonpolitical, such groups engaged in various activities to reduce purchasing costs, increase crop production, and secure favorable markets.

Direct economic action failed to bring the desired results, however, and farmers turned to political action. Beginning in December, 1890, they held a series of meetings and conventions which led to the formation of the People's (or Populist) party in 1892. Polling over a million popular votes, almost ten per cent of the total, presidential candidate James B. Weaver made what the party interpreted as a respectable showing. Then, when a severe depression after 1893 brought with it a marked increase in social and economic unrest, the People's party looked forward to a corresponding increase in membership. Indeed, agrarian leaders optimistically anticipated the achievement of major party status.

Whatever Populist hopes may have been, the silver lining in the dark cloud of hard times was subject to economic as well as political interpretation. Farmers had long believed that the post-Civil War decline in agricultural prices was at least in part attributable to a contraction of the currency. Populists accepted that explanation and called for a stable dollar that would not vary in purchasing power. In the meantime, other groups had begun successfully to agitate for the free and unlimited coinage of silver. Hoping to capitalize on what was becoming a popular issue, People's party spokesmen made much of the silver plank in their platform.

It was their undoing. Instead of winning acceptance of a broad reform program, Populists found themselves outmaneuvered by the very groups they had hoped to attract. In 1896 silverites gained control of the Democratic party and nominated William Jennings Bryan. To avoid splitting the forces of reform, Populists supported Bryan as a silver candidate, even though he refused to endorse the Populist platform in its entirety. Compromising to win half a loaf, they did not win even that. After the fusion of 1896—and the defeat of Bryan by McKinley—the People's party was never the same. As an organization it continued into the twentieth century, but the old vitality was gone.

What was the significance of the Populist experience? Historians, political analysts, and students of American culture have long concerned themselves with the question. Scholarly investigation of Populism began in the 1920's, and the writing that came out of it revealed considerable sympathy for the movement. The first historians to consider nineteenth-century agricultural problems were men who clearly shared the Jeffersonian, agrarian biases on which the People's party built. The interpretation of Populism began to undergo revision when the United States passed through the depression crisis of the thirties and faced new challenges at home and abroad during the forties and fifties. Fascism and McCarthyism seemed to demonstrate the malevolent and oppressive possibilities in mass movements. Struck by the similarities between Populism and McCarthyism, some historians in the years after World War II saw Populism as a precursor of illiberal twentieth-century fanaticism. It was a convincing interpretation, but it did not persuade those historians who were sympathetic to a fundamental reconstruction of American society in the sixties. Such men were inclined to defend the earlier agrarian radicals; they saw in the Populist movement a precedent for their own criticism of established institutions and elites.

I. EARLY INTERPRETATION

John D. Hicks, one of the first historians to investigate the Populist movement, published his classic study, *The Populist Revolt*, in 1931. The work examines in sympathetic detail the formation of the People's party and the party's demise. In his concluding chapter, from which the following selection has been taken, Hicks presents what he considers the essence of Populist philosophy and the nature of the Populist contribution. He argues that although the People's party met defeat, its cause went marching on to victory. Populism must therefore be seen as occupying an important place in a long reform continuum.

JOHN D. HICKS

Early in 1890, when the People's party was yet in the embryo stage, a farmer editor from the West set forth the doctrine that "the cranks always win." As he saw it,

The cranks are those who do not accept the existing order of things, and propose to change them. The existing order of things is always accepted by the majority, therefore the cranks are always in the minority. They are always progressive thinkers and always in advance of their time, and they always win. Called fanatics and fools at first, they are sometimes persecuted and abused. But their reforms are generally righteous, and time, reason and argument bring men to their side. Abused and ridiculed, then tolerated, then respectfully given a hearing, then supported. This has been the gauntlet that all great reforms and reformers have run, from Galileo to John Brown.[1]

The writer of this editorial may have overstated his case, but a backward glance at the history of Populism shows that many of the reforms that the Populists demanded, while despised and rejected for a reason, won triumphantly in the end. The party itself did not survive, nor did many of its leaders, although the number of contemporary

politicians whose escutcheons should bear the bend sinister of Populism is larger than might be supposed; but Populistic doctrines showed an amazing vitality.

In formulating their principles the Populists reasoned that the ordinary, honest, willing American worker, be he farmer or be he laborer, might expect in this land of opportunity not only the chance to work but also, as the rightful reward of his labor, a fair degree of prosperity. When, in the later eighties and in the "heart-breaking nineties," hundreds of thousands—perhaps millions—of men found themselves either without work to do or, having work, unable to pay their just debts and make a living, the Populists held that there must be "wrong and crime and fraud somewhere." What was more natural than to fix the blame for this situation upon the manufacturers, the railroads, the moneylenders, the middlemen—plutocrats all, whose "colossal fortunes, unprecedented in the history of mankind," grew ever greater while the multitudes came to know the meaning of want. Work was denied when work might well have been given, and "the fruits of the toil of millions were boldly stolen."[2]

And the remedy? In an earlier age the hard-pressed farmers and laborers might have fled to free farms in the seemingly limitless lands of the West, but now the era of free lands had passed. Where, then, might they look for help? Where, if not to the govern-

[1] *Farmers' Alliance* (Lincoln), February 15, 1890. This chapter follows in the main an article on "The Persistence of Populism," *Minnesota History*, 12:3–20 (March, 1931).

Reprinted from John D. Hicks, THE POPULIST REVOLT *(Minneapolis: University of Minnesota Press, 1931), Copyright 1931 by the University of Minnesota, renewed 1959 by John D. Hicks; pp. 404–422, by permission of the publisher.*

[2] Donnelly's preamble to the St. Louis and Omaha platforms stated not unfairly the Populist protest.

ment, which alone had the power to bring the mighty oppressors of the people to bay? So to the government the Populists turned. From it they asked laws to insure a full redress of grievances. As Dr. Turner puts it, "the defences of the pioneer democrat began to shift from free land to legislation, from the ideal of individualism to the ideal of social control through regulation by law." [3] Unfortunately, however, the agencies of government had been permitted to fall into the hands of the plutocrats. Hence, if the necessary corrective legislation were to be obtained, the people must first win control of their government. The Populist philosophy thus boiled down finally to two fundament propositions; one, that the government must restrain the selfish tendencies of those who profited at the expense of the poor and needy; the other, that the people, not the plutocrats, must control the government. . . .

To list [Populist] demands is to cite the chief political innovations made in the United States during recent times. The Australian system of voting, improved registration laws, and other devices for insuring "a free ballot and a fair count" have long since swept the country. Woman suffrage has won an unqualified victory. The election of United States senators by direct vote of the people received the approval of far more than two-thirds of the national House of Representatives as early as 1898; it was further foreshadowed by the adoption, beginning in 1904, of senatorial primaries in a number of states, the results of which were to be regarded as morally binding upon the legislatures concerned; and it became a fact in 1913 with the ratification of

the seventeenth amendment to the constitution. . . .

Direct legislation by the people became almost an obsession with the Populists, especially the middle-of-the-road faction, in whose platforms it tended to overshadow nearly every other issue; and it is perhaps significant that the initiative and referendum were first adopted by South Dakota, a state in which the Populist party had shown great strength, as close on the heels of the Populist movement as 1898. Other states soon followed the South Dakota lead, and particularly in Oregon the experiment of popular legislation was given a thorough trial.[4] New constitutions and numerous amendments to old constitutions tended also to introduce much popularly made law, the idea that legislation in a constitution is improper and unwise receiving perhaps its most shattering blow when an Oklahoma convention wrote for that state a constitution of fifty thousand words. The recall of elected officials has been applied chiefly in municipal affairs, but some states also permit its use for state officers and a few allow even judges, traditionally held to be immune from popular reactions, to be subjected to recall. Thus many of the favorite ideas of the Populists, ideas that had once been "abused and ridiculed," were presently "respectfully given a hearing, then supported." [5] . . .

The control of the government by the people was to the thoughtful Popu-

[3] Frederick J. Turner, *The Frontier in American History* (New York, 1921), 277.

[4] Ellis P. Oberholtzer, *The Referendum in America together with Some Chapters on the Initiative and the Recall* (New York, 1912).

[5] For satisfactory general discussions of these reforms see Charles A. Beard, *American Government and Politics*, 4th ed., ch. 24; Charles and Mary R. Beard, *The Rise of American Civilization*, Vol. 2, ch. 27; and David S. Muzzey, *The United States of America*, Vol. 2, ch. 7.

list merely a means to an end. The next step was to use the power of the government to check the iniquities of the plutocrats. When the Populists at Omaha were baffled by the insistence of the temperance forces, they pointed out that before this or any other such reform could be accomplished they must "ask all men to first help us to determine whether we are to have a republic to administer." The inference is clear. Once permit the people really to rule, once insure that the men in office would not or could not betray the popular will, and such regulative measures as would right the wrongs from which the people suffered would quickly follow. The Populist believed implicitly in the ability of the people to frame and enforce the measures necessary to redeem themselves from the various sorts of oppression that were being visited upon them. They catalogued in their platform the evils from which society suffered and suggested the specific remedies by which these evils were to be overcome. . . .

The Populists observed with entire accuracy that the currency of the United States was both inadequate and inelastic. They criticized correctly the part played by the national banking system in currency matters as irresponsible and susceptible of manipulation in the interest of the creditor class. They demanded a stabilized dollar, and they believed that it could be obtained if a national currency "safe, sound, and flexible" should be issued direct to the people by the government itself in such quantities as the reasonable demands of business should dictate. Silver and gold might be issued as well as paper, but the value of the dollar should come from the fiat of government and not from the "intrinsic worth" of the metal.

It is interesting to note that since the time when Populists were condemned as lunatics for holding such views legislation has been adopted that, while by no means going the full length of an irredeemable paper currency, does seek to accomplish precisely the ends that the Populists had in mind. . . .

Probably no item in the Populist creed received more thorough castigation at the hands of contemporaries than the demand for subtreasuries, or government warehouses for the private storage of grain; but the subtreasury idea was not all bad, and perhaps the Populists would have done well had they pursued it further than they did.

. . .

To the middle western Populist the railway problem was as important as any other—perhaps the most important of all. Early Alliance platforms favored drastic governmental control of the various means of communication as the best possible remedy for the ills from which the people suffered, and the first Populist platform to be written called for government ownership and operation only in case "the most rigid, honest, and just national control and supervision" should fail to "remove the abuses now existing." Thereafter the Populists usually demanded government ownership, although it is clear enough from their state and local platforms and from the votes and actions of Populist officeholders that, pending the day when ownership should become a fact, regulation by state and nation must be made ever more effective.

Possibly government ownership is no nearer today than in Populist times, but the first objective of the Populists, "the most rigid, honest, and just national control," is as nearly an accomplished fact as carefully drawn legislation and highly efficient administration can make it. Populist misgivings about governmental control arose from the knowledge that the Interstate Commerce Act of 1887, as well as most regulatory state legislation, was wholly ineffectual during the nineties; but beginning with the Elkins Act of 1903, which struck at the practice of granting rebates, a long series of really workable laws found their way into the statute books. The Hepburn Act of 1906, the Mann-Elkins Act of 1910, and the Transportation Act of 1920, not to mention lesser laws, placed the Interstate Commerce Commission upon a high pinnacle of power. State laws, keeping abreast of the national program, supplemented national control with state control; and through one or the other agency most of the specific grievances of which the Populists had complained were removed.[6] The arbitrary fixing of rates by the carriers, a commonplace in Populist times, is virtually unknown today. If discriminations still exist between persons or places, the Interstate Commerce Commission is apt to be as much to blame as the railroads. Free passes, so numerous in Populist times as to occasion the remark that the only people who did not have passes were those who could not afford to pay their own fare, have virtually ceased to be issued except to railways employes. Railway control of state governments, even in the old Granger states, where in earlier days party bosses took their orders directly from railways officials, has long since become a thing of the past. The railroads still may have an influence in politics, but the railroads do not rule. Governmental control of telephones, telegraphs, and pipe lines, together

with such later developments as the radio and the transmission of electric power, is accepted today as a matter of course, the issues being merely to what extent control should go and through what agencies it should be accomplished.

For the trust problem, as distinguished from the railroad problem, the Populists had no very definite solution. They agreed, however, that the power of government, state and national, should be used in such a way as to prevent "individuals or corporations fastening themselves, like vampires, on the people and sucking their substance."[7] Antitrust laws received the earnest approval of Alliancemen and Populists and were often initiated by them. The failure of such laws to secure results was laid mainly at the door of the courts, and when Theodore Roosevelt in 1904 succeeded in securing an order from the United States Supreme Court dissolving the Northern Securities Company, it was hailed as a great victory for Populist principles. Many other incidental victories were won. Postal savings banks "for the safe deposit of the earnings of the people" encroached upon the special privileges of the bankers. An amendment to the national constitution in 1913, authorizing income taxes, recalled a contrary decision of the Supreme Court, which the Populists in their day had cited as the best evidence of the control of the government by the trusts; and income and inheritance taxes have ever since been levied. The reform of state and local taxation so as to exact a greater proportion of the taxes from the trusts and those who profit from them has also been freely undertaken. Labor demands, such as the right of labor to

[6] William Z. Ripley, *Railroads; Rates and Regulation;* Homer B. Vanderblue and Kenneth F. Burgess, *Railroads. Rates—Service—Management;* David Philip Locklin, *Railroad Regulation since 1920.*

[7] See the Cincinnati platform in the *American*, 27:167 (September 10, 1898).

organize, the eight-hour day, limitation of injunctions in labor disputes, and restrictions on immigration were strongly championed by the Populists as fit measures for curbing the power of the trusts and were presently treated with great consideration. The Clayton Antitrust Act and the Federal Trade Commission Act, passed during the Wilson régime, were the products of long experience with the trust problem. The manner in which these laws have been enforced, however, would seem to indicate that the destruction of the trusts, a common demand in Populist times, is no longer regarded as feasible and that by government control the interests of the people can best be conserved.[8]

On the land question the Populist demands distinctly foreshadowed conservation. "The land," according to the Omaha declaration, "including all the natural resources of wealth, is the heritage of all the people and should not be monopolized for speculative purposes." Land and resources already given away were of course difficult to get back, and the passing of the era of free lands could not be repealed by law, but President Roosevelt soon began to secure results in the way of the reclamation and irrigation of arid western lands, the enlargement and protection of the national forests, the improvement of internal waterways, and the withdrawal from entry of lands bearing mineral wealth such as coal, oil, and phosphates. At regular intervals, since 1908, the governors of the states have met together in conference to discuss the conservation problem, and this once dangerous Populist doctrine has now won all but universal acceptance.[9]

It would thus appear that much of the Populist program has found favor in the eyes of later generations. Populist plans for altering the machinery of government have, with but few exceptions, been carried into effect. Referring to these belated victories of the Populists, William Allen White, the man who had once asked, "What's the matter with Kansas?" wrote recently, "They abolished the established order completely and ushered in a new order."[10] Mrs. Mary E. Lease looked back proudly in 1914 on her political career:

In these later years I have seen, with gratification, that my work in the good old Populist days was not in vain. The Progressive party has adopted our platform, clause by clause, plank by plank. Note the list of reforms which we advocated which are coming into reality. Direct election of senators is assured. Public utilities are gradually being removed from the hands of the few and placed under the control of the people who use them. Woman suffrage is now almost a national issue. . . . The seed we sowed out in Kansas did not fall on barren ground.[11]

Thanks to this triumph of Populist principles, one may almost say that, in so far as political devices can insure it, the people now rule. Political dishonesty has not altogether disappeared and the people may yet be betrayed by the men they elect to office, but on the whole the acts of government have come to reflect fairly clearly the will of the people. Efforts to assert this

[8] Eliot Jones, *The Trust Problem in the United States;* Henry R. Seager and Charles A. Gulick, *Trust and Corporation Problems;* Myron W. Watkins, *Industrial Combinations and Public Policy.*

[9] Theodore Roosevelt, *Autobiography*, ch. 11; Charles R. Van Hise, *The Conservation of Natural Resources in the United States.*

[10] White, in *Scribner's Magazine*, 79:564.

[11] *Kansas City Star*, March 29, 1931.

newly won power in such a way as to crush the economic supremacy of the predatory few have also been numerous and not wholly unsuccessful. The gigantic corporations of today, dwarfing into insignificance the trusts of yesterday, are, in spite of their size, far more circumspect in their conduct than their predecessors. If in the last analysis "big business" controls, it is because it has public opinion on its side and not merely the party bosses.

To radicals of today, however, the Populist panaceas, based as they were upon an essentially individualistic philosophy and designed merely to insure for every man his right to "get ahead" in the world, seem totally inadequate. These latter-day extremists point to the perennial reappearance of such problems as farm relief, unemployment, unfair taxation, and law evasion as evidence that the Populist type of reform is futile, that something more drastic is required. Nor is their contention without point. It is reasonable to suppose that progressivism itself must progress; that the programs that would provide solutions for the problems of one generation might fall far short of meeting the needs of a succeeding generation. Perhaps one may not agree with the view of some present-day radicals that only a revolution will suffice and that the very attempt to make existing institutions more tolerable is treason to any real progress, since by so doing the day of revolution is postponed; but one must recognize that when the old Populist panaceas can receive the enthusiastic support of Hooverian Republicans and Alsmithian Democrats these once startling demands are no longer radical at all. One is reminded of the dilemma that Alice of Wonderland encountered when she went through the looking-glass into the garden of live flowers. On and on she ran with the Red Queen, but however fast they went they never seemed to pass anything.

"Well, in our country," said Alice, still panting a little, "you'd generally get to somewhere else—if you ran very fast for a long time as we've been doing."

"A slow sort of country!" said the Queen. "Now here, you see, it takes all the running you can do to keep in the same place. If you want to get somewhere else, you must run twice as fast as that!"

II. DOCUMENTS

1. A Proclamation and a Platform

This section of documents begins with a proclamation from the pen of Lorenzo D. Lewelling, who was elected governor of Kansas on the Populist ticket in 1892. He sent the proclamation to police commissioners of the cities of Kansas in December, 1893. Almost immediately the document won recognition as the "Tramp Circular," for it dealt with the unemployed and vagabond poor. Lewelling here came to grips with a problem that many Populists attributed to a harsh industrial system, and his Tramp Circular provides a good example of radical Populist thought.

No consideration of Populism would be complete without reference to the platform adopted at the Omaha convention of the People's party in 1892, and it is therefore included here. The persuasive and eloquent Populist from Minnesota, Ignatius Donnelly, wrote into the preamble a succinct justification for third-party action. The platform itself contains those demands that Populists considered basic.

LORENZO D. LEWELLING'S "TRAMP CIRCULAR"

In the reign of Elizabeth the highways were filled with the throngs of the unemployed poor, who were made to "move on," and were sometimes brutally whipped, sometimes summarily hanged as "sturdy vagrants" or "incorrigible vagabonds." In France, just previous to the revolution, the punishment of being poor and out of work was, for the first offense, a term of years in the galleys; for the second offense, the galleys for life. In this country, the monopoly of labor-saving machinery and its devotion to selfish instead of social use have rendered more and more human beings superfluous, until we have a standing army of the unemployed numbering, even in the most prosperous times, not less than one million able-bodied men; yet, until recently, it was the prevailing notion, as it is yet the notion of all but the work-people themselves, and those of other classes given to thinking, that whosoever being able-bodied and willing to work, can always find work to do, and section 571 of the General Statutes of 1889 is a disgraceful reminder how savage, even in Kansas, has been our treatment of the most unhappy of our human brothers.

The man out of work and penniless is, by this legislation, classed with "con-

Reprinted from TRANSACTIONS OF THE KANSAS STATE HISTORICAL SOCIETY, *VII (1901–1902), 125–126. The "Omaha Platform" is from the same source.*

fidence men." Under this statute, and city ordinances of similar import, thousands of men, guilty of no crime but poverty, intent upon no crime but seeking employment, have languished in the city prisons of Kansas or performed unrequited toil on "rock piles" as municipal slaves, because ignorance of economic conditions had made us cruel. The victims have been the poor and humble, for whom police courts are the courts of last resort. They cannot give bond and appeal. They have been unheeded and uncared for by the busy world, which wastes no time visiting prisoners in jail. They have been too poor to litigate with their oppressors, and thus no voice from this underworld of human woe has ever reached the ear of the appellate court, because it was nobody's business to be his brother's keeper.

But those who sit in the seats of power are bound by the highest obligation to especially regard the cause of the oppressed and helpless poor. The first duty of the government is to the weak. Power becomes fiendish if it be not the protector and sure reliance of the friendless, to whose complaints all other ears are dulled. It is my duty to see that the laws are faithfully executed, and among those laws is the constitutional provision that no instrumentality of the state "shall deny to any person within its jurisdiction the equal protection of the laws." And who needs to be told that equal protection of the laws does not prevail where this inhuman vagrancy law is enforced? It separates men into two distinct classes, differentiated as those who are penniless and those who are not, and declare the former criminals. Only the latter are entitled to the liberty guaranteed by the constitution. To be found in a city "without some visible means of support or some legitimate business" is the involuntary condition of some millions at this moment, and we proceed to punish them for being victims of conditions which we, as a people, have forced upon them.

I have noticed in police court reports that "sleeping in a box car" is among the varieties of this heinous crime of being poor. Some police judges have usurped a sovereign power not permitted by highest functionaries of the states or of the nation, and victims of the industrial conditions have been peremptorily "ordered to leave town." The right to go freely from place to place in search of employment, or even in obedience to a mere whim, is part of that personal liberty guaranteed by the constitution of the United States to every human being on American soil. If voluntary idleness is not forbidden; if a Diogenes preferred poverty; if a Columbus choose hunger and the discovery of a new race, rather than seek personal comfort by engaging in "some legitimate business," I am aware of no power in the legislature or in city councils to deny him the right to seek happiness in his own way, so long as he harms no other, rich or poor; but let simple poverty cease to be a crime.

In some cities it is provided by ordinance that if police court fines be not paid or secured the culprit shall be compelled to work out the amount as a municipal slave, and "rock piles" and "bull pens" are provided for the enforcement of these ordinances. And so it appears that this slavery is not imposed as a punishment, but solely as a means of collecting a debt.

Such city ordinances are in flagrant violation of constitutional prohibition. The rock pile and the bull pen have only been used in degrading friendless and poor, and are relics of a departed auction-block era [which have not] ceased to disgrace the cities of Kansas.

And let the dawn of Christmas day find the rock pile and the bull pen, and the crime of being homeless and poor, obsolete in all the cities of Kansas governed by the metropolitan police act.

It is confidently expected that their own regard for constitutional liberty and their human impulses will induce police commissioners to carry out the spirit as well as the letter of the foregoing suggestions.

L. D. Lewelling, Governor

THE OMAHA PLATFORM

Assembled upon the 116th anniversary of the Declaration of Independence, the People's Party of America in their first national convention, invoking upon their action the blessing of Almighty God, put forth in the name and on behalf of the people of this country, the following preamble and declaration of principles:

PREAMBLE

The conditions which surround us best justify our co-operation; we meet in the midst of a nation brought to the verge of moral, political, and material ruin. Corruption dominates the ballot-box, the Legislatures, the Congress, and touches even the ermine of the bench. The people are demoralized; most of the States have been compelled to isolate the voters at the polling places to prevent universal intimidation and bribery. The newspapers are largely subsidized or muzzled, public opinion silenced, business prostrated, homes covered with mortgages, labor impoverished, and the land concentrated in the hands of capitalists. The urban workmen are denied the right to organize for self-protection; imported pauperized labor beats down their wages, a hireling standing army, unrecognized by our laws, is established to shoot them down, and they are rapidly degenerating into European conditions. The fruits of the toil of millions are boldly stolen to build up colossal fortunes for a few, unprecedented in the history of mankind; and the possessors of these, in turn despise the Republic and endanger liberty. From the same prolific womb of governmental injustice we breed the two great classes—tramps and millionaires.

The national power to create money is appropriated to enrich bond-holders; a vast public debt payable in legal tender currency has been funded into gold-bearing bonds, thereby adding millions to the burdens of the people.

Silver, which has been accepted as coin since the dawn of history, has been demonetized to add to the purchasing power of gold by decreasing the value of all forms of property as well as human labor, and the supply of currency is purposely abridged to fatten usurers, bankrupt enterprise, and enslave industry. A vast conspiracy against mankind has been organized on two continents, and it is rapidly taking possession of the world. If not met and overthrown at once, it forebodes terrible social convulsions, the destruction of civilization, or the establishment of an absolute despotism.

We have witnessed for more than a quarter of a century the struggles of the two great political parties for power and plunder, while grievous wrongs have been inflicted upon the suffering people. We charge that the controlling influence dominating both these parties have permitted the existing dreadful conditions to develop without serious effort to prevent or restrain them. Neither do they now promise us any substantial reform. They have agreed together to ignore, in the coming campaign, every issue but one. They propose to drown the outcries of a plundered people with the uproar of a sham battle over the tariff, so that capitalists, corporations, national banks, rings, trusts, watered stock, the demonetization of silver and the oppressions of the usurers may all be lost sight of. They propose to sacrifice our homes, lives, and children on the altar of mammon; to destroy the multitude in order to secure corruption funds from the millionaires.

Assembled on the anniversary of the birthday of the nation, and filled with the spirit of the grand general and chief who established our independence, we seek to restore the government of the Republic to the hands of "the plain people," with which class it originated. We assert our purposes to be identical with the purposes of the National Constitution, to form a more perfect union and establish justice, insure domestic tranquility, provide for the common defense, promote the general welfare, and secure the blessings of liberty for ourselves and our posterity.

We declare that this Republic can only endure as a free government while built upon the love of the whole people for each other and for the nation; that it cannot be pinned together by bayonets; that the civil war is over and that every passion and resentment which grew out of it must die with it, and that we must be in fact, as we are in name, one united brotherhood of freemen.

Our country finds itself confronted by conditions for which there is no precedent in the history of the world; our annual agricultural productions amount to billions of dollars in value, which must, within a few weeks or months be exchanged for billions of dollars' worth of commodities consumed in their production; the existing currency supply is wholly inadequate to make this exchange; the results are falling prices, the formation of combines and rings, the impoverishment of the producing class. We pledge ourselves that, if given power, we will labor to correct these evils by wise and reasonable legislation, in accordance with the terms of our platform.

We believe that the power of government—in other words, of the people—should be expanded (as in the case of the postal service) as rapidly and as far as the good sense of an intelligent people and the teachings of experience shall justify, to the end that oppression, injustice and poverty, shall eventually cease in the land.

While our sympathies as a party of reform are naturally upon the side of every proposition which will tend to make men intelligent, virtuous and temperate, we nevertheless regard these questions, important as they are, as secondary to the great issues now pressing for solution, and upon which not only our individual prosperity, but the very existence of free institutions depend; and we ask all men to first help us to determine whether we are to have a republic to administer, before we differ as to the conditions upon which it is to be administered, believing that the forces of reform this day organized will never cease to move forward, until every wrong is remedied, and equal rights and equal privileges securely established for all the men and women of this country.

PLATFORM

We declare, therefore,

First—That the union of the labor forces of the United States this day consummated shall be permanent and perpetual; may its spirit enter into all hearts for the salvation of the Republic and the uplifting of mankind.

Second—Wealth belongs to him who creates it, and every dollar taken from industry without an equivalent is robbery. "If any will not work, neither shall he eat." The interests of rural and civic labor are the same; their enemies are identical.

Third—We believe that the time has come when the railroad corporations will either own the people or the people must own the railroads, and should the government enter upon the work of owning and managing all railroads, we should favor an amendment to the Constitution by which all persons engaged in the government service shall be placed under a civil service regulation of the most rigid character, so as to prevent the increase of the power of the national administration by the use of such additional government employees.

Finance—We demand a national currency, safe, sound, and flexible, issued by the general government only, a full legal tender for all debts, public and private, and that without the use of banking corporations, a just, equitable and efficient means of distribution direct to the people, at a tax not to exceed 2 per cent per annum, to be provided as set forth by the sub-treasury plan of the Farmers' Alliance, or a better system; also by payments in discharge of its obligations for public improvements.

1. We demand free and unlimited coinage of silver and gold at the present legal ratio of 16 to 1.

2. We demand that the mount of circulating medium be speedily increased to not less than $50 per capita.

3. We demand a graduated income tax.

4. We believe that the money of the country should be kept as much as possible in the hands of the people, and hence we demand that all State and national revenues shall be limited to the necessary expenses of the government, economically and honestly administered.

5. We demand that postal savings banks be established by the government for the safe deposit of the earnings of the people and to facilitate exchange.

Transportation—Transportation being a means of exchange and a public necessity, the government should own and operate the railroads in the interest of the people. The telegraph and telephone, like the post office system, being a necessity for the transmission of news, should be owned and operated by the government in the interest of the people.

Land—The land, including all the natural sources of wealth, is the heritage of the people, and should not be monopolized for speculative purposes, and alien ownership of land should be prohibited. All land now held by railroads and other corporations in excess of their actual needs, and all lands now owned by aliens, should be reclaimed by the government and held for actual settlers only.

2. The Campaign of 1892

A major portion of the Omaha platform dealt with transportation and asserted that railroads should be government owned and operated. This attack on railroad iniquities comes from an 1892 campaign book written by Thomas E. Watson. An intrepid, "middle-of-the-road" (uncompromising) Populist from Georgia, Watson received the People's party vice-presidential nomination in 1896.

In 1892 the Populist candidate for President, James B. Weaver, published a book entitled A Call to Action. *Weaver later played a vital role in bringing about fusion with the Democrats in 1896, a development that many devoted Populists bitterly resented. The book was, nevertheless, an important political tract, and a portion of it is reproduced here.*

THOMAS E. WATSON

In a speech made in Congress, March 11, 1884, Hon. Wm. S. Holman sums up the Land Grant business as follows:

Number of acres donated to 58 Rail

Reprinted from Thomas E. Watson, THE PEO-PLE'S PARTY CAMPAIGN BOOK, *1892 (Washington, D.C., 1892), pp. 48–51.*

Road Corporations, 85,000,000 acres.

Number of acres given to the Pacific Rail Roads, 139,403,000.

How many brave men died in battle with Mexico when we tore from her that territory of 334,000,000 acres?

How much money belonging to all the people was poured out like water in defraying the expenses of that war?

Who to-day holds the lion's share of the land which we thus obtained at so terrible a price?

The Rail Roads.

But the chapter is not yet ended.

They were not satisfied with land alone. They asked for money also. They got it. They generally get it.

The Government guaranteed the interest on the Bonds of the Rail Roads.

On July 1, 1876, the roads owed the people $25,000,000, which the government had paid as interest on these Bonds.

On January 1, 1883, the sum had grown to $41,000,000.

By the last official statement of the Secretary of the Treasury, the amount due by these Corporations to the Tax-payers of this country is nearly SEVENTY MILLIONS OF DOLLARS—for interest already paid.

That's a very neat sum. It is what Joe Gargery would pronounce "cool."

Jay Gould and Huntingdon (sic) and Stanford and millionaires of that stripe control the Corporations which owe the people this money. These men and a score of others have made colossal fortunes out of this magnificent property.

Yet the Tax-payers whose land and whose money built those Roads find it impossible to collect the debt.

Why?

Corrupt legislators; venal judges; subsidized newspapers!

That's the answer; none other is possible.

Who is responsible for this fearful outrage upon public justice?

Both the Old Parties. Democrats and Republicans ran over each other in their haste to vote these subsidies.

The National Platforms of both the Parties, as has already been shown, pledged Government aid to these Corporations. The pledge was most fully kept.

The Corporations had a contingent in each Party sufficiently strong to compel a redemption of the political pledge so readily given.

That National scandals should have grown out of these transactions was quite natural. I do not care to go into them. It is sufficient to remind the reader of the Credit Mobilier stench of a few years ago. It was a most noisome scandal. Statesmen, lawyers, judges, editors were implicated in a gigantic fraud and conspiracy, and the name of Oakes Ames became a byword in all the land.

How Stanford and Huntington made their "piles" may be seen from one quotation from the Official Report made during Cleveland's Administration, known as the Pattison Report:

"On the face of the books the barren fact appeared that Leland Stanford and C. P. Huntingdon (sic) have taken from assets of this Company, over which they have absolute control, the sum aforesaid, $4,818,355."

Precisely. That's what they took at that special time and in that special way.

It's not all they took, by a jug full.

At this good hour Huntington, instead of being behind the bars as a convicted thief, is one of the Grandees of Plutocracy, and Stanford, instead of being in jail, is in the United States Senate!

Of course. Had these men stolen a bunch of cattle, they would have been shot down without ceremony.

Had they robbed a "Smoke House" in Georgia or Tennessee to get food (perhaps for hungry children), they would have been slaving in the Convict Camp of those precious Democrats, Joe Brown and Calvin Brice.

But they showed better judgment.

They stole enough to buy Judges, corrupt Legislators, and muzzle the Press.

Net result:—One is a Grandee, and lives in clover; the other is Senator, and makes laws for the people.

Jay Gould, another of the Gang has no political ambition like Stanford.

He is a modest sort of a Buccaneer.

It satisfies him to ride over the Seas in a dandy yacht which a king might envy; or to whirl along the rails in a palace car, all brilliant with gildings of silver and gold and rich in tapestries of velvets and silks.

He has robbed the public in a more skilful manner than Boss Tweed—therefore he is in no fear of having to run away.

He has been more artistic in his marauding than Jesse James, therefore he has no apprehension that a price will be set upon his head.

Quite the reverse! When he approaches a city in his palational (sic) car he expects a royal reception—and gets it!

Merchants, editors, officials, and a general miscellany of flunkeyism crowd and push, and cringe and fawn, in the promiscuous competition of cowardice and servility and meanness and Golden-Calf-ism!

Decency veils her face, and the man in the moon stuffs cotton in his nose!

The very buzzards hurry by with impatient and nervous wing.

Even a buzzard knows when it has enough!

Flunkeyism never does.

JAMES B. WEAVER

The man who originated the word *mortgage* and applied it to real estate which is pledged for the payment of debt, was a philologist and a philosopher. The first part of the word—*mort*—was originally derived from a

Reprinted from James B. Weaver, A CALL TO ACTION *(Des Moines, Iowa, 1892), pp. 349–52.*

latin word which signifies death. The word murder is from the same ultimate root. The last half of the word—*gage* —is from the Old French, and signifies to pledge, pawn or stake. We get the whole word from the Old English, where it was used to mean a dead pledge. It was probably employed to distinguish the pledge of lands from the pawn of chattels—the latter being movable; but this would not sufficiently account for the selection of the word *mort,* which is suggestive of death and the departure of the mortgager from the earth. Having pledged his source of subsistence, when that is gone he is liable to perish. Hence in its last analysis, the mortgage rests upon the life of him who gives the pledge and upon those who are dependent upon him for support. It is creditable to the savage tribes that they have never committed this abominable crime.

As we have seen, the effects of an insufficient volume of money, are, to depress the price of real estate in the market, drive it into pledge, force it to sale and to greatly reduce the number and increase the extent of individual holdings. By such means the land passes rapidly into the hands of a small class of persons whose means enable them to retain the title. These influences have been at high tide in this country for more than twenty years. The effects are seen in the rapid increase of urban and corresponding decrease of rural population as shown by our late census.

But the most disastrous and appalling manifestation of this deplorable policy has yet to be mentioned. The decline in the price of lands, in the very nature of things, can be but temporary. Two influences unite to make this certain: First, the increase of population, and second, that as titles pass into the hands of capitalists the land is withdrawn from sale except to persons of like means. Such landholders can wait for still further advance in prices.

It may be suggested that this increase in value will result in relief to those who are mortgaged and cultivating the soil. A moment's reflection will show this to be an error. No one but a land speculator or some one wishing to escape from the curse of debt can be interested in having real estate advance in price, for the reason that an increase in price means heavier taxes. What the farmer most wants is a good price for the products of his farm rather than an advance in the value of the farm itself. This can only be brought about by increasing consumption, and this, in turn, by enabling the consumer to supply his wants. It is plain that an advance in the price of real estate which is not caused by an increase in the value of its products, while it may enable a few debt-ridden citizens to escape from their burdens, is nevertheless, upon the whole, a serious evil to the community at large. It shuts the door of opportunity against the people and deprives them of the hope of securing homes. It is not high priced lands that we want, but high priced products; and this can never be realized until those who are engaged in other pursuits are furnished with employment at wages which will enable them to fully supply their wants.

We have now reached the period in the history of this country when the secondary effects of our financial system are beginning to be seriously felt. Land values are rising, but the prices of farm products, taking the years together are seriously declining. The great body of mortgaged farmers will make heroic struggles to save their homes but they will, unless relief be extended, in most instances be forced at last to yield to the inevitable and part with their lands. The increased price of land is only an additional inducement for them to relax their efforts. This is exactly the effect which has been realized in Great Britain where the ante-type of our financial system has been in undisturbed (sic) operation for nearly three-quarters of a century. In England the result has been large holdings wholly disproportionate to the wants of the proprietors, while the great body of the people are left homeless and hopeless in a country which they are expected to love and defend.

The reader has doubtless learned from his own observation that the same deplorable state of affairs is rapidly taking place in our own country. It seems incredible that a people possessing the boon of free Government and an unobstructed ballot could be thus despoiled and subjugated by a few selfish speculators and monopolists in a single Century. And more lamentable still the fact that up to a very recent period the majority of the people seem to have been unmindful of the fact that these evil influences and laws, fashioned to beggar themselves and their posterity, have been in full operation before their eyes.

3. Silver

The following document is part of a speech by William Jennings Bryan, one of the most important he made during his two terms in the United States House of Representatives. In arguing against repeal of the Sherman Silver Purchase Act, he voiced sentiments similar to those Populists had expressed, and the speech helps to account for the political strength that Bryan demonstrated in 1896.

WILLIAM JENNINGS BRYAN

I am on sound and scientific ground, therefore, when I say that a dollar approaches honesty as its purchasing power approaches stability. If I borrow a thousand dollars today and next year pay the debt with a thousand dollars which will secure exactly as much of all things desirable as the one thousand which I borrowed, I have paid in honest dollars. If the money has increased or decreased in purchasing power, I have satisfied my debt with dishonest dollars. While the Government can say that a given weight of gold or silver shall constitute a dollar, and invest that dollar with legal-tender qualities, it cannot fix the purchasing power of the dollar. That must depend upon the law of supply and demand, and it may be well to suggest that this Government never tried to fix the exchangeable value of a dollar until it began to limit the number of dollars coined.

If the number of dollars increases more rapidly than the need for dollars —as it did after the gold discoveries of 1849—the exchangeable value of each dollar will fall and prices rise. If the demand for dollars increases faster than the number of dollars—as it did after 1800—the price of each dollar will rise and prices generally will fall. The relative value of the dollar may be changed by natural causes or by legislation. An increased supply—the demand remaining the same—or a decreased demand— the supply remaining the same—will reduce the exchangeable value of each dollar. Natural causes may act on both supply and demand; as, for instance, by increasing the product from the mines or by increasing the amount consumed in the arts. Legislation acts

Reprinted from William Jennings Bryan, THE FIRST BATTLE *(Chicago, 1896), pp. 80–82.*

directly on the demand, and thus affects the price, since the demand is one of the factors in fixing the price.

If by legislative action the demand for silver is destroyed and the demand for gold is increased by making it the only standard, the exchangeable value of each unit of that standard, or dollar, as we call it, will be increased. If the exchangeable value of the dollar is increased by legislation the debt of the debtor is increased, to his injury and to the advantage of the creditor. And let me suggest here, in reply to the gentleman from Massachusetts (Mr. McCall), who said that the money loaner was entitled to the advantages derived from improved machinery and inventive genius, that he is mistaken. The laboring man and the producer are entitled to these benefits, and the money loaner by every law of justice, ought to be content with a dollar equal in purchasing power to the dollar which he loaned, and any one desiring more than that desires a dishonest dollar, it matters not what name he may give to it. Take an illustration: John Doe, of Nebraska, has a farm worth $2,000 and mortgages it to Richard Roe, of Massachusetts, for $1,000. Suppose the value of the monetary unit is increased by legislation which creates a greater demand for gold. The debt is increased. If the increase amounts to 100 per cent. the Nebraska farmer finds that the price of his products have fallen one-half and his land loses one-half its value, unless the price is maintained by the increased population incident to a new country.

The mortgage remains nominally the same, though the debt has actually become twice as great. Will he be deceived by the cry of "honest dollar?" If he should loan a Nebraska neighbor a hog weighing 100 pounds and the next spring demand in return a hog weighing 200 pounds he would be called dishonest, even though he contended that he was only demanding one hog—just the number he loaned. Society has become accustomed to some very nice distinctions. The poor man is called a socialist if he believes that the wealth of the rich should be divided among the poor, but the rich man is called a financier if he devises a plan by which the pittance of the poor can be converted to his use.

The poor man who takes property by force is called a thief, but the creditor who can by legislation make a debtor pay a dollar twice as large as he borrowed is lauded as the friend of a sound currency. The man who wants the people to destroy the Government is an anarchist, but the man who wants the Government to destroy the people is a patriot.

The great desire now seems to be to restore confidence, and some have an idea that the only way to restore confidence is to coax the money loaner to let go of his hoard by making the profits too tempting to be resisted. Capital is represented as a shy and timid maiden who must be courted, if won. Let me suggest a plan for bringing money from Europe. If it be possible, let us enact a law "whereas confidence must be restored; and whereas money will always come from its hiding place if the inducement is sufficient, Therefore, be it enacted, That every man who borrows $1 shall pay back $2 and interest (the usury law not to be enforced)."

Would not English capital come "on the swiftest ocean greyhounds?" The money loaner of London would say: "I will not loan in India or Egypt or in South America. The inhabitants of those countries are a wicked and ungodly people and refuse to pay more than they borrowed. I will loan in the United States, for there lives an honest people, who delight in a sound currency and pay in an honest dollar." Why does not some one propose that plan? Because no one would dare to increase by law the number of dollars which the debtor must pay, and yet by some it is called wise statesmanship to do indirectly and in the dark what no man has the temerity to propose directly and openly.

4. An Echo from '76

Whatever the Populists may have lacked in experience they made up in enthusiasm. An indication of that enthusiasm is the large number of People's party song books appearing in the nineties. The following song is unusual in that it reveals not only the Populist attitude toward the silver question, but the political strategy advocated by many party leaders after that question assumed overwhelming importance.

"THE POPS ARE MARCHING"

TUNE—*"Tramp, tramp, tramp, the boys are marching."*

Sturdy populists are we,
And united we agree

That to us belongs the wealth that we create,
And that he who will not toil
Has no title to the soil,
But his land must be surrendered to the state.

Chorus
Tramp, tramp, tramp, the pops are marching,

Reprinted from Charles A. Sheffield, ECHOES FROM '76 *(Minneapolis, 1896), p. 28.*

Labor's rights have got to come,
All the land is ours to share,
Free as water, sun or air
   Every freeman is entitled to a home.

Silver free, sixteen to one,
Is not all we stand upon,
   Though we mean to split old parties
      with that wedge,
But our platform shall abide
When the wedge is thrown aside,
   Then the gold and silver kings will
      have to "hedge".

Chorus: Tramp, tramp, tramp, etc.

Uncle Sam should not refuse
All the scrip we need to use,
   And without the intervention of a
      bank,
'Tis a very shameful way
Double interest to pay,
   So we're standing on a legal tender
      plank.

Chorus: Tramp, tramp, tramp, etc.

"We the people" now demand
Every railroad in the land,
   To be *freemen* we must own the
      right of way;
All the telegraphic lines
All the forests and the mines,
   Must be ours to keep forever and a
      day!

Chorus: Tramp, tramp, tramp, etc.

Vast estates will melt as wax
When we get the income-tax,
   And we'll have it yet in spite of venal
      courts;
Referendum shall be law,
Where no judge can pick a flaw,
   Then we'll batter down the last of
      Shylock's forts.

Chorus: Tramp, tramp, tramp, etc.

III. RECENT INTERPRETATIONS

In the years since World War II, the rereading of sources and rethinking of the place of Populism in American history have produced some new evaluations of the movement. An important critical reassessment of the Populist experience—one that incorporates insights from findings of social psychologists—appeared in Richard Hofstadter's Pulitzer Prize book, *The Age of Reform,* published in 1955. Unlike Hicks, who saw Populism as part of a liberal reform tradition, Hofstadter and others identified it as a mass movement that in its romanticism, acceptance of conspiracy theories, and anti-Semitism foreshadowed a twentieth-century trend toward totalitarianism.

    Another recent analysis of Populism, one that takes issue with Hofstadter without returning full circle to the earlier position of Hicks, may be found in Norman Pollack's provocative essay, *The Populist Response to Industrial America.* In Pollack's view, Populism was a truly radical reaction to evils accompanying industrialization. While it was in no sense influenced by Karl Marx, Populist thought at several points ran parallel to Marxist thought, or so Pollack contends in his essay.

RICHARD HOFSTADTER

The utopia of the Populists was in the past, not the future. According to the agrarian myth, the health of the state was proportionate to the degree to which it was dominated by the agricultural class, and this assumption pointed to the superiority of an earlier age. The Populists looked backward with longing to the lost agrarian Eden, to the republican America of the early years of the nineteenth century in which there were few millionaires and, as they saw it, no beggars, when the laborer had excellent prospects and the farmer had abundance, when statesmen still responded to the mood of the people and there was no such thing as the money power.[1] What they meant—though they did not express themselves in such terms—was that they would like to restore the conditions prevailing before the development of industrialism and the commercialization of agriculture. . . . There was something about the Populist imagination that loved the secret plot and the conspiratorial meeting. There was in fact a widespread Populist idea that all American history since the Civil War could be understood as a sustained conspiracy of the international money power.

The pervasiveness of this way of

looking at things may be attributed to the common feeling that farmers and workers were not simply oppressed but oppressed deliberately, consciously, continuously, and with wanton malice by "the interests." It would of course be misleading to imply that the Populists stand alone in thinking of the events of their time as the results of a conspiracy. This kind of thinking frequently occurs when political and social antagonisms are sharp. Certain audiences are especially susceptible to it—particularly, I believe, those who have attained only a low level of education, whose access to information is poor,[2] and who are so completely shut out from access to the centers of power that they feel themselves completely deprived of self-defense and subjected to unlimited manipulation by those who wield power. There are, moreover, certain types of popular movements of dissent that offer special opportunities to agitators with paranoid tendencies, who are able to make a vocational asset out of their psychic disturbances.[3] Such persons have an opportunity to impose their own style of thought upon the movements they lead. It would of course be misleading to imply that there are no such things as conspiracies in history. Anything that partakes of political strategy may need, for a time at least, an element of secrecy, and is thus vulnerable to being dubbed conspiratorial. Corruption itself has the character of conspiracy. In this sense the Crédit Mobilier was a conspiracy, as was the Teapot Dome affair. If we

[1] Thomas E. Watson: *The Life and Times of Andrew Jackson* (Thomson, Ga., 1912), p. 325: "All the histories and all the statesmen agree that during the first half-century of our national existence, we had no poor. A pauper class was unthought of: a beggar, or a tramp never seen." Cf. Mrs. S. E. V. Emery: *Seven Financial Conspiracies which have Enslaved the American People* (Lansing, ed. 1896), pp. 10–11.

[2] In this respect it is worth pointing out that in later years, when facilities for realistic exposure became more adequate, popular attacks on "the money power" showed fewer elements of fantasy and more of reality.

[3] See, for instance, the remarks about a mysterious series of international assassinations with which Mary E. Lease opens her book *The Problem of Civilization Solved* (Chicago, 1895).

tend to be too condescending to the Populists at this point, it may be necessary to remind ourselves that they had seen so much bribery and corruption, particularly on the part of the railroads, that they had before them a convincing model of the management of affairs through conspiratorial behavior. Indeed, what makes conspiracy theories so widely acceptable is that they usually contain a germ of truth. But there is a great difference between locating conspiracies *in* history and saying that history *is,* in effect, a conspiracy, between singling out those conspiratorial acts that do on occasion occur and weaving a vast fabric of social explanation out of nothing but skeins of evil plots.

· · ·

The financial argument behind the conspiracy theory was simple enough. Those who owned bonds wanted to be paid not in a common currency but in gold, which was at a premium; those who lived by lending money wanted as high a premium as possible to be put on their commodity by increasing its scarcity. The panics, depressions, and bankruptcies caused by their policies only added to their wealth; such catastrophes offered opportunities to engross the wealth of others through business consolidations and foreclosures. Hence the interests actually relished and encouraged hard times. The Greenbackers had long since popularized this argument, insisting that an adequate legal-tender currency would break the monopoly of the "Shylocks." Their demand for $50 of circulating medium per capita, still in the air when the People's Party arose, was rapidly replaced by the less "radical" demand for free coinage of silver. But what both the Greenbackers and free-silverites held in common was the idea that the contraction of currency was a de-

liberate squeeze, the result of a long-range plot of the "Anglo-American Gold Trust." Wherever one turns in the Populist literature of the nineties one can find this conspiracy theory expressed. It is in the Populist newspapers, the proceedings of the silver conventions, the immense pamphlet literature broadcast by the American Bimetallic League, the Congressional debates over money; it is elaborated in such popular books as Mrs. S. E. V. Emery's *Seven Financial Conspiracies which have Enslaved the American People* or Gordon Clark's *Shylock: as Banker, Bondholder, Corruptionist, Conspirator. . . .*

One feature of the Populist conspiracy theory that has been generally overlooked is its frequent link with a kind of rhetorical anti-Semitism. The slight current of anti-Semitism that existed in the United States before the 1890's had been associated with problems of money and credit.[4] During the closing years of the century it grew noticeably.[5] While the jocose and rather heavy-handed anti-Semitism that can be found in Henry Adams's letters of

---

[4] Anti-Semitism as a kind of rhetorical flourish seems to have had a long underground history in the United States. During the panic of 1837, when many states defaulted on their obligations, many of which were held by foreigners, we find Governor McNutt of Mississippi defending the practice by baiting Baron Rothschild: "The blood of Judas and Shylock flows in his veins, and he unites the qualities of both his countrymen. . . ." Quoted by George W. Edwards: *The Evolution of Finance Capitalism* (New York, 1938), p. 149. Similarly we find Thaddeus Stevens assailing "the Rothschilds, Goldsmiths, and other large money dealers" during his early appeals for greenbacks. See James A. Woodburn: *The Life of Thaddeus Stevens* (Indianapolis, 1913), pp. 576, 579.

[5] See Oscar Handlin: "American Views of the Jew at the Opening of the Twentieth Century," *Publications of the American Jewish Historical Society,* no. 40 (June 1951), pp. 323–44.

the 1890's shows that this prejudice existed outside Populist literature, it was chiefly Populist writers who expressed that identification of the Jew with the usurer and the "international gold ring" which was the central theme of the American anti-Semitism of the age. The omnipresent symbol of Shylock can hardly be taken in itself as evidence of anti-Semitism, but the frequent references to the House of Rothschild make it clear that for many silverites the Jew was an organic part of the conspiracy theory of history.

A paradox pervades modern interpretations of the agrarian revolt of the nineties. On one hand the failure of the revolt has been described again and again as the final defeat of the American farmer. John Hicks, in his history of the movement, speaks of the Populists as having begun "the last phase of a long and perhaps a losing struggle—the struggle to save agricultural America from the devouring jaws of industrial America," while another historian calls Populism "the last united stand of the country's agricultural interest . . . the final attempt made by the farmers of the land to beat back an industrial civilization whose forces had all but vanquished them already." [6] On the other hand, it has been equally common to enumerate, as evidence of the long-range power of Populism, the substantial list of once derided Populist proposals that were enacted within less than twenty years after the defeat of Bryan, and to assign to the agrarian agitations of the Populist era an important influence on the golden age of Progressive reform.[7] How can a movement whose program was in the long run so generally successful be identified with such a final and disastrous defeat for the class it was supposed to represent?

There is something valid in both these views. Populism and Bryanism were the last attempt to incorporate what I have called the "soft" side of the farmer's dual character into a national mass movement. But the further conclusion that the eclipse of this sort of reform represents the total and final defeat of agriculture is no more than the modern liberal's obeisance to the pathos of agrarian rhetoric. After the defeat of Populism and Bryanism and the failure of the agrarian catchwords, the "hard" side of the farmers' movements, based upon the commercial realities of agriculture, developed more forcefully and prosperously than ever. It was during the twenty years after McKinley routed Bryan that American agriculture enjoyed its greatest prosperity under modern peacetime conditions, prior to 1945-55; and it was the same twenty years that saw agriculture make the greatest gains it had ever made in the sphere of national legislation.

The failure of a political movement based upon the old phrases of agrarian ideology must not be identified with the failure of commercial agriculture as an economic interest. Certainly no one would maintain that even a victory for Bryan in 1896 could have seriously delayed the industrialization of the country and the relative shrinkage of the rural farm population. But it can be said that the Populist movement, despite its defeat, activated a stream of agrarian organization and

---

[6] John D. Hicks: *The Populist Revolt* (Minneapolis, 1931); Louis Hacker in Hacker and Kendrick: *The United States since 1865* (New York, ed. 1949), p. 253. For a similar view see C. Vann Woodward: *Tom Watson* (New York, 1938), p. 330.

[7] Hicks: *The Populist Revolt*, chapter XV; Hacker and Kendrick, op. cit., pp. 257, 352–3.

protest that subsequently carried point after point. Before these victories could be won it was necessary that both the market situation of agriculture and the political climate of the country should change. The attempt to make agrarianism into a mass movement based upon third-party ideological politics also had to be supplanted by the modern methods of pressure politics and lobbying within the framework of the existing party system. Populism was the expression of a transitional stage in the development of our agrarian politics: while it reasserted for the last time some old ways of thought, it was also a harbinger of the new. American agricultural leaders were spurred by its achievements and educated by its failures. Far from being the final defeat of the farmer, it was the first uncertain step in the development of effective agrarian organization.

NORMAN POLLACK

Populism was certainly not Marxism; its vision of America was not socialized production and the collective farm. Yet, comparing the two, one finds such remarkable similarities as to suggest further proof that Populism was radical. For each, industrial capitalism meant alienated man—man divorced from himself, his product, and humanity. The *Farmers' Alliance* and Marx's *Economic and Philosophic Manuscripts* point up these same aspects of alienation. "The materialism of today," stated the *Farmers' Alliance*, "does all the time segregate human

Reprinted by permission of the publishers from Norman Pollack, THE POPULIST RESPONSE TO INDUSTRIAL AMERICA *(Cambridge, Mass.: Harvard University Press, copyright 1962 by the President and Fellows of Harvard College), pp. 68–72, 82–83.*

lives." The issue is more than physical hardship: Man "is brutalized both morally and physically" so that the "divine spark" becomes "torpid in his soul." This dichotomized person also appears in Marx: "The worker . . . only feels himself outside his work, and in his work feels outside himself." Thus "what is animal becomes human and what is human becomes animal." On man's relation to his product, the *Farmers' Alliance* was concerned not with the sense of workmanship but with an exploitative productive system: "He knows that it is greed that enforces the material labor that is crushing him down." Further, the economy is an opposing force which makes the worker's position that "of a machine to its director." For Marx, "The *alienation* of the worker in his product means not only that his labour becomes an object, an *external* existence, but that it exists *outside* him, independently, as something alien to him, and that it becomes a power on its own confronting him." And the Populist paper saw man separated from his fellow men in these terms: "The tendency of the competitive system is to antagonize and disassociate men." The bonds of humanity are broken; man is in "a state of war." Marx likewise held that man is turned from "the *life of the species* into a means of individual life." Capitalism therefore "is the *estrangement of man* from *man*." Nor was the similarity confined to a critique of the problem. The *Farmers' Alliance*, while not calling for the abolition of private property, did pose some leading questions: "How is he to have more time and more energy to develop his faculties except by lessening his hours of labour and increasing his wages? Can this be done under the present system?" Its reply clearly suggests the potential for a radical solution, one perhaps awaiting greater awareness or harder times: "There *must* be a better one." [1]

The second area of convergence deals with the creation of tramps and vagabonds: Lewelling's "Tramp Circular" and Marx on original accumulation in *Capital* see this as a central feature of capitalist development. Taking enclosures in Elizabethan England as the type-form, each finds men uprooted from a position of independence, forced as tramps to wander in search of work, and kept in a dependent condition through legal means. "In the reign of Elizabeth," Lewelling began, "the highways were filled with the throngs of the unemployed poor, who were made to 'move on,' and were sometimes brutally whipped, sometimes summarily hanged, as 'sturdy vagrants' or 'incorrigible vagabonds.'" Marx agreed; the unemployed "were turned *en masse* into beggars, robbers, vagabonds, partly from inclination, in most cases from stress of circumstances." Even his words were similar: "Hence at the end of the 15th and during the whole of the 16th century, throughout Western Europe a bloody legislation against vagabondage . . . Legislation treated them as 'voluntary' criminals, and assumed that it depended on their goodwill to go on working under the old conditions that no longer existed." Lewelling in turn denied that the unemployed were at fault; it was ridiculous to assume that anyone "being able bodied and willing to work can always find work to do." Further, both maintained that the change was monumental; man had become totally transformed. For Lewelling this "rendered more and more human beings superfluous," while for Marx it separated "the labourers from all property in the means by which they can realise their labour." Hence, it was "the historical process of divorcing the producer from the means of production." Yet, the remedies differed markedly, Lewelling contending only that poverty should "cease to be a crime." [2]

Nor does the resemblance end here; each treated ideology as a reflection of dominant group interests. For Populism the success myth was a fraud: "No effort of the people . . . could have averted these results." Hence, "While the cause exists the evils *must* and *will* remain." Social Darwinism was no better; it meant "not the survival of the fittest, but the survival of the strongest." And laissez faire brought about "the plutocracy of today," where "the corporation has absorbed the community." These ideologies, by denying social protest, sought to preserve the status quo; they could not be taken at face value. Thus, Populism expressed in practice what Marx observed in the *German Ideology:* "The ideas of the ruling class are in every epoch the ruling ideas." Even basic values had become perverted by current ideologies; freedom was now a mere shibboleth. Populism insisted that freedom could not be meaningful unless founded upon *"industrial* freedom, without which there can be no political freedom." Marx in *Capital* also regarded freedom as a fiction; in its present guise freedom was the right of a man to "dispose of his labour-power as his own commodity." A positive statement was therefore needed, one piercing through ideological subterfuges: For Populism individuality could only

---

[1] See Pollack, *The Populist Response,* pp. 25–27; Karl Marx, *Economic and Philosophic Manuscripts of 1844* (Moscow, 1956), pp. 72–73, 70, 75, 77.

[2] See Pollack, *The Populist Response,* pp. 33–35; Karl Marx, *Capital* (Modern Library, New York, n.d.), I, 806, 785–786, 786.

mean "the divinity of humanity," and freedom, human existence "devoted to rest, to mental culture, to social intercourse and recreation." Marx held up the same standard for judging freedom —the multi-faceted man who would be able "to hunt in the morning, fish in the afternoon, rear cattle in the evening, criticize after dinner . . . without ever becoming hunter, fisherman, shepherd or critic." [3]

Yet, Populism and Marxism differed on ideology in a notable respect: Marx sought the relation between ideological and material factors in society, delineating the role of capitalism, division of labor, and commodity fetishism in the rise of ideology. For Populism this was unknown territory. Lloyd spoke instead of manipulation: Dominant groups were "the most strenuous in urging" workers to protest, for the economic power of these groups insured their political dominance as well. While Marx agreed with this on two counts—the primacy of economic over political factors, and the superficiality of reform politics—he studiously avoided the treatment of manipulation for its own sake. Even the famous statement on religion as "the opium of the people," in Marx's *A Criticism of the Hegelian Philosophy of Right,* was a complicated analysis of ideology, not a simplistic variation of conspiracy theory. "Man makes religion, religion does not make man. Religion indeed is man's self-consciousness and self-estimation while he has not found his feet in the universe. But Man is no abstract being, squatting outside the world. Man is the world of men, the State, society." Thus, "This State, this

society produces religion, which is an inverted world. Religion is the general theory of this world, its encyclopaedic compendium, its logic in popular form . . ." In a word, Populism described the results of ideology, and Marx its causation. Still, Lloyd too rejected conspiracy theory: Personal intentions are irrelevant, for "the main point is the simple issue of monopoly." [4]

But the greatest affinity between Populism and Marxism lies in still a fourth area. Each pointed to the same economic features as defining capitalism. On the concentration of wealth, Populism held that capitalism transformed "the common property of all" into "the monopoly of the few." Hence, "the present cruelly unjust system" was "fast working the hopeless pauperization and degradation of the toiling masses." The "people have produced but they possess not," for now "the means of subsistence are monopolized." In sum, "more are reduced to dependence than rise to independence." Throughout volume one, part seven, of *Capital,* Marx noted the accumulation of wealth coupled with "the mass of misery, oppression, slavery," and other forms of hardship. More succinctly, he stated in *Capital:* "Accumulation of capital is, therefore, increase of the proletariat." For Populism labor became "merely a commodity" in this system, no more than "sponges to be squeezed and rats to be shot." Marx also regarded labor in this light; man was known by "this peculiar commodity, labour-power." Further, capitalism produced cyclical fluctuations: It drives down wages to the subsistence level, affirmed Populism, for "the

---

[3] See Pollack, *The Populist Response,* pp. 18–20, 15, 13, 31; Karl Marx, *German Ideology* (New York, 1947), p. 39; Marx, *Capital,* I, 188; Marx, *German Ideology,* p. 22.

[4] See Pollack, *The Populist Response,* pp. 40, 21; Karl Marx, *Selected Essays* (London, 1926), pp. 11–12.

workers are in constant want." And it "destroys the commercial equilibrium, makes the seller unable to buy back as much labor value as he sold, and so leads to glutted markets." Populism therefore offered an underconsumption theory for economic crisis, a view Marx maintained in volume three of *Capital:* "The last cause of all real crises always remains the poverty and restricted consumption of the masses" as compared to the development of productive forces "in such a way that only the absolute power of consumption of the entire society would be their limit." [5]

Yet, an important difference in scope emerges here: Marxism, unlike Populism, analyzed business cycles through the falling tendency of the rate of profit. Still, the difference is not as great as it seems. While Populism had no conception of rates of profit, its emphasis on underconsumption raises an interesting possibility. If Populism and Marxism did in fact agree on other essential points in economics, perhaps underconsumption is more central to the latter than is generally recognized. One economist argues precisely this— working, of course, from Marx, and not Populism: "Marx was giving advance notice of a line of reasoning which, if he had lived to complete his work, would have been of primary importance." It could not be otherwise—for Populism *or* Marxism. The basic social and economic fact in each is the surplus worker, one who by definition cannot adequately consume the products of society.[6]

For Populism capitalism depended

upon the surplus worker: "The army of destitute unemployed is the source of its power." Hence, "It is in the interest of the capitalist class to have as many men as possible out of work and seeking it in order to keep and force wages down by making competition fierce." And the mechanism insuring this is "labor-saving machinery," from which the "capitalist has been the chief beneficiary." Since there was a "monopoly of machinery and other means of production and distribution," technological improvements could be specifically "used to displace labor." The fault lay with capitalism; under "a proper use of the instrumentalities of modern production and distribution" labor would not be cast down into poverty. The unemployed were thus "the natural product of a false and vicious system." Marx likewise focused in *Capital* on surplus labor and the role of technology: "Relative surplus-population is therefore the pivot upon which the law of demand and supply of labour works." Here machinery is crucial in displacing the worker, whether in the "form of the repulsion of labourers already employed, or the less evident but not less real form of the more difficult absorption of the additional labouring population through the usual channels." Marx concluded, "this surplus population becomes . . . the lever of capitalistic accumulation, nay, a condition of existence of the capitalist mode of production." This reliance upon the surplus worker suggests, then, the strong place of underconsumption in Marx. Nor did his view of machinery differ from that of Populism. He observed in the *Manifesto,* "The bourgeoisie cannot exist without constantly revolutionising the instruments of production," and added in *Capital,* the bourgeois must "keep constantly extending his capital, in

---

[5] See Pollack, *The Populist Response,* pp. 17, 27–29; Marx, *Capital,* I, 836, 673, 189, III, 568. The last citation is quoted as part of an extremely interesting analysis in Paul M. Sweezy, *The Theory of Capitalist Development* (London, 1942), p. 177.

[6] *Ibid.,* p. 178.

order to preserve it." Increased surplus labor therefore promotes surplus value; and capital accumulation merely renews the process, making possible "revolutions in the technical composition of capital, which . . . thereby reduce the relative demand for labor." [7]

Finally, each believed that capitalism developed through a dialectical process. Populism saw the tramp not only as "a natural product" but a basic trend of society: "The tendency of the times is to force the masses into a propertyless condition." The result is "a pivotal or turning point" in which "every element for good or *evil* is *developed to a* ripened maturity of forces." Since dominant groups "will NEVER consent" to fundamental reform, the crisis is fast approaching: "Without a complete eradication of this system the people cannot for once hope for relief of a permanent character." But Marx went further, a fact suggesting again that Populism and Marxism were concerned with different levels of the problem. While each might agree on the opening sentence of the *Manifesto,* class struggle was only the surface of dialectics for Marx. Hence, one does not find the Populist equivalent for Marx's preface to *A Contribution to the Critique of Political Economy:* "At a certain stage of their development, the material productive forces of society come in conflict with the existing relations of pro-

duction. . ." Yet, the problem for each was still class struggle.[8]

• • •

What, therefore, emerges from the comparison of Populism and Marxism? Since the similarities concern not superficial points but total views of capitalism, the following is clear: Populism, measured by Marx's own writings, offered a highly radical critique. Further, Populism can also be seen as more than an agrarian movement; its critique was possessed neither with the agrarian question nor the desire to turn back the clock on industrial development. But the comparison suggests even more; it provides fertile ground for historical imagination. Thus, the question immediately becomes, how can the similarities of totally independent systems of thought be explained—especially when lines of communication are absent, and intellectual roots so totally different? There are only two logical possibilities: chance, and the existence of similar historical contexts. Rejecting the first as unlikely, one confronts an extremely exciting prospect, perhaps even a new working hypothesis for determining the course of American history: If, in their respective periods, Populism and Marxism pointed to the same features of capitalism, it follows that capitalist development assumed the same pattern in the United States and Western Europe. In a word, the Populist experience might well challenge a basic proposition in historical writing—the uniqueness of America.

[7] See Pollack, *The Populist Response,* pp. 29–31; Marx, *Capital,* I, 701, 691–692, 693; Karl Marx and Frederick Engels, *Manifesto of the Communist Party,* in their *Selected Works* (Moscow, 1955), I, 37; Marx, *Capital,* I, 649, 689.

[8] See Pollack, *The Populist Response,* pp. 37, 28; Karl Marx, *A Contribution to the Critique of Political Economy,* in *Selected Works,* I, 363.

HISTORIOGRAPHICAL NOTE

What, then, was the significance of the Populist experience? Most of the early literature on Populism was polemic, and filled with abusive epithets. After World War I, however, professional historians began to write sympathetically of the movement. Reacting against the values of a business culture that emerged triumphant in the twenties, they looked back on nineteenth-century agrarian movements with a mixture of nostalgia and regret. Books such as Solon J. Buck's *The Agrarian Crusade: A Chronicle of the Farmer in Politics* (New Haven, 1920), Alex M. Arnett's *The Populist Movement in Georgia* (New York, 1922), and John D. Hicks' *The Populist Revolt* (Minneapolis, 1931) by and large accepted the Populist indictment of the American economic system. Hicks, especially, found in the People's party the values of a Jeffersonian liberal tradition accompanied by a willingness to use the state as an instrument for social and economic welfare. In the failure of that party he saw the triumph of industry over agriculture. At the same time, he accorded a measure of success to Populism, for other parties incorporated into their programs the demands of the People's party platform of 1892. *The Populist Revolt* had a long-lasting influence, an influence evident in Fred A. Shannon's *The Farmer's Last Frontier* (New York, 1945) and in Theodore Saloutos' *Farmer Movements in the South, 1865–1933* (Berkeley, 1960). But it was in the depression years of the 1930's, when historians often implied that the historical roots of the New Deal could be discovered in the Populist movement, that the Hicks interpretation became standard.

This was the view that prevailed until a new school of historians—led by Richard Hofstadter and Oscar Handlin—gained prominence after World War II. Profoundly impressed by the disastrous consequences of fascism, and deeply concerned with the force that brought it about, the new school applied some of the findings of sociologists and social psychologists to the study of history. The antics of Senator Joseph R. McCarthy, and the apparent ease with which he won a fanatical popular following, seemed to suggest that American democracy was not immune to the illiberal emotionalism which had characterized totalitarian states such as Nazi Germany. The new school of historians—urban in outlook and unable to identify with nineteenth-century agrarianism—saw similarities between the psychology of Populism and that of McCarthyism. Exploring the unlovely side of agrarian radicalism in *The Age of Reform* (New York, 1955), Hofstadter never went so far as did some others in identifying Populism with fascism. Victor Ferkiss, for example, made the connection explicit in "Populist Influences on American Fascism," *Western Political Quarterly,* (June, 1957). Nevertheless, Hofstadter did find a marked tendency among Populists to see nefarious conspiracy as the basic cause of the farmers' plight. This tendency, he suggested, helps to account for the strain of nativism and anti-Semitism in Populist writing and oratory.

The new criticism of Populism did not go unchallenged. In "The Populist Heritage and the Intellectual," published in *The American Scholar* (Winter, 1959–1960), and republished in *The Burden of Southern History* (Baton Rouge, 1960), C. Vann Woodward comments on the historiography of the movement from the point of view of one in sympathy with the older liberal interpretation. In short order several historians sought to rehabilitate the Populists. Walter Nugent studied Kansas Populists and wrote *The Tolerant Populists* (Chicago, 1963). His conclusion, suggested by his title, is that Populists were no more anti-Semitic and nativistic than other groups in American society. They were, in fact, much more tolerant than most. Norman Pollack went even further in *The Populist Response to Industrial Society* (Cambridge, Mass., 1962). He contends that Populism was by no means an attempt to return to an agrarian order, rather it was a realistic effort to meet the problems of industrialization. The failure of the People's party meant nothing less than the failure of American society to recognize the potential in a genuinely radical alternative to an exploitative economic system.

Pollack's interpretation elaborated on some of the ideas suggested earlier by Chester M. Destler in *American Radicalism, 1865–1901* (New London, 1946). But Pollack's work is also characteristic of the sixties—with its awakening interest in radical causes—just as Hicks' interpretation is characteristic of the twenties and thirties. Another study, Michael Rogin's *The Intellectuals and McCarthy: The Radical Specter* (Cambridge, Mass., and London, 1967), provides fresh evidence in support of Pollack and Nugent. Rogin employs quantitative analysis to show that McCarthyism bore little relationship to Populism, and in the process he displays none of the fear of mass movements that marked the intellectuals' response to McCarthy. The view that Populism was a radical force did not, however, sweep the field. In *The Climax of Populism: The Election of 1896* (Lexington, 1965), Robert F. Durden takes issue with the suggestion that Populism meant radicalism of any sort. The People's party, he argues in his sympathetic account, operated in a fashion remarkably similar to other political parties. In recent work, then, Populism has found its champions, but they have defended Populism on such different grounds that the historiographical dialogue has not become submerged in consensus.

12. Expansionism and the Exercise of World Power

INTRODUCTION

The American people have often identified expansion with progress and immensity with greatness. In the United States growth and size are popular criteria for measuring the success of social and educational as well as economic institutions. "The bigger, the better" suggests a major strain in American thought, however much it might be countered with "The bigger they are, the harder they fall." Gutzon Borglum, the sculptor, carved up a mountain in the Black Hills because he believed that only statuary of colossal proportions could adequately express the American spirit. Small wonder, then, that historians have found American expansion a subject of absorbing interest.

The nation's development, from a scattering of sparsely settled colonies on the eastern seaboard to a continental republic with global interests, has doubtless conditioned popular thought. So argued Frederick Jackson Turner in 1893 when he suggested that the national character took form and substance out of the three-hundred-year westward movement of the frontier. Turner profoundly influenced twentieth-century historiography, but his frontier hypothesis was only one variation on the expansionist theme. Many of his contemporaries were impressed by the economic growth that by 1900 made the United States a leading industrial producer and justified their thinking of it as a great power. Many were even more impressed by the manner in which the American government took an increasingly active part in world affairs.

The salient facts of that overseas involvement are familiar. In 1889–1890 Congress threatened war against Germany to protect American rights in the Samoan Islands. President Harrison made the first moves toward annexation of Hawaii in 1893. Grover Cleveland, although he temporarily thwarted the Hawaiian project, intervened in the Venezuela boundary dispute of 1895. Under William McKinley's leadership the United States in 1898 waged a titillating three months' war against Spain. For their pains—which were minimal—the American people acquired a protectorate over Cuba and outright possession of Puerto Rico, Guam, and the Philippines.

When Theodore Roosevelt entered the White House in 1901, he acted on the assumption that the United States had every right to consider itself a great power. His "big stick" diplomacy helped to bring about a revolution in Panama and construction of the interoceanic canal. In the "Roosevelt Corollary" to the Monroe Doctrine, the President in effect announced that the United States would police the western hemisphere. But Roosevelt's interests extended far beyond the Americas. In 1905 he used his good offices to end the Russo-Japanese War and a Franco-German dispute over Morocco. In 1907, when he sent the battle fleet on a demonstration cruise around the world, his action symbolized the achievement of great power status by the United States.

Yet Americans did not all thrill to Roosevelt's accomplishments. Many had grave reservations about expansionist moves, and others disliked the foreign entanglements to which those moves led. Anti-imperialists feared that gaining control of colonies overseas would endanger democracy at home. More significantly, however, those who favored expansion differed on what form it should take. Some believed that great power status created an obligation to build a colonial empire and to share with Britain the "white man's burden." Others, including some who associated themselves with the anti-imperialist movement, were less concerned with colonial imperatives and more interested in economic growth. Feeling themselves threatened by periodic economic depression, they urged the development of overseas markets rather than the acquisition of overseas colonies.

Differing economic interests and differing conceptions of America's mission at the turn of the century helped to produce a vacillating policy; political leaders and opinion makers seemed unable to agree on how the power of the United States ought to be exercised. Initially, the predominant group in policy formation favored economic penetration of underdeveloped areas. Following the war with Spain, emphasis shifted to colonial acquisition, but empire building after the British model was soon abandoned. In place of colonies the United States established protectorates in the western hemisphere, and Secretary of State John Hay promulgated the Open Door in China. Applied on an increasingly broader scale, the Open Door concept eventually came to mean a return to market expansionist views.

For several years, then, divergent opinions on what constituted legitimate and desirable foreign policy objectives may have limited the degree to which the United States was capable of fulfilling its promise as a great power. Nevertheless, in the early struggles between expansionists and their opponents, the expansionists won out. During the years from Roosevelt to Roosevelt, choice of policy was largely limited to expansionist alternatives; but it was the expansion of trade, rather than the expansion of political control, that had the greater appeal. Erratically perhaps, though nonetheless certainly, the United States moved toward increasingly wider participation in world affairs.

I. EARLY INTERPRETATION

One of the most perceptive of the early works dealing with American foreign policy at the turn of the century was *The United States as a World Power* by Archibald Cary Coolidge, professor of modern European history at Harvard University. In the following selection, Coolidge accepts the idea that 1898 marked a turning point in relations between the United States and the rest of the world. After the Spanish-American War, he contends, the nation occupied a new position in international affairs. Probing for the influences that led to that new position, he examines the economic foundations of American world power.

ARCHIBALD CARY COOLIDGE

Early in the year 1901, a foreign ambassador at Washington remarked in the course of conversation that, although he had been in America only a short time, he had seen two different countries,—the United States before the war with Spain, and the United States since the war with Spain. This was a picturesque way of expressing the truth, now generally accepted, that the war of 1898 was a turning-point in the history of the American republic. The reason therefor is usually summed up in the phrase that since that date the United States has been a world power. This assertion is, however, vigorously disputed by two sets of opponents, and on exactly opposite grounds. Some writers labor to prove that the United States is not, or if it is, ought not to be, a world power to-day; others maintain that it has always been one, because ever since its independence it has been interested in affairs in many parts of the world,—which is also true of Holland. Evidently the term has not the same meaning to the two parties. But

Reprinted from Archibald Cary Coolidge, THE UNITED STATES AS A WORLD POWER *(New York, 1908), pp. 121–122, 130–133, 174–181, 183.*

without entering into discussion, we can confine ourselves to the indisputable fact that the Spanish War brought about in American public feeling a change important enough to mark the beginning of an epoch.

When we come to analyze the causes of this sudden evolution, we must concede that at first sight the magnitude of the result seems out of all proportion to that of the military operations. The war was a short, bloodless one between two nations of very unequal resources. There were but three battles worthy of the name,—two on the water and one on the land. The two sea-fights were brilliantly conducted, and the completeness of the success, coupled with the almost entire absence of loss on the part of the Americans, constituted a pleasing testimony to the efficiency of their new navy; but the difference in the strength between the combatants made the victory a foregone conclusion. The one battle on land was marked by creditable fighting on both sides, rather than by any display of generalship, and the forces engaged and the losses incurred were too small for the encounter to deserve the name of a great battle. Though the United States had good reason to be satisfied with the outcome, there was, when all is said, no cause for undue elation; nor had there been any severe strain on the country.

. . .

The liberation of Cuba was not the only result of the Spanish War; the effects on the United States were many and important. Considering how little fighting took place, the territorial changes brought about by the conflict were very large. They gave the Americans a stronger strategic position in the Gulf of Mexico and in the Caribbean Sea, coaling stations in the Pacific, and a base of operations in the Far East. But, though they made the United States stronger for offensive purposes, in some ways they weakened it for defensive ones. Up to 1898 Alaska was the only possession which could be seized by a foe with a superior fleet; now Hawaii, the Philippines, and other Pacific islands, as well as Porto Rico, could hardly be defended against an adversary who controlled the sea. None the less, however the gain and the loss may balance, they both represent far-reaching changes in the military position of the country; yet even these are not sufficient to account for the difference in the American attitude before and after the war.

Like so many other things, an attitude has two faces, a subjective and an objective one. The people of the republic, if not actually transformed by their short victorious conflict, were much affected by it, both as they saw themselves and as others saw them. To the greater part of Europe the war itself, and the course which it took, came as an unpleasant surprise. During most of the nineteenth century the United States had enjoyed a remarkable popularity abroad. Many Englishmen were well disposed toward it because it was inhabited by their kin; Frenchmen were proud of it because they had as-

sisted in its creation; Russia was a traditional friend; liberals all over Europe sympathized with its democratic institutions; zealous Roman Catholics were pleased with the flourishing condition of their church across the water. Countless European children had delighted in the Indians of Fenimore Cooper, and millions of kindly souls had read and wept over *Uncle Tom's Cabin*. Travelling Americans, though sometimes forth-putting, were open-handed and good-natured. In the later years of the century American students in numbers had frequented the art schools in Paris and the universities in Germany, and had given a good account of themselves. The fame of the country's wealth and prosperity, of the ingenuity and practical abilities of its inhabitants, and especially of their eagerness to make money, was wide-spread. But in the great game of international politics they took little part. European statesmen could usually leave them out of their reckonings. Well-informed persons were aware that the United States was a power of great resources,—how great in a military way had been shown by the Civil War,—and that, as the Mexican, and quite lately the Venezuelan, incident had proved, it was resolved to stand by its traditional policy. But if one let that policy alone and kept clear of the Monroe Doctrine, in which most of Europe had small interest, then in practice the United States need not often be taken into consideration. It belonged, so to speak, to a different world.

All this was changed by the Spanish War. Continental Europe, without defending Spanish misgovernment in Cuba, regarded the action of the Americans as brutal aggression against a smaller nation. How could it be pleased with the cry, so often raised across the sea, that European rule in the western hemisphere ought to be brought to an end? But the Americans did more than expel the Spaniards from Cuba and Porto Rico: they proved that they possessed a most efficient modern fleet, they crossed the Pacific and established themselves in the Far East, they threatened to send ships to attack Spain in her own waters. It was evident that they had assumed a new position among nations; that henceforth they would have to be counted with as one of the chief forces in international affairs. Although, as usually happens for the victorious, a revulsion of sentiment soon took place in their favor, and many persons hastened to testify that they had always been on their side, still the appearance of a new factor of such magnitude interfered with many old calculations. The former easy popularity of the United States was gone, probably never to return. Some idealists mournfully declared that what the Union had gained in political importance it had lost in moral greatness; that it had forfeited its real eminence, and was now only one more huge, aggressive, selfish power. Be this as it may, its situation, for better or for worse, was radically changed in the eyes of the outside world.

The change was equally decisive in the consciousness of the Americans themselves. The war aroused within them a feeling of strength which had until then been latent. It opened their eyes to new horizons, suggested new outlets for their energies, and made them confident that they could deal with problems which had never before attracted their attention. They had always been proud of their country,—aggressively so, foreigners thought, —but they had regarded it as something different from the others, and leading its own life apart. Now, all at once, they were willing to give up their isolation and plunge into the fray. They felt that the day had come when they were called upon to play a part in the broader affairs of mankind even at the cost of sacrificing some of their cherished ideals. They were indeed unable, as well as unwilling, to return to their earlier point of view. Full of joyous self-reliance, they were prepared to meet all the difficulties and to accept all the burdens of their new position.

. . . Americans had long been accustomed to proclaim that theirs was the "greatest country on earth," and after 1898 it seemed as if facts were coming to their aid in a way that must convince all doubters. Throughout the nineteenth century the United States furnished to Europe several of the staples necessary to the support of mankind and to the development of modern industry. In the export of wheat and petroleum its sole rival was Russia; in that of cotton it had been supreme for many generations; in that of sheep and wool it came next to Australia; in the number of its cattle it was ahead even of Argentina. Of late it has taken the lead in one after another of the chief industrial commodities: in the production of both iron and coal it has surpassed Great Britain, which so long led in those staples that her primacy seemed unassailable; in copper the American output is more than a half of the world's supply. But it is not only in raw materials that the country has made such startling progress; its manufactures have developed with even more wonderful rapidity: the American silk industry is second to none but the French; the cotton is inferior to that of Great Britain only; the iron and steel leads the world. Between 1896 and 1906 American exports almost doubled in value, passing in 1901 those of England, which, since the creation of modern mechanical industry, had been the first exporting nation on the globe. The huge immigration, which has risen to over a million a year, has been insufficient to supply the demand for labor; and the railway system, though larger than that of all Europe, is inadequate to the needs of transportation. All this contributed to a prosperity which was not confined to one part of the land, or to one class of the community. Both capitalists and laborers shared in the dispensation. The Americans would, in truth, be more than human if they had not at times lost their heads in the midst of their unparalleled achievements.

In 1898 this new era had only just begun, but it had got enough of a start for the people, with their inborn optimism, to be full of confidence in their powers. What in ordinary times might have seemed prudence now passed for cowardice; any arguments based on caution were out of keeping with the popular temper; hostile criticism from a foreign source was attributed to jealousy or fear, and was thus more flattering than praise. The whole country was bursting with a consciousness of strength. It could, then, scarcely be expected to give up its hold on the Philippines, which seemed to offer a new field for enterprise, and a base for the expansion of trade in the Far East. America was now in a position to take up her share of "the white man's burden," with all its incidental advantages.

The economic progress of the United States in the last few years has inevitably influenced the national policy in various ways, and will continue to do so. Until a short time ago the country belonged to the debtor rather than to the creditor class of states. It was well off, but it had no investments of consequence beyond its borders, and it owed the development of its resources in part to foreign capital. To-day the situation is radically different: the

Americans have bought back much of their paper formerly held abroad, and, though they are continually borrowing afresh in order to carry out the countless undertakings in which they are engaged, they are no longer in the same situation as before. There is a distinction between the poor man who has to ask for a loan from a well-to-do neighbor in order to set his business going, and the wealthy financier who invites others to take shares in a profitable enterprise; and the United States is now in the position of the latter. It still needs foreign capital; but the Americans are themselves the greatest capitalists in the world, and though as yet they find uncertain ventures at a distance—as in the Philippines—less attractive than investments at home, where they do see an alluring prospect, —as in Cuba and Mexico,—they are not backward in risking their money.

Another element affecting the international relations of the United States is the transformation which is taking place in its export trade. Greatly as its exports of raw materials have increased, those of manufactured goods have grown faster still. In 1880 they formed but twelve and one-half per cent of the total, in 1896 they were twenty-six and one-half per cent, in 1906 thirty-four and one-half per cent, and the future appears to belong to them. With the growth of the population at home, the supply of wheat for exportation must diminish, and may soon disappear altogether. The development of an immense cotton industry which makes an increasing home demand on the crop leaves less and less for foreign countries, several of which are to-day making strenuous efforts to find an independent source of supply in their own colonies. On the other hand, South America, Africa, and Asia produce sufficient food for their own wants and are rich in metals, and in raw materials —Argentine wheat, Indian and Egyptian cotton, and Burmese petroleum. It is obvious that exports to such regions must consist chiefly of manufactured articles.

The political consequences of this change are already felt. In the days when the United States sent abroad nothing but the great staples which all the world needed, when its rivals were mostly backward states, and it had little to fear from hostile tariffs, it could tax as it pleased the imports from foreign countries without much danger of retaliation. Now it finds itself competing on equal terms with the highly developed industries of England, Germany, France, and other manufacturing countries,—and every civilized country to-day aspires to be a manufacturing one. Each of these countries pushes its trade by every means in its power, and most of them protect their industries by high duties wherever they are able to impose them.

• • •

When American statesmen set themselves to face the situation, they perceived that the policy of aiding and protecting the national exports must be adapted to circumstances. In dealing with the European powers and their colonies, no originality was required: the United States was meeting equals and, in most cases, rivals. There was room for a mighty development of trade, but the government could do little to further it except by insisting on fair treatment, by improving its consular service, and lastly, by concluding profitable commercial treaties,—a matter in which it was less hampered by the demands of foreign countries than it was by the unreasonableness of the ultra-protectionists at home. Since the larger half of Asia, almost all of Africa, and the whole of Australia were in the hands of European peoples, a good part of the world was accounted for. There remained, however, two regions where the Americans believed they saw splendid possibilities for the future. But to make the most of these possibilities they must take decided action.

In the republics of Latin America there was no highly developed native industry to be feared as a rival. There was nothing but the competition of Europe, which had too long had the field to itself, and the Americans were convinced that they could meet this competition victoriously if only they made the best of their natural advantages. A first step was to draw closer to these fellow-republicans to the south, for the benefit of all concerned. This led to the policy known as Pan-Americanism.

• • •

The other tempting field for American enterprise was in the Far East, where hundreds of millions of human beings were just waking up, at the rude contact of the outside world, to the advantages of dealing with and imitating the hated foreigner. Here, indeed, were magnificent opportunities. Ardent imaginations pictured the countless population of the Middle Kingdom lighted by American petroleum, working with American tools, dressed in American cottons. The competition of Japan and the new activity of the Chinese themselves had not yet come to mar these fair visions. Unfortunately, even as it was, they were already threatened with destruction.

Ever since the war with Japan, China had seemed on the point of breaking up, and in danger of partition among foreign powers, who would probably introduce preferential tariffs for their own manufactures, and then—good-by to the dreams of American trade. The peril appeared extreme, and difficult to meet. Single-handed, the United States could not maintain the integrity of the Chinese Empire against the rest of the world, especially if that empire insisted on going to pieces of itself. It might, to be sure, take part in the general scramble and claim a sphere of influence of its own; but it had come into the field rather late to get a good share, and public opinion at home would never tolerate such a proceeding. The Americans' only other course was to take up and echo the newly invented British cry of the "open door." On the face of it, there was something rather ludicrous in the spectacle of the nation which had just voted the Dingley Bill waxing so enthusiastic over the justice of equal commercial opportunities for all. This attitude might be natural enough in Great Britain, which for half a century had been the free-trade power of the world, and could well assert that she had consistently stood for the "open door" policy; it was hard to see exactly how the Americans had done so, except in forcing the door open in Japan. But nations are guided in such matters not by logic, but by their interests. When the English, with intelligent appreciation of the value of American aid in the Far East, proclaimed that the two peoples had always been the defenders of the "open door," the latter cheerfully assented. It mattered not that the door which they wished to keep open was that of somebody else, not their own, and that, as in the case of most tariff doors, it was to open but one way. They did not stop for abstract considerations. Unless they were prepared to see many of the possible outlets for their trade closed against them at short notice, it behooved them to take a firm stand. Accordingly they fell into line with Great Britain and demanded the "open door" of equal chances for all, whatever territorial rearrangements might take place.

. . .

To-day the "open door" idea is no longer confined to Asia, since it has been accepted at Algeciras as one of the conditions of Morocco. True, it is not applicable everywhere. The United States, for instance, will take good care that it never penetrates to the western hemisphere, where it might interfere with Pan-Americanism. Still, it is, within the geographical limits to which it applies, one of the cardinal principles of American policy. Its maintenance involves trouble and responsibilities; but, with the expansion of the national trade and the keen commercial rivalry which this brings, such trouble and responsibilities are unavoidable: they are part of the price which the country has to pay for its new greatness.

II. DOCUMENTS

1. Rationales for Expansion

Among political leaders William McKinley was always a great favorite of the National Association of Manufacturers. As governor of Ohio he addressed the Association's organizing convention held at Cincinnati in 1895. The United States was experiencing one of the worst depressions in its history, and the Governor's remarks struck a note of hope and inspiration that manufacturers wanted to hear. In 1898, after he had become President and after prosperity had returned, McKinley journeyed to New York where the NAM marked the beginning of its fourth year with a banquet at the plush Waldorf-Astoria. Featured speaker on that memorable occasion, the President emphasized economic recovery and actions required to insure continued prosperity. Following McKinley's assassination in 1901, American Trade, *organ of the National Association of Manufacturers, published a commemorative article containing excerpts from his two speeches. A portion of that article is included here as the first of four documents pointing up the relationship between economic development and America's posture in world affairs.*

In his first annual message to Congress in 1901, Theodore Roosevelt recognized that the dynamics of international relations required institutional adjustment on the part of the United States. In some detail he also discussed American policy in China following the Boxer Rebellion. That he should treat both matters in the same speech suggests a relationship between the sort of administrative and military reform he recommended and the course of action he proposed to follow in the Far East. It was a course he thought would lead to increased commercial opportunities.

Begun as an organization devoted to increasing American exports, the National Association of Manufacturers broadened its activities in the first decade of the twentieth century, but it never lost sight of its original objective. In 1911, American Industries *published an article by James L. Ewell reiterating arguments that had by then become standard NAM liturgy. Ewell's central point was as profound as it was simple: American capitalists must have the "great world's market" to offset recurrent cycles of growth and depression at home.*

"McKINLEY TO THE MANUFACTURERS"

On two memorable occasions President McKinley was the honored guest of the National Association of Manufacturers, and his utterances in both cases were characteristic of his devotion to the industrial interests of the country and his concern for the nation's material welfare. When a convention of representative manufacturers was held in Cincinnati on January 22, 1895, to consider the expediency of forming a national organization of manufacturers for the purpose of advancing the industrial interests of the country, it was Governor William McKinley, of Ohio, who sounded the keynote of that convention and furnished the inspiration which gave life and impetus to the National Association of Manufacturers. From his speech on that occasion the following extracts are given as significant of the times and the man:

"I congratulate the business men of Cincinnati for having inaugurated the movement which has brought here this great body of business men from every

Reprinted from "McKinley to the Manufacturers," AMERICAN TRADE, *IV (September 15, 1901), pp. 177–178.*

part of the country. I congratulate you and them upon the representative character of this convention. What it represents and stands for can scarcely be appreciated. What it may be able to accomplish for business and commerce if wise counsel prevails cannot be overstated. Any association of this character, well conducted, cannot fail to have a bright future and a great field of usefulness. I do not think that even you, who constitute such a large part of the business world, appreciate the full magnitude of the manufacturing interests of the United States. The fabled wealth of the Indies and the vast projects of empire and conquest that filled the minds of the rulers of old are as nothing in comparison with the trophies of your peaceful and practical pursuits.

"You touch every business interest of the country, every hamlet and household—every delicate thread of trade is interwoven with the transactions you represent. To those who do not come into immediate contact with trade as well as to all of us, some reference to the enormous volume of our manufactures will be timely and interesting. It is only when we contemplate these interests as a whole that we can properly appreciate what vast concerns our business men have constantly in their care and keeping, and what grave responsibilities they have constantly resting upon them. It is a mighty problem to keep the wheels of industry in motion. They cannot be kept in motion without markets. They will not long produce beyond consumption.

"Think of the immense capital invested in manufactures in this country, and what skill and watchfulness are required to keep it at work. Capital is not willingly idle for a moment. It is ever seeking steady employment. It is hourly solicitous for profitable investment,

and more than solicitous to keep at work what is already invested. Capital always wants to work, but it will not work long with waste or loss to principal if it can help it. If we realize the magnitude of your enterprises we begin to understand the necessity of wise and fair treatment and even generous encouragement in all legislation affecting these interests.

"I can well see why you should meet to exchange views and discuss with one another subjects of common interest and for the common good. Your meeting, if conducted in the right spirit, can result only in good. All that our manufacturing interests have asked for is fair play and equal rights with their outside competitors. More they have never demanded, and they surely should not have and will not long consent to have less. Indeed it is highly humiliating that they should ever be brought to contest at all for these plain and natural rights. If we are wise or even ordinarily prudent as a patriotic, progressive people, our care must be constant and supreme that nothing is ever permitted to impair, much less destroy, our great manufacturing interests. Consider what they mean to the masses of the people. Their prosperity and happiness are both involved in them.

"What lessons of progress the figures of our industries proclaim! But you are far more interested in a general revival of trade and manufactures than in any review, however creditable, of what has already been accomplished. In a government like ours no class of business men can be permanently prosperous unless all are prosperous. Our business interests are interdependent and mutual. The prosperity of one, to be permanent and enduring, must not impair or sacrifice any other. If commerce would thrive, manufactures must flourish. If agriculture would enjoy active markets and good prices, there must be conceded to enterprise and skill in manufactures just return for hazard and outlay. If artisans would receive good wages, they must be willing to pay fair prices to merchants and farmers. The moral of our present situation is that the prostration of manufactures is the downfall of all other business interests.

"The policy which seeks to cripple or advance one interest regardless of every other is pernicious in the extreme, and if persisted in will prove destructive of all. It will lower and degrade our civilization, and instead of the United States being in the forefront of the nations of the world, it will drive her into the ranks of the second or third rate governments, neither prosperous at home nor respected abroad.

"What a magnificent tribute are the figures I quote to the business ability of the men of the United States. I am sure there has been no decadence in either enterprise or ability among the active business men of the country. Their push and pluck and perseverance, integrity and skill, are still here and will assert themselves in future industrial triumphs.

"For are we not to recover the ground we have lost in the last two years? This is one of the subjects doubtless which will engage our attention during the deliberations of your convention. For myself, I believe we will reoccupy the field temporarily lost to us, and go out to the peaceful conquest of new and greater fields for trade and manufactures. The American people have no idea of surrendering or resting upon past achievements. We propose to do our own work at home and widen our fields of production. For example: Why should we not produce our own sugar? Are we less enterprising than Germany? This great country cannot be permanently kept in a state of relapse. It is too great, too resourceful, and its people too enterprising and progressive to permit any reverse long to retard its progress. The recovery will come, and when it does, we will be steadier and will better know how to avoid exposure hereafter and keep the great interests of the country robust and healthy.

"We want our own markets for our manufactures and agricultural products; we want a foreign market for our surplus products which will not surrender our markets and will not degrade our labor to hold our markets. We want a reciprocity which will give us foreign markets for our surplus products, and in turn that will open our markets to foreigners for those products which they produce and which we do not.

"I bespeak for your sessions the highest wisdom. May you be able to devise some plan to improve our industrial situation and start this great country once more upon its march of triumph for the welfare of our own people and for the good of mankind everywhere."

Again, in 1898, when the famous banquet of the National Association of Manufacturers was held at the Waldorf-Astoria in New York City on January 27, it was President McKinley who delivered the most memorable speech of the occasion, uttering words which clearly defined the nation's sound money policy, a speech that was read with interest the world over. What he said on that occasion is given in full below:

"For the cordial character of this greeting I return my grateful thanks. The genuineness of your welcome is full compensation for having left Washington at an unusually busy season in order to participate in this interesting meeting.

"I scarcely need remind you that we do not meet as strangers. Neither your business organization nor your social reunions are altogether unfamiliar to me. I have been with you before, not a guest as now, but rather in the capacity of host. I recall that as Governor of the State of Ohio it was my pleasure to welcome you to the city of Cincinnati on January 22, 1895, at the initial convention of the Manufacturers' Association.

"I well remember the occasion. It was a cold, cold day. You had lost everything but your pluck, or thought you had. Courage was the only friend your grief could call its own. I note with satisfaction your improved appearance now. You are more cheerful in countenance, more buoyant in spirit, more hopeful in manner and more confident in purpose. Then, too, there are more of you here than there were at your first meeting. Distances are, of course, the same, but traveling has been resumed. Your speeches and resolutions at that first convention were directed mainly to the question of how to regain what you had lost in the previous years, or, if that was found impossible, then how to stop further loss. But your object now, as I gather it, is to go out and possess what you have never had before. You want to extend, not your notes, but your business. I sympathized with your purposes then; I am in full accord with your intentions now.

"I ventured to say at the gathering referred to, as reported in your published proceedings, speaking both for your encouragement and from a profound conviction—

" 'This great country cannot be permanently kept in a state of relapse. I believe we will reoccupy the field temporarily lost to us, and go out to the peaceful conquest of new and greater fields of trade and commerce. The recovery will come slowly, perhaps, but

it will come, and when it does we will be steadier and will better know how to avoid exposure hereafter.'

"I have abated none of the faith I then expressed, and you seem to have regained yours.

"National policies can encourage industry and commerce, but it remains for the people to protect and carry them on. If these policies stimulate industrial development and energy, the people can be safely trusted to do the rest.

"The government, however, is restricted in its power to promote industry. It can aid commerce, but not create it. It can widen and deepen its rivers, improve its harbors and develop its great national waterways, but the ships to sail and the traffic to carry the people must supply. The government can raise revenues by taxation in such a way as will discriminate in favor of domestic enterprises, but it cannot establish them. It can make commercial treaties, opening to our manufacturers and agriculturists the ports of other nations. It can enter into reciprocal arrangements to exchange our products with those of other countries.

"It can aid our merchant marine by encouraging our people to build ships of commerce. It can assist in every lawful manner private enterprise to unite the two oceans with a great canal. It can do all these things, and ought to do them; but with all this accomplished the result will still be ineffectual unless supplemented by the energy, enterprise and industry of the people. It is they who must build and operate the factories, furnish the ships and cargoes for the canal and the rivers and the seas. It is they who must find the consumers and obtain trade by going forth to win it.

"Much profitable trade is still unenjoyed by our people because of their present insufficient facilities for reaching desirable markets. Much of it is lost because of a lack of information, and ignorance of the conditions and needs of other nations. We must know just what other people want before we can supply their wants. We must understand exactly how to reach them with least expense if we would enter into the most advantageous business relations with them. The ship requires the shipper, but the shipper must have assured promise that his goods will have a sale when they reach their destination. It is a good rule, if buyers will not come to us, for us to go to them.

"It is our duty to make American enterprise and industrial ambition, as well as achievement, terms of respect and praise not only at home, but among the family of nations the world over. . . ."

THEODORE ROOSEVELT

Probably no other great nation in the world is so anxious for peace as we are. There is not a single civilized power which has anything whatever to fear from aggressiveness on our part. All we want is peace; and toward this end we wish to be able to secure the same respect for our rights from others which we are eager and anxious to extend to their rights in return, to insure fair treatment to us commercially, and to guarantee the safety of the American people.

Our people intend to abide by the Monroe Doctrine and to insist upon it as the one sure means of securing the peace of the Western Hemisphere. The Navy offers us the only means of

Reprinted from Theodore Roosevelt, Annual Message to Congress, December 3, 1901, in CONGRESSIONAL RECORD, *57 Cong. 1st sess., 1901, XXXV, 88–92.*

making our insistence upon the Monroe Doctrine anything but a subject of derision to whatever nation chooses to disregard it. We desire the peace which comes as of right to the just man armed; not the peace granted on terms of ignominy to the craven and the weakling.

It is not possible to improvise a navy after war breaks out. The ships must be built and the men trained long in advance. Some auxiliary vessels can be turned into makeshifts which will do in default of any better for the minor work, and a proportion of raw men can be mixed with the highly trained, their shortcomings being made good by the skill of their fellows; but the efficient fighting force of the Navy when pitted against an equal opponent will be found almost exclusively in the war ships that have been regularly built and in the officers and men who through years of faithful performance of sea duty have been trained to handle their formidable but complex and delicate weapons with the highest efficiency. In the late war with Spain the ships that dealt the decisive blows at Manila and Santiago had been launched from two to fourteen years, and they were able to do as they did because the men in the conning towers, the gun turrets, and the engine-rooms had through long years of practice at sea learned how to do their duty.

Our present Navy was begun in 1882. At that period our Navy consisted of a collection of antiquated wooden ships, already almost as out of place against modern war vessels as the galleys of Alcibiades and Hamilcar—certainly as the ships of Tromp and Blake. Nor at that time did we have men fit to handle a modern man-of-war. Under the wise legislation of the Congress and the successful administration of a succession of patriotic Secretaries of the Navy, belonging to both political parties, the work of upbuilding the Navy went on, and ships equal to any in the world of their kind were continually added; and what was even more important, these ships were exercised at sea singly and in squadrons until the men aboard them were able to get the best possible service out of them. The result was seen in the short war with Spain, which was decided with such rapidity because of the infinitely greater preparedness of our Navy than of the Spanish Navy.

While awarding the fullest honor to the men who actually commanded and manned the ships which destroyed the Spanish sea forces in the Philippines and in Cuba, we must not forget that an equal meed of praise belongs to those without whom neither blow could have been struck. The Congressmen who voted years in advance the money to lay down the ships, to build the guns, to buy the armor-plate; the Department officials and the business men and wage-workers who furnished what the Congress had authorized; the Secretaries of the Navy who asked for and expended the appropriations; and finally the officers who, in fair weather and foul, on actual sea service, trained and disciplined the crews of the ships when there was no war in sight—all are entitled to a full share in the glory of Manila and Santiago, and the respect accorded by every true American to those who wrought such signal triumph for our country. It was forethought and preparation which secured us the overwhelming triumph of 1898. If we fail to show forethought and preparation now, there may come a time when disaster will befall us instead of triumph; and should this time come, the fault will rest primarily, not upon those whom the accident of events puts in supreme command at the moment, but upon those who have failed to prepare in advance.

. . .

The American people must either build and maintain an adequate navy or else make up their minds definitely to accept a secondary position in international affairs, not merely in political, but in commercial matters. It has been well said that there is no surer way of courting national disaster than to be "opulent, aggressive, and unarmed."

It is not necessary to increase our Army beyond its present size at this time. But it is necessary to keep it at the highest point of efficiency. The individual units who as officers and enlisted men compose this Army are, we have good reason to believe, at least as efficient as those of any other army in the entire world. It is our duty to see that their training is of a kind to insure the highest possible expression of power to these units when acting in combination.

. . .

A general staff should be created. As for the present staff and supply departments, they should be filled by details from the line, the men so detailed returning after a while to their line duties. It is very undesirable to have the senior grades of the Army composed of men who have come to fill the positions by the mere fact of seniority. A system should be adopted by which there shall be an elimination grade by grade of those who seem unfit to render the best service in the next grade. Justice to the veterans of the Civil War who are still in the Army would seem to require that in the matter of retirements they be given by law the same privileges accorded to their comrades in the Navy.

The process of elimination of the least fit should be conducted in a manner that would render it practically impossible to apply political or social pressure on behalf of any candidate, so that each man may be judged purely on his own merits. Pressure for the promotion of civil officials for political reasons is bad enough, but it is tenfold worse where applied on behalf of officers of the Army or Navy. Every promotion and every detail under the War Department must be made solely with regard to the good of the service and to the capacity and merit of the man himself. No pressure, political, social, or personal, of any kind, will be permitted to exercise the least effect in any question of promotion or detail; and if there is reason to believe that such pressure is exercised at the instigation of the officer concerned, it will be held to militate against him. In our Army we cannot afford to have rewards or duties distributed save on the simple ground that those who by their own merits are entitled to the rewards get them, and that those who are peculiarly fit to do the duties are chosen to perform them.

. . .

Much good has already come from the act reorganizing the Army, passed early in the present year. The three prime reforms, all of them of literally inestimable value, are, first, the substitution of four-year details from the line for permanent appointments in the so-called staff divisions; second, the establishment of a corps of artillery with a chief at the head; third, the establishment of a maximum and minimum limit for the Army. It would be difficult to overestimate the improvement in the efficiency of our Army which these three reforms are making, and have in part already effected.

. . .

The consular service is now organized under the provisions of a law passed in 1856, which is entirely inadequate to existing conditions. The interest shown by so many commercial bodies throughout the country in the reorganization of the service is heartily commended to your attention. Several bills providing for a new consular service have in recent years been submitted to the Congress. They are based upon the just principle that appointments to the service should be made only after a practical test of the applicant's fitness, that promotions should be governed by trustworthiness, adaptability, and zeal in the performance of duty, and that the tenure of office should be unaffected by partisan considerations.

The guardianship and fostering of our rapidly expanding foreign commerce, the protection of American citizens resorting to foreign countries in lawful pursuit of their affairs, and the maintenance of the dignity of the Nation abroad, combine to make it essential that our consuls should be men of character, knowledge, and enterprise. It is true that the service is now, in the main, efficient, but a standard of excellence cannot be permanently maintained until the principles set forth in the bills heretofore submitted to the Congress on this subject are enacted into law.

. . .

Owing to the rapid growth of our power and our interests on the Pacific, whatever happens in China must be of the keenest national concern to us.

The general terms of the settlement of the questions growing out of the antiforeign uprisings in China of 1900, having been formulated in a joint note addressed to China by the representatives of the injured powers in December last, were promptly accepted by the Chinese Government. After protracted conferences the plenipotentiaries of the several powers were able to sign a final protocol with the Chinese plenipotentiaries on the 7th of last September, setting forth the measures taken by China in compliance with the demands of the joint note, and expressing their satisfaction therewith. It will be laid before the Congress, with a report of the plenipotentiary on behalf of the United States, Mr. William Woodville Rockhill, to whom high praise is due for the tact, good judgment, and energy he has displayed in performing an exceptionally difficult and delicate task.

The agreement reached disposes in a manner satisfactory to the powers of the various grounds of complaint, and will contribute materially to better future relations between China and the powers. Reparation has been made by China for the murder of foreigners during the uprising and punishment has been inflicted on the officials, however high in rank, recognized as responsible for or having participated in the outbreak. Official examinations have been forbidden for a period of five years in all cities in which foreigners have been murdered or cruelly treated, and edicts have been issued making all officials directly responsible for the future safety of foreigners and for the suppression of violence against them.

Provisions have been made for insuring the future safety of the foreign representatives in Peking by setting aside for their exclusive use a quarter of the city which the powers can make defensible and in which they can if necessary maintain permanent military guards; by dismantling the military works between the capital and the sea; and by allowing the temporary maintenance of foreign military posts along this line. An edict has been issued by the Emperor of China prohibiting for two years the importation of arms and ammunition into China. China has agreed to pay adequate indemnities to the states, societies, and individuals for the losses sustained by them and for the expenses of the military expeditions sent by the various powers to protect life and restore order.

Under the provisions of the joint note of December, 1900, China has agreed to revise the treaties of commerce and navigation and to take such other steps for the purpose of facilitating foreign trade as the foreign powers may decide to be needed.

The Chinese Government has agreed to participate financially in the work of bettering the water approaches to Shanghai and to Tientsin, the centers of foreign trade in central and northern China, and an international conservancy board, in which the Chinese Government is largely represented, has been provided for the improvement of the Shanghai River and the control of its navigation. In the same line of commercial advantages a revision of the present tariff on imports has been assented to for the purpose of substituting specific for *ad valorem* duties, and an expert has been sent abroad on the part of the United States to assist in this work. A list of articles to remain free of duty, including flour, cereals, and rice, gold and silver coin and bullion, has also been agreed upon in the settlement.

During these troubles our Government has unswervingly advocated moderation, and has materially aided in bringing about an adjustment which tends to enhance the welfare of China and to lead to a more beneficial intercourse between the Empire and the modern world; while in the critical period of revolt and massacre we did our full share in safeguarding life and property, restoring order, and vindicating the national interest and honor. It behooves us to continue in these paths, doing what lies in our power to foster feelings of good will, and leaving no effort untried to work out the great policy of full and fair intercourse between China and the nations, on a footing of equal rights and advantages to all. We advocate the "open door" with all that it implies; not merely the procurement of enlarged commercial opportunities on the coasts, but access to the interior by the waterways with which China has been so extraordinarily favored. Only by bringing the people of China into peaceful and friendly community of trade with all the peoples of the earth can the work now auspiciously begun be carried to fruition. In the attainment of this purpose we necessarily claim parity of treatment, under the conventions, throughout the Empire for our trade and our citizens with those of all other powers.

JAMES L. EWELL

With the great change in the House of Representatives in Congress and the possible tariff tinkering by the Democratic wing of the House, with a consequent decrease in domestic business, any reference to the immediate development of foreign markets is being received with increasing interest by all manufacturers able to take care of foreign orders.

To be perfectly candid and honest with ourselves, the average manufacturer has not got to the point where he is willing to admit the necessity of cultivating foreign markets. He must dissipate the fond idea that he has so long cherished, namely that the harvest of a great prosperous home business, so seductive with a large and immediate return of profits, cannot be experienced

Reprinted from James L. Ewell, "Developing Export Markets," AMERICAN INDUSTRIES, *XI (May, 1911), p. 22.*

in any other market on the globe. He hangs on too tenaciously to the hope that the conditions in the home market may remain rosy and productive of large returns. His better judgment tells him, away down deep in his heart, that with the enormous growth that the manufacturers of the United States have experienced in the last ten years, instead of complaining about the strange little burdens that are imposed by handling foreign shipments, he must bend his energies to surmounting these little molehills and reap the harvest of a great world's market which awaits him. Instead of being content to weather the storms of recurring depressions he should secure the great balance wheel of a world's market to overcome the gap occasioned by local conditions.

The panic of 1907–08 is perhaps the first occasion of the kind in the history of this country when American manufacturers recognized that though business conditions are paralyzed here, the business of the various foreign markets of the world is generally normal and capable of taking goods in large quantities. In 1907–08 manufacturers who had consistently and persistently cultivated the development of foreign markets for a period of ten to twenty years were able to testify in not a few cases that if it had not been for the checks and drafts accompanying orders for merchandise from foreign countries, which they used in paying off their help, that in the latter months of 1907 and the early months of 1908 they would have been compelled to close their factories.

There is criticism from many quarters with regard to reciprocity with Canada, but after all that can be said and done, is it not desirable that we enhance the possibilities of our trade relations with Canada as rapidly as possible? She is one of our largest customers after Great Britain. She is also our nearest neighbor and her conditions are almost the same as our own. Is there any commodity that she can produce more cheaply than the United States? If we buy more of her wheat, will she not buy more of our machinery and agricultural implements? Might it not be wise to have better and more reciprocal trade relations with the Latin-American republics as well? There is a great purchasing power in Argentina which is anxious to buy of us. These splendid markets, as we have been told by representatives of the United States abroad who have talked to the various members of our Association of Brazil and Venezuela, coming closer home, are open to increase their trade relations with us. Particularly important are the west coast states of South America, Chile, Peru and Colombia; the last not a manufacturing nation but developing her country entirely with machinery, implements and tools of every kind secured from foreign countries, makes less than one-sixth of her purchases through us, the balance from Europeans, who are much further away.

The time is past when our manufacturers may ask each other or the American consuls, what kind of products we can sell to these people, because the answer now is that almost everything that is manufactured in this country is capable of developing a foreign demand which will grow increasingly profitable to the manufacturer who will go after the business.

It is but natural that we should have this temporary lull in business, with the threatened changes in the tariff, and the promised reciprocity with Canada, together with the Supreme Court decisions fraught with such importance to some of the largest indus-

trial interests of our country. But in the end these will not count for much in the face of the best crop prospects that the country has ever known, and with a long series of wonderful crop years that can only be described in superlatives, for the past six or seven years. At worst it will only hold back the advance of commerce and trade in 1911 to a point where the railroads can handle the tonnage without complaining about car-shortage. With the increased foreign demand and with the prosperous home conditions, even with legislation by the most radical democracy and tariff revision, there can be but a temporary check upon the advance of commerce and trade in this great republic, which is looking now, as never before, to the four corners of the world.

Therefore let the American manufacturers face the situation and challenge the competition of the world. They can do it. There is no nation in the world, even with cheap pauper labor, that can hope to compete with them in controlling in the near future the markets of the world. If they but take heart with enthusiasm and put their shoulder to the wheel, the great progress of commerce and trade of this great republic will continue to advance to its manifest destiny. That being the case, let us use the means at hand. Those who cannot afford personal representation and send their travelers abroad, can utilize the next best thing offered by the greatest industrial organization in the world, that is, the official international organ of the National Association of Manufacturers, which is now reaching over 73,000 buyers in the world's markets and is able to carry them with the proper introduction to the furthermost outposts of civilization where business may be developed.

2. Anti-Imperialism

William Graham Sumner was a man of firm convictions, and he never shunned controversy when those convictions were involved. The champion of a self-regulating economic system and an implacable foe of bureaucratic government, he fought against all forces that might limit individual freedom of action. In this essay, first published in 1896, Sumner explained why he considered territorial expansion unnecessary and foolish.

WILLIAM GRAHAM SUMNER

The traditional belief is that a state aggrandizes itself by territorial extension, so that winning new land is gaining in wealth and prosperity, just as an individual would gain if he increased his land possessions. It is undoubtedly true that a state may be so small in territory and population that it cannot serve the true purposes of a state for its citizens, especially in international relations with neighboring states which control a large aggregate of men and capital. There is, therefore, under given circumstances, a size of territory and population which is at the maximum of advantage for the civil unit. The unification of Germany and Italy was apparently advantageous for the people affected. In the nineteenth century there has been a tendency to create national states, and nationality has been advocated as the true basis of state unity. The cases show, however, that the national unit does not necessarily coincide with the most advantageous state unit, and that the principle of nationality cannot override the historical accidents which have made the states. Sweden and Nor-

Reprinted from William Graham Sumner, "The Fallacy of Territorial Extension," WAR AND OTHER ESSAYS *(New Haven, 1911), pp. 285–289.*

way, possessing unity, threaten to separate. Austro-Hungary, a conglomerate of nationalities largely hostile to each other, will probably be held together by political necessity. The question of expedient size will always be one for the judgment and good sense of statesmen. The opinion may be risked that Russia has carried out a policy of territorial extension which has been harmful to its internal integration. For three hundred years it has been reaching out after more territory and has sought the grandeur and glory of conquest and size. To this it has sacrificed the elements of social and industrial strength. The autocracy has been confirmed and established because it is the only institution which symbolizes and maintains the unity of the great mass, and the military and tax burdens have distorted the growth of the society to such an extent as to produce disease and weakness.

Territorial aggrandizement enhances the glory and personal importance of the man who is the head of a dynastic state. The fallacy of confusing this with the greatness and strength of the state itself is an open pitfall close at hand. It might seem that a republic, one of whose chief claims to superiority over a monarchy lies in avoiding the danger of confusing the king with the state, ought to be free from this fallacy of national greatness, but we have plenty of examples to prove that the traditional notions are not cut off by changing names and forms.

The notion that gain of territory is gain of wealth and strength for the state, after the expedient size has been won, is a delusion. In the Middle Ages the beneficial interest in land and the jurisdiction over the people who lived on it were united in one person. The modern great states, upon their formation, took to themselves the jurisdiction, and the beneficial interest turned into full property in land. The confusion of the two often reappears now, and it is one of the most fruitful causes of fallacy in public questions. It is often said that the United States owns silver-mines, and it is inferred that the policy of the state in regard to money and currency ought to be controlled in some way by this fact. The "United States," as a subject of property rights and of monetary claims and obligations, may be best defined by calling it the "Fiscus." This legal person owns no silver-mines. If it did, it could operate them by farming them or by royalties. The revenue thus received would lower taxes. The gain would inure to all the people in the United States. The body politic named the United States has nothing to do with the silver-mines except that it exercises jurisdiction over the territory in which they lie. If it levies taxes on them it also incurs expenses for them, and as it wins no profits on its total income and outgo, these must be taken to be equal. It renders services for which it exacts only the cost thereof. The beneficial and property interest in the mines belongs to individuals, and they win profits only by conducting the exploitation of the mines with an expenditure of labor and capital. These individuals are of many nationalities.

They alone own the product and have the use and enjoyment of it. No other individuals, American or others, have any interest, right, duty, or responsibility in the matter. The United States has simply provided the protection of its laws and institutions for the mine-workers while they were carrying on their enterprise. Its jurisdiction was only a burden to it, not a profitable good. Its jurisdiction was a boon to the mine-workers and certainly did not entail further obligation.

It is said that the boundary between Alaska and British America runs through a gold field, and some people are in great anxiety as to who will "grab it." If an American can go over to the English side and mine gold there for his profit, under English laws and jurisdiction, and an Englishman can come over to the American side and mine gold there for his profit, under American laws and jurisdiction, what difference does it make where the line falls? The only case in which it would make any difference is where the laws and institutions of the two states were not on equal stages of enlightenment.

This case serves to bring out distinctly a reason for the old notion of territorial extension which is no longer valid. In the old colonial system, states conquered territories or founded colonies in order to shut them against all other states and to exploit them on principles of subjugation and monopoly. It is only under this system that the jurisdiction is anything but a burden.

If the United States should admit Hawaii to the Union, the Fiscus of the former state would collect more taxes and incur more expenses. The circumstances are such that the latter would probably be the greater. The United States would not acquire a square foot of land in property unless it paid for it. Individual Americans would get no land to till without paying for it and would win no products from it except by wisely expending their labor and capital on it. All that they can do now. So long as there is a government on the islands, native or other, which is competent to guarantee peace, order, and security, no more is necessary, and for any outside power to seize the jurisdiction is an unjustifiable aggression. That jurisdiction would be the best founded which was the most liberal and enlightened, and would give the best security to all persons who sought the islands upon their lawful occasions. The jurisdiction would, in any case, be a burden, and any state might be glad to see any other state assume the burden, provided that it was one which could be relied upon to execute the charge on enlightened principles for the good of all. The best case is, therefore, always that in which the resident population produce their own state by the institutions of self-government.

What private individuals want is free access, under order and security, to any part of the earth's surface, in order that they may avail themselves of its natural resources for their use, either by investment or commerce. If, therefore, we could have free trade with Hawaii while somebody else had the jurisdiction, we should gain all the advantages and escape all the burdens. The Constitution of the United States establishes absolute free trade between all parts of the territory under its jurisdiction. A large part of our population was thrown into indignant passion because the Administration rejected the annexation of Hawaii, regarding it like the act of a man who refuses the gift of a farm. These persons were generally those who are thrown into excitement by any proposition of free trade. They will not, therefore, accept free trade with the islands while somebody else has the trouble and burden of the jurisdiction, but they would accept free trade with the islands eagerly if they could get the burden of the jurisdiction too.

III. RECENT INTERPRETATION

The following selection, taken from William A. Williams' interpretive essay, *The Great Evasion,* provides a novel treatment of economic influences on foreign policy. It differs in several ways from the work of Archibald Cary Coolidge, who saw economic prosperity as a major cause of overseas expansion after 1898. Unlike Coolidge, Williams draws heavily on the writings of Karl Marx in developing his analysis. This furnishes him with a vehicle for arguing a number of points: that the United States has always been a colonial power; that both industrial productivity and fear of depression gave rise to the strategy of building an informal, commercial empire; and that the Open Door notes represented a succinct statement of that strategy. This selection is in large measure a summary of ideas Williams has explored more fully elsewhere, particularly in *The Tragedy of American Diplomacy.*

WILLIAM A. WILLIAMS

Marx's particular emphasis on foreign policy as a way to generate recovery in the context of economic crisis is also verified by American behavior. The trans-Appalachian depression that developed between 1808 and 1811, and which hit the farmers hard, had a direct causative connection with the agitation that elected the War Hawks and led to the War of 1812. Expansion into Mexico began in the downturn after the War of 1812, and matured into an imperial clash ultimately involving war during the panics and the depression of the late 1830's. The same pattern appears in the late 1860's and the 1870's, though it is somewhat camouflaged by taking the form, at least primarily, of the North's extension of its economic control over the South and the West.

Americans again began to react more explicitly and generally to depressions by turning to economic expansion during the business troubles of the 1880's, a decade when surplus production began to pose a problem in some industries as well as in agriculture. This response crystallized during the panic and depression of the 1890's and prompted the appearance of a good many general theories about the necessity of such expansion. Such ideas played a double role: they served as an explanation of what was happening, and they offered a solution for the difficulties of the system. As a result, they were a primary causative force in the imperial expansion of the period.

This emphasis on overseas economic expansion, through both exports and

Reprinted from William Appleman Williams, THE GREAT EVASION *(Chicago: Quadrangle Books, 1964), pp. 36–45.*

investments, was an integral part of the New Deal program for recovery from the Great Depression. And it was the central theme of the discussions during 1943–1945 concerning the best way to handle the depression that was expected to develop at the end of World War II. The same approach has been increasingly emphasized during the series of postwar recessions. The New Frontier's stress on the expansion of exports and the creation of regional markets tied to the American system is candidly explained and defended as a solution for the specific difficulties of the domestic economy and the more general problems incident to the breakdown of the nineteenth-century imperial system.

Marx recognized and understood that the imperial relationship that evolved out of such economic expansion could take several forms. One of these is colonialism, which involves the seizure or conquest of empty, or lightly populated, real estate and the subsequent transfer of other people into the new area. It is accompanied by direct and extensive controls over the new society, as well as over the displaced or conquered population. Americans take great pride, of course, in denying any colonial blemish upon their historical record. This case is debatable even if colonialism is defined or thought of, as it usually is by Americans, as involving action across the open sea.

But there is no serious justification for making the crossing of water a necessary condition of colonialism. The essential definition is the control of territory and resources, and the displacement, re-establishment, and control of human beings. American policy toward the Indian, and toward the Negro from 1650 to 1863, certainly satisfies those criteria and therefore belies the assertion that the United States has never been a colonial power. It is customary and accurate to talk about the Negro during those years as a slave, but slavery is only the most extreme form of colonial exploitation. In any event, the Negro was transported across the sea in the course of being colonized.

There was also a significant degree of colonialism involved in the economic and political controls exercised by the American Metropolis over the Western territories. Jefferson's attitude toward the non-English settlers in the region acquired through the Louisiana Purchase is symbolic, not only of the discrepancy between his rhetoric and his policy, but also of the general attitude of the East toward the new settlements across the mountains. The foreigners could acquiesce or leave, Jefferson announced; otherwise force would be used against them.

The process by which the settlements beyond the Appalachians were ultimately accepted as full members of the federal commonwealth does not offer as great an exception to the usual colonial pattern as latter-day Americans are inclined to assume. For one thing, the final agreement to admit such areas as states was not achieved without overt resistance by the territories against being treated as colonies. The agitation of the 1780's, for example, had a great deal to do with overcoming Easterners who wanted to handle the trans-Appalachian region as a colony in the traditional British manner.

In the final plan, moreover, the Metropolis was given many explicit controls over a territory until it was admitted as a state, and these opened the way for outsiders to establish their power and authority in less formal ways. It often took a generation (if not longer) for the new state to break free of the resulting institutionalized influence. Nor was statehood granted by the Metropolis with any noticeable dispatch. After the Civil War, for example, only two territories (Nebraska and Colorado) gained legal equality during a period of twenty-four years. As might be imagined, this artificial and protracted delay reinforced and intensified other causes involved in the West's antagonism and resistance toward outsiders.

A second kind of imperial relationship that Marx recognized and discussed is the form of administrative colonialism evolved by the British in India during and after the 1850's. This pattern is characterized by the effective control by an outside minority, through force and the threat of force, of alien territory and population, and by its concurrent establishment of economic predominance. It does not involve, as with colonialism per se, the large-scale transfer of population under the direction and control of the Metropolis. There is emigration from the Metropolis, but it is strictly limited both in numbers and direct function. Its object is to provide a military force in being in support of the leadership necessary for the effective control and management of the political economy of the subject society. The emigrants thus comprise an absolute and a relatively small group of army and naval personnel, political administrators, and economic directors. The success of the system, and of the agents of the Metropolis, is measured by the degree to which absentee control of crucial decisions is institutionalized within the framework of native self-government in local affairs, and routinely maintained domestic political and social peace.

American administrative colonialism appears most classically in the cases of Cuba and the Philippines. All the features of the system were apparent: the colony's own internal cleavage between town and country, its imbalanced, limited, and skewed development, and the improvement purchased at the price of drastic costs in human and material resources, and in harmful consequences to the social fabric itself. The same pattern, with variations appropriate to the circumstances, has emerged in American relations with Liberia and many Latin-American countries, such as Nicaragua and Guatemala. And the current American relationships with Okinawa, South Korea, and Vietnam follow the main outlines of such administrative colonial empire.

The third principal form of the imperial relationship emerges in the evolution of the inherent nature of the marketplace connection between a Metropolis and a backward, underdeveloped region or society. It arises out of the imbalance between the two societies which produces the situation so aptly described by Adam Smith: "The revenue of a trading and manufacturing country must, other things being equal, always be much greater than that of one without trade or manufactures. . . . A country without trade or manufactures is generally obliged to purchase, at the expense of a great part of its rude produce, a very small part of the manufactured produce of other countries." Or as described by Karl Marx: "The favored country recovers more labor in exchange for less labor." Or, to phrase it in the language of our own time, the price received by the underdeveloped country for its goods and services does not suffice to pay for the goods and services it requires to initiate and sustain its own development. For that matter, in many cases the prices set by the Metropolis for such goods decline so much that the loss to the underdeveloped country is not even made up by grants or loans provided by the Metropolis.

Even under the most favorable circumstances, therefore, the gap between the rich and the poor remains constant or decreases only in tiny and sporadic increments. At worst (and more usually), the increases take the form of creeping impoverishment in the poorer nation. Or, as Marx put it, in a kind of increasing misery and increasing proletarianization. It is essential to realize that, whatever the evidence indicates as to increasing misery within the Metropolis, the facts of the world capitalist marketplace support Marx's analysis. He was correct. The poor are poorer and more miserable.

While force is periodically employed, and formal agents from the Metropolis occasionally take a direct hand in managing the affairs of the weaker society, neither action is a routine, institutionalized part of this variant of the imperial relationship. British historians have recently used the phrases, "the imperialism of free trade" and "informal empire," to describe this pattern, and their suggestions seem astute, accurate, and convenient. As Marx clearly understood, the system evolves from the basic capitalist conception of the market and the marketplace as the Metropolis expands into the backward area.

The marketplace is an integrated, two-way relationship involving access to raw materials as well as export markets for goods, services, and investment capital. Marx understood these reasons that lay behind the expansionist arguments developed by American farmers and industrial leaders. They pointed out the marginal utility of foreign operations and explained why it was rational to sell at a loss overseas in order to avoid the economic and social costs of shutting down when the domestic demand was satisfied. In addition to saving capital and avoiding labor unrest, such practices offered an effective strategy for entering and winning control of foreign markets.

American foreign relations since 1895 provide the central historical illustration of this kind of imperial expansion. The informal empire of the United States in the twentieth century offers an example of the character, dynamism, and consequences of the capitalist marketplace that is even purer in form and substance than the one provided by British expansion after the middle of the nineteenth century. The famous Open Door Notes of 1899 and 1900 were consciously and brilliantly formulated on the assumption that America possessed the necessary and overwhelming economic power vis-à-vis other advanced industrial powers, as well as the weaker, poorer countries, and on the conviction that Adam Smith was correct in holding that such strength would enable the United States to control the world marketplace if it was defined as a fair field with favor to none.

Given this belief in the fundamental economic preponderance of their system, American policy-makers designed their imperial strategy with a view to creating and maintaining the conditions which would enable their nation's power to produce the desired economic and political victories. Since they viewed war as the great disrupter of economic progress, and as the night-rider of political and social regression, their broad objective was to establish rules of the game which would prevent the struggle in the marketplace from becoming a trial by arms.

The Open Door Notes sought to do this in Asia (and later, in other regions, such as Africa) by committing America's industrial rivals to the following principles of policy and action: (1) a prohibition on further division and colonization of such areas as China; (2) existing and subsequent regulations within established spheres of interest

to apply equally to all competitors; and (3) equal opportunity to be afforded to all rivals in all future economic activity.

While the strategy did not succeed in preventing subsequent wars, it is crucial to realize that the United States entered such conflicts to defend and to re-establish the Open Door Policy. In an important degree, moreover, America was drawn into those wars because of antagonisms arising out of the effectiveness of its performance within the limits set by the principles of the Open Door Policy. This was true in the positive sense of American economic penetration and influence in the world marketplace after 1900, as well as in the negative sense that the Open Door Policy appeared to competitors as an obstacle to their own progress. In this respect, at any rate, the policy was effective enough in its actual or potential economic operation to subvert its political and military objectives.

The evolution and adoption of the Open Door Policy involved one of the truly majestic ironies of American—and perhaps even Western—history. Men like Theodore Roosevelt and Henry Cabot Lodge initially favored a vigorous kind of administrative colonialism as the proper strategy of American expansion. Not unjustly, therefore, they came to be known as Imperialists. Their critics and opponents, men like Andrew Carnegie, William Jennings Bryan, and Edward Atkinson, claimed and were known by the label of Anti-Imperialists. This likewise was true and fair enough as a description of their position on traditional colonialism, or even formal and extensive administrative colonialism.

But the Anti-Imperialists were actually men who understood and advocated the very kind of informal empire that Adam Smith and Karl Marx maintained was created by the inherent imbalance of the marketplace relationship between the advanced industrial Metropolis and the poor, backward, agrarian societies. To begin with, the Anti-Imperialists argued that the economic and other institutional requirements of colonialism or widespread administrative colonialism would slow down and limit the accumulation of capital at home, would progressively limit essential bourgeois freedoms, and would breed social unrest. They added that such a strategy of expansion would also encourage and sustain resistance movements in the dependencies and lead to wars with other advanced nations. Taken together, such consequences would be very apt to subvert economic and political liberty at home, and might even bring about the destruction of the empire itself. To avoid such dangers, yet enjoy the necessary expansion of the marketplace, the Anti-Imperialists rested their strategy of empire on the very principle that Adam Smith advanced.

The Anti-Imperialists and Smith were correct. The Open Door Policy worked magnificently for half a century —surely as effectively as the European forms of colonialism and administrative colonialism. American economic power expanded throughout the world, into the other advanced countries as well as into the underdeveloped regions (including European colonies and spheres of interest), and came ultimately and literally to dominate the world capitalist marketplace. And, measured either in absolute terms or relatively against the performance of the older patterns of empire, the United States was required to employ but small amounts of force between 1900 and 1950 in order to maintain its imperial relationship with the weaker countries. Within the assumptions of the system, American

economic power as deployed with considerably more astuteness, and managed with more finesse and sophistication, than either its advocates or its critics are often prone to admit. In addition to the huge profits returned to the United States, the result was the creation of a pattern of domestic politics within the "country" side of the empire that sustained pro-American rulers in power for the great majority of the years since 1900.

But Karl Marx was also correct. The inherent drive within the advanced countries to accumulate capital and to expand and control the marketplace, and the resulting increasing proletarianization and misery in the subject half of the empire, has led to more and increasingly violent conflict. American entry into World War I was at bottom predicated upon the conclusion, reached by both top economic and high political leaders, that the United States could not risk being excluded from what appeared to be the probable reorganization of the world marketplace on terms that would seriously restrict, if not actually subvert, the operation of the Open Door Policy.

Both the Allies and the Central powers had made it clear by 1916 that they would transform a military and political victory into an economic system strongly favorable to themselves. Wilson's emphasis on his famous Fourteen Points, and his insistence on the Covenant of the League of Nations, involved far more than transcendental idealism. Those programs were designed to apply the axioms of the Open Door Policy to the world and, through the crucial Article X of the Covenant, to guarantee their observance for an indefinite future. The same considerations, even more explicitly avowed, lie at the heart of American involvement in World War II and the Cold War.

HISTORIOGRAPHICAL NOTE

That the years between the close of the Civil War and the coming of World War I marked the emergence of the United States as a great power is a conventional—not to say trite—observation. Contemporary historians made much of the nation's changing relationship to other parts of the world. The seventh volume of the *Cambridge Modern History* (London and New York, 1903) contains an essay by John Bassett Moore under the title "The United States as a World Power (1885–1902)." Lecturing at the Sorbonne in the winter of 1906–07, Archibald Cary Coolidge undertook development of the same theme, and shortly thereafter he published his book, *The United States as a World Power* (New York, 1908). In the meantime, John H. Latane had written the final volume of A. B. Hart's "American Nation" series, *America as a World Power* (New York, 1907). A concept so generally and emphatically enunciated was not to be lightly renounced or easily refuted; that the United States entered the twentieth century as the newest of the great powers became, in fact, a common assumption of monographs and textbooks alike.

Recognizing the great power status of the United States was not, however, the same as *approving* of that status or the means by which it was achieved. In the period after World War I especially, when disillusionment with political and military involvement in world affairs ran high, historians took a critical backward look at earlier American policy. Walter Millis wrote *The Martial Spirit* (Boston, 1931) to show that the United States entered the conflict against Spain in 1898 because the jingoism of the yellow press had aroused war hysteria. Julius W. Pratt in *The Expansionists of 1898* (Baltimore, 1936) saw enthusiasm for expansion arising out of social Darwinism and ethnocentric missionary zeal. Henry F. Pringle's *Theodore Roosevelt* (New York, 1931) sneered at Roosevelt's imperialistic bluster. Another biography, Tyler Dennett's *John Hay: From Poetry to Politics* (New York, 1933), considered the Open Door policy in China a misfortune and an embarrassment. And A. Whitney Griswold, in *The Far Eastern Policy of the United States* (New York, 1938), found that the Open Door idea had actually originated with an Englishman and that it did not represent the best interests of the United States.

But if the isolationist sentiment of the period between world wars found its way into historical studies, so also did the changing American mood of the late thirties and the forties. After the failure of attempts to placate Hitler at Munich, the use of force no longer seemed so reprehensible. Strongly affected by the struggle against Nazi Germany and by development of the Cold War, many historians began to take what they believed to be a more realistic approach to the study of foreign policy. Robert S.

Osgood, for example, in *Ideals and Self-Interest in America's Foreign Relations* (Chicago, 1953), argued that appeals to national honor and moral duty were responsible not only for aberrations in American foreign relations but for later disillusionment as well. A realistic assessment of the national interest, he argued, was the only safe guide in foreign-policy-making. The most influential historian of the realist school, however, was George F. Kennan whose ideas as expressed in *American Diplomacy, 1900–1950* (Chicago, 1951) were to have a profound influence on American policy during the Truman-Eisenhower era.

While such historians as Osgood and Kennan were more concerned with shaping policy than with accounting for the rise of the United States to world power, Ernest R. May took what he described as a Rankean stance. That is to say, in *Imperial Democracy: The Emergence of America as a Great Power* (New York, 1961), he sought to explain what actually happened, not what course of action the United States should have taken. Exploring archives in London, Paris, Madrid, Vienna, and the United States, he uncovered abundant evidence that European diplomats had come to recognize the United States as a great power by the 1890's. Yet he saw little conscious planning on the part of those responsible for American policy; the nation, he concluded, had greatness thrust upon it.

Such an argument failed to satisfy other investigators who found a good measure of understanding on the part of both political and business leaders. Especially important in advancing this viewpoint was William Appleman Williams, whose *The Tragedy of American Diplomacy* (Cleveland, 1959) contended that the essence of American policy was market expansion, not acquisition of colonies. Indeed, the United States followed a program of "imperial anticolonialism" which found expression in the Open Door and remained the basic American strategy for half a century. Many of Williams' insights found corroboration in Walter LaFeber's *The New Empire: An Interpretation of American Expansion, 1860–1898* (Ithaca, 1963) and in Thomas J. McCormick's *China Market* (Chicago, 1967). Far from being the result of momentary enthusiasm, LaFeber and McCormick suggested, expansionism was the consequence of long and careful planning, and it was based on the idea that foreign markets were essential to American well-being. Whatever the merits of the Williams thesis, however, it has won acceptance from only a portion of the historical profession. Thus the historical debate about the foundations of American foreign policy continues with a vigor that parallels the passion of controversies arising from the Cold War.

13. Progressivism: New Nationalism, New Freedom, and New Era

INTRODUCTION

The years from the Spanish-American War to World War I were years of prosperity, but the typical American sought more than material well-being. Profound social and economic changes forced him to pursue accommodation to a dynamic society. An urban revolution accompanied the growth of industry; people from scattered farms and rural hamlets, together with immigrants from the Old World, flocked to the great cities. Back in 1896, when William Jennings Bryan warned that the destruction of agriculture would precipitate a national calamity and cause grass to grow in city streets, census returns indicated that less than 40 per cent of the population could be classified as urban. By 1920, on the other hand, the Bureau of the Census reported that for the first time in the nation's history more people lived in urban than in rural areas. This demographic change coincided with an expansion of intellectual and commercial horizons. New institutions of learning, new methods of teaching, and a rigorous new scholarship helped to produce an exciting period in the development of higher education. At the same time military successes in the war with Spain and the prospect of opening markets overseas brought to many Americans a sense of power, a consciousness of world-wide interest.

A generation that took seriously the homilies of preachers and the platitudes of politicians tended to view in a moral perspective the adjustments made necessary by changing patterns of life. Connotations of the word "progressive"—the term eventually used to describe the period of adaptation—in themselves suggest an ordering of change to values implicit in the inherited popular culture. Many currents of thought ran through the early years of the twentieth century, of course, and ideas jostled one another. Those who regarded themselves as progressives did so out of a variety of motives: some felt guilty about the iniquities that industrialism produced; some resented a loss of the influence they believed to be slipping into the hands of *nouveaux riches;* some opportunistically seized on progressivism as a means of satisfying ambitions for public office; some accepted a measure of reform as the least of many possible evils. But whatever form progressivism took, and whatever might be said about its psychological or sociological roots, progressives themselves at some point al-

188

ways justified with moral arguments the numerous projects they undertook.

The moralism of the progressives, which found expression in rhetorical generalization, provided a sense of coherence for a movement that had little programmatic unity. Penetrating the generalizations and probing the substratum of progressive thought leads to the discovery of protean multiformity. When faced with what seemed at the time to be problems of immediate importance, such as what to do about business combinations and monopolies, progressives tended to divide. One group, believing in the benefits of competition and fearing that concentrated economic power would destroy the essential structure of democracy, urged legislation to restrain the growth of "trusts." Another aligned itself with Theodore Roosevelt, who thought such legislation represented a retrograde "rural toryism." This school of progressives held that the twentieth century had ushered in a new era of business organization and that while big business should be made to behave, it should not be destroyed.

The debate over industrial organization revealed equivocation and obscurity on both sides. Participants at times seemed uncertain in their own minds about what they wanted. There was, for example, considerable ambiguity in Woodrow Wilson's remark, "I am for big business and I am against the trusts." The uncertainty of progressives themselves, perhaps as much as Wilsonian decline or business ascendancy, brought a waning of interest in trust regulation and half-hearted enforcement of measures already enacted. But the debates on business and industrial organization had results that were not simply negative. More and more the protagonists tended to converge on the question of efficiency, and concern with efficiency led a large number of progressives to accept the rationale of a new era of business enterprise in the 1920's. Using leaders as symbols, one could argue that the conflict between Theodore Roosevelt and Woodrow Wilson produced Herbert Hoover.

I. EARLY INTERPRETATIONS

The historiography of progressivism has never been static; the two selections that follow illustrate an early modification in the interpretation of pre-World War I reform. The first is from Benjamin Parke De Witt's *The Progressive Movement,* one of the initial studies of progressive reform agitation, published in 1915. Here De Witt discerns three tendencies that underlay the movement and gave it cohesion.

The second selection appeared twelve years after De Witt's *Progressive Movement.* Taken from *The Rise of American Civilization* by Charles A. Beard, it contains a hint of the disillusionment that was to influence later scholars. Yet the two authors, the one optimistic and confident that justice would be achieved and the other saddened by the ineffectiveness of reform effort, had at least one common characteristic: both sympathized with the objectives of the progressives. In this sense Beard, as much as De Witt, wrote from within a progressive frame of reference.

BENJAMIN PARKE DE WITT

The term "progressive movement" has been so widely used, so much discussed, and so differently interpreted that any exposition of its meaning and principles, to be adequate, must be prefaced by careful definition. To some —comparatively few—the progressive movement stands for the attempt of one man, disappointed in his efforts to control his political party, to found another and return himself to power. To others, who are willing to concede that the movement is not confined to a single leader, it represents the efforts of a small body of self-seeking politicians to gain position and influence by making capital of a movement that is temporarily popular. To others, the movement expresses the effort of a few sincere but misguided enthusiasts to carry out an impossible and chimerical program of social reform through government and legislation. Some believe that the movement is partisan, limited to the party that bears its name; others believe that it is broader than any single party and that its supporters are found in political parties everywhere. Some believe it is new, fleeting, and evanescent, destined to disappear quickly from our political life; others hold that it is permanent, deep-seated, and fundamental, involving a modification and readjustment of our political theories and institutions.

Whatever difference of opinion may exist concerning the meaning of the progressive movement, every thinking man and woman must be convinced that the nation today is passing through a severe political crisis. After a period of unprecedented industrial and commercial expansion, during which time little or no attention has been given to the problems of government, the people have suddenly realized that government is not functioning properly and that radical changes are needed. Manifestations of this excitement and unrest are seen on every hand. Men write of a new democracy [1] and a new freedom.[2] In 1912 the vote of the Socialist party—the party of protest against existing conditions—almost reached the million mark; and in the same year a new political party, appealing to new ideals and new standards, polled four million votes. The Democratic party in the nation, after a stormy convention, nominated and elected as President, in 1912, a leader who insists upon high standards of public service; and the Republican party, chastened by defeat, and forced to recognize the present political tendencies, has already set about the work of party regeneration in many states. Everywhere there are evidences that the nation has passed into a new political era.

In this widespread political agitation that at first sight seems so incoherent and chaotic, there may be distinguished upon examination and analysis three tendencies. The first of these tenden-

Reprinted from Benjamin Parke De Witt, THE PROGRESSIVE MOVEMENT (New York, 1915), pp. 3–5, 13–25.

[1] Weyl, The New Democracy.
[2] Wilson, The New Freedom.

cies is found in the insistence by the best men in all political parties that special, minority, and corrupt influence in government—national, state, and city—be removed; the second tendency is found in the demand that the structure or machinery of government, which has hitherto been admirably adapted to control by the few, be so changed and modified that it will be more difficult for the few, and easier for the many, to control; and, finally, the third tendency is found in the rapidly growing conviction that the functions of government at present are too restricted and that they must be increased and extended to relieve social and economic distress. These three tendencies with varying emphasis are seen today in the platform and program of every political party; they are manifested in the political changes and reforms that are advocated and made in the nation, the states, and the cities; and, because of their universality and definiteness, they may be said to constitute the real progressive movement.

. . .

At the close of the [Civil] war, the Democratic party, the party that advocated limited federal powers, lay prostrate, discredited, the party of rebellion. The Republicans, unmolested, began to build up a strong party organization. All things were favorable to the preëmption of the government. The temptation was not long in coming. It had come before the war even. Railroads sprang up all over the country; industrial corporations of Brobdingnagian proportions put in their appearance. Strong men were behind the railroads and the corporations; they were also behind the Republican party. Here was an opportunity to extend the powers of government—to use government. Here was a government designed by its makers to be controlled by a wealthy minority. The wealthy minority were not slow in seizing the opportunity. Land grants, franchise steals, favorable court decisions, supple politicians, appeared in a bewildering array. Long before the country realized it, the government was being *used* —not in the interests of the many, but in the interests of the few.

Instinctively, men turned to each other for support. They did not at first turn to the government for relief. They were still under the delusion that the government was a dispassionate, fair arbiter; and that was what they desired it to be. The workmen of the country tried to fight their own fight. They formed labor unions and attempted to force all those engaged in a certain craft to join. Capitalists had joined together: labor would join together, too; and united labor would oppose a solid front to united capital.

But the fight was too unequal. Capital, wealth, and the corporations did not play fair. The government was theirs and they used it with deadly effect. They secured what their opponents bitterly called government by injunction; they had laws limiting the number of hours a day a man might work declared unconstitutional; they fought factory regulation. Meanwhile, they strengthened their own resources. Stolen franchises were ratified; inflated capitalization was given legal confirmation; the tariff was adjusted to meet their needs.

The idea that permanent relief from oppressive conditions could be obtained only through governmental intervention slowly gained ground. Those who proposed the idea at first were called revolutionists and socialists and were regarded as visionaries. Soon, however, the government was appealed to in various ways to change existing conditions. Railroads could be curbed by commissions, the tariff could be lowered, corporations could be dissolved, incomes could be taxed. The people were under the delusion that they owned the government; they had used it little: now, they thought, it would have to succor them. Government and legislation would bring in the millennium.

Singularly enough, the government was not sensitive to popular appeal. Sometimes, indeed, it openly defied the people. For a long time, the people could not realize what had happened —the people could not understand that their government had passed beyond their control. They came to the government which they had made, intending to use it, and they found that it was already in use.

The people paused in their search for remedial legislation to discover what was wrong with their government. They found that the government was run in strict accordance with the famous dictum attributed to Andrew Jackson, "To the victor belong the spoils." Incompetent, self-seeking, venal politicians were directing the affairs of the country. The people began to study the origin, history, and effect of the spoils system. They found that the spoils system had not always existed. The revolutionary presidents made honesty, capability, and fidelity the tests of fitness. "With Jackson's administration in 1830, the deluge of the spoils system burst over our national politics." [3] As time went on and the number of offices increased, the system grew worse. Startling disclosures of dishonesty were made in Grant's administration. Some of the President's secretaries were found guilty of bribery and corruption. General Babcock, the Presi-

dent's private secretary, narrowly escaped conviction on the charge of corruptly aiding the Whisky Ring to avoid the payment of revenues. It was proved that Belknap, Secretary of War, had received a portion of an annual payment of from six to twelve thousand dollars of bribe money given by a post trader at Fort Sill to retain his place.[4] The people clamored for reform. In response to the popular cry for civil service reform, based upon the belief that much of the corruption in government had its basis in the spoils system, President Grant in 1871 appointed a commission to investigate the subject. A second commission was appointed in 1883. Backed by popular sentiment, these and succeeding commissions placed under the protection of civil service hundreds of thousands of government employees.

The search for the source of special influence in government soon passed from individual corruption in other directions. Railroads began to be searchingly investigated. It was time attention was directed toward the railroads and their relation to special influence in government. "The progress of the construction of railroads in the United States was comparatively slow until assistance was granted by Congress. This was given under the form of donations of the public lands, for the first time, in 1850." [5] The first of these grants of land was made to the Illinois Central, and embraced 2,595,053 acres. Between 1850 and 1870 the total area granted to roads through the various states exceeded 60,000,000 acres. In addition to these grants, extensive grants were made later to the three Pacific railroads. These latter amounted to 135,-

[3] Curtis, Speech on Spoils System, *Harper's Encyclopaedia of United States History*, Vol. 2.

[4] Hart, *The American Nation—A History*, Vol. 22, pp. 281 *et seq.*

[5] Appleton's *American Annual Cyclopaedia*, 1871, pp. 672 *et seq.*

000,000 acres or about 200,000 square miles.

The mania for building railroads and granting lands abated somewhat about 1875, and people began to direct their attention to the control of the roads already in existence. As far back as 1852 we find a provision in the platform of a minor political party, the Free Soil Democrats, "that the public lands of the United States belong to the people, and should not be sold to individuals nor granted to corporations." These protests continued until finally all the important parties joined in the protest against any further grants. In a convention of the National Association of Transportation and Commerce held in Chicago in 1875, the vice-president of the association in his opening address emphasized the need of inquiring "whether there is less danger in leaving the property and industrial interests of the people thus wholly at the mercy of a few men who recognize no responsibility but to their stockholders and no principle of action but personal and corporate aggrandizement, than in adding somewhat to the power and patronage of a government directly responsible to the people, and entirely under their control." [6] The convention appointed a committee of seven to present their resolution to Congress. The resolution provided generally for national supervision of rates, capitalization, passes, etc.

Meanwhile, the states were taking similar action. In 1879 the State Grange at a meeting held at Montpelier, Vermont, framed and sent a set of resolutions to Congress asking relief from "the giant monopolies." In 1871 Illinois had passed a law creating the Railroad and Warehouse Commission.[7] In speaking of the reasons for the appointment of that commission, the governor, in a message to the state legislature, said: "They (the railroads) discriminated against persons and places. Citizens protested against these abuses in vain. The railroad corporations, when threatened with the power of the government, indulged in the language of defiance, and attempted to control legislation to their own advantage. At last, public indignation became excited against them. They did not heed it; they believed that the courts would be their refuge from popular fury."

The form of control usually adopted by the states was that of a commission to regulate rates and other matters connected with the railroads. The first of these state commissions was appointed in Massachusetts in 1869. Then came the Illinois Commission in 1871. Iowa, Minnesota, and Wisconsin soon followed. The railroads appealed to the highest courts in the states to declare the laws regulating rates unconstitutional. When they were defeated in the states, they carried their cases to the United States Supreme Court, only to be again defeated in a famous line of decisions known as the "Granger Cases." [8]

State regulation, of necessity, proved ineffectual. Many of the largest and most offensive railroads did business in several states and could not be controlled by state laws or state commissions. An appeal was therefore made to Congress to pass a law providing for a commission similar to the various state commissions to control interstate commerce as the individual states controlled intra-state commerce. In the

[6] Appleton's *American Annual Cyclopaedia,* 1875, p. 672. The last part of the statement is very naïve.

[7] *Ibid.,* 1879, p. 483.
[8] 94 U.S., pp. 113 *et seq.*

House of Representatives on January 5, 1881, the bill to establish a board of commissioners of interstate commerce was taken up. The bill apparently had few advocates and many opponents. The activity of the railroad interests was everywhere apparent. Mr. Reagan, representative from Texas, in closing his speech in favor of federal control, but not in favor of a commission, said: "I know, sir, in all preceding discussion here in this House, in our committee, in the committee of the Senate, the lawyers and managers of railroads have attempted to confuse this subject by saying that members of Congress, by their vocation were not qualified to regulate railroad traffic. . . . They have said that none can do it but experts. God deliver this country if its interests are placed in the hands of railroad experts, in the interest of railroad companies, under the dictation of railroad officers!" [9] The account of the debate in Congress closes with the significant words, "Subsequently, on March 1st, the House refused further to consider the bill." [10]

In the first session of the Forty-ninth Congress, which convened Monday, Dec. 7, 1885, as usual, a bill to regulate interstate commerce came up, and as usual no final action was taken.[11] The next year, however, the opposition had to yield. A bill providing for an Interstate Commerce Commission to control common carriers engaged in interstate commerce passed through Congress in that year. The act has since been substantially amended and made more effective, but even then it was a great step in advance. It is significant that among those who opposed the measure to the very end were Senator Aldrich of Rhode Island, Senator Evarts of New York, and Senator Hoar of Massachusetts.[12]

The passage of the Interstate Commerce Act and the appointment of the Interstate Commerce Commission marked the end of the first period of the attacks of the people upon the railroads as the chief source of organized corruption. An investigation into the railroads had revealed startling causes of their corruption and malpractices and showed that they were at least as much sinned against as sinning. The gigantic industrial corporations, of which the Standard Oil Company was the first to occupy a conspicuous place, had in many instances forced the railroads to discriminate in their favor. A company like the Standard Oil Company could easily exact any favors. Backed by its powerful interests, it could say to a recalcitrant railroad, "You must carry our oil on our terms if you carry it at all. And if you do not wish to carry it, we will build a railroad or a pipe line of our own and run you out of business." And, in some instances, they made good their threat. Too often, however, the railroads yielded to their demands and the most shameful discrimination resulted. The cry against trusts and monopolies had long since been raised. They were denounced in some of the early state constitutions. But the idea that the government should oversee industrial corporations and direct their affairs was repugnant to the minds of a people who favored as little government as possible. It was therefore not strange that Congress did not pass until 1890 a law forbidding combinations in restraint of trade.

[9] Appleton's *American Annual Cyclopaedia*, 1881, p. 176.

[10] *Ibid.*

[11] Appleton's *American Annual Cyclopaedia*, 1886, p. 264.

[12] *Ibid.*, 1887, p. 177. For provisions of this act, *ibid.*, p. 173.

While the people were engaged in the search for corruption and its sources, the need of governmental interference to relieve social conditions became more and more pressing. In order to pass laws of this kind, the people had found it necessary to find and remove the corrupt influences which had so vigorously opposed any ameliorative measures. They *now* found it necessary, in order to keep out this corrupt influence and at the same time to make the government more responsive to their demands, to modify it in many important particulars. These modifications of the machinery of government constitute the second of the three phases of the progressive movement.

The point at which the government was most vulnerable under the attacks of special interests was in the elections known as the primaries. The primary elections, strangely enough, have always been considered secondary. They were, for a long time, uncontrolled by law. These primary elections determined who was to control the party, who were to be the delegates to the various conventions which nominated men for office. The easiest and least expensive method of controlling the government was to control the man who controlled the primaries. That man could control the selection of delegates; and, by consequence, the delegates themselves. The delegates controlled the nominations and therefore the nominees. The nominees—the governor, the legislators, the judges—controlled the government.

If the corrupting interests failed to dominate the primaries; if candidates, by some miracle, were nominated who were known to oppose them, the next step was to prevent the election of these candidates. The ways of accomplishing this result were many. If necessary, men could be bought to vote against the dangerous candidate. But such extremes were not always necessary. The newspapers could be induced to print scurrilous attacks upon the integrity of the candidate. His past record could be interpreted in a malign way. He could, in general, be discredited in the minds of people too little informed to know the real merits of the case and too busy to care.

But if the candidate, in spite of all his opponents could contrive, succeeded in winning, the special interests might be supposed to be at the end of their rope. Far from it. The next step was to prevent any law injurious to their welfare from passing through the legislature. As the student of American government knows, practically all important measures are referred to committees to be discussed and reported. To corrupt some member of the committee, to induce the committee by specious arguments advanced by well-trained and well-paid lawyers, to "kill the bill" by not reporting it, was not always impossible. If the committee and the legislature proved intractable and impervious to gold and favors, the governor might be induced to see things in the right light. Unfortunately, not even our governors have been wholly free from suspicion.

If by some accident the special interests lost in the primaries, in the elections, in the legislature, and in the governor's office, there still remained the courts. Under our peculiar system of government, courts have the power to declare laws unconstitutional. The state courts are first appealed to. If, after long litigation, they decide against the special interests, the case may, if the federal constitution is involved, be taken to the federal courts. The constitution of the United States has been twisted, mutilated, rendered almost absurd in some instances, to allow special interests to appeal from state to federal courts. The fourteenth amendment, an amendment primarily concerned with the negro problem, has under the powerful alchemy of the well-paid corporation and railroad lawyers, been transformed into a bulwark of the corporation.

Special interests, then, have seized the government at these different points, and reformers before they can enact laws in the interests of the people must strengthen the government at these points. To wrest government from the hands of the bosses and corrupt interests and keep it free, it is proposed to use direct primaries, a system which allows the people directly to nominate their candidates for office. To diminish the power of the special interests to defeat a good candidate, corrupt practices acts are being passed. In some states an attempt is being made to control the newspapers by requiring them to mark as advertising any political matter which they print for money, together with the source of the material. It has been proposed to compel the newspapers to publish any article which is of vital interest to a reasonably large portion of the population. Under some plans, the state itself enables the candidate to print at public expense arguments in his favor. To abolish the domination of the legislature by special interests, reform in legislative procedure has been suggested; and better still, in many states, the people themselves, whether the legislature wills it or not, are being given the power to pass laws which they desire and to reject those which they do not. The governmental device which gives the people the right to pass laws over the head of the legislature is called the initiative; that which enables them to reject laws is known as the referendum.

If the legislators continue to display too great apathy toward the interests of the people and too great predilection for the special interests, a device known as the recall is used to expel the legislators. The recall may be used also to remove from office any executive officials who are tainted through too close contact with the privilege-seeking class; to control unfaithful judges; and, perhaps even more important, to recall judicial decisions that declare a law unconstitutional. With these and other similar measures in effective operation, a great step will have been taken toward removing permanently organized corrupt influence from government and toward making the machinery of government more responsive to the people.

The third and last phase of the government has to do with the extension of the functions of government—city, state, and national—to relieve, as far as possible, the distress caused by social and economic conditions. Many persons think that the progressive movement proposes to usher in the millennium by legislation. Nothing could be farther from the minds of the men and women who call themselves progressive. What they do propose to do is to bring the United States abreast of Germany and other European countries in the matter of remedial legislation. They propose to regulate the employment of women and children in factories; to impose a maximum number of hours of work a day for men under certain conditions; to provide for workingmen in their old age and for their widows and orphans when their support is taken from them; to reduce or remove the tariff and substitute in its stead a system of taxation which will fall most heavily on those best able to bear it; to adopt a minimum wage law to strengthen the needy against temptation; to strike at poverty, crime, and disease; to do everything that government can do to make our country better, nobler, purer, and life more worth living.

CHARLES A. BEARD

Abridgement of the incomes enjoyed by common carriers was only one phase of the general assault upon the chief beneficiaries of the prevailing system of acquisition and enjoyment. Vast as it was, the capital invested in the railroads, real and fictitious, represented the finances of only a minor portion of the complex mechanism employed in producing and distributing wealth in the United States. Indeed, the railways were simply strands of a larger network of corporate business enterprise—an enterprise impersonal in form and centralizing in tendency, that continued to occupy, with the passing years, an ever larger area of the economic field.

In the path of the rolling ball of accumulation, the Sherman Anti-Trust Act of 1890, penalizing combinations which restrained trade in the sphere of interstate and foreign commerce, proved no barrier at all. The Act was vague in language and not enforced in practice. During Harrison's administration there were three indictments under the law; during Cleveland's second term two indictments; under McKinley not one. Roosevelt, although he believed and said publicly that anti-trust legislation was about as effective as a papal bull against a comet, instituted twenty-five indictments; and Taft, his successor, placed forty-five to

Reprinted by permission of The Macmillan Company from Charles A. Beard, THE RISE OF AMERICAN CIVILIZATION *(New York: Copyright 1927 by The Macmillan Company, renewed 1955 by Mary R. Beard), II, 569–573.*

his credit. Considering the multitude of combinations and the fact that each act in restraint of trade was an indictable offense, the prosecutions in the days of highest tension were few in number.

What is more to the point the most severe judicial decisions, if they caused a furor in the news, made small impression on the captains of industry. The latter paused now and then to cry out against "Theodore the meddler" or to direct an editor to write a double-shotted leader on the inspiring topic of "Let us alone"; but ordinarily they had their minds fixed on things more substantial than the verbiage of the conflict.

As a matter of fact the years that followed the enactment of the Sherman law witnessed the formation of combinations on a daring scale that would have amazed the promoters of the seventies and eighties. In 1899, the Standard Oil Company took the place of the old trust; about the same time the Copper Trust and the Smelters' Trust were formed under the beneficent laws of New Jersey. The next year the National Sugar Refining Company came into existence with a capital greater than the total national debt in Washington's day; and at the opening of the new century that towering genius of finance, J. P. Morgan, completed the edifice of the United States Steel Corporation with more than a billion dollars in outstanding paper. As the chief element in these operations was the ability to float huge issues of stocks and bonds, primacy in such matters passed to large banking houses and heavy investors. So an immense collection of great and small interests was knit into a compact fabric under the management of two or three potent financial groups in New York.

This course in human events was

naturally alarming to the middle classes, to philosophers of the cross-roads store and isolated factory, and to all the armchair speculators who saw a certain incongruity between political democracy and financial concentration. Inevitably also a mass of discontent accumulated among the people at large. Normal grievances were aggravated by untoward incidents which seemed to indicate a want of foresight and consideration on the part of the masters of the capitalist ceremony. For example, hundreds of petty manufacturers were frozen out by high-handed competitive methods and driven to raise plaintive voices about their vanished rights. Useless plants, offices, and mills were closed in many communities, causing resentment among local merchants. For one reason or another the general level of prices seemed to be rising and this produced anxiety among consumers. To make matters worse, leaders in the formation of great combinations often showed an arrogant severity in dealing with those who came across their path, a quarterdeck bluntness that savored of the methods applied by stalwart characters, like Drake and Hawkins, to Spanish sea-captains who objected to being robbed in the days of the Virgin Queen.

Even the investors who relied with child-like faith on the legerdemain of financial wizards had grounds for complaints. Either through inadvertence or calculation, some of the gigantic corporate structures revealed distressing flaws in their masonry. For instance, the New York, New Haven and Hartford Railway combination, effected under Morgan's tutelage, was so loaded with stocks and bonds that it collapsed with an awful crash, spreading ruin far and wide among widows, orphans, and other security holders in New England and giving an awful shock to those who had bought common shares at a high figure in the old days of prudence. In other cases thousands of small investors who tried to partake of the feast likewise found themselves reduced to scanty fare; those enthusiasts who bought common stock at the inception of the United States Steel Corporation were fated to see their paper fall to eight and not a few perished in the hour of disenchantment. In fact when everything seemed possible to the titans, huge quantities of water had been injected into the system of corporate finance, and, except where monopoly or good fortune attended the operation, the commonalty was called upon to pay the bill. All such things awakened emotions of hurt surprise among four influential classes of American citizens: petty investors who had tried without avail to turn an honest penny; bystanders who had merely been permitted to view the lucrous combat from afar; consumers, particularly farmers and planters, who could not raise their incomes by organization and suspected that they bore some share of the expense; and philosophic politicians who entertained misgivings about the safety of the republic.

So, as the new century dawned, a demand for more legislation against the trusts arose on all sides. Having in mind western farmers, southern planters, people of the smaller towns, and workingmen of the cities, Democratic chieftains with a radical cast of thought inveighed against the trusts as a matter of course and conviction. Socialists hailed the new giants as proof that competition destroyed itself and prepared the economic structure for the inevitable Marxian transition. Feeling the solid earth tremble under their feet, Republican leaders spoke in favor of cutting away the "evils" of the trusts by regulation. Even the astute Hanna, on whom fell the burden of collecting campaign funds in "the high places of Wall Street," thinking that the Republicans should break their reticence in 1900, approved a cautious anti-trust plank drafted by Senator Foraker for the party platform of that year. Unwittingly, therefore, Theodore Roosevelt, raised to the presidency by a stroke of Atropos, was furnished a canonical text for many prolix messages and impetuous speeches on the trust question and given the color of justification for instituting several prosecutions against corporations accused of restraining trade. His successor, Taft, pressed forward along similar lines and in 1911 actually secured at the hands of the Supreme Court a dissolution of the Standard Oil and the American Tobacco companies into several individual but friendly concerns.

Still the Democrats were not appeased. Their spokesman, Woodrow Wilson, in proclaiming the New Freedom, promised to restore the old and happy days of competition when every person with a little capital could go into business and taste the wine of liberty—and profits—for himself. So on coming to power, the Democrats proceeded to enact the Clayton anti-trust law of 1914, an elaborate measure which in letter at least threatened to tear apart all combinations large enough to control prices in their respective areas. But the mild fright that it immediately caused in business circles was allayed in time by a decision of the Supreme Court, to the effect that so great a giant as the United States Steel Company was not proscribed by the terms of the law.

In truth, grave doubts existed in many places as to whether pains and penalties of any kind could restore the era of petty industry and unrestrained competition. Though appealing to the masses, the Democrats came to think more kindly of federal regulation; for they supplemented the Clayton Act by a bill which contemplated the control rather than the destruction of huge industrial combinations. Besides declaring unfair methods of competition illegal, the law in question created a federal trade commission and authorized it to coöperate with business men in establishing equitable practices.

As the new century advanced, intransigent hostility to great organizations of capital seemed to be on the wane. At any rate, the threat of horrible dissolution almost vanished as their securities flowed out into the hands of small investors, profit-sharing employees, savings banks, and endowed institutions. Socialistic proposals to transform the new leviathans into national property produced practically no response. Price-fixing devices, similar to those used with such effect against railways, apparently could not be brought into play against the trusts, perhaps partly for the reason that attempts of farmers to apply regulation to corporations or to break them asunder received no material support from industrial shippers as in the case of the joint war on common carriers. Neither could the trade unions get a grip on the basic industries comparable to their hold on systems of transportation, for the want, they alleged, of effective barriers against the flood of European immigrants ready to work at any price on any terms. After forty years of political campaigning therefore, the solid structure of manufacturing enterprise remained intact throughout the land.

II. DOCUMENTS

1. Progressive Ideologies

In the progressive period Louis D. Brandeis became famous as a persuasive proponent of business competition. Here he presents some of his reasons for opposing monopoly. In developing his argument he discusses the relationship of progress, efficiency, and the business structure.

Such arguments in favor of competition in business met sturdy resistance from those who believed that, rather than insuring progress, a policy of scaling down business units would hamper progress. Among the most important of those who pleaded for another alternative, one that would permit the growth of big business, was Herbert Croly. In this selection from The Promise of American Life, *Croly explains why large business combinations have come into existence and why he believes that government agencies for business regulation—though necessary—should consider matters other than the size of corporations.*

In 1914, when Walter Lippmann published Drift and Mastery, *progressives were still debating the relative merits of large and small business. A brash young man of 25, Lippmann laid down a barrage of invective on the competitive ideal for which Brandeis and Wilson spoke. Lippmann, who had already made a name for himself with* A Preface to Politics, *was au courant. The argument he presented—in part reproduced here—was one certain to please those who looked backward with irreverence, confident that their own ideas would bring about a bright, new world.*

LOUIS D. BRANDEIS

Shall we abandon as obsolete the long-cherished policy of competition, and accept in its place the long-detested policy of monopoly? The issue is not (as it is usually stated by advocates of monopoly), "Shall we have unrestricted competition or regulated monopoly?" It is, "Shall we have regulated competition or regulated monopoly?"

Regulation is essential to the preservation and development of compe-

Reprinted from Louis D. Brandeis, THE CURSE OF BIGNESS *(Port Washington, N.Y.: Kennikat Press, 1965), pp. 104–107, 109–110.*

tition, just as it is necessary to the preservation and best development of liberty. We have long curbed physically the strong, to protect those physically weaker. More recently we have extended such prohibitions to business. We have restricted theoretical freedom of contract by factory laws. The liberty of the merchant and manufacturer to lie in trade, expressed in the fine phrase of *caveat emptor,* is yielding to the better conceptions of business ethics, before pure-food laws and postal-fraud prosecutions. Similarly, the right to competition must be limited in order to preserve it. For excesses of competition lead to monopoly, as excesses of liberty lead to absolutism. The extremes meet.

This issue, therefore, is: Regulated competition *versus* regulated monopoly. The policy of regulated competition is distinctly a constructive policy. It is the policy of development as distinguished from the destructive policy of private monopoly.

It is asserted that to persist in the disintegration of existing unlawful trusts is to pursue a policy of destruction. No statement could be more misleading. Progress demands that we remove the obstacles in the path of progress; and private monopoly is the most serious obstacle.

One has heard of late the phrases: "You can't make people compete by law." "Artificial competition is undesirable."

These are truisms, but their implication is false. The suggestion is not that traders be compelled to compete, but that they be prevented from killing competition. Equally misleading is the phrase, "Natural monopolies should not be interfered with." There are no natural monopolies today in the industrial world. The Oil Trust and the Steel Trust have been referred to as natural monopolies, but they are both most unnatural. The Oil Trust acquired its control of the market by conduct which involved flagrant violations of law. Without the aid of criminal rebating, of bribery and corruption, the Standard Oil would never have acquired the vast wealth and power which enabled it to destroy its small competitors by price-cutting and similar practices.

The Steel Trust acquired control not through greater efficiency, but by buying up existing plants and ore supplies at fabulous prices. It is believed that not a single industrial monopoly exists today which is the result of natural growth. Competition has been suppressed either by ruthless practices or by an improper use of inordinate wealth and power. If the law prohibiting such practices is clearly defined and enforced, as it is the purpose of the La Follette Bill to accomplish, no similar trust will arise in the future.

The only argument that has been seriously advanced in favor of private monopoly is that competition involves waste, while the monopoly prevents waste and leads to efficiency. This argument is essentially unsound. The wastes of competition are negligible. The economies of monopoly are superficial and delusive. The efficiency of monopoly is at the best temporary.

Undoubtedly competition involves waste. What human activity does not? The wastes of democracy are among the greatest obvious wastes, but we have compensations in democracy which far outweigh that waste and make it more efficient than absolutism. So it is with competition. The waste is relatively insignificant. There are wastes of competition which do not develop, but kill. These the law can and should eliminate, by regulating competition.

It is true that the unit in business may be too small to be efficient. It is also true that the unit may be too large to be efficient, and this is no uncommon incident of monopoly.

Whenever trusts have developed efficiency, their fruits have been absorbed almost wholly by the trusts themselves. From such efficiency as they have developed, the community has gained substantially nothing.

The proposed Government commission to fix prices would not greatly relieve the evils attendant upon monopoly. It might reduce a trust's profits, but it would fail materially to reduce the trust's prices; because the limitation of the monopoly's profits would, by lessening this incentive, surely reduce the monopoly's efficiency.

To secure successful management of any private business, reward must be ,proportionate to success. The establishment of any rule fixing a maximum return on capital would, by placing a limit upon the fruits of achievement, tend to lessen efficiency.

No selling price for monopoly products could be set constitutionally at a point lower than that which would allow a reasonable return on capital. And in the absence of comparative data from any competing businesses producing the same article at less cost, it would be virtually impossible to determine that the cost should be lower.

The success of the Interstate Commerce Commission has been invoked as an argument in favor of licensing and regulating monopoly.

But the Interstate Commerce Commission has been effective principally in preventing rate increases and in stopping discrimination. In those instances where the Commission has reduced rates (as distinguished from preventing increases) the Commission rested its decisions largely on the ground that existing rates amounted to discriminations against particular places or articles, or the lower rates were justified by a comparison with other rates of the same or other companies. Price-fixing of that nature applied to industrial trusts would afford little protection to the public.

In the second place, there is a radical difference between attempts to fix rates for transportation and similar public services, and fixing prices in industrial businesses. Problems of transportation, while varying infinitely in detail, are largely the same throughout the whole country, and they are largely the same yesterday, today, and tomorrow. In industry we have, instead of uniformity, infinite variety; instead of stability, constant change.

In the third place, the problems of the Interstate Commerce Commission, relatively simple as they are, already far exceed the capacity of that or any single board. Think of the infinite questions which would come before an industrial commission seeking to fix rates, and the suffering of the community from the inability of that body promptly and efficiently to dispose of them.

Every business requires for its business health the *memento mori* of competition from without. It requires likewise a certain competition from within, which can exist only where the ownership and management, on the one hand, and the employees, on the other, shall each be alert, hopeful, self-respecting, and free to work out for themselves the best conceivable conditions.

The successful, the powerful trusts, have created conditions absolutely inconsistent with these—America's—industrial and social needs. It may be true that as a legal proposition mere size is not a crime, but mere size may become an industrial and social menace, because it frequently creates as against possible competitors and as against the employees conditions of such gross inequality, as to imperil the welfare of the employees and of the industry.

. . .

A large part of the American people realize today that competition is in no sense inconsistent with large-scale production and distribution. They realize that the maintenance of competition does not necessarily involve destructive and unrestrained competition, any more than the maintenance of liberty implies license or anarchy. We learned long ago that liberty could be preserved only by limiting in some way the freedom of action of individuals; that otherwise liberty would necessarily lead to absolutism and in the same way we have learned that unless there be regulation of competition, its excesses will lead to the destruction of competition, and monopoly will take its place.

A large part of our people have also learned that efficiency in business does not grow indefinitely with the size of the business. Very often a business grows in efficiency as it grows from a small business to a large business; but there is a unit of greatest efficiency in every business at any time, and a business may be too large to be efficient, as well as too small. Our people have also learned that these profits are not due in the main to efficiency but are due to control of the market, to the exercise by a small body of men of the sovereign taxing power. Nothing has helped so much to make this clear to our people as an incident in the life of the Tobacco Trust. When the Spanish War came on and we needed additional revenue, Congress properly increased the tax on tobacco' products. Three years later, when our country no longer needed that additional revenue, Congress sought to remove the burden which it had placed upon the people, but Congress found itself powerless to remove the burden it had imposed. And when Congress reduced the tax, the effect was merely to transfer, from the Treasury of the United States to the treasury of the Trust, the several millions of dollars a year which represented the reduction in the tax; because the tobacco-products market was controlled by the Trust, which held the selling price practically unchanged.

The history of the Tobacco Trust also showed in the history of its detailed operations how control made for profit, for the degree of control exercised by that great Trust was very different in the various departments of its business and, as the commissioner of corporations found, the ratio of profit was ordinarily in direct relation to the ratio of control. Where the trusts had a high degree of control, the profits were great; where they had a small degree of control the profits were small. In the cigar business, in which the Trust had no control of the market, in which it was merely a large concern, doing perhaps one-eighth of the cigar business of the country, the Trust's profits were not only small, but they were very much smaller than would be satisfactory to the ordinary manufacturer. In the same year in which some of the subsidiary corporations of the Trust were earning fifty, sixty, eighty, or one hundred per cent upon the tangible assets, the Trust was earning in its cigar department only four to six per cent, although the ultimate management of all departments of the Trust's business rested with the same able men and was supplied with the same great resources. Such facts as these have made men realize that while trusts are sometimes efficient, it is not their efficiency but the fact that they control the market, that accounts for the huge profits of trusts.

And people have learned also another fact of perhaps even greater importance. They have come to realize the effect of monopoly in arresting progress, arresting that advance in industry without which a great industrial future is unattainable.

HERBERT CROLY

The central government in its policy toward the large corporations must adopt one of two courses. Either it

Reprinted from Herbert Croly, THE PROMISE OF AMERICAN LIFE *(New York, 1909), pp. 357, 363, 367–368.*

must discriminate in their favor or it must discriminate against them. The third alternative—that of being what is called "impartial"—has no real existence; and it is essential that the illusory nature of a policy of impartiality should in the beginning be clearly understood.

A policy of impartiality is supposed to consist in recognizing the existence of the huge industrial and railroad organizations, while at the same time forbidding them the enjoyment of any of those little devices whereby they have obtained an unfair advantage over competitors. It would consist, that is, of a policy of recognition tempered by regulation; and a policy of this kind is the one favored by the majority of conservative and fair-minded reformers. Such a policy has unquestionably a great deal to recommend it as a transitional means of dealing with the problem of corporate aggrandizement, but let there be no mistake: it is not really a policy of strict neutrality between the small and the large industrial agent. Any recognition of the large corporations, any successful attempt to give them a legal standing as authentic as their economic efficiency, amounts substantially to a discrimination in their favor.

The whole official programme of regulation does not in any effective way protect their competitors. Unquestionably these large corporations have in the past thrived partly on illegal favors, such as rebates, which would be prevented by the official programme of regulation; but at the present time the advantage which they enjoy over their competitors is independent of such practices. It depends upon their capture and occupation of certain essential strategic positions in the economic battle-field. It depends upon abundant capital, which enables it to take ad-

vantage of every opportunity, and to buy and sell to the best advantage. It depends upon the permanent appropriation of essential supplies of raw materials, such as iron ore and coal, or of terminals in large cities, which cannot now be duplicated. It depends upon possibilities of economic industrial management and of the systematic development of individual industrial ability and experience which exist to a peculiar degree in large industrial enterprises. None of these sources of economic efficiency will be in any way diminished by the official programme of regulation. The corporations will still possess substantially all of their existing advantages over their competitors, while to these will be added the additional one of an unimpeachable legal standing. Like the life insurance companies after the process of purgation, they will be able largely to reduce expenses by abolishing their departments of doubtful law.

Thus the recognition of the large corporation is equivalent to the perpetuation of its existing advantages. It is not an explicit discrimination against their smaller competitors, but it amounts to such discrimination. If the small competitor is to be allowed a chance of regaining his former economic importance, he must receive the active assistance of the government. Its policy must become, not one of recognition, but one of recognition under conditions which would impair the efficiency of the large industrial organizations. Mr. William J. Bryan's policy of a Federal license granted only under certain rigid conditions as to size, is aimed precisely at the impairment of the efficiency of the "trusts," and the consequent active discrimination in favor of the small competitor; but the Roosevelt-Taft programme allows the small competitor only such advantages as he is capable of earning for himself; and it must be admitted that these advantages are, particularly in certain dominant industries, not of a very encouraging nature.

Nevertheless, at the last general election the American people cast a decisively preponderant vote in favor of the Roosevelt-Taft programme; and in so doing they showed their customary common sense. The huge corporations have contributed to American economic efficiency. They constitute an important step in the direction of the better organization of industry and commerce. They have not, except in certain exceptional cases, suppressed competition; but they have regulated it; and it should be the effort of all civilized societies to substitute coöperative for competitive methods, wherever coöperation can prove its efficiency. Deliberately to undo this work of industrial and commercial organization would constitute a logical application of the principle of equal rights, but it would also constitute a step backward in the process of economic and social advance. The process of industrial organization should be allowed to work itself out. Whenever the smaller competitor of the large corporation is unable to keep his head above water with his own exertions, he should be allowed to drown. That the smaller business man will entirely be displaced by the large corporation is wholly improbable. There are certain industries and lines of trade in which he will be able to hold his own; but where he is not able to hold his own, there is no public interest promoted by an expensive attempt to save his life.

The Sherman Anti-Trust Law constitutes precisely such an attempt to save the life of the small competitor; and in case the Roosevelt-Taft policy of recognition tempered by regulation is to prevail, the first step to be taken is the repeal or the revision of that law. As long as it remains on the statute books in its existing form, it constitutes an announcement that the national interest of the American people demands active discrimination in favor of the small industrial and commercial agent. It denies the desirability of recognizing what has already been accomplished in the way of industrial and commercial organization; and according to prevalent interpretations, it makes the legal standing of all large industrial combinations insecure—no matter how conducive to economic efficiency their business policy may be.

Assuming, however, that the Sherman Anti-Trust Law can be repealed, and that the Roosevelt-Taft policy of recognition tempered by regulation be adopted, the question remains as to the manner in which such a policy can best be carried out. Certain essential aspects of this question will not be discussed in the present connection. The thorough carrying out of a policy of recognition would demand a Federal incorporation act, under which all corporations engaged in anything but an exclusively local business would be obliged to organize; but, as we have already seen, such an act would be unconstitutional as applied to many technically domestic corporations, and it would probably be altogether unconstitutional, except, perhaps, under limitations which would make it valueless. It may be that some means will be found to evade these Constitutional difficulties, or it may not be. These are matters on which none but the best of Constitutional lawyers have any right to an opinion. But in any event, I shall assume that the Federal government can eventually find the legal means to make its policy of recognition effective and to give the "trust" a definite legal standing. What sort of regulation should supplement such emphatic recognition?

The purpose of such supervision is, of course, to prevent those abuses which have in the past given the large corporation an illegal or an "unfair" advantage over its competitors; and the engine which American legislatures, both Federal and state, are using for the purpose is the commission. The attempt to define in a comprehensive statute just what corporations may do, or must in the public interest be forbidden from doing, is not being tried, because of the apparent impossibility of providing in advance against every possible perversion of the public interest in the interest of the private corporation. The responsibility of the legislature for the protection of the public interest is consequently delegated to a commission whose duties are partly administrative and partly either legislative or judicial. The most complete existing type of such a delegated power is not the Federal Interstate Commerce Commission, but the Public Service Commissions of New York State; and in considering the meaning and probable effects of this kind of supervision I shall consider only the completed type. A Federal Inter-state Commerce Commission which was fully competent to supervise all inter-state commerce and all commerce competing therewith would necessarily possess powers analogous to those bestowed upon the New York Public Service Commissions.

The powers bestowed upon these commissions are based upon the assumption that the corporations under their jurisdiction cannot be trusted to take any important decision in respect to their business without official approval. All such acts must be known to the commission, and be either expressly or tacitly approved, and the official body has the power of ordering their wards to make any changes in their service or rates which in the opinion of the commission are desirable in the public interest. Thus the commission is required not only to approve all agreements among corporations, all mergers, all issues of securities, but they are in general responsible for the manner in which the corporations are operated. The grant of such huge powers can be explained only on the ground that the private interest of these corporations is radically opposed to the interest of their patrons. Public opinion must have decided that if left to themselves, the corporations will behave, on the whole, in a manner inimical to the public welfare; and their business must consequently be actually or tacitly "regulated" in every important detail.

One may well hesitate wholly to condemn this government by commission, because it is the first emphatic recognition in American political and economic organization of a manifest public responsibility. In the past the public interests involved in the growth of an extensive and highly organized industrial system have been neither recognized nor promoted. They have not been promoted by the states, partly because the states neither wanted to do so, nor when they had the will, did they have the power. They have not been promoted by the central government because irresponsibility in relation to national economic interest was, the tariff apart, supposed to be an attribute of the central authority. Any legislation which seeks to promote this neglected public interest is consequently to be welcomed; but the welcome accorded to these commissions should not be very enthusiastic. It should not be any more enthusiastic than the welcome accorded by the citizens of a kingdom to the birth of a first child to the reigning monarchs,—a child who turns out to be a girl, incapable under the law of inheriting the crown. A female heir is under such circumstances merely the promise of better things; and so these commissions are merely an evidence of good will and the promise of something better. As initial experiments in the attempt to redeem a neglected responsibility, they may be tolerated; but if they are tolerated for too long, they may well work more harm than good.

The constructive idea behind a policy of the recognition of semi-monopolistic corporations, is, of course, the idea that they can be converted into economic agents which will make unequivocally for the national economic interest; and it is natural that in the beginning legislators should propose to accomplish this result by rigid and comprehensive official supervision. But such supervision, while it would eradicate many actual and possible abuses, would be just as likely to damage the efficiency which has been no less characteristic of these corporate operations. The only reason for recognizing the large corporations as desirable economic institutions is just their supposed economic efficiency; and if the means taken to regulate them impair that efficiency, the government is merely adopting in a roundabout way a policy of destruction. Now, hitherto, their efficiency has been partly the product of the unusual freedom they have enjoyed. Unquestionably they cannot continue to enjoy any similar freedom hereafter; but in restricting it care should be taken not to destroy with the freedom the essential condition of the efficiency. The essential condition of efficiency is always concentration of responsibility; and the decisive objection to government by commission as any sufficient solution of the corporation problem is

the implied substitution of a system of divided for a system of concentrated responsibility.

This objection will seem fanciful and far-fetched to the enthusiastic advocates of reform by commission. They like to believe that under a system of administrative regulation abuses can be extirpated without any diminution of the advantages hitherto enjoyed under private management; but if such proves to be the case, American regulative commissions will establish a wholly new record of official good management. Such commissions, responsible as they are to an insistent and uninformed public opinion, and possessed as they inevitably become of the peculiar official point of view, inevitably drift or are driven to incessant, vexatious, and finally harmful interference. The efficient conduct of any complicated business, be it manufacturing, transportation, or political, always involves the constant sacrifice of an occasional or a local interest for the benefit of the economic operation of the whole organization. But it is just such sacrifices of local and occasional to a comprehensive interest which official commissions are not allowed by public opinion to approve. Under their control rates will be made chiefly for the benefit of clamorous local interests; and little by little the economic organization of the country, so far as affected by the action of commission government, would become the increasing rigid victim of routine management. The flexibility and enterprise, characteristic of our existing national economic organization, would slowly disappear; and American industrial leaders would lose the initiative and energy which has contributed so much to the efficiency of the national economic system. Such a result would, of course, only take place gradually; but it would none the less be the eventual result of any complete adoption of such a method of supervision. The friends of commission government who expect to discipline the big corporations severely without injuring their efficiency are merely the victims of an error as old as the human will. They "want it both ways." They want to eat their cake and to have it. They want to obtain from a system of minute official regulation and divided responsibility the same economic results as have been obtained from a system of almost complete freedom and absolutely concentrated responsibility.

. . .

The American corporation problem will never be understood in its proper relations and full consequences until it is conceived as a sort of an advanced attack on the breastworks of our national economic system by this essential problem of the distribution of wealth. The current experiments in the direction of corporate "regulation" are prompted by a curious mixture of divergent motives. They endeavor to evade a fundamental responsibility by meeting a superficial one. They endeavor to solve the corporation problem merely by eradicating abuses, the implication being that as soon as the abuses are supervised out of existence, the old harmony between public and private interest in the American economic system will be restored, and no more "socialistic" legislation will be required. But the extent to which this very regulation is being carried betrays the futility of the expectation. And as we have seen, the intention of the industrial reformers is to introduce public management into the heart of the American industrial system; that is, into the operation of railroads and public service corporations, and in this way to bring about by incessant official interference that harmony between public and private interest which must be the object of a national economic system. But this proposed remedy is simply one more way of shirking the ultimate problem; and it is the logical consequence of the persistent misinterpretation of our unwholesome economic inequalities as the result merely of the abuse, instead of the legal use, of the opportunities provided by the existing economic system.

An economic organization framed in the national interest would conform to the same principles as a political organization framed in the national interest. It would stimulate the peculiarly efficient individual by offering him opportunities for work commensurate with his abilities and training. It would grant him these opportunities under conditions which would tend to bring about their responsible use. And it would seek to make the results promote the general economic welfare. The peculiar advantage of the organization of American industry which has gradually been wrought during the past fifty years is precisely the opportunity which it has offered to men of exceptional ability to perform really constructive economic work. The public interest has nothing to gain from the mutilation or the destruction of these nationalized economic institutions. It should seek, on the contrary, to preserve them, just in so far as they continue to remain efficient; but it should at the same time seek the better distribution of the fruits of this efficiency. The great objection to the type of regulation constituted by the New York Public Service Commission Law is that it tends to deprive the peculiarly capable industrial manager of any sufficient opportunity to turn his abilities and experience to good account. It places him under the tutelage of public officials, responsible to a public opinion which has not yet been sufficiently nationalized in spirit or in purpose, and in case this tutelage fails of its object (as it assuredly will) the responsibility for the failure will be divided. The corporation manager will blame the commissions for vexatious, blundering, and disheartening interference. The commissions will blame the corporation manager for lack of cordial coöperation. The result will be either the abandonment of the experiment or the substitution of some degree of public ownership. But in either event the constructive economic work of the past two generations will be in some measure undone; and the American economic advance will be to that extent retarded. Such obnoxious regulation has been not unjustly compared to the attempt to discipline a somewhat too vivacious bull by the simple process of castration. For it must be substituted an economic policy which will secure to the nation and the individual the opportunities and the benefits of the existing organization, while at the same time seeking the diffusion of those benefits over a larger social area.

WALTER LIPPMANN

It has been said that no trust could have been created without breaking the law. Neither could astronomy in the time of Galileo. If you build up foolish laws and insist that invention is a crime, well—then it is a crime. That is undeniably true, but not very interesting. Of course, you can't possibly treat the trusts as crimes. First of all, nobody knows what the trust laws mean. The spectacle of an enlightened people trying in vain for twenty-five years to find out the intention of a statute that it has enacted—that is one of those episodes that only madmen can appreciate. You see, it is possible to sympathize with the difficulties of a scholar trying to decipher the hieroglyphics of some ancient people, but when statesmen can't read the things they've written themselves, it begins to look as if some imp had been playing pranks. The men who rule this country to-day were all alive, and presumably sane, when the Sherman Act was passed. They all say in public that it is a great piece of legislation— an "exquisite instrument" someone called it the other day. The highest paid legal intelligence has concentrated on the Act. The Supreme Court has interpreted it many times, ending with the enormous assumption that reason had something to do with the law.[1] The Supreme Court was denounced for this: the reformers said that if there was any reason in the law, the devil himself had got hold of it. As I write, Congress is engaged in trying to define what it thinks it means by the Act. . . .[2]

. . .

If the anti-trust people really grasped the full meaning of what they said, and if they really had the power or the courage to do what they propose, they would be engaged in one of the most destructive agitations that America has known. They would be breaking up the beginning of a collective organization, thwarting the possibility of coöperation, and insisting upon submitting industry to the wasteful, the planless

Reprinted from Walter Lippmann, DRIFT AND MASTERY: AN ATTEMPT TO DIAGNOSE THE CURRENT UNREST, *ed. William E. Leuchtenburg (Englewood Cliffs, N.J.: Prentice-Hall, Inc., © 1961), pp. 77–85, by permission of Prentice-Hall, Inc., Englewood Cliffs, N.J.*

[1] In *Standard Oil Co. v. United States*, 221 U.S. 1 (1911), Chief Justice Edward D. White enunciated the "rule of reason"; the Sherman Act, he insisted, prohibited only unreasonable restraints of trade.

[2] Congress's attempt to redefine the anti-trust law resulted in the enactment of the Clayton law on October 15, 1914.

scramble of little profiteers. They would make impossible any deliberate and constructive use of our natural resources, they would thwart any effort to form the great industries into coordinated services, they would preserve commercialism as the undisputed master of our lives, they would lay a premium on the strategy of industrial war, —they would, if they could. For these anti-trust people have never seen the possibilities of organized industries. They have seen only the obvious evils, the birth-pains, the undisciplined strut of youth, the bad manners, the greed, and the trickery. The trusts have been ruthless, of course. No one tried to guide them; they have broken the law in a thousand ways, largely because the law was such that they had to.

At any rate, I should not like to answer before a just tribunal for the harm done this country in the last twenty-five years by the stupid hostility of anti-trust laws. How much they have perverted the constructive genius of this country it is impossible to estimate. They have blocked any policy of welcome and use, they have concentrated a nation's thinking on inessentials, they have driven creative business men to underhand methods, and put a high money value on intrigue and legal cunning, demagoguery and waste. The trusts have survived it all, but in mutilated form, the battered make-shifts of a trampled promise. They have learned every art of evasion—the only art reformers allowed them to learn.

It is said that the economy of trusts is unreal. Yet no one has ever tried the economies of the trust in any open, deliberate fashion. The amount of energy that has had to go into repelling stupid attack, the adjustments that had to be made underground—it is a wonder the trusts achieved what they did to bring order out of chaos, and forge an instrument for a nation's business. You have no more right to judge the trusts by what they are than to judge the labor movement by what it is. Both of them are in that preliminary state where they are fighting for existence, and any real outburst of constructive effort has been impossible for them.

But revolutions are not stopped by blind resistance. They are only perverted. And as an exhibition of blind resistance to a great promise, the trust campaign of the American democracy is surely unequalled. Think of contriving correctives for a revolution, such as ordering business men to compete with each other. It is as if we said: "Let not thy right hand know what thy left hand doeth; let thy right hand fight thy left hand, and in the name of God let neither win." Bernard Shaw remarked several years ago that "after all, America is not submitting to the Trusts without a struggle. The first steps have already been taken by the village constable. He is no doubt preparing a new question for immigrants" . . . after asking them whether they are anarchists or polygamists, he is to add " 'Do you approve of Trusts?' but pending this supreme measure of national defense he has declared in several states that trusts will certainly be put in the stocks and whipped."

There has been no American policy on the trust question: there has been merely a widespread resentment. The small local competitors who were wiped out became little centers of bad feeling: these nationally organized industries were looked upon as foreign invaders. They were arrogant, as the English in Ireland or the Germans in Alsace, and much of the feeling for local democracy attached itself to the revolt against these national despotisms. The trusts made enemies right and left: they squeezed the profits of the farmer, they made life difficult for the shopkeeper, they abolished jobbers and travelling salesmen, they closed down factories, they exercised an enormous control over credit through their size and through their eastern connections. Labor was no match for them, state legislatures were impotent before them. They came into the life of the simple American community as a tremendous revolutionary force, upsetting custom, changing men's status, demanding a readjustment for which people were unready. Of course, there was anti-trust feeling; of course, there was a blind desire to smash them. Men had been ruined and they were too angry to think, too hard pressed to care much about the larger life which the trusts suggested.

. . .

Woodrow Wilson is an outsider capable of skilled interpretation. He is an historian, and that has helped him to know the older tradition of America. He is a student of theory, and like most theorists of his generation he is deeply attached to the doctrines that swayed the world when America was founded.

But Woodrow Wilson at least knows that there is a new world. "There is one great basic fact which underlies all the questions that are discussed on the political platform at the present moment. That singular fact is that nothing is done in this country as it was done twenty years ago. We are in the presence of a new organization of society. . . . We have changed our economic conditions, absolutely, from top to bottom; and, with our economic society, the organization of our life." You could not make a more sweeping statement of the case. The President is perfectly aware of what has happened, and he says at the very outset that "our laws still deal with us on the basis of the old system . . . the old positive formulas do not fit the present problems."

You wait eagerly for some new formula. The new formula is this: "I believe the time has come when the governments of this country, both state and national, have to set the stage, and set it very minutely and carefully, for the doing of justice to men in every relationship of life." Now that is a new formula, because it means a willingness to use the power of government much more extensively.

But for what purpose is this power to be used? There, of course, is the rub. It is to be used to *"restore* our politics to their full spiritual vigor *again,* and our national life, whether in trade, in industry, or in what concerns us only as families and individuals, to its purity, its self-respect, and its *pristine* strength and freedom." The ideal is the old ideal, the ideal of Bryan, the method is the new one of government interference.

That, I believe, is the inner contradiction of Woodrow Wilson. He knows that there is a new world demanding new methods, but he dreams of an older world. He is torn between the two. It is a very deep conflict in him between what he knows and what he feels.

His feeling is, as he says, for "the man on the make." "For my part, I want the pigmy to have a chance to come out" . . . "Just let some of the youngsters I know have a chance and they'll give these gentlemen points. Lend them a little money. They can't get any now. See to it that when they have got a local market they can't be squeezed out of it." Nowhere in his speeches will you find any sense that it may be possible to organize the fundamental industries on some deliberate plan for national service. He is thinking always about somebody's chance to build up a profitable business; he likes the idea that somebody can beat somebody else, and the small business man takes on the virtues of David in a battle with Goliath.

"Have you found trusts that thought as much of their men as they did of their machinery?" he asks, forgetting that few people have ever found competitive textile mills or clothing factories that did. There isn't an evil of commercialism that Wilson isn't ready to lay at the door of the trusts. He becomes quite reckless in his denunciation of the New Devil—Monopoly—and of course, by contrast the competitive business takes on a halo of light. *It is amazing how clearly he sees the evils that trusts do, how blind he is to the evils that his supporters do. You would think that the trusts were the first oppressors of labor; you would think they were the first business organization that failed to achieve the highest possible efficiency.* The pretty record of competition throughout the Nineteenth Century is forgotten. Suddenly all that is a glorious past which we have lost. You would think that competitive commercialism was really a generous, chivalrous, high-minded stage of human culture.

"We design that the limitations on private enterprise shall be removed, so that the next generation of youngsters, as they come along, will not have to become protégés of benevolent trusts, but will be free to go about making their own lives what they will; so that we shall taste again the full cup, not of charity, but of liberty,—the only wine that ever refreshed and renewed the spirit of a people." That cup of liberty —we may well ask him to go back to Manchester, to Paterson to-day, to the garment trades of New York, and taste it for himself.

The New Freedom means the effort of small business men and farmers to use the government against the larger collective organization of industry. Wilson's power comes from them; his feeling is with them; his thinking is for them. Never a word of understanding for the new type of administrator, the specialist, the professionally trained

business man; practically no mention of the consumer—even the tariff is for the business man; no understanding of the new demands of labor, its solidarity, its aspiration for some control over the management of business; no hint that it may be necessary to organize the fundamental industries of the country on some definite plan so that our resources may be developed by scientific method instead of by men "on the make"; no friendliness for the larger, collective life upon which the world is entering, only a constant return to the commercial chances of young men trying to set up in business. That is the push and force of this New Freedom, a freedom for the little profiteer, but no freedom for the nation from the narrowness, the poor incentives, the limited vision of small competitors,—no freedom from clamorous advertisement, from wasteful selling, from duplication of plants, from unnecessary enterprise, from the chaos, the welter, the strategy of industrial war.

There is no doubt, I think, that President Wilson and his party represent primarily small business in a war against the great interests. Socialists speak of his administration as a revolution within the bounds of capitalism. Wilson doesn't really fight the oppressions of property. He fights the evil done by large property-holders to small ones. The temper of his administration was revealed very clearly when the proposal was made to establish a Federal Trade Commission. It was suggested at once by leading spokesmen of the Democratic Party that corporations with a capital of less than a million dollars should be exempted from supervision. Is that because little corporations exploit labor or the consumer less? Not a bit of it. It is because little corporations are in control of the political situation.

But there are certain obstacles to the

working out of the New Freedom. First of all, there was a suspicion in Wilson's mind, even during the campaign, that the tendency to large organization was too powerful to be stopped by legislation. So he left open a way of escape from the literal achievement of what the New Freedom seemed to threaten. *"I am for big business,"* he said, *"and I am against the trusts."* That is a very subtle distinction, so subtle, I suspect, that no human legislation will ever be able to make it. The distinction is this: big business is a business that has survived competition; a trust is an arrangement to do away with competition. But when competition is done away with, who is the Solomon wise enough to know whether the result was accomplished by superior efficiency or by agreement among the competitors or by both?

The big trusts have undoubtedly been built up in part by superior business ability, and by successful competition, but also by ruthless competition, by underground arrangements, by an intricate series of facts which no earthly tribunal will ever be able to disentangle. And why should it try? These great combinations are here. What interests us is not their history but their future. The point is whether you are going to split them up, and if so into how many parts. Once split, are they to be kept from coming together again? Are you determined to prevent men who could coöperate from cooperating? Wilson seems to imply that a big business which has survived competition is to be let alone, and the trusts attacked. But as there is no real way of distinguishing between them, he leaves the question just where he found it: he must choose between the large organization of business and the small.

It's here that his temperament and his prejudices clash with fact and necessity. He really would like to disintegrate large business. "Are you not eager for the time," he asks, "when your sons shall be able to look forward to becoming not employees, but heads of some small, it may be, but hopeful business . . . ?" But to what percentage of the population can he hold out that hope? How many small but hopeful steel mills, coal mines, telegraph systems, oil refineries, copper mines, can this country support? A few hundred at the outside. And for these few hundred sons whose "best energies . . . are inspired by the knowledge that they are their own masters with the paths of the world before them," we are asked to give up the hope of a sane, deliberate organization of national industry brought under democratic control.

I submit that it is an unworthy dream. I submit that the intelligent men of my generation can find a better outlet for their energies than in making themselves masters of little businesses. They have the vast opportunity of introducing order and purpose into the business world, of devising administrative methods by which the great resources of the country can be operated on some thought-out plan. They have the whole new field of industrial statesmanship before them, and those who prefer the egotism of some little business are not the ones whose ambitions we need most to cultivate.

2. The Persistence of Progressivism

The decade of the twenties has often been seen as one in which Americans took their bearings from a materialistic constellation and set their course away from progressive reform. But the twenties can just as easily be seen in another sort of relationship to progressivism. Many men in the administrations of Coolidge and Hoover were as interested as Brandeis, Croly or Lippmann in "progress" and "efficiency," and shared the progressives' confidence in a democracy built on industrial plenty. The following document illustrates the way that parts of the progressive ethic persisted through the twenties. It was written in 1927 by one of Herbert Hoover's subordinates in the Department of Commerce, under the revealing title, "Progress in National Efficiency."

E. DANA DURAND

There has been an extraordinary increase in the production of American industry during recent years, with a consequent corresponding advance in standards of living. This reflects not merely recovery from the dislocation caused by the war, nor from the low point of the postwar slump—it represents in large part an advance beyond the highest pre-war levels and marks a trend which we may well consider of a permanent character. The country may from time to time in the future suffer the depressions of the business cycle, but there is no reason to anticipate any continuing recession from the present general productivity of industry, and on the contrary much reason to believe that progressively higher levels will be attained.

Recent careful calculations made by the Department of Commerce with reference to the quantitative output

Reprinted from E. Dana Durand, "Progress in National Efficiency," FIFTEENTH ANNUAL REPORT OF THE SECRETARY OF COMMERCE, *1927 (Washington, D.C.: United States Government Printing Office, 1927), pp. xxvii–xxxiii.*

(eliminating the effect of price changes) of the major branches of industry show an immense increase since the beginning of the century, a great part of which has taken place in the few years since the war. Between 1899 and 1925 the output of agricultural products increased about 47 per cent, that of mining about 248 per cent, and that of manufactures about 178 per cent, while the volume of railway service increased by 199 per cent. The weighted total for these four branches of industry shows an increase of 140 per cent for the quarter century. Meantime population had grown only about 55 per cent, so that per capita output rose also by about 55 per cent.

Even this figure does not measure fully the progress in production for the reason that the number of workers in these four branches has increased much less than the total working population, a relative shift having taken place into the mercantile, professional, and personal-service pursuits. The increase in efficiency of older industries has freed great numbers of persons to undertake new industries, and thus add new articles and services to the standard of living. The most familiar evidence of such a shift is the great number now employed in occupations connected with motor vehicles, quite apart from those manufacturing them. From two and one-half to three millions of persons—perhaps even more—are engaged in selling automobiles and automobile supplies, including gasoline, in repairing them, in constructing good roads, and in driving trucks, taxicabs, and the like. Far the greater part of this number represents an increase above any corresponding occupations in the days preceding the automobile.

duction per worker amounting to nearly 80 per cent. The increase has been shared by all the major branches. It is scarcely less conspicuous in agriculture than in manufactures and railway transportation, while the higher gain in mining has been due almost solely to the extraordinary expansion of the petroleum industry, in which the value of product per person employed is exceptionally high. It may be noted that the increase in output per worker for the four branches combined is greater than for all but one of the individual branches. The reason is that there has

INCREASE IN PRODUCTION OF MAJOR BRANCHES OF INDUSTRY

[Manufactures indexes are computed from data for 1899, 1919, and 1925; other data are based on averages of three years, with a few exceptions]

PERIOD AND BRANCH	NUMBER OF WORKERS		INDEX FOR END OF PERIOD; BEGINNING = 100		
				OUTPUT, QUANTITY	
	BEGINNING OF PERIOD	END OF PERIOD	NUMBER OF WORKERS	OF GOODS OR SERVICES	OUTPUT PER WORKER
1898–1900 to 1924–1926:					
Agriculture	10,700,000	10,700,000	100	147	147
Mining	600,000	1,050,000	175	348	199
Manufactures	5,300,000	1 9,900,000	187	278	149
Railways	970,000	1,860,000	192	299	156
Total or weighted average	17,570,000	23,510,000	134	240	179
1918–1920 to 1924–1926:					
Agriculture	11,300,000	10,700,000	95	112½	118
Mining	1,050,000	1,050,000	100	127	127
Manufactures	10,670,000	1 9,770,000	91½	128½	140½
Railways	2,035,000	1,860,000	91½	100	109
Total or weighted average	25,055,000	23,380,000	93	120	129

1 The two figures given for the number employed in manufactures in 1925 differ in order to make them comparable with the figures for 1899 and 1919, respectively, which were reported on a slightly different basis.

The progress in efficiency is brought into sharp relief by comparing the increase in the product of agriculture, mining, manufactures, and railways with the increase in the number of persons employed in these branches. The addition of 140 per cent to their output between 1899 and 1925 was achieved by adding only 34 per cent to the number of workers. This means a gain in pro-

been a relative shift of workers from agriculture to other fields in which the amount of capital and power employed is greater so that the output is higher than in farming.

Statistics for different periods indicate that during the first decade of the century there was a steady increase in output per worker in the four major branches of industry. The shift of vast numbers to new jobs during the war and the general dislocation resulting from it brought down the efficiency of manufacturing industry so that the increase in combined output of the four branches between 1909 and 1919 was less than from 1899 to 1909. On the other hand, the combined output of goods and services in agriculture, mining, manufactures, and transportation during 1925 (some of the figures are averages for the three years 1924 to 1926) was 20 per cent greater than in 1919, the increase in population meanwhile being not more than 10 per cent. The average output per worker increased no less than 29 per cent during this short interval. The number of persons employed in these fields is not merely relatively but absolutely less at the present time than at the close of the World War. This is a change unprecedented in our history or in that of almost any country growing in population. The shift into other pursuits has been much more rapid than ever before. The decline in the number of employees in agriculture, mining, manufactures, and railway transport is far from being an indication of business depression or of lack of employment. It is due to the advance in income which enables the people to devote a larger share of effort to services of distribution and to professional and personal services, reflecting a higher standard of living. If the reduction in workers in these four branches had meant unemployment, the great gain in output would have been impossible, since it could not have found a market.

That the marked recent advance in production is only in smaller part due to the relatively low efficiency of 1919, or to recovery from the slump of 1921, is evidenced by the increase that has taken place even since 1923, itself a year of high prosperity and activity.

Between 1923 and 1925, when the last census of manufactures was taken, the number of factory workers decreased 4½ per cent, while the output (always in terms of quantity, not value) increased about 6 per cent. The monthly index of production of major manufactured commodities shows still further advance down to the present time, while there has also been a further reduction in the number of factory employees. The statistics also prove that the railways have continued to date to gain in efficiency and no doubt the same is true in agriculture and mining.

The increase in production per worker during the past quarter century has taken place in the face of a decided reduction in working hours. On the average, working time per week in manufacturing industries is to-day about 11 per cent less than in 1909, the first year for which comprehensive data were collected. It is probable that since 1899 the average working day in all branches of industry considered together has been shortened fully 15 per cent. The workers have reaped double advantage from expanding output—by increase of their wage and by reduction in their hours of labor.

THE CAUSES OF PROSPERITY AND PROGRESS

The causes which have made for the rapid advance in American industry are fortunately of an enduring and cumulative character. The idea that our present high prosperity is the result of the World War is wholly without foundation. The war cut down the efficiency of our industry besides wasting an important fraction of its production. The increase in exports during the war was far less than the Government expenditures on war. Marked as has been the gain in the last few years in our export of manufactures, which alone competes with Europe, it shows less increase over the immediate pre-war period than that in turn showed over the opening years of the century. Exports at the present time are not a larger proportion of our production than before the war. Export trade in any case represents barely 10 per cent of our production of movable commodities.

The true causes of the prosperity and economic progress of the United States are not difficult to discern. At the foundation lie the rich resources of the country, not taxed by an excessive population, and the energy and intelligence and attitude toward work of the producing population. In our earlier days advance was in considerable measure attributable to the opening up of new resources, but during the past quarter century this has not been a major influence. There have been some discoveries of minerals, notably of petroleum, but these have been largely offset by the using up of other resources; for example, of the more conveniently located forest reserves. The principal factors of the recent increase in productivity are what may be called human as distinguished from natural factors.

These basic causes of economic progress translate themselves into a number of more specific and directly working causes. Among these may be mentioned especially the advance in education, scientific research, and invention; the growing use of mechanical power, machinery, and other forms of capital; the larger scale of production; the conscious and concerted effort to eliminate waste and reduce costs; the high scale of wages, with consequent general high buying power; and the relative stability of prices, money, and credit.

Taking into account both the enrollment and the length of attendance, the amount of instruction in elementary and secondary schools has increased, relatively to the total number of children, over 90 per cent since 1890. Pupils in high schools represented 5½ per cent of the total number of children of high-school age in 1890, and 35 per cent in 1926. The proportion of young men and women attending colleges, universities, and professional schools was 1½ per cent in 1890 and 9 per cent in 1926. At the same time instruction has become more effective, more practical; it does more to develop thinking than formerly. Our colleges and universities, moreover, have expanded enormously in their research work. Their activity has been supplemented by that of industrial concerns, many of which in recent years have established well-equipped and well-manned technical laboratories in which systematic efforts are made to improve methods, invent machinery, and devise new products. Added to advance in physical sciences and invention has been the marked expansion of economic and statistical research and application of the results.

An immense increase has taken place in the capital employed in American industry. On the average each wage earner in our mines is now aided by more than $10,000 of capital, each factory employee by more than $5,000, and each railway worker by more than $8,000. It has been roughly estimated that the annual savings in the United States amount to about ten billions of dollars or approximately one-ninth of the national income. New issues of capital securities alone totalled more than six billions of dollars in 1926.

The accumulation of capital is reflected in the great and increasing application of mechanical power. On the average each factory wage earner today is aided by 4.3 horsepower of prime movers, a figure about double that in 1900. A similar great increase has taken place in the power of locomotives as compared with the number of railway employees. On farms the decline in the number of horses and mules is more than offset by the larger employment of mechanical tractors; as a consequence the number of acres tilled per worker is steadily rising. The United States now consumes in fuel and water power the equivalent of from 7 to 8 tons of coal per capita annually, as against less than 5 tons at the beginning of the century. The increase would be much greater but for the marked improvements in economizing fuel. The increasing use of mechanical power means, of course, a correspondingly greater use of machinery. Moreover, the machines themselves have been made more efficient so that the growth of power equipment does not fully measure the gain in productive capacity of machinery.

One of the most profound modern tendencies is the swiftly expanding use of electric current both in the household and in industry. We are adding 10 or 12 per cent to the output of electricity every year. Approximately two-thirds of our factory machinery is now operated by electric motors as compared with 15 per cent 20 years ago. The electric stations are rapidly advancing in technical efficiency. The amount of fuel converted to coal units burned in fuel-using electric plants has fallen from about 3.2 pounds per kilowatt hour in 1919 to about 1.9 pounds in 1927. There is little doubt that three times as much current is obtained from a given quantity of fuel at the present time as 15 or 20 years ago.

Industrial units in the United States are much larger than anywhere else in the world and are steadily growing in size. Manufacturing plants with an annual output exceeding $1,000,000 each represent only about 5 per cent of the total number of establishments, but they contribute two-thirds of the total value of factory products. Adjusting for change in the buying power of money, the corresponding proportion 20 years ago was only about 45 per cent. Large-scale production is particularly conducive to low costs where processes are repetitive. Specialized machinery is used in such "mass production," whereas with a smaller output it would be necessary to use machines designed for more general purposes and less adapted to the particular task. The workers likewise can develop highly specialized efficiency. The immense domestic market of the United States makes possible repetitive production in numbers of units far greater than are produced in plants abroad.

At the close of the World War prices of commodities fell sharply. Wages, however, were maintained. This situation put on employers unprecedented pressure to cut down costs in every direction possible. Individual business concerns, trade associations, research organizations, private and public, and universities have entered upon serious and concerted study of problems of production. One of the several important directions taken has been in the simplification of products. In scores of branches of industry agreements have been reached to cut out unnecessary sizes, shapes, and varieties of articles and to concentrate production on a limited number of standard types.

The high and advancing level of real wages has also served directly to advance the efficiency of industry. It has meant an immensely wide and even wider market for commodities, and this has tended greatly to lower unit costs. It has also made for good health and contentment on the part of the workers and thereby increased their productive capacity. There is little tendency to restrict output or to oppose labor-saving machinery and methods. Labor very generally recognizes that large product tends to high wages.

The evidence of advance in wages is clear. By dividing the total amount paid in wages by the average number of wage earners as reported by the census of manufacturers, the average annual wage for 1925 is found to have been $1,280. This average is for both sexes, all ages, and all degrees of skill. Adjusting for changes in the buying power of money the figure was at least 35 per cent higher in 1925 than in 1914, and that in the face of a considerable shortening of the working day. Many more detailed statistics of wages and of earnings likewise demonstrate the marked recent advance.

A factor of importance in our recent economic progress has been the relative stability of prices. Since the sharp break following the post-armistice boom, the general index of wholesale prices has changed relatively little. The general downward tendency during the past two years has apparently been due largely to the greater volume of commodities to be bought and sold, an increase attributable to the progress in the efficiency of industry. The relative stability of prices contrasts strikingly with the wide, often enormous, variations from which most countries of Europe have suffered since the war. The abundance of new capital and the soundness of the currency and banking system have facilitated business by making available ample credit, both short term and long term, at low and fairly stable rates.

All these specific factors in the prosperity and progress of the United States, as well as the more basic factors of abundant natural resources and a capable population, are of such a character that we may well hope for continuance of our economic progress. Indeed, these favorable factors tend to work cumulatively; each forward step makes another forward step easier. The fact that our national income is already high makes it possible for us readily to add to our capital equipment and to improve educational standards and to carry further scientific and technical research.

III. RECENT INTERPRETATION

In 1964, Samuel Haber provided students of history with a fresh look at the progressive period. *Efficiency and Uplift* is an examination of the ideas and impact of the cult of scientific management promoted by men such as Frederick W. Taylor. Haber found that an efficiency craze, stimulated by the cult, swept through the ranks of progressives as well as through other segments of society. Progressives, in fact, were particularly susceptible to the efficiency appeal. In this selection Haber shows how Brandeis, Croly, and Lippmann each incorporated ideas about efficiency into his social and economic analysis. Unlike De Witt or Beard, Haber assumes no obvious moral posture in developing his theme. He writes with a detachment foreign to the earlier historians.

SAMUEL HABER

Louis D. Brandeis, Herbert Croly, and Walter Lippmann picked up scientific management at the time of the efficiency craze but did not put it down quite as easily as many others did. Though all three men were prominent intellectual leaders of the progressive movement, they were actually of different generations. Brandeis came of age politically when Rutherford B. Hayes was in the White House, and Civil Service versus "the Stalwart ruffians" was the new issue of the day. When Croly came to politics, the Sherman Act had just been placed on the statute books, and business wildcatting was nearing its end. Lippmann cast his first vote amid the excitement of the insurgent Republican revolt, when many bright young men were predicting that socialism was the coming thing. Each reached intellectual maturity and made his first commitments (commitments which were never completely left behind) in very different times. Considered together, these three men reveal some of the different layers of experience that were reflected in the progressive thought of the years before 1917. All three were affected by scientific management. Their interpretation of its doctrines was important not only for scientific management but for their own social outlook as well.

Louis D. Brandeis was the son of Jewish refugees from the defeated European liberal revolution of 1348. His family settled and prospered in Louisville, Kentucky, where Brandeis was born. After starting his education in local private schools, he went on to

Reprinted from Samuel Haber, EFFICIENCY AND UPLIFT (Chicago: University of Chicago Press, © 1964), pp. 75–98, by permission of the publisher.

study at a German *Gymnasium* and finally at the Harvard Law School.[1] Apparently Brandeis met with no anti-Jewish prejudice, and his brilliance admitted him to the circles of the Back Bay cultural elite. He heard Ralph Waldo Emerson at a private reading of his "Education" and later knew and visited with such important and representative figures as William Dean Howells and Barrett Wendell. "Those years were among the happiest of my life," he remembered. "For me, the world's center was Cambridge." [2]

Brandeis accepted New England ideals, and his speech even borrowed the regional twang. His law partner, Samuel D. Warren, wrote that in many ways Brandeis was a better example of New England virtues than the natives. And few were surprised when this son of immigrants (but member of the exclusive Dedham Polo Club as well) advised Bostonians to protect "the great heritage of an honorable, glorious past, handed down to us by our fathers." [3]

Brandeis' politics, at first, were also New England. A Republican until the Cleveland-Blaine election, he became a mugwump in 1884. Once having stepped out of the fold, however, Brandeis moved closer to the Democrats than most New Englanders, and gave his support to the Olney wing of the party. This was still considered

[1] Alpheus Thomas Mason, *Brandeis: A Free Man's Life* (New York: Viking Press, 1946), chaps. i, ii, and iii.

[2] Elizabeth Glendower Evans, "Mr. Justice Brandeis: The People's Tribune," *Survey,* LXVII (Nov. 1, 1931), 141; Mason, pp. 42–43, 76; Ernest Poole, "Brandeis, a Remarkable Record of Unselfish Work Done in the Public Interest," *American Magazine,* LXXI (February, 1911), 482.

[3] Louis D. Brandeis, *The Curse of Bigness: Miscellaneous Papers of Justice Brandeis,* ed. Osmond K. Frankel (New York: Viking Press, 1934), p. 263; Mason, pp. 329, 389.

quite reputable and conservative. When the rumblings of Populism reached Boston, Brandeis was recommending the establishment of law courses for laymen, since "the conservatism which the study of law engenders would be invaluable." [4]

By the time of the Eastern Rate Case, however, Brandeis had earned a national reputation as a proponent and defender of social legislation; he had found one of the currents of reform which moved from mugwumpery to progressivism. This current was formed by the admonitions and achievements of the social workers, muckrakers, and social gospel sociologists. The public health, safety, and morals, they asserted, were not adequately protected by moral teaching and liberty of contract in a competitive market economy. Brandeis started from a limited concept of "police power," and gradually found increasing need for government control. "The Government must keep order not only physically but socially." [5] The mugwump ideal social order of moderate-sized enterprise, personal independence, and social responsibility was to be preserved not by opposing government power but by using it.

In addition to a growing acceptance of active government, there was a change in Brandeis' social perspective. He came to look upon the working classes through the eyes of the social worker rather than the political economist. Labor appeared more as a category of humanitarianism and even philanthropy and less as a category of economics and politics. Stronger trade unions were necessary to protect the worker from the greed of the employer and to provide a training ground in the spirit of brotherhood and altruism. Occasionally Brandeis expounded the doctrine of the middle ground—that society must be protected from the excesses of both capital and labor—but it is apparent that he found less to fear from below than from above. [6]

His opposition to "plutocracy" took two forms. He condemned the power of the trusts, proposing a regime of publicly regulated and sustained competition as substitute; and he scorned "commercialism," offering the professional ethic in its place. Brandeis shared the characteristic mugwump disdain for "mere money making" and "the vulgar satisfaction which is experienced in the acquisition of money." Yet the longing for old ways and old families, often an important component in the mugwump response to a rapidly changing America, was not readily available to Brandeis. His family was not old and his way to

---

[4] Louis D. Brandeis to Charles W. Eliot, March 20, 1893, quoted in *The Brandeis Guide to the Modern World,* ed. Alfred Lief (Boston: Little, Brown, 1941), p. 75; Alfred Lief, *Brandeis: The Personal History of an American Ideal* (Harrisburg, Pa.: Stackpole Sons, 1936), p. 30.

[5] Ernest Poole, *loc. cit.,* p. 492. Moving into progressive currents, he supported Theodore Roosevelt in 1904, Taft in 1908, Wilson in 1912, and 1916, and was "100% for Hoover" in 1920. Alpheus Thomas Mason, "Variations on the Liberal Theme," *Publications of the Brandeis Lawyers Society,* I (1947), 2.

[6] Louis D. Brandeis, *Business—a Profession* (Boston: Small, Maynard, 1914), pp. 18–21, 83–84, 152–53, 321; Mason, *Brandeis: A Free Man's Life,* chap. x; Louis D. Brandeis to Paul U. Kellogg, Dec. 19, 1911, in *Brandeis Guide,* p. 129; Mason, *Brandeis: Lawyer and Judge in the Modern State,* (Princeton, N.J.: Princeton University Press, 1933), p. 75. Yet when the economic results of the growth of unionism were thrust upon him, Brandeis could not discard his early-formed belief in economic individualism. He favored strong unions but opposed the closed shop. Louis D. Brandeis to Ray Stannard Baker, Feb. 26, 1912, in *Brandeis Guide,* pp. 139–40; Mason, *Brandeis: A Free Man's Life,* pp. 294–301.

prominence had been through the legal profession.[7]

It is understandable, therefore, that Brandeis came to place a special emphasis upon the virtues of professionalism. Moreover, where most engineers would have been happy to establish (and most lawyers happy to re-establish) the influence of professional ideals within their own occupation, Brandeis carried the teachings of professionalism to business itself. His efforts paralleled Taylor's. Brandeis' proposal for transforming business into a profession meant the rejection of financial return as the primary measure of success and the development of a technical knowledge, training, and discipline which would eliminate the charlatans and establish the leadership of the competent. The new graduate schools of business were to play an important part. The university would subdue and civilize the market place.[8]

Brandeis' belief in the leadership of the competent extended to the realm of politics as well. When the movement to "give government back to the people" was already well under way,

Brandeis was still calling for a leadership of those with "greatest ability and intelligence" to act as a brake upon democracy. He accepted neither Robert M. LaFollette's program of direct government nor Theodore Roosevelt's "recall of judicial decisions." [9] Nevertheless, as Brandeis himself rose to a position of political influence, his confidence in the people's ability to select capable guides increased. Leadership was important, but now Brandeis stressed that it must be leadership by consent. He became optimistic about the fruitful interaction of expert and public opinion.[10]

---

[7] Brandeis, *The Curse of Bigness*, pp. 104–36; Mason, *Brandeis: A Free Man's Life*, chap. xxii; Brandeis, *Business—a Profession*, pp. 1–12; John C. Van Dyke, *The Money God* (New York: Charles Scribner's Sons, 1908). This book provides a synoptic example of mugwump attacks upon commercialism. It traces the disease through the American social organism and incidentally points to the Jew as a principal carrier. Van Dyke was a professor of art history at Rutgers University and the author of *Art for Art's Sake* (1893) and even *Nature for Its Own Sake* (1898). He was from an old family and did recommend the return to old ways (the Ten Commandments) as an antidote.

[8] Brandeis' view of the role of business colleges was often shared by their deans. Harlow Stafford Person, *Industrial Education* (Boston: Houghton Mifflin, 1907), pp. 22–26, 27. Herbert Heaton, *A Scholar in Action: Edwin F. Gay* (Cambridge, Mass.: Harvard University Press, 1952), p. 76.

[9] Brandeis, *Curse of Bigness*, p. 41; Mason, *Brandeis: A Free Man's Life*, pp. 94, 124, 368; Brandeis, *Business—a Profession*, pp. 341–42; Louis D. Brandeis to Roger Sherman Hoar [no date given], 1911, File Box NMF45, Louis D. Brandeis Collection, University of Louisville Law School, Louisville, Ky.; Louis D. Brandeis and others, *Preliminary Report on Efficiency in Administration of Justice* (Boston: National Economic League [1914]), pp. 6, 11, 15, 29. There were three principal reactions of those who accepted the progressive discovery that the courts made political decisions: (1) recall of judicial decisions (Theodore Roosevelt); (2) judicial reticence (Holmes and later Frankfurter); (3) sociological jurisprudence (Roscoe Pound and Brandeis). Brandeis' endorsement of sociological jurisprudence did not involve diminishing the position of the judiciary, but rather broadening its training. Brandeis, *Business—a Profession* (rev. ed., 1933), pp. 358–63, liv. Roscoe Pound liked to quote Sir Edward Coke on this issue—that judges are responsible only to God. Morris Cohen, "A Critical Sketch of Legal Philosophy in America," *Law: A Century of Progress* (New York: New York University Press, 1937), II, 299.

[10] Louis D. Brandeis to Morris L. Cooke, July 24, 1916, in *Brandeis Guide*, p. 71; Mason, *Brandeis: A Free Man's Life*, p. 602. In January, 1913, Felix Frankfurter, then an important link joining Brandeis, Croly, and Lippmann, asked for Brandeis' comment on a proposed organization of a small group of experts to draw up plans for the remodeling of the social system. Brandeis answered that such a group would be "of great assistance to the forward movement," but reliance could not be placed

Brandeis prescribed the "logic of facts" to pry open outmoded precedents and theories and to provide a social understanding free from bias.[11] In this era of naturalism in the arts and new inductive techniques in the social sciences, there seemed to be much to support his belief that many large issues could be reduced to matters of fact. On a more sophisticated level, this belief was paralleled by John Dewey's attempt to provide an ethical outlook based on the methods of the descriptive sciences. And if Dewey's ethical pronouncements often turned out to be those of liberal Christianity, one should not be surprised that in the Brandeis brief, as in Frank Norris' *The Octopus* and the Pittsburgh Survey, the "facts" turned out to be on the side of the underdog.[12]

Related to this invocation of "the facts" was an eagerness to deal with conditions rather than motives. This was a reform without an appeal to conscience and without the usual struggle between the forces of good and evil. To stand at Armageddon was proof of failure. The reformer, rather than siding with any of the contending forces as he found them, was to discover harmonizing devices which would be to the interests of the antagonists and to the benefit of the general public. Reform was primarily an act of "social invention." [13]

Scientific management was just such a "social invention." At the time of the Eastern Rate Case it promised to preserve the shippers' current rates, the railroads' profits, and the union's wage increase and also hold down the cost of living for the public. Brandeis need not blame any of the parties. The railroad managers were not incompetent, for, as Brandeis pointed out, scientific management was so new that one could hardly have expected them to have adopted it earlier.[14]

Brandeis' fervor for scientific management persisted long after the Eastern Rate Case. Scientific management spoke to Brandeis' mugwump belief in the virtue of hard work and the strength of character which hard work fostered. Scientific management converted haphazard and unskilled jobs into precise and methodical tasks that permitted the worker to appraise his individual achievement and compete against a standard. Hard work need not be devitalizing work, Brandeis assured his social worker friends. In fact, he stressed the connection between reduced fatigue and increased production. The industrious were rewarded by rapid promotion, and the less able workers were shown the way to improvement through the intensified supervision

---

in any one small group. *Brandeis Guide*, p. 281. Often, in these later years, Brandeis seemed to echo Jefferson's belief in a natural aristocracy. The crucial difference was that Jefferson held his view when many believed in an aristocracy of property, and Brandeis held his amid cries for direct democracy.

11 *Brandeis Guide*, pp. 121, 160, 209–10.

12 The major exception was the famous Report of the Immigration Commission which required 47 volumes to recommend a literacy test. After World War I, beginning with the Army intelligence tests and their findings that the average American was a moron, "the facts" were usually on the other side. After the war, the technique of the Brandeis brief was used to strike down social legislation. Mason, *Brandeis: Lawyer and Judge*, pp. 117–22.

13 For Brandeis' most direct statement of this approach see "Testimony of Louis D. Brandeis," *U.S. Commission on Industrial Relations*, 64th Cong., 1st Sess., Sen. Doc. 415 (Ser. Vol. 6936), Jan. 23, 1915, p. 7669; Brandeis, *Curse of Bigness*, p. 40; Poole, *loc. cit.*, p. 492; *Brandeis Guide*, pp. 210, 280–85.

14 Louis D. Brandeis, "Brief Submitted to the Interstate Commerce Commission," *Evidence in Matter of Proposed Advances in Freight Rates*, U.S., 61st Cong., 3d Sess., Sen. Doc. 725 (Ser. Vol. 5911), pp. 4752, 4759, 5262.

provided under Taylor's system of functional foremen. These functional foremen, and the planning department to which they were responsible, provided a new type of leadership for the factory. It was a leadership based on knowledge and could provide means toward the professionalization of business. This technical knowledge was not elicited from abstract or *a priori* principles but from hundreds of thousands of industrial trial-and-error experiments. Taylor, like Brandeis, based his law on facts.[15]

Scientific management offered extraordinary proof for Brandeis' prediction of the professionalization of business. Before the Eastern Rate Case, he had discussed this idea only parenthetically, but afterward he extended and elaborated upon it. Scientific management also led Brandeis to shift his emphasis from questions of the distribution of wealth to those of its production. Furthermore, it added to his stock of "social inventions," thereby providing for more varied and flexible reform campaigns.[16]

Brandeis agreed with the Bull Moosers that bigness should be handled as a condition and not a crime. However, his insistence that the trusts were inefficient and that efficiency must prevail turned their own type of argument against them. The plants in which scientific management had been applied most thoroughly, Brandeis pointed out, were medium-sized. Too great a distance from the diversity of fact which made up the actual operation of a plant was destructive of sound judgment. The huge profits of the trusts, Brandeis insisted, owed more to control of the market than to efficiency in production. He admitted that free and unrestricted competition was a failure; but he did not accept the trusts as the inevitable alternative. Brandeis gave his support to resale price maintenance, co-operatives and the trade associations which could preserve medium-sized enterprises and (with the aid of scientific management) efficiency as well.[17]

Brandeis was that special type of progressive whose chief ideals remained those of a New England mugwump but whose manner became that of a social engineer. This manner seemed devious

[15] Louis D. Brandeis, *Scientific Management and the Railroads* (New York: Engineering Magazine, 1911), pp. 11–14, 25–29, 37–42; "Testimony of Louis D. Brandeis," *U.S. Commission on Industrial Relations*, 64th Cong., 1st Sess., Sen. Docs. Vol. 26 (Ser. Vol. 6929), pp. 1003–4; Brandeis, *Business—A Profession*, pp. 48–9; *Curse of Bigness*, p. 56; Josephine Goldmark, *Fatigue and Efficiency: A Study in Industry* (New York: Charities Publication Committee, 1912), chap. vii; *Business—A Profession* (rev. ed., 1933), p. 317; Louis D. Brandeis, "What Is the Relation between Efficiency and Modern Trusts?" *Efficiency Magazine*, II (November, 1912), 6, 16; Louis D. Brandeis to A. J. Portenar, Jan. 22, 1917, File Box MMF8, Brandeis Collection.

[16] "Testimony of Louis D. Brandeis," *U.S. Commission on Industrial Relations*, 64th Cong., 1st Sess., Sen. Doc. Vol. 19 (Ser. Vol. 6929), pp. 991, 1008–9; Vol. 26 (Ser. Vol. 6936), p. 7666; *Curse of Bigness*, p. 51. When Brandeis did support some redistribution of income, it was in terms of increased incentives to production. Louis D. Brandeis to Arthur T. Morey, Feb. 14, 1912, *Brandeis Guide*, pp. 230–31.

[17] Louis D. Brandeis, "What Is the Relation between Efficiency and Modern Trusts?" p. 6. Louis D. Brandeis to Robert M. La Follette, Sr., May 26, 1913, *Brandeis Guide*, p. 55. Mason, *Brandeis: A Free Man's Life*, chap. xxii. But what if the trusts somehow did turn out to be more efficient? When cornered with this question, Brandeis fell back upon the argument that the social and political ills resulting from trustfication make medium-sized enterprise the more desirable form. "Testimony of Louis D. Brandeis," *Hearings before the Senate Committee on Interstate Commerce Pursuant to S. Res. 98*, 62d Cong., 1st Sess. (1911), I, 1168, 1174.

to many of his early allies in reform. In the tangled battle over Brandeis' appointment to the Supreme Court, some of his fellow reformers testified to what they thought was his fickleness to principles. For New Dealers, his failing was often precisely the opposite. "Brandeis was a wolf in sheep's clothing— more accurately a doctrinaire parading as an instrumentalist," thought Rexford Tugwell; and David Reisman, Brandeis' law clerk in the thirties, was of a similar opinion. Yet out of his dual outlook, Brandeis created a popular image of scientific management in the years before World War I that seemed public-spirited and humane but also modern, technical, and morally neutral.[18]

Though his immediate audience was more limited than Brandeis', Herbert D. Croly's influence on progressive thought was not less important. Croly came from a family dedicated to reform. His mother was a prominent feminist and his father a journalist with an itch for unusual causes.[19]

Young Croly was closely tutored in Conte's ritualistic and hierarchical Religion of Humanity—once described by T. H. Huxley as Catholicism minus Christianity—but broke with those doctrines in the search for more rigorous belief. During his much interrupted college education at the City College of New York and Harvard, which allowed for two years of study and travel in Europe, Croly drifted from an early interest in teaching philosophy to a career in serious journalism and art criticism. He established himself at the art colony in Cornish, New Hampshire (which had been founded by Augustus Saint-Gaudens and his admirers), and joined the staff of the *Architectural Record,* where he remained for thirteen years, serving as editor for six years.[20]

Croly came to the field of American architecture when there was an increasing concern for professionalism, similar to that which Taylor witnessed in engineering and Brandeis observed in law. American colleges of architecture were growing in number and the many students trained at the Ecole des Beaux Arts in Paris were beginning to influence the American scene. The special training which infused Ameri-

---

[18] Among those who testified against the Brandeis appointment were Clifford Thorne, midwestern reformer and Brandeis' associate in the Eastern Rate Case; Hollis R. Bailey, who aided Brandeis in inaugurating his savings-bank life insurance plan; William S. Youngman, an ally in the Boston Elevated Fight; and Edward P. Warren, a fellow reformer in the Public Franchise League. Rexford G. Tugwell, *The Art of Politics* (Garden City, N.Y.: Doubleday, 1958), p. 247. Samuel J. Konefsky, *The Legacy of Holmes and Brandeis: A Study in the Influence of Ideas* (New York: Macmillan, 1956), p. 163.

[19] Oswald Garrison Villard, "Herbert David Croly," *Dictionary of American Biography,* ed. Harris E. Starr (New York: Charles Scribner's, Sons, 1944), XXI, 209. Croly's father campaigned against the use of black and white print, expressed sympathy for race improvement through stirpiculture, for polygamy, and for the idea of transforming prostitution into a proper vocation for women. David Goodman Croly, *Glimpses of the Future* (New York:

G. P. Putnam's Sons, 1888), pp. 48–54, 55–61, 171–73; Carl Bode, "Columbia's Carnal Bed," *American Quarterly,* XV (Spring, 1963), 57–60. However, many of the father's less unusual ideas appear again in the works of the son. For example, the advocacy of an active, centralized state, strong trade unions, regulated trusts, and the rejection of equality in democracy, of deliberative legislatures, etc. D. G. Croly, pp. 10–17, 20–21, 25–26, 110–12, 138.

[20] Eric F. Goldman, *Rendezvous with Destiny* (New York: Alfred A. Knopf, 1953), p. 191; Villard, "Croly," DAB, XXI, 209; Jesse Lynch Williams, "Herbert Croly," *Metropolitan Magazine,* XXXIII (March, 1911), 742–44; Philip Littell, "A Look at Cornish," *Independent,* LXXIV (June 5, 1913), 1297–98.

can architecture drew its rules not so much from science as from the arts, and the importance of this training was often not recognized by the architect's client. The architect's posture, therefore, was more self-conscious and self-justifying than the engineer's.[21]

In his work for the *Architectural Record,* Croly did much to supply justification for the professionalization of architecture. There was little instinctive love of art in America, Croly declared. The great mass of building in this country was directed by men who were simply trying to build for as little money as possible something which would sell or rent. Even those who seemed concerned with beauty had the most barbarous taste. Art, which in most countries grew almost unconsciously, in America had to be pursued consciously if at all. This required a trained elite. In architecture, progress depended absolutely upon increasing the authority of the architect with his client—upon the ability of the architect to get his own way.

Yet Croly did not adopt an unqualified aesthetic elitism. For he also believed that art was a social expression, and in its greatest periods a thoroughly popular growth. Somehow the American architect must be popular and influential without surrendering to the demands of business and popular taste, and without compromising the integrity of his work.[22]

How was this to be done? How could the artist be "good" and yet "formative in a large way" while America "resents exclusive technical standards and refuses to trust men who through their training have earned the right to represent such standards?" In his writings on architecture and his similar discussion of literature, Croly never resolved the dilemma. Yet when he generalized the problem and placed it in a broader social and historical setting, he did find what he thought to be the answer.[23]

That answer was embodied in *The Promise of American Life,* Croly's most important work. This book, the author wrote, was "an attempt to justify the specialized contemporary intellectual discipline and purposes against the tyranny of certain aspects of our democratic tradition." The way to that justification lay in the formula, "a constructive relation between democracy and nationality." Democracy could not realize itself without a strong state, a strong executive, and an efficient administrative apparatus. The more democratic institutions were used to provide for the needs of the people, the more the people must resort to nationalized government organization.

---

pp. 256, 258–61, "Rich Men and Their Houses," *ibid.,* XII (1902), 28, "What Is Indigenous Architecture?" *ibid.,* XXI (1907), 437–38, "Art and Life," *ibid.,* I (1891–92), 227, and "The New World and the New Art," *ibid.,* XII (1902), 151.

23 Herbert D. Croly, "Henry James and His Countrymen," *The Lamp: A Review and Record of Current Literature,* XXVIII (February, 1904), 47–53, and "The Architect in Recent Fiction," *Architectural Record,* XVII (Feb. 1905), 138. "The Case of the statesman, the man of letters, the philanthropist, or the reformer does not differ essentially from that of the architect." Herbert D. Croly, *The Promise of American Life* (New York: Macmillan, 1909), p. 446.

---

21 For example, compare Barr Ferree, "What Is Architecture?" *Architectural Record,* I (1891–92), 199, and A. D. F. Hamlin, "The Difficulties of Modern Architecture," *ibid.,* (1892–93), p. 137, with R. H. Thurston, "President's Inaugural Address," in *Trans. ASME,* I (1880), 13, or Oberlin Smith, "The Engineer as a Scholar and a Gentleman," *ibid.,* XII (1891), 42.

22 Herbert D. Croly, "Criticism That Counts," *Architectural Record,* X (1901), 404, "American Artists and Their Public," *ibid.,*

This organization would make use of men's varying individual abilities by giving each a sufficient sphere of exercise. Individualism and distinction were to be rescued not by smallness, as Brandeis thought, but by bigness and the specialized competence that bigness required. The commercialism which Croly condemned as destructive of individuality was precisely the small competitive model which Brandeis was trying to modify and preserve.[24]

Croly saw Theodore Roosevelt as America's exemplary political leader. He used strong government action for social purposes and "exhibited his genuinely national spirit in nothing so clearly as his endeavor to give men of special ability, training and eminence a better opportunity to serve the public." Croly's ideal was a democracy with an emphasis on distinction rather than equality, on "exceptional men" rather than "the popular average." It was a government which would use democratic organization "for the joint benefit of individual distinction and social improvement."[25]

Croly's vigorous state was also designed to prevent the social divisions within America from dissolving society. The magnitude and specialization which he urged upon government had already been realized in society at large. Since the Civil War, America had changed from a nation which was agricultural and relatively homogeneous to one which was industrial and highly differentiated. The unconscious social bonds of a homogeneous society had been shattered, Croly observed, and must be replaced by a conscious national ideal which would harness the special interests and purposes of the country to the general welfare.[26] Croly's new nationalism would fulfill the people's needs, provide sanction for individual excellence, and maintain social order. These themes were carried through almost all of his subsequent writings.

His next book, *Progressive Democracy*, was clearly less impressive than the *Promise of American Life*. Already in the *Promise* Croly had suggested a belief that the center of experience was moral and even mystical, but he had carefully restrained this feeling. He wished to avoid the usual reformer's vice of recklessly cutting through complexities with simple moral verities. Croly's moralism was always more abstract and even abstracted. Yet in *Progressive Democracy*, these leanings brought him to a faith which was "emancipated . . . from bondage to a mechanical conception of social causation." [27] He came to neglect those circumstances and forces which condition and constrict the operation of the human will. The importance of social understanding, therefore, decreased and exhortation increased. *Progressive Democracy* is laced with calls to sacrifice, social righteousness, moral stamina, and risk, and with glorifications of the creative power of the will, the moral value of democracy, and the mystical unity of human nature. At some points it sounds like Friedrich Nietzsche presiding as a YMCA discussion leader.

Croly projected his mixture of moralism and mysticism into society

---

24 Herbert D. Croly, "Why I Wrote My Latest Book: My Aim in 'The Promise of American Life,'" *World's Work*, XX (June, 1910), 13086, and *The Promise of American Life*, pp. 33–34, 185–214, 272–79, 408–15.

25 Croly, *The Promise of American Life*, pp. 170, 207, 409–15.

26 *Ibid.*, pp. 138–40.

27 *Ibid.*, pp. 452–54, 145–46; Herbert D. Croly, *Progressive Democracy* (New York: Macmillan, 1914), p. 174.

as a "moving democratic faith." This faith, which was to provide a new social cement, temporarily diminished the role of the national ideal and even the state in his writings. *Progressive Democracy*, however, gave Croly's other guiding concepts—expertism and popular entry into and use of government—even more extreme application. The "moving democratic faith" downgraded law, constitutions, deliberating legislatures, and the party system, while it exalted direct democracy. The extension of direct government allowed for fluid majorities which would quickly and easily register their desires. But this very fluidity made necessary an enlarged and powerful administrative division of experts to "discover and define better methods of social behavior and . . . secure cooperation in the use of such methods by individuals and classes." [28] Croly's proposal was for some sort of plebiscitarian administocracy.

The first issue of the *New Republic*, with Croly as its editor-in-chief, was on the newsstands about a month after the publication of *Progressive Democracy*. It was to be a political journal with high intellectual standards, addressed to that select audience interested in serious but unconventional social inquiry. "We shall be radical without being socialistic," wrote Croly. "We are seeking to build a body of public opinion believing in a more thoughtful and radical form of progressivism." The financial support came from Willard and Dorothy Straight. They had become interested in Croly's ideas through the *Promise of American Life* and were willing to subsidize the new magazine with almost no strings

attached.[29] The very existence of the *New Republic* could be seen as support for Croly's belief that America would find place for professional competence and integrity. It seemed to prove that he who paid the piper need not call the tune, providing the piper played exceedingly well.

The *New Republic* quickly won a reputation for fresh comment on current events in the light of much cleverness and information. The enthusiastic mysticism and exalted moralism of *Progressive Democracy* were not reflected in its pages, nor even in Croly's signed articles. At this point, Croly seems to have been less interested in their direct relevance to politics. The *New Republic* reached for intelligence rather than moralism and science rather than mysticism. As "the facts" were to provide Brandeis with the basis of a social program free from bias, so the scientific method was to do something similar for Croly and his staff. The *New Republic* championed expert administration and social control through active government. Within this context it also supported "radical democracy" but often in such a manner as purportedly to save democracy from itself.[30]

---

[28] *Ibid.*, pp. 44–62, 236–37, 284–302, 330–31, 349–77, 368.

[29] Herbert Croly to Randolph Bourne, June 3, 1914, in the Randolph Bourne Collection, Butler Library, Columbia University. Herbert D. Croly, *Willard Straight* (New York: Macmillan, 1924), pp. 473–74.

[30] For the *New Republic*'s views on expert administration see "The Expert and American Society," *New Republic*, XV (May 4, 1918), 5–7, IV (Sept. 25, 1915), 194–95, VI (March 18, 1916), 170, VII (July 8, 1916), 240–41, XV (June 8, 1918), 160; Herbert Croly, "Unregenerate Democracy," *ibid.*, VI (Feb. 5, 1915), 18. See also George Santayana, "Natural Leadership," *ibid.*, III (July 31, 1915), 333–34; "Philonous," "Intellectual Leadership in America," *ibid.*, I (Nov. 14, 1914), 17. On social control through active government see "Innocuous Frankenstein," *ibid.*, II (May 20, 1915), 169–70; "The

An odd and interesting illustration of the *New Republic*'s line of thought was its support for the Cincinnati Unit Plan. This scheme, for which Croly won Dorothy Straight's financial backing, set up geographically based bicameral councils of consumers and professional groups which would "break down the barriers between the expert and the community," provide for various local needs, and even replace conventional political forms. The Social Unit Plan combined efficiency and democracy; it wed the experts to the masses. "Bosses" were to give way to "leaders," and the usual political party, in which the sincere efforts of the "college-bred" too often came to naught, was to be replaced by this new type of organization, in which such efforts would gain importance. After some tentative successes, the Social Unit Plan was overwhelmed and crushed in the Red Scare and the mass rush for normalcy.[31]

From its first issues, the *New Republic* seemed to be drawn to scientific management. "Mr. Taylor and his followers," a leading article asserted, "have made a major contribution to civilization." The *New Republic* not only condemned the AFL campaign against Taylorism but urged the application of scientific management to diverse social issues.[32] One editorial, presumably written by Croly, proposed setting up industrial colonies under the charge of a corps of expert scientific managers to which tramps and loafers would be committed. These camps would provide training in industrial habits and "disembarrass society of the work-shy." Another editorial reported that many manufacturers were not efficient enough to pay their workers a decent salary and still stay in business. It recommended that the State Industrial Commission hire efficiency experts to inspect the factories' efficiency (just as it provided inspectors for safety and sanitation) and impose business efficiency upon all employers. In the pages of the *New Republic* the problem of industrial peace was often seen primarily as a question of business organization.[33]

Future of the Two Party System," *ibid.*, I (Nov. 14, 1914), 10–11; "Municipal Ownership versus Regulation," *ibid.* (Nov. 28, 1914), pp. 12–14; *New Republic*, V (Nov. 6, 1915), 6. On democracy see "True Democracy," *ibid.*, III (June 26, 1915), 186; H. G. Wells, "What Democracy Means," *ibid.*, XIV (April 13, 1918), 316–18. After the smash-up of progressivism, when Croly began to lose interest in politics and became disillusioned with the social engineer, mysticism and moralism often reappeared in his writings. Herbert D. Croly, "Disordered Christianity," *ibid.*, XXI (Dec. 31, 1919), 136–39, "Regeneration," *ibid.*, XXIII (June 9, 1920), 40–47, and "Better Prospect," *ibid.*, XXVII (Aug. 24, 1921), 344–49. For Croly's disillusionment with the social engineer, see the introduction to Eduard C. Lindeman's *Social Discovery* (New York: Republic Publishing Co., 1924), pp. v–xx.

31 A description of the Cincinnati Unit Plan is found in its inventor's autobiography. Wilbur C. Phillips, *Adventuring for Democracy* (New York: Social Unit Press, 1940), pp. 148–259, 370. For the enthusiastic support given to the Cincinnati Unit Plan by the New Republic

see "The Expert and American Society," *New Republic*, XV (May 4, 1918), 7; "Who Makes Bolshevism in Cincinnati," *ibid.*, XVIII (April 19, 1919), 365–67. See also E. T. Devine, "Social Unit in Cincinnati: An Experiment in Organization," *Survey*, XLIII (Nov. 15, 1919), 115–26.

32 "Trade Unions and Productive Efficiency," *New Republic*, XV (May 11, 1918), 40–41; "Anti-Efficiency in War," *ibid.* (May 4, 1918), 8–9; *ibid.*, IX (Dec. 23, 1916), 204; *ibid.*, VII (May 27, 1916), 75; *ibid.*, VI (April 18, 1916), 252.

33 "Salvaging the Unemployable," *New Republic*, IV (Oct. 2, 1915), 221–23; "Beyond Arbitration," *ibid.*, IX (Jan. 20, 1917), 315–17; *ibid.*, (Nov. 25, 1916), 84; *ibid.*, (Dec. 23, 1916), 204–05.

The basis for the support of scientific management becomes apparent in Croly's own writings. Croly singled out the planning department for special attention. It was to replace the "adventurers" and "amateurs" with experts and substitute broad social purposes for selfish and hidebound goals. It was in the planning department that the college-bred man, in a position of influence, could impose technical standards for the general good. The discerning reader, Croly admitted, would note the parallel between the program of scientific management for the factory and his own suggestions for an enlarged administrative body for the state.

The parallelism is, as a matter of fact, extremely close. The successful conduct of both public and private business is becoming more and more a matter of expert administration, which demands similar methods and is confronted by the solution of similar problems.

Moreover, Taylor's vision of the harmony of the classes through a common commitment to production afforded an economic analogy to the national ideals which would stand above class and avert social dissolution.[34]

The *New Republic's* interest in scientific management did not hinge solely upon Croly's influence. Walter Lippmann, a brilliant young member of the editorial board, had come to these interests largely without Croly's help and followed them to somewhat different uses. Lippmann, like Brandeis, came from a well-to-do German-Jewish family and, like him, had made an outstanding record at Harvard. Yet while Brandeis embraced New England

traditions and was, at least in the early years, accepted by its heirs, Lippmann kept and was kept at a distance. He was on good terms with the faculty but worked most closely with such outsiders as Graham Wallas and George Santayana.[35]

At Harvard, Lippmann became a socialist. Socialism in the America of the day was a various and loosely defined movement containing many contrasts in belief and temperament. Lippmann's youthful career in socialism consisted in a rapid sampling of its many varieties. He was influenced by the Fabianism of Graham Wallas, dipped into settlement work, served for four months as secretary to Rev. George R. Lumm, socialist mayor of Schenectady, and at one point led a left-wing local of the Socialist party.[36]

These rapidly succeeding socialisms had at least two connecting themes: a desire to bring a better life to the lower classes and a desire to bring order out of the disorder of capitalism. It was particularly among those socialists who laid special stress on setting things in order that a predisposition for elite leadership appeared. For a while, Lippmann took James MacKaye's *Economy of Happiness,* a learned socialist trea-

---

[34] Croly, *Progressive Democracy*, pp. 395–97, 399, 400, 403–05.

[35] David Elliott Weingast, *Walter Lippmann* (New Brunswick, N.J.: Rutgers University Press, 1949), p. 6.

[36] *Ibid.*, pp. 7–11. For a while, Lippmann was an assistant muckraker to Lincoln Steffens. Though some of Steffens' "discoveries" were dazzling, he provided no consistent constructive program. Perhaps sensing his young assistant's dissatisfaction, Steffens wrote a friend, "We have been the blind leading the blind, but we have led. . . . I suppose that some young fellow like Lippmann will expose us some day, and I say let 'em expose." Lincoln Steffens to Francis J. Heney, December 23, 1910 in Francis J. Heney Papers, Bancroft Library, University of California, Berkeley.

tise on political engineering, as his bible.[37]

With one hand Lippmann held to science and order, but he stretched to grasp indeterminacy, emotion, imagination, and even mysticism with the other. He praised the city planners and the efficiency experts, but he also praised the William James, who respected the findings of the spiritualists, and Henri Bergson, who taught the doctrine of Life Force. Lippmann became a regular visitor at Mabel Dodge's famous Fifth Avenue salon of artists, reformers, and radicals where a cheerful gospel of passionate living was preached.[38]

[37] Carl Binger, "A Child of the Enlightenment," *Walter Lippmann and His Times*, ed. Marquis Childs and James Reston (New York: Harcourt, Brace, 1959), p. 34. Walter Lippmann, "Basic Sanity," *New Republic*, II (April 3, 1915), 241. MacKaye had presented five lectures at Harvard on "An Outline of Political Engineering" while Lippmann was there as a student. "James MacKaye," *National Cyclopedia of American Biography*, XIV (New York: White, 1917), 159. Lippmann's clearest description of his brand of socialism was in his articles for the *New Review*. See Walter Lippmann, "The I.W.W.—Insurrection or Revolution," *New Review*, I (August, 1913), 701–6, and "Walling's 'Progressivism and After,'" *ibid.*, II (June, 1914), 340–44. The elitist currents in American socialism of the day and the stress on the rational restraints of socialism have not been discussed by the historians of the movement; however, these both become apparent in even a cursory glance at socialist literature. See for example Lena Morrow Lewis, "Jeffersonian vs. Social Democracy," *Masses*, III (April, 1912), 17; Rufus W. Weeks, "The Socialized Efficiency Expert To Be," *ibid.* (May, 1912), 16. Max Schrabisch, "Is American Democracy a Failure? Its Evils and the Way Out," *New York Call*, May 26, 1912, p. 13; "By the Editor," *Metropolitan Magazine*, XXXVII (April, 1913), 4. The *New Review*, which strained to avoid any taint of the Marxist "Classics" and Marxist orthodoxy, featured Engels' hard-boiled essay "The Principle of Authority" II [April, 1914], 222.

[38] Walter Lippmann, "Lewis Jerome Johnson," *Amer. Mag.*, LXXIII (Feb. 1912), 418,

Lippmann respected both the non-rational and the rational, impulse and order, art and politics. He attempted to reconcile these apparently conflicting allegiances in his first two books, *Preface to Politics* and *Drift and Mastery*. In the *Preface* not only did the perspectives of the statesman and the artist sometimes merge, as in Croly's writings, but, more radically, the underlying forces of art and politics were held to be one and the same. Man was a bundle of desires. In politics as well as art, emotion, will, and fantasy bubbled beneath. The statesman was to recognize these forces. Though they were initially destructive, the statesman should not suppress them, but rather direct them toward socially constructive paths. The state was not the effect of the agreement of rational men; it was the supreme instrument of civilization.[39]

But who would wield the instrument? Lippmann left this and other important issues unclear. He did emphasize the role of leaders and experts but placed them in a broad frame of a popular government. Lippmann's insistence upon the importance of the irrational also threatened the standing of objective knowledge itself. He liked the arguments of Nietzsche, Bergson, and Sorel that ideas were disguised impulses. Yet, if ideas were disguised impulses, did not that apply to this idea as well? Was anything safe from sub-

"More Brains—Less Sweat," *Everybody's Magazine*, XXV (Dec. 1911), 827–28, "An Open Mind: William James," *ibid.*, XXIII (Dec. 1910), 800–801, and "The Most Dangerous Man in the World," *ibid.*, XXVII (July, 1912), 100–101. For a discussion of the Mabel Dodge salon and its importance for the young intellectuals of the prewar years see May, *The End of American Innocence*, pp. 310–14.

[39] Walter Lippmann, *A Preface to Politics* (New York: Mitchell Kennerley, 1913), pp. 47–52, 77–85, 112–21, 266–67.

jectivism? At some points the *Preface to Politics* threatened to turn into a postscript.[40]

Actually Lippmann only flirted with this radical form of irrationalism. It seemed to be out of character for him. Mabel Dodge described the Lippmann of those days as always rational, well-balanced, and in complete possession of himself. She recalled that he even felt the need for more organization to eliminate chaos and confusion at her soirées. And in fact, already within the *Preface to Politics* was a path from the quagmire of subjectivism, which he followed in his later *Drift and Mastery* and his articles in the *New Republic*. This path was the scientific method. Scientific method, to Lippmann, was a practical device which was free from bias and could provide a discipline for intellectual order and social co-operation.[41]

Lippmann's social Freudianism was the model of his proposed integration of science and irrationality. For Lippmann, Freud was a scientist who provided an objective guide to the realm of the unconscious. He called upon Freud to prove the folly of suppression of basic instincts. Yet, unlike the other members of the Mabel Dodge circle, Lippmann emphasized the sublimation of desire rather than its gratification. One should not surrender to impulse nor suppress it, but direct it toward a higher aim. Lippmann believed that

Freud had emphasized the repressed impulses rather than the repressive mechanism, simply because his interests were primarily therapeutic. Therefore, to make Freudianism available for social progress, Lippmann proposed a scientific understanding of the nature and possibilities of the "psychic censor." [42]

From this viewpoint, social reform appeared as a problem of social control. It involved a strong and active state, like Croly's, which would use its powers to minimize social conflict and promote the development of social harmony. This state would be dedicated to a social program "carried out against the active opposition of class interest and sectional prejudices." The trusts were to be regulated vigorously, and the labor movement was not to become "the plaything of its own vision." Both must be disciplined and joined to the other interests of civilization.[43]

Lippmann believed that as part of the increased scale and complexity of all social and economic life, reform had shifted from moral to technical issues. Political problems derived not from corruption and dishonesty but rather from lack of insight and intelligence. One must, therefore, appeal less to honesty and more to expertise. All efficient organizations produced natural pyramids of power, thought Lippmann; therefore, a strong and active

40 *Ibid.*, pp. 18, 155, 195–96, 212–13, 225–36, 302. H. Stuart Hughes, in *Consciousness and Society* (New York: Alfred A. Knopf, 1958), discusses the European origins of the irrationalist thought reflected in Lippmann's work.

41 Mabel Dodge Luhan, *Intimate Memories: Movers and Shakers*, II (New York: Harcourt, Brace, 1936), pp. 92, 118; Lippmann, *Preface to Politics*, p. 301; *Drift and Mastery* (New York: Mitchell Kennerley, 1914), pp. 274–76, 281–85, 289–334; "Unrest," *New Republic*, XX (Nov. 12, 1919), 320–21.

42 Walter Lippmann, "An Epic of Desire," *New Republic*, VII (May 6, 1916), 21–22, *Preface to Politics*, pp. 51–52, *Drift and Mastery*, pp. 258, 271–72, and "Trotter and Freud," *New Republic*, IX (Nov. 18, 1916), Supp. 18.

43 Lippmann, *Drift and Mastery*, pp. 72–76, 145–46, 169, 327, 328, and "Integrated America," *New Republic*, VI (Feb. 19, 1916), 63–65. Lippmann was later to propose a plan to eliminate strikes, which he felt caused too much economic disruption. "Can the Strike Be Abandoned?" *New Republic*, XXI (Jan. 21, 1920), 224–27.

state must have strong leadership. This leadership, as Croly had advised, would be tempered by the forms of direct democracy. Yet the leaders would create issues with a view to the needs of the people and organize for popular support.[44]

Such issues were the nationalization of the railroads and comprehensive social insurance. These would give the country a basis for order, purpose, and discipline. They would serve as Hamiltonian devices in the twentieth century, just as funding the national debt had served in the eighteenth. However, it was the broad mass of the people rather than the rich and well-born who would be given a vested interest in their government. The nation's misfortune was that the rudderless rich, "untrained and uneducated," were born to power. Lippmann's nationalized America, given direction and discipline by expert administrators, would rectify this.[45]

[44] Lippmann, *Drift and Mastery*, pp. 10–26, 35–37, 261, *Preface to Politics*, pp. 16, 18, 59, 97–103, 115–16, 195–97, 250–51, 261, 263, 301–2, "Insiders and Outsiders," *New Republic*, V (Nov. 13, 1915), 35; "The puzzle of Hughes," *ibid.*, VIII (Sept. 30, 1916), 213. Lippmann greatly admired H. G. Wells's novel, *The New Machiavelli*, which described a "student of social conditions and political theory" who entered Parliament and found little hope in radicalism, socialism, or the Liberal Party. He became a Tory in order to bring social regeneration from the top down.

[45] Lippmann, "Integrated America," pp. 62 ff., "Albert, The Male," *New Republic*, VII (July 23, 1916), 301, and "Mr. Rockefeller on the Stand," *ibid.*, I (Jan. 30, 1915), 13. Lippmann's foreign policy was a program of social control projected upon the world of nations. Abstract justice was irrelevant. The fundamental problem was one of diplomatic anarchy, and "the ideal condition of the world would, of course, be the concentration of power in the hands of those whose purposes were civilized." Walter Lippmann, *The Stakes of Diplomacy* (New York: Henry Holt, 1915), pp. 220–21, 82 ff.

Lippmann's attachment to scientific management was to be expected. While the Eastern Rate Case was still in progress, he wrote an article praising the scientific management experts who were "setting the world in order" and "humanizing" work. He saw them as the logical culmination of the muckraking movement, which had begun with questions of honesty and ended with questions of efficiency. The increased production which their discoveries yielded would provide the funds of progress. In addition, scientific management would help create a new type of business leader who could forsake the "cesspool of commercialism" for the independence and dignity of professionalism. Lippmann thought that the graduate schools of business, which Brandeis had praised, would play an important role in the new collective business organization in which the profiteer would give way to the "industrial statesman." [46]

Lippmann's concept of professionalism, like Croly's, was tied to bigness. The managers of the big corporations stood outside of "the higgling of the market" and could rise above the profit motive. The bigness of the corporations permitted the development of specialized competence which could be exercised independent of the shareholders, "the most incompetent constituency conceivable." In the great mass-production industries, "private property will melt away; its functions will be taken over by the salaried men who direct them, by government commissions, by developing labor unions." This socialized managerial revolution was to make big business cultured,

[46] Lippmann, "More Brains—Less Sweat," pp. 827–28, *Drift and Mastery*, pp. 10–11, 23–26, 46–49, 115–17, 119–20, 328, and "Wilson and Little Business," *Metropolitan Magazine*, XL (August 1914), 23–25.

234

magnanimous, and aware of "the larger demands of civilized life." [47]

Of course, there was the objection that bigness yielded inefficiency. Brandeis, using in part the facts of scientific management (the fact that the plants where it was used were of medium size), cast doubt upon the efficiency of bigness. Lippmann, using the logic of scientific management (the logic of the planning department and its generalized laws), came to the aid of bigness. Administration, Lippmann explained, was becoming a science capable of dealing with tremendous units.[48]

Lippmann, Croly, and Brandeis evolved social programs in which both scientific management and the trade union movement had important places. One of the difficulties in this position was that organized labor rejected scientific management, and most efficiency experts rejected trade unionism. This did not prove discouraging, however, for Lippmann, Croly, and Brandeis believed that science, expertism, and some form of democracy could be made to work together both in society and in the factory.

Their programs for the factory they usually called "industrial democracy." This term had been used earlier to describe the various shop-representation plans of the industrial betterment workers. These devices included "suggestion box" techniques and profit-sharing and even management-sharing plans based on stock purchases by

workmen. Brandeis' "industrial democracy" derived directly from these schemes. Though stock-holding workers were not part of his program, shop representation in itself was a substitute for it. Property ownership, Brandeis believed, developed independence and responsibility. (This was one of the reasons for his support for smallness.) The worker, who could not own property, would gain his independence through his union and his sense of responsibility by having a say in shop affairs. Industrial democracy would eliminate the objections to scientific management on the part of the worker. The conflict between the unions and the efficiency engineers, Brandeis said, was based upon misunderstanding. Those aspects of management to which the laws of science did not as yet apply were to be subject to collective bargaining. Where science did apply, a union representative might serve as a watchdog to make sure that it was the laws of science and not class interest which was obeyed. That the laws of science might serve class interest did not seem to be a possibility.[49]

The whiff of guild socialism which was added to the already vaporous formula of "industrial democracy" in the years just before the war gave nothing to its precision but did make it more interesting to the younger reformers. Lippmann, who thought that guild socialism was a way to "ride the forces of syndicalism and use them for constructive purpose," incorporated some of its suggestions into his version of "industrial democracy." [50] The unions, as well as the managers and the state,

[47] Lippmann, *Drift and Mastery*, pp. 35–36, 38–39, 46, 48–49, 57–59, 60, 63. The romance of bigness occasionally pops up in progressive novels as part of the protest against acquisitiveness. Robert Herrick's *The Memoirs of An American Citizen* (1905) points out that little business is sordid and mean while big business may be poetic. Van Harrington, the hero, breaks with traditional commercial ethics, but his work is justified by its creativeness and its service to humanity.

[48] Lippmann, *Drift and Mastery*, pp. 39–42.

[49] "Testimony of Louis D. Brandeis," *U.S. Commission on Industrial Relations*, 64th Cong. 1st Sess. (Ser. Vol. 6936), pp. 7660 ff., and (Ser. Vol. 6929), pp. 991–92, 1004; Brandeis, *Curse of Bigness*, pp. 35 ff., and *Business—a Profession* (1933 ed.), pp. 53–56.

[50] Lippmann, *Preface to Politics*, pp. 287–89. Robert Grosvenor Valentine provided a link

were to have a voice in the running of industry. The union with a say in management would protect the workers from exploitation and give them the discipline and interest in efficiency necessary for industrial advance. The real peril to the nation was not labor with power and responsibility but workers with "nothing to lose but their chains." For Croly, a form of co-management would not only protect the worker and bring him to accept efficiency methods, but would also preserve some dignity in the subordinate position he held in the factory. There was no loss of self-respect, Croly argued, when subordination was self-imposed. Industrial democracy became a staple program for the *New Republic*. A young Chicago lawyer, Donald Richberg, who later became better known as chief administrator of the NRA, suggested that industrial democracy might even lead the unions to lay aside the strike.[51]

Brandeis, Croly, and Lippmann shared a broad congruence of outlook. Stepping outside the dominant modes of progressivism, they tried to construct reform programs which could be fulfilled without a direct appeal to conscience. They attacked commercialism and acquisitiveness and wished to substitute the non-pecuniary posture of the professional. Acceptance of the age of mass participation in politics was balanced by an attachment to the expert and his guiding role in an active government. Scientific management, especially when placed within the conditions of industrial democracy, embodied in the factory the regime these progressive thinkers envisioned within society at large.

Their differences were often expressive of the changes taking place in American intellectual and social life. While Brandeis and Croly rejected the simple moralism prevalent in progressive reform, they clearly retained a belief that the ultimate direction of reform was toward moral improvement in a traditional sense. With Lippmann, this was much less clear. Brandeis' support for scientific management was accompanied by advocacy of resale price maintenance and open-price trade associations, devices for small business survival in an age of industrial giants. In contrast, Croly's and Lippmann's support of scientific management was accompanied by advocacy of bigness, and specialization and by a moderate anti-property bias.[52] Brandeis' reform program spoke to an old middle class. Croly's and Lippmann's spoke to the new.

---

between Brandeis and the *New Republic* on the issues of scientific management and industrial democracy. Though affected by the guild socialist notions which had influenced the *New Republic* version of industrial democracy, he also worked with Brandeis to introduce scientific management techniques into the New York garment industry within the system of "industrial self-government" which Brandeis had set up. Louis Levine, *The Women's Garment Workers* (New York: B. W. Huebsch, 1924), pp. 306–9; "Robert Grosvenor Valentine," *New Republic*, IX (Nov. 25, 1916), 84 ff.

[51] Lippmann, *Drift and Mastery*, pp. 92–100; Croly, *Progressive Democracy*, p. 402, chap. xviii; "Tolerated Unions," *New Republic*, I (Nov. 7, 1914), 12; "Substitute for Violence," *ibid.* (Dec. 12, 1914), p. 9; "Another Cassandra," *New Republic*, III (July 17, 1915), 271; Donald R. Richberg, "Democratization of Industry," *ibid.*, XI (May 12, 1917), 50. Robert F. Hoxie's *Scientific Management and Labor* (New York:

D. Appleton, 1915), which sympathized with the aspirations but was sharply critical of some of the practices of scientific management, led the *New Republic* to be more insistent on workers' consultation in scientific management. See Alvin S. Johnson, "Hoxie's *Scientific Management and Labor*," *New Republic*, V (Dec. 4, 1915), 127; "Democratic Control of Scientific Management," *ibid.*, IX (Dec. 23, 1916), 264.

[52] Croly, *Progressive Democracy*, p. 385; Lippmann, *Drift and Mastery*, pp. 50–65.

HISTORIOGRAPHICAL NOTE

The first historians of the progressive movement saw it largely as a reaction to changes that came with industrial development. In particular they thought of it as part of a long-term effort to limit or reduce the economic power accumulated by a business elite. Humane and liberal, most of them sympathized with progressive aims, and they enlisted in the struggle against injustice. Benjamin De Witt and others wrote books to show that progressivism was but a continuation of earlier battles against privilege. Few scholars thought of the progressive movement as an isolated phenomenon; to them it represented one phase of a long and honorable tradition. Thus, with the passage of time, it was easy for many historians to associate the New Deal of the thirties with progressivism, just as they associated progressivism with late-nineteenth-century reform agitation.

This approach to the progressive years, with its emphasis on continuities, unfortunately left too many questions unanswered and too many apparent inconsistencies unexplained. Why, for example, did Theodore Roosevelt, a Republican who never cared very much for the Populist reformers, attract an enthusiastic progressive following? Why did many of the old progressives later turn against Franklin Roosevelt and the New Deal? Clearly progressivism—and the reform tradition of which it was supposed to have been a part—demanded more sophisticated analysis.

Gradually historians began to undertake intensive studies of cities and states, hoping to find clues that would lead them to a fuller understanding of the progressive movement. One of the first and most important of such studies is George Mowry's *The California Progressives* (Berkeley and Los Angeles, 1951). After careful analysis, Mowry concludes that progressives typically belonged to the middle or professional classes of cities; imbued with middle-class values, they were obviously troubled by the growing power of organized business and labor. Another regional study is Arthur Mann's *Yankee Reformers in the Urban Age* (Cambridge, Mass., 1954). Although arguing that immigrants could be reformers too, Mann corroborates Mowry's suggestion that progressivism was to a very large degree urban rather than rural in origin.

In the meantime, as various monographic studies made their appearance, intellectual historians set themselves to writing syntheses of reform thought. Perhaps the most important of such syntheses is Richard Hofstadter's *The Age of Reform, From Bryan to F.D.R.* (New York, 1955). Drawing on the insights of social scientists as well as the findings of other scholars, Hofstadter focuses attention on social groups rather than on individual thinkers. He takes into consideration political moods as well as political ideas, and he recognizes the nonrational character of much progressive sentiment. His book clearly represents a degree of detachment from the reform tradition that had not characterized earlier work.

Following the publication of *The Age of Reform,* few historians continued to write of progressivism from the viewpoint of involved participants. The liberal historical consensus disintegrated as studies of the movement shifted toward criticism—and even deprecation—on the one hand, and dispassionate analysis on the other. Three recent books, in particular, reflect the new critical attitude toward progressivism. In *The Crossroads of Liberalism* (New York, 1961), Charles Forcey examines the thought of Herbert Croly, Walter Lippmann, and Walter Weyl. He finds their progressivism wanting in the exigencies of the period before the American entry into World War I, and he contends that their failure to cope with harsh realities of power was symptomatic of progressive decline. Gabriel Kolko's *The Triumph of Conservatism* (New York, 1963) elaborates on the ways in which leaders of business and finance adapted portions of the progressive program to their own purposes and gained control of regulatory agencies. Christopher Lasch, in *The New Radicalism in America* (New York, 1965), deals with the political failure of the intellectuals. In his view, they were unable to create reality from their hopes and visions.

These three studies are matched by three others that are less indignant, but equally detached, in their treatment of progressivism. Robert Wiebe takes as the theme of *Businessmen and Reform* (Cambridge, Mass., 1962) the participation of businessmen in the framing of progressive legislation. Samuel Haber, concentrating on both the thought of progressives and the ideas and activities of businessmen in *Efficiency and Uplift* (Chicago, 1964), concludes that the cult of efficiency had an enormous influence on the directions taken by the reform movement. And finally, Otis Graham's *An Encore for Reform* (New York, 1967) provides a study of those progressives who survived into the thirties. Concerned especially with their reactions to the New Deal, Graham finds hostility as well as support.

The recent works by scholars such as Forcey, Kolko, Lasch, Wiebe, Haber, and Graham, written outside the liberal consensus that prevailed for a generation or more, have cast the progressive period in new terms. While students of Populism have tended to view the farmers' movement as more radical than was once thought, students of twentieth-century reform have been inclined to see progressivism as more conservative and less effective than their predecessors had seen it. These new assessments, along with re-interpretations of the thirties, have seriously weakened the case for continuity of reform from Populism to the New Deal. On the other hand, Michael Rogin, in *The Intellectuals and McCarthy* (Cambridge, Mass., and London, 1967), suggests that throughout the twentieth century liberalism and conservatism have each rested upon a remarkably stable power base. While Rogin is especially critical of those who saw in Populism the roots of McCarthyism, his argument and his statistical analysis lead to an emphasis on continuities. Voters who supported the Populists and progressives had much in common with those who oppose McCarthy, while voters who supported McCarthy had distinctly anti-progressive antecedents.

14. Darwinism, Pragmatism, Science, and Power

INTRODUCTION

In his famous essay, written in 1911, the philosopher George Santayana wrote that America was a nation with a divided mind. On one side, there was the practical, efficient, exploiting American mentality, occupied with pioneering and business affairs. On the other side, there was an inherited concern with abstract and "higher" things—ideals, religion, ceremonies, and doctrines—matters that Santayana called "genteel." American culture was distinctive, according to Santayana, because of the long separation between these two halves of a national personality, between intellect and experience, between what he called "Sabbath" and "weekday" attitudes. Santayana went on to say,

> The truth is that one-half of the American mind, that not occupied intensely in practical affairs . . . has floated gently in the back-water, while, alongside, in invention and industry and social organization, the other half of the mind was leaping down a sort of Niagara rapids. This division may be found symbolized in American architecture: a neat reproduction of the colonial mansion . . . stands beside the sky-scraper. The American Will inhabits the sky-scraper; the American Intellect inhabits the colonial mansion.

The intellectual history of the period between the Civil War and World War I can be best understood as the history of attempts to cure the situation that Santayana diagnosed. One after another, American intellectuals recognized the symptoms of the separation between thought and work, ideas and actions, ideals and actualities. This recognition was an uncomfortable experience because it threatened intellectuals with irrelevance. Unless the separation between culture and social realities could be bridged somehow, the lives and careers of men of letters would become mere decoration on the humming engines of American civilization.

Some intellectuals, such as Henry Adams in his famous autobiography, *The Education of Henry Adams*, met the situation with announcements of failure and chaos. Others dreamed utopias. Edward Bellamy, in his best-selling novel, *Looking Backward,* painted a picture of Boston in the year 2000 as a society in which practical achievements and ideals were closely tied. Some others, such as Henry James, turned to Europe for relief from the "complex fate" of being an artist in a country whose loyalties were to production and efficiency. But Adams, Bellamy, and Henry James, brilliant as they were and enduring as their work has been, were not really in step with the majority of their intellectual contemporaries. For most men of learning and talent, the lesson of Santayana's essay was fairly simple: conceptions of intellect ought to be revised to bring them into touch with American realities. This did not mean an abandonment of ideals and an embracing of mere practicality. It meant, instead, an attempt to discover new ideals that might give meaning and direction to experience

This attempt took a variety of forms. In literature, for example, it resulted in "realism" and "naturalism," styles that tried to bring reality— either commonplace or ugly and evil—to fiction. For writers like William Dean Howells or Theodore Dreiser, the novel was not just a pleasing alternative to life but a creative effort to portray and penetrate life as it actually was. The outcome, especially after about 1890, was dozens of novels whose purpose it was to promote social reforms. Literature, within such a program, not only could be related to real life, but might exercise a certain amount of control over it.

The discipline of history was transformed during the period in similar ways. During the first three-quarters of the nineteenth century, historians had written about the American past with what Santayana called a "Sabbath" attitude, interpreting national history as the career of certain elevated ideals such as democracy or liberty. Toward the end of the century, young historians began to study the ways in which concrete realities had determined national character and public policy. In 1893, Frederick Jackson Turner announced his influential theory that the experience of settling the frontier had determined the ways Americans thought about such elevated notions as equality and individualism. Charles Beard, just as influential as Turner in the long run, published in 1913 his *An Economic Interpretation of the Constitution,* which attempted to show how the specific interests of men of property had dictated some of the most important provisions of the federal Constitution. What was true for literature and for history was true as well for every other field of learning. Psychology, sociology, anthropology, political science, economics, and philosophy were all under the same pressure to devise methods and to reach conclusions that would have relevant consequences in the real world.

The most familiar intellectual expression of this shift in attitudes was the philosophy that came to be known as pragmatism. There always seemed to be a certain embarrassment about the name of the school. Charles Sanders Peirce, the logician whom William James credited with being the founder of pragmatism, eventually called his version of it pragmati*cism.* James finally seized on the phrase "radical empiricism." John Dewey, the third principal figure in the movement, called himself an "instrumentalist" and sometimes a "scientific humanist." This superfluity of names was a result of the fact that "pragmatism" was not so much a philosophy as a style, a generalized intellectual stance. James summed it up as neatly as anyone ever has:

> The pragmatist turns away from abstraction and insufficiency, from verbal solutions, from bad *a priori* reasons, from fixed principles, closed systems, and pretended absolutes and origins. He turns towards concreteness and adequacy, towards facts, towards action and towards power.

In this description of the pragmatic style, James might well have been speaking not just for a few philosophers but for intellectuals in every field of inquiry. James and Dewey simply launched in philosophy very much the same kind of program as that pursued by Thorstein Veblen in economics, Beard in history, and William Graham Sumner in sociology.

A great deal of emphasis has been placed on the influence of James' and Dewey's pragmatism on intellectuals in other disciplines. It would be more accurate to say that intellectuals in all fields were making similar responses to the same sorts of challenges. There were two general causes for intellectuals' concern with concreteness, adequacy, action, and power. The first was a theory, Charles Darwin's theory of evolution. Darwin's *Origin of Species,* which was published in 1859, frightened some men because it challenged Scripture. A few others tried to use the theory to justify business competition and the accumulation of great fortunes—based on the idea that "survival of the fittest" was just as much a fact of human experience as of biology. But for most intellectuals, the meaning of the theory had nothing important to do with Scripture or with business practices. Darwinism was important to the generation of American thinkers who matured after the Civil War because of two other messages it seemed to contain. The first of these was that man, since he was descended from the beasts, occupied no permanently special place in nature. His reason, then, rather than being a gift of the Creator that set man finally apart from the rest of nature, was the outcome of a purely natural process. Darwinism seemed to say that man's highest aspirations and ideals—conscience, art, religion, and so on—would have to be studied in terms of their practical uses and survival values. The second lesson that seemed implicit in Darwinism was that science, and with it all forms of inquiry, should examine factual states of affairs rather than play intellectual games with what ought to be. The *Origin of Species* seemed to mean that men ought to be concerned with changing realities rather than with perfect, unrealized ideals.

The second general cause of the heightened concern with action and power was not a theory but a set of facts. The revolutions in industrial technology and business organization created enormous new pools of unfamiliar power. Old assurances, built on agrarian and village realities, had to give way. The secondary effects of industrialism—the breaking up of local culture, the enormous new immigration of southern and eastern Europeans, the rise of cities and of their slums—were as frightening as they were exciting. The great danger seemed to almost everyone in America to be loss of control. Reformers feared the uncontrolled power of trusts. Voters feared political bosses and machines over which they could exercise no control. Businessmen feared the power of agrarian and labor protest and the threat of "anarchy." Native Americans feared the new urban ghettos, where uncontrolled ignorance, disease, and violence festered. Most of the intellectuals of the period came from small towns and from native families with English, German, or Scandinavian backgrounds. Given the new situation they confronted, it was no accident that words such as power, control, discipline, restraint, and action composed so large a part of their conceptual vocabulary.

I. EARLY INTERPRETATION

The finest book on American history published between the 1880's and the 1930's was probably *Main Currents in American Thought* by Vernon Louis Parrington. Parrington did not live to complete this three-volume masterpiece, but he did sketch out much of the third volume, which he planned to call *The Beginnings of Critical Realism in America, 1860–1920*. In this volume, as it was published posthumously, there was included the following selection—a sardonic eulogy for Parrington's own liberal generation. Parrington's chapter provides a nice example of what was to be the prevailing modern interpretation of the intellectual history of the late-nineteenth and early-twentieth centuries. He links the intellectual experience of his generation closely to politics; he assumes that his contemporaries' liberalism was an expression of the "real" American spirit which had been waiting patiently for an opportunity to show itself; and he supposes that the defeat of the forces of pragmatism and democracy came because "the war intervened and the green fields shriveled in an afternoon."

VERNON LOUIS PARRINGTON

Liberals whose hair is growing thin and the lines of whose figures are no longer what they were, are likely to find themselves today in the unhappy

Reprinted from Vernon Louis Parrington, THE BEGINNINGS OF CRITICAL REALISM IN AMERICA, *1860–1920, Vol. III of* MAIN CURRENTS IN AMER- ICAN THOUGHT *(New York: Harcourt, Brace & World, Inc., 1927–1930), pp. 401–413, by permission of the publisher.*

predicament of being treated as mourners at their own funerals. When they pluck up heart to assert that they are not yet authentic corpses, but living men with brains in their heads, they are pretty certain to be gently chided and led back to the comfortable armchair that befits senility. Their counsel is smiled at as the chatter of a belated post-Victorian generation that knew not Freud, and if they must go abroad they are bidden take the air in the garden where other old-fashioned plants—mostly of the family *Demo-cratici*—are still preserved. It is not pleasant for them. It is hard to be dispossessed by one's own heirs, and especially hard when those heirs, in the cheerful ignorance of youth, forget to acknowledge any obligations to a hardworking generation that laid by a very substantial body of intellectual wealth, the income from which the heirs are spending without even a "Thank you." If therefore the middle-aged liberal occasionally grows irritable and indulges in caustic comment on the wisdom of talkative young men it may be set down as the prerogative of the armchair age and lightly forgiven.

Yet in sober fact there are the solidest reasons for such irritation. The younger liberals who love to tweak the nose of democracy are too much enamored of what they find in their own mirrors. They are indisputably clever, they are spouting geysers of smart and cynical talk, they have far outrun their fathers in the free handling of ancient tribal totems—but they are afflicted with the short perspective of youth that finds a vanishing-point at the end of its own nose. There is no past for them beyond yesterday. They are having so good a time playing with ideas that it does not occur to them to question the validity of their intellectual processes or to inquire into the origins of the ideas they have adopted so blithely. Gaily engaged in smashing *bourgeois* idols, the young intellectuals are too busy to realize that it was the older generation that provided them with a hammer and pointed out the idols to be smashed. It is the way of youth.

Middle-aged liberals—let it be said by way of defense—at least know their history. They were brought up in a great age of liberalism—an age worthy to stand beside the golden forties of the last century—and they went to school to excellent teachers. Darwin, Spencer, Mill, Karl Marx, Haeckel, Taine, William James, Henry George, were masters of which no school in any age need feel ashamed; nor were such tutors and undermasters as Ruskin, William Morris, Matthew Arnold, Lester Ward, Walt Whitman, Henry Adams, to be dismissed as incompetent. To the solution of the vexing problems entailed by industrialism—in America as well as in Europe—was brought all the knowledge that had been accumulating for a century. It was a time of reëvaluations when much substantial thinking was done; when the flood of light that came with the doctrine of biological evolution lay brilliant on the intellectual landscape and the dullest mind caught some of the reflection. Few of the young scholars attended the lectures of Friedrich Nietzsche, and behavioristic psychology had not yet got into the curriculum; but Ladd and James were inquiring curiously into the mechanism of the brain, and animal psychology was preparing the way for the later Freudians. It was the end of an age perhaps, the rich afterglow of the Enlightenment, but the going down of the sun was marked by sunset skies that gave promise of other and greater dawns.

To have spent one's youth in such a school was a liberal education. The mind opened of its own will. Intellectual horizons were daily widening and the new perspectives ran out into cosmic spaces. The cold from those outer spaces had not yet chilled the enthusiasms that were a heritage from the Enlightenment, and the social idealism begotten by the democratic nature school still looked confidently to the future. They were ardent democrats—the young liberals of the nineties—and none doubted the finality or sufficiency of the democratic principle, any more than Mill or Spencer had doubted it. All their history and all their biology justified it, and the business of the times was to make it prevail in the sphere of economics as it prevailed in the realm of the political. The cure for the evils of democracy was held to be more democracy, and when industrialism had been brought under its sway —when America had become an economic democracy—a just and humane civilization would be on the threshold of possibility. To the achievement of that great purpose the young liberals devoted themselves and the accomplishments of the next score of years were the work of their hands. Certain intellectuals had been democrats— Paine and Jefferson and Emerson and Thoreau and Whitman and Melville— but they were few in comparison with the skeptical Whigs who professed democracy only to bind its hands. The Republican party had not been democratic since former days—and as Henry Adams said in 1880, it was accounted foolishness to believe in it in 1880. Autocracy was a toy to distract the voting man from the business of money-getting.

It was from such a school—richer in intellectual content, one might argue, than any the younger liberals have frequented—that the ferment of twenty years ago issued; a school dedicated to the ideals of the Enlightenment and bent on carrying through the unfulfilled program of democracy. Democratic aspirations had been thwarted hitherto by the uncontrolled play of the acquisitive instinct; the immediate problem of democracy was the control of that instinct in the common interest. Economics had controlled the political state to its narrow and selfish advantage; it was for the political state to resume its sovereignty and extend its control over economics. So in the spirit of

the Enlightenment the current liberalism dedicated itself to history and sociology, accepting as its immediate and particular business a reëxamination of the American past in order to forcast an ampler democratic future. It must trace the rise of political power in America in order to understand how that power had fallen into the unsocial hands of economics. The problem was difficult. American political history had been grossly distorted by partisan interpretation and political theory had been dissipated by an arid constitutionalism. The speculative thinker had long been dispossessed by the eulogist and the lawyer, both of whom had subsisted on a thin gruel of patriotic myths. Even the social historians, though dealing in materials rich in suggestion, had been diffident in the matter of interpretation, without which history is no more than the dry bones of chronicle. Inheriting no adequate philosophy of historical evolution, the young school of historians must first provide themselves with one, in the light of which the American past should take on meaning, and the partisan struggles, hitherto meaningless, should fall into comprehensible patterns.

That necessary work was to engage them for years, but in the meanwhile, as critical realists, their immediate business was with facts and the interpretation of facts. John Fiske a few years before had essayed to interpret the rise of democracy in America by analogy from biological evolution, tracing the source of American democracy to the New England town meeting, which he explained as a resurgence of ancient Teutonic folk-ways. The theory was tenuous and it was not till Professor Turner drew attention to the creative influence of the frontier on American life that the historians were provided with a suggestive working hypothesis. Before that hypothesis could be adequately explored, however, and brought into just relations to a comprehensive philosophy of history, the rise of liberalism was well under way, marked by a rich ferment of thought that made the early years of the new century singularly stimulating. That ferment resulted from pouring into the vial of native experience the reagent of European theory—examining the ways of American industrialism in the light of continental socialism; and the result was an awakening of popular interest in social control of economics, a widespread desire to bring an expanding industrialism into subjection to a rational democratic program, that was to provide abundant fuel to the social unrest that had burst forth in sporadic flames for a generation. The great movement of liberalism that took possession of the American mind after the turn of the century—a movement not unworthy to be compared with the ferment of the eighteen forties—was the spontaneous reaction of an America still only half urbanized, still clinging to ideals and ways of an older simpler America, to an industrialism that was driving its plowshare through the length and breadth of the familiar scene, turning under the rude furrows what before had been growing familiarly there. It was the first reaction of America to the revolutionary change that followed upon the exhaustion of the frontier—an attempt to secure through the political state the freedoms that before had come from unpreempted opportunity.

For a quarter of a century following the great westward expansion of the late sixties America had been drifting heedlessly towards a different social order. The shambling frontier democracy that had sufficed an earlier time was visibly breaking down in presence of the imperious power of a centralizing capitalism. The railways were a dramatic embodiment of the new machine civilization that was running head on into a primitive social organism fashioned by the old domestic economy, and the disruptions and confusions were a warning that the country was in for vast changes. New masters, new ways. The rule of the captain of industry had come. The farmers had long been in ugly mood, but their great rebellion was put down in 1896, and never again could they hope to wrest sovereignty from capitalism. The formal adoption of the gold standard in 1900 served notice to the world that America had put away its democratic agrarianism, that a shambling Jacksonian individualism had had its day, and that henceforth the destiny of the country lay in the hands of its business men. Capitalism was master of the country and though for the present it was content to use the political machinery of democracy it was driving towards an objective that was the negation of democracy.

The immediate reaction to so broad a shift in the course of manifest destiny was a growing uneasiness amongst the middle class—small business and professional men—who looked with fear upon the program of the captains of industry. Industrialization brought its jars and upsets. The little fish did not enjoy being swallowed by the big, and as they watched the movement of economic centralization encroaching on the field of competition they saw the doors of opportunity closing to them. It was to this great body of *petite bourgeoisie* that members of the lesser intellectuals—journalists, sociologists, reformers—were to make appeal. The work was begun dramatically with the spectacularly advertised *Frenzied Finance,* written by Thomas W. Lawson, and appearing as a series in *McClure's*

Magazine in 1903. The immense popular success of the venture proved that the fire was ready for the fat, and at once a host of volunteer writers fell to feeding the flames. The new ten-cent magazines provided the necessary vehicle of publicity, and enterprising editors were soon increasing their circulations with every issue. As it became evident how popular was the chord that had been struck, more competent workmen joined themselves to the group of journalists: novelists—a growing army of them—essayists, historians, political scientists, philosophers, a host of heavy-armed troops that moved forward in a frontal attack on the strongholds of the new plutocracy. Few writers in the years between 1903 and 1917 escaped being drawn into the movement—an incorrigible romantic perhaps, like the young James Branch Cabell, or a cool patrician like Edith Wharton; and with such popular novelists as Winston Churchill, Robert Herrick, Ernest Poole, David Graham Phillips, Upton Sinclair, and Jack London embellishing the rising liberalism with dramatic heroes and villains, and dressing their salads with the wickedness of Big Business; with such political leaders as Bob La Follette and Theodore Roosevelt and Woodrow Wilson beating up the remotest villages for recruits; with such scholars as Thorstein Veblen, Charles A. Beard,ꞌ and John Dewey, and such lawyers as Louis Brandeis, Frank P. Walsh, and Samuel Untermyer, the movement gathered such momentum and quickened such a ferment as had not been known before in the lands since the days of the Abolition controversy. The mind and conscience of America were stirred to their lowest sluggish stratum, and a democratic renaissance was all aglow on the eastern horizon.

At the core it was a critical realistic movement that spread quietly amongst intellectuals, but the nebulous tail of the comet blazed across the sky for all to wonder at: and it was the tail rather than the core that aroused the greatest immediate interest. Lincoln Steffens, Charles Edward Russell, Ida Tarbell, Gustavus Myers, and Upton Sinclair were read eagerly because they dealt with themes that many were interested in—the political machine, watered stock, Standard Oil, the making of great fortunes, and the like—and they invested their exposures with the dramatic interest of a detective story. Up to 1910 it was largely a muckraking movement—to borrow President Roosevelt's picturesque phrase; a time of brisk housecleaning that searched out old cobwebs and disturbed the dust that lay thick on the antiquated furniture. The Gilded Age had been slovenly and such a housecleaning was long overdue. There was a vast amount of nosing about to discover bad smells, and to sensitive noses the bad smells seemed to be everywhere. Evidently some hidden cesspool was fouling American life, and as the inquisitive plumbers tested the household drains they came upon the source of infection—not one cesspool but many, under every city hall and beneath every state capitol—dug secretly by politicians in the pay of respectable business men. It was these cesspools that were poisoning the national household, and there would be no health in America till they were filled in and no others dug.

It was a dramatic discovery and when the corruption of American politics was laid on the threshold of business—like a bastard on the doorsteps of the father—a tremendous disturbance resulted. There was a great fluttering and clamor amongst the bats and owls, an ominous creaking of the machine as the wrenches were thrown into the well-oiled wheels, and a fierce sullen anger at the hue and cry set up. To many honest Americans the years between 1903 and 1910 were abusive and scurrilous beyond decency, years when no man and no business, however honorable, was safe from the pillory; when wholesale exposure had grown profitable to sensation-mongers, and great reputations were lynched by vigilantes and reputable corporations laid under indictment at the bar of public opinion. Respectable citizens did not like to have their goodly city held up to the world as "corrupt and contented"; they did not like to have their municipal housekeeping brought into public disrepute no matter how sluttish it might be. It was not pleasant for members of great families to read a cynical history of the origins of their fortunes, or for railway presidents seeking political favors to find on the newsstand a realistic account of the bad scandals that had smirched their roads. It was worse than unpleasant, it was hurtful to business. And so quietly, and as speedily as could be done decently, the movement was brought to a stop by pressure put on the magazines that lent themselves to such harmful disclosures. Then followed a campaign of education. Responding to judicious instruction, conducted in the columns of the most respectable newspapers, the American public was soon brought to understand that it was not the muck that was harmful, but the indiscretion of those who commented in print on the bad smells. It was reckoned a notable triumph for sober and patriotic good sense.

So after a few years of amazing activity the muckraking movement came to a stop. But not before it had done its work; not before the American middle class had been indoctrinated in the elementary principles of political real-

ism and had rediscovered the social conscience lost since the days of the Civil War. Many a totem had been thrown down by the irreverent hands of the muckrakers, and many a fetish held up to ridicule, and plutocracy in America would not recover its peace of mind until at great cost the totems should be set up again and the fetishes reanointed with the oil of sanctity. The substantial result of the movement was the instruction it afforded in the close kinship between business and politics —a lesson greatly needed by a people long fed on romantic unrealities. It did not crystallize for the popular mind in the broad principle of economic determinism; that remained for certain of the intellectuals to apply to American experience. But with its sordid object—service—it punished the flabby optimism of the Gilded Age, with its object-lessons in business politics; it revealed the hidden hand that was pulling the strings of the political puppets; it tarnished the gilding that had been carefully laid on our callous exploitation, and it brought under common suspicion the captain of industry who had risen as a national hero from the muck of individualism. It was a sharp guerilla attack on the sacred American System, but behind the thin skirmish-line lay a volunteer army that was making ready to deploy for a general engagement with plutocracy.

With the flood of light thrown upon the fundamental law by the historians, the movement of liberalism passed quickly through successive phases of thought. After the first startled surprise it set about the necessary business of acquainting the American people with its findings in the confident belief that a democratic electorate would speedily democratize the instrument. Of this first stage the late Professor J. Allen Smith's *The Spirit of American Gov-*

ernment (1907) was the most adequate expression, a work that greatly influenced the program of the rising Progressive Party. But changes came swiftly and within half a dozen years the movement had passed from political programs to economic, concerned not so greatly with political democracy as with economic democracy. Of this second phase Professor Beard's notable study, *An Economic Interpretation of the Constitution* (1913), was the greatest intellectual achievement. Underlying this significant work was a philosophy of politics that set it sharply apart from preceding studies—a philosophy that unsympathetic readers were quick to attribute to Karl Marx, but that in reality derived from sources far earlier and for Americans at least far more respectable. The current conception of the political state as determined in its form and activities by economic groups is no modern Marxian perversion of political theory; it goes back to Aristotle, it underlay the thinking of Harrington and Locke and the seventeenth-century English school, it shaped the conclusions of Madison and Hamilton and John Adams, it ran through all the discussions of the Constitutional Convention, and it reappeared in the arguments of Webster and Calhoun. It was the main-traveled road of political thought until a new highway was laid out by French engineers, who, disliking the bog of economics, surveyed another route by way of romantic equalitarianism. The logic of the engineers was excellent, but the drift of politics is little influenced by logic, and abstract equalitarianism proved to be poor material for highway construction. In divorcing political theory from contact with sobering reality it gave it over to a treacherous romanticism. In seeking to avoid the bog of economics it ran into an arid desert.

To get back once more on the main-traveled road, to put away all profitless romanticisms and turn realist, taking up again the method of economic interpretation unused in America since the days of Webster and Calhoun, became therefore the business of the second phase of liberalism to which Professor Beard applied himself. The earlier group of liberals were ill equipped to wage successful war against plutocracy. Immersed in the traditional equalitarian philosophy, they underestimated the strength of the enemies of democracy. They did not realize what legions of Swiss Guards property can summon to its defense. They were still romantic idealists tilting at windmills, and it was to bring them to a sobering sense of reality that *The Economic Interpretation of the Constitution* was written. If property is the master force in every society one cannot understand American institutional development until one has come to understand the part property played in shaping the fundamental law. Interpreted thus the myths that had gathered about the Constitution fell away of themselves and the document was revealed as English rather than French, the judicious expression of substantial eighteenth-century realism that accepted the property basis of political action, was skeptical of romantic idealisms, and was more careful to protect title-deeds to legal holdings than to claim unsurveyed principalities in Utopia. If therefore liberalism were to accomplish any substantial results it must approach its problems in the same realistic spirit, recognizing the masterful ambitions of property, recruiting democratic forces to overmaster the Swiss Guards, leveling the strongholds that property had erected within the organic law, and taking care that no new strongholds should rise.

The problem confronting liberalism was the problem of the subjection of property to social justice.

Yet interesting as was the muckraking tail of the comet, far more significant was the core—the substantial body of knowledge gathered by the scholars and flung into the scale of public opinion. The realities of the American past had been covered deep with layers of patriotic myths, provided in simpler days when the young Republic, suffering from a natural inferiority complex, was building up a defense against the acrid criticism of Tory Europe. Those myths had long since served their purpose and had become a convenient refuge for the bats and owls of the night; it was time to strip them away and apply to the past objective standards of scholarship, and to interpret it in the light of an adequate philosophy of history. To this work, so essential to any intelligent understanding of the American experiment, a group of historians and political scientists turned with competent skill, and the solid results of their labor remained after the popular ferment subsided, as a foundation for later liberals to build on.

The journalistic muckrakers had demonstrated that America was not in fact the equalitarian democracy it professed to be, and the scholars supplemented their work by tracing to its historical source the weakness of the democratic principle in governmental practice. America had never been a democracy for the sufficient reason that too many handicaps had been imposed upon the majority will. The democratic principle had been bound with withes like Samson and had become a plaything for the Philistines. From the beginning—the scholars discovered—democracy and property had been at bitter odds; the struggle invaded the Constitutional Convention, it gave form to the party alignment between Hamilton and Jefferson, Jackson and Clay, and then during the slavery struggle, sinking underground like a lost river, it nevertheless had determined party conflicts down to the present. In this ceaseless conflict between the man and the dollar, between democracy and property, the reasons for persistent triumph of property were sought in the provisions of the organic law, and from a critical study of the Constitution came a discovery that struck home like a submarine torpedo—the discovery that the drift toward plutocracy was not a drift away from the spirit of the Constitution, but an inevitable unfolding from its premises; that instead of having been conceived by the fathers as a democratic instrument, it had been conceived in a spirit designedly hostile to democracy; that it was, in fact, a carefully formulated expression of eighteenth-century property consciousness, erected as a defense against the democratic spirit that had got out of hand during the Revolution, and that the much-praised system of checks and balances was designed and intended for no other end than a check on the political power of the majority—a power acutely feared by the property consciousness of the times.

It was a startling discovery that profoundly stirred the liberal mind of the early years of the century; yet the really surprising thing is that it should have come as a surprise. It is not easy to understand today why since Civil War days intelligent Americans should so strangely have confused the Declaration of Independence and the Constitution, and have come to accept them as complementary statements of the democratic purpose of America. Their unlikeness is unmistakable: the one a classical statement of French humanitarian democracy, the other an organic law designed to safeguard the minority under republican rule. The confusion must be charged in part to the lawyers who had taken over the custodianship of the Constitution, and in part to the florid romantic temper of the middle nineteenth century. When the fierce slavery struggle fell into the past, whatever honest realism had risen from the passions of the times was buried with the dead issue. The militant attacks on the Constitution so common in Abolitionist circles after 1835, and the criticism of the Declaration that was a part of the southern argument, were both forgotten, and with the Union reestablished by force of arms, the idealistic cult of the fundamental law entered on a second youth. In the blowsy Gilded Age the old myths walked the land again, wrapped in battle-torn flags and appealing to the blood shed on southern battlefields. It was not till the advent of a generation unblinded by the passions of civil war that the Constitution again was examined critically, and the earlier charge of the Abolitionists that it was designed to serve property rather than men, was heard once more. But this time with far greater weight of evidence behind it. As the historians dug amongst the contemporary records they came upon a mass of fact the Abolitionists had been unaware of. The evidence was written so plainly, in such explicit and incontrovertible words—not only in *Elliott's Debates,* but in the minutes of the several State Conventions, in contemporary letters and memoirs, in newspapers and pamphlets and polite literature—that it seemed incredible that honest men could have erred so greatly in confusing the Constitution with the Declaration.

With the clarification of its philosophy the inflowing waters of liberalism reached flood-tide; the movement would either recede or pass over into radicalism. On the whole it followed the latter course, and the years immediately preceding 1917 were years when American intellectuals were immersing themselves in European collectivistic philosophies—in Marxianism, Fabianism, Syndicalism, Guild Socialism. New leaders were rising, philosophical analysts like Thorstein Veblen who were mordant critics of American economics. The influence of socialism was fast sweeping away the last shreds of political and social romanticism that so long had confused American thinking. The doctrine of economic determinism was spreading widely, and in the light of that doctrine the deep significance of the industrial revolution was revealing itself for the first time to thoughtful Americans. In its reaction to industrialism America had reached the point Chartist England had reached in the eighteen-forties and Marxian Germany in the eighteen-seventies. That was before a mechanistic science had laid its heavy discouragements on the drafters of democratic programs. Accepting the principle of economic determinism, liberalism still clung to its older democratic teleology, convinced that somehow economic determinism would turn out to be a fairy godmother to the proletariat and that from the imperious drift of industrial expansion must eventually issue social justice. Armed with this faith liberalism threw itself into the work of cleaning the Augean stables, and its reward came in the achievements of President Wilson's first administration.

Then the war intervened and the green fields shriveled in an afternoon. With the cynicism that came with postwar days the democratic liberalism of 1917 was thrown away like an empty whiskey-flask. Clever young men began to make merry over democracy. It was preposterous, they said, to concern one-self about social justice; nobody wants social justice. The first want of every man, as John Adams remarked a hundred years ago, is his dinner, and the second his girl. Out of the muck of the war had come a great discovery—so it was reported—the discovery that psychology as well as economics has its word to say on politics. From the army intelligence tests the moron emerged as a singular commentary on our American democracy, and with the discovery of the moron the democratic principle was in for a slashing attack. Almost overnight an army of enemies was marshaled against it. The eugenist with his isolated germ theory flouted the perfectional psychology of John Locke, with its emphasis on environment as the determining factor in social evolution—a psychology on which the whole idealistic interpretation was founded; the beardless philosopher discovered Nietzsche and in his pages found the fit master of the moron—the biological aristocrat who is the flower that every civilization struggles to produce; the satirist discovered the flatulent reality that is middle-class America and was eager to thrust his jibes at the complacent denizens of the Valley of Democracy. Only the behaviorist, with his insistence on the plasticity of the new-born child, offers some shreds of comfort to the democrat; but he quickly takes them away again with his simplification of conduct to imperious drives that stamp men as primitive animals. If the mass—the raw materials of democracy—never rises much above sex appeals and belly needs, surely it is poor stuff to try to work up into an excellent civilization, and the dreams of the social idealist who forecasts a glorious democratic future are about as substantial as moonshine. It is a discouraging essay. Yet it is perhaps conceivable that our current philosophy —the brilliant coruscations of our younger intelligentsia—may indeed not prove to be the last word in social philosophy. Perhaps—is this *lèse-majesté*—when our youngest liberals have themselves come to the armchair age they will be smiled at in turn by sons who are still cleverer and who will find their wisdom as foolish as the wisdom of 1917 seems to them today. But that lies on the knees of the gods.

II. DOCUMENTS

1. Pragmatism: A Definition

There has been so much disagreement about pragmatism that the usefulness of calling it a school is in serious doubt. But almost anyone who ever called himself a pragmatist would agree with the following selection, an eloquent statement of the pragmatic attitude by William James. James states very clearly the basic ingredient of the pragmatic style: "Theories thus become instruments, not answers to enigmas, in which we can rest." *It is important to notice James' explicit reference to the "anti-intellectualist tendencies" of pragmatism, tendencies that have bothered some historians more recent than Parrington.*

WILLIAM JAMES

Some years ago, being with a camping party in the mountains, I returned from a solitary ramble to find every one engaged in a ferocious metaphysical dispute. The *corpus* of the dispute was a squirrel—a live squirrel supposed to be clinging to one side of a tree-trunk; while over against the tree's opposite side a human being was imagined to stand. This human witness tries to get sight of the squirrel by moving rapidly round the tree, but no matter how fast he goes, the squirrel moves as fast in the opposite direction, and always keeps the tree between himself and the man, so that never a glimpse of him is caught. The resultant metaphysical problem is this: *Does the man go round the squirrel or not?* He goes round the tree, sure enough, and the squirrel is on the tree; but does he go round the squirrel? In the unlimited leisure of the wilderness, discussion had been worn threadbare. Every one had taken sides, and was obstinate; and the numbers on both sides were even. Each side, when I appeared, therefore appealed to me to make it a majority. Mindful of the scholastic adage that whenever you meet a contradiction you must make a distinction, I immediately sought and found one, as follows: "Which party is right," I said, "depends on what you *practically mean* by 'going round' the squirrel. If you mean passing from the north of him to the east, then to the south, then to the west, and then to the north of him again, obviously the man does go round him, for he occupies these successive positions. But if on the contrary you mean being first in front of him, then on the right of

Reprinted from William James, PRAGMATISM *(New York, 1908), pp. 43–65.*

him, then behind him, then on his left, and finally in front again, it is quite as obvious that the man fails to go round him, for by the compensating movements the squirrel makes, he keeps his belly turned towards the man all the time, and his back turned away. Make the distinction, and there is no occasion for any further dispute. You are both right and both wrong according as you conceive the verb 'to go round' in one practical fashion or the other."

Although one or two of the hotter disputants called my speech a shuffling evasion, saying they wanted no quibbling or scholastic hair-splitting, but meant just plain honest English "round," the majority seemed to think that the distinction had assuaged the dispute.

I tell this trivial anecdote because it is a peculiarly simple example of what I wish now to speak of as *the pragmatic method.* The pragmatic method is primarily a method of settling metaphysical disputes that otherwise might be interminable. Is the world one or many?—fated or free?—material or spiritual?—here are notions either of which may or may not hold good of the world; and disputes over such notions are unending. The pragmatic method in such cases is to try to interpret each notion by tracing its respective practical consequences. What difference would it practically make to any one if this notion rather than that notion were true? If no practical difference whatever can be traced, then the alternatives mean practically the same thing, and all dispute is idle. Whenever a dispute is serious, we ought to be able to show some practical difference that must follow from one side or the other's being right.

A glance at the history of the idea will show you still better what pragmatism means. The term is derived from the same Greek word πραγμα, meaning action, from which our words "practice" and "practical" come. It was first introduced into philosophy by Mr. Charles Peirce in 1878. In an article entitled "How to Make Our Ideas Clear," in the *Popular Science Monthly* for January of that year Mr. Peirce, after pointing out that our beliefs are really rules for action, said that, to develop a thought's meaning, we need only determine what conduct it is fitted to produce: that conduct is for us its sole significance. And the tangible fact at the root of all our thought-distinctions, however subtle, is that there is no one of them so fine as to consist in anything but a possible difference of practice. To attain perfect clearness in our thoughts of an object, then, we need only consider what conceivable effects of a practical kind the object may involve—what sensations we are to expect from it, and what reactions we must prepare. Our conception of these effects, whether immediate or remote, is then for us the whole of our conception of the object, so far as that conception has positive significance at all.

This is the principle of Peirce, the principle of pragmatism. It lay entirely unnoticed by any one for twenty years, until I, in an address before Professor Howison's Philosophical Union at the University of California, brought it forward again and made a special application of it to religion. By that date (1898) the times seemed ripe for its reception. The word "pragmatism" spread, and at present it fairly spots the pages of the philosophic journals. On all hands we find the "pragmatic movement" spoken of, sometimes with respect, sometimes with contumely, seldom with clear understanding. It is evident that the term applies itself conveniently to a number of tendencies that hitherto have lacked a collective name, and that it has "come to stay."

To take in the importance of Peirce's principle, one must get accustomed to applying it to concrete cases. I found a few years ago that Ostwald, the illustrious Leipzig chemist, had been making perfectly distinct use of the principle of pragmatism in his lectures on the philosophy of science, though he had not called it by that name.

"All realities influence our practice," he wrote me, "and that influence is their meaning for us. I am accustomed to put questions to my classes in this way: In what respects would the world be different if this alternative or that were true? If I can find nothing that would become different, then the alternative has no sense."

That is, the rival views mean practically the same thing, and meaning, other than practical, there is for us none. Ostwald in a published lecture gives this example of what he means. Chemists have long wrangled over the inner constitution of certain bodies called "tautomerous." Their properties seemed equally consistent with the notion that an instable hydrogen atom oscillates inside of them, or that they are instable mixtures of two bodies. Controversy raged, but never was decided. "It would never have begun," says Ostwald, "if the combatants had asked themselves what particular experimental fact could have been made different by one or the other view being correct. For it would then have appeared that no difference of fact could possibly ensue; and the quarrel was as unreal as if, theorizing in primitive times about the raising of dough by yeast, one party should have invoked a 'brownie,' while another insisted on an 'elf' as the true cause of the phenomenon."

It is astonishing to see how many

philosophical disputes collapse into insignificance the moment you subject them to this simple test of tracing a concrete consequence. There can *be* no difference anywhere that doesn't *make* a difference elsewhere—no difference in abstract truth that doesn't express itself in a difference in concrete fact and in conduct consequent upon that fact, imposed on somebody, somehow, somewhere, and somewhen. The whole function of philosophy ought to be to find out what definite difference it will make to you and me, at definite instants of our life, if this world-formula or that world-formula be the true one.

There is absolutely nothing new in the pragmatic method. Socrates was an adept at it. Aristotle used it methodically. Locke, Berkeley, and Hume made momentous contributions to truth by its means. Shadworth Hodgson keeps insisting that realities are only what they are "known as." But these forerunners of pragmatism used it in fragments: they were preluders only. Not until in our time has it generalized itself, become conscious of a universal mission, pretended to a conquering destiny. I believe in that destiny, and I hope I may end by inspiring you with my belief.

Pragmatism represents a perfectly familiar attitude in philosophy, the empiricist attitude, but it represents it, as it seems to me, both in a more radical and in a less objectionable form than it has ever yet assumed. A pragmatist turns his back resolutely and once for all upon a lot of inveterate habits dear to professional philosophers. He turns away from abstraction and insufficiency, from verbal solutions, from bad *a priori* reasons, from fixed principles, closed systems, and pretended absolutes and origins. He turns towards concreteness and adequacy, towards facts, towards action and to-wards power. That means the empiricist temper regnant and the rationalist temper sincerely given up. It means the open air and possibilities of nature, as against dogma, artificiality, and the pretence of finality in truth.

At the same time it does not stand for any special results. It is a method only. But the general triumph of that method would mean an enormous change in what I called in my last lecture the "temperament" of philosophy. Teachers of the ultra-rationalistic type would be frozen out, much as the courtier type is frozen out in republics, as the ultramontane type of priest is frozen out in protestant lands. Science and metaphysics would come much nearer together, would in fact work absolutely hand in hand.

Metaphysics has usually followed a very primitive kind of quest. You know how men have always hankered after unlawful magic, and you know what a great part in magic *words* have always played. If you have his name, or the formula of incantation that binds him, you can control the spirit, genie, afrite, or whatever the power may be. Solomon knew the names of all the spirits, and having their names, he held them subject to his will. So the universe has always appeared to the natural mind as a kind of enigma, of which the key must be sought in the shape of some illuminating or power-bringing word or name. That word names the universe's *principle,* and to possess it is after a fashion to possess the universe itself. "God," "Matter," "Reason," "the Absolute," "Energy," are so many solving names. You can rest when you have them. You are at the end of your metaphysical quest.

But if you follow the pragmatic method, you cannot look on any such word as closing your quest. You must bring out of each word its practical cash-value, set it at work within the stream of your experience. It appears less as a solution, then, than as a program for more work, and more particularly as an indication of the ways in which existing realities may be *changed.*

Theories thus become instruments, not answers to enigmas, in which we can rest. We don't lie back upon them, we move forward, and, on occasion, make nature over again by their aid. Pragmatism unstiffens all our theories, limbers them up and sets each one at work. Being nothing essentially new, it harmonizes with many ancient philosophic tendencies. It agrees with nominalism, for instance, in always appealing to particulars; with utilitarianism in emphasizing practical aspects; with positivism in its disdain for verbal solutions, useless questions and metaphysical abstractions.

All these, you see, are *anti-intellectualistic* tendencies. Against rationalism as a pretension and a method pragmatism is fully armed and militant. But, at the outset, at least, it stands for no particular results. It has no dogmas, and no doctrines save its method. As the young Italian pragmatist Papini has well said, it lies in the midst of our theories, like a corridor in a hotel. Innumerable chambers open out of it. In one you may find a man writing an atheistic volume; in the next some one on his knees praying for faith and strength; in a third a chemist investigating a body's properties. In a fourth a system of idealistic metaphysics is being excogitated; in a fifth the impossibility of metaphysics is being shown. But they all own the corridor, and all must pass through it if they want a practicable way of getting into or out of their respective rooms.

No particular results then, so far, but only an attitude of orientation, is what

the pragmatic method means. *The attitude of looking away from first things, principles, "categories," supposed necessities; and of looking towards last things, fruits, consequences, facts.*

So much for the pragmatic method! You may say that I have been praising it rather than explaining it to you, but I shall presently explain it abundantly enough by showing how it works on some familiar problems. Meanwhile the word pragmatism has come to be used in a still wider sense, as meaning also a certain *theory of truth.* I mean to give a whole lecture to the statement of that theory, after first paving the way, so I can be very brief now. But brevity is hard to follow, so I ask for your redoubled attention for a quarter of an hour. If much remains obscure, I hope to make it clearer in the later lectures.

One of the most successfully cultivated branches of philosophy in our time is what is called inductive logic, the study of the conditions under which our sciences have evolved. Writers on this subject have begun to show a singular unanimity as to what the laws of nature and elements of fact mean, when formulated by mathematicians, physicists and chemists. When the first mathematical, logical, and natural uniformities, the first *laws*, were discovered, men were so carried away by the clearness, beauty and simplification that resulted, that they believed themselves to have deciphered authentically the eternal thoughts of the Almighty. His mind also thundered and reverberated in syllogisms. He also thought in conic sections, squares and roots and ratios, and geometrized like Euclid. He made Kepler's laws for the planets to follow; he made velocity increase proportionally to the time in falling bodies; he made the law of the sines for light to obey when refracted; he established the classes, orders, families and genera of plants and animals, and fixed the distances between them. He thought the archetypes of all things, and devised their variations; and when we rediscover any one of these his wondrous institutions, we seize his mind in its very literal intention.

But as the sciences have developed further, the notion has gained ground that most, perhaps all, of our laws are only approximations. The laws themselves, moreover, have grown so numerous that there is no counting them; and so many rival formulations are proposed in all the branches of science that investigators have become accustomed to the notion that no theory is absolutely a transcript of reality, but that any one of them may from some point of view be useful. Their great use is to summarize old facts and to lead to new ones. They are only a man-made language, a conceptual shorthand, as some one calls them, in which we write our reports of nature; and languages, as is well known, tolerate much choice of expression and many dialects.

Thus human arbitrariness has driven divine necessity from scientific logic. If I mention the names of Sigwart, Mach, Ostwald, Pearson, Milhaud, Poincaré, Duhem, Ruyssen, those of you who are students will easily identify the tendency I speak of, and will think of additional names.

Riding now on the front of this wave of scientific logic Messrs. Schiller and Dewey appear with their pragmatistic account of what truth everywhere signifies. Everywhere, these teachers say, "truth" in our ideas and beliefs means the same thing that it means in science. It means, they say, nothing but this, *that ideas (which themselves are but parts of our experience) become true just in so far as they help us to get into satisfactory relation with other parts of our experience,* to summarize them and

get about among them by conceptual short-cuts instead of following the interminable succession of particular phenomena. Any idea upon which we can ride, so to speak; any idea that will carry us prosperously from any one part of our experience to any other part, linking things satisfactorily, working securely, simplifying, saving labor; is true for just so much, true in so far forth, true *instrumentally*. This is the "instrumental" view of truth taught so successfully at Chicago, the view that truth in our ideas means their power to "work," promulgated so brilliantly at Oxford.

Messrs. Dewey, Schiller, and their allies, in reaching this general conception of all truth, have only followed the example of geologists, biologists and philologists. In the establishment of these other sciences, the successful stroke was always to take some simple process actually observable in operation—as denudation by weather, say, or variation from parental type, or change of dialect by incorporation of new words and pronunciations—and then to generalize it, making it apply to all times, and produce great results by summating its effects through the ages.

The observable process which Schiller and Dewey particularly singled out for generalization is the familiar one by which any individual settles into *new opinions.* The process here is always the same. The individual has a stock of old opinions already, but he meets a new experience that puts them to a strain. Somebody contradicts them; or in a reflective moment he discovers that they contradict each other; or he hears of facts with which they are incompatible; or desires arise in him which they cease to satisfy. The result is an inward trouble to which his mind till then had been a stranger, and from which he seeks to escape by modifying his previous mass of opinions. He saves as much of it as he can, for in this matter of belief we are all extreme conservatives. So he tries to change first this opinion, and then that (for they resist change very variously), until at last some new idea comes up which he can graft upon the ancient stock with a minimum of disturbance of the latter, some idea that mediates between the stock and the new experience and runs them into one another most felicitously and expediently.

This new idea is then adopted as the true one. It preserves the older stock of truths with a minimum of modification, stretching them just enough to make them admit the novelty, but conceiving that in ways as familiar as the case leaves possible. An *outrée* explanation, violating all our preconceptions, would never pass for a true account of a novelty. We should scratch round industriously till we found something less excentric. The most violent resolutions in an individual's beliefs leave most of his old order standing. Time and space, cause and effect, nature and history, and one's own biography remain untouched. New truth is always a go-between, a smoother-over of transitions. It marries old opinion to new fact so as ever to show a minimum of jolt, a maximum of continuity. We hold a theory true just in proportion to its success in solving this "problem of maxima and minima." But success in solving this problem is eminently a matter of approximation. We say this theory solves it on the whole more satisfactorily than that theory; but that means more satisfactorily to ourselves, and individuals will emphasize their points of satisfaction differently. To a certain degree, therefore, everything here is plastic.

The point I now urge you to observe particularly is the part played by the older truths. Failure to take account of

it is the source of much of the unjust criticism levelled against pragmatism. Their influence is absolutely controlling. Loyalty to them is the first principle—in most cases it is the only principle; for by far the most usual way of handling phenomena so novel that they would make for a serious rearrangement of our preconception is to ignore them altogether, or to abuse those who bear witness for them.

You doubtless wish examples of this process of truth's growth, and the only trouble is their superabundance. The simplest case of new truth is of course the mere numerical addition of new kinds of facts, or of new single facts of old kinds, to our experience—an addition that involves no alteration in the old beliefs. Day follows day, and its contents are simply added. The new contents themselves are not true, they simply *come* and *are*. Truth is *what we say about* them, and when we say that they have come, truth is satisfied by the plain additive formula.

But often the day's contents oblige a rearrangement. If I should now utter piercing shrieks and act like a maniac on this platform, it would make many of you revise your idea as to the probable worth of my philosophy. "Radium" came the other day as part of the day's content, and seemed for a moment to contradict our ideas of the whole order of nature, that order having come to be identified with what is called the conservation of energy. The mere sight of radium paying heat away indefinitely out of its own pocket seemed to violate that conservation. What to think? If the radiations from it were nothing but an escape of unsuspected "potential" energy, pre-existent inside of the atoms, the principle of conservation would be saved. The discovery of "helium" as the radiation's outcome, opened a way to this belief. So Ramsay's view is generally held to be true, because, although it extends our old ideas of energy, it causes a minimum of alteration in their nature.

I need not multiply instances. A new opinion counts as "true" just in proportion as it gratifies the individual's desire to assimilate the novel in his experience to his beliefs in stock. It must both lean on old truth and grasp new fact; and its success (as I said a moment ago) in doing this, is a matter for the individual's appreciation. When old truth grows, then, by new truth's addition, it is for subjective reasons. We are in the process and obey the reasons. That new idea is truest which performs most felicitously its function of satisfying our double urgency. It makes itself true, gets itself classed as true, by the way it works; grafting itself then upon the ancient body of truth, which thus grows much as a tree grows by the activity of a new layer of cambium.

Now Dewey and Schiller proceed to generalize this observation and to apply it to the most ancient parts of truth. They also once were plastic. They also were called true for human reasons. They also mediated between still earlier truths and what in those days were novel observations. Purely objective truth, truth in whose establishment the function of giving human satisfaction in marrying previous parts of experience with newer parts played no rôle whatever, is nowhere to be found. The reasons why we call things true is the reason why they *are* true, for "to be true" *means* only to perform this marriage-function.

The trail of the human serpent is thus over everything. Truth independent; truth that we *find* merely; truth no longer malleable to human need; truth incorrigible, in a word; such truth exists indeed superabundantly—or is supposed to exist by rationalistically minded thinkers; but then it means only the dead heart of the living tree, and its being there means only that truth also has its paleontology, and its "prescription," and may grow stiff with years of veteran service and petrified in men's regard by sheer antiquity. But how plastic even the oldest truths nevertheless really are has been vividly shown in our day by the transformation of logical and mathematical ideas, a transformation which seems even to be invading physics. The ancient formulas are reinterpreted as special expressions of much wider principles, principles that our ancestors never got a glimpse of in their present shape and formulation.

2. The Influence of Darwinism

In an essay on "The Influence of Darwinism on Philosophy," John Dewey goes well beyond the kinds of surface realities discussed by Parrington's essay. Dewey's essay is not only a revealing document, but is itself a fine piece of intellectual history. He sums up brilliantly the ways in which Darwinism undercut older ways of looking at reality. He also illustrates one of the characteristics of his generation: its acute self-consciousness of itself as a generation cut free from the faiths of its fathers and striking out in radical new directions. It is important to notice, also, that Dewey does not refer to any problems of politics or to any social evils that Darwinism might il-

luminate or help solve. Dewey was interested in politics and social progress, but he was also, always, a professional philosopher.

Dewey's "Influence of Darwinism on Philosophy" has a parallel in Thorstein Veblen's "Why is Economics Not an Evolutionary Science?" Veblen makes a near-perfect statement of the contrast between pre-evolutionary and post-evolutionary concepts of human nature. The concept of man used in classical economics, according to Veblen, was essentially that of a passive "homogeneous globule of desire." The new economics must recognize the fact that it is "characteristic of man to do something." Veblen also insisted, in stronger terms than Dewey, on the necessity of scientific detachment. It is not the business of the intellectual, according to Veblen, to discover whether the universe is tending toward a good or a bad end. Unlike the abstract liberal described by Parrington, Veblen has abandoned the ideas of the Enlightenment.

JOHN DEWEY

When Descartes said: "The nature of physical things is much more easily conceived when they are beheld coming gradually into existence, than when they are only considered as produced at once in a finished and perfect state," the modern world became self-conscious of the logic that was henceforth to control it, the logic of which Darwin's *Origin of Species* is the latest scientific achievement. Without the methods of Copernicus, Kepler, Galileo, and their successors in astronomy, physics, and chemistry, Darwin would have been helpless in the organic sciences. But prior to Darwin the impact of the new scientific method upon life, mind, and politics, had been arrested, because between these ideal or moral interests and the inorganic world intervened the kingdom of plants and animals. The gates of the garden of life were barred to the new ideas; and only through this garden was there access to mind and politics. The influence of Darwin upon

Reprinted from John Dewey, THE INFLUENCE OF DARWINISM ON PHILOSOPHY *(New York, 1910)*, pp. 8–19.

philosophy resides in his having conquered the phenomena of life for the principle of transition, and thereby freed the new logic for application to mind and morals and life. When he said of species what Galileo had said of the earth, *e pur se muove,* he emancipated, once for all, genetic and experimental ideas as an organon of asking questions and looking for explanations.

The exact bearings upon philosophy of the new logical outlook are, of course, as yet, uncertain and inchoate. We live in the twilight of intellectual transition. One must add the rashness of the prophet to the stubbornness of the partizan to venture a systematic exposition of the influence upon philosophy of the Darwinian method. At best, we can but inquire as to its general bearing— the effect upon mental temper and complexion, upon that body of half-conscious, half-instinctive intellectual aversions and preferences which determine, after all, our more deliberate intellectual enterprises. In this vague inquiry there happens to exist as a kind of touchstone a problem of long historic currency that has also been much discussed in Darwinian literature. I refer to the old problem of design *versus* chance, mind *versus* matter, as the causal explanation, first or final, of things.

As we have already seen, the classic notion of species carried with it the idea of purpose. In all living forms, a specific type is present directing the earlier stages of growth to the realization of its own perfection. Since this purposive regulative principle is not visible to the senses, it follows that it must be an ideal or rational force. Since, however, the perfect form is gradually approximated through the sensible changes, it also follows that in and through a sensible realm a rational ideal force is working out its own ultimate manifestation. These inferences were extended to nature: (*a*) She does nothing in vain; but all for an ulterior purpose. (*b*) Within natural sensible events there is therefore contained a spiritual causal force, which as spiritual escapes perception, but is apprehended by an enlightened reason. (*c*) The manifestation of this principle brings about a subordination of matter and sense to its own realization, and this ultimate fulfillment is the goal of nature and of man. The design argument thus operated in two directions. Purposefulness accounted for the intelligibility of nature and the possibility of science, while the absolute or cosmic character of this purposefulness gave sanction and worth to the moral and religious endeavors of man. Science was underpinned and morals authorized by one and the same principle, and their mutual agreement was eternally guaranteed.

This philosophy remained, in spite of sceptical and polemic outbursts, the official and regnant philosophy of Europe for over two thousand years. The expulsion of fixed first and final causes

from astronomy, physics, and chemistry had indeed given the doctrine something of a shock. But, on the other hand, increased acquaintance with the details of plant and animal life operated as a counterbalance and perhaps even strengthened the argument from design. The marvelous adaptations of organisms to their environment, of organs to the organism, of unlike parts of a complex organ—like the eye—to the organ itself; the foreshadowing by lower forms of the higher; the preparation in earlier stages of growth for organs that only later had their functioning—these things were increasingly recognized with the progress of botany, zoology, paleontology, and embryology. Together, they added such prestige to the design argument that by the late eighteenth century it was, as approved by the sciences of organic life, the central point of theistic and idealistic philosophy.

The Darwinian principle of natural selection cut straight under this philosophy. If all organic adaptations are due simply to constant variation and the elimination of those variations which are harmful in the struggle for existence that is brought about by excessive reproduction, there is no call for a prior intelligent causal force to plan and preordain them. Hostile critics charged Darwin with materialism and with making chance the cause of the universe.

. . .

So much for some of the more obvious facts of the discussion of design *versus* chance, as causal principles of nature and of life as a whole. We brought up this discussion, you recall, as a crucial instance. What does our touchstone indicate as to the bearing of Darwinian ideas upon philosophy? In the first place, the new logic outlaws, flanks, dismisses—what you will—one type of problems and substitutes for it another type. Philosophy forswears inquiry after absolute origins and absolute finalities in order to explore specific values and the specific conditions that generate them.

Darwin concluded that the impossibility of assigning the world to chance as a whole and to design in its parts indicated the insolubility of the question. Two radically different reasons, however, may be given as to why a problem is insoluble. One reason is that the problem is too high for intelligence; the other is that the question in its very asking makes assumptions that render the question meaningless. The latter alternative is unerringly pointed to in the celebrated case of design *versus* chance. Once admit that the sole verifiable or fruitful object of knowledge is the particular set of changes that generate the object of study together with the consequences that then flow from it, and no intelligible question can be asked about what, by assumption, lies outside. To assert—as is often asserted—that specific values of particular truths, social bonds and forms of beauty, if they can be shown to be generated by concretely knowable conditions, are meaningless and in vain; to assert that they are justified only when they and their particular cause and effects have all at once been gathered up into some inclusive first cause and some exhaustive final goal, is intellectual atavism. Such argumentation is reversion to the logic that explained the extinction of fire by water through the formal essence of aqueousness and the quenching of thirst by water through the final cause of aqueousness. Whether used in the case of the special event or that of life as a whole, such logic only abstracts some aspect of the existing course of events in order to reduplicate it as a petrified eternal principle by which to explain the very changes of which it is the formalization.

When Henry Sidgwick casually remarked in a letter that as he grew older his interest in what or who made the world was altered into interest in what kind of a world it is anyway, his voicing of a common experience of our own day illustrates also the nature of that intellectual transformation effected by the Darwinian logic. Interest shifts from the wholesale essence back of special changes to the question of how special changes serve and defeat concrete purposes; shifts from an intelligence that shaped things once for all to the particular intelligences which things are even now shaping; shifts from an ultimate goal of good to the direct increments of justice and happiness that intelligent administration of existent conditions may beget and that present carelessness or stupidity will destroy or forego.

In the second place, the classic type of logic inevitably set philosophy upon proving that life *must* have certain qualities and values—no matter how experience presents the matter—because of some remote cause and eventual goal. The duty of wholesale justification inevitably accompanies all thinking that makes the meaning of special occurrences depend upon something that once and for all lies behind them. The habit of derogating from present meanings and uses prevents our looking the facts of experience in the face; it prevents serious acknowledgment of the evils they present and serious concern with the goods they promise but do not as yet fulfill. It turns thought to the business of finding a wholesale transcendent remedy for the one and guarantee for the other. One is reminded of the way many moralists and theologians greeted Herbert Spencer's recognition of an unknowable energy from which welled up the phenomenal physical processes without and the conscious operations within. Merely because Spencer labeled his unknowable energy "God," this faded piece of metaphysical goods was greeted as an important and grateful concession to the reality of the spiritual realm. Were it not for the deep hold of the habit of seeking justification for ideal values in the remote and transcendent, surely this reference of them to an unknowable absolute would be despised in comparison with the demonstrations of experience that knowable energies are daily generating about us precious values.

The displacing of this wholesale type of philosophy will doubtless not arrive by sheer logical disproof, but rather by growing recognition of its futility. Were it a thousand times true that opium produces sleep because of its dormitive energy, yet the inducing of sleep in the tired, and the recovery to waking life of the poisoned, would not be thereby one least step forwarded. And were it a thousand times dialectically demonstrated that life as a whole is regulated by a transcendent principle to a final inclusive goal, none the less truth and error, health and disease, good and evil, hope and fear in the concrete, would remain just what and where they now are. To improve our education, to ameliorate our manners, to advance our politics, we must have recourse to specific conditions of generation.

Finally, the new logic introduces responsibility into the intellectual life. To idealize and rationalize the universe at large is after all a confession of inability to master the courses of things that specifically concern us. As long as mankind suffered from this impotency, it naturally shifted a burden of responsibility that it could not carry over to the more competent shoulders of the transcendent cause. But if insight into specific conditions of value and into specific consequences of ideas is possible, philosophy must in time become a method of locating and interpreting the more serious of the conflicts that occur in life, and a method of projecting ways for dealing with them: a method of moral and political diagnosis and prognosis.

The claim to formulate *a priori* the legislative constitution of the universe is by its nature a claim that may lead to elaborate dialectic developments. But it is also one that removes these very conclusions from subjection to experimental test, for, by definition, these results make no differences in the detailed course of events. But a philosophy that humbles its pretensions to the work of projecting hypotheses for the education and conduct of mind, individual and social, is thereby subjected to test by the way in which the ideas it propounds work out in practice. In having modesty forced upon it, philosophy also acquires responsibility.

Doubtless I seem to have violated the implied promise of my earlier remarks and to have turned both prophet and partisan. But in anticipating the direction of the transformations in philosophy to be wrought by the Darwinian genetic and experimental logic, I do not profess to speak for any save those who yield themselves consciously or unconsciously to this logic. No one can fairly deny that at present there are two effects of the Darwinian mode of thinking. On the one hand, there are making many sincere and vital efforts to revise our traditional philosophic conceptions in accordance with its demands. On the other hand, there is as definitely a recrudescence of absolutistic philosophies; an assertion of a type of philosophic knowing distinct from that of the sciences, one which opens to us another kind of reality from that to which the sciences give access; an appeal through experience to something that essentially goes beyond experience. This reaction affects popular creeds and religious movements as well as technical philosophies. The very conquest of the biological sciences by the new ideas has led many to proclaim an explicit and rigid separation of philosophy from science.

Old ideas give way slowly; for they are more than abstract logical forms and categories. They are habits, predispositions, deeply engrained attitudes of aversion and preference. Moreover, the conviction persists—though history shows it to be a hallucination—that all the questions that the human mind has asked are questions that can be answered in terms of the alternatives that the questions themselves present. But in fact intellectual progress usually occurs through sheer abandonment of questions together with both of the alternatives they assume—an abandonment that results from their decreasing vitality and a change of urgent interest. We do not solve them: we get over them. Old questions are solved by disappearing, evaporating, while new questions corresponding to the changed attitude of endeavor and preference take their place. Doubtless the greatest dissolvent in contemporary thought of old questions, the greatest precipitant of new methods, new intentions, new problems, is the one effected by the scientific revolution that found its climax in the *Origin of Species*.

THORSTEIN VEBLEN

The men of the sciences that are proud to own themselves "modern"

Reprinted from Thorstein Veblen, "Why Is Economics Not an Evolutionary Science?" QUARTERLY JOURNAL OF ECONOMICS, XII (1898), 373–397.

find fault with the economists for being still content to occupy themselves with repairing a structure and doctrines and maxims resting on natural rights, utilitarianism, and administrative expediency. This aspersion is not altogether merited, but is near enough to the mark to carry a sting. These modern sciences are evolutionary sciences, and their adepts contemplate that characteristic of their work with some complacency. Economics is not an evolutionary science—by the confession of its spokesmen; and the economists turn their eyes with something of envy and some sense of baffled emulation to those rivals that make broad their phylacteries with the legend, "Up to date."

Precisely wherein the social and political sciences, including economics, fall short of being evolutionary sciences, is not so plain.

. . .

Of the achievements of the classical economists, recent and living, the science may justly be proud; but they fall short of the evolutionist's standard of adequacy, not in failing to offer a theory of a process or of a developmental relation, but through conceiving their theory in terms alien to the evolutionist's habits of thought. . . .

The difference is a difference of spiritual attitude or point of view in the two contrasted generations of scientists. . . . The modern scientist is unwilling to depart from the test of causal relation or quantitative sequence. When he asks the question, Why? he insists on an answer in terms of cause and effect. . . . The great deserts of the evolutionist leaders—if they have great deserts as leaders—lie, on the one hand, in their refusal to go back of the colorless sequence of phenomena and seek higher ground for their ultimate syntheses, and, on the other hand, in their having shown how this colorless impersonal sequence of cause and effect can be made use of for theory proper, by virtue of its cumulative character.

For the earlier natural scientists, as for the classical economists, this ground of cause and effect is not definitive. Their sense of truth and substantiality is not satisfied with a formulation of mechanical sequence. The ultimate term in their systematisation of knowledge is a "natural law." This natural law is felt to exercise some sort of a coercive surveillance over the sequence of events, and to give a spiritual stability and consistence to the causal relation at any given juncture. To meet the high classical requirement, a sequence —and a developmental process especially—must be apprehended in terms of a consistent propensity tending to some spiritually legitimate end. When facts and events have been reduced to these terms of fundamental truth and have been made to square with the requirements of definitive normality, the investigator rests his case. . . .

The standpoint of the classical economists, in their higher or definitive syntheses and generalisations, may not inaptly be called the standpoint of ceremonial adequacy. The ultimate laws and principles which they formulated were laws of the normal or the natural, according to a preconception regarding the ends to which, in the nature of things, all things tend. In effect, this preconception imputes to things a tendency to work out what the instructed common sense of the time accepts as the adequate or worthy end of human effort. It is a projection of the accepted ideal of conduct. This ideal of conduct is made to serve as a canon of truth, to the extent that the investigator contents himself with an appeal to its legitimation for premises that run back of the facts with which he is immediately dealing, for the "controlling principles"

that are conceived intangibly to underlie the process discussed, and for the "tendencies" that run beyond the situation as it lies before him. . . .

. . . If economics is to follow the lead or the analogy of the other sciences that have to do with a life process, the way is plain so far as regards the general direction in which the move will be made. . . . The psychological and anthropological preconceptions of the economists have been those which were accepted by the psychological and social sciences some generations ago. The hedonistic conception of man is that of a lightning calculator of pleasures and pains, who oscillates like a homogeneous globule of desire of happiness under the impulse of stimuli that shift him about the area, but leave him intact. He has neither antecedent nor consequent. He is an isolated, definitive human datum, in stable equilibrium except for the buffets of the impinging forces that displace him in one direction or another. Self-imposed in elemental space, he spins symmetrically about his own spiritual axis until the parallelogram of forces bears down upon him, whereupon he follows the line of the resultant. When the force of the impact is spent, he comes to rest, a self-contained globule of desire as before. Spiritually, the hedonistic man is not a prime mover. He is not the seat of a process of living, except in the sense that he is subject to a series of permutations enforced upon him by circumstances external and alien to him.

The later psychology, reënforced by modern anthropological research, gives a different conception of human nature. According to this conception, it is the characteristic of man to do something, not simply to suffer pleasures and pains through the impact of suitable forces. He is not simply a bundle of desires that are to be saturated by being placed in the path of the forces of the environment, but rather a coherent structure of propensities and habits which seeks realisation and expression in an unfolding activity. According to this view, human activity, and economic activity among the rest, is not apprehended as something incidental to the process of saturating given desires. The activity is itself the substantial fact of the process, and the desires under whose guidance the action takes place are circumstances of temperament which determine the specific direction in which the activity will unfold itself in the given case. These circumstances of temperament are ultimate and definitive for the individual who acts under them, so far as regards his attitude as agent in the particular action in which he is engaged. But, in the view of the science, they are elements of the existing frame of mind of the agent, and are the outcome of his antecedents and his life up to the point at which he stands. They are the products of his hereditary traits and his past experience, cumulatively wrought out under a given body of traditions, conventionalities, and material circumstances; and they afford the point of departure for the next step in the process. The economic life history of the individual is a cumulative process of adaptation of means to ends that cumulatively change as the process goes on, both the agent and his environment being at any point the outcome of the last process. His methods of life to-day are enforced upon him by his habits of life carried over from yesterday and by the circumstances left as the mechanical residue of the life of yesterday.

What is true of the individual in this respect is true of the group in which he lives. All economic change is a change in the economic community,—a change in the community's methods of turning material things to account. The change is always in the last resort a change in habits of thought. This is true even of changes in the mechanical processes of industry. A given contrivance for effecting certain material ends becomes a circumstance which affects the further growth of habits of thought—habitual methods of procedure—and so becomes a point of departure for further development of the methods of compassing the ends sought and for the further variation of ends that are sought to be compassed. In all this flux there is no definitively adequate method of life and no definitive or absolutely worthy end of action, so far as concerns the science which sets out to formulate a theory of the process of economic life. What remains as a hard and fast residue is the fact of activity directed to an objective end. Economic action is teleological, in the sense that men always and everywhere seek to do something. What, in specific detail, they seek, is not to be answered except by a scrutiny of the details of their activity; but, so long as we have to do with their life as members of the economic community, there remains the generic fact that their life is an unfolding activity of a teleological kind.

It may or may not be a teleological process in the sense that it tends or should tend to any end that is conceived to be worthy or adequate by the inquirer or by the consensus of inquirers. Whether it is or is not, is a question with which the present inquiry is not concerned; and it is also a question of which an evolutionary economics need take no account. The question of a tendency in events can evidently not come up except on the ground of some preconception or prepossession on the part of the person looking for the tendency. In order to search for a tendency, we must be possessed of some notion of a definitive end to be sought, or some notion as to what is the legitimate trend of events. The notion of a legitimate trend in a course of events is an extra-evolutionary preconception, and lies outside the scope of an inquiry into the causal sequence in any process. The evolutionary point of view, therefore, leaves no place for a formulation of natural laws in terms of definitive normality, whether in economics or in any other branch of inquiry. Neither does it leave room for that other question of normality, What should be the end of the developmental process under discussion?

3. The Science of Society

One of the most interesting figures of the post-Civil War period was the sociologist, William Graham Sumner. Sumner was a tough-minded intellectual who did as much as James or Dewey to further the cause of a scientific and relativistic conception of inquiry. But he does not fit Parrington's categories at all. Politically, he was what we have come to call a "conservative," though in his own time he was considered a radical of sorts. Sumner's essay on "Sociology," is interesting for its preoccupation with professional sociologists, as against amateur theorists. He seemed to be conscious of the intellectual as a member of a social group, an awareness that has prompted some of the recent reinterpretations of the period.

Edward Alsworth Ross' Social Control was one of the most popular statements of the preoccupation with concrete problems of power and control. He was nostalgic for the older situation in which positive forms of social control had not been necessary, but he was aware that industrial realities demanded a positive application of social "science" to the human situation. This awareness made Ross politically a progressive. But his book is interesting as well because of its racism, a feature of turn-of-the-century American thought which Parrington ignored, but which has been rediscovered by more recent historians.

WILLIAM GRAHAM SUMNER

Each of the sciences which, by giving to man greater knowledge of the laws of nature, has enabled him to cope more intelligently with the ills of life, has had to fight for its independence of metaphysics. . . . Sociology, however, the latest of this series of sciences, is rather entering upon the struggle

Reprinted from *William Graham Sumner,* COLLECTED ESSAYS IN POLITICAL AND SOCIAL SCIENCE *(New York, 1885), pp. 77–86.*

than emerging from it. Sociology threatens to withdraw an immense range of subjects of the first importance from the dominion of *a priori* speculation and arbitrary dogmatism, and the struggle will be severe in proportion to the dignity and importance of the subject. . . . I know of nothing more amusing in these days than to see an old-fashioned metaphysician applying his tests to the results of scientific investigation, and screaming with rage because men of scientific training do not care whether the results satisfy those tests or not.

Sociology is the science of life in society. It investigates the forces which come into action wherever a human society exists. It studies the structure and functions of the organs of human society, and its aim is to find out the laws in subordination to which human society takes its various forms, and social institutions grow and change. Its practical utility consists in deriving the rules of right social living from the facts and laws which prevail by nature in the constitution and functions of society. It must, without doubt, come into collision with all other theories of right living which are founded on authority, tradition, arbitrary invention, or poetic imagination.

Sociology is perhaps the most complicated of all the sciences, yet there is no domain of human interest the details of which are treated ordinarily with greater facility. Various religions have various theories of social living, which they offer as authoritative and final. It has never, so far as I know, been asserted by anybody that a man of religious faith (in any religion) could not study sociology or recognize the existence of any such science; but it is incontestably plain that a man who accepts the dogmas about social living which are imposed by the authority of any religion must regard the subject of right social living as settled and closed, and he cannot enter on any investigation the first groundwork of which would be doubt of the authority which he recognizes as final. Hence social problems and social phenomena present no difficulty to him who has only to cite an authority or obey a prescription.

Then again the novelists set forth "views" about social matters. To write and read novels is perhaps the most royal road to teaching and learning which has ever been devised. The proceeding of the novelists is kaleidoscopic. They turn the same old bits of colored glass over and over again into new combinations. There is no limit, no sequence, no bond of consistency. The romance-writing social philosopher always proves his case just as a man always wins who plays chess with himself.

Then again the utopians and socialists make easy work of the complicated phenomena with which sociology has to deal. These persons, vexed with the intricacies of social problems, and revolting against the facts of the social order, take upon themselves the task of inventing a new and better world. They brush away all which troubles us men, and create a world free from annoying limitations and conditions—in their imagination. In ancient times, and now in half-civilized countries, these persons have been founders of religions. Something of that type always lingers around them still and among us, and is to be seen amongst the reformers and philanthropists who never contribute much to the improvement of society in any actual detail, but find a key principle for making the world anew and regenerating society. I have even seen faint signs of the same mysticism in social matters in some of the greenbackers who have "thought out" in bed, as they relate, a scheme of wealth by paper money, as Mahomet would have received a Surah, or Joe Smith a revelation about polygamy. Still there are limits to this resemblance, because in our nineteenth-century American life a sense of humor, even if defective, answers some of the purposes of commonsense.

Then again all the whimsical people who have hobbies of one sort or another, and who cluster around the

Social Science Association, come forward with projects which are the result of a strong impression, an individual misfortune, or an unregulated benevolent desire, and which are therefore the product of a facile emotion, not of a laborious investigation.

Then again the *dilettanti* make light work of social questions. Every one, by the fact of living in society, gathers some observations of social phenomena. The belief grows up, as it was expressed some time ago by a professor of mathematics, that everybody knows about the topics of sociology. Those topics have a broad and generous character. They lend themselves easily to generalizations. There are as yet no sharp tests formulated. Above all, and worst lack of all as yet, we have no competent criticism. Hence it is easy for the aspirant after culture to venture on this field without great danger of being brought to account, as he would be if he attempted geology, or physics, or biology. Even a scientific man of high attainments in some other science, in which he well understands what special care, skill, and training are required, will not hesitate to dogmatize about a topic of sociology. A group of half-educated men may be relied upon to attack a social question and to hammer it dead in a few minutes with a couple of commonplaces and a sweeping *a priori* assumption. Above all other topics, social topics lend themselves to the purposes of the diner-out.

. . .

Let us then endeavor to define the field of sociology. Life in society is the life of a human society on this earth. Its elementary conditions are set by the nature of human beings and the nature of the earth. We have already become familiar, in biology, with the transcendent importance of the fact that life on earth must be maintained by a struggle against nature, and also by a competition with other forms of life. In the latter fact biology and sociology touch. Sociology is a science which deals with one range of phenomena produced by the struggle for existence, while biology deals with another. The forces are the same, acting on different fields and under different conditions. The sciences are truly cognate. Nature contains certain materials which are capable of satisfying human needs, but those materials must, with rare and mean exceptions, be won by labor, and must be fitted to human use by more labor. As soon as any number of human beings are each struggling to win from nature the material goods necessary to support life, and are carrying on this struggle side by side, certain social forces come into operation. The prime condition of this society will lie in the ratio of its numbers to the supply of materials within its reach. For the supply at any moment attainable is an exact quantity, and the number of persons who can be supplied is arithmetically limited. If the actual number present is very much less than the number who might be supported, the condition of all must be ample and easy. Freedom and facility mark all social relations under such a state of things. If the number is larger than that which can be supplied, the condition of all must be one of want and distress, or else a few must be well provided, the others being proportionately still worse off. Constraint, anxiety, possibly tyranny and repression mark social relations. It is when the social pressure due to an unfavorable ratio of population to land becomes intense that the social forces develop increased activity. Division of labor, exchange, higher social organization, emigration, advance in the arts, spring from the necessity of contending against the harsher conditions of existence which are continually reproduced as the population surpasses the means of existence on any given status.

The society with which we have to deal does not consist of any number of men. An army is not a society. A man with his wife and his children constitutes a society, for its essential parts are all present, and the number more or less is immaterial. A certain division of labor between the sexes is imposed by nature. The family as a whole maintains itself better under an organization with division of labor than it could if the functions were shared so far as possible. From this germ the development of society goes on by the regular steps of advancement to higher organization, accompanied and sustained by improvements in the arts. The increase of population goes on according to biological laws which are capable of multiplying the species beyond any assignable limits, so that the number to be provided for steadily advances, and the status of ease and abundance gives way to a status of want and constraint. Emigration is the first and simplest remedy. By winning more land the ratio of population to land is once more rendered favorable. It is to be noticed, however, that emigration is painful to all men. To the uncivilized man, to emigrate means to abandon a mass of experiences and traditions which have been won by suffering, and to go out to confront new hardships and perils. To the civilized man migration means cutting off old ties of kin and country. The earth has been peopled by man at the cost of this suffering.

On the side of the land also stands the law of the diminishing return as a limitation. More labor gets more from the land, but not proportionately more. Hence, if more men are to be supported, there is need not of a proportionate increase of labor, but of a disproportionate increase of labor. The law of population, therefore, combined with the law of the diminishing return constitutes the great underlying condition of society. Emigration, improvements in the arts, in morals, in education, in political organization, are only stages in the struggle of man to meet these conditions, to break their force for a time, and to win room under them for ease and enlargement. Ease and enlargement mean either power to support more men on a given stage of comfort or power to advance the comfort of a given number of men. Progress is a word which has no meaning save in view of the laws of population and the diminishing return, and it is quite natural that any one who fails to understand those laws should fall into doubt which way progress points, whether towards wealth or poverty. The laws of population and the diminishing return, in their combination, are the iron spur which has driven the race on to all which it has achieved, and the fact that population ever advances, yet advances against a barrier which resists more stubbornly at every step of advance, unless it is removed to a new distance by some conquest of man over nature, is the guarantee that the task of civilization will never be ended, but that the need for more energy, more intelligence, and more virtue will never cease while the race lasts. If it were possible for an increasing population to be sustained by proportionate increments of labor, we should all still be living in the original home of the race on the spontaneous products of the earth. Let him, therefore, who desires to study social phenomena first learn the transcendent importance for the whole social organization, industrial, political, and civil, of the ratio of population to land.

. . .

The sentimental philosophy starts from the first principle that nothing is true which is disagreeable, and that we must not believe anything which is "shocking" no matter what the evidence may be. There are various stages of this philosophy. It touches on one side the intuitional philosophy which proves that certain things must exist by proving that man needs them, and it touches on the other side the vulgar socialism which affirms that the individual has a right to whatever he needs, and that this right is good against his fellowmen. To this philosophy in all its grades the laws of population and the diminishing return have always been very distasteful. The laws which entail upon mankind an inheritance of labor cannot be acceptable to any philosophy which maintains that man comes into the world endowed with natural rights, and an inheritor of freedom. It is a death-blow to any intuitional philosophy to find out, as an historical fact, what diverse thoughts, beliefs, and actions man has manifested, and it requires but little actual knowledge of human history to show that the human race has never had any ease which it did not earn, or any freedom which it did not conquer. Sociology, therefore, by the investigations which it pursues dispels illusions about what society is or may be, and gives instead knowledge of facts which are the basis of intelligent effort by man to make the best of his circumstances on earth. Sociology, therefore, which can never accomplish anything more than to enable us to make the best of our situation, will never be able to reconcile itself with those philosophies which are trying to find

out how we may arrange things so as to satisfy any ideal of society.

EDWARD ALSWORTH ROSS

A condition of order at the junction of crowded city thoroughfares implies primarily an absence of collisions between men or vehicles that interfere one with another. Order cannot be said to prevail among people going in the same direction at the same pace, because there is no interference. It does not exist when persons are constantly colliding one with another. But when all who meet or overtake one another in crowded ways take the time and pains needed to avoid collision, the throng is *orderly*. Now, at the bottom of the notion of social order lies the same idea. The members of an orderly community do not go out of their way to aggress upon one another. Moreover, whenever their pursuits interfere they make the adjustment necessary to escape collision, and make it according to some conventional rule. If the weaker of two hunters that have brought down the same stag avoids a fight by yielding up the game, there is peace, but no order. But if the dispute is settled according to the rule that "first struck" decides the ownership of game, the solution is an orderly one. Similarly, there is order when teamsters shun collision by conforming to "the law of the road," or miners settle the ownership of claims according to priority of "pegging out."

The denser the traffic that is handled without confusion at a busy corner, the higher is the grade of order. Likewise, the more that the smooth running of social machinery implies the fre-

Reprinted from Edward Alsworth Ross, SOCIAL CONTROL: A SURVEY OF THE FOUNDATIONS OF ORDER *(New York, 1901), pp. 1–5, 432–437.*

quent breaking off or turning aside of individual activities, the more perfect is the social order. *Successful coöperation,* therefore, bespeaks a high grade of social order, inasmuch as each of the coöperators must unfold specific activities within precise limits, and the results therefrom are enjoyed or shared according to some recognized principle. *Hierarchical organization* is still more a test of orderliness, inasmuch as in the sharing of unlike burdens and the division of unequal benefits men are more apt to fall afoul of one another.

The severest test of the régime of order occurs when, as in war or government, individuals are incited to a common effort, the benefits of which are shared in common. The sacrificing of one corps of an army to save the rest, or the placing of the public burdens upon the non-governing classes, is recognized as putting the severest strain on discipline. In general, the absence of hostile encounter is a mark of social order, since it implies that interferences are adjusted according to some rule. But extreme division of social labor and high organization is the surest sign of order, since it requires the nice adjustment of multifarious activities according to some prearranged plan.

The readiness of men to disturb the peace or to violate rules in the pursuit of their personal interests depends upon their mental make-up. The peaceable turn aside from collision, while the pugnacious welcome it. The easily contented readily accommodate their desires and actions to the customary restrictions, but the enterprising are always pressing against and trampling upon barriers. The passive strive only to satisfy old wants, and are therefore much stronger in resistance than in offence. The aggressive are insatiate and put forth as much energy to seize what they have not, as to keep what

they have. In a passive race, once order is established, the individual keeps to his prescribed orbit from sheer inertia. In an aggressive race order is perpetually endangered by the unruliness of the individual, and can be maintained only through the unremitting operation of certain social forces.

Now, it is the purpose of this inquiry to ascertain how men of the West-European breed are brought to live closely together, and to associate their efforts with that degree of harmony we see about us. Social order, even among the passive, unambitious Hindoos, presents a problem for solution. But it is a much more serious problem among the dolichocephalic blonds of the West. The restless, striving, doing Aryan, with his personal ambition, his lust for power, his longing to wreak himself, his willingness to turn the world upside down to get the fame, or the fortune, or the woman, he wants, is under no easy discipline. The existence of order among men of this daring and disobedient breed challenges explanation. Especially is this true of the European man in America or Australia. The same selective migrations that made the Teuton more self-assertive than the docile Slav or the quiescent Hindoo, have made the American more strong-willed and unmanageable than even the West-European.

To many, no doubt, a survey of the foundations of social order will appear superfluous. Most of us take order for granted, and are hardly more aware of it than we are of the air we breathe. Order being the universal and indispensable condition of all our social structures, we give no more thought to it than to the force of cohesion that keeps our machinery from flying into bits. Those to whom the fact is brought home by the persistence of a delinquent class assume, nevertheless, that the social fabric rests on a law-abiding disposition which is natural to all but the slant-browed few.

But it would be, in truth, much juster to assume a state of disorder. We ought to take for granted that men living in propinquity will continually fall afoul of one another. We ought to expect in the normal person not, it is true, the malice, lust, or ferocity of the born criminal, but certainly a natural unwillingness to be checked in the hot pursuit of his ends. Whenever men swarm in new places,—Dutch Flat, Kimberley, Siberia, Skagway,—the man-to-man struggle stands out naked and clear, and the slow emergence of order out of disorder and violence presents itself as the attainment of a difficult and artificial condition. Could we abstract from such communities the training received in older societies, the thrift that recognizes disorder as a blight upon prosperity, and the ready revolver which discourages aggression by equalizing men, we might arrive at a notion of the state in which the men of today, despite their high facial angle, would find themselves, if they were remanded to the zero point of social development. Starting from this point, we must face the problem. By what means is the human struggle narrowed and limited? How has violence been purged away from it? How has the once brawling torrent of conflicting personal desires been induced to flow smoothly in the channels of legitimate rivalry, or even for a time to vanish underground in those numerous coöperations where conflict is absent until it comes to dividing the results?

It is a common delusion that order is to be explained by the person's inherited equipment for good conduct, rather than by any control that society exercises over him. Once it was held that normal human beings are born with a set of commandments etched upon the soul. When evidence accumulated as to the startling contrasts in the moral ideas of different times and peoples, the moralists contented themselves with declaring that the soul is, at least, endowed with a sense of *ought-ness*. When the emptiness of this theory was demonstrated, and formalism was convicted of overlooking the emotional elements that lie behind conduct, there arose the theory that man's nature is constituted out of egoism and altruism. This in time was seen to be much the same as defining milk as a combination of whey and curd. Then came the charming tales of the mutual aid of ants, beavers, and prairie dogs, suggesting the existence of certain social instincts which moralists found it very convenient to use in explaining human society.

We are not yet sure, however, that man is the "good ape" Buffon supposed him to be. There is reason to believe that our social order is by no means a mere hive or herd order. It seems to be a *fabric,* rather than a *growth*.

• • •

Here certain questions press upon us. Is there any prospect that humanity, having sown its wild oats, will now settle down and be good? Is there any reason to believe that in the years to come social control will be less necessary than now?

Probably not. On the contrary it is likely that certain of the more searching and pervasive means of control will grow in favor. . . . The ground for this surmise is the fact that powerful forces are more and more transforming *community* into *society,* that is, replacing living tissue with structures held together by rivets and screws. In the *community* the secret of order is not so much *control* as *concord*. So far as community extends people keep themselves in order, and there is no need to put them under the yoke of an elaborate discipline. The lively sense of a common life enables mates, kinsfolk, neighbors, and comrades to love and understand one another, to yield to one another, and to observe those forbearances and good offices that make associate life a success. In such a case the group does not make the ties; the ties make the group. To people living in such relations the apparatus of control seems a nuisance and an impertinence. Reciprocal constraint, indeed, shows itself even among kinsmen and neighbors; but of control, definite and organized, there is little trace.

Now these natural bonds, that were many and firm when the rural neighborhood or the village community was the type of aggregation, no longer bind men as they must be bound in the huge and complex aggregates of today. Kinship has lost its old sacred significance. Social erosion has worn down the family until now it consists of only parents and young. From being a sacrament marriage has become a contract terminable almost at pleasure. Nearness of dwelling means less in the country and nothing in the town. For the intimacy of the countryside the city offers only a "multitudinous desolation." Frequent change of domicile hinders the growth of strong local feelings. The householder has become a tenant, the working-man a bird of passage. Loose touch-and-go acquaintanceships take the place of those close and lasting attachments that form between neighbors that have long lived, labored, and pleasured together. The power of money rends the community into classes incapable of feeling keenly with one another. Even while we are welding it, the social mass laminates. Everywhere we see the march of differentiation. Everywhere we see the local group—the parish, commune, neighborhood, or village—decaying, or else developing beyond the point of real community.

Of course this is not all the story. If the molecules of the local group are jarred asunder, it is partly because they fall under influences which make them vibrate in vaster unisons. Local solidarity perishes because bonds of fellowship are woven which unite a man to distant co-religionists, or fellow-partisans, or fellow-craftsmen, or members of the same social class. In this way fresh social tissue forms and replaces, perhaps, the tissue that dies.

. . .

After all is said, however, it is doubtful if *community* has grown as fast as *society*. . . . The neighborhood or village communities that have been eaten away by the currents of change, were probably more serviceable to social order than are the great civic or national communities that take their place. It is perhaps safe to say that we are relying on artificial rather than natural supports to bear the increasing weight of our social order, and that a return to the natural basis of social partnership is about as likely as a return to raw food or skin garments.

The reader may shudder at the thought of modern society precariously rearing its huge bulk above the devouring waves of selfishness like a Venice built on piles. But it is perhaps no worse than man's depending upon cultivated instead of wild fruits, or removing the seats of his civilization to climates where only houses and stoves can keep him alive through the winter. So long as there is bread and wool and coal enough, what matters it that we depend on art instead of nature! And so long as society can stamp its standards and values upon its members, what matters our dependence on forms of control!

Not that the future is secure. The grand crash may yet come through the strife of classes, each unable to master the others by means of those influences that enable society to subdue the individual. But if it comes, it will be due to the thrust of new, blind, economic forces we have not learned to regulate, and will no more discredit the policy of social control than the failure of the water in the mountain reservoir discredits the policy of irrigation.

The better adaptation of animals to one another appears to be brought about by accumulated changes in body and brain. The better adaptation of men to one another is brought about, not only in this way, but also by the improvement of the instruments that constitute the *apparatus of social control*. In the same way that the improvement of optical instruments checks the evolution of the eye, and the improvement of tools checks the evolution of the hand, the improvement of instruments of control checks the evolution of the social instincts. The goal of social development is not, as some imagine, a Perfect Love, or a Perfect Conscience, but *better adaptation;* and the more this adaptation is artificial, the less need it be natural.

4. The Mastery of Politics

Herbert Croly, more than any other man of his time, tried to apply the philosophical approach of James and Dewey directly to American politics. His The Promise of American Life *was an electrifying book to his generation—though today it seems a little obvious, overlong, and even somewhat boring. It was exciting in its day because it announced a fact that has by now become commonplace: America's "destiny" and "promise" would not be fulfilled automatically, but would have to be won in what a President of the 1960's would call a "long, twilight struggle." The following selection illustrates the odd mixture of pessimism and optimism about the American situation which was characteristic of many intellectuals and which tended to set them apart from the rest of their contemporaries.*

HERBERT CROLY

All the conditions of American life have tended to encourage an easy, generous, and irresponsible optimism. As compared to Europeans, Americans have been very much favored by circumstances. Had it not been for the

Reprinted from Herbert Croly, THE PROMISE OF AMERICAN LIFE *(New York, 1910), pp. 7–8, 17–18, 20–25.*

Atlantic Ocean and the virgin wilderness, the United States would never have been the Land of Promise. . . . The United States was divided from the mainland of Europe not by a channel but by an ocean. Its dimensions were continental rather than insular. We were for the most part freed from alien interference, and could, so far as we dared, experiment with political and social ideals. The land was unoccupied, and its settlement offered an unprecedented area and abundance of economic opportunity. After the Revolution the whole political and social organization was renewed, and made both more serviceable and more flexible. Under such happy circumstances the New World was assuredly destined to become to its inhabitants a Land of Promise,—a land in which men were offered a fairer chance and a better future than the best which the Old World could afford.

. . .

The fault in the vision of our national future possessed by the ordinary American does not consist in the expectation of some continuity of achievement. It consists rather in the expectation that the familiar benefits will continue to accumulate automatically. In his mind the ideal Promise is identified with the processes and conditions which hitherto have very much simplified its fulfillment, and he fails sufficiently to realize that the conditions and processes are one thing and the ideal Promise quite another. Moreover, these underlying social and economic conditions are themselves changing, in such wise that hereafter the ideal Promise, instead of being automatically fulfilled, may well be automatically stifled. For two generations and more the American people were, from the economic point of view, most happily situated. They were able, in a sense, to slide down hill into the valley of fulfillment. Economic conditions were such that, given a fair start, they could scarcely avoid reaching a desirable goal. But such is no longer the case. Economic conditions have been profoundly modified, and American political and social problems have been modified with them. The Promise of American life must depend less than it did upon the virgin wilderness and the Atlantic Ocean, for the

virgin wilderness has disappeared, and the Atlantic Ocean has become merely a big channel. The same results can no longer be achieved by the same easy methods. Ugly obstacles have jumped into view, and ugly obstacles are peculiarly dangerous to a person who is sliding down hill. The man who is clambering up hill is in a much better position to evade or overcome them. Americans will possess a safer as well as a worthier vision of their national Promise as soon as they give it a house on a hill-top rather than in a valley.

. . .

A numerous and powerful group of reformers has been collecting whose whole political policy and action is based on the conviction that the "common people" have not been getting the Square Deal to which they are entitled under the American system; and these reformers are carrying with them a constantly increasing body of public opinion. A considerable proportion of the American people is beginning to exhibit economic and political, as well as personal, discontent. A generation ago the implication was that if a man remained poor and needy, his poverty was his own fault, because the American system was giving all its citizens a fair chance. Now, however, the discontented poor are beginning to charge their poverty to an unjust political and economic organization, and reforming agitators do not hesitate to support them in this contention. Manifestly a threatened obstacle has been raised against the anticipated realization of our national Promise. Unless the great majority of Americans not only have, but believe they have, a fair chance, the better American future will be dangerously compromised.

The conscious recognition of grave national abuses casts a deep shadow across the traditional American patriotic vision. The sincere and candid reformer can no longer consider the national Promise as destined to automatic fulfillment. The reformers themselves are, no doubt, far from believing that whatever peril there is cannot be successfully averted. They make a point of being as patriotically prophetic as the most "old-fashioned Democrat." They proclaim even more loudly their conviction of an indubitable and a beneficent national future. But they do not and cannot believe that this future will take care of itself. As reformers they are bound to assert that the national body requires for the time being a good deal of medical attendance, and many of them anticipate that even after the doctors have discontinued their daily visits the patient will still need the supervision of a sanitary specialist. He must be persuaded to behave so that he will not easily fall ill again, and so that his health will be permanently improved. Consequently, just in so far as reformers they are reformers they are obliged to abandon the traditional American patriotic fatalism. The national Promise has been transformed into a closer equivalent of a national purpose, the fulfillment of which is a matter of conscious work.

The transformation of the old sense of a glorious national destiny into the sense of a serious national purpose will inevitably tend to make the popular realization of the Promise of American life both more explicit and more serious. As long as Americans believed they were able to fulfill a noble national Promise merely by virtue of maintaining intact a set of political institutions and by the vigorous individual pursuit of private ends, their allegiance to their national fulfillment remained more a matter of words than of deeds; but now that they are being aroused from their patriotic slumber, the effect is inevitably to disentangle the national idea and to give it more dignity. The redemption of the national Promise has become a cause for which the good American must fight, and the cause for which a man fights is a cause which he more than ever values. The American idea is no longer to be propagated merely by multiplying the children of the West and by granting ignorant aliens permission to vote. Like all sacred causes, it must be propagated by the Word and by that right arm of the Word, which is the Sword.

The more enlightened reformers are conscious of the additional dignity and value which the popularity of reform has bestowed upon the American idea, but they still fail to realize the deeper implications of their own programme. In abandoning the older conception of an automatic fulfillment of our national destiny, they have abandoned more of the traditional American point of view than they are aware. The traditional American optimistic fatalism was not of accidental origin, and it cannot be abandoned without involving in its fall some other important ingredients in the accepted American tradition. Not only was it dependent on economic conditions which prevailed until comparatively recent times, but it has been associated with certain erroneous but highly cherished political theories. It has been wrought into the fabric of our popular economic and political ideas to such an extent that its overthrow necessitates a partial revision of some of the most important articles in the traditional American creed.

The extent and the character of this revision may be inferred from a brief consideration of the effect upon the substance of our national Promise of an alteration in its proposed method of fulfillment. The substance of our national Promise has consisted, as we have seen, of an improving popular economic condition, guaranteed by democratic political institutions, and resulting in moral and social amelioration. These manifold benefits were to be obtained merely by liberating the enlightened self-interest of the American people. The beneficent result followed inevitably from the action of wholly selfish motives—provided, of course, the democratic political system of equal rights was maintained in its integrity. The fulfillment of the American Promise was considered inevitable because it was based upon a combination of self-interest and the natural goodness of human nature. On the other hand, if the fulfillment of our national Promise can no longer be considered inevitable, if it must be considered as equivalent to a conscious national purpose instead of an inexorable national destiny, the implication necessarily is that the trust reposed in indivdual self-interest has been in some measure betrayed. No preëstablished harmony can then exist between the free and abundant satisfaction of private needs and the accomplishment of a morally and socially desirable result. The Promise of American life is to be fulfilled—not merely by a maximum amount of economic freedom, but by a certain measure of discipline; not merely by the abundant satisfaction of individual desires, but by a large measure of individual subordination and self-denial. And this necessity of subordinating the satisfaction of individual desires to the fulfillment of a national purpose is attached particularly to the absorbing occupation of the American people,—the occupation, viz.: of accumulating wealth. The automatic fulfillment of the American national Promise is to be abandoned, if at all, precisely because the traditional American confidence in individual freedom has resulted in a morally and socially undesirable distribution of wealth.

In making the concluding statement of the last paragraph I am venturing, of course, upon very debatable ground. Neither can I attempt in this immediate connection to offer any justification for the statement which might or should be sufficient to satisfy a stubborn skeptic. I must be content for the present with the bare assertion that the prevailing abuses and sins, which have made reform necessary, are all of them associated with the prodigious concentration of wealth, and of the power exercised by wealth, in the hands of a few men. I am far from believing that this concentration of economic power is wholly an undesirable thing, and I am also far from believing that the men in whose hands this power is concentrated deserve, on the whole, any exceptional moral reprobation for the manner in which it has been used. In certain respects they have served their country well, and in almost every respect their moral or immoral standards are those of the great majority of their fellow-countrymen. But it is none the less true that the political corruption, the unwise economic organization, and the legal support afforded to certain economic privileges are all under existing conditions due to the malevolent social influence of individual and incorporated American wealth; and it is equally true that these abuses, and the excessive "money power" with which they are associated, have originated in the peculiar freedom which the American tradition and organization have granted to the individual. Up to a certain point that freedom has been and still is beneficial. Beyond that point it is not merely harmful; it is by way of being fatal. Efficient regulation there must be; and it must be regulation which will strike, not at the symptoms of the evil, but at its roots. The existing concentration of wealth and financial power in the hands of a few irresponsible men is the inevitable outcome of the chaotic individualism of our political and economic organization, while at the same time it is inimical to democracy, because it tends to erect political abuses and social inequalities into a system. The inference which follows may be disagreeable, but it is not to be escaped. In becoming responsible for the subordination of the individual to the demand of a dominant and constructive national purpose, the American state will in effect be making itself responsible for a morally and socially desirable distribution of wealth.

The consequences, then, of converting our American national destiny into a national purpose are beginning to be revolutionary. When the Promise of American life is conceived as a national ideal, whose fulfillment is a matter of artful and laborious work, the effect thereof is substantially to identify the national purpose with the social problem. What the American people of the present and the future have really been promised by our patriotic prophecies is an attempt to solve that problem. They have been promised on American soil comfort, prosperity, and the opportunity for self-improvement; and the lesson of the existing crisis is that such a Promise can never be redeemed by an indiscriminate individual scramble for wealth. The individual competition, even when it starts under fair conditions and rules, results, not only, as it should, in the triumph of the strongest, but in the attempt to perpetuate the victory; and it is this attempt which must be recognized and forestalled in the interest of the American national purpose. The way to realize a purpose is, not to leave it to chance, but to keep it loyally in mind, and adopt means proper to the importance and the difficulty of the task. No voluntary association of individuals, resourceful and disinterested though they be, is competent to assume the responsibility. The problem belongs to the American national democracy, and its solution must be attempted chiefly by means of official national action.

Neither can its attemped solution be escaped. When they are confronted by the individual sacrifices which the fulfillment of their national Promise demands, American political leaders will find many excuses for ignoring the responsibility thereby implied; but the difficulty of such an attempted evasion will consist in the reënforcement of the historical tradition by a logical and a practical necessity. The American problem is the social problem partly because the social problem is the democratic problem. American political and social leaders will find that in a democracy the problem cannot be evaded. The American people have no irremediable political grievances. No good American denies the desirability of popular sovereignty and of a government which should somehow represent the popular will. While our national institutions may not be a perfect embodiment of these doctrines, a decisive and a resolute popular majority has the power to alter American institutions and give them a more immediately representative character. Existing political evils and abuses are serious enough; but inasmuch as they have come into being, not against the will, but with the connivance of the American people, the latter are responsible for their persistence. In the long run, consequently, the ordinary American will have nothing irremediable to complain about except economic and social inequalities. In Europe such will not be the case. The several European peoples have, and will continue to have, political grievances, because such grievances are the inevitable consequence of their national history and their international situation; and as long as these grievances remain, the more difficult social problem will be subordinated to an agitation for political emancipation. But the American people, having achieved democratic institutions, have nothing to do but to turn them to good account. In so far as the social problem is a real problem and the economic grievance a real grievance, they are bound under the American political system to come eventually to the surface and to demand express and intelligent consideration. A democratic ideal makes the social problem inevitable and its attempted solution indispensable.

III. RECENT INTERPRETATION

One of the most controversial young historians to emerge in the 1960's is Christopher Lasch. His book, *The New Radicalism in America,* offended a great many historians who were still attached to Parrington's perception of the experience of his generation. Lasch examined the careers of intellectuals who are still heroic figures to men of liberal persuasion. He claimed to find that their ideas were molded by highly subjective experiences—such as the collapse of middle-class family patterns—and by their interests as a social "class." Lasch did accept one of Parrington's primary assumptions: the period ought to be interpreted in terms of the political activities of the intellectuals. For Lasch, however, this was not a cause for celebration but for criticism. He accused Parrington's liberals of a fatal confusion of culture and politics, and of a search for political solutions to what were really cultural and intellectual problems.

CHRISTOPHER LASCH

The main argument of this book is that modern radicalism or liberalism can best be understood as a phase of the social history of the intellectuals. In the United States, to which this study is confined, the connection is particularly clear. There, the rise of the new radicalism coincided with the emergence of the intellectual as a distinctive social type.

Reprinted from Christopher Lasch, THE NEW RADICALISM IN AMERICA, 1889–1963 *(New York: Alfred A. Knopf, Inc., 1965), pp. ix–xvii, by permission of the publisher.*

The intellectual may be defined, broadly, as a person for whom thinking fulfills at once the function of work and play; more specifically, as a person whose relationship to society is defined, both in his eyes and in the eyes of the society, principally by his presumed capacity to comment upon it with greater detachment than those more directly caught up in the practical business of production and power. Because his vocation is to be a critic of society, in the most general sense, and because the value of his criticism is presumed to rest on a measure of detachment from the current scene, the intellectual's relation to the rest of society is never entirely comfortable; but it has not always been as uncomfortable as it is today in the United States. "Anti-intellectualism" offers only a partial explanation of the present tension between intellectuals and American society. The rest of the explanation lies in the increased sensitivity of intellectuals to attacks on themselves as a group. It lies in the intellectuals' own sense of themselves, not simply as individuals involved in a common undertaking, the somewhat hazardous business of criticism, but as members of a beleaguered minority. The tension is a function, in other words, of the class-consciousness of the intellectuals themselves.

Intellectuals have existed in all literate societies, but they have only recently come to constitute a kind of subculture. In fact, the word "intellectual" does not seem to have found its way into American usage much before the turn of the century. Before that, most intellectuals belonged to the middle class, and though they may sometimes have felt themselves at odds with the rest of the community, they did not yet conceive of themselves as a class apart. The modern intellectual, even when he chooses to throw himself into the service of his country or attempts to embrace the common life about him, gives himself away by the very self-consciousness of his gestures. He agonizes endlessly over the "role of the intellectuals." A hundred years ago these discussions, and the passion with which they are conducted, would have been incomprehensible.

The growth of a class (or more accurately, a "status group") of intellectuals is part of a much more general development: the decline of the sense of community, the tendency of the mass society to break down into its component parts, each having its own autonomous culture and maintaining only the most tenuous connections with the general life of the society—which as a consequence has almost ceased to exist. The most obvious victims of this process in our own time are adolescents, who live increasingly in a world all their own. The emergence of the intellectual class in the first couple of decades of the present century reveals the workings of the same process at a somewhat earlier period in time.

The intellectual class, then, is a distinctively modern phenomenon, the product of the cultural fragmentation that seems to characterize industrial and postindustrial societies. It is true that in the United States the agencies of social cohesion (church, state, family, class) were never very strong in the first place. Nevertheless, there existed during the first two and a half centuries of American history a sort of cultural consensus at the heart of which was a common stake in capitalism and a common tradition of patriarchal authority. There were social classes but, compared to Europe or even to American society during the colonial period, remarkably little class-consciousness; and whatever the real opportunities for social advancement, the myth of equal opportunity was sufficiently strong to minimize the tensions and resentments which later came to characterize American society. "The whole society," wrote Tocqueville in 1831, "seems to have melted into a middle class. . . . All the Americans whom we have encountered up to now, even to the simplest *shop salesman,* seem to have received, or wish to appear to have received, a good education. Their manners are grave, deliberate, reserved, and they all wear the same clothes. All the customs of life show this mingling of the two classes which in Europe take so much trouble to keep apart." Divisive influences tended to be local and regional rather than social; and the very intensity of local and regional rivalries enhanced the social solidarity of each particular part of the country, so that Southerners, for instance, found what seemed to be a common interest in resisting the encroachments of the Yankee. Under these conditions men of intellectual inclination had very little sense of themselves as a class. The South—the preindustrial society par excellence—offers a particularly striking example of the degree to which such men shared the general aspirations of the *bourgeoisie,* the highest form of which, as is customary in bourgeois societies, was to set up as country gentlemen on lordly estates.

It was only in the North that writers and thinkers began to acquire a sense of being at odds with the rest of society. The transcendentalists and reformers of the 1830's and 1840's, in their protest against the materialism of a society dominated by the Cotton Whigs, in some respects anticipated the attacks of modern intellectuals on the middle class. But the truth of the matter is suggested by the ease with which the reforming impulse after the Civil War was reabsorbed into the stream of genteel culture. The war itself had a unifying effect on New England, as on the South. Abolitionism petered out in mugwumpery, a form of extreme sectional particularism. Indeed, the whole New England tradition—with which American reform until the twentieth century was so completely bound up—precisely embodied everything against which later intellectuals were in rebellion, everything associated with the cultural ascendancy of the middle class.

The term "middle class" seems nowadays to encounter as much resistance, among historians at least, as the term "intellectual." I have been told by historians that the term means nothing, that indeed the "middle class" is a myth. It is true that the term has often been loosely used. But I do not understand why that should prevent its being used quite precisely. I have used it here simply as a synonym for *bourgeoisie,* to describe a class of people which derives its income from the ownership of property and in particular from trade and commerce—a definition, when applied to American society in the nineteenth century, which includes most of the farming population as well as the bulk of those who lived in towns. It does not include the salaried employees (clerks, salesmen, managers, professionals), whom C. Wright Mills has called the "new" middle class—itself a creation of the twentieth century. The cultural style of the old as distinguished from the new middle class was characterized by that combination of patriarchal authority and the sentimental veneration of women which is the essence of the genteel tradition. Everything I mean to catch up in the phrase "middle-class culture" seems to me ultimately to derive from these characteristic familial arrangements. It is no wonder that the revolt of the intellectuals so often took the form of a rebellion against the conventional family. The family was the agency which transmitted from generation to generation—and not only transmitted but embodied down to the last detail of domestic architecture—the enormous weight of respectable culture; as its defenders would have said, of civilization itself.

Everyone who has studied the history of American reform agrees that the reform tradition underwent a fundamental change around 1900. Some people identify the change with a changing attitude toward government, a new readiness to use government (particularly the federal government) as an instrument of popular control. Others associate it with an abandonment of the old populistic distrust of large-scale institutions, like corporations, and an acceptance of the inevitability of the concentration of wealth and power. Still others define the change as a movement away from the dogma of natural rights toward a relativistic, environmentalist, and pragmatic view of the world. All of these developments, in truth, were going on at the same time, and all of them contributed to the emergence of the new radicalism. Equally important was a tendency to see cultural issues as inseparable from political ones; so that "education," conceived very broadly, came to be seen not merely as a means of raising up an enlightened electorate but as an instrument of social change in its own right. Conversely, the new radicals understood the end of social and political reform to be the improvement of the quality of American culture as a whole, rather than simply a way of equalizing the opportunities for economic self-advancement. It is precisely this confusion of politics and culture, so essential to the new radicalism, that seems to me to betray its origins in the rise of the intellectual class; for such a program, with its suggestion that men of learning occupy or ought to occupy the strategic loci of social control, has an obvious appeal to intellectuals, and particularly to intellectuals newly conscious of their own common ties and common interests.

What I have called the new radicalism was not the same thing as the so-called progressive movement, though it took shape during the "progressive era." Progressivism was influenced by the new radicalism, but it was more deeply indebted to the populism of the nineteenth century. It was for the most part a purely political movement, whereas the new radicals were more interested in the reform of education, culture, and sexual relations than they were in political issues in the strict sense. Many of them, in fact, rejected progressivism; they saw in "uplift" only another manifestation of middle-class morality. Even those like Jane Addams who did not embrace socialism, and whose political position therefore has to be described, for lack of a better word, as "progressive" (or "liberal"), had more in common with socialists than with the kind of progressives one associates with the initiative and referendum, the campaign against the trusts, and the crusade for "good government." What distinguished her from them was not only her insistence on the preeminence of "education" but her sense of kinship with the "other half" of humanity. The intellectual in his estrangement from the middle class identified himself with other outcasts and tried to look at the world from their point of view. This radical reversal of perspective was still another distinguishing feature of the new radicalism, socialist or progressive. The particular political labels are of little importance. What matters is the point of view such people deliberately cultivated.

That point of view—the effort to see society from the bottom up, or at least from the outside in—seems to me to account for much of what was valuable and creative in the new radicalism. On the other hand, the very circumstance which made this feat possible—the estrangement of intellectuals, as a class, from the dominant values of American culture—also accounted for what seems to me the chief weakness of the new radicalism, its distrust not only of middle-class culture but of intellect itself. Detachment carried with it a certain defensiveness about the position of intellect (and intellectuals) in American life; and it was this defensiveness, I think, which sometimes prompted intellectuals to forsake the role of criticism and to identify themselves with what they imagined to be the laws of historical necessity and the working out of the popular will. At certain points in the history of the twentieth century, notably during the First World War, American intellectuals seemed too eager to participate in national crusades, too little inclined to wonder precisely how such crusades would serve the values they professed to cherish; and such episodes, together with the more recent appearance of a cold-war liberalism determined not to be outdone in its devotion to the "national purpose," have left me somewhat skeptical of "pragmatic liberalism" in its more militant and affirmative moods. I have not attempted to disguise my skepticism, or for that matter my admiration for whatever was negative and critical in the new radicalism; but I have not wished to write a tract, . . . and I state my own prejudices here only in order to make it clear what they are, not because this book is intended to document them.

I am much less interested, in short, in praising or condemning the new radicalism than in understanding where it came from. Even the effort to understand where it came from, unfortunately, will strike some readers as an insidious attempt to discredit the ideas of radicals and reformers by "psychologizing" them away. For some people, it is enough to say that the reformers were moved by the spectacle of human injustice; to say anything more is to deny the fact of injustice. I am unable to understand this argument, nor do I know quite how to meet it (since I cannot understand it), except to say that the reformers themselves did not share this reluctance of their admirers to examine their own motives. They wrote about their motives with all the enthusiasm, and all the honesty, with which they wrote about social injustice, and I have relied very heavily on what they wrote. Of course it would be possible to ignore what they wrote about themselves, and to write instead about the evils of capitalism. But that is not the book I have chosen to write. I have written instead about some of the critics of capitalism, in the hope that their history would tell something, if not specifically about capitalism, about the peculiarly fragmented character of modern society, and beyond that, about what it means to pursue the life of reason in a world in which the irrational has come to appear not the exception but the rule.

HISTORIOGRAPHICAL NOTE

During the first quarter of this century, young progressives created what became the traditional view of the intellectual history of the late-nineteenth and early-twentieth centuries. According to this interpretation, the central meaning of the history of the period was the struggling to the surface of the progressive outlook. Historians such as Beard and Parrington, themselves part of the progressive movement, took up this interpretation and made it into something approaching an orthodoxy among professional historians. In books such as Henry Steele Commager's *The American Mind: an Interpretation of American Thought and Character since the 1880's* (New Haven, 1950), this point of view has had an impressive and widening number of restatements.

This traditional point of view has several distinct characteristics. First of all, it has always insisted that a marked break with tradition occurred someplace around 1890 or 1900, thus making a sharp distinction between the progressive period and the Gilded Age. Second, this dominant liberal interpretation has discussed intellectual history in political terms. It has paid attention to those intellectuals who seem to have had influence on political and social policy. For this reason, there is considerable overlap in intellectual and political histories of the progressive period (see pp. 236–37). Third, this political emphasis has been clearly partisan. Most American historians have been enthusiastic supporters of progressive intellectuals against outmoded, conservative "formalism" or "absolutism." Fourth, most historians have, until recently, assumed that the conditions against which progressive intellectuals reacted were objectively bad. According to this view, progressive intellectuals simply surveyed their world dispassionately and reacted against objectively existing political corruption, industrial license, and a wornout intellectual "genteel tradition." Finally, liberal historians have usually argued that the failures of the movement were caused by conditions which were not within the control of the progressives. The overwhelming power of the masters of industry, or the coming of World War I, turned Americans aside from reform and brought on the disastrous "return to normalcy" of the 1920's.

After World War II, this prevailing interpretation came under cautious but serious criticism. In the main, the critics were the self-conscious heirs of liberalism and not its enemies, but in a piecemeal way they began to notice difficulties in both the liberal ideology and in the traditional interpretation of it. Richard Hofstadter, in *The Age of Reform,* suggested that intellectuals might have become progressives because of difficulties in their own *subjective* situation, and not merely because of the objective existence of political and economic evils. Morton White, in *Social Thought in America: the Revolt against Formalism* (New York, 1949), subjected the ideas of men such as Beard, Dewey, and Veblen to systematic analysis. White, himself a philosopher in the pragmatic tradition, was sympathetic; but he noticed internal difficulties in the pragmatic scheme of things which made him uneasy. A similar kind of uneasiness over the internal patterns of liberal thought prompted David Noble's *Paradox of Progressive Thought* (Minneapolis, 1958). In a very influential book, Henry F. May has dissected *The End of American Innocence: a Story of the First Years of Our Time, 1912–1917* (New York, 1959). May challenged several of the leading ideas of the traditional interpretation. He did not link intellectual history so closely to politics and he suggested a considerable amount of continuity between progressive thought and the ideas of the Gilded Age. May also picked out a large number of internal divisions in what had usually been interpreted as a close-knit movement.

More recently, younger historians have turned sharply against the traditional interpretation. Lasch's *The New Radicalism* is part of the beginning of a wholesale reassessment of the intellectual history of the period. Charles Peter Forcey, in *The Crossroads of Liberalism*, raised very serious questions about the strength and durability of the liberal ideology. Samuel Haber, in *Efficiency and Uplift*, went further and argued that liberal intellectuals were committed to a very unattractive and undemocratic set of ideas and that World War I was actually a moment of great opportunity for them rather than a defeat. There is every reason to suppose that the lines laid out by Lasch, Forcey, and Haber will become the prevailing interpretation during the 1970's.

15. The Depression
and the New Deal

INTRODUCTION

The New Deal, greatly increasing the powers and responsibilities of the central government, established itself as one of the major developments of the twentieth century. The changes brought about under its auspices seemed so important that many observers—including some historians—associated Franklin D. Roosevelt with revolution. While there is some truth to assertions that those changes were on their way before the advent of the worst depression Americans had yet experienced, the fact remains that the New Deal occurred in an atmosphere of acute economic and social unrest.

By every economic measurement the depression was a disaster. The gross national product fell from $104.4 billion in 1929 to $74.2 billion in 1933. American imports dropped from nearly $5.5 billion in 1929 to $1.735 billion in 1932, while exports declined from $4.625 billion to $1.497 billion. The *New York Times* "Weekly Index of Business Activity" plummeted from its high of 114.8 in June, 1929, to a low of 63.7 in March, 1933. In the frightening years from 1929 through 1933, national income shrank from $87.8 billion to $40.2 billion. Total income from labor decreased 40 per cent, and total income from property decreased 31 per cent. Unemployment mounted steadily as factories and businesses laid off men. By April, 1930, 3 million were unemployed, and by the time F.D.R. took office somewhere between 12 and 15 million were out of work.

Yet the impact of the Great Depression cannot be determined by statistics alone. The crisis was perhaps even more severe than the figures would indicate, for it followed closely upon a period of unusual business optimism. Government and business leaders of the New Era after World War I encouraged Americans to believe that they had penetrated the mysteries of a modern economic utopia. There were soft spots in the economy, to be sure, but prosperity in the 1920's indicated that under the tutelage of a benign government, business was moving in the right direction. Secretary of Commerce Herbert Hoover busied himself with the promotion of various co-operative activities to increase efficiency of production and distribution and to insure continued economic progress. "We in America today are nearer to the final triumph over poverty than ever before in the history of any land," Hoover announced in accepting the Republican party's nomination in 1928. "The poorhouse is vanishing from among us. We have not yet reached the goal, but, given a chance to go forward with the policies of the last eight years, we shall soon with the help of God be in sight of the day when poverty will be banished from this nation."

The New Era, then, appeared to have resolved a centuries old dilemma of capitalism. In destroying the closed society of the Middle Ages, a society in which every man had known his place, capitalism had helped to bring about a new freedom. Yet the economic transformation of the western world had also brought with it a profound psychological uncertainty. As the regimentation of the medieval corporative system disappeared, man lost his sense of unity with the universe. From time to time conditions seemed to restore some of the old ties, some of the old consciousness of place and identity. Nineteenth-century American agrarianism—emphasizing the idea of partnership between man and God in the cyclical process of planting, nurture, and harvest—may be seen as a response to the terrifying isolation of the individual in modern society. With the rapid growth of cities in the twentieth century, however, agrarian concepts no longer appeared adequate or even relevant. Thus the rationale of the New Era, its blending of individual with associational activities, met the deepest of psychological needs. Here was a system under which a man was free to achieve as much as his abilities warranted, and here too was a system in which he functioned as part of a cooperative society.

What the depression destroyed was not so much the structure of the American economy, for New Deal tinkering and manipulation left that structure basically unchanged. What the depression destroyed was the mythology of the New Era, the congeries of ideas by which it sought to justify itself. The bright and rosy optimism of the 1920's provided subject matter for bitter jokes in the 1930's. Humor did not conceal a loss of confidence, nor did bitterness conceal the pathos that accompanied a loss of identity. On every hand men displayed a reluctance to trust their own judgments. The truth had taken on characteristics of grim fantasy, and systems of social thought had proved themselves unreliable.

Reality was hard to find and difficult to recognize, but Americans groped for it amongst the wreckage. Whatever else it may have been, the New Deal was an effort to discard hoary mythology and to discover the realities that, properly understood, would lead to a more durable prosperity than that of the New Era. F.D.R. and the New Dealers were unsuccessful in their quest for economic recovery in the 1930's, perhaps in part because Roosevelt was ready to try many proposals yet could not bring himself to follow the logic of any single formula. The New Deal was therefore internally inconsistent. And in discarding old myths, New Dealers created new ones—myths not necessarily closer to ultimate reality than the old, but at least more plausible in those years of the locust. In the meantime the President's warmth, his apparent concern for the unfortunate, and his willingness to experiment with a profusion of new governmental agencies mitigated the crisis of identity for millions of people.

I. EARLY INTERPRETATION

The following appreciation of the New Deal by Henry Steele Commager was published at the time of Roosevelt's death in April, 1945. The author evaluates what he considers the major achievements of F.D.R.'s administration, and he comments on what he is confident will be Roosevelt's place in history.

HENRY STEELE COMMAGER

Now that the bitter controversies over New Deal policies have been drowned out by the clamor of war, it is possible to evaluate those policies in some historical perspective. And now that the outcome of this war which is to determine the future of democracy and of America's rôle in world affairs, is certain, it is possible to interpret something of the significance of the foreign policy, or program, of the Roosevelt administrations. Those policies, domestic and foreign, have been four times decisively endorsed by large popular majorities: so fully have they been translated into accomplished and irrevocable facts that controversy about them is almost irrelevant. It should be possible to fix, if not with finality, at least with some degree of accuracy, the place occupied by Roosevelt in American history.

That this place still seems clouded by controversy and bitterness cannot be denied. Yet this, too, is part of the

Reprinted from Henry Steele Commager, "Twelve Years of Roosevelt," AMERICAN MERCURY, *LX (April, 1945), 391–397, 400–401, by permission of* AMERICAN MERCURY, *Torrance, Calif.*

picture and has its own significance. The Washington, the Jefferson, the Jackson, the Lincoln, the Wilson administrations, too, were characterized by controversy and bitterness; it is only the administrations of mediocre men like Monroe, Arthur, Harrison, that are memorable for placidity. The explanation of the controversy and especially of the bitterness is, however, less rational. It is a two-fold one: contemporaries tended to see in both the domestic and foreign policies of Roosevelt an abrupt and even revolutionary break with the past; they tended to personalize those policies, to regard them as largely an expression of Roosevelt's character, to focus all their attention— both their devotion and their hatred— on the man in the White House rather than on the groundswell of opinion to which he gave expression.

We can see now that the "Roosevelt revolution" was no revolution, but rather the culmination of half a century of historical development, and that Roosevelt himself, though indubitably a leader, was an instrument of the popular will rather than a creator of, or a dictator to, that will. Indeed, the two major issues of the Roosevelt administration—the domestic issue of the extension of government control for democratic purposes, and the international issue of the rôle of America as a world power—emerged in the 1890's, and a longer perspective will see the half-century from the 1890's to the present as an historical unit. The roots of the New Deal, the origins of our participation in this war, go deep down into our past, and neither development is comprehensible except in terms of that past.

What was really but a new deal of the old cards looked, to startled and dismayed contemporaries, like a revolution for two reasons: because it was carried through with such breathless rapidity, and because in spirit at least it contrasted so sharply with what immediately preceded. But had the comparison been made not with the Coolidge-Hoover era, but with the Wilson, the Theodore Roosevelt, even the Bryan era the contrast would have been less striking than the similarities. Actually, precedents for the major part of New Deal legislation was to be found in these earlier periods. Regulation of railroads and of business dated back to the Interstate Commerce Act of 1887 and the Sherman Act of 1890, and was continuous from that time forward. The farm relief program of the Populists, and of Wilson anticipated much that the Roosevelt administrations enacted. The beginnings of conservation can be traced to the Carey Act of 1894 and the Reclamation Act of 1902, and the first Roosevelt did as much as the second to dramatize—though less to solve—the problem of conserving natural resources.

Power regulation began with the Water Power Act of 1920; supervision over securities exchanges with grain and commodities exchange acts of the Harding and Coolidge administrations; while regulation of money is as old as the Union, and the fight which Bryan and Wilson waged against the "Money Power" and Wall Street was more bitter than anything that came during the New Deal. The policy of reciprocity can be traced to the Republicans, Blaine and McKinley. Labor legislation had its beginnings in such states as Massachusetts and New York over half a century ago, while much of the program of social security was worked out in Wisconsin and other states during the second and the third decades of the new century.

There is nothing remarkable about this, nor does it detract in any way from the significance of President Roosevelt's achievements and contributions. The pendulum of American history swings gently from right to left, but there are no sharp breaks in the rhythm of our historical development; and it is to the credit of Roosevelt that he worked within the framework of American history and tradition.

What, then, are the major achievements, the lasting contributions, of the first three Roosevelt administrations? First, perhaps, comes the restoration of self-confidence, the revivification of the national spirit, the reassertion of faith in democracy. It is irrelevant to argue whether these things were achieved by Roosevelt, or whether they came, rather, as a result of extraneous forces—as needless as to argue whether Jackson really was concerned with the rise of the common man, or Lincoln with abolition, or the first Roosevelt with reform. These things are irrevocably associated with their administrations, and it is safe to prophesy that the revival of faith in democracy, after a long decade of materialism and cynicism, will be associated with Franklin Roosevelt.

More, a strong case can be made out for the propriety of that association.

"The only thing we need to fear," said Mr. Roosevelt on assuming the Presidency, "is fear itself. . . . We face the arduous days that lie before us in the warm courage of national unity; with the clear consciousness of seeking old and precious moral values; with the clean satisfaction that comes from the stern performance of duty." And during twelve years of office, Mr. Roosevelt did not abate his confidence in "the future of essential democracy" or in the capacity of the American people to rise to any challenge, to meet any crisis, domestic or foreign. Those who lived through the electric spring of 1933 will remember the change from depression and discouragement to excitement and hope; those able to compare the last decade with previous decades will agree that interest in public affairs has rarely been as widespread, as alert, or as responsive.

All this may be in the realm of the intangible. If we look to more tangible things, what does the record show? Of primary importance has been the physical rehabilitation of the country. Notwithstanding the splendid achievements of the Theodore Roosevelt administrations, it became clear, during the twenties and thirties, that the natural resources of the country—its soil, forests, water power—were being destroyed at a dangerous rate. The development of the Dust Bowl, and the migration of the Oakies to the Promised Land of California, the tragic floods on the Mississippi and the Ohio, dramatized to the American people the urgency of this problem.

Roosevelt tackled it with energy and boldness. The Civilian Conservation Corps enlisted almost three million young men who planted seventeen million acres in new forests, built over six million check dams to halt soil erosion, fought forest fires and plant and animal diseases. To check erosion the government organized a co-operative program which enlisted the help of over one-fourth the farmers of the country and embraced 270 million acres of land, provided for the construction of a series of huge dams and reservoirs, and planned the creation of a hundred-mile-wide shelter belt of trees on the high plains. The Resettlement Administration moved farmers off marginal lands and undertook to restore these to usefulness. More important than all this, was the TVA, a gigantic laboratory for regional reconstruction. Though much of this program owes its inspiration to the past, the contrast between the New Deal and what immediately preceded it cannot be better illustrated than by reference to Hoover's characterization of the Muscle Shoals bill of 1931 as not "liberalism" but "degeneration."

Equally important has been the New Deal achievement in the realm of rehabilitation. Coming into office at a time when unemployment had reached perhaps fourteen million, and when private panaceas had ostentatiously failed, it was perhaps inevitable that Roosevelt should have sponsored a broad program of government aid. More important than bare relief, was the acceptance of the principle of the responsibility of the state for the welfare and security of its people—for employment, health and general welfare.

That this principle was aggressively and bitterly opposed now seems hard to believe: its establishment must stand as one of the cardinal achievements of the New Deal. Beginning with emergency legislation for relief, the Roosevelt program in the end embraced the whole field of social security—unemployment assistance, old age pensions, aid to women and children, and public health. Nor did it stop with formal "social security" legislation. It entered the domains of agriculture and labor, embraced elaborate programs of rural rehabilitation, the establishment of maximum hours and minimum wages, the prohibition of child labor; housing reform, and, eventually, enlarged aid to education. Under the New Deal the noble term "commonwealth" was given a more realistic meaning than ever before in our history.

That to Roosevelt the preservation of democracy was closely associated with this program for social and economic security is inescapably clear. He had learned well the moral of recent continental European history: that given a choice between liberty and bread, men are sorely tempted to choose bread. The task of democracy, as he conceived it, was to assure both. In a fireside chat of 1938 he said:

Democracy has disappeared in several other great nations, not because the people of those nations disliked democracy, but because they had grown tired of unemployment and insecurity, of seeing their children hungry while they sat helpless in the face of government confusion and government weakness through lack of leadership in government. Finally, in desperation, they chose to sacrifice liberty in the hope of getting something to eat. We in America know that our democratic institutions can be preserved and made to work. But in order to preserve them we need . . . to prove that the practical operation of democratic government is equal to the task of protecting the security of the people. . . . The people of America are in agreement in defending their liberties at any cost, and the first line of that defense lies in the protection of economic security.

In the political realm the achievements of the New Deal were equally notable. First we must note the steady trend towards the strengthening of government and the expansion of government activities—whether for weal or for woe only the future can tell. As yet no better method of dealing with the crowding problems of modern economy and society has revealed itself, and it can be said that though government today has, quantitatively, far greater responsibilities than it had a generation or even a decade ago, it has, qualitatively, no greater power. For our Constitutional system is intact, and all power still resides in the people and their representatives in Congress, who can at any moment deprive their government of any power.

But we seem to have solved, in this country, the ancient problem of the reconciliation of liberty and order; we seem to have overcome our traditional distrust of the state and come to a realization that a strong state could be used to benefit and advance the commonwealth. That is by no means a New Deal achievement, but it is a development which has gained much from the experience of the American people with their government during the Roosevelt administrations.

It has meant, of course, a marked acceleration of the tendency towards Federal centralization. This tendency had been under way for a long time before Roosevelt came to office: a century ago liberals were deploring the decline of the states and the growth of the power of the national government. That under the impact first of depression and then of war it has proceeded at a rapid rate since 1933 cannot be denied. It is apparent in the administrative field, with the growth of bureaus and departments and civil servants—and of the budget! It is apparent in the legislative field, with the striking extension of Federal authority into the fields of labor, agriculture, banking, health, education and the arts. It is apparent in the executive field with the immense increase in the power of the President. And it has been ratified by the judiciary with the acceptance and application of a broad construction of the Constitution.

Yet it cannot be said that this Federal centralization has weakened the states or local communities. What we are witnessing is a general increase in governmental activities—an increase in which the states share—witness any state budget at present. And it can be argued, too, that political centralization strengthens rather than weakens local government and the health of local communities. For if we look below forms to realities we can see that during the last decade Federal aid to farmers, to home-owners, to labor, Federal assistance in road-building, education and public health, has actually restored many communities to financial and economic health. It is by no means certain that community sentiment is weaker today than it was a generation ago.

Along with Federal centralization has gone a great increase in the power of the executive. The charge that Roosevelt has been a dictator can be dismissed, along with those hoary charges that Jefferson, Jackson, Lincoln, Theodore Roosevelt, and Wilson were dictators. American politics simply doesn't run to dictators. But Roosevelt has been a "strong" executive—as every great democratic President has been a strong executive. There is little doubt that the growing complexity of government plays into the hands of the executive; there is little doubt that Roosevelt accepted this situation cheerfully. Today Roosevelt exercises powers far vaster than those contemplated by the Fathers of the Constitution, as vast, indeed, as those exercised by the head of any democratic state in the world.

Yet it cannot fairly be asserted that any of these powers has been exercised arbitrarily, or that the liberties of Americans are not so safe today as at any other time.

Two other political developments under the New Deal should be noted. The first is the revitalization of political parties; the second the return of the Supreme Court to the great tradition of Marshall, Story, Miller and Holmes. Four observations about political parties during the last decade are in order. First, the danger that our parties might come to represent a particular class or section or interest was avoided: both major parties retained —after the election of 1936—a broad national basis. Second, minor parties all but disappeared: in the elections of 1940 and 1944 the minor parties cast less than 1 per cent of the total vote— the first time this happened since 1872. Third, legislation such as the Hatch Act diminished the possibility that any party might come to be controlled by powerful vested interests or by patronage. And finally, with the organization of the PAC in the campaign of 1944, labor for the first time in our history became an important factor in elections; and labor chose to work within the framework of existing parties rather than, as elsewhere, to organize its own party.

The New Deal, as far as can be foreseen, is here to stay: there seems no likelihood of a reversal of any of the major developments in politics in the last twelve years. This was recognized by the Republicans in 1940 and again in 1944, for both platforms endorsed all the essentials of the New Deal and confined criticism to details and administration. How far the reforms and experiments of the Roosevelt era will be carried is a hazardous question. That the program of conservation will be continued and enlarged seems obvious. A recent Congress, to be sure, cavalierly ended the life of the National Resources Planning Board, but the present Congress seems disposed to undertake a Missouri Valley development along the lines of the TVA, and doubtless other "little TVA's" are ahead. Social security, too, will be maintained and possibly enlarged: whether it will come to embrace socialized medicine or a broad rehousing program is more dubious.

There may be a reaction against some of the labor legislation of the New Deal, but labor's newly discovered political power would seem to make that unlikely. It is improbable that there will be any relaxation of governmental peacetime controls over business, banking, securities, power, though here a change in taxation policies may do much to stimulate private enterprise and create an appearance of a shift away from New Deal practices. Federal centralization, which has been under way so long, is doubtless here to stay; planning, imperatively required by war, will in all probability wear off its faintly pink tinge, and flourish as a peacetime technique. And, finally, it seems probable that the restoration of the dignity of politics and statecraft, which came with 1933, will survive.

Today it is foreign affairs rather than domestic policy that commands our most agitated attention. Here, too, the large outlines of the Roosevelt achievements are clear, though the details are blurred and the future projection uncertain.

. . .

And what, finally, of Roosevelt himself? It may seem too early to fix his position in our history, yet that position is reasonably clear. He takes his place in the great tradition of American liberalism, along with Jefferson, Jackson, Lincoln, Theodore Roosevelt and Wilson. Coming to office at a time when the very foundations of the republic seemed threatened and when men were beginning to despair of the ability of a constitutional democracy to meet a crisis, he restored confidence and proved that democracy could act as effectively in crisis as could totalitarian governments. A liberal, he put government clearly at the service of the people; a conservative, he pushed through reforms designed to strengthen the natural and human resources of the nation, restore agriculture and business to its former prosperity, and save capitalism. He saw that problems of government were primarily political, not economic; that politics should control economy—not economy, politics; and that politics was an art as well as a science. He repudiated isolationism, demanded for America once more her proper station and responsibility in world affairs, and, after unifying the American people on the major issues of aid to the democracies and war, furnished a war leadership bold, energetic and successful.

In all this Roosevelt was an opportunist—but an opportunist with a philosophy. He was the same kind of opportunist that Jefferson—that earlier "traitor to his class"—had been. The close view of Roosevelt has discovered numerous inconsistencies. But if we look back over Roosevelt's long career in politics—beginning with his fight on the Tammany machine in 1910, we can see that amidst the hurly-burly of politics he has been unfalteringly consistent in his fundamental social and political philosophy. He has sought ends, and cheerfully adopted the "quarterback" technique with respect to means. And as the bitterness of particular controversies dies away, the larger outlines of his achievements during the past twelve years emerge with striking clarity. We can see that the promises of the New Deal platform of 1932 were carried out, more fully perhaps than those of any party platform since that of Polk a century ago. We can see that the promises of the inaugural address were fulfilled. We can see that the democratic philosophy which Roosevelt asserted was applied and implemented. Under his leadership the American people withstood the buffetings of depression and the fearful trial of war, and emerged strong and respected, refreshed in their faith in democracy and in the ultimate triumph of justice in human affairs.

"The only sure bulwark of continuing liberty," Roosevelt said, "is a government strong enough to protect the interests of the people, and a people strong enough and well enough informed to maintain its sovereign control over its government."

The Roosevelt administration proved once more that it was possible for such a government to exist and such a people to flourish, and restored to the United States its position as "the hope of the human race."

II. DOCUMENTS

1. The New Deal

In 1932, Rexford Guy Tugwell—soon to become a member of Roosevelt's Brain Trust—believed, as did millions of Americans, that Herbert Hoover had misunderstood the causes of depression and had failed to discover the measures that would lead to recovery. The most striking feature of the selection from Mr. Hoover's Economic Policy *is Tugwell's explanation of the fallacies in Hoover's thinking.*

Tugwell was certain about the mistaken "theology" of the past. The New Deal was less certain about the course which ought to be pursued in the future. In an essay of 1955, Gilbert Burck and Charles E. Silberman examined some of the hesitations and inconsistencies which plagued Roosevelt's politics of "recovery."

If the grim realities of the depression were difficult to control, this provided part of the context of foreign-policy discussions in the New Deal era. Some observers convinced themselves that F.D.R., having failed to lead the nation out of depression, would turn to foreign affairs as an escape. In international crisis—and especially in war—the American course would be clearly marked: the United States would become the champion of "freedom" and "democracy." Should war come, in other words, the President could call into service an emotional mythology to save both the New Deal and himself. Such considerations led Charles A. Beard to make a gloomy prediction in 1935 that "the Pacific war awaits."

REXFORD GUY TUGWELL

Mr. Hoover believes that he proceeds from particulars to generals; in reality he proceeds from generals to particulars. Once this is seen, new meaning is given to his policy. Furthermore the tragedy of his pitilessly exposed position in the Presidency begins to recommend him to human clemency. For no one with a series of fixed ideas, inherited from a vanished past, ever had to apply them under more difficult circumstances. And added to that, in his case, is the convinced belief that he is *par excellence* the engineer pragmatist, the examiner of reality, the man of action guided by fact. The two together have ravaged his mind and spirit.

No one without this peculiar inner turmoil could act quite as he does. Failure to understand it is the source of much of the disaffection among his former supporters. Only the politicians were realists about him all along; and that, of course, was because they were specialists in human nature. Most unforgivable were the liberals, now unhappy and disillusioned, who thought, without any reason at all, that their cause might find a champion in the author of *American Individualism.* Their romantic conception of Hoover the engineer left wholly out of account what should have been obvious: that Mr. Hoover only thinks he subsists on an engineer's diet of fact. He has a mania for facts and an obsession for acting on them—if only they will behave! It is not difficult to imagine much recent wringing of Presidential hands over misguided experts and un-

Reprinted from Rexford Guy Tugwell, MR. HOOVER'S ECONOMIC POLICY *(New York: The John Day Company, Inc.,* © *1932 by Rexford Guy Tugwell), pp. 5–7, 10, 11, 13–14, 18–19, by permission of The John Day Company, Inc.*

amenable information. For time after time it has been quite impossible to evade a show-down. And always principles have won: facts, experts, never. Sometimes humiliation has been complete: witness the 1000 economists who petitioned against the signing of the Hawley-Smoot tariff bill—which nevertheless, in a smothered silence, Mr. Hoover signed.

That the President fancies his pragmatic logic there can be no doubt. He has said so numbers of times. For instance, at the Edison celebration, he likened civilization to a garden—"It is to be apprised (*sic*) by the quality of its blooms." This is a full acceptance of the test of consequence. But the really numerous instances of these commitments ought not to be accepted at their face value until their orientation is understood. For in the same passages in which these things are said, there are usually references of another sort to be found. When he spoke of the blooms in civilization's garden, he went on, with no more than a period between, to show how such blooms are always produced—"as we fertilize the soil with liberty, as we maintain diligence in cultivation and guardianship against destructive forces." What the passage means, then, taken as a whole, is that we judge by fruits, so long as their production requires no change in our customary attitudes. That these attitudes of his are particularly strong in the economic field is amply demonstrated by habitual allusion. In his acceptance speech he said: "With impressive proof on all sides of magnificent progress, no one can rightly deny the fundamental correctness of our economic system." Whether rightly or wrongly, most, perhaps, of the experts seriously question just this "fundamental correctness." He appeals to our progress as proof, which is quite all right provided there is a willingness to show the relations between cause and effect. But in no instance, in all his public remarks, has Mr. Hoover followed through in this way. There is always a citation of pleasant fact, and an immediate attribution of cause to those certain elements in our system which seem to him so unassailable but to most of us so open to serious doubt.

The question of real interest is whether this faith is produced by hoping that all this is true and by recognizing that the only policy available to a Republican president must be based on it, or whether it really arises from some analysis of evidence. Perhaps the King's Mountain speech may tell something. Here, it will be remembered, Mr. Hoover was speaking within a few miles of Gastonia, and at the height of the troubles there, which, one would have said, illustrated in rather lurid fashion, the virtues of the courageous and independent businessman.

In the large sense we have maintained open the channels of opportunity . . . we have no class or caste or aristocracy whose privilege limits the hopes and opportunities of our people.

This unparallelled rise of the American man and woman was not alone the result of riches in lands or forests or mines; it sprang from ideas and ideals, which liberated the mind and stimulated the exertion of a people. . . . Some have called it individualism, but it is not an individualism which permits men to override the equal opportunity of others. By its enemies it has been called capitalism, and yet under its ideals capital is but an instrument, not a master.

In the American system . . . we train the runners . . . the winner is he who shows the most conscientious training, the greatest ability, the strongest character.

If there were any strikers in that region whose radios still belonged to them and who were tuned in on that October day, they must have listened in some amazement, both to the recitation of history and to the attribution of cause. It is just not true, of course, that Mr. Hoover is really guided by facts or that he has other than a collector's respect for them. Many of us are collectors, some of pictures, some of old furniture, some—and we are locked up when we go this far—of shiny pebbles or odd pieces of string. Mr. Hoover collects facts in the same spirit and hides them under his bed.

. . .

No one could undergo the psychological ordeal involved in these struggles between ideals and reality and come out of it undamaged; and especially a humorless man who is *both* clumsy and earnest. It has left its mark on Mr. Hoover. He is less and less able to face reality. He succumbs gradually to the dangerous prestige of the presidency, the tendency to believe that what he says may be true because he says it.

Perhaps the best illustration of the progress of Mr. Hoover's disease is furnished by the events of the depression during his presidential years. He began by attributing our post-war prosperity to Republican policies in his speech of acceptance; he went on to a systematic whittling down of the damaging reality and a deliberate twisting of evidence which might reflect upon the basis of his policy; and he ended by stamping his feet, beating tom-toms, ballyhooing for better business, and hurling invectives at "pessimists."

. . .

It was when he was Secretary of Commerce that he initiated the series of studies which gave us our first good information about unemployment. Everyone expected that these studies would mature into a plan for prevention or, at least, relief. The years have gone by, the tide of unemployment has risen and fallen and risen again. Mr. Hoover's reaction has been characteristically protective. It consisted (1) of denying or shading the facts, (2) evading administrative responsibility, and (3) making false gestures toward relief. His single contribution to the whole problem of depression and unemployment during the first two years was the calling together of certain business leaders to whom he preached "teamwork," postulating a solidarity of social interests to which they must have listened with amazement—not to say amusement. They applauded his denunciations of government action, went back to their offices, and acted exactly as they have always done in pursuit of those aims which seemed to them to meet their individual interests best.

Relief by these methods was bound to fail dismally; that it had failed was immediately apparent in the deepening of the depression, the vast enlargement of the numbers of unemployed, and the systematic reduction of wages. He persisted in his faith that these measures were sufficient and valiantly resisted all attempts to do anything more or anything different—even to the point of vetoing Senator Wagner's well-conceived measure for establishing employment exchanges which afterward he tried to copy in ineffective form. Several quotations from addresses made during the height of the depression reveals his psychological difficulty and the consequent orientation of his policy.

. . .

In spite of the general malaise of hard times, all this volubility of the President served to tickle American risibilities. The stock market about that time began also to react in strange inverse fashion to White House optimism, which added to the general gayety. This naturally irritated Mr. Hoover who not only was a faith-professor but also thought he knew reality at first hand. He began to speak of the hair shirt any president must wear; and with heavy whimsicality he said to the Bankers' Association:

There are a few folks in business and several folks in the political world who resent the notion that things will ever get better and who wish to enjoy our temporary misery. To recount to these persons the progress of co-operation between the people and the Government in amelioration of this situation, or to mention that we are suffering far less than other countries, or that savings are piling up in the banks, or that our people are paying off installment purchases, that abundant capital is now pressing for new ventures and employment, only inspires the unkind retort that we should fix our gaze solely upon the unhappy features of the decline.

It is in such a passage as this that he displays how deeply he is troubled. His determination to believe in the goodness of our system had been assailed on every side. Even a system which produces depressions may produce them for our good. They teach us lessons: "From this one we shall gain stiffening and economic discipline." He now sought that last refuge of the mentally troubled: the attribution to those who thought otherwise of a lack of balance.

. . .

Americans usually have liked to view economics as a matter of common sense, a clear exposition of the principles of business relations, government being restricted to policing duties. This is the Hoover tradition. Any nineteenth century textbook—McVickar, Wayland, Perry, Bowen, Walker—could be used as well as Mr. Hoover's speeches for excerpting the chief rules of economic conduct and the relation to them of the Government. Because they are theological in origin and dogmatic in form, they are generally a consistent well-rounded body of principles. They become confused only from contact with unholy reality. For a clergyman or a college professor this is not important: the consistency of doctrine, within itself, can, with patience, be worked out. But a President of the Federal Union in the 1930's is not so lucky. Hobgoblin reality reaches for him from behind every bush; but received theology, however deep its sanctions, comes to be suspect. He must be an acute and clever apologist who would save such a doctrinal system from ridicule. Sometimes the attempted enforcement of outworn dogma has precipitated crises; they have not been infrequent, in our social history.

GILBERT BURCK
AND
CHARLES E. SILBERMAN

When Roosevelt took office his advisers were full of ideas, many conflicting, about what had gone wrong—the nation's capital stock had been overexpanded, prices had been "managed," labor hadn't got a fair share of income, public utilities had been antisocial, and so on. But at first Roosevelt and his Administration had one important broad, fixed objective: to raise production by stimulating purchasing power, and to achieve this objective they were willing to try anything plausible. In a press conference Roosevelt compared himself to a football quarterback who can call only one play at a time, and must decide each play on the basis of how the previous one worked.

Reprinted from Gilbert Burck and Charles E. Silberman, "Why the Depression Lasted So Long," FORTUNE, LI (March, 1955), 192–200, by permission of the publisher.

This pragmatic, experimental approach was perhaps the only intelligent one in those early days of the New Deal, and for a time it worked very well. Roosevelt's cheerful ignorance of economics, far from being a handicap, was if anything an advantage, for it made him receptive to the new and unorthodox. The trouble came later on, when it became necessary to stop improvising and choose a sound approach to the nation's problems and stick to it.

But the earliest measures of the new Administration, in March, 1933, were consistent enough. In his 1932 campaign Roosevelt had, much to his later embarrassment, argued eloquently against an unbalanced budget. "Stop the deficits," he had implored. "I accuse the Administration of being the biggest spending Administration in peacetimes in all our history." And the first thing the New Deal had to do, after reopening the solvent banks, was to "restore confidence" by demonstrating that it could cut expenditures and balance the budget. An economy act was passed, and federal salaries and other costs were cut. What would have happened if this deflationary course had been followed to the bitter end is hard to say, but even most businessmen by this time were afraid to let it happen.

At all events, the Administration reversed itself and moved rapidly toward credit expansion, monetary inflation, price and wage rises, relief payments, and public works. The most important decision was to go off gold, and the decision was in effect forced on Roosevelt by an inflation-minded Congress. On April 20, 1933, Roosevelt placed an embargo on gold, and thus in effect took the country off the gold standard.

There followed, between 1933 and 1937, a continuous avalanche of congressional acts and executive orders dealing with recovery. There were steps primarily designed to raise prices and boost purchasing power—though some of them involved various reforms. There was, of course, pump priming by means of a bewildering succession of public works and relief measures. There was the Federal Emergency Relief Administration, the Civilian Conservation Corps, the Civil Works Administration, and PWA, which under "Honest" Harold Ickes spent so little money that WPA had to be formed under Harry Hopkins. Partly as a result of these measures, . . . federal expenditures rose from $3.7 billion in 1932 to $8.2 billion in 1936 (in 1929 dollars).

There was TVA, which got the government into the power business in a colossal way. There were aids to agriculture like "parity" prices and the AAA, which raised prices by paying farmers to restrict production. There were several labor measures, discussed later, which raised union membership from about two million in 1932 to over 11 in 1941. There were a variety of measures easing home and farm mortgages. And there was the social-security system, founded in 1936.

Among the solidest early achievements of the New Deal were the laws reforming and strengthening the banking system, such as the Banking Act of 1933, which provided for deposit insurance and for the divorce of investment and commercial banking; the Bank Act of 1935, which centralized Federal Reserve power, particularly over open-market operations; and the Securities and Exchange Acts of 1934–35, which reformed the issuing and buying and selling of securities. Sidney Weinberg, who fought hard against the Securities and Exchange Acts, now says he would go on a crusade against any move to repeal them. And Professor

Milton Friedman of the University of Chicago, one of the leading orthodox economists, argues that the Federal Deposit Insurance Corporation is by all odds the most important of the changes affecting the cyclical characteristics of the American economy, perhaps even more important than the establishment of the Federal Reserve.

The most inconsistent New Deal creation, the one that remains the supreme example of the Administration's let's-give-it-a-try, all-things-to-all-men approach, was NRA, or the Natoinal Recovery Administration, created in 1933. NRA was a kind of state-run supercartel, with a genially ferocious dictator in the person of General Hugh ("Ironpants") Johnson in charge and a new national flag in the form of the "bright badge" of the Blue Eagle. Had NRA survived and succeeded, it would have accomplished publicly all that any group of European cartelists, meeting behind closed doors and puffing big cigars, has ever been able to accomplish. It would have wiped out the antitrust acts and committed the whole nation to planned restrictionism, with government, capital, management, and labor restricting together.

NRA's immediate genesis seems to have been a 1933 memo by Gerard Swope, president of General Electric, who advanced industry's plausible argument that cut-throat competition in a depression would make things worse rather than better. NRA put a floor under wages and hours, and through Section 7a guaranteed labor the right to organize and bargain collectively. Since productivity had been rising, this was long overdue. But NRA also allowed business to get together and adopt codes that incorporated price-fixing and production-restriction agreements, which might well have hamstrung the increase of American productivity. Hundreds of businessmen took their codes before the red-faced, wisecracking Johnson, who assured them he would crack down unmercifully on the chiselers. "May God Almighty," he roared, "have mercy on anyone who attempts to trifle with that bird [the Blue Eagle]." Fortunately for the U.S., there were too many chiselers in business even for General Johnson. Long before May, 1935, when the Supreme Court declared the NRA unconstitutional, the codes were being violated all across the nation.

The labor provisions of the act started a wave of unionization, and they, too, encountered employer resistance. Section 7a of the dead NRA, however, was quickly replaced by the National Labor Relations Act (the Wagner Act), which specifically authorized collective bargaining, defined unfair employer practices, and set up the National Labor Relations Board to help enforce the act.

For all their inconsistencies, the New Deal's early measures did achieve their major aim: they raised farm and industrial prices and wages, and so stimulated consumption and industrial production. Gross national product, . . . rose just about as fast as it had declined, and by the third quarter of 1937 stood 5 per cent above its mid-1929 level. Industrial production had also passed the 1929 peak, and volume of consumer non-durables was 10 per cent above 1929. This, however, was not full recovery. Because the national working force had increased 10 per cent and its productivity 15 per cent, true recovery, that is, fairly full employment, would have meant a G.N.P. at least 25 per cent higher than in 1929. As it was, there were still more than seven million unemployed early in 1937.

What blocked full recovery, and so perpetuated mass unemployment, was the fact that the durables sector of the economy hardly recovered at all. By 1937 the volume of residential construction was still 40 per cent below its 1929 level, industrial and commercial construction . . . was 50 per cent below 1929, and producer and consumer durables were 5 and 6 per cent below 1929, respectively. Why did they lag?

The story of residential construction may be told simply. There had been considerable overbuilding in the 1920's, and the low incomes and low household formation of the Thirties created little additional demand. The birth rate fell 19 per cent, and people doubled up. And so long as lenders feared that new houses would have to compete with houses on which they had foreclosed, or held shaky mortgages, they were reluctant to give mortgages for new construction. Then, too, building costs did not fall so much as costs in general.

The stagnation in capital spending —on industrial and commercial construction and producers' goods—is not so simple a story. The volume of commercial construction was so great in 1929 that it was not equaled again until 1954; thus the overbuilding and speculative real-estate inflation of the 1920's were among the main reasons why 1937's volume remained only half of 1929's volume. Then, too, commercial construction is closely related to the rate of home building, which was low.

Even the fact that the 1937 volume of producers' goods was only 5 per cent below its 1929 volume was disappointing. For there was (and is) occurring a long-term shift in capital spending from plant to equipment, and thus the volume of producers' equipment relative to the trend was actually low. And why did not this capital spending on equipment and plant recover?

One answer popular in the late 1930's was Alvin Hansen's theory of secular stagnation, which blamed oversaving at a time when investment opportunities were declining, thanks to the economy's "maturity." What seems today a more plausible reason is that business probably was not able to adjust to all the changes that confronted it in a few short years:

—The reform of the credit system, as well as SEC regulations, were badly needed, but probably discouraged new-issue flotation.

—Legalized unionization elevated wage rates 41 per cent in 1933–37. Even harder to accept, for many businessmen, was that unions had to be recognized and bargained with.

—Increasingly higher taxes altered the calculations on which investments had been based. In his attempts to balance the budget, Hoover had raised tax *rates* drastically in 1932. The New Deal raised them further, and added new taxes—e.g., excess-profits taxes, social-security taxes, and the undistributed-profits tax. It had also closed many loopholes, such as personal holding companies. As business and income picked up, therefore, tax payments rose even more. Federal receipts more than tripled between 1932 and 1937, rising (in 1929 dollars) from $2 billion to $6.8 billion, or nearly double the 1929 figure of $3.8 billion.

Banking regulations, unionization, and higher taxes, of course, are commonplace enough today. But the speed with which business had to adjust to them had a lot to do with its reluctance to make capital investment. Its adjustment problems were not eased by the increasingly uncompromising attitude of President Roosevelt. He had provocation, it is true. Some businessmen were venting a virtually psychopathic hatred of "that man." Roosevelt went on to assume that all businessmen, save a few New Deal "captives," were enemies of the people. His 1936 message to Congress was studded with such fighting phrases as "entrenched greed" and "resplendent economic autocracy," and his campaign speeches were even less conciliatory. "They are unanimous in their hate of me," he boasted with a certain accuracy of those who opposed him. But then he added childishly: "I welcome their hate."

Yet there remains one other important circumstance that probably contributed greatly to the lag in capital goods. What really shapes business decisions to buy capital goods is not a vague sense of confidence or doubt, not necessarily even an inflationary or deflationary government policy, but the outlook for sales and profits. Partly because of rising wages, partly because of rising taxes (and partly because 1929 profits were unusually high), profits in the 1930's did not recover so fast as wages and production. Corporate profits in 1937, after taxes, were 43 per cent below their 1929 level, and the sales outlook for the durable industries was still bad. But could anything have been done about *that*? The government could have kept taxes down by running somewhat bigger deficits. And why didn't this high-spending government run bigger deficits? Simply because Roosevelt was constantly plagued by the ideal of a balanced budget and by congressional advocates of sound money, and never seemed to understand quite how an unbalanced budget need not be inflationary (though he actually needed some inflation). Thus is irony defined.

And it was the lack of a consistent New Deal fiscal policy that was partly if not largely responsible for the disheartening recession of 1937–38, the steepest economic descent on record. In a few months the nation lost half the ground it had gained since 1932; industrial production fell 30 per cent, unemployment passed ten million. Stocks plummeted; e.g., New York Central declined from 41½ to 10 in about six months.

The reasons for the recession seem clear enough today. The 1936–37 boom, fed by the 1936 soldier's bonus, pushed up industrial production, commercial loans, and stock prices. Settlement of the automobile sitdown and other strikes led to a rash of wage increases. Businessmen, fearing that rising wages would mean higher prices, and expecting the government to continue to run a deficit, put their money into goods, speculatively placing orders for both current and future needs, and touching off an inventory boom. Yet rising wages did not increase consumption enough to stabilize the economy, and they did not because the government's irresolute fiscal policy in 1937 reduced its contribution to the nation's buying power by $3.2 billion, or more than the inventory accumulation and more than the aggregate wage increase.

How did this happen? It happened because in 1936 Roosevelt had begun to worry about inflation and the mounting pressures of business and the press, and had tried to balance the budget. He had even vetoed the 1936 soldier's bonus. But Congress had passed a $1.7-billion bonus over his veto, so in 1936 the government ran a deficit of $3.4 billion (1929 dollars).

In 1937, however, the government had no bonus to pay, and so spent $1.2 billion less than it did in 1936. At the same time, moreover, it collected $1.5 billion in new social-security taxes, practically none of which it disbursed. So for all practical purposes Roosevelt and Secretary of the Treasury Morgenthau balanced the budget. And thus it was that they reduced the government's contribution to the nation's buying power by more than $3 billion. Businessmen, seeing their inventories mount while sales (especially of durables) fell, curtailed orders. By the late summer of 1937, the landslide began to gather way.

Franklin Roosevelt, who had been so hospitable to the new economics (up to a point), now found himself in the same frustrating, discouraging position that Herbert Hoover had been in five and six years before. For the first time in his associates' memory, Roosevelt was unable to make up his mind quickly on an important issue. Even while Secretary Morgenthau was promising another balanced budget, Roosevelt was conferring and discussing and mulling over the problem. Finally, on April 14, 1938, a full seven months after the recession began, he countermanded Morgenthau and asked Congress to appropriate $3 billion for relief, public works, housing, and flood control. The economy revived quickly as inventories were rebuilt, and by late 1939 most of the lost ground was recovered. But full employment was not restored until 1942, when World War II was in full swing.

CHARLES A. BEARD

Out of the war of 1917, as out of the war of 1812 and the war of 1861, the party of business enterprise emerged more triumphant than ever. It had a new national banking system, sanctioned by Democrats, despite Andrew Jackson. Fortunes had multiplied. War profiteers had heaped up a mountain of accumulated capital. A Republican House had been elected in 1918 and was at work on a new tariff bill. In 1920 the party of the New Freedom was hurled headlong out of Washington in a combination of Waterloo and Sedan.

Reprinted from Charles A. Beard, "National Politics and War," SCRIBNER'S MAGAZINE, *XCVII (February, 1935), 69–70, by permission of the publisher.*

From 1921 to 1933, the party of wealth and talents, still bearing Jefferson's old title, Republican, continued to rule the country, despite all agitations and threats on the left, despite agrarian discontents voiced in Congress. Its regime looked like a permanent order of things. It might have been if the economic base could have been kept intact, if that high level of "permanent prosperity" could have been maintained. But for various reasons, business enterprise and a Republican administration could not make the system work. It broke down on their very hands, and all the economists and witch doctors in the country could not get it running again by 1932.

Then came the great Democratic upheaval, under the direction of Franklin D. Roosevelt. And to the surprise of hardened politicians the upheaval became more of an upheaval in 1934.

Is this the permanent revolution at last—the utter and final discomfiture of the party of wealth and talents?

That calls for prophecy, which is a dangerous trade. Judging by the past, we may be sure that the "permanent" is not permanent. There has been no great shift in the economic base since 1933. The party of wealth and talents as an economic order has not been decimated. Banks have not been nationalized, nor the railways taken over by the Government. Not a single instrumentality of economic power has been wrested from this party. The public debt has been increased, and its members hold bonds representing that debt. Even the financing of farmers has been assumed by the Federal Government on the basis of tax-exempt bonds. This operation has strengthened, not weakened, the party of wealth and talents; in the place of defaulted and decaying farm mortgages, it holds bonds guaranteed by the Federal Government. In the process of liquidation now going on, all signs indicate a swift concentration of defaulted and distress paper in the hands of the shrewd and enterprising. There is no hint whatever of any change in the old practices of reorganizing bankrupt concerns. The "little fellow" is being frozen out as usual. At the end of the depression, if it ever ends, the concentration of wealth in the United States will doubtless mark a new high point in the evolution of American economy. The party of wealth and talents survived the Jeffersonian revolution, and the Jacksonian revolution. If it has not lost its talents, it will survive the Roosevelt revolution.

Yet the future is veiled.

If we seek to penetrate it, what instruments can we use? Only knowledge of the past, including the latest moment. What knowledge is relevant? And how far does it take us?

Certainly we cannot foreclose on the future. We may divine its alternatives and catch a dim vision of its contours, but we cannot bring any equation of forecast to a mathematical conclusion, a Q. E. D.

We can be reasonably sure that the depression will relax or deepen. If from obscure causes it does relax and President Roosevelt is in power at the time, the Democratic party is likely to reap the reward of appreciation at the polls, to the long-time discomfiture of the Republicans. If the crisis deepens, the Democratic administration may resort to strong measures. It may nationalize banks, especially the business of issuing notes. This is not impossible, but it seems improbable. Still more likely is inflation on a large scale, an orgy of paper money, such as we had after the destruction of the United States Bank in 1836. But if anything is known at all, large-scale inflation will aggravate the crisis and thus deliver into the hands of some strong party a mandate to rehabilitate the disordered finances of the country.

Other measures, well known, are also at the disposal of the President. Will he make use of them in an hour of deeper crisis? Nobody knows. Not even the President, unless, like Lincoln in the summer of 1862, he has already made up his mind. Critics may say that he is going to the left or to the right, but this is a meaningless phrase until the words are defined in terms of concrete measures.

If there is anything in American tradition and practices to guide us, it is that a wider spread of economic calamity will culminate in a foreign war, rather than in a drastic reorganization of domestic economy. President Roosevelt has given no indication that this alternative will be rejected. He has, to be sure, spoken of peace with his wonted geniality, but Herr Hitler has done as much. The gentlemen who stumbled into war in 1914 had been celebrating peace for a quarter of a century, while they feverishly prepared for war. Deeds speak louder than words. President Roosevelt has adopted the biggest navy program in the history of the country in peace time, and Secretary Swanson was not going beyond the record when he declared that the Democratic victory last November was an endorsement of this program. President Roosevelt has not given any indication whatever that he intends to relax the competition of the United States with Great Britain and Japan for prestige and "sea power." Judging by the past and by his actions, war will be his choice—and it will be a "war for Christianity against Paganism" this time.

At once the cry will go up that "nations do not deliberately make war." Nations as such never do anything. Statesmen in power make decisions for nations. Seldom if ever do statesmen deliberately "make" war, but they often prefer "strong" foreign policies to "strong" domestic policies. It is well known, except to innocence, that it is a favorite device of statesmen to attempt the adjustment of domestic dissensions by resort to diplomatic fulminations, war scares, and war itself. The Department of State under Cleveland and Olney was well aware that the threat against Great Britain over the Venezuela episode was calculated to reduce the inflammation of "the anarchistic, socialistic, and populistic boil." The Spanish War was in many quarters regarded as a welcome relief from the domestic conflict—an effective damper on the populistic movement. This is not saying that President Roosevelt will deliberately plunge the country into a Pacific war in his efforts to escape the economic crisis. There will be an "incident," a "provocation." Incidents and provocations are of almost daily occurrence. Any government can quickly magnify one of them into a "just cause for war."

Confronted by the difficulties of a deepening domestic crisis and by the comparative ease of a foreign war, what will President Roosevelt do? Judging by the past history of American politicians, he will choose the latter, or, perhaps it would be more accurate to say, amid powerful conflicting emotions he will "stumble into" the latter. The Jeffersonian party gave the nation the War of 1812, the Mexican War, and its participation in the World War. The Pacific war awaits.

Beyond that lies the Shadowy Shape of Things to Come.

2. A Troubled Society

Whatever confusion may have existed within the New Deal about exactly what should be done, the view from Washington was clear about one thing: the nation's problems were economic and the purpose of politics was "recovery." Out in the society, however, the landscape was more uncertain; reality was difficult enough to discover, much less to manipulate. In a very influential book, The Folklore of Capitalism, *Thurman Arnold satirized the kinds of "mythologies" which he thought prevented the leaders of American business from seeing even the simplest economic facts as they really were.*

On Halloween night of 1938, for thousands of Americans, the "facts" suddenly became not merely uncertain but terrifying. That evening, Orson Welles and his "Mercury Theatre of the Air" broadcast a version of War of the Worlds, *a science-fiction fantasy by H. G. Wells. The radio play portrayed a Martian invasion, and despite four announcements which identified the program as dramatic fiction, thousands of listeners were stricken with terror. Shortly after the broadcast, a social psychologist, Hadley Cantril, made a study of the panic and published* The Invasion from Mars, *an interesting contemporary analysis of the sources of social uncertainty and fear.*

THURMAN ARNOLD

The logical content of creeds never realistically describes the institutions to which the creeds are attached. Every phrase in the Constitution designed to protect the submerged individual has become an instrument for the protection of large organizations. There is not time to develop here this commonplace theme. To illustrate we use again the development of the due process clause because it has been referred to so frequently that it is familiar to everyone. Due process of law under the Fifth Amendment unquestionably referred to

Reprinted from Thurman Arnold, THE FOLKLORE OF CAPITALISM *(New Haven: Yale University Press, 1937), pp. 33–39, 48–51, by permission of the publisher.*

arbitrary criminal prosecution of individuals. The words are:

No person shall be held to answer for a capital, or otherwise infamous crime, unless on a presentment or indictment of a grand jury, except in cases arising in the land or naval forces, or in the militia, when in actual service in time of war or public danger; nor shall any person be subject for the same offense to be twice put in jeopardy of life or limb; nor be compelled in any criminal case to be witness against himself, nor be deprived of life, liberty, or property, without due process of law; nor shall private property be taken for public use, without just compensation.

Today this amendment is one of the reasons why railroads are protected from a Federal pension system. Public control of business becomes the same as taking away property. Great national organizations become individuals. Only a short time ago nobody saw anything strange or out of the way in the change. Scholars in law schools proved that it was not a change at all and were generally believed.

It is therefore not the content of the governmental creed which molds institutions, but the imaginary personalities which make up the national mythology. Every culture has its hierarchy of divinities, like the ancient Greeks. This hierarchy is never recognized as a mythology during the period when it is most potent. It is only the myths of other peoples or other times that we label as myths. The power of any currently accepted mythology lies in the fact that its heroes are thought to have a real existence. There is always a large number of them because each mood and aspiration must be represented. Every institution tries to represent all of these heroes at once. Thus the American industrial organization is a hard-boiled trader, a scholar, a patron of modern architecture, a thrifty housewife, a philanthropist, a statesman preaching sound principles of government, a patriot, and a sentimental protector of widows and orphans at the same time. Let me designate the heroes of a nation and I care not who writes its constitution.

In the days of chivalry national heroes were princes of the Church or warriors seeking high adventure for a holy motive. These imaginary personalities gave form and logic to governmental structure. King Richard went to the Crusades in an unconscious response to the demand that the Government of England imitate its myths, just as the ruling class of every time unconsciously imitates the little ideal pictures to which it owes its prestige.

In the United States the mythology used to be very simple. The predominant figure was the American Businessman. Warriors were respected, but they had a distinctly minor place. The National Government had to imitate the American Businessman. Whenever it failed, people became alarmed. A businessman balances his budget. Hence the unbalanced budget which was actually pulling us out of the depression was the source of greater alarm than administrative failures which were actually much more dangerous. The American Businessman bosses his employees. Hence the encouragement of the C.I.O. was thought to be the forerunner of a revolution, in spite of the fact that never had industrial unrest been followed with less actual disorder.

The creed of the American Businessman was celebrated in our institutions of learning. Since the American Scholar was a minor divinity, some of his characteristics had to be assumed by the great industrial organization. Therefore colleges were endowed to prove that the predominant divinity was supported by reason and scholarship. All the Christian virtues were also ascribed to him—for the selfishness of business was an enlightened selfishness which resulted in the long run in unselfish conduct if it were only let alone.

The American Businessman was independent of his fellows. No individual could rule him. Hence the "rule of law above men" was symbolized by the Constitution. This meant that the American Businessman was an individual who was free from the control of any other individual and owed allegiance only to the Constitution. However, he was the only individual entitled to this kind of freedom. His employees were subject to the arbitrary control of this divinity. Their only freedom consisted in the supposed opportunity of laborers to become American businessmen themselves.

It is this mythology, operating long after the American Businessman has disappeared as an independent individual, which gives the great industrial organization an established place in our temporal government. Every demand on these great industrial structures is referred to the conception of the American Businessman as a standard.

Thus pension systems for great corporations are all right provided businessmen inaugurate them. Economic coercion is permitted provided these heroes accomplish it. Boondoggling of every kind is subject to no criticism if businessmen finance it. Charity and welfare work, provided they are used to portray businessmen in their softer and more sentimental moods, are lovely things. When undertaken by the Government, they are necessary evils because such activity impairs the dignity and prestige of our great national ideal type. The businessman is the only divinity supposed to conduct such affairs. Therefore one never hears a community chest spoken of as a necessary evil as the dole is. Private charity even in times when it is an obvious failure is supposed to be more efficient than government relief.

In this mythology are found the psychological motives for the decisions of courts, for the timidity of humanitarian action, for the worship of states rights and for the proof by scholars that the only sound way of thinking about government is a fiscal way of thinking. Move Communism or any other kind of creed into this country, keep the present national hierarchy of tutelary divinities, and one would soon find that the dialecticians and priests were ingenious enough to make communistic principles march the same way as the old ones. So long as the American Businessman maintains his present place in this mythological hierarchy, no practical inconvenience is too great to be sacrificed to do him honor—every humanitarian impulse which goes counter to the popular conception of how the businessman should act is soft and effeminate.

Coupled with the national heroes in every institutional mythology is the national Devil. Our Devil is governmental interference. Thus we firmly believe in the inherent malevolence of government which interferes with business. Here are people who are not to be trusted—they are the bureaucrats, the petty tyrants, the destroyers of a rule of law. Organizations always tend to assume the characters given to them by popular mythology. Hence the government is no career for an up-and-coming young man. Governmental institutions are not to be trusted to hire their employees. We must control their inherent malevolence by Civil Service rules. Civil Service is a great protection for mediocrity and thus tends to make the government fit the bureaucratic preconceptions. Thus the powerful influence of the national hierarchy of gods moves institutions into patterns from which they cannot escape until the attitudes change.

Germany is a country which loves to wear uniforms. It is said that it is difficult to keep even German railway conductors from wearing out their uniforms at home. The national hero is a soldier. Therefore, no economic principles ever designed have prevented Germany from assuming the atmosphere of at best a military academy with a scholarly faculty, and at worst an armed camp.

How far nations can be induced to revise their mythologies is a psychological problem not unlike the problem of how to change the admiration and dislikes of the individual. The politician does not attempt to change the mythology. He works with it unscrupulously to get results. The trouble with him is not that his technique is bad but that his ends are not broad or humanitarian. Yet in our present medieval atmosphere it is his techniques which are condemned. His ends, in so far as they are selfish, are supposed to work for the greatest benefit of all in a free economic system.

Probably the only way in which mythologies actually change is through the rise to power of a new class whose traditional heroes are of a different mold. Nothing seems clearer than that the attitudes of any given ruling class are so set that all the arguments in the world will not change them.

This can be observed in revolutions of all kinds, peaceful as well as violent. A ruling class ceases to perform the functions necessary to distribute goods according to the demands of a people. A new class appears to satisfy those demands. At first it is looked down on. Gradually it accumulates a mythology and a creed. Finally all searchers for universal truth, all scholars, all priests (except, of course, unsound radicals), all educational institutions of standing, are found supporting that class and everyone feels that the search for legal and economic truth has reached a successful termination. We can observe the rise of a race of traders and money lenders against the system of law and economics of chivalry and feudalism which today looks incredibly romantic, but which then looked like the very bedrock of reality. No one would have dreamed in the Middle Ages that the despised creed of the trader and the money lender—a creed of selfishness and worship of the then lowest material values—should rise to be a compendium of everything most respectable in temporal affairs.

Today we can observe the rise of a class of engineers, salesmen, minor executives, and social workers—all engaged in actually running the country's temporal affairs. Current mythology puts them in the rôle of servants, not rulers. Social workers are given a subordinate rôle. For purposes of governmental policy their humanitarian ideas are positively dangerous, because they put consideration of actual efficiency in the distribution of goods above reverence for the independence and dignity of the businessman. It is as if a usurer attempted to sit at the table in social equality with the medieval baron to whom he was lending money.

Nevertheless, it is this great class of employees, working for salaries, which distributes the goods of the world. Traders still are possessed of the symbols of power. The new class, however, has already shown signs of developing a creed of its own and a set of heroes. In our universities it is represented by a group of younger economists, political scientists, and lawyers. True, these men are often branded as unsound. Older universities look at their new economic thinking with suspicion, but its prestige grows with the prestige of the class of business and social technicians which it represents. Its mythology does not include the worship of the American Businessman. So far it is destructive only. On the positive side it is as yet undeveloped. However, one should remember that a fully developed creed and mythology are not found until the class which they support is securely in power. Adam Smith did not think up principles by which the merchant and manufacturer gained power. He supplied them with a philosophy after they had taken charge of the temporal government.

. . .

In the spring of 1936 the writer heard a group of bankers, businessmen, lawyers, and professors, typical of the learned and conservative thinkers of the time, discussing a crisis in the affairs of the bankrupt New York, New Haven, and Hartford Railroad—once the backbone of New England, the support of its institutions and its worthy widows and orphans. They were expressing indignation that a bureaucratic Interstate Commerce Commission, operating from Washington, had decreed that passenger rates be cut almost in half. Every man there would directly benefit from the lower rate. None were stockholders. Yet all were convinced that the reduction in rate should be opposed by all conservative citizens and they were very unhappy about this new outrage committed by a government bent on destroying private business by interfering with the free judgment of its managers.

This sincere indignation and gloom had its roots not in selfishness nor the pursuit of the profit of the moment, but in pure idealism. These men, though they owned no stock, were willing to forego the advantage of lower fares to save the railroad from the consequences of economic sin. They took a long-range view and decided that in the nature of things the benefits of the lower rates would be only temporary, because they had been lowered in violation of the great principle that government should not interfere with business. Some sort of catastrophe was bound to result from such an action. The writer tried to get the picture of the impending catastrophe in clearer detail. Did the gentlemen think that, under the new rates, trains would stop running and maroon them in the City of Elms? It appeared that no one quite believed this. The collapse which they feared was more nebulous. Trains would keep on running, but with a sinister change in the character of the service. Under government influence, it would become as unpleasant as the income taxes were unpleasant. And in the background was an even more nebulous fear. The Government would, under such conditions, have to take over the railroad, thus ushering in bureaucracy and regimentation. Trains would run, but there would be no pleasure in riding on them any more.

There was also the thought that investors would suffer. This was difficult to put into concrete terms because investors already had suffered. The railroad was bankrupt. Most of the gentlemen present had once owned stock, but had sold it before it had reached its present low. Of course, they wanted the stock to go up again, along with everything else, provided, of course, that the Government did not put it up by "artificial" means, which would be inflation.

The point was raised as to whether the Interstate Commerce Commission was right in believing that the road would actually be more prosperous under the lower rates. This possibility was dismissed as absurd. Government commissions were always theoretical. This was a tenet of pure faith about which one did not even argue.

In addition to faith, there were figures. One gentleman present had the statistical data on *why* the railroad would suffer. In order to take care of the increased traffic, new trains would have to be added, new brakemen and conductors hired, more money put into permanent equipment. All such expenditures would, of course, reflect advantageously on the economic life of New Haven, remove persons from relief rolls, stimulate the heavy goods industries, and so on. This, however, was argued to be unsound. Since it was done in violation of sound principle it would damage business confidence, and actually result in less capital goods expenditures, in spite of the fact that it appeared to the superficial observer to be creating more. And besides, where was the money coming from? This worry was also somewhat astonishing, because it appeared that the railroad actually could obtain the necessary funds for the present needed improvements. However, the answer to that was that posterity would have to pay through the nose.

And so the discussion ended on a note of vague worry. No one was happy over the fact that he could travel cheaper. No one was pleased that employment would increase, or that the heavy industries would be stimulated by the reduction of rates. Out of pure mystical idealism, these men were opposing every selfish interest both of themselves and the community, because the scheme went counter to the folklore to which they were accustomed. And since it went counter to that folklore, the same fears resulted from every other current scheme which violated traditional attitudes, whether it was relief, housing, railroad rates, or the Securities Exchange Act. Anything which could be called governmental interference in business necessarily created bureaucracy, regimentation, inflation and put burdens on posterity.

All this discussion was backed by much learning and theory. Yet it was easy to see its emotional source. These men pictured the railroad corporation as a big man who had once been a personal friend of theirs. They were willing to undergo financial sacrifice in order to prevent injustice being done to that big man. The personality of the corporation was so real to them that it was impossible to analyze the concept into terms of selfish interest. Does one think of personal gain when a member of one's family is insulted? With that

emotional beginning, the balance of the discussion flowed out of the learned myths of the time, and ended where all the economic arguments of the time ended, in a parade of future horrors. The thinking was as primitive and naïve as all such thinking must be when it is divorced from practical issues and involved in prevailing taboos. As to the merits of the rate reduction from a practical point of view, neither the writer, nor any member of the group, knew anything. Yet such was the faith of these men in the formula they recited, that they felt that knowledge of details was completely unnecessary in having a positive and unchangeable opinion.

The way of thinking illustrated by the above incident is a stereotype. Its pattern is the same to whatever problems it is applied. It starts by reducing a situation, infinitely complicated by human and political factors, to a simple parable which illustrates fundamental and immutable principles. It ends by proving that the sacrifice of present advantage is necessary in order to protect everything we hold most dear. All such discussions end with arguments based on freedom, the home, tyranny, bureaucracy, and so on. All lead into a verbal crusade to protect our system of government. In this way certainty of opinion is possible for people who know nothing whatever about the actual situation. They feel they do not have to know the details. They know the principles.

HADLEY CANTRIL

When a culture is highly stable and in a state of complete equilibrium, it

Reprinted from Hadley Cantril, THE INVASION FROM MARS *(Princeton: Princeton University Press, 1940), pp. 153–155, 157–159, 161–164, by permission of Princeton University Press.*

means that the frames of reference of the individuals constituting the culture are in complete conformity with the norms of that culture. It means, furthermore, that the frames of reference of individuals are, for them, completely adequate pathways in an environment that is satisfying their needs. Such an ideal state of affairs has certainly never existed for long in any large cultural group. Unrest, change, frustration, dissatisfaction are the rule. For at least a segment of the population current norms are inadequate to meet personal physical and psychological needs. Individual frames of reference either do not conform to accepted norms, as in the case with the radical thinker, or do not adequately explain to the individual the dissatisfaction he is experiencing, as is the case with those who frankly confess they don't know what the remedy is, those who try one remedy after another, or those who land in the camp of a leader, such as Dr. Townsend, who has an oversimplified but understandable solution.

At the time of the Martian invasion many social norms, with the corresponding personal habits, were in a state of flux and change, many of the previously accepted social standards were either proving themselves inadequate to accommodate human needs or were in danger of being overthrown by outside ideologies. In either case many of the individuals who composed the culture were perplexed and confused.

UNSETTLED CONDITIONS

Particularly since the depression of 1929, a number of people have begun to wonder whether or not they will ever regain any sense of economic security. The complexity of modern finance and government, the discrepancies shown in the economic and political proposals of the various "experts," the felt threats of Fascism, Communism, prolonged unemployment among millions of Americans—these together with a thousand and one other characteristics of modern living—create an environment which the average individual is completely unable to interpret. Not only do events occur that he is unable to understand, but almost all of these events seem to be completely beyond his own immediate control, even though his personal life may be drastically affected by them. He feels that he is living in a period of rapid social change, but just what direction the change should take and how it may be peacefully accomplished he does not know. For the most part, the potential consequences of forthcoming events are unpredictable.

This situation is not something known only to the public official, the big businessman, or the social scientist. The masses of people themselves know all this most poignantly. The material consequences of a disturbed economic order are not difficult for anyone to recognize. And most important for our purposes are the psychological consequences in terms of personal anxieties, ambitions, and insecurities of this awareness that all is not right with the world. . . .

In the case of certain listeners to this broadcast, the general confusion in economic, political and social conditions does seem to have been a major cause of fantastic interpretation. And it was the people who were closest to the borderline of economic disaster who were most apt to take the program as news. We have already shown the high relationship between education and economic status and have seen that people of low education oriented themselves least adequately. But even when we equate people by their educational level and then compare their adjustment to the broadcast according to their economic circumstances, we find that poorer people tended to assume a false standard of judgment more frequently than others, irrespective of education.

PROPORTION OF PEOPLE IN DIFFERENT EDU-
CATIONAL AND ECONOMIC GROUPS WHO
INTERPRETED THE PROGRAM AS
NEWS (CBS SURVEY)

	Education		
Economic Status	COLLEGE	HIGH SCHOOL	GRAMMAR SCHOOL
High	28%	31%	43%
Average	25	34	45
Low	0	44	53

A few comments from the case studies will show how people felt, and why they were suggestible to news which perhaps seemed little less confused than the confused world they already knew.

"Everything is so upset in the world that *anything might happen.*"

"Things have happened so thick and fast since my grandfather's day that *we can't hope to know what might happen now.* I am all balled up."

"Ever since my husband lost his job a few years ago, *things seem to have gone from bad to worse.* I don't know when everything will be all right again."

"*Being we are in a troublesome world, anything is liable to happen.* We hear so much news every day—so many things we hear are unbelievable. Like all of a sudden 600 children burned to death in a school house, or a lot of people being thrown out of work. Everything seems to be a shock to me."

For many persons another bewildering characteristic of our present civilization is the mystery of science. For certain people without scientific training or without sufficient personal ability, initiative or opportunity to investigate the mechanisms surrounding them, the telephone, the airplane, poison gas, the radio, the camera are but specific manifestations of a baffling power. The principles by which such things operate are completely unknown. Such devices come from a world outside and lie within a universe of discourse completely foreign to the perplexed layman. Scientists in general are frequently referred to as "they." Many variations of this theme are found in the case studies. If science can create the things we have, why can't it create rocket ships and death rays?

"*I hear they are experimenting* with rocket ships and it seems possible that we will have them."

"So many odd things are happening in the world. *Science has progressed so far* that we don't know how far it might have gone on Mars. The way the world runs ahead anything is possible."

WAR SCARE

This broadcast followed closely on the heels of a European war crisis. Not only did the crisis seem to be a very real one, but it was perhaps at the time a more widely known one than any in history—thanks to the medium of radio and the ingenuity and resourcefulness of the large broadcasting companies who had special reporters on the spot. During August, September and part of October 1938 millions of Americans were listening regularly to their radios, to the latest stories of a developing international crisis. Probably never before in the history of broadcasting had so many people in this country been glued to their sets. Stations at all hours were willing to interrupt prearranged programs for the latest news broadcast. Hence both the technique and the content of this broadcast tended to fit into the existing mental context which had resulted from world events of the previous weeks.

When our interviewers asked, "What major catastrophe could happen to the American people?" three-fourths of those in the frightened group as contrasted to half of those in the nonfrightened group answered war or revolution. Evidence of the same feeling is seen in answer to the question, "What sort of a catastrophe did you think it was?" Here the largest single category of response, except that of a Martian invasion, was the belief that the catastrophe actually was an act of war or some foreign attack. Over a fourth of the people who were disturbed or frightened by the broadcast gave such answers. . . .

THE THRILL OF DISASTER

It is a well known fact that people who suffer deeply or whose lot in life is generally miserable frequently compensate for their situations by seeking some temporary change or escape from their troubles. Dull lives may be cheered with bright clothing or gaudy furniture, harassed breadwinners may become fixtures at the local beer hall, worried housewives may zealously participate in religious orgies, repressed youths may identify themselves for a few hours with the great lovers or gangsters of the silver screen. There are many socially accepted ways of escape from the responsibilities, worries, and frustrations of life—the movies, the pulp magazines, fraternal organizations, and a host of other devices thrive partially because their devotees want surcease from their woes.

In addition to these more obvious escapes, there are two other conditions that may resolve the problems such persons face. In the first place, some social upheaval may dissipate the circumstances that create the frustration. The early days after a revolution generally bring with them freedom and license. Sometimes the upheaval may be of such a nature that the individual will in the end be in a worse situation than he was before. But because of the intense worries or anxieties he has, he may consciously or unconsciously welcome the cataclysm. Take, for example, a bank clerk who has embezzled certain funds to help a needy family. His conscience may bother him and he may always have the dread that some day he will be caught. But one day the bank is blown up, all the records are destroyed and he himself is badly injured. It is not hard to imagine that such a man would greet such a catastrophe. A few persons represented in the case studies showed signs of welcoming the invasion and their consequent extermination because of the relief it would give them.

"I was looking forward with some pleasure to the destruction of the entire human race and the end of the world. If we have Fascist domination of the world, there is no purpose in living anyway."

"My only thought involving myself as a person in connection with it was a delight that if it spread to Stelton *I would not have to pay the butcher's bill."*

"I looked in the icebox and saw some chicken left from Sunday dinner that I was saving for Monday night dinner. I said to my nephew, '*We may as well eat this chicken*—we won't be here in the morning.' "

"The broadcast had us all worried but I knew *it would at least scare ten years' life out of my mother-in-law."*

Another way in which people may get relief from their troubles is by submerging their own responsibilities and worries into a battle their whole society is having with some threatening force. We know, for example, that the suicide rate decreases in war time, presumably because potential suicides gain new securities and feel new responsibilities that are socially valued. Some of the frightened persons to the broadcast had a feeling of self-importance while they were listening or relaying vital information regarding the invasion to uninformed friends whom they thought they were helping. They were temporarily a member of the "in" group.

"I urged my husband to listen and said *it was an historical moment* possibly and he would be sorry afterwards to have missed it."

"*It was the thrill of a lifetime*—to hear something like that and think it's real."

"I had never heard anything like it before and I was excited even after I knew what it was about. *I felt like telling somebody all about it.*"

Others seemed to enjoy the broadcast despite their fear because the event was aligning them with other people in a conflict for rights, privileges, or ideals they had been carrying on alone or with a minority group. A Jewish woman reported, for example:

"I realized right away that *it was*

something that was affecting everybody, not only the Jews, and I felt relieved. *As long as everybody was going to die, it was better.*"

Although comparatively rare, these instances of an ambivalent attitude to the ensuing destruction do serve as a mirror of the times. Such persons would probably not have experienced any pleasure or relief from their worries had they lived in a more ideal social order where democracy was secure, where every person played a rôle, or where money, food, or houses were plentiful.

So far we have indicated that the broadcast would not have aroused an extensive panic if people had enjoyed greater educational advantages which they might have followed through with satisfying jobs, sufficiently rewarding to accommodate more of their needs. The times also seemed out of joint because of the threat of an impending war in which this country might become involved. These dislocations in the culture probably account in large measure for the emotional insecurity we have found so important and for the lack of critical ability discovered especially in the lower education and income brackets of the population.

III.   RECENT INTERPRETATIONS

The following selections from recent studies suggest a new assessment of the New Deal, one that differs markedly from Henry Steele Commager's 1945 evaluation. In the first, Richard Hofstadter explains why he believes Thurman Arnold was representative of important trends in New Deal thought. In the second selection, Arthur M. Schlesinger, Jr., who has established his place among historians of the New Deal with his multivolume study, *The Age of Roosevelt,* provides a capsule summary of relationships between the ideas and the economic programs of the period. He touches on the differences between the first New Deal and the second, and he concludes with a comment on "unconscious Platonists," those who in the thirties confused abstract models with reality.

RICHARD HOFSTADTER

The New Deal, and the thinking it engendered, represented the triumph of economic emergency and human needs over inherited notions and inhibitions. It was conceived and executed above all in the spirit of what Roosevelt called "bold, persistent experimentation," and what those more critical of the whole enterprise considered crass opportunism. In discussing Progressivism I emphasized its traffic in moral absolutes, its exalted moral tone. While something akin to this was by no means entirely absent from the New Deal, the later movement showed a strong and candid awareness that what was happening was not so much moral reformation as economic experimentation. Much of this experimentation seemed to the conservative opponents of the New Deal as not only dangerous but immoral.

The high moral indignation of the critics of the New Deal sheds light on another facet of the period—the relative reversal of the ideological roles of conservatives and reformers. Naturally in all ideologies, conservative or radical, there is a dual appeal to ultimate moral principles and to the practical necessities of institutional life. Classically, however, it has been the strength of conservatives that their appeal to institutional continuities, hard facts, and the limits of possibility is better founded; while it has usually been the strength of reformers that they arouse moral sentiments, denounce injustices, and rally the indignation of the community against intolerable abuses. Such had been the alignment of arguments

Reprinted from Richard Hofstadter, THE AGE OF REFORM (New York: Alfred A. Knopf, Inc., © 1955 by Richard Hofstadter), pp. 314–326, by permission of Alfred A. Knopf, Inc.

during the Progressive era. During the New Deal, however, it was the reformers whose appeal to the urgent practical realities was most impressive—to the farmers without markets, to the unemployed without bread or hope, to those concerned over the condition of the banks, the investment market, and the like. It was the conservatives, on the other hand, who represented the greater moral indignation and rallied behind themselves the inspirational literature of American life; and this not merely because the conservatives were now the party of the opposition, but because things were being done of such drastic novelty that they seemed to breach all the inherited rules, not merely of practicality but of morality itself. Hence, if one wishes to look for utopianism in the 1930's, for an exalted faith in the intangibles of morals and character, and for moral indignation of the kind that had once been chiefly the prerogative of the reformers, one will find it far more readily in the editorials of the great conservative newspapers than in the literature of the New Deal. If one seeks for the latter-day equivalent of the first George Kennan, warning the people of San Francisco that it would do them no good to have a prosperous town if in gaining it they lost their souls, one will find it most readily in the 1930's among those who opposed federal relief for the unemployed because it would destroy their characters or who were shocked by the devaluation of the dollar, not because they always had a clear conception of its consequences, but above all because it smacked to them of dirtiness and dishonesty. In the past it had been the conservatives who controlled the settlement of the country, set up its great industrial and communications plant, and founded the fabulous system of production and distribution upon which the country prided itself, while the reformers pointed to the human costs, the sacrifice of principles, and drew blueprints to show how the job could be better done. Now, however, it was the reformers who fed the jobless or found them jobs, saved the banks, humanized industry, built houses and schools and public buildings, rescued farmers from bankruptcy, and restored hope—while the conservatives, expropriated at once from their customary control of affairs and from their practical role, invoked sound principles, worried about the Constitution, boggled over details, pleaded for better morals, and warned against tyranny.

Lamentably, most of the conservative thinking of the New Deal era was hollow and cliché-ridden. What seems most striking about the New Deal itself, however, was that all its ferment of practical change produced a very slight literature of political criticism. While the changes of the Progressive era had produced many significant books of pamphleteering or thoughtful analyses of society—the writings of such men as Croly, Lippmann, Weyl, Brooks Adams, Brandeis, the muckrakers, Socialist critics like W. J. Ghent and William English Walling—the New Deal produced no comparable body of political writing that would survive the day's headlines. In part this was simply a matter of time: the Progressive era lasted over a dozen years, and most of the significant writing it engendered came during its later phases, particularly after 1910; whereas the dynamic phase of the New Deal was concentrated in the six hectic years from 1933 to 1938. Perhaps still more important is the fact that the New Deal brought with it such a rapid bureaucratic expansion and such a complex multitude of problems that it created an immense market for the skills of reform-minded Americans from law, journalism, politics, and the professoriat. The men who might otherwise have been busy analyzing the meaning of events were caught up in the huge expanding bureaucracy and put to work drafting laws that would pass the courts, lobbying with refractory Congressmen, or relocating sharecroppers.

To this generalization there is one noteworthy exception: in his two books, *The Symbols of Government* and *The Folklore of Capitalism*, Thurman Arnold wrote works of great brilliance and wit and considerable permanent significance—better books, I believe, than any of the political criticism of the Progressive era.[1] But what do we find in these works, the most advanced of the New Deal camp? We find a sharp and sustained attack upon ideologies, rational principles, and moralism in politics. We find, in short, the theoretical equivalent of F. D. R.'s opportunistic virtuosity in practical politics—a theory that attacks theories. For Arnold's books, which were of course directed largely against the ritualistic thinking of the conservatives of the 1930's, might stand equally well as an attack upon that moralism which we found so insistent in the thinking of Progressivism.

Arnold's chief concern was with the disparities between the way society actually works and the mythology through which the sound lawyers, economists, and moralists attempt to understand it. His books are an explanation of the ritualistic and functionally irrational character of most of the superficially rational principles by

[1] Thurman W. Arnold: *The Symbols of Government* (New Haven, 1935), *The Folklore of Capitalism* (New Haven, 1937). By 1941 the first of these works had gone through five printings; the second, fourteen.

which society lives. At the time his books were written, the necessity of coping with a breakdown in the actual workings of the economy had suddenly confronted men with the operational uselessness of a great many accepted words and ideas. The language of politics, economics, and law had itself become so uncertain that there was a new vogue of books on semantics and of works attempting to break "the tyranny of words," a literature of which Arnold's books were by far the most important. The greater part of Arnold's task was to examine, and to satirize, the orthodox conservative thinking of the moment. This is not our main concern, but what is of primary interest here is the extent to which Arnold's thinking departs from, and indeed on occasion attacks, earlier Progressivism. The deviation of Arnold's system of values from the classic values of American Progressivism was clear from his very terminology. I noted, in discussing the Progressive climate of opinion, the existence of a prevailing vocabulary of civic morals that reflected the disinterested thinking and the selfless action that was expected of the good citizen. The key words of Progressivism were terms like *patriotism, citizen, democracy, law, character, conscience, soul, morals, service, duty, shame, disgrace, sin,* and *selfishness*—terms redolent of the sturdy Protestant Anglo-Saxon moral and intellectual roots of the Progressive uprising. A search for the key words of Arnold's books yields: *needs, organization, humanitarian, results, technique, institution, realistic, discipline, morale, skill, expert, habits, practical, leadership*—a vocabulary revealing a very different constellation of values arising from economic emergency and the imperatives of a bureaucracy.

Although primarily concerned with the conservatives of the present, Arnold paid his respects to the reformers of the past often enough to render a New Dealer's portrait of earlier Progressivism. He saw the reformers of the past as having occupied themselves with verbal and moral battles that left the great working organizations of society largely untouched. "Wherever the reformers are successful—whenever they see their direct primaries, their antitrust laws, or whatever else they base their hopes on, in actual operation —the great temporal institutions adapt themselves, leaving the older reformers disillusioned, like Lincoln Steffens, and a newer set carrying on the banner." [2] Respectable people with humanitarian values, Arnold thought, had characteristically made the mistake of ignoring the fact that "it is not logic but organizations which rule an organized society"; therefore they selected logical principles, rather than organizations, as the objects of their loyalties. Most liberal reform movements attempt to make institutions practice what they preach, in situations where, if this injunction were followed, the functions of the institutions could not be performed.[3] Where the Progressives had been troubled about the development of institutions and organizations, Arnold's argument often appeared to be an apotheosis of them.

At one point or another, Arnold had critical observations to make on most of the staple ideas of Progressive thinking. *The Folklore of Capitalism* opened with a satire on "the thinking man," to whom most of the discourse of rational politics was directed; and the thinking man was hardly more than a caricatured version of the good citizen who was taken as the central figure in

[2] *The Symbols of Government,* p. 124.
[3] *The Folklore of Capitalism,* pp. 375, 384.

most Progressive thinking. While Progressive publicists had devoted much of their time to preachments against what they called "lawlessness," one of the central themes of Arnold's books was an analysis of law and legal thinking showing that law and respectability were so defined that a good many of the real and necessary functions of society had to go on outside the legal framework.[4] Similarly anti-Progressive was his attack on the anti-trust laws—a source of some amusement when he was later put in charge of the enforcement of these laws. But Arnold did not deny that the laws, as they had been interpreted by reformers, had had some use. Their chief use, as he saw it, had been that they permitted the organization of industry to go on while offering comfort to those who were made unhappy by the process. They had, then, a practical significance, but a far different one from that which the reformers had tried to give them. The reformers, however, had had no real strategy with which to oppose the great trusts: "The reason why these attacks [against industrial organizations] always ended with a ceremony of atonement, but few practical results, lay in the fact that there were no new organizations growing up to take over the functions of those under attack. The opposition was never able to build up its own commissary and its service of supply. It was well supplied with orators and economists, but it lacked practical organizers. A great cooperative movement in America might have changed the power of the industrial empire. Preaching against it, however, simply resulted in counterpreaching. And the reason for this was that the reformers themselves were caught in the same creeds which supported the institutions they were trying to reform. Obsessed with a moral attitude toward society, they thought in Utopias. They were interested in systems of government. Philosophy was for them more important than opportunism and so they achieved in the end philosophy rather than opportunity." [5]

Arnold professed more admiration for the tycoons who had organized American industry and against whom the Progressives had grown indignant than he did for the reformers themselves. He spoke with much indulgence of Rockefeller, Carnegie, and Ford, and compared John L. Lewis with such men as examples of skillful organizers who had had to sidestep recognized ·scruples. "Actual observation of human society . . . indicates that great constructive achievements in human organization have been accomplished by unscrupulous men who violated most of the principles which we cherish." [6] The leaders of industrial organization ignored legal, humanitarian, and economic principles. "They built on their mistakes, their action was opportunistic, they experimented with human material and with little regard for social justice. Yet they raised the level of productive capacity beyond the dreams of their fathers." [7]

Not surprisingly Arnold also had a good word for the politicians, who, for all their lack of social values and for all the imperfections in their aims and

---

4 Cf. *The Symbols of Government*, p. 34: "It is part of the function of 'Law' to give recognition to ideals representing the exact opposite of established conduct . . . the function of law is not so much to guide society as to comfort it. Belief in fundamental principles of law does not necessarily lead to an orderly society. Such a belief is as often at the back of revolt or disorder."

5 *The Folklore of Capitalism*, p. 220.
6 *The Symbols of Government*, p. 5.
7 Ibid., p. 125.

vision, are "the only persons who understand the techniques of government." One would prefer a government in the hands of disinterested men, to be sure, but such men are so devoted to and satisfied with the development of good principles that they fail to develop skills, and hence fail to constitute "a competent governing class." Hence society is too often left with a choice between demagogues and psychopaths on one side, or, on the other, "kindly but uneducated Irishmen whose human sympathies give them an instinctive understanding of what people like." [8] Several pages of *The Folklore of Capitalism* were given to a defense of the political machines for the common sense with which they attack the task of government and for the humanitarian spirit in which their work is conducted.[9]

Taken by itself, Arnold's work, with its skepticism about the right-thinking citizen, its rejection of fixed moral principles and disinterested rationality in politics, its pragmatic temper, its worship of accomplishment, its apotheosis of organization and institutional discipline, and its defense of the political machines, may exaggerate the extent of the difference between the New Deal and pre-war Progressivism, but it does point sharply to the character of that difference.[10]

[8] Ibid., pp. 21–2.

[9] *The Folklore of Capitalism*, pp. 367–72; cf. pp. 43, 114–15; cf. *The Symbols of Government*, pp. 239–40.

[10] There are many points at which Arnold yields to the need to seem hard-boiled and at which (rather like F. D. R. himself) he becomes flippant over serious questions. While such lapses have a good deal of symptomatic importance, I do not wish to appear to portray his writing as an attack upon political morality as such: it was not an effort to destroy political morality, but to satirize a particular code of morality that he considered obsolescent and obstructive, and to substitute for it a new one,

To emphasize, as I have done, the pragmatic and "hard" side of the New Deal is not to forget that it had its "soft" side. Not all its spokesmen shared Arnold's need to pose as hardboiled.[11] No movement of such scope

the precise outlines of which were obviously vague. In my judgment, Arnold did not even successfully pose, much less answer, the very real and important questions that were suggested by his books concerning the relations between morals and politics, or between reason and politics. For a searching criticism see the essay by Sidney Hook in his *Reason, Social Myths, and Democracy* (New York, 1950), pp. 41–51 and the ensuing exchange between Hook and Arnold, pp. 51–61, which to my mind succeeds only in underscoring Arnold's philosophical difficulties. The great value of Arnold's books lies not in the little they have to say about political ethics, but in their descriptive, satirical, and analytical approach to the political thinking of his time, and in their statement of the working mood of a great many New Dealers.

I should perhaps add that my own comments in this area are not intended to be more than descriptive, for there are large questions of political ethics that I too have not attempted to answer. In contrasting the pragmatic and opportunistic tone of the New Deal with the insistent moralism of the Progressives, it has not been my purpose to suggest an invidious comparison that would, at every point, favor the New Deal. Neither is it my purpose to imply that the political morals of the New Dealers were inferior to those of their opponents. My essential interest is in the fact that the emergency that gave rise to the New Deal also gave rise to a transvaluation of values, and that the kind of moralism that I have identified with the dominant patterns of thought among the Progressives was inherited not so much by their successors among the New Dealers, who tended to repudiate them, as by the foes of the New Deal.

[11] I have been referred to David Lilienthal's *TVA: Democracy on the March* (New York, 1944) as an illustration of the idealism and inspirational force of the New Deal, and as a work more representative of its spirit than the writings of Thurman Arnold. Lilienthal's book is indeed more unabashedly humanitarian, more inspirational, more concerned with maintaining democracy in the face of technical and

and power could exist without having its ideals and its ideologies, even its sentimentalities. The New Deal had its literature of inspiration and indignation, its idealistic fervor, its heroes and villains. The difference I hope to establish is that its indignation was directed far more against callousness and waste, far less against corruption or monopoly, than the indignation of the Progressives, and that its inspiration was much more informed by engineering, administration, and economics, considerably less by morals and uplift. For the New Deal not only brought with it a heartening rediscovery of the humane instincts of the country; it also revived the old American interest in practical achievement, in doing things with the physical world, in the ideal that had inspired the great tycoons and industry-builders of the Gilded Age but that afterwards had commonly been dismissed by sensitive men as the sphere only of philistines and money-grubbers.

At the core of the New Deal, then,

---

administrative change, more given to idealization of the people. It also shows, however, a dedication to certain values, readily discernible in Arnold, that would have been of marginal importance to all but a few of the Progressives. Like Arnold, Lilienthal is pleading the cause of organization, engineering, management, and the attitudes that go with them, as opposed to what he calls the "fog" of conventional ideologies. He appeals to administrative experience, technology, science, and *expertise*, finds that efficient devices of management "give a lift to the human spirit," and asserts that "there is almost nothing, however fantastic that (given competent organization) a team of engineers, scientists, and administrators cannot do today." (Pocket Book ed., New York, 1945, pp. ix, x, 3, 4, 8, 9, 79, 115.) In the light of this philosophy it is easier to see that Lilienthal's more recent defense of big business does not represent a conversion to a new philosophy but simply an ability to find in private organization many of the same virtues that as TVA administrator he found in public enterprise.

was not a philosophy (F. D. R. could identify himself philosophically only as a Christian and a democrat), but an attitude, suitable for practical politicians, administrators, and technicians, but uncongenial to the moralism that the Progressives had for the most part shared with their opponents. At some distance from the center of the New Deal, but vital to its public support, were other types of feeling. In some quarters there was a revival of populistic sentiment and the old popular demonology, which F. D. R. and men like Harold Ickes occasionally played up to, chiefly in campaign years, and which Harry Truman later reflected in his baiting of Wall Street. Along with this came another New Deal phenomenon, a kind of pervasive tenderness for the underdog, for the Okies, the share-croppers, the characters in John Steinbeck's novels, the subjects who posed for the FSA photographers, for what were called, until a revulsion set in, "the little people." With this there came, too, a kind of folkish nationalism, quickened no doubt by federal patronage of letters and the arts, but inspired at bottom by a real rediscovery of hope in America and its people and institutions. For after the concentration camps, the Nuremberg Laws, Guernica, and (though not everyone saw this so readily) the Moscow trials, everything in America seemed fresh and hopeful, Main Street seemed innocent beyond all expectation, and in time Babbitt became almost lovable. Where Progressivism had capitalized on a growing sense of the ugliness under the successful surface of American life, the New Deal flourished on a sense of the human warmth and the technological potentialities that could be found under the surface of its inequities and its post-depression poverty. On the far fringe there was also a small number of real ideologues, aroused not only by the battle over domestic reform but by the rise of world fascism. Although many of them were fellow travelers and Communists, we stand in serious danger of misunderstanding the character of the New Deal if we overemphasize the influence of this fringe either upon the New Deal core or upon the American people at large. It has now become both fashionable and, for some, convenient to exaggerate the impact of the extreme left upon the thinking of the country in the 1930's. No doubt it will always be possible to do so, for Marxism had a strong if ephemeral impact upon many intellectuals; but the amateur Marxism of the period had only a marginal effect upon the thought and action of either the administrative core of the New Deal or the great masses of Americans.[12] For the people at large —that is, for those who needed it most —the strength of the New Deal was based above all upon its ability to get results.

The New Deal developed from the

[12] Granville Hicks, in his *Where We Came Out* (New York, 1954), chapter iv, makes a sober effort to show how limited was the Communist influence even in those circles which were its special province. A complementary error to the now fashionable exaggeration of the Communist influence is to exaggerate its ties to the New Deal. Of course Communists played an active part in the spurt of labor organization until the experienced labor leaders expelled them, and in time Communists also succeeded in infiltrating the bureaucracy, with what shocking results we now know. But it was the depression that began to put American Communism on its feet and the New Deal that helped to kill it. The Communists, as consistent ideologues, were always contemptuous of the New Deal. At first they saw fascism in it, and when they gave up this line of criticism during the Popular Front period, they remained contemptuous of its frank experimentalism, its lack of direction, its unsystematic character, and of course its compromises.

beginning under the shadow of totalitarianism, left and right. F. D. R. and Hitler took office within a few months of each other, and from that time down to the last phases of the New Deal reforms, not a year went by without some premonition of the ultimate horror to come. In the earliest days of the Roosevelt administration a great many of its critics, influenced by such models of catastrophe as they could find abroad, saw in it the beginnings of fascism or Communism. Critics from the left thought, for instance, that the NRA was a clear imitation of Mussolini's corporate state. And—though this is now all but forgotten—critics from the right at first thought they saw fascist tendencies in the "violations" of fundamental liberties with which they regularly charged the architects of the New Deal. Only later did they find it more congenial to accuse the New Deal of fostering Communism.

To a sober mind all of this rings false today, for it is easier to see now that Roosevelt and his supporters were attempting to deal with the problems of the American economy within the distinctive framework of American political methods—that in a certain sense they were trying to continue to repudiate the European world of ideology. Between the London Economic Conference and Roosevelt's "quarantine" speech of 1937, the New Deal, for all its tariff-reduction agreements, was essentially isolationist. What it could not escape was the reality of what even some of the Republican leaders later began to characterize as "one world." After 1939 that reality was the dominant force in American life. The beginning of the war meant that Americans, with terrible finality, had been at last torn from that habitual security in which their domestic life was merely interrupted by crises in the foreign world, and thrust into a situation in which their domestic life is largely determined by the demands of foreign policy and national defense. With this change came the final involvement of the nation in all the realities it had sought to avoid, for now it was not only mechanized and urbanized and bureaucratized but internationalized as well. Much of America still longs for—indeed, expects again to see—a return of the older individualism and the older isolation, and grows frantic when it finds that even our conservative leaders are unable to restore such conditions. In truth we may well sympathize with the Populists and with those who have shared their need to believe that somewhere in the American past there was a golden age whose life was far better than our own. But actually to live in that world, actually to enjoy its cherished promise and its imagined innocence, is no longer within our power.

ARTHUR M. SCHLESINGER, JR.

The depression supplied the laboratory which tested and discarded one after another of the competing economic approaches. Andrew Mellon's *laissez faire* ("Liquidate labor, liquidate stocks, liquidate the farmers, liquidate real estate") was an immediate casualty; Herbert Hoover's dilution of *laissez faire* by appeals to the voluntary efforts of private groups solved nothing. The remaining recourse was positive action by the national government. To some in the early thirties the

Reprinted from Arthur M. Schlesinger, Jr., "Ideas and the Economic Process," in Seymour Harris, AMERICAN ECONOMIC HISTORY *(New York: © 1961 by McGraw-Hill Book Company, Inc.), pp. 20–25, by permission of McGraw-Hill Book Company, Inc.*

invocation of the affirmative state seemed to violate the American way of life. But it actually violated only the precepts of Herbert Spencer, and it had, in fact, deeper antecedents than Spencer in the American tradition—from Hamilton, Jackson, and Carey to Patten, Veblen, Bryan, Theodore Roosevelt, and Wilson.

The thirties were a welter of experiment. As in the eighteenth century technology outran science—so that science made its theoretical breakthroughs by explaining what practical men had already achieved—so in the early part of the twentieth century, under the stress of the Great Depression, economics lagged behind politics, and economists made their mark by explaining what politicians were already doing. Franklin D. Roosevelt's New Deal enlisted economists of various schools united only by a zest for experiment, and, as usual, experiment furnished a better means of verifying doctrine than mathematical analysis. The virtue of Roosevelt himself was his relative freedom from the constraint of dogma. His policy was action tempered by compassion: When a program justified itself by its human results, it was acceptable, whatever the affront to economic orthodoxy; when it failed to meet human needs, it had to go. If his opponents (correctly) characterized this as opportunism, they may have forgotten that opportunism is more likely than dogmatism to serve the purposes of a free democracy.

The job of the economists was to rationalize what the New Deal could not escape from doing. One basic difference divided the New Deal economists. Those in the institutionalist tradition demanded structural changes in the economy; in particular they proposed a revision of traditional modes of decision over resources allocation, production, and price. R. G. Tugwell, A. A. Berle, Jr., and their associates were far from Veblen, Commons, and Mitchell; they were more practical, more experimental, and more eclectic, but they did share with the older institutionalists the conviction that capitalism would not work without basic institutional reconstruction. The opposing group was less concerned about the structure of the capitalist engine than about its fuel. Their antecedents could perhaps be traced to the soft-money tradition which had contributed so much to American economic development, but their reliance was, not on a crude recourse to the printing press, but on the modern ingenuities of fiscal policy. Some of them, like Marriner Eccles, had been influenced by the American monetary heretics, William Trufant Foster and Waddill Catchings; others were disciples of the Englishmen J. A. Hobson and, above all, John Maynard Keynes. Whatever their inspiration, they counted far more on government action to increase spending in the economy than on government action to reconstruct the pattern of economic decision. The statistical inventions of Simon Kuznets and others, especially in the field of national-income measurement, happily now appeared to make Keynesian manipulation of economic aggregates administratively practicable.

The First New Deal—the National Recovery Administration, the Agricultural Adjustment Administration, and the like—expressed the belief in structural reform and national planning. By 1935 this first initiative had run its course. In the next years, the New Deal sought to pursue the will-o'-the-wisp of small-unit competition and price flexibility until, after the recession of 1937, it settled more or less on the gospel of compensatory spending. Dis-

tinctions should not be made too absolute; the advocates of fiscal policy, Keynes among them, certainly counted on a measure of institutional readjustment. But the central weapons in what came to be known as contracyclical policy were the budget and the management of the national debt; structural reform had its role as a means of preventing future depressions rather than of getting out of the present one. The fact that fiscal policy minimized interference with structure, markets, and individual economic decision was, of course, one of its appeals.

But the next generation's experience began to reveal difficulties with the purely fiscal approach. For one thing, contracyclical management seemed easier in principle than it has turned out to be in practice. The compensatory method of control, as Walter Lippmann pointed out as early as 1934, required that the state act almost continually contrary to the prevailing opinion in the business world:

In substance, the state undertakes to counteract the mass errors of the individualist crowd by doing the opposite of what the crowd is doing; it saves when the crowd is spending too much, it borrows when the crowd is saving too much; it economizes when the crowd is extravagant, and it spends when the crowd is afraid to spend; . . . it taxes when the crowd is borrowing, and borrows when the crowd is hoarding; it becomes an employer when there is private unemployment, and it shuts down when there is work for all.

Thus it proved politically difficult to bring about a tax increase in a time of prosperity, as the contracyclical approach required.

More than that, the emphasis on aggregates of spending tended toward a neglect of social priorities; the contracyclical approach, in other words, concentrated on the volume rather than on the distribution of income. This meant that the increased income did not necessarily go to those sectors of the economy where it was most needed, from the viewpoint of either social welfare or economic growth. This became apparent with the rising concern in the late 1950s over the growth problem. Analysis of growth per se was a relatively late economic preoccupation for Americans. As late as 1955, Prof. Edward S. Mason could remark on the continuing American conviction that growth took place automatically. He then wrote:

It is a little difficult for Americans to understand why the attainment of some rate of economic growth is a difficult matter or why it should be the object of action either by this government or by any other government. . . . No one either inside or outside of government conceives it to be his function to tinker with this rate. There are no "great debates" on the subject of the United States rate of economic growth.

In a few years, under the stress both of Soviet economic competition and of the decline in American growth rates in 1957 and 1958, all this was transformed. The result was to place the problems of the national economy in a new perspective. First growth and then allocation of resources emerged as insistent issues. Their resolution called for a fusion of the fiscal and structural approaches. While fiscal policy remained the central weapon against depression, its advocates were now forced to recognize the reality of a host of institutional elements which lay outside the strict bounds of the compensatory system and which growth and allocation were bringing into the spotlight: the problem, for example, of the division of resources between the public and private sectors; the problem of productivity; various prob-

lems touching the relation of inflation and growth (e.g., wage rises in excess of productivity not absorbable by reduction of excess profits; administered price policies of concentrated industrial sectors of the economy where such policies induce inflation and restrict output; the differential impact of interest-rate manipulation on small and large business); the problem of depressed areas and industries; the special problems of agriculture and of resources and energy development. The belated awareness that this range of problems was largely beyond the reach of fiscal, monetary, and budgetary policies confronted economic thought with the urgent challenge of uniting compensatory and institutional elements in a more comprehensive and precise economic strategy. The responsibility facing mid-century economists was first to work out the new synthesis and then to instruct both political leaders and the electorate in its application.

As late as the 1950s the laissez-faire faith of the post-Civil War period still had nominal devotees. An influential Secretary of the Treasury, George Humphrey, said that, in case of depression, he would favor a reduction of public spending; he would cut taxes only if prosperity yielded surpluses in the budget. The national government in this period proudly divested itself of a significant measure of control over monetary policy. The President of the United States seemed more concerned with diminishing than with exercising public control over the economy.

Yet, to many observers, this seemed a form of fair-weather piety. The American people, it was evident, had crossed the great divide. If anything were to go seriously wrong with the economy, the demand for public action would surely be irresistible. Spencer was dead beyond recall. In affirming the inability of unassisted "free private enterprise" to achieve the national economic goals, the United States was not abandoning its traditions in order to pursue foreign "isms"; it was, in fact, returning to the earliest traditions of the republic. The conceptions of the role of government, of the proper mix between public and private enterprise, of the need for a national economic policy—all these were more alike in 1790 and 1960 than any were like the conceptions of 1880.

The "mixed economy" of the mid-twentieth century represented an advance not only beyond classical *laissez faire* but beyond classical socialism. The advocates of both these classical creeds had agreed in rejecting the notion of a half-way house between them. The economy, they said, could be entirely private, or it could be entirely public, but one could never, never mix freedom and control. As Ogden Mills, Herbert Hoover's last Secretary of the Treasury, put it,

We can have a free country or a socialistic one. We cannot have both. Our economic system cannot be half free and half socialistic. . . . There is no middle ground between governing and being governed, between absolute sovereignty and liberty, between tyranny and freedom.

And Hoover himself added, "Even partial regimentation cannot be made to work and still maintain live democratic institutions." In this respect, at least, the men of the right commanded the wholehearted assent of the men on the left. The *New Republic* characteristically stated in 1935:

Either the nation must put up with the confusions and miseries of an essentially unregulated capitalism, or it must prepare to supersede capitalism with socialism. There is no longer a feasible middle course.

The great battle of the 1930s was to dispel this ideological superstition; it was the battle of American pragmatism against all forms of economic dogmatism, of the right and of the left. Whether conservatives or radicals, the dogmatists saw themselves as hardheaded realists. But they were really unconscious Platonists, confusing abstract models with practical reality and thereby committing what Whitehead called the "fallacy of misplaced concreteness." In their private realm of essences, capitalism was, by definition, one thing, socialism another, and so doctrinaire capitalists agreed with doctrinaire socialists that no compromise between the two was possible. But economics properly should deal, not with essence, but with existence; in fact, the very sort of mixed economy whose viability the dogmatists of the thirties denied turned out to be the salvation of the free system. The lesson is plain: The worst enemy of intelligent adaptation is ideology.

The American record thus shows the potency of ideas in economic development. It also shows the danger when ideas harden into all-encompassing, rigid systems. Americans have characteristically regarded ideas as efficient tools, not as sacred truths. Throughout American history ideas have served as a means of releasing economic initiative and then as a means of chastening economic arrogance; as a means of stimulating private energy and then as a means of reasserting public responsibility. One set of ideas helped to launch American economic growth. Another assisted in the great phase of private accumulation. When the passion for private accumulation threatened the values of democracy, another set of ideas prepared for public supervision and regulation. When private enterprise proved inadequate to maintain national growth, further ideas accustomed the nation to a new national commitment for economic development. What mattered was the philosophical flexibility, the intellectual resilience, of the people—the capacity to face new problems relatively unencumbered by the cults and clichés of the past. One must say "relatively": America, in face of every new crisis, has had to fight its way out of the "conventional wisdom" (in the valuable phrase of J. K. Galbraith) which would otherwise condemn it to repeating the same old mistakes. Yet in the end reality has generally triumphed over dogma. The ability to change one's mind (which is easier in a society in which people have the freedom to think, inquire, and speculate) turns out, on last analysis, to be the secret of American economic growth, without which resources, population, climate, and the other favoring factors would have been of no avail. If the American experience bequeathes anything to nations facing today even more formidable problems of economic self-development, it is that nothing counts more than a faith in thought combined with an instinct for empirical reality—and an understanding that reality is forever changing.

HISTORIOGRAPHICAL NOTE

Any development as multifaceted and as rich in documentation as the New Deal requires prodigious effort on the part of the historical researcher. But the New Deal—at once opportunistic and humane, adventuresome and temporizing, theoretical in its parts and unsystematic in its entirety—poses an especially difficult conceptual problem for historians confronting it. Many of those who lived through the depression years agreed with Henry Steele Commager that the election of Roosevelt brought the resurgence of a progressivism that had all but disappeared in the twenties. By comparison with Nazi Germany, often presented as a frightening alternative to the direction taken by F.D.R. and his administration, the New Deal seemed all the more liberal, democratic, and decent. But granted that the New Deal came off well in contrast to National Socialism, the simple truism that it avoided totalitarian extremes did not really say very much about it.

The first historian to develop an adequate formula for understanding the complex politics of the depression was Basil Rauch. His book, *The New Deal* (New York, 1944), contended that there were actually two New Deals. The first one, based on NRA and AAA, Rauch portrayed as a tentative and cautious effort to meliorate the effects of the depression. The second came in 1934–35 as Roosevelt moved to the left in concentrating on reform rather than recovery. For a dozen years historians followed the general outlines of Rauch's analysis; that is to say, they assumed that there were two New Deals and that the second was more radical than the first. Modifications or qualifications sometimes appeared. James M. Burns, for example, argued in *Roosevelt: The Lion and the Fox* (New York, 1956) that F.D.R. shifted to the left not because of any new ideological commitment but because of circumstances. Burns did not, however, question the essential correctness of Rauch's analysis.

The two New Deals concept, as expounded by Rauch and others, did not significantly challenge the old idea that the Roosevelt administration brought about a resurgence of progressivism. What it did was suggest that the resurgence came with the second New Deal, not the first. And in making that suggestion, the concept exhibited a very limited view of what constituted progressivism or liberalism; it assumed that "conservative" meant a program favorable to business, and "liberal" or "progressive" meant one favorable to labor. Significantly, two members of Roosevelt's 1933 Brain Trust, Raymond Moley and Rexford G. Tugwell, could not agree with such an interpretation. Moley's *After Seven Years* (New York, 1939) had already taken an approach different from that of Rauch. Tugwell, in *The Democratic Roosevelt* (Garden City, 1959), challenged more explicitly Rauch's understanding of the second New Deal. Identified as he was with a New Nationalist strain of thought, which placed emphasis on the necessity of planning and control rather than on competition, Tugwell contended that the really significant innovations were made during the first New Deal.

We can now see that early interpretations of the New Deal hinged on interpretations of progressivism; suggestions that the shift in New Deal strategy in 1934–35 represented a swing to the left involved a Brandeisian–New Freedom set of assumptions. As historians began to revise their views of the progressive movement, and as they began to see it as more complex than once had been thought, it was inevitable that interpretations of the New Deal would undergo modification. Richard Hofstadter's *The Age of Reform* (New York, 1955) therefore assumed an important place in New Deal as well as progressive historiography. Although he did not address himself to the problems posed by the two New Deals concept, he did recast thinking about progressivism. No longer did the small-enterprise, New Freedom, Brandeis variety of progressivism seem so radical. It took on a conservative hue in Hofstadter's treatment, and the second New Deal appeared a reversion to a bygone age rather than a crusading step into the future. The New Deal that had started out to operate on the basis of new realities, Hofstadter's readers might easily conclude, ended up returning to old myths that had served as props for what was by now an antiquated system.

Studies of the New Deal completed since publication of *The Age of Reform* have recognized the need for reappraisal of the traditional Rauchian view. Arthur Schlesinger, Jr., in *The Politics of Upheaval* (New York, 1960), the third volume of *The Age of Roosevelt*, expanded on Tugwell's interpretation. The first New Deal, he admitted, had been much more novel and far-reaching than its concern for business interests had led historians to believe. William E. Leuchtenberg, in *Franklin D. Roosevelt and the New*

Deal (New York, 1963), played down the significance of the two New Deals concept which he thought had been exaggerated out of proportion to its significance. The New Deal, Leuchtenberg insisted, was from beginning to end as skeptical about Utopias and ultimate solutions as it was suspicious of the peculiar wisdom associated with the marketplace. Always experimental, it avoided wholehearted commitment to any all-encompassing theory of society.

In what direction, then, is New Deal historiography moving? The day of the broad interpretive essay, the Roosevelt biography, or the synthesis has not passed. But the great need at this point is for detailed treatment of specific facets of the New Deal. A model for such monographs is Ellis Hawley's *The New Deal and the Problem of Monopoly* (Princeton, 1966). Focusing on a single problem, Hawley came to the conclusion that the New Deal did not undergo a fundamental reversal of policy. Throughout its existence it contained two strains of thought about business organization and planning, and what actually occurred was vacillation from one set of policies to the other. In the end neither one side nor the other—neither the planners nor the advocates of small business competition—was able to dominate. And as a result the conflict in American policy continued into the post-New Deal era. The gap between ideals and myths on the one hand, and realities on the other, was never closed. The New Deal was, in a sense, a poignant phase of an unfulfilled quest for control in the rapidly changing world of the twentieth century.

16. The Cold War

INTRODUCTION

Two stern facts of overwhelming importance became apparent at the close of World War II. The first was that the conflict had eliminated five nations from the ranks of the mighty. Germany, Japan, Italy, France, and Great Britain were all but destroyed in the holocaust. Of the several powers that had exercised a marked influence on international relations before the war, only two—the U.S. and the U.S.S.R.—remained in positions of strength. The second fact, demonstrated at Hiroshima and Nagasaki, was that modern science had given men the capacity to obliterate an entire city in a split second. These two facts established the basic conditions under which the Cold War came to be waged. Both limited the alternatives available to leaders of the two great powers; both severely restricted the flexibility of policy in their rivalry with each other.

This is not to say, of course, that Russian-American relations were always cordial before 1945, for they were not. More than a century earlier, Alexis de Tocqueville had made some astute observations about the two countries. "Their starting-point is different, and their courses are not the same," he wrote in a flash of prophetic insight, "yet each of them seems marked out by the will of Heaven to sway the destinies of half the globe." Thus the possibility of antagonism had long existed and had long been recognized. Not until after the triumph of Bolshevism in 1917, however, did severe tensions between the two countries develop. Revolutionary Russian ideologues dedicated to the overthrow of capitalism and western traditionalists equally dedicated to its preservation each made their contributions to the growth of ill feeling. And the mutual distrust was but little relieved by belated American recognition of the U.S.S.R. in 1933. In the Russian view, failure of the western powers to take a firm stand against Hitler during the troubled thirties seemed only a cynical use of Nazi Germany to thwart Soviet development. The West, for its part, experienced moral revulsion to the Nazi-Soviet Pact of 1939. Then, *mirabile dictu,* Hitler in his megalomania attacked the U.S.S.R. and immediately made a Russian-American alliance appear desirable.

Wartime cooperation, however, was directed principally toward defeating the Axis. Conferences of Allied leaders left unresolved certain problems of long-term interest, especially those stemming from the Soviet desire for hegemony over Slavic Europe. Although the United States opposed establishment of such a sphere of influence, the U.S.S.R. achieved it as a result of military operations during the war. With postwar western reluctance to accept the Soviet penetration of eastern Europe, Allied unity began to disintegrate, and from Stettin on the Baltic to Trieste on the Adriatic an iron curtain began to form.

Intransigence on both sides marked the early years of the Cold War. In the United States three possible courses of action—other than accommodation and negotiated settlement—won adherents. Some idealists, adopting a Wilsonian logic, urged settlement of international conflicts through a system of world government. Some superpatriotic moralists clamored for preventive war against forces of the communist evil. Some who regarded themselves as realists urged a policy aimed at the containment of Soviet expansive tendencies. Of these three alternatives, the first seemed impossibly visionary and the second insanely destructive. It was the third that won acceptance as official American policy, and the Truman administration set about implementing it through military alliances and economic aid programs. But containment worked better in Europe than elsewhere. Communist success in China in 1949 and the outbreak of war in Korea in 1950 posed an internal as well as an external threat to the policy. Proponents of aggressive action denounced Truman's "no-win" program and exercised a major influence in turning the White House over to the first Republican President since Herbert Hoover. More responsible than many of his supporters, Dwight Eisenhower helped to bring about a truce in Korea and refused to follow a strategy of aggressive military action. At the same time, he and Secretary of State John Foster Dulles talked about the liberation of Soviet satellites and the use of atomic retaliatory power if American interests were violated. The Cold War's peculiar rhythm—brinksmanship followed by moderating diplomacy—began to assume an institutional character. An Orwellian world seemed to be moving rapidly toward 1984.

Then came John F. Kennedy, urging Americans to close the missile gap and to prepare more adequately for limited conventional wars. Several major confrontations—arising out of the abortive invasion of the Bay of Pigs, the sealing off of East Berlin, and, above all, the Cuban missile crisis of 1962—disturbed Kennedy's days in the White House. Nevertheless, the threat of atomic war in the fall of 1962, together with unrest in China and the divergence of Chinese from Soviet communism, prompted moves to reduce international tensions. Kennedy himself advised his countrymen to re-examine their attitudes toward the U.S.S.R. and the Cold War. Hopefully, yet skeptically, Americans waited to see whether a new rapprochement, symbolized by the nuclear test-ban treaty of 1963, would become permanent.

In the meantime, while Russian-American relations improved, civil war in Vietnam claimed increasing attention. As the United States became deeply involved in that conflict, hopes for peace evaporated. Voices of dissent began to cry out. In an atmosphere of controversy and discord American Cold War policies came under attack, and historiography of the Cold War itself began to show signs of revision.

I. EARLY INTERPRETATION

That great and fundamental changes characterized the middle of the twentieth century was obvious to anyone who looked at the world of 1950. One of the most clearly written analyses of changing conditions of life and their influence on international relations was Hans Morgenthau's *In Defense of the National Interest: A Critical Examination of American Foreign Policy*. A significant chapter of the book describes "the three revolutions of our age," those that marked "the definite and radical end of the political, technological, and moral conditions under which the Western world lived for centuries." This selection presents Morgenthau's assessment of the political revolution.

HANS J. MORGENTHAU

Since the Renaissance and Reformation, the two great revolutions of the sixteenth century, the Western world has almost continuously lived in fear or expectation of some kind of revolution. Since the French Revolution of 1789, this state of mind has become endemic in the Western world, and since the end of the First World War it has become a commonplace to say that we live in a revolutionary age. However, the three great revolutions confronting the United States in the aftermath of the Second World War are different not only in magnitude but also in kind from those that preceded them. They mark the definite and radical end of the political, technological, and moral conditions under

Reprinted from Hans J. Morgenthau, IN DE-FENSE OF THE NATIONAL INTEREST: A CRITICAL EXAMINATION OF AMERICAN FOREIGN POLICY *(New York: Alfred A. Knopf, Inc., copyright 1950, 1951 by Hans J. Morgenthau), pp. 40–52, by permission of Alfred A. Knopf, Inc.*

which the Western world lived for centuries. It is not too much to say that our age has broken with the traditions in these areas of life which have dominated the West for at least four hundred years. The revolutions of that break have been long in the making, yet only the cataclysm of the Second World War has made their destructive effects fully plain.

The political revolution signifies the end of the state system which has existed since the sixteenth century in the Western world. This state system was characterized by continuous conflicts among a multiplicity of nations of approximately equal strength, all located in Europe. They protected and promoted their national interests and, more particularly, safeguarded their independence by joining together in alliances and counteralliances in an unending succession of attempts to equalize and, if possible, to surpass the strength of their enemies. This system was called the balance of power.

Within this system Great Britain

played a unique and vital part. It so happened that for four centuries Great Britain was both powerful enough in comparison with the other European Nations and detached enough from the power struggles of the continent to be able to play the role of the stabilizer or, in technical parlance, the "holder" of the balance, the "balancer" of the Western state system. While other European nations strove for the succession to a throne, the acquisition of a strategic frontier, the annexation of a town or province, Great Britain had only one interest on the continent of Europe: that no nation or combination of nations gain such a preponderance of power as to be able to dominate the whole of the continent. In other words, the only interest Great Britain pursued consistently in Europe throughout the centuries was the maintenance of the balance of power itself.

The relationship of the non-European world to this European state system was one of isolation or subordination. That is to say, to the extent to which non-European nations came in contact with European ones, they were dominated by them. The non-European possessions were for the European nations a source of power and wealth and, hence, became a source of rivalry among them. Yet it must be borne in mind that the colonial rivalries of European nations were but the reflection and extension in space of those power relations, centered in Europe, which we call the balance of power.

Of this state system, nothing is left today. Five radical transformations signify its end. First of all, the European state system has been transformed into a worldwide system. This development started when the American colonies declared their independence from the British Crown and President Monroe proclaimed the mutual political independence of Europe and the Western Hemisphere as a principle of American foreign policy. Thus the world, whose one political center until then had been in Europe, was divided into two political systems and the groundwork laid for the subsequent transformation of the European into a worldwide balance-of-power system. This transformation was accomplished when the United States, through the Spanish-American War, and Japan, through the Russo-Japanese War of 1904–5, became active participants in the worldwide struggle for power. The consummation of this development became obvious in the First World War—the very designation of that war as a "World War" is significant in this respect—in which virtually all nations of the world participated actively on one or the other side. The aftermath of the Second World War has seen an accentuation of this development in the emancipation of most of the former Asiatic colonies of European nations and their entrance as independent factors into the arena of world politics. The colonial pawns of Asia not only became independent of their European masters, as did the American colonies in the eighteenth and nineteenth centuries, but with their independence they also immediately assumed an active role in the affairs of the world.

More important for American foreign policy than this quantitative expansion of the European state system is its qualitative transformation. Europe has lost is political predominance in the world, and the center of political gravity has shifted since the beginning of the century—first imperceptibly, then with ever greater momentum—away from Europe into either completely or predominantly non-European areas. This development began with the First World War and was consummated with the Second. The issues of the First World War were still exclusively confined to Europe, and it was only the temporary intervention of a non-European power, the United States, which decided the issues. The issues of the Second World War were no longer confined to Europe, but were shared by Asia, and it was the intervention of two completely or predominantly non-European powers, the United States and the Soviet Union, which decided them.

Since the end of the Second World War, the relation between the European and the non-European world has been reversed. Europe has become the object of the power struggle of non-European forces, upon whose outcome its fate depends. For not only have the centers of power shifted from London, Paris, Berlin, and Rome to Washington and Moscow; the power concentrated in the latter capitals is also so superior to that of any other nation or possible combination of nations as to reduce the former great powers of Europe to the rank of second or third rate powers. The third aspect of the revolutionary transformation of the Western state system, then, consists in the substitution of a bipolar political world for a system composed of a multiplicity of states of approximately equal strength. In the various periods of modern history preceding the Second World War the political world consisted of six or eight or ten power centers, as the case might be, which would deal with each other on an equal footing and around which second- or third-rate powers would group themselves. Today only two power centers of first-rate magnitude remain, drawing the other nations of the world into their orbits.

The fourth aspect of the political revolution of our time is the inevitable by-product of the preceding one. It is the decline of British power in comparison with that of the United States and the Soviet Union and, as a result, Britain's inability to continue to play the decisive role with respect to the balance of power which it played for four centuries. The key position of Britain was founded upon its naval supremacy and its virtual immunity from foreign attack. Today, the United States has far surpassed Great Britain in naval strength, and the modern technology of war has deprived navies of uncontested mastery of the seas. Modern instruments of warfare have not only put an end to the invulnerability of the British Isles, but have also transformed from an advantage into a liability the concentration of population and industries on a relatively small territory in close proximity to a continent.

What in the long run is even more important than this decline of British power is the inability of any other nation to take over the heritage of Great Britain in this respect. There is much talk of the neutrality of Europe in the struggle between East and West and of the establishment of a third force either in Europe or in Asia. This is no more than talk, for there is no power center, besides Washington and Moscow, that could even approximate the ability to perform that vital and decisive function which Great Britain has performed for so long. Thus it is not so much that the power of the traditional occupant of that key position has declined, incapacitating it for its tradi- no longer exists. With two giants strong tional role, as that the position itself enough to determine the position of the scales with their own weight alone, there can be no chance for a third power to exert a decisive influence. Thus it is not only the decline of British power but the disappearance of the function itself, performed by Great Britain, which constitutes the fourth revolutionary change in the modern state system.

Finally, the decline of Europe as the power center of the world has brought in its wake a fundamental change in the relations between the white and the colored races. The political pre-eminence of Europe throughout modern times was primarily the result of its predominance over the colored races. It was the cultural, technological, and political differential between the white man of Europe and the colored man of Africa and Asia which allowed Europe to acquire and keep its domination over the world. At least in so far as Asia is concerned, this dominion has come to an end. With it has dried up the main source of strength—military, economic, political—upon which the European nations could draw in order to make up for their inferiority in numbers, space, and natural resources. Furthermore, with the disappearance of the colonial frontier, the European nations have lost the opportunity for relatively effortless and profitable expansion without necessarily interfering with each other's interests. This holds true for the United States and the Soviet Union as well, in view of the consummation of their transcontinental expansion.

Much that is new and disturbing in the present world situation is the result of these political changes. They all have brought about an unprecedented concentration of power in two governments in whose hands lies truly the fate of the world. Because of the enormous disparity of power which now exists between the two superpowers and even their closest competitors, the flexibility that characterized the old state system, with its ever changing alignments and alliances, has given place to the rigidity of a two-bloc system, divided by an iron curtain that prevents a crossing of the dividing line either way. Thus the United States and the Soviet Union enjoy a freedom from restraint by other nations which no nation in modern times has enjoyed for any length of time.

During those centuries when there existed a multiplicity of nations of approximately equal strength, no player in the game of power politics could go very far in his aspirations for power without being sure of the support of at least one or the other of his co-players, and nobody could generally be too sure of that support. There was virtually no nation in the eighteenth and nineteenth centuries which was not compelled to retreat from an advanced position and retrace its steps because it did not receive the diplomatic or military support from other nations upon which it had counted.

The greater the number of active players, the greater the number of possible combinations and the greater also the uncertainty as to the combinations that would actually oppose each other and as to the roles the individual players would actually perform. Both Wilhelm II in 1914 and Hitler in 1939 refused to believe that Great Britain, and ultimately the United States, too, would join the ranks of their enemies, and both discounted the effect of American intervention. It is obvious that these miscalculations as to who would fight whom meant for Germany the difference between victory and defeat. Whenever coalitions of nations comparable in power confront each other, calculations of this kind will of necessity be close, since the defection of one prospective member or the addition of an unexpected one cannot fail to affect the balance of power considerably, if not decisively. Consequently, the extreme flexibility of the balance of power resulting from the utter unreliability of alliances made it imperative for all players to be cautious in their moves on the international chessboard and, since risks were hard to calculate, to take as small risks as possible.

In the Second World War, the decisions of such countries as Italy, Spain, or Turkey, or even France, to join or not to join one or the other side were mere episodes, welcomed or feared, to be sure, by the belligerents, but in no way even remotely capable of transforming victory into defeat, or vice versa. The disparity in the power of nations of the first rank, such as the United States, the Soviet Union, Great Britain, Japan, and Germany on the one hand, and all the remaining nations on the other, was then already so great that the defection of one, or the addition of another ally could no longer overturn the balance of power and thus materially affect the outcome of the struggle. Under the influence of changes in alignments one scale might rise somewhat and the other sink still more under a heavier weight, yet these changes could not reverse the relation of the scales, which was determined by the preponderant weight of the first-rate powers. It was only the position of the major countries—the United States, the Soviet Union, and Great Britain on the one hand, Germany and Japan on the other—that really mattered. This situation, first noticeable in the Second World War, is now accentuated in the polarity between the United States and the Soviet Union and has become the paramount feature of international politics. The power of the United States and of the Soviet Union in comparison with the power of their actual or prospective allies has become so overwhelming that through their own preponderant weight they determine the balance

of power between them. That balance cannot be decisively affected by changes in the alignments of their allies, at least in the foreseeable future.

As a result, both the flexibility of the balance of power and its restraining influence upon the power aspirations of the main protagonists on the international scene have disappeared. Two great powers, each incomparably stronger than any other power or possible combination of other powers, oppose each other. Neither of them need fear surprises from actual or prospective allies. The disparity of strength between major and minor powers is so great that the minor powers have not only lost their ability to tip the scales, they have also lost that freedom of movement which in former times enabled them to play so important and often decisive a role in the balance of power. What was formerly true of a relatively small number of nations, such as certain Latin-American countries in their relations with the United States, and Portugal in its relations with Great Britain, is true now of most of them: they are in the orbit of one or the other of the two giants whose political, military, and economic preponderance can hold them there even against their will. If France, for instance, does not like American policy with regard to Germany, there is little it can do about it. In times past, if France did not find what it wanted with one alliance it would simply cross over to the other side and make a pact with another nation or group of nations. Today this has become impossible. France has no place to go. It can protest; it can try to retard the inevitable or to modify it in some minor particulars. But it has lost effective control over the matters that concern its vital interest. More particularly, it has lost that freedom of maneuver which was one of the main characteristics of the state system now at an end. It has lost the ability to change sides. What is true of France is true of all nations with the exception of the two super-powers. The Iron Curtain is not only a dividing line in the military and ideological sense; it is also a dividing line in the political sense. It denotes a rigid, inflexible line of separation which resembles two opposing battle lines rather than the traditional diplomatic constellation with its ever changing alignments.

The apparent recent changing of sides by Yugoslavia bears this analysis out rather than contradicts it. It was not of its own volition that Yugoslavia left the Russian camp; it did not go voluntarily over to the other side of the Iron Curtain. Yugoslavia was, as it were, thrown over the Iron Curtain by the Soviet Union because it refused to subordinate its national interests and those of its ruling group to the interests of the Soviet Union. Its crime in the eyes of the Soviet Union was the refusal to accept that satellite status which conquest by the Red Army had imposed upon the other nations of eastern Europe. Thus, whether it wanted it or not, Yugoslavia found itself on the other side of the Iron Curtain. Even if it wanted to go back to the Russian side, it could not do so short of giving up its very independence as a nation. Appearances to the contrary, it, too, has lost its freedom of movement.

The disappearance of Great Britain's key position as the "holder" of the balance is but a special—and the most important—case of the loss of that flexibility and restraint which were the characteristics of the state system for four centuries. In that period of history, Great Britain was able to play the controlling and restraining role of the balancer because it was strong enough in comparison with the contenders and their allies to make likely the victory of whichever side it joined. No nation would knowingly dare to oppose Great Britain, and all nations would compete for its support. Thus Great Britain could always say: "If you want to have our support, you can go thus far but no farther." Today Great Britain's friendship is no longer of decisive importance. Its role as the "holder" of the balance has come to an end, leaving the modern state system without the benefits of restraint and pacification which it bestowed upon that system in former times. Even as late as the Second World War, the neutrality of Great Britain or its alignment with Germany and Japan instead of with the United Nations might easily have meant for the latter the difference between victory and defeat. Now, in view of the probable trends in the technology of warfare and the distribution of power between the United States and the Soviet Union, it may well be that the attitude of Great Britain in an armed conflict between these two powers would not decisively affect the outcome. Let us assume rather crudely that, while in the Russian scale there is a weight of seventy, the weight of the American scale amounts to a hundred, of which seventy is the United States' own strength, ten that of Great Britain, and the remainder that of the other actual or prospective allies. Thus, even if the British weight were removed from the American scale and placed in the Russian scale, the heavier weight would still be in the American scale.

These two super-powers and their allies and satellites face each other like two fighters in a short and narrow lane. They can advance and meet in what is likely to be combat, or they can retreat and allow the other side to advance into what to them is precious ground. Those manifold and variegated maneuvers through which the masters of the balance of power tried to either stave off armed conflicts altogether or at least make them brief and decisive, yet limited in scope—the alliances and counteralliances, the shifting of alliances according to whence the greater threat or the better opportunity might come, the sidestepping and postponement of issues, the deflection of rivalries from the exposed frontyard into the colonial backyard—these are things of the past. Into oblivion with them have gone the peculiar finesse and subtlety of mind, the calculating and versatile intelligence and bold yet circumspect decisions which were required of the players in that game. And with those modes of action and intellectual attitudes there has disappeared that self-regulating flexibility, that automatic tendency of disturbed power relations either to revert to their old equilibrium or to establish a new one.

Today there stands nothing in the way of either the Russian or American governments attempting to reach their aims with any means at hand except the self-restraint they might be able to exert upon themselves (a very weak type of restraint indeed) or the fear with which either side watches the power of the other (a much more potent restraint). For the two giants that today determine the course of world affairs only one policy seems to be left, that is, to increase their own strength and that of their satellites. All the players that count have taken sides, and in the foreseeable future no switch from one side to the other is likely to take place, nor, if it were to take place, would it be very likely to upset the existing balance. Since the issues everywhere boil down to retreat from, or advance into, areas that both sides regard as of vital interest to themselves, positions must be held, and the give and take of compromise becomes a weakness neither side is able to afford.

While formerly war was regarded, according to the classic definition of Clausewitz, as the continuation of diplomacy by other means, the art of diplomacy is now transformed into a variety of the art of warfare. That is to say, we live in the period of "cold war," where the aims of warfare are being pursued, for the time being, with other than violent means. In such a situation the peculiar qualities of the diplomatic mind are useless, for it has nothing to operate with and is consequently superseded by military thinking. The balance of power, once disturbed, can be restored only, if at all, by an increase in the weaker side's military strength. Yet, since there are no important variables in the picture aside from the inherent strength of the two giants themselves, either side must fear that the temporarily stronger contestant will use its superiority to eliminate the threat from the other side by shattering military and economic pressure or by a war of annihilation.

Thus the international situation is reduced to the primitive spectacle of two giants eyeing each other with watchful suspicion. They bend every effort to increase their military potential to the utmost, since this is all they have to count on. Both prepare to strike the first decisive blow, for if one does not strike it the other might. Thus, to contain or be contained, to conquer or be conquered, to destroy or be destroyed, become the watch words of the new diplomacy. Total victory, total defeat, total destruction seem to be the alternatives before the two great powers of the world.

II. DOCUMENTS

1. "Hiroshima Today"

In August, 1945, the world became suddenly aware of having entered the atomic age when the United States dropped the first—and by more recent standards tiny—atomic bombs on Hiroshima and Nagasaki. Twenty years later, A M. Rosenthal visited the city of Hiroshima. He found nearly all the hibakusha *(survivors of the bomb) trapped in the lingering horror of that August day that marked the beginning of a new era. Here he deftly draws comparisons between the outlook of those who experienced the bomb and the outlook of those who did not.*

A. M. ROSENTHAL

In the city of Hiroshima, which sits with its back to soft hills and faces the green islands of the Inland Sea, a Japanese businessman smiled a huge golden smile as he talked of the future.

"Our city," he said, "will go further and further; there is no plateau for us. More and more industry will come, more and more." He thought of a symbolic piece of news and leaned forward on the sofa in his office when he told it: "Our new Chamber of Commerce building. It will be as big as the one in Tokyo!"

On the same day, in the same city, burgeoning with more and more—more factories, more bars, more buildings, more bank deposits, more cinemas, more dreams of more and more—a man who had been an engineer sat on the *tatami*-covered floor of a back-street

Reprinted from A. M. Rosenthal, "Hiroshima Today," in HIROSHIMA PLUS 20, prepared by The New York Times (New York: Delacorte Press, 1965; copyright © 1945, 1951, 1963, 1964, 1965 by The New York Times Company), pp. 49–51, by permission of Delacorte Press.

house and said: "We are like prisoners, convicted and sentenced to death, but we do not know when. We think illness waits in us and it has been difficult to think of a future and work for it."

The two men were about the same age, in their late fifties, both well educated, both raised in Hiroshima. The only difference between them was that on August 6, 1945, the businessman was serving in the Army in northern Japan and the engineer was in Hiroshima.

The taste of life in Hiroshima today is in the thoughts and feelings of the businessman and of the engineer and in that difference between them—the taste of life and also whatever meaning is to be found here.

Two decades after that millionth of a second that changed the world and left this city not quite dead but in an unknown kind of continuing dying, more than 2,000,000 Japanese and about 70,000 foreigners come to Hiroshima every year to look.

From early morning until long after dark, convoy after convoy of buses unloads Japanese at the museum, a long modern crackerbox on stilts, where the bits of seared clothing and the pictures of men roasted and children's faces without skin are preserved. They walk around the park, rather gaily toll the great bronze Peace Bell, picnic on the scraggly lawns, line up for group pictures and then go home in their buses.

Foreigners as a rule stay longer—two or three days. What do they seek? What do they find? Hiroshima is a city of 517,000 with 562 bars and 363 teahouses, and 13,385 retail and wholesale businesses, two warring gangs of racketeers and one ball park. It is also a frame of mind and usually visitors find what they have come to find.

If their minds are filled with the guilt or shame of being part of the human race, they find what they seek in the museum or in the beds of the Atomic Bomb Hospital.

If they come seeking solace in the knowledge that life does go on, they find that in the noisy commerce of the city or in some piece of symbolism— at night, young men, shouting raucously, use the road around the museum as a drag strip for racing their cars, and the sound of the engines is much louder than the occasional mellow boom of the bronze bell.

If they come seeking spiritual truth or comfort, some few find that, too.

"Why do I, an American, have a special feeling for Hiroshima? What is there that keeps pulling me back, no matter where I may go?"

Mrs. Barbara Reynolds, an American Quaker who has set up a Friendship Center in Hiroshima, asked herself that, and this was part of her answer: "Because I believe that God has revealed himself here and that he is working mightily in the hearts of men."

On a hill overlooking the city, American doctors find what they seek in the stacks of statistics that are put through the computer, statistics analyzing the illnesses and deaths of scores of thousands of *hibakusha,* the atomic-bomb survivors, and proving conclusively that radiation can be bad for you.

A brilliant young American psychiatrist finds it in months of long interviews with *hibakusha* and in two discoveries—one that their great illness is that they are never free of the sense of being death's captives, the other that he himself, trained in scientific detachment, found himself weary, shocked and spent and then discovered that the repetition of horror upon horror upon horror had an enclosing effect, helped build a protective wall around him.

Sometimes Hiroshima seems like a pair of binoculars that each person has to adjust to his own eyes for focus. But beyond the seeking of strangers there is the reality of the city and what has happened here over the past 20 years. There are three components in that reality—those who came after August 6; those who were here then; the difference.

The real Hiroshima for that businessman is glass and concrete, growth, joy of endeavor. The engineer acknowledges the existence of that Hiroshima but it can never fill him with the juice of life. The difference: the businessman thinks of himself as a free man, the engineer as a captive waiting to be claimed. He is a special kind of victim of a special kind of weapon; for him the millionth of a second never really ends.

2. The Cold War

In 1948 Leonard S. Cottrell, Jr., and Sylvia Eberhart published the results of a public opinion poll designed to gauge the main currents of American thinking about foreign affairs. Their selection is an indication of popular attitudes toward other countries, especially the Soviet Union, during initial phases of the Cold War.

As a foreign service expert on the U.S.S.R., George Frost Kennan had great influence during the Truman years. In 1946 he became chairman of the policy planning staff within the Department of State, and in that capacity he was responsible for foreign policy analyses on which several important decisions were based. When he published "The Sources of Soviet Conduct" in 1947, Kennan provided a succinct summary of his point of view. In essence he argued for the containment of Soviet expansionist tendencies as a means of alleviating international tensions.

Kennan and others of his persuasion never conceived of "containment" in military terms only. To prevent Soviet expansion effectively required removal of causes for dissatisfaction in a western Europe still suffering from the results of war and close to economic collapse. To bring about the economic rehabilitation of Europe was the main objective of the plan outlined by Secretary of State George C. Marshall in his address at the Harvard University commencement exercises in 1947.

Although success seemed to crown American efforts to contain communist expansion in Europe, other parts of the world proved more troublesome. Communist victories in China and the withdrawal of Chiang Kai-shek to Taiwan in 1949 aroused considerable uneasiness in the United States, and after the outbreak of war in Korea some of that uneasiness developed into criticism of the Truman administration. Particularly irksome to many of the critics was Truman's insistence on maintaining limits to the Korean conflict and refusing to expand the war by attacking China. When General MacArthur publicly expressed his irritation with such restrictions, the President dismissed him. MacArthur then became a symbol for the dissatisfied groups urging more aggressive prosecution of the war, and the nation fell into bitter wrangling over policy. Such was the situation when James Reston wrote the fantasy which concludes this chapter.

LEONARD S. COTTRELL, JR., AND SYLVIA EBERHART

In the main, people felt dissatisfied with the state of world affairs in 1946. Asked in our intensive survey, "Now that the war is over, how do you feel about the way the countries of the world are getting along these days?" seven out of ten expressed themselves as dissatisfied. When asked what they thought of "the way the UN has worked out so far"—even though most of them had just expressed strong approval of "the idea of having such an organization"—half thought UN was functioning unsatisfactorily, and most of the more favorable verdicts were qualified or unenthusiastic. The nations are "bickering and squabbling." They "don't seem to be getting anywhere."

Their own country, on the other hand, seemed to them to be trying steadfastly to achieve justice and harmony. It was, if anything, too generous with its material goods, and too lenient toward those governments which place obstacles in the road toward these goals. Thus, although only 15 percent said they were satisfied with "the way the countries of the world are getting along," almost two-thirds expressed themselves as at least fairly well-satisfied with the way the United States was behaving toward other countries. They felt that "we are making every effort," "doing the best we can." Among the 26 percent who expressed dissatisfaction with our own behavior toward other countries, the main criticisms were that we had been sending too

Reprinted from Leonard S. Cottrell, Jr., and Sylvia Eberhart, AMERICAN OPINION ON WORLD AFFAIRS *(Princeton, N.J.: Princeton University Press, 1948), pp. 45–52, by permission of Princeton University Press.*

much material aid abroad, and that we had been too lenient in our policies:

"I don't think we're tough enough, to tell you the truth. You can call any American a sucker."

"We are too soft. With Russia our attitude has been more appeasement than anything else. We should have taken a different stand in the beginning."

"I feel the United States has been more than lenient. She has tried to see everybody's point of view, has tried to work things out, and hasn't walked out [of the UN]. I feel other nations are not cooperating as they should, and they have more to gain than we have. It was organized for them, not us."

"I just think we have been pretty lenient with all of them. We are consistently handing out money and food to them and depriving ourselves. There is no use in that. . . . I believe in helping out, but they shouldn't strip us down."

Asked directly, "Do you think the United States has made any mistakes in dealing with other countries since the end of the war?" although only 30 percent (mainly among those least informed about world affairs) were willing to say that we had made no mistakes, more than half were unable to think of any such mistakes. The only criticisms of any prominence were that we had not been firm enough (especially toward Russia—a view then receiving prominent official sanction within the government) and that we were sending too much material aid abroad.

. . .

The people's belief in the generous motives of their own government stands in decided contrast to their skepticism regarding the motives that underlie the behavior of other countries. . . .

The people's view of Russia was extremely unfavorable. As of August 1946, only 25 percent believed that we could perhaps "count on the Russian Government to be friendly with us," on the grounds that Russia does not want war, or is afraid of us, or will find it profitable to stay on good terms with us. Responses to this question show a definite fluctuation in feeling from time to time, but the view that we can count on a friendly Russia remains steadily a minority one: In June 1946, 36 percent said yes to the question (or yes with qualifications); in August, 25 percent; in December, 39 percent. Although this form of question has not been repeated in subsequent surveys, it is probably safe to say that the proportion of those answering yes would have dropped again in the summer of 1947. The question, "Do you think the Russian Government is trying to cooperate with the rest of the world as much as it can?" was asked in our intensive survey in June and August 1946, and in another survey of the same type in December. In each case an overwhelming majority answered no; there was a tendency to be less emphatic in this opinion in June and December than in August, but at no time were as many as 20 percent willing to say, even with qualifications, that Russia might be trying to cooperate. Scarcely two percent explained Russia's behavior as stemming from fear of other countries—from a desire to increase her security. People simply argued that Russia wants to increase her power and will do anything to that end, or just that Russia is arbitrary, self-willed, and generally untrustworthy. National polls conducted by other agencies about the same time as our surveys found that from a quarter to a third of the public expressed the view that Russia was primarily interested in security rather than in imperialist expansion. But this opinion seemed to play almost no part in the spontaneous moral appraisals of Russia expressed in answer to open questions in our intensive surveys.

If people's failure to see the *quid pro quo* of international cooperation stands in the way of their supporting it, their moral rating of foreign countries stands in the way of their believing cooperation is feasible. In our extensive survey people were asked:

"With which of these four statements do you come closest to agreeing?"

"It is very important to keep on friendly terms with Russia, and we should make every effort to do so."   13%

"It is important for the U.S. to be on friendly terms with Russia, but not so important that we should make too many concessions to her."   50

"If Russia wants to keep on friendly terms with us, we shouldn't discourage her, but there is no reason why we should make any special effort to be friendly."   17

"We shall be better off if we have just as little as possible to do with Russia."   16

No opinion.   4

100%

Among those who chose the first statement—"we should make every effort" to keep on good terms with Russia— 36 percent said in reply to another question that a system of international control and supervision of atomic energy production would not work. Among those who chose any of the other statements regarding our official position toward Russia, more than half said international control would not work. Among those who favored "making every effort," 32 percent favored putting "the secret of making atomic bombs" under UN control; in the groups choosing each of the other statements about policy toward Russia, that proposal was favored by 22, 12, and 7 percent respectively. . . .

It is understandable enough that people should be averse to entering into critical cooperative enterprises with partners whom they distrust. But it must not be overlooked that the contrast the people drew between their own government and other governments was based not on approval or disapproval of specific policies or actions, but on generalized "feelings." In spite of the fluctuations of opinion shown by trend questions about Russia—fluctuations that undoubtedly reflect the variations in the news of Russian behavior in international councils —intensive surveys show a very low level of awareness of just what it is that Russia and the others are differing about.

. . .

But it has by now become apparent that international problems in general receive disappointingly little careful attention. We can elicit opinions in surveys by asking people direct questions, but on re-examination we find that many of these are not questions the people are asking themselves. As with the problem of what to do about the atomic bomb, the people are apparently letting the government do the worrying. And they appear to accept as a matter of course that, if the government errs, unlike other governments it will not err in the direction of too great self-interest.

GEORGE F. KENNAN

It is clear that the United States cannot expect in the foreseeable future

Reprinted from George F. Kennan, "The Sources of Soviet Conduct," FOREIGN AFFAIRS, XXV (July, 1947; copyright by the Council on Foreign Relations, Inc., New York), pp. 580–582, by special permission of FOREIGN AFFAIRS.

to enjoy political intimacy with the Soviet régime. It must continue to regard the Soviet Union as a rival, not a partner, in the political arena. It must continue to expect that Soviet policies will reflect no abstract love of peace and stability, no real faith in the possibility of a permanent happy coexistence of the Socialist and capitalist worlds, but rather a cautious, persistent pressure toward the disruption and weakening of all rival influence and rival power.

Balanced against this are the facts that Russia, as opposed to the western world in general, is still by far the weaker party, that Soviet policy is highly flexible, and that Soviet society may well contain deficiencies which will eventually weaken its own total potential. This would of itself warrant the United States entering with reasonable confidence upon a policy of firm containment, designed to confront the Russians with unalterable counterforce at every point where they show signs of encroaching upon the interests of a peaceful and stable world.

But in actuality the possibilities for American policy are by no means limited to holding the line and hoping for the best. It is entirely possible for the United States to influence by its actions the internal developments, both within Russia and throughout the international Communist movement, by which Russian policy is largely determined. This is not only a question of the modest measure of informational activity which this government can conduct in the Soviet Union and elsewhere, although that, too, is important. It is rather a question of the degree to which the United States can create among the peoples of the world generally the impression of a country which knows what it wants, which is coping successfully with the problems of its internal life and with the responsibilities of a World Power, and which has a spiritual vitality capable of holding its own among the major ideological currents of the time. To the extent that such an impression can be created and maintained, the aims of Russian Communism must appear sterile and quixotic, the hopes and enthusiasm of Moscow's supporters must wane, and added strain must be imposed on the Kremlin's foreign policies. For the palsied decrepitude of the capitalist world is the keystone of Communist philosophy. Even the failure of the United States to experience the early economic depression which the ravens of the Red Square have been predicting with such complacent confidence since hostilities ceased would have deep and important repercussions throughout the Communist world.

By the same token, exhibitions of indecision, disunity and internal disintegration within this country have an exhilarating effect on the whole Communist movement. At each evidence of these tendencies, a thrill of hope and excitement goes through the Communist world; a new jauntiness can be noted in the Moscow tread; new groups of foreign supporters climb on to what they can only view as the band wagon of international politics; and Russian pressure increases all along the line in international affairs.

It would be an exaggeration to say that American behavior unassisted and alone could exercise a power of life and death over the Communist movement and bring about the early fall of Soviet power in Russia. But the United States has in its power to increase enormously the strains under which Soviet policy must operate, to force upon the Kremlin a far greater degree of moderation and circumspection than it has had to observe in recent years, and in this way to promote tendencies which must eventu-

ally find their outlet in either the break-up or the gradual mellowing of Soviet power. For no mystical, Messianic movement—and particularly not that of the Kremlin—can face frustration indefinitely without eventually adjusting itself in one way or another to the logic of that state of affairs.

Thus the decision will really fall in large measure in this country itself. The issue of Soviet-American relations is in essence a test of the over-all worth of the United States as a nation among nations. To avoid destruction the United States need only measure up to its own best traditions and prove itself worthy of preservation as a great nation.

Surely, there was never a fairer test of national quality than this. In the light of these circumstances, the thoughtful observer of Russian-American relations will find no cause for complaint in the Kremlin's challenge to American society. He will rather experience a certain gratitude to a Providence which, by providing the American people with this implacable challenge, has made their entire security as a nation dependent on their pulling themselves together and accepting the responsibilities of moral and political leadership that history plainly intended them to bear.

GEORGE C. MARSHALL

I need not tell you gentlemen that the world situation is very serious. That must be apparent to all intelligent people. I think one difficulty is that the problem is one of such enormous complexity that the very mass of facts presented to the public by press and radio make it exceedingly difficult for

Reprinted from George C. Marshall, Commencement Address, Harvard University, June 5, 1947, in THE DEPARTMENT OF STATE BULLETIN, *XVI (June 15, 1947), pp. 1159–1160.*

the man in the street to reach a clear appraisement of the situation. Furthermore, the people of this country are distant from the troubled areas of the earth and it is hard for them to comprehend the plight and consequent reactions of the long-suffering peoples, and the effect of those reactions on their governments in connection with our efforts to promote peace in the world.

In considering the requirements for the rehabilitation of Europe, the physical loss of life, the visible destruction of cities, factories, mines, and railroads was correctly estimated, but it has become obvious during recent months that this visible destruction was probably less serious than the dislocation of the entire fabric of European economy. For the past 10 years conditions have been highly abnormal. The feverish preparation for war and the more feverish maintenance of the war effort engulfed all aspects of national economies. Machinery has fallen into disrepair or is entirely obsolete. Under the arbitrary and destructive Nazi rule, virtually every possible enterprise was geared into the German war machine. Long-standing commercial ties, private institutions, banks, insurance companies, and shipping companies disappeared, through loss of capital, absorption through nationalization, or by simple destruction. In many countries, confidence in the local currency has been severely shaken. The breakdown of the business structure of Europe during the war was complete. Recovery has been seriously retarded by the fact that two years after the close of hostilities a peace settlement with Germany and Austria has not been agreed upon. But even given a more prompt solution of these difficult problems, the rehabilitation of the economic structure of Europe quite evidently will require a much longer time and greater effort than had been foreseen.

There is a phase of this matter which is both interesting and serious. The farmer has always produced the foodstuffs to exchange with the city dweller for the other necessities of life. This division of labor is the basis of modern civilization. At the present time it is threatened with breakdown. The town and city industries are not producing adequate goods to exchange with the food-producing farmer. Raw materials and fuel are in short supply. Machinery is lacking or worn out. The farmer or the peasant cannot find the goods for sale which he desires to purchase. So the sale of his farm produce for money which he cannot use seems to him an unprofitable transaction. He, therefore, has withdrawn many fields from crop cultivation and is using them for grazing. He feeds more grain to stock and finds for himself and his family an ample supply of food, however short he may be on clothing and the other ordinary gadgets of civilization. Meanwhile people in the cities are short of food and fuel. So the governments are forced to use their foreign money and credits to procure these necessities abroad. This process exhausts funds which are urgently needed for reconstruction. Thus a very serious situation is rapidly developing which bodes no good for the world. The modern system of the division of labor upon which the exchange of products is based is in danger of breaking down.

The truth of the matter is that Europe's requirements for the next three or four years of foreign food and other essential products—principally from America—are so much greater than her present ability to pay that she must have substantial additional help or face economic, social, and political deterioration of a very grave character.

The remedy lies in breaking the vicious circle and restoring the confidence of the European people in the economic future of their own countries and of Europe as a whole. The manufacturer and the farmer throughout wide areas must be able and willing to exchange their products for currencies the continuing value of which is not open to question.

Aside from the demoralizing effect on the world at large and the possibilities of disturbances arising as a result of the desperation of the people concerned, the consequences to the economy of the United States should be apparent to all. It is logical that the United States should do whatever it is able to do to assist in the return of normal economic health in the world, without which there can be no political stability and no assured peace. Our policy is directed not against any country or doctrine but against hunger, poverty, desperation, and chaos. Its purpose should be the revival of a working economy in the world so as to permit the emergence of political and social conditions in which free institutions can exist. Such assistance, I am convinced, must not be on a piecemeal basis as various crises develop. Any assistance that this Government may render in the future should provide a cure rather than a mere palliative. Any government that is willing to assist in the task of recovery will find full cooperation, I am sure, on the part of the United States Government. Any government which maneuvers to block the recovery of other countries cannot expect help from us. Furthermore, governments, political parties, or groups which seek to perpetuate human misery in order to profit therefrom politically or otherwise will encounter the opposition of the United States.

It is already evident that, before the United States Government can proceed much further in its efforts to alleviate the situation and help start the European world on its way to recovery, there must be some agreement among the countries of Europe as to the requirements of the situation and the part those countries themselves will take in order to give proper effect to whatever action might be undertaken by this Government. It would be neither fitting nor efficacious for this Government to undertake to draw up unilaterally a program designed to place Europe on its feet economically. This is the business of the Europeans. The initiative, I think, must come from Europe. The role of this country should consist of friendly aid in the drafting of a European program and of later support of such a program so far as it may be practical for us to do so. The program should be a joint one, agreed to by a number, if not all, European nations.

An essential part of any successful action on the part of the United States is an understanding on the part of the people of America of the character of the problem and the remedies to be applied. Political passion and prejudice should have no part. With foresight, and a willingness on the part of our people to face up to the vast responsibility which history has clearly placed upon our country, the difficulties I have outlined can and will be overcome.

JAMES RESTON

"In that direction," said the Cheshire Cat, waving its right paw round, *"lives*

Reprinted from James Reston, *"Alice Seeks for Light in Wonderland, D.C.,"* NEW YORK TIMES (April 15, 1951; © 1951 by The New York Times Company), by permission of the publisher.

a Hatter; and in that direction," waving the other paw, "lives a March Hare. Visit either you like; they're both mad."

"But I don't want to go among mad people," Alice remarked.

"Oh, you can't help that," said the Cat. *"We're all mad here. . . ."*

—From "Alice's Adventures in Wonderland."

The Mad Hatter was sitting on the big black couch in the Senate press gallery this morning when Miss Alice walked in.

Alice: Why is everybody here out of sorts with everybody else?

Hatter: It's the war, child. The Chinese are killing our soldiers in Korea. The Russians are threatening our friends all over Asia and Europe, so the Republicans are naturally angry with the Democrats and the Democrats are angry with the Republicans. Surely you understand that?

Alice: No, I don't think I do. For if our men are being killed and our countries threatened, everybody should be working together.

Hatter: The Supreme Commander's been dismissed. That's what disturbs and divides us. Man by the name of MacArthur. Great general.

Alice: Oh, dear, that is a pity! But if he was really the "supreme" commander, who could dismiss him?

Hatter: It's the Constitution, Miss! The Supreme Commander in this country is not really "supreme." The "supreme" commander is the Commander in Chief. That is President Truman, and he has an absolute right to dismiss General MacArthur if the general is not carrying out his orders.

Alice: Wasn't he carrying out the President's orders?

Hatter: Apparently not, so under the Constitution, the President replaced him.

Alice: Then why are the Republi-

cans angry? Don't they believe in the Constitution?

Hatter: Of course they do. The Republican party is the party of Abraham Lincoln and Senator Taft. It is devoted to the Constitution. Anybody knows that. It prides itself in the conservation of great principles of Government procedure. If you had been here earlier you wouldn't have to ask. For four months the Republicans fought in the troops-to-Europe debate for the constitutional principle of civilian control of the military. Good show, too!

Alice: Then what made them change so quickly? If they wanted civilian control of the military for four months, why don't they want civilian control of General MacArthur now?

(This young woman is taking a decidedly un-American attitude, thought the Mad Hatter.)

Alice: And why, if things are so serious, couldn't the Commander in Chief and the Supreme Commander get together?

Hatter: This naive confidence in reason is entirely out of the question. General MacArthur was 7,000 miles away. He had a war to direct. He had communiqués to write and cablegrams from correspondents to answer and Senators to receive and trips to far-off places such as Formosa to make.

Alice: When was he back here last?

Hatter: In 1937.

Alice: I'm sorry, but I don't see why, if the President had the power to dismiss him, he didn't have the power to order him home for a little chat. Does the President always dismiss men who are naughty?

Hatter: Certainly not! But he always dismisses men who are naughty to *him.*

Alice: What do the Republicans think he should do?

Hatter: You must simply read the

statements of Senators Taft and Wherry and Representative Martin. The one from Massachusetts. They're all in the papers.

Alice: That's precisely what confuses me.

Hatter: Now see here. Here is a detailed account of a speech by Senator Taft at the Yale Club Thursday night. No Yale man would seek to deceive another Yale man. The speech is entirely clear. The Senator says the war in Korea has "no purpose whatsoever." He points out that the influence of freedom in the Far East can be built up only by the believers in freedom among the Far Eastern powers themselves. And Senator Wherry says . . .

Alice: Just a minute, please. Senator Taft also says in that same speech that he favors extending the Korean war to China. If it has no purpose, why make it bigger?

Hatter: The way to end a war is to end it. Bomb the "privileged sanctuary" in Manchuria, I say!

Alice: Wouldn't that make the Communists cross? And wouldn't they then bomb our "privileged sanctuary" in Japan? I am confused about all this. The only advantage I can see in the whole thing is that we must be stronger than the Russians now.

Hatter: What do you mean stronger than the Russians now? We are far weaker. They can take Korea or Japan or Western Europe anytime they like. We won't be strong enough to deal with them for fifteen months or two years.

Alice: Then why do we want to provoke them now? If we are silly enough to risk a big war, why not wait a couple of years?

Hatter: Confound it, because these little untidy wars are the very mischief! Partial war, partial peace, partial controls, partial mobilization, total inflation, total fiddlesticks! Appeasement's

the trouble. That's what causes the confusion. When you get into any kind of war you must use all the power you have; otherwise you're an appeaser!

Alice: I suppose that's what we should have done with the Russians when they blockaded Berlin and with the Yugoslavs when they shot down the American planes, and the . . .

Hatter: Don't make foolish remarks. Korea is not Berlin and Communist China is not Yugoslavia . . .

Alice: Wouldn't it be nice if they were?

Hatter: Appeasement is what we were talking about. Mr. Wherry charges the Truman Administration with appeasement. So does Mr. Taft. So does Mr. Martin. They want an end of this slaughter in Korea. They want a second front in South China. They want to cut our losses and they want to operate in Manchuria. They want peace and unconditional surrender. And no more nonsense! What more could you ask?

Alice: A little common sense would not hurt! And, incidentally, whatever happened to the United Nations?

Hatter: The United Nations is a failure. Senator Taft said so Thursday night.

. . .

Alice: Just the same, the Republicans are backing MacArthur?

Hatter: Well, not precisely. You see, they want to take advantage of all the fuss without really going along with General MacArthur's ideas.

Alice: I say, this is a peculiar country, isn't it? Tell me one other thing before I go. Mr. Martin said that the future of this country was at stake now and that if America was to be saved Congress must do it. You don't really believe that, do you?

Hatter: Oh, no, child. I'm not *that* mad.

3. Disarmament and Disengagement

In the fifties, the Cold War in a sense became institutionalized. Tensions continued, but each of the two major powers learned to recognize the limits beyond which the other could not be driven. Despite U.S. emphasis on nuclear deterrence—some people would say because of it—a Soviet-American modus vivendi became recognizable. Following John F. Kennedy's election in 1960, a series of crises threatened the peace of the world. Those crises, frightening though they were, did not lead to a hot war between the U.S. and the U.S.S.R., such was the degree to which the two great powers came to understand each other. Yet many Americans, contemplating possible consequences of Cold War games, began to have serious doubts about the wisdom of maintaining Cold War institutions. Edmund Wilson, among others, questioned both the ethics and the efficacy of American military expenditures. Wilson's The Cold War and the Income Tax, *from which the following selection has been taken, was a vigorous protest against what he considered an immoral and increasingly burdensome armaments program.*

That accommodation with the Soviet Union was not beyond the realm of possibility, and that such accommodation could lead to disarmament, was the burden of President Kennedy's address at the American University commencement exercises, June 10, 1963.

EDMUND WILSON

Our own spree of spending on nuclear weapons—that is, our government's spree—and the public's indifference to it is one of the most remarkable phenomena—if it does not prove to be one of the last—in the history of Western civilization. We inaugurated atomic warfare in 1945, when we wiped out the two Japanese towns—gratuitously, and in disregard of an officially appointed committee which had predicted that this would make us unpopular and recommended a non-lethal demonstration which would convince the Japa-

Reprinted from Edmund Wilson, THE COLD WAR AND THE INCOME TAX *(New York: Farrar, Straus & Giroux, Inc., 1963), pp. 68–81, by permission of the author.*

nese of the effectiveness of our weapons. It has been known for a long time now that, before the Hiroshima attack, Stalin had been notified by the Japanese of their willingness to negotiate peace, but it had always been said that Stalin, in a desire to prolong the conflict long enough to give the Russians a chance to participate in the defeat of Japan, had concealed this news from President Truman. It now appears, however, that Truman was fully informed. A conversation at Potsdam between Stalin and Truman was recorded by Charles Bohlen, who has revealed, in a recent statement, that the President would not take this peace feeler seriously, declaring that he could not trust the Japanese. When the offer was repeated ten days later, he still declined to talk terms and immediately had the bomb dropped. It has also been revealed, in an article in *Look* magazine of August 13,[1] that a considerable body of scientific opinion was opposed to the unannounced use of the bomb. General George C. Marshall wrote, "We must offset by . . . warning methods the opprobrium which might follow from an ill-considered employment of such force." James B. Conant foresaw "super-super bombs" delivered by guided missiles and urged Secretary of War Stimson to first demonstrate "Little Boy" and "Fat Man," as the bombs were affectionately known, before unloading them on the Japanese. . . . An atomic productions man named O. C. Brewster wrote to President Truman: "This thing must not be permitted to exist upon earth. We must not be the most hated and feared people on earth, however good our intent may be. So long as the threat against Germany existed, we had to proceed with all speed to accomplish this end. With the threat of Germany removed, we must stop this project." Leo Szilard and seventy of his colleagues petitioned Truman to consider the "moral responsibilities" involved in the use of the bomb and not to use it unless terms of surrender had been definitely rejected by the Japanese. But this petition and others were not allowed to reach the President. They were side-tracked by Major General Leslie R. Groves, the Army engineer who built the Pentagon, who put through the project of constructing the bomb and who was firmly in favor of dropping it.

President Truman, Major General Groves is quoted in this article as saying, "was like a little boy on a toboggan," who never had a real chance to say yes. But how can we explain the eagerness of Major General Groves and others to annihilate these Japanese cities when there was no necessity for doing so, regardless of the obvious danger of terrifying and antagonizing the rest of the world? The fact that the Japanese had fought us in the fiercest way and savagely tortured our soldiers ought to have been irrelevant for a nation which boasted itself in the advance guard of civilization. How, then, did we champions of freedom, with our mission to protect the world, come to spend enormous sums of money on enthusiastically developing these weapons? This can only, I believe, be explained by an irrepressible combination, on our part, of the instinctive impulsion to power, which in a state implies the power to crush, and the technological passion which is undoubtedly, among the workings of the human creative, or inventive, genius, the predominant one of the age. We claimed, of course, that we were defending ourselves against the Russians. But why did we have to fear them? We had no border in common with them. It was absurd to imagine that they wanted to invade us. They had already quite enough to think about with their recalcitrant captive nations in Europe. As for the Communist Party in the United States, it was so tiny that it would have been absurd to take it seriously as a subversive influence, and its membership, it seems, is now largely composed of FBI agents. There was, to be sure, the old business man's nightmare of being robbed of his profits by the Socialist State (which, ironically, is now being done on the pretext of protecting him against socialism); and this does partly account for our fear of the Soviets. There is also the periodical American panic, which dates from the

[1] This article, by Fletcher Knebel and Charles W. Bailey, is based on new material unearthed from the official files. The authors have had these facts for two years but permission to make them public has only just been given by the State Department.

Revolution, at the thought of being dominated by a foreign power. And then there are commercial interests: oil in Iran, rubber in Vietnam, sugar plantations in Cuba, etc. All this may be enough, I suppose, to produce the national nightmare of a United States first surrounded—Cuba, Canada, South America—by the insidious Soviet forces, then annexed by a Communist power and our inhabitants reduced to the status of slave labor. In any case, many Americans were shaken by a horrible shudder when Khrushchev, in one of his speeches for home consumption, predicted that Communism would "bury" us—perhaps because we were already half-buried by income tax extortions, official bamboozlement and suppression of civil rights.

Yet the whole world had reason to shudder when we detonated the first atomic bombs. The Soviets soon came to be as scared of us as we have come to be of them. It was not without plausibility that they began to denounce us as "warmongers"—since we proceeded from the "nominal atomic bomb" that obliterated Hiroshima and disintegrated its inhabitants by radio-activity to a hydrogen bomb of twenty megatons that could devastate Moscow at a single blast; and there has been talk of a cobalt bomb which, from the point of view of radiation casualties as distinguished from burning and blasting, would be found even more effective. Our government has also been working on a project for a neutron bomb which would have the immense advantage of destroying the human beings while leaving the buildings intact. What could be neater than this? We incinerate the people and take over the plant. That, as a result of this radio-activity, our race may degenerate later, cannot be taken into consideration in our contest with the Soviet Union to show ourselves technologically top

man. Now, the Russians, on their side, have been genuinely alarmed ever since their Revolution—much as we were after ours in regard to England and France—lest the "capitalist" world should gang up on them and suppress their "Marxist-Leninist" state; and if the United States was piling up mega-ton bombs after Germany had been crushed and divided, what else could they have in mind? Had not loud American voices declared war to the death on the Communist world? Were we not encircling this world by air bases in England, Spain, Turkey and Japan? Were we not, with this end in view, sending troops to assure our ascendancy over South Korea, Laos and Vietnam? The Russians began to race us, and the race ran to long-distance missiles. We can launch these now from specially constructed and very expensive submarines, and the Soviets now assert that they can pulverize our cities without ever leaving Russia. At one point, we were wailing about a "missile gap" between our resources and the Russians' in as ludicrously juvenile a way—and our opponents sounded equally juvenile—as if we were a freshwater college which had lost the big game of the season and was in danger of forfeiting its championship. When the stakes in games become so serious—when everybody's life is at stake—they ought not to be played at all, and the taxpayers should not support them.

But the taxpayers do support them, and that is why we cannot halt these activities. How much do the taxpayers know about the objects that their money is going for? About nuclear weapons, something. But they confuse nuclear weapons with sputniks and putting a man on the moon, as they are encouraged to do—see The Budget in Brief—by being told that the mastery of space is important for the world supremacy, the real Big League championship, at which we are supposed to be aiming.

. . .

On June 26 of this year [1963], a bill was passed by the House for the second largest annual defense appropriation in peacetime in the history of the United States: over forty-seven billion dollars; the largest was last year's: over forty-eight billion. This was followed on June 30, however, by an announcement that "The administration is giving serious consideration to ordering the first substantial cutback in the production of atomic weapons since the United States began building up its nuclear arsenal after World War II. Behind the current study is a belief that the United States, with an arsenal of tens of thousands of atomic weapons, has a sufficient and perhaps an excessive number of nuclear arms to meet its military needs. There also is rising concern in high Administration circles over the multiplying number of warheads that have been assigned to the military forces in the last five years. The major fear is that a continuing profusion would only increase the chances of accidental explosion or unauthorized use of the weapon." It now appeared, from recent statements of the Joint Congressional Committee on Atomic Energy, that a suspicion had arisen in the minds of "many committee members that the production of atomic weapons was coming to be based more on the capabilities of the Atomic Energy Commission to manufacture them than on the actual requirements of the military." But why is it, one is tempted to ask, that we taxpayers and newspaper-readers, who now have impositions to complain of on the part of our own government far heavier and infinitely more dangerous than the American colonists did when they revolted against the Crown—why is it that we citizens of the United States, who established our independence only a

century and three quarters ago, have not rebelled against these impositions and refused to provide further funds for a hypothetical war that there was no reason to fear in the first place? What, however, one should really be asking—since we no longer have taxation *without* representation—is why the voters should keep on sending to Congress representatives who are willing to vote for such a monstrous allocation of these funds. The forty-seven billion dollar defense appropriation passed the House, for example, by 410 to 1, and the only man who voted against it explained that he did not disapprove of the purposes of the bill, but merely believed that the amount should be somewhat reduced because "we haven't got the money." Two reasons for this acquiescence are no doubt, as I have already suggested, a failure to grasp what is happening and the appeal of our contest with Russia to the sporting imagination. But before going into the matter further, I want to point out some features of our defense policy which do not have a sporting appeal and of which the general public has hardly become even conscious, both because they have been little publicized and because they are so disagreeable that one has been glad to disregard this publicity. The gigantic mushroom-shaped cloud has a certain heroic grandeur, but there is nothing heroic or grand about chemical and biological weapons.

JOHN F. KENNEDY

Total war makes no sense in an age when great powers can maintain large

Reprinted from John F. Kennedy, "Toward a Strategy of Peace," Commencement Address, The American University, June 10, 1963, published in THE DEPARTMENT OF STATE BULLETIN, *XLIX (July 1, 1963), pp. 2–6.*

and relatively invulnerable nuclear forces and refuse to surrender without resort to those forces. It makes no sense in an age when a single nuclear weapon contains almost 10 times the explosive force delivered by all of the Allied air forces in the Second World War. It makes no sense in an age when the deadly poisons produced by a nuclear exchange would be carried by the wind and water and soil and seed to the far corners of the globe and to generations yet unborn.

Today the expenditure of billions of dollars every year on weapons acquired for the purpose of making sure we never need to use them is essential to keeping the peace. But surely the acquisition of such idle stockpiles—which can only destroy and never create—is not the only, much less the most efficient, means of assuring peace.

I speak of peace, therefore, as the necessary rational end of rational men. I realize that the pursuit of peace is not as dramatic as the pursuit of war, and frequently the words of the pursuer fall on deaf ears. But we have no more urgent task.

Some say that it is useless to speak of world peace or world law or world disarmament—and that it will be useless until the leaders of the Soviet Union adopt a more enlightened attitude. I hope they do. I believe we can help them do it. But I also believe that we must reexamine our own attitude, as individuals and as a nation, for our attitude is as essential as theirs. And every graduate of this school, every thoughtful citizen who despairs of war and wishes to bring peace, should begin by looking inward—by examining his own attitude toward the possibilities of peace, toward the Soviet Union, toward the course of the cold war, and toward freedom and peace here at home.

First: Let us examine our attitude toward peace itself. Too many of us think it is impossible. Too many think it unreal. But that is a dangerous, defeatist belief. It leads to the conclusion that war is inevitable, that mankind is doomed, that we are gripped by forces we cannot control.

We need not accept that view. Our problems are manmade; therefore they can be solved by man. And man can be as big as he wants. No problem of human destiny is beyond human beings. Man's reason and spirit have often solved the seemingly unsolvable, and we believe they can do it again.

. . .

So let us persevere. Peace need not be impracticable, and war need not be inevitable. By defining our goal more clearly, by making it seem more manageable and less remote, we can help all peoples to see it, to draw hope from it, and to move irresistibly toward it.

Second: Let us reexamine our attitude toward the Soviet Union. It is discouraging to think that their leaders may actually believe what their propagandists write. It is discouraging to read a recent authoritative Soviet text on military strategy and find, on page after page, wholly baseless and incredible claims—such as the allegation that "American imperialist circles are preparing to unleash different types of wars . . . that there is a very real threat of a preventive war being unleashed by American imperialists against the Soviet Union . . . [and that] the political aims of the American imperialists are to enslave economically and politically the European and other capitalist countries . . . [and] to achieve world domination . . . by means of aggressive wars."

Truly as it was written long ago: "The wicked flee when no man pursueth." Yet it is sad to read these Soviet statements—to realize the extent of the gulf between us. But it is also a warning—a warning to the American people not to fall into the same trap as the Soviets, not to see only a distorted and desperate view of the other side, not to see conflict as inevitable, accommodation as impossible, and communication as nothing more than an exchange of threats.

No government or social system is so evil that its people must be considered as lacking in virtue. As Americans we find communism profoundly repugnant as a negation of personal freedom and dignity. But we can still hail the Russian people for their many achievements—in science and space, in economic and industrial growth, in culture and in acts of courage.

Among the many traits the peoples of our two countries have in common, none is stronger than our mutual abhorrence of war.

· · ·

So let us not be blind to our differences, but let us also direct attention to our common interests and to the means by which those differences can be resolved. And if we cannot end now our differences, at least we can help make the world safe for diversity. For in the final analysis our most basic common link is that we all inhabit this planet. We all breathe the same air. We all cherish our children's future. And we are all mortal.

Third: Let us reexamine our attitude toward the cold war, remembering that we are not engaged in a debate, seeking to pile up debating points. We are not here distributing blame or pointing the finger of judgment. We must deal with the world as it is and not as it might have been had the history of the last 18 years been different.

We must, therefore, persevere in the search for peace in the hope that constructive changes within the Communist bloc might bring within reach solutions which now seem beyond us. We must conduct our affairs in such a way that it becomes in the Communists' interest to agree on a genuine peace. Above all, while defending our own vital interests, nuclear powers must avert those confrontations which bring an adversary to a choice of either a humiliating retreat or a nuclear war. To adopt that kind of course in the nuclear age would be evidence only of the bankruptcy of our policy—or of a collective death wish for the world.

· · ·

Speaking of other nations, I wish to make one point clear. We are bound to many nations by alliances. Those alliances exist because our concern and theirs substantially overlap. Our commitment to defend Western Europe and West Berlin, for example, stands undiminished because of the identity of our vital interests. The United States will make no deal with the Soviet Union at the expense of other nations and other peoples, not merely because they are our partners but also because their interests and ours converge.

Our interests converge, however, not only in defending the frontiers of freedom but in pursuing the paths of peace. It is our hope—and the purpose of Allied policies—to convince the Soviet Union that she, too, should let each nation choose its own future, so long as that choice does not interfere with the choices of others. The Communist drive to impose their political and economic system on others is the primary cause of world tension today. For there can be no doubt that, if all nations could refrain from interfering in the self-determination of others, the peace would be much more assured.

This will require a new effort to achieve world law, a new context for world discussions. It will require increased understanding between the Soviets and ourselves. And increased understanding will require increased contact and communication. One step in this direction is the proposed arrangement for a direct line between Moscow and Washington, to avoid on each side the dangerous delays, misunderstandings, and misreadings of the other's actions which might occur at a time of crisis.

We have also been talking in Geneva about other first-step measures of arms control, designed to limit the intensity of the arms race and to reduce the risks of accidental war. Our primary long-range interest in Geneva, however, is general and complete disarmament, designed to take place by stages, permitting parallel political developments to build the new institutions of peace which would take the place of arms. The pursuit of disarmament has been an effort of this Government since the 1920's. It has been urgently sought by the past three administrations. And however dim the prospects may be today, we intend to continue this effort—to continue it in order that all countries, including our own, can better grasp what the problems and possibilities of disarmament are.

The one major area of these negotiations where the end is in sight, yet where a fresh start is badly needed, is in a treaty to outlaw nuclear tests. The conclusion of such a treaty—so near and yet so far—would check the spiraling arms race in one of its most dangerous areas. It would place the nuclear powers in a position to deal more effectively with one of the greatest hazards which man faces in 1963, the further spread of nuclear arms. It would increase our security; it would decrease the prospects of war. Surely this goal is sufficiently important to require our steady pursuit, yielding neither to the temptation to give up the whole effort nor the temptation to give up our insistence on vital and responsible safeguards.

I am taking this opportunity, therefore, to announce two important decisions in this regard.

First: Chairman Khrushchev, Prime Minister Macmillan, and I have agreed that high-level discussions will shortly begin in Moscow looking toward early agreement on a comprehensive test ban treaty. Our hopes must be tempered with the caution of history, but with our hopes go the hopes of all mankind.

Second: To make clear our good faith and solemn convictions on the matter, I now declare the United States does not propose to conduct nuclear tests in the atmosphere so long as other states do not do so. We will not be the first to resume. Such a declaration is no substitute for a formal binding treaty, but I hope it will help us achieve one. Nor would such a treaty be a substitute for disarmament, but I hope it will help us achieve it.

Finally, my fellow Americans, let us examine our attitude toward peace and freedom here at home. The quality and spirit of our own society must justify and support our efforts abroad. We must show it in the dedication of our own lives, as many of you who are graduating today will have a unique opportunity to do, by serving without pay in the Peace Corps abroad or in the proposed National Service Corps here at home.

But wherever we are, we must all, in our daily lives, live up to the age-old faith that peace and freedom walk together. In too many of our cities today the peace is not secure because freedom is incomplete.

. . .

The United States, as the world knows, will never start a war. We do not want a war. We do not now expect a war. This generation of Americans has already had enough—more than enough—of war and hate and oppression. We shall be prepared if others wish it. We shall be alert to try to stop it. But we shall also do our part to build a world of peace where the weak are safe and the strong are just. We are not helpless before that task or hopeless of its success. Confident and unafraid, we labor on—not toward a strategy of annihilation but toward a strategy of peace.

III. RECENT INTERPRETATIONS

Unfortunately, the promise of Kennedy's American University address reached only partial fulfillment. In the meantime civil strife in Vietnam demanded an increasingly heavy commitment of American troops. As President Johnson pursued a course leading to further escalation of the Vietnamese conflict, voices of dissent began to be heard. The dissenters condemned Johnson's policy in part because they thought it exploited popular misunderstanding of the Cold War. They attacked the view that rivalry between the U.S. and the U.S.S.R. developed out of communist aggression and they went on to assert that after 1945 the United States, too, had assumed an offensive and intimidating posture. Advanced by "revisionists" such as William Appleman Williams, David Horowitz, Gar Alperovitz, Carl Oglesby, and Richard Shaull, such arguments raised fundamental questions not only about American policy but also about the very nature of American society. Professional historians, many of whom taught in strife-torn universities, found themselves unavoidably drawn into discussions stimulated by revisionist interpretations. In the first selection Arthur M. Schlesinger, Jr., who as an advisor to President Kennedy was a more active participant in public affairs than most of his colleagues, presents a counter-revisionist analysis of the origins of the Cold War.

The most succinct response to Schlesinger's attack on "revisionism" was written by a younger historian—himself a political activist—Christopher Lasch. In his essay, Lasch attempts not only to answer Schlesinger's points but also to raise new issues.

The selection by C. Vann Woodward, which concludes this volume, makes no attempt to settle the problems raised by the Cold War. It is an older statement than Lasch's or Schlesinger's, but it is one of most balanced efforts by an historian to assess the effects of the Cold War on the way in which historians look at their world and their past.

ARTHUR SCHLESINGER, JR.

The Cold War in its original form was a presumably mortal antagonism, arising in the wake of the Second World War, between two rigidly hostile blocs, one led by the Soviet Union, the other by the United States. For nearly two somber and dangerous decades this antagonism dominated the fears of mankind; it may even, on occasion, have come close to blowing up the planet. In recent years, however, the once implacable struggle has lost its familiar clarity of outline. With the passing of old issues and the emergence of new conflicts and contestants, there is a natural tendency, especially on the part of the generation which grew up during the Cold War, to take a fresh look at the causes of the great contention between Russia and America.

Some exercises in reappraisal have merely elaborated the orthodoxies promulgated in Washington or Moscow during the boom years of the Cold War. But others, especially in the United States (there are no signs, alas, of this in the Soviet Union), represent what American historians call "revisionism"—that is, a readiness to challenge official explanations. No one should be surprised by this phenomenon. Every war in American history has been followed in due course by skeptical reassessments of supposedly sacred assumptions. So the War of 1812, fought at the time for the freedom of the seas, was in later years ascribed to the expansionist ambitions of Congressional war hawks; so the Mexican War became a slaveholders' conspiracy. So the Civil War has been

Reprinted from Arthur Schlesinger, Jr., "Origins of the Cold War," FOREIGN AFFAIRS, XLVI *(October, 1967; copyright 1967 by the Council on Foreign Relations, Inc., New York), 22–52, by special permission of* FOREIGN AFFAIRS.

pronounced a "needless war," and Lincoln has even been accused of manœuvring the rebel attack on Fort Sumter. So too the Spanish-American War and the First and Second World Wars have, each in its turn, undergone revisionist critiques. It is not to be supposed that the Cold War would remain exempt.

In the case of the Cold War, special factors reinforce the predictable historiographical rhythm. The outburst of polycentrism in the communist empire has made people wonder whether communism was ever so monolithic as official theories of the Cold War supposed. A generation with no vivid memories of Stalinism may see the Russia of the forties in the image of the relatively mild, seedy and irresolute Russia of the sixties. And for this same generation the American course of widening the war in Viet Nam—which even non-revisionists can easily regard as folly—has unquestionably stirred doubts about the wisdom of American foreign policy in the sixties which younger historians may have begun to read back into the forties.

It is useful to remember that, on the whole, past exercises in revisionism have failed to stick. Few historians today believe that the war hawks caused the War of 1812 or the slaveholders the Mexican War, or that the Civil War was needless, or that the House of Morgan brought America into the First World War or that Franklin Roosevelt schemed to produce the attack on Pearl Harbor. But this does not mean that one should deplore the rise of Cold War revisionism.[1] For revisionism is an essential part of the process by which history, through the posing of new problems and the in-

[1] As this writer somewhat intemperately did in a letter to *The New York Review of Books,* October 20, 1966.

vestigation of new possibilities, enlarges its perspectives and enriches its insights.

More than this, in the present context, revisionism expresses a deep, legitimate and tragic apprehension. As the Cold War has begun to lose its purity of definition, as the moral absolutes of the fifties become the moralistic clichés of the sixties, some have begun to ask whether the appalling risks which humanity ran during the Cold War were, after all, necessary and inevitable; whether more restrained and rational policies might not have guided the energies of man from the perils of conflict into the potentialities of collaboration. The fact that such questions are in their nature unanswerable does not mean that it is not right and useful to raise them. Nor does it mean that our sons and daughters are not entitled to an accounting from the generation of Russians and Americans who produced the Cold War.

The orthodox American view, as originally set forth by the American government and as reaffirmed until recently by most American scholars, has been that the Cold War was the brave and essential response of free men to communist aggression. Some have gone back well before the Second World War to lay open the sources of Russian expansionism. Geopoliticians traced the Cold War to imperial Russian strategic ambitions which in the nineteenth century led to the Crimean War, to Russian penetration of the Balkans and the Middle East and to Russian pressure on Britain's "lifeline" to India. Ideologists traced it to the Communist Manifesto of 1848 ("the violent overthrow of the bourgeoisie lays the foundation for the sway of the proletariat"). Thoughtful observers (a phrase meant to exclude those who speak in Dullese about the unlimited

evil of godless, atheistic, militant communism) concluded that classical Russian imperialism and Pan-Slavism, compounded after 1917 by Leninist messianism, confronted the West at the end of the Second World War with an inexorable drive for domination.[2]

The revisionist thesis is very different.[3] In its extreme form, it is that,

[2] Every student of the Cold War must acknowledge his debt to W. H. McNeill's remarkable account, "America, Britain and Russia: Their Cooperation and Conflict, 1941–1946" (New York, 1953) and to the brilliant and indispensable series by Herbert Feis: "Churchill, Roosevelt, Stalin: The War They Waged and the Peace They Sought" (Princeton, 1957); "Between War and Peace: The Potsdam Conference" (Princeton, 1960); and "The Atomic Bomb and the End of World War II" (Princeton, 1966). Useful recent analyses include André Fontaine, "Histoire de la Guerre Froide" (2 v., Paris, 1965, 1967); N. A. Graebner, "Cold War Diplomacy, 1945–1960" (Princeton, 1962); L. J. Halle, "The Cold War as History" (London, 1967); M. F. Herz, "Beginnings of the Cold War" (Bloomington, 1966) and W. L. Neumann, "After Victory: Churchill, Roosevelt, Stalin and the Making of Peace" (New York, 1967).

[3] The fullest statement of this case is to be found in D. F. Fleming's voluminous "The Cold War and Its Origins" (New York, 1961). For a shorter version of this argument, see David Horowitz, "The Free World Colossus" (New York, 1965); the most subtle and ingenious statements come in W. A. Williams' "The Tragedy of American Diplomacy" (rev. ed., New York, 1962) and in Gar Alperovitz's "Atomic Diplomacy: Hiroshima and Potsdam" (New York, 1965) and in subsequent articles and reviews by Mr. Alperovitz in *The New York Review of Books*. The fact that in some aspects the revisionist thesis parallels the official Soviet argument must not, of course, prevent consideration of the case on its merits, nor raise questions about the motives of the writers, all of whom, so far as I know, are independent-minded scholars.

I might further add that all these books, in spite of their ostentatious display of scholarly apparatus, must be used with caution. Professor Fleming, for example, relies heavily on newspaper articles and even columnists. While Mr. Alperovitz bases his case on official docu-

after the death of Franklin Roosevelt and the end of the Second World War, the United States deliberately abandoned the wartime policy of collaboration and, exhilarated by the possession of the atomic bomb, undertook a course of aggression of its own designed to expel all Russian influence from Eastern Europe and to establish democratic-capitalist states on the very border of the Soviet Union. As the revisionists see it, this radically new American policy—or rather this resumption by Truman of the pre-Roosevelt policy of insensate anti-communism—left Moscow

---

ments or authoritative reminiscences, he sometimes twists his material in a most unscholarly way. For example, in describing Ambassador Harriman's talk with President Truman on April 20, 1945, Mr. Alperovitz writes, "He argued that a reconsideration of Roosevelt's policy was necessary" (p. 22, repeated on p. 24). The citation is to p. 70–72 in President Truman's "Years of Decision." What President Truman reported Harriman as saying was the exact opposite: "Before leaving, Harriman took me aside and said, 'Frankly, one of the reasons that made me rush back to Washington was the fear that you did not understand, as I had seen Roosevelt understand, that Stalin is breaking his agreements.' " Similarly, in an appendix (p. 271) Mr. Alperovitz writes that the Hopkins and Davies missions of May 1945 "were opposed by the 'firm' advisers." Actually the Hopkins mission was proposed by Harriman and Charles E. Bohlen, who Mr. Alperovitz elsewhere suggests were the firmest of the firm—and was proposed by them precisely to impress on Stalin the continuity of American policy from Roosevelt to Truman. While the idea that Truman reversed Roosevelt's policy is tempting dramatically, it is a myth. See, for example, the testimony of Anna Rosenberg Hoffman, who lunched with Roosevelt on March 24, 1945, the last day he spent in Washington. After luncheon, Roosevelt was handed a cable. "He read it and became quite angry. He banged his fists on the arms of his wheelchair and said, 'Averell is right; we can't do business with Stalin. He has broken every one of the promises he made at Yalta.' He was very upset and continued in the same vein on the subject."

no alternative but to take measures in defense of its own borders. The result was the Cold War.

. . .

Peacemaking after the Second World War was not so much a tapestry as it was a hopelessly raveled and knotted mess of yarn. Yet, for purposes of clarity, it is essential to follow certain threads. One theme indispensable to an understanding of the Cold War is the contrast between two clashing views of world order: the "universalist" view, by which all nations shared a common interest in all the affairs of the world, and the "sphere-of-influence" view, by which each great power would be assured by the other great powers of an acknowledged predominance in its own area of special interest. The universalist view assumed that national security would be guaranteed by an international organization. The sphere-of-interest view assumed that national security would be guaranteed by the balance of power. While in practice these views have by no means been incompatible (indeed, our shaky peace has been based on a combination of the two), in the abstract they involved sharp contradictions.

The tradition of American thought in these matters was universalist—*i.e.* Wilsonian. Roosevelt had been a member of Wilson's subcabinet; in 1920, as candidate for Vice President, he had campaigned for the League of Nations. It is true that, within Roosevelt's infinitely complex mind, Wilsonianism warred with the perception of vital strategic interests he had imbibed from Mahan. Moreover, his temperamental inclination to settle things with fellow princes around the conference table led him to regard the Big Three—or Four—as trustees for the rest of the world. On occasion, as this narrative will show, he was beguiled into flirtation with the sphere-of-influence heresy. But in principle he believed in joint action and remained a Wilsonian. His hope for Yalta, as he told the Congress on his return, was that it would "spell the end of the system of unilateral action, the exclusive alliances, the spheres of influence, the balances of power, and all the other expedients that have been tried for centuries—and have always failed."

Whenever Roosevelt backslid, he had at his side that Wilsonian fundamentalist, Secretary of State Cordell Hull, to recall him to the pure faith. After his visit to Moscow in 1943, Hull characteristically said that, with the Declaration of Four Nations on General Security (in which America, Russia, Britain and China pledged "united action . . . for the organization and maintenance of peace and security"), "there will no longer be need for spheres of influence, for alliances, for balance of power, or any other of the special arrangements through which, in the unhappy past, the nations strove to safeguard their security or to promote their interests."

Remembering the corruption of the Wilsonian vision by the secret treaties of the First World War, Hull was determined to prevent any sphere-of-influence nonsense after the Second World War. He therefore fought all proposals to settle border questions while the war was still on and, excluded as he largely was from wartime diplomacy, poured his not inconsiderable moral energy and frustration into the promulgation of virtuous and spacious general principles.

.   .   .

The Kremlin, on the other hand, thought *only* of spheres of interest; above all, the Russians were determined to protect their frontiers, and especially their border to the west, crossed so often and so bloodily in the dark course of their history. These western frontiers lacked natural means of defense—no great oceans, rugged mountains, steaming swamps or impenetrable jungles. The history of Russia had been the history of invasion, the last of which was by now horribly killing up to twenty million of its people. The protocol of Russia therefore meant the enlargement of the area of Russian influence. Kennan himself wrote (in May 1944), "Behind Russia's stubborn expansion lies only the age-old sense of insecurity of a sedentary people reared on an exposed plain in the neighborhood of fierce nomadic peoples," and he called this "urge" a "permanent feature of Russian psychology."

.   .   .

The unconditional surrender of Italy in July 1943 created the first major test of the Western devotion to universalism. America and Britain, having won the Italian war, handled the capitulation, keeping Moscow informed at a distance. Stalin complained:

The United States and Great Britain made agreements but the Soviet Union received information about the results . . . just as a passive third observer. I have to tell you that it is impossible to tolerate the situation any longer. I propose that the [tripartite military-political commission] be established and that Sicily be assigned . . . as its place of residence.

Roosevelt, who had no intention of sharing the control of Italy with the Russians, suavely replied with the suggestion that Stalin send an officer "to General Eisenhower's headquarters in connection with the commission." Unimpressed, Stalin continued to press for a tripartite body; but his Western allies were adamant in keeping the Soviet Union off the Control Commission for Italy, and the Russians in the end had to be satisfied with a seat, along with minor Allied states, on a meaningless Inter-Allied Advisory Council. Their acquiescence in this was doubtless not unconnected with a desire to establish precedents for Eastern Europe.

Teheran in December 1943 marked the high point of three-power collaboration. Still, when Churchill asked about Russian territorial interests, Stalin replied a little ominously, "There is no need to speak at the present time about any Soviet desires, but when the time comes we will speak." In the next weeks, there were increasing indications of a Soviet determination to deal unilaterally with Eastern Europe—so much so that in early February 1944 Hull cabled Harriman in Moscow:

Matters are rapidly approaching the point where the Soviet Government will have to choose between the development and extension of the foundation of international cooperation as the guiding principle of the postwar world as against the continuance of a unilateral and arbitrary method of dealing with its special problems even though these problems are admittedly of more direct interest to the Soviet Union than to other great powers.

As against this approach, however, Churchill, more tolerant of sphere-of-influence deviations, soon proposed that, with the impending liberation of the Balkans, Russia should run things in Rumania and Britain in Greece. Hull strongly opposed this suggestion but made the mistake of leaving Washington for a few days; and Roosevelt, momentarily free from his Wilsonian conscience, yielded to Churchill's plea for a three-months' trial. Hull resumed the fight on his return, and Churchill postponed the matter.

. . .

Meanwhile Eastern Europe presented the Alliance with still another crisis

that same September. Bulgaria, which was not at war with Russia, decided to surrender to the Western Allies while it still could; and the English and Americans at Cairo began to discuss armistice terms with Bulgarian envoys. Moscow, challenged by what it plainly saw as a Western intrusion into its own zone of vital interest, promptly declared war on Bulgaria, took over the surrender negotiations and, invoking the Italian precedent, denied its Western Allies any role in the Bulgarian Control Commission. In a long and thoughtful cable, Ambassador Harriman meditated on the problems of communication with the Soviet Union. "Words," he reflected, "have a different connotation to the Soviets than they have to us. When they speak of insisting on 'friendly governments' in their neighboring countries, they have in mind something quite different from what we would mean." The Russians, he surmised, really believed that Washington accepted "their position that although they would keep us informed they had the right to settle their problems with their neighbors unilaterally." But the Soviet position was still in flux: "the Soviet Government is not one mind." The problem, as Harriman had earlier told Harry Hopkins, was "to strengthen the hands of those around Stalin who want to play the game along our lines." The way to do this; he now told Hull, was to

be understanding of their sensitivity, meet them much more than half way, encourage them and support them wherever we can, and yet oppose them promptly with the greatest of firmness where we see them going wrong. . . . The only way we can eventually come to an understanding with the Soviet Union on the question of non-interference in the internal affairs of other countries is for us to take a definite interest in the solution of the problems of each individual country as they arise.

As against Harriman's sophisticated universalist strategy, however, Churchill, increasingly fearful of the consequences of unrestrained competition in Eastern Europe, decided in early October to carry his sphere-of-influence proposal directly to Moscow. Roosevelt was at first content to have Churchill speak for him too and even prepared a cable to that effect. But Hopkins, a more vigorous universalist, took it upon himself to stop the cable and warn Roosevelt of its possible implications. Eventually Roosevelt sent a message to Harriman in Moscow emphasizing that he expected to "retain complete freedom of action after this conference is over." It was now that Churchill quickly proposed—and Stalin as quickly accepted—the celebrated division of southeastern Europe: ending (after further haggling between Eden and Molotov) with 90 percent Soviet predominance in Rumania, 80 percent in Bulgaria and Hungary, fifty-fifty in Jugoslavia, 90 percent British predominance in Greece.

Churchill in discussing this with Harriman used the phrase "spheres of influence." But he insisted that these were only "immediate wartime arrangements" and received a highly general blessing from Roosevelt. Yet, whatever Churchill intended, there is reason to believe that Stalin construed the percentages as an agreement, not a declaration; as practical arithmetic, not algebra. For Stalin, it should be understood, the sphere-of-influence idea did not mean that he would abandon all efforts to spread communism in some other nation's sphere; it did mean that, if he tried this and the other side cracked down, he could not feel he had serious cause for complaint. . . .

No one, of course, can know what really was in the minds of the Russian leaders. The Kremlin archives are locked; of the primary actors, only Molotov survives, and he has not yet indicated any desire to collaborate with the Columbia Oral History Project. We do know that Stalin did not wholly surrender to sentimental illusion about his new friends. In June 1944, on the night before the landings in Normandy, he told Djilas that the English "find nothing sweeter than to trick their allies. . . . And Churchill? Churchill is the kind who, if you don't watch him, will slip a kopeck out of your pocket. Yes, a kopeck out of your pocket! . . . Roosevelt is not like that. He dips in his hand only for bigger coins." But whatever his views of his colleagues it is not unreasonable to suppose that Stalin would have been satisfied at the end of the war to secure what Kennan has called "a protective glacis along Russia's western border," and that, in exchange for a free hand in Eastern Europe, he was prepared to give the British and Americans equally free hands in their zones of vital interest, including in nations as close to Russia as Greece (for the British) and, very probably—or at least so the Jugoslavs believe—China (for the United States). In other words, his initial objectives were very probably not world conquest but Russian security.

It is now pertinent to inquire why the United States rejected the idea of stabilizing the world by division into spheres of influence and insisted on an East European strategy. One should warn against rushing to the conclusion that it was all a row between hard-nosed, balance-of-power realists and starry-eyed Wilsonians. Roosevelt, Hopkins, Welles, Harriman, Bohlen, Berle, Dulles and other universalists were tough and serious men. Why then did they rebuff the sphere-of-influence solution?

The first reason is that they regarded this solution as containing within itself the seeds of a third world war. The balance-of-power idea seemed inherently unstable. It had always broken down in the past. It held out to each power the permanent tempation to try to alter the balance in its own favor, and it built this temptation into the international order. It would turn the great powers of 1945 away from the objective of concerting common policies toward competition for postwar advantage. As Hopkins told Molotov at Teheran, "The President feels it essential to world peace that Russia, Great Britain and the United States work out this control question in a manner which will not start each of the three powers arming against the others." "The greatest likelihood of eventual conflict," said the Joint Chiefs of Staff in 1944 (the only conflict which the J.C.S., in its wisdom, could then glimpse "in the foreseeable future" was between Britain and Russia), ". . . would seem to grow out of either nation initiating attempts to build up its strength, by seeking to attach to herself parts of Europe to the disadvantage and possible danger of her potential adversary." The Americans were perfectly ready to acknowledge that Russia was entitled to convincing assurance of her national security—but not this way. "I could sympathize fully with Stalin's desire to protect his western borders from future attack," as Hull put it. "But I felt that this security could best be obtained through a strong postwar peace organization."

Hull's remark suggests the second objection: that the sphere-of-influence approach would, in the words of the State Department in 1945, "militate against the establishment and effective functioning of a broader system of general security in which all countries will have their part." The United Nations, in short, was seen as the alternative to the balance of power. Nor did the universalists see any necessary incompatibility between the Russian desire for "friendly governments" on its frontier and the American desire for self-determination in Eastern Europe. Before Yalta the State Department judged the general mood of Europe as "to the left and strongly in favor of far-reaching economic and social reforms, but not, however, in favor of a left-wing totalitarian regime to achieve these reforms." Governments in Eastern Europe could be sufficiently to the left "to allay Soviet suspicions" but sufficiently representative "of the center and *petit bourgeois* elements" not to seem a prelude to communist dictatorship. The American criteria were therefore that the government "should be dedicated to the preservation of civil liberties" and "should favor social and economic reforms." A string of New Deal states—of Finlands and Czechoslovakias—seemed a reasonable compromise solution.

Third, the universalists feared that the sphere-of-interest approach would be what Hull termed "a haven for the isolationists," who would advocate America's participation in Western Hemisphere affairs on condition that it did not participate in European or Asian affairs. Hull also feared that spheres of interest would lead to "closed trade areas or discriminatory systems" and thus defeat his cherished dream of a low-tariff, freely trading world.

Fourth, the sphere-of-interest solution meant the betrayal of the principles for which the Second World War was being fought—the Atlantic Charter, the Four Freedoms, the Declaration of the United Nations. Poland summed up the problem. Britain, having gone to war to defend the independence of Poland from the Germans, could not easily conclude the war by surrendering the independence of Poland to the Russians. Thus, as Hopkins told Stalin after Roosevelt's death in 1945, Poland had "become the symbol of our ability to work out problems with the Soviet Union." Nor could American liberals in general watch with equanimity while the police state spread into countries which, if they had mostly not been real democracies, had mostly not been tyrannies either. The execution in 1943 of Ehrlich and Alter, the Polish socialist trade union leaders, excited deep concern. "I have particularly in mind," Harriman cabled in 1944, "objection to the institution of secret police who may become involved in the persecution of persons of truly democratic convictions who may not be willing to conform to Soviet methods."

Fifth, the sphere-of-influence solution would create difficult domestic problems in American politics. Roosevelt was aware of the six million or more Polish votes in the 1944 election; even more accurately, he was aware of the broader and deeper attack which would follow if, after going to war to stop the Nazi conquest of Europe, he permitted the war to end with the communist conquest of Eastern Europe. As Archibald MacLeish, then Assistant Secretary of State for Public Affairs, warned in January 1945, "The wave of disillusionment which has distressed us in the last several weeks will be increased if the impression is permitted to get abroad that potentially totalitarian provisional governments are to be set up without adequate safeguards as to the holding of free elections and the realization of the principles of the Atlantic Charter." Roosevelt believed that no administration could survive which did not try everything short of war to save Eastern Europe, and he was the supreme American politician of the century.

Sixth, if the Russians were allowed to overrun Eastern Europe without

argument, would that satisfy them? Even Kennan, in a dispatch of May 1944, admitted that the "urge" had dreadful potentialities: "If initially successful, will it know where to stop? Will it not be inexorably carried forward, by its very nature, in a struggle to reach the whole—to attain complete mastery of the shores of the Atlantic and the Pacific?" His own answer was that there were inherent limits to the Russian capacity to expand—"that Russia will not have an easy time in maintaining the power which it has seized over other people in Eastern and Central Europe unless it receives both moral and material assistance from the West." Subsequent developments have vindicated Kennan's argument, By the late forties, Jugoslavia and Albania, the two East European states farthest from the Soviet Union and the two in which communism was imposed from within rather than from without, had declared their independence of Moscow. But, given Russia's success in maintaining centralized control over the international communist movement for a quarter of a century, who in 1944 could have had much confidence in the idea of communist revolts against Moscow?

Most of those involved therefore rejected Kennan's answer and stayed with his question. If the West turned its back on Eastern Europe, the higher probability, in their view, was that the Russians would use their security zone, not just for defensive purposes, but as a springboard from which to mount an attack on Western Europe, now shattered by war, a vacuum of power awaiting its master. "If the policy is accepted that the Soviet Union has a right to penetrate her immediate neighbors for security," Harriman said in 1944, "penetration of the next immediate neighbors becomes at a certain time equally logical." If a row with Russia were inevitable, every consideration of prudence dictated that it should take place in Eastern rather than Western Europe.

Thus idealism and realism joined in opposition to the sphere-of-influence solution. The consequence was a determination to assert an American interest in the postwar destiny of all nations, including those of Eastern Europe. In the message which Roosevelt and Hopkins drafted after Hopkins had stopped Roosevelt's initial cable authorizing Churchill to speak for the United States at the Moscow meeting of October 1944, Roosevelt now said, "There is in this global war literally no question, either military or political, in which the United States is not interested." After Roosevelt's death Hopkins repeated the point to Stalin: "The cardinal basis of President Roosevelt's policy which the American people had fully supported had been the concept that the interests of the U.S. were worldwide and not confined to North and South America and the Pacific Ocean."

. . .

Yalta remains something of an historical perplexity less, from the perspective of 1967, because of a mythical American deference to the sphere-of-influence thesis than because of the documentable Russian deference to the universalist thesis. Why should Stalin in 1945 have accepted the Declaration on Liberated Europe and an agreement on Poland pledging that "the three governments will jointly" act to assure "free elections of governments responsive to the will of the people"? There are several probable answers: that the war was not over and the Russians still wanted the Americans to intensify their military effort in the West; that one clause in the Declaration premised action on "the opinion of the three governments" and thus implied a Soviet veto, though the Polish agreement was more definite; most of all that the uni-versalist algebra of the Declaration was plainly in Stalin's mind to be construed in terms of the practical arithmetic of his sphere-of-influence agreement with Churchill the previous October. Stalin's assurance to Churchill at Yalta that a proposed Russian amendment to the Declaration would not apply to Greece makes it clear that Roosevelt's pieties did not, in Stalin's mind, nullify Churchill's percentages. He could well have been strengthened in this supposition by the fact that *after* Yalta, Churchill himself repeatedly reasserted the terms of the October agreement as if he regarded it, despite Yalta, as controlling.

Harriman still had the feeling before Yalta that the Kremlin had "two approaches to their postwar policies" and that Stalin himself was "of two minds." One approach emphasized the internal reconstruction and development of Russia; the other its external expansion. But in the meantime the fact which dominated all political decisions—that is, the war against Germany—was moving into its final phase. In the weeks after Yalta, the military situation changed with great rapidity. As the Nazi threat declined, so too did the need for coöperation. The Soviet Union, feeling itself menaced by the American idea of self-determination and the borderlands diplomacy to which it was leading, skeptical whether the United Nations would protect its frontiers as reliably as its own domination in Eastern Europe, began to fulfill its security requirements unilaterally.

In March Stalin expressed his evaluation of the United Nations by rejecting Roosevelt's plea that Molotov come to the San Francisco conference, if only for the opening sessions. In the next weeks the Russians emphatically and crudely worked their will in Eastern Europe, above all in the test country of Poland. They were ignoring the Declaration on Liberated Europe, ignoring the Atlantic Charter, self-determination, human freedom and everything else the Americans considered essential for a stable peace. "We must clearly recognize," Harriman wired Washington a few days before Roosevelt's death, "that the Soviet program is the establishment of totalitarianism, ending personal liberty and democracy as we know and respect it."

At the same time, the Russians also began to mobilize communist resources in the United States itself to block American universalism. In April 1945 Jacques Duclos, who had been the Comintern official responsible for the Western communist parties, launched in *Cahiers du Communisme* an uncompromising attack on the policy of the American Communist Party. Duclos sharply condemned the revisionism of Earl Browder, the American Communist leader, as "expressed in the concept of a long-term class peace in the United States, of the possibility of the suppression of the class struggle in the postwar period and of establishment of harmony between labor and capital." Browder was specifically rebuked for favoring the "self-determination" of Europe "west of the Soviet Union" on a bourgeois-democratic basis. The excommunication of Browderism was plainly the Politburo's considered reaction to the impending defeat of Germany; it was a signal to the communist parties of the West that they should recover their identity; it was Moscow's alert to communists everywhere that they should prepare for new policies in the postwar world.

The Duclos piece obviously could not have been planned and written much later than the Yalta conference— that is, well before a number of events which revisionists now cite in order to demonstrate American responsibility for the Cold War: before Allen Dulles, for example, began to negotiate the surrender of the German armies in Italy (the episode which provoked Stalin to charge Roosevelt with seeking a separate peace and provoked Roosevelt to denounce the "vile misrepresentations" of Stalin's informants); well before Roosevelt died; many months before the testing of the atomic bomb; even more months before Truman ordered that the bomb be dropped on Japan. William Z. Foster, who soon replaced Browder as the leader of the American Communist Party and embodied the new Moscow line, later boasted of having said in January 1944, "A post-war Roosevelt administration would continue to be, as it is now, an imperialist government." With ancient suspicions revived by the American insistence on universalism, this was no doubt the conclusion which the Russians were reaching at the same time. The Soviet canonization of Roosevelt (like their present-day canonization of Kennedy) took place after the American President's death.

· · ·

The Cold War . . . was the product not of a decision but of a dilemma. Each side felt compelled to adopt policies which the other could not but regard as a threat to the principles of the peace. Each then felt compelled to undertake defensive measures. Thus the Russians saw no choice but to consolidate their security in Eastern Europe. The Americans, regarding Eastern Europe as the first step toward Western Europe, responded by asserting their interest in the zone the Russians deemed vital to their security. The Russians concluded that the West was resuming its old course of capitalist encirclement; that it was purposefully laying the foundation for anti-Soviet régimes in the area defined by the blood of centuries as crucial to Russian survival. Each side believed with passion that future international stability depended on the success of its own conception of world order. Each side, in pursuing its own clearly indicated and deeply cherished principles, was only confirming the fear of the other that it was bent on aggression.

Very soon the process began to acquire a cumulative momentum. The impending collapse of Germany thus provoked new troubles: the Russians, for example, sincerely feared that the West was planning a separate surrender of the German armies in Italy in a way which would release troops for Hitler's eastern front, as they subsequently feared that the Nazis might succeed in surrendering Berlin to the West. This was the context in which the atomic bomb now appeared. Though the revisionist argument that Truman dropped the bomb less to defeat Japan than to intimidate Russia is not convincing, this thought unquestionably appealed to some in Washington as at least an advantageous side-effect of Hiroshima.

. . .

Up to this point, the discussion has considered the schism within the wartime coalition as if it were entirely the result of disagreements among national states. Assuming this framework, there was unquestionably a failure of communication between America and Russia, a misperception of signals and, as time went on, a mounting tendency to ascribe ominous motives to the other side. It seems hard, for example, to deny that American postwar policy created genuine difficulties for the Russians and even assumed a threatening aspect for them. All this the revisionists have rightly and usefully emphasized.

But the great omission of the revisionists—and also the fundamental explanation of the speed with which the Cold War escalated—lies precisely in the fact that the Soviet Union was *not* a traditional national state.[4] This is where the "mirror image," invoked by some psychologists, falls down. For the Soviet Union was a phenomenon very different from America or Britain: it was a totalitarian state, endowed with an all-explanatory, all-consuming ideology, committed to the infallibility of government and party, still in a somewhat messianic mood, equating dissent with treason, and ruled by a dictator who, for all his quite extraordinary abilities, had his paranoid moments.

Marxism-Leninism gave the Russian leaders a view of the world according to which all societies were inexorably destined to proceed along appointed roads by appointed stages until they achieved the classless nirvana. Moreover, given the resistance of the capitalists to this development, the existence of any noncommunist state was *by definition* a threat to the Soviet Union. "As long as capitalism and socialism exist," Lenin wrote, "we cannot live in peace: in the end, one or the other will triumph—a funeral dirge will be sung either over the Soviet Republic or over world capitalism."

Stalin and his associates, whatever

---

[4] This is the classical revisionist fallacy—the assumption of the rationality, or at least of the traditionalism, of states where ideology and social organization have created a different range of motives. So the Second World War revisionists omit the totalitarian dynamism of Nazism and the fanaticism of Hitler, as the Civil War revisionists omit the fact that the slavery system was producing a doctrinaire closed society in the American South. For a consideration of some of these issues, see "The Cause of the Civil War: A Note on Historical Sentimentalism" in my "The Politics of Hope" (Boston, 1963).

Roosevelt or Truman did or failed to do, were bound to regard the United States as the enemy, not because of this deed or that, but because of the primordial fact that America was the leading capitalist power and thus, by Leninist syllogism, unappeasably hostile, driven by the logic of its system to oppose, encircle and destroy Soviet Russia. Nothing the United States could have done in 1944–45 would have abolished this mistrust, required and sanctified as it was by Marxist gospel—nothing short of the conversion of the United States into a Stalinist despotism; and even this would not have sufficed, as the experience of Jugoslavia and China soon showed, unless it were accompanied by total subservience to Moscow. So long as the United States remained a capitalist democracy, no American policy, given Moscow's theology, could hope to win basic Soviet confidence, and every American action was poisoned from the source. So long as the Soviet Union remained a messianic state, ideology compelled a steady expansion of communist power.

. . .

Paradoxically, of the forces capable of bringing about a modification of ideology, the most practical and effective was the Soviet dictatorship itself. If Stalin was an ideologist, he was also a pragmatist. If he saw everything through the lenses of Marxism-Leninism, he also, as the infallible expositor of the faith, could reinterpret Marxism-Leninism to justify anything he wanted to do at any given moment. No doubt Roosevelt's ignorance of Marxism-Leninism was inexcusable and led to grievous miscalculations. But Roosevelt's efforts to work on and through Stalin were not so hopelessly naïve as it used to be fashionable to think. With the extraordinary instinct of a great political leader, Roosevelt intuitively understood that Stalin was

the *only* lever available to the West against the Leninist ideology and the Soviet system. If Stalin could be reached, then alone was there a chance of getting the Russians to act contrary to the prescriptions of their faith. The best evidence is that Roosevelt retained a certain capacity to influence Stalin to the end; the nominal Soviet acquiescence in American universalism as late as Yalta was perhaps an indication of that. It is in this way that the death of Roosevelt was crucial—not in the vulgar sense that his policy was then reversed by his successor, which did not happen, but in the sense that no other American could hope to have the restraining impact on Stalin which Roosevelt might for a while have had.

Stalin alone could have made any difference. Yet Stalin, in spite of the impression of sobriety and realism he made on Westerners who saw him during the Second World War, was plainly a man of deep and morbid obsessions and compulsions. When he was still a young man, Lenin had criticized his rude and arbitrary ways. A reasonably authoritative observer (N. S. Khrushchev) later commented, "These negative characteristics of his developed steadily and during the last years acquired an absolutely insufferable character." His paranoia, probably set off by the suicide of his wife in 1932, led to the terrible purges of the mid-thirties and the wanton murder of thousands of his Bolshevik comrades. "Everywhere and in everything," Khrushchev says of this period, "he saw 'enemies,' 'double-dealers' and 'spies.'" The crisis of war evidently steadied him in some way, though Khrushchev speaks of his "nervousness and hysteria . . . even after the war began." The madness, so rigidly controlled for a time, burst out with new and shocking intensity in the postwar years. "After the war," Khrushchev testifies, the situation became even more complicated. Stalin became even more capricious, irritable and brutal; in particular, his suspicion grew. His persecution mania reached unbelievable dimensions. . . . He decided everything, without any consideration for anyone or anything.

Stalin's wilfulness showed itself . . . also in the international relations of the Soviet Union. . . . He had completely lost a sense of reality; he demonstrated his suspicion and haughtiness not only in relation to individuals in the USSR, but in relation to whole parties and nations.

A revisionist fallacy has been to treat Stalin as just another Realpolitik statesman, as Second World War revisionists see Hitler as just another Stresemann or Bismarck. But the record makes it clear that in the end nothing could satisfy Stalin's paranoia. His own associates failed. Why does anyone suppose that any conceivable American policy would have succeeded?

An analysis of the origins of the Cold War which leaves out these factors—the intransigence of Leninist ideology, the sinister dynamics of a totalitarian society and the madness of Stalin—is obviously incomplete. It was these factors which made it hard for the West to accept the thesis that Russia was moved only by a desire to protect its security and would be satisfied by the control of Eastern Europe; it was these factors which charged the debate between universalism and spheres of influence with apocalyptic potentiality.

Leninism and totalitarianism created a structure of thought and behavior which made postwar collaboration between Russia and America—in any normal sense of civilized intercourse between national states—inherently impossible. The Soviet dictatorship of 1945 simply could not have survived such a collaboration. Indeed, nearly a quarter-century later, the Soviet régime, though it has meanwhile moved a good distance, could still hardly survive it without risking the release inside Russia of energies profoundly opposed to communist despotism. As for Stalin, he may have represented the only force in 1945 capable of overcoming Stalinism, but the very traits which enabled him to win absolute power expressed terrifying instabilities of mind and temperament and hardly offered a solid foundation for a peaceful world.

   . . .

In retrospect, if it is impossible to see the Cold War as a case of American aggression and Russian response, it is also hard to see it as a pure case of Russian aggression and American response. "In what is truly tragic," wrote Hegel, "there must be valid moral powers on both the sides which come into collision. . . . Both suffer loss and yet both are mutually justified." In this sense, the Cold War had its tragic elements. The question remains whether it was an instance of Greek tragedy—as Auden has called it, "the tragedy of necessity," where the feeling aroused in the spectator is "What a pity it had to be this way"—or of Christian tragedy, "the tragedy of possibility," where the feeling aroused is "What a pity it was this way when it might have been otherwise."

Once something has happened, the historian is tempted to assume that it had to happen; but this may often be a highly unphilosophical assumption. The Cold War could have been avoided only if the Soviet Union had not been possessed by convictions both of the infallibility of the communist word and of the inevitability of a communist world. These convictions transformed an impasse between national states into a religious war, a tragedy of possibility into one of necessity. One might wish that America had preserved the poise and proportion of the first years of the Cold War and had not in time succumbed to its own forms of self-righteousness. But the most rational of American policies could hardly have averted the Cold War. Only today, as Russia begins to recede from its messianic mission and to accept, in practice if not yet in principle, the permanence of the world of diversity, only now can the hope flicker that this long, dreary, costly contest may at last be taking on forms less dramatic, less obsessive and less dangerous to the future of mankind.

CHRISTOPHER LASCH

More than a year has passed since Arthur Schlesinger Jr. announced that the time had come "to blow the whistle before the current outburst of revisionism regarding the origins of the cold war goes much further." Yet the outburst of revisionism shows no signs of subsiding. On the contrary, a growing number of historians and political critics, judging from such recent books as Ronald Steel's "Pax Americana" and Carl Oglesby's and Richard Shaull's "Containment and Change," are challenging the view, once so widely accepted, that the cold war was an American response to Soviet expansionism, a distasteful burden reluctantly shouldered in the face of a ruthless enemy bent on our destruction, and that Russia, not the United States, must therefore bear the blame for shattering the world's hope that two world wars in

Reprinted from Christopher Lasch, "The Cold War, Revisited and Re-Visioned," THE NEW YORK TIMES MAGAZINE, *January 14, 1968 (© 1968 by The New York Times Company), by permission of the publisher and the author.*

the 20th century would finally give way to an era of peace.

"Revisionist" historians are arguing instead that the United States did as much as the Soviet Union to bring about the collapse of the wartime coalition. Without attempting to shift the blame exclusively to the United States, they are trying to show, as Gar Alperovitz puts it, that "the cold war cannot be understood simply as an American response to a Soviet challenge, but rather as the insidious interaction of mutual suspicions, blame for which must be shared by all."

Not only have historians continued to re-examine the immediate origins of the cold war—in spite of attempts to "blow the whistle" on their efforts— but the scope of revisionism has been steadily widening. Some scholars are beginning to argue that the whole course of American diplomacy since 1898 shows that the United States has become a counterrevolutionary power committed to the defense of a global status quo. Arno Mayer's monumental study of the Conference of Versailles, "Politics and Diplomacy of Peacemaking," which has recently been published by Knopf and which promises to become the definitive work on the subject, announces in its subtitle what a growing number of historians have come to see as the main theme of American diplomacy: "Containment and Counterrevolution."

Even Schlesinger has now admitted, in a recent article in Foreign Affairs, that he was "somewhat intemperate," a year ago, in deploring the rise of cold-war revisionism. Even though revisionist interpretations of earlier wars "have failed to stick," he says, "revisionism is an essential part of the process by which history . . . enlarges its perspectives and enriches its insights." Since he goes on to argue that "postwar collaboration between Russia and America [was] . . . inherently impossible" and that "the most rational of American policies could hardly have averted the cold war," it is not clear what Schlesinger thinks revisionism has done to enlarge our perspective and enrich our insights; but it is good to know, nevertheless, that revisionists may now presumably continue their work (inconsequential as it may eventually prove to be) without fear of being whistled to a stop by the referee.

The orthodox interpretation of the cold war, as it has come to be regarded, grew up in the late forties and early fifties—years of acute international tension, during which the rivalry between the United States and the Soviet Union repeatedly threatened to erupt in a renewal of global war. Soviet-American relations had deteriorated with alarming speed following the defeat of Hitler. At Yalta, in February, 1945, Winston Churchill had expressed the hope that world peace was nearer the grasp of the assembled statesmen of the great powers "than at any time in history." It would be "a great tragedy," he said, "if they, through inertia or carelessness, let it slip from their grasp. History would never forgive them if they did."

Yet the Yalta agreements themselves, which seemed at the time to lay the basis of postwar cooperation, shortly provided the focus of bitter dissension, in which each side accused the other of having broken its solemn promises. In Western eyes, Yalta meant free elections and parliamentary democracies in Eastern Europe, while the Russians construed the agreements as recognition of their demand for governments friendly to the Soviet Union.

The resulting dispute led to mutual mistrust and to a hardening of positions on both sides. By the spring of 1946 Churchill himself, declaring that "an iron curtain has descended" across Europe, admitted, in effect, that the "tragedy" he had feared had come to pass. Europe split into hostile fragments, the eastern half dominated by the Soviet Union, the western part sheltering nervously under the protection of American arms. NATO, founded in 1949 and countered by the Russian-sponsored Warsaw Pact, merely ratified the existing division of Europe.

From 1946 on, every threat to the stability of this uneasy balance produced an immediate political crisis— Greece in 1947, Czechoslovakia and the Berlin blockade in 1948—each of which, added to the existing tensions, deepened hostility on both sides and increased the chance of war. When Bernard Baruch announced in April, 1947, that "we are in the midst of a cold war," no one felt inclined to contradict him. The phrase stuck, as an accurate description of post-war political realities.

Many Americans concluded, moreover, that the United States was losing the cold war. Two events in particular contributed to this sense of alarm—the collapse of Nationalist China in 1949, followed by Chiang Kai-shek's flight to Taiwan, and the explosion of an atomic bomb by the Russians in the same year. These events led to the charge that Americans leaders had deliberately or unwittingly betrayed the country's interests. The Alger Hiss case was taken by some people as proof that the Roosevelt Administration had been riddled by subversion.

Looking back to the wartime alliance with the Soviet Union, the American Right began to argue that Roosevelt, by trusting the Russians, had sold out the cause of freedom. Thus Nixon and McCarthy, aided by historians like Stefan J. Possony, C. C. Tansill and others, accused Roosevelt of handing Eastern Europe to the Russians and of giving them a preponderant interest in China which later enabled the Communists to absorb the entire country.

The liberal interpretation of the cold war—what I have called the orthodox interpretation—developed partly as a response to these charges. In liberal eyes, the right-wingers made the crucial mistake of assuming that American actions had been decisive in shaping the postwar world. Attempting to rebut this devil theory of postwar politics, liberals relied heavily on the argument that the shape of postwar politics had already been dictated by the war itself, in which the Western democracies had been obliged to call on Soviet help in defeating Hitler. These events, they maintained, had left the Soviet Union militarily dominant in Eastern Europe and generally occupying a position of much greater power, relative to the West, than the position she had enjoyed before the war.

In the face of these facts, the United States had very little leeway to influence events in what were destined to become Soviet spheres of influence, particularly since Stalin was apparently determined to expand even if it meant ruthlessly breaking his agreements—and after all it was Stalin, the liberals emphasized, and not Roosevelt or Truman, who broke the Yalta agreement on Poland, thereby precipitating the cold war.

These were the arguments presented with enormous charm, wit, logic and power in George F. Kennan's "American Diplomacy" (1951), which more than any other book set the tone of cold-war historiography. For innumerable historians, but especially for those who were beginning their studies in the fifties, Kennan served as the model of what a scholar should be—committed yet detached—and it was through the perspective of his works that a whole generation of scholars came to see not only the origins of the cold war, but the entire history of 20th century diplomacy.

It is important to recognize that Kennan's was by no means an uncritical perspective—indeed for those unacquainted with Marxism it seemed the only critical perspective that was available in the fifties. While Kennan insisted that the Russians were primarily to blame for the cold war, he seldom missed an opportunity to criticize the excessive moralism, the messianic vision of a world made safe for democracy, which he argued ran "like a red skein" through American diplomacy.

•   •   •

The revisionist view of the origins of the cold war, as it emerges from the works of Williams, Alperovitz, Marzani, Fleming, Horowitz, and others, can be summarized as follows. The object of American policy at the end of World War II was not to defend Western or even Central Europe but to force the Soviet Union out of Eastern Europe. The Soviet menace to the "free world," so often cited as the justification of the containment policy, simply did not exist in the minds of American planners. They believed themselves to be negotiating not from weakness but from almost unassailable superiority.

Nor can it be said that the cold war began because the Russians "broke their agreements." The general sense of the Yalta agreements—which were in any case very vague—was to assign to the Soviet Union a controlling influence in Eastern Europe. Armed with the atomic bomb, American diplomats tried to take back what they had implicitly conceded at Yalta.

The assumption of American moral

superiority, in short, does not stand up under analysis.

The opponents of this view have yet to make a very convincing reply. Schlesinger's recent article in Foreign Affairs, referred to at the outset of this article, can serve as an example of the kind of arguments which historians are likely to develop in opposition to the revisionist interpretation. Schlesinger argues that the cold war came about through a combination of Soviet intransigence and misunderstanding. There were certain "problems of communication" with the Soviet Union, as a result of which "the Russians might conceivably have misread our signals." Thus the American demand for self-determination in Poland and other East European countries "very probably" appeared to the Russians "as a systematic and deliberate pressure on Russian's western frontiers."

Similarly, the Russians "could well have interpreted" the American refusal of a loan to the Soviet Union, combined with cancellation of lend-lease, "as deliberate sabotage" of Russia's postwar reconstruction or as "blackmail." In both cases, of course, there would have been no basis for these suspicions; but "we have thought a great deal more in recent years," Schlesinger says, ". . . about the problems of communication in diplomacy," and we know how easy it is for one side to misinterpret what the other is saying.

This argument about difficulties of "communications" at no point engages the evidence uncovered by Alperovitz and others—evidence which seems to show that Soviet officials had good reason to interpret American actions exactly as they did: as attempts to dictate American terms.

. . .

When pressed on the matter of "communications," Schlesinger retreats to a second line of argument, namely that none of these misundertandings "made much essential difference," because Stalin suffered from "paranoia" and was "possessed by convictions both of the infallibility of the Communist word and of the inevitability of a Communist world."

The trouble is that there is very little evidence which connects either Stalin's paranoia or Marxist-Leninist ideology or what Schlesinger calls "the sinister dynamics of a totalitarian society" with the actual course of Soviet diplomacy during the formative months of the cold war. The only piece of evidence that Schlesinger has been able to find is an article by the Communist theoretician Jacques Duclos in the April, 1945, issue of Cahiers du communisme, the journal of the French Communist party, which proves, he argues, that Stalin had already abandoned the wartime policy of collaboration with the West and had returned to the traditional Communist policy of world revolution.

Even this evidence, however, can be turned to the advantage of the revisionists. Alperovitz points out that Duclos did not attack electoral politics or even collaboration with bourgeois governments. What he denounced was precisely the American Communists' decision, in 1944, to withdraw from electoral politics. Thus the article, far from being a call to world revolution, "was one of many confirmations that European Communists had decided to abandon violent revolutionary struggle in favor of the more modest aim of electoral success." And while this decision did not guarantee world peace, neither did it guarantee 20 years of cold war.

Schlesinger first used the Duclos article as a trump card in a letter to The New York Review of Books, Oct. 20, 1966, which called forth Alperovitz's rejoinder. It is symptomatic of the general failure of orthodox historiography to engage the revisionist argument that Duclos's article crops up again in Schlesinger's more recent essay in Foreign Affairs, where it is once again cited as evidence of a "new Moscow line," without any reference to the intervening objections raised by Alperovitz.

Sooner or later, however, historians will have to come to grips with the revisionist interpretation of the cold war. They cannot ignore it indefinitely. When serious debate begins, many historians, hitherto disposed to accept without much question the conventional account of the cold war, will find themselves compelled to admit its many inadequacies. On the other hand, some of the ambiguities of the revisionist view, presently submerged in the revisionists' common quarrel with official explanations, will begin to force themselves to the surface. Is the revisionist history of the cold war essentially an attack on "the doctrine of historical inevitability," as Alperovitz contends? Or does it contain an implicit determinism of its own?

. . .

Pushed to what some writers clearly regard as its logical conclusion, the revisionist critique of American foreign policy thus becomes the obverse of the cold-war liberals' defense of that policy, which assumes that nothing could have modified the character of Soviet policy short of the transformation of the Soviet Union into a liberal democracy—which is exactly the goal the containment policy sought to promote. According to a certain type of revisionism, American policy has all the rigidity the orthodox historians attribute to the U.S.S.R., and this inflexibility made the cold war inevitable.

Moreover, Communism really did threaten American interests, in this view. Oglesby argues that, in spite of its obvious excesses, the "theory of the International Communist Conspiracy is not the hysterical old maid that many leftists seem to think it is." If there is no conspiracy, there is a world revolution and it *"does* aim itself at America" —the America of expansive corporate capitalism.

Revisionism, carried to these conclusions, curiously restores cold-war anti-Communism to a kind of intellectual respectability, even while insisting on its immorality. After all, it concludes, the cold warriors were following the American national interest. The national interest may have been itself corrupt, but the policy-makers were more rational than their critics may have supposed.

In my view, this concedes far too much good sense to Truman, Dulles and the rest. Even Oglesby concedes that the war in Vietnam has now become irrational in its own terms. I submit that much of the cold war has been irrational in its own terms—as witness the failure, the enormously costly failure, of American efforts to dominate Eastern Europe at the end of World War II. This is not to deny the fact of American imperialism, only to suggest that imperialism itself, as J. A. Hobson and Joseph Schumpeter argued in another context long ago, is irrational—that even in its liberal form it may represent an archaic social phenomenon having little relation to the realities of the modern world.

At the present stage of historical scholarship, it is of course impossible to speak with certainty about such matters. That very lack of certainty serves to indicate the direction which future study of American foreign policy might profitably take.

The question to which historians must now address themselves is whether

American capitalism really depends, for its continuing growth and survival, on the foreign policy its leaders have been following throughout most of the 20th century. To what extent are its interests really threatened by Communist revolutions in the Third World? To what extent can it accommodate itself to those revolutions, reconciling itself to a greatly diminished role in the rest of the world, without undergoing a fundamental reformation—that is, without giving way (after a tremendous upheaval) to some form of Socialism?

Needless to say, these are not questions for scholars alone. The political positions one takes depends on the way one answers them. It is terribly important, therefore, that we begin to answer them with greater care and precision than we can answer them today.

C. VANN WOODWARD

Innumerable influences have inspired the reinterpretation of history. The most common of late would appear to have been those originating within the intellectual community, or within the historical guild itself, rather than with the impact of historical events. Influences of the predominant sort include new theories, new methods, and new sources. Of special importance in recent years has been the example of other disciplines and sciences, old ones such as philosophy and biology with new theories, or new ones such as psychology and sociology with new approaches to old problems.

With no intended disparagement for prevailing and recent types of revision, the present essay concerns itself almost exclusively with reinterpretations

Reprinted from C. Vann Woodward, "The Age of Reinterpretation," AMERICAN HISTORICAL REVIEW, LXVI (October, 1960), 1–19, by permission of the author.

that are inspired by historical events and have little to do with new theories, new methods, or new disciplines. The suggested opportunities for reinterpretation are, in fact, related to historical events so recent that nearly all of them have occurred since the summer of 1945. As responsible human beings we are rightly concerned first of all with the impact of these events upon the present and immediate future. But as historians we are, or we should be, concerned with their effect upon our view of the past as well. These events have come with a concentration and violence for which the term "revolution" is usually reserved. It is a revolution, or perhaps a set of revolutions, for which we have not yet found a name. My thesis is that these developments will and should raise new questions about the past and affect our reading of large areas of history, and my belief is that future revisions may be extensive enough to justify calling the coming era of historiography, an age of reinterpretation. The first illustration happens to come mainly from American history, but this should not obscure the broader scope of the revolution, which has no national limitations.

Throughout most of its history the United States has enjoyed a remarkable degree of military security, physical security from hostile attack and invasion. This security was not only remarkably effective, but it was relatively free. Free security was based on nature's gift of three vast bodies of water interposed between this country and any other power that might constitute a serious menace to its safety. There was not only the Atlantic to the east and the Pacific to the west, but a third body of water, considered so impenetrable as to make us virtually unaware of its importance, the Arctic Ocean and its great ice cap to the north. The security thus provided was free in the sense that it was enjoyed as a bounty of nature in place of the elaborate and costly chains of fortifications and even more expensive armies and navies that took a heavy toll of the treasuries of less fortunate countries and placed severe tax burdens upon the backs of their people. The costly navy that policed and defended the Atlantic was manned and paid for by British subjects for more than a century, while Americans enjoyed the added security afforded without added cost to themselves. In 1861 the United States was maintaining the second largest merchant marine in the world without benefit of a battle fleet. At that time there were only 7,600 men in the United States Navy as compared with more than ten times that number in the British Navy.[1]

Between the second war with England and the Second World War, the United States was blessed with a security so complete and so free that it was able virtually to do without an army and for the greater part of the period without a navy as well. Between the world war that ended in 1763 and the world wars of the twentieth century the only major military burdens

[1] During Andrew Jackson's administration Alexis de Tocqueville described the situation in the following terms: "The President of the United States is the commander-in-chief of the army, but of an army composed of only six thousand men; he commands the fleet, but the fleet reckons but few sails; he conducts the foreign relations of the Union, but the United States are a nation without neighbors. Separated from the rest of the world by the ocean, and too weak as yet to aim at the dominion of the seas, they have no enemies, and their interests rarely come into contact with those of any other nation of the globe." *Democracy in America*, ed. Henry Reeve (2 vols., New York, 1904), I, 120.

placed upon the people were occasioned not by foreign threats but by domestic quarrels, the first to establish independence for the American colonies and the second to thwart independence for the southern states. After each of these civil wars, as after all the intervening wars, Americans immediately dismantled their military establishment. They followed the same procedure after every succeeding war, down to World War II, and even after that they carried demobilization to dangerous extremes before reversing the policy.

The end of the era of free security has overtaken Americans so suddenly and swiftly that they have not brought themselves to face its practical implications, much less its bearing upon their history. Conventional aircraft and jet propulsion had shrunk the time dimensions of the Atlantic and Pacific from weeks to hours by the mid-fifties. But before military adjustment could be properly made to that revolution, the development of ballistic missiles shrank the two oceans further from hours to minutes. In the same period the hitherto impenetrable Arctic Ocean has not only been navigated by atomic-powered submarines under the ice cap, but has been shrunk in time width to dimensions of minutes and seconds by which we now measure the other oceans. The age of security and the age of free security ended almost simultaneously.

The proposition was advanced before a meeting of the American Historical Association in 1893 that "the first period of American history," a period of four centuries, was brought to an end by the disappearance of free land. Perhaps it is not premature to suggest that another epoch of American history was closed even more suddenly sixty years later by the disappearance of free security. It may be objected that security was never completely free and that the period when it came nearest to being so did not last very long. But one can reasonably ask as much latitude to speak in comparative and relative terms about free security as the theorists of free land enjoyed in their generalizations. Land was of course never completely free either, and the period when it came nearest to being so only dated from the Homestead Act of 1862, less than three decades before the end of the frontier era. In a comparative sense land may nevertheless be said to have been relatively free for a much longer period. In similar terms security may also be said to have been free until quite recently.

Military expenditures of the federal government have, of course, increased greatly and almost continuously since the last decade of the eighteenth century. Until very recently, however, they have not increased so rapidly as the government's nonmilitary expenditures. During the first century of the Republic's history, save in war years, annual military expenditures rarely came to as much as 1 per cent of the gross national product, returned to that level a few years after the First World War, and remained there until the Great Depression cut production back drastically. In the decade preceding Pearl Harbor, the percentage of federal expenditures devoted to military purposes fell lower than ever before in our history.[2]

Another measure of free security is the small demand that military service has made upon national manpower. Before World War I, apart from actual war periods and their immediate aftermath, it was an extremely rare year in which as many as 1 per cent of the total male population between the ages of twenty and thirty-nine saw military service. Between Reconstruction and the Spanish-American War there was no year in which as many as one-half of 1 per cent served in the armed forces.[3] The handful of men who made up the regular army during the nineteenth century were not employed in patrolling frontiers against foreign invasion, but chiefly in coping with a domestic police problem posed by the Indians. Upon the outbreak of the Civil War the United States Army numbered a few more than sixteen thousand men, and 183 of its 198 companies were spread among seventy-nine posts on the Indian frontier. The remaining fifteen companies were available for "defense" of the Canadian and Atlantic frontiers, and the incipient Confederate frontier.[4] The southern constabulary that patrolled the slaves was organized on military lines, but like the regular army it was concerned with a domestic police problem.

The contrast between free security and security costs of the present era scarcely requires emphasis. Military expenditures in 1957 and the years since

[2] M. Slade Kendrick, *A Century and a Half of Federal Expenditures*, Occasional Paper 48, National Bureau of Economic Research (New York, 1955), 10–12, 28, 38, 40–42. For comparisons between military appropriations of the United States and other powers, 1820–1937, see Quincy Wright, *A Study of War* (2 vols., Chicago, 1942), I, 666–72, Appendix XXII, esp. Tables 58, 59, and 60. The significant index of comparison is the proportion between military appropriations and national income. That proportion rose in the United States from 0.8 in

1914 to 1.5 in 1937, while in the same years it stood in Great Britain at 3.4 and 5.7; in France at 4.8 and 9.1; in Japan at 4.8 and 28.2; in Germany at 4.6 and 23.5; and in Russia at 6.3 and 26.4. This was the only period for which figures are given for all these powers.

[3] Kendrick, *A Century and a Half of Federal Expenditures*, 89–90. Before 1865 only white males of military age are included in these figures.

[4] Theodore Ropp, *War in the Modern World* (Durham, N. C., 1959), 157.

have amounted to 10 per cent of the gross national product. By way of comparison, military expenditures in the 1880's were never over four-tenths of 1 per cent. In spite of the vast increase of the gross national product during the last century, military costs have increased far faster and now represent ten to twenty times the percentage of the gross national product they represented in the peace years of the previous century.[5] Not counting payments to veterans, they now account for nearly 70 per cent of the federal budget. The more advanced and improved military machinery paradoxically requires more instead of less manpower, both military and civilian. The Department of Defense and its branches employ more civilian workers now than did the entire federal government before the Great Depression. Indications are that we are only at the beginning instead of the culmination of expansion in costs and manpower for military purposes and that future expenditures will be larger still.

If historians waited until the disappearance of free land to recognize fully the influence of the frontier-and-free-land experience on American history, perhaps the even more sudden and dramatic disappearance of free security will encourage them to recognize the effect of another distinguishing influence upon our national history. I am not prepared to make any claims about the comparative importance of the two themes, nor do I wish to make or inspire any exaggerations of the influence of free security. But if the influence of free land may be considered significant in the shaping of American character

and national history, it is possible that the effect of free security might profitably be studied for contributions to the same ends.

Certain traits that Americans generally regard as desirable, such as democracy, individualism, self-reliance, inventiveness have been attributed in some measure to the frontier-and-free-land experience. It might be that the sunnier side of the national disposition—the sanguine temperament, the faith in the future,[6] what H. G. Wells once called our "optimistic fatalism" —is also related to a long era of habituation to military security that was effective, reliable, and virtually free. Optimism presupposes a future that is unusually benign and reliably congenial to man's enterprises. Anxieties about security have kept the growth of optimism within bounds among other peoples, but the relative absence of such anxieties in the past has helped, along with other factors, to make optimism a national philosophy in America. The freedom of American youth from the long period of training in military discipline that left its mark upon the youth of nations where it was a routine requirement could hardly have failed to make some contribution to the distinctiveness of national character.

Free security is related at various points to the development of the American economy. So long as an economy of scarcity prevailed in the land the gross national product was not far above the level of subsistence. While the margin was narrow, the demands of an expensive military establishment could have consumed so large a proportion of the surplus above subsistence

[5] Simon Kuznets in Committee for Economic Development, *Problems of United States Economic Development* (2 vols., New York, 1958), I, 29.

[6] Boyd C. Shafer, "The American Heritage of Hope," *Mississippi Valley Historical Review*, XXXVII (Dec. 1950), 422–50.

as to retard seriously the formation of capital. Relative immunity from this drain, on the other hand, enlarged opportunities for the formation of capital and the increase of productivity. Free security was certainly related to light taxes and a permissive government, and they in turn had much to do with the development of the famous Amercan living standard.

Not all the historic influences of free security have been so benign. Tocqueville's classic study of the national character attributes to democracy some familiar patterns of military conduct that might be profitably reexamined in the light of the free security thesis. Tocqueville finds, for example, that "the private soldiers remain most like civilians" in a democracy, that they chafe under discipline with "a restless and turbulent spirit," and that they are "ever ready to go back to their homes" when the fighting is over. With regard to the officer corps he observes that "among a democratic people the choicer minds of the nation are gradually drawn away from the military profession, to seek by other paths distinction, power, and especially wealth." He adds that "among democratic nations in time of peace the military profession is held in little honor and indifferently followed. This want of public favor is a heavy discouragement to the army." [7] Tocqueville may be correct in suggesting democracy as one explanation for these attitudes and patterns of behavior, but no explanation of American attitudes is complete that neglects a national disposition to look upon security as a natural right. What a people half consciously comes to regard as a free gift of nature they are with difficulty persuaded to purchase at high cost in treasure, incon-

[7] Tocqueville, *Democracy in America,* II, 761–68.

venience, and harsh discipline. To reward with high honors, prestige, and secure status the professional military men who insist upon these sacrifices in time of peace comes hard to such people.

The heritage of free and easy security can also be detected behind the disposition to put living standard, private indulgence, and wasteful luxury ahead of vital security requirements. The same heritage can almost certainly be discerned at work in the tendency to plunge into wars first and prepare for them later. The historic background of security might help to explain, even if it cannot excuse, the irresponsibility of political leaders who make foreign commitments, coin bellicose slogans, and indulge in wild threats and promises without first providing the military means to back them up.

There are other aspects of American history besides demagogic diplomacy and military shortcomings that are not to be fully understood without reference to the history of free security. Among these surely is the American Civil War. The United States is the only major country since Cromwellian England that could afford the doubtful luxury of a full-scale civil war of four years without incurring the evils of foreign intervention and occupation. Had such evils been as much a foregone conclusion as they have been among other nations, it is doubtful that Americans would have proved as willing as they were to fall upon each other's throats.

It is doubtful, also, that Americans could have developed and indulged with the freedom they have their peculiar national attitudes toward power, had it not been for their special immunity from the more urgent and dire demands for the employment of power to assure national security and survival. Having this relative immunity, they were able to devise and experiment with elaborate devices to diffuse and atomize power. They divided it among the states and later among business corporations. They used such devices as checks and balances, separation of powers, and division of powers to deadlock power and to thwart positive action for long periods. The experience probably encouraged the tendency to regard power as bad in itself and any means of restraining or denying it as a positive good.

The national myth that America is an innocent nation in a wicked world is associated to some degree in its origins and perpetuation with the experience of free security. That which other nations had of necessity to seek by the sword and defend by incurring the guilt of using it was obtained by the Americans both freely and innocently, at least in their own eyes. They disavowed the engines and instruments of the power they did not need and proclaimed their innocence for not using them, while at the same time they passed judgment upon other nations for incurring the guilt inevitably associated with power. "We lived for a century," writes Reinhold Niebuhr, "not only in the illusion but in the reality of innocency in our foreign relations. We lacked the power in the first instance to become involved in the guilt of its use." But we sought to maintain the innocence of our national youth after acquiring power that was incompatible with it. We first concealed from ourselves the reality of power in our economic and technological might, but after it became undeniable, and after military strength was added to it, as Niebuhr says, "we sought for a time to preserve innocency by disavowing the responsibilities of power." [8]

8 Reinhold Niebuhr, *The Irony of American History* (New York, 1952), 35.

The urge to return to a free security age of innocence and the flight from responsibility and from the guilt of wielding power may be traced in elaborate efforts to maintain neutrality, in desperate struggles for isolationism and "America First," as well as in the idealistic plans of religious and secular pacifists.

So long as free land was fertile and arable, and so long as security was not only free but strong and effective, it is no wonder that the world seemed to be America's particular oyster. Now that both free land and free security have disappeared, it is not surprising that the American outlook has altered and the prospect has darkened. The contrast with the past was even sharper in the case of free security than in the instance of free land, for the transition was almost immediate from a security that was both free and effective to an attempt at security that was frightfully costly and seemed terrifyingly ineffective. The spell of the long past of free security might help to account for the faltering and bewildered way in which America faced its new perils and its new responsibilities.

This discussion leads naturally to a second and more extensive field of opportunity for reinterpretation, that of military history. In this field there are no national limitations and few limits of time and period. Military subjects have traditionally occupied a large share of the historian's attention, a disproportionate share in the opinion of some critics. Yet the military historian is now faced with the challenge of relating the whole history of his subject to the vast revolution in military weapons and strategic theory that has occurred in the past fifteen years. Primarily this revolution involves two phases: first, explosives, and second, the means of delivering them upon a target. Both phases were inaugurated toward the end of the Second World War.

The revolution in explosives began when the primitive A bomb was exploded by American forces over Hiroshima on August 6, 1945.[9] This was the first and, so far, the last such weapon but one ever fired in anger. That event alone marked the lurid dawn of a new age. But the entirely unprecedented pace of change in the weapons revolution has swept us far beyond the primitive dawn and broken the continuity of military tradition and history. Since 1945 we have passed from bombs reckoned in kilotons of TNT to those computed in megatons, the first of which was the hydrogen bomb exploded at Bikini on March 1, 1954, less than a decade after the A-bomb innovation. The twenty kiloton atomic bomb dropped over Nagasaki in 1945 had a thousand times the explosive power of the largest blockbuster used in World War II, but the twenty megaton thermonuclear bomb represents a thousand-fold increase over the Nagasaki bomb. One bomb half the twenty megaton size is estimated by Henry A. Kissinger to represent *"five times the explosive power of all the bombs dropped on Germany during the five years of war and one hundred times those dropped on Japan."* [10] And according to Oskar Morgenstern, "One single bomb can harbor a force greater than all the explosives used by all belligerents in World War II or even greater than all the energy ever used in any form in all previous wars of

mankind put together." [11] But this would still not appear to be the ultimate weapon, for it is now said that a country capable of manufacturing the megaton bomb is conceivably capable, should such madness possess it, of producing a "begaton" bomb. Reckoned in billions instead of millions of tons of TNT, it would presumably represent a thousand-fold increase, if such a thing is conceivable, over the megaton weapon.

The revolution in the means of delivering explosives upon targets, like the revolution in explosives, also began during the Second World War. Before the end of that war, the jet-propelled aircraft, the snorkel submarine, the supersonic rocket, and new devices for guiding ships, aircraft, or missiles were all in use. But also as in the case of the revolution in explosives, the revolution in agents of delivery accelerated at an unprecedented pace during the fifteen years following the war. The new jet aircraft became obsolescent in succeeding models before they were in production, sometimes before they came off the drafting boards. The snorkel submarine acquired atomic power and a range of more than fifty thousand miles without refueling. The expansion of rockets in size, range, and speed was even more revolutionary. The German V-2 in use against London during the last year of the war had a range of only about two hundred miles and a speed of only about five times that of sound. The intermediary range ballistic missile, capable of carrying a thermonuclear warhead, has a range of around fifteen hundred miles, and the intercontinental missile with similar capabilities has a range in excess of five thousand miles and flies at a rate

---

[9] Two rival dates for the opening of the nuclear age are December 2, 1942, when Enrico Fermi established a chain reaction in the Chicago laboratory, and July 16, 1945, when the test bomb was exploded in New Mexico.

[10] Henry A. Kissinger, *Nuclear Weapons and Foreign Policy* (New York, 1957), 70–71. Italics in the original.

[11] Oskar Morgenstern, *The Question of National Defense* (New York, 1959), 10.

on the order of twenty times the speed of sound. To appreciate the pace and extent of the revolution in agents of delivery, one should recall that in the long history of firearms, military technology was only able to increase the range of cannon from the few hundred yards of the primitive smoothbore to a maximum of less than thirty miles in the 1940's with the mightiest rifled guns. Then in less than fifteen years ranges became literally astronomical.

In all these measurements and samples of change in military technology it should be kept in mind that the revolution is still in progress and in some areas may well be only in its beginning stages. The line between the intercontinental rockets and some of the space rockets would seem to be a rather arbitrary one. The race for the development of the nuclear-powered plane may produce a craft capable of ranges limited in a practical way only by the endurance of the crew. The technological breakthrough has become a familiar phenomenon of the military revolution, and there is no justification for the assumption that we have seen the last of these developments.

To seek the meaning of this revolution in a comparison with that worked by the advent of firearms is misleading. The progress of the revolution brought on by gunpowder, first used in military operations in the early fourteenth century, was glacial by comparison. Only very gradually did the gun replace the sword, the arrow, the spear, and the battering ram. Flintlocks did not arrive until the seventeenth century, field artillery of significance until the eighteenth century, and it was not until the middle of the last century, more than five hundred years after the first military use of gunfire, that the era of modern firearms really opened. Military doctrine changed even more slowly.

The nuclear revolution is of a different order entirely. If strategic bombing with thermonuclear weapons occurs on an unrestricted scale now entirely possible with existing forces, it is quite likely to render subsequent operation of armies, navies, and air forces not only superfluous but unfeasible. It is not simply that huge concentrations of forces such as were used in major amphibious and land operations in the last world war present a vulnerable target themselves. Of more elemental importance is the fact that such armies, navies, and air forces require thriving industrial economies and huge bases and cannot operate when the cities of their home territories are smoking craters and their ports and bases are piles of radioactive rubble. As for the military effectiveness of survivors in the home territory, according to Bernard Brodie, "the *minimum* destruction and disorganization that one should expect from an unrestricted thermonuclear attack in the future is likely to be too high to permit further meaningful mobilization of war-making capabilities over the short term." [12] Faith in the wartime potential of the American industrial plant would appear to be another casualty of the revolution.

Historic changes in weapons, tactics, and strategy between one war and the next, or even one century or one era and the next in the past, become trivial in importance by comparison with the gulf between the preatomic and the nuclear age of strategic bombing. We are now able to view the past in a new perspective. We can already see that the vast fleets that concentrated off the Normandy beaches and at Leyte Gulf,

[12] Bernard Brodie, *Strategy in the Missile Age* (Princeton, N.J., 1959), 167. See also 147–49 on the comparison with the firearms revolution.

or the massed armies that grappled in the Battle of the Bulge or across the Russian Steppes, or for that matter the old-fashioned bomber squadrons that droned back and forth across the English Channel year after year dropping what the air force now contemptuously calls "iron bombs" were more closely related to a remote past than to a foreseeable future. They did not, as they seemed at the time, represent the beginning of a new age of warfare. They represented instead the end of an old age, a very old age.

This is not to assume that unrestricted nuclear war is the only type of military operations that are any longer conceivable, nor that wars of limited objectives, limited geographic area, and limited destructiveness are no longer possible. To make such assumptions, indeed, would be either to despair of the future of civilized man or to subscribe to the theory that national differences will thenceforth be settled without resort to force. Even assuming that limited wars may still be fought with "conventional" weapons, tactics, and strategy of the old era, there will still be an important difference setting them apart from prenuclear wars. Where major powers are directly or indirectly involved, at least, limited wars will be fought under an umbrella of nuclear power. The effects of that conditioning environment have yet to be tested, but it can scarcely be assumed that they will be inconsiderable.

Instead of making military history irrelevant or unimportant, the sudden transition from the old to the new age of warfare should actually enhance the role of the historian. We stand desperately in need of historical reinterpretation. The men who now have responsibility for determining policy, strategy, and tactics in the new age of warfare are inevitably influenced by

their experience and training grounded on an earlier age of warfare and an outmoded interpretation of its history. The fact is that many of the precepts, principles, and values derived from past experience in wars can be tragically misleading in the new age. These include some of the so-called "unchanging principles of war" that are imbibed during training and discipline until they become almost "second nature" to the professional military man. Traditions that associate the new type of war with honor, valor, and glory are no longer quite relevant. The sacred doctrine of concentration and mass, applied at the critical point, has lost its traditional meaning.

The age-old assumption of a commander's freedom of choice once war was started can no longer be made. In previous ages, one could start a war and assume that his objectives, methods, or degree of commitment could be altered according to changing prospects of success or failure, or according to whether probable gains outweighed probable losses. Even as late as World War II one could still approach the abyss of barbarism or annihilation, take a look and turn back, settle for an armistice or a compromise, and bide one's time. Once resort is made to unrestricted nuclear war, there is no turning back.

The underpinnings of logic that have served historically to justify resort to war as the lesser of several evils have shifted or, in their traditional form, quite disappeared. Victory has been deprived of its historical meaning in total war with the new weapons, for the "victor" is likely to sustain such devastation as to lack the means of imposing his will upon the "vanquished." And yet to accomplish this end, according to Karl von Clausewitz, is the only rational motive of war. Democratic participation or consent in a war decision is rendered most unmeaningful at the very time popular involvement in the devastation of war has reached an unprecedented maximum.

The history of war and man's attitudes about it should be reexamined in the light of these developments. Attention has already been profitably directed in particular to the question of how and why total war came to appear the "normal" type of conflict between major powers.[13] Such investigation might reveal how military planning became divorced from political planning and war became an end in itself rather than a means of achieving more or less rational political ends. Given the destructive military capabilities presently at the disposal of major powers, it would seem to be more interesting than it has ever been before to learn how and why powers have been willing at some times in history to wage wars with more limited objectives than unconditional surrender, total victory, or complete annihilation of the enemy.

That mankind should have carried the values and precepts of the age of firearms into the thermonuclear age represents a far greater anachronism than the one represented by his carrying the values and precepts of the age of chivalry into the age of firearms. Anachronisms are preeminently the business of historians. The historic service that Cervantes performed with mockery in 1605, when he published the first volume of *Don Quixote,* three centuries after the advent of firearms, cannot with safety be deferred that long after the advent of nuclear weapons. Lacking a Cervantes, historians

might with their own methods help to expose what may well be the most perilous anachronism in history.

On a grander scale, a third field of opportunity for historical reinterpretation has opened up since 1945. Too complex to be attributed to an event, it might better be ascribed to an avalanche of events, or a combination of avalanches. These avalanches go under such names as the collapse of Western imperialism, the revolt of the colored peoples of Asia and Africa, the rise of Eastern nationalism, the westward advance of the frontier of Russian hegemony, and the polarization of power between the Russian and American giants. All these developments and more have contributed to the shrinkage of Europe in power and relative importance, and thus to what is probably the greatest of all opportunities for historical reinterpretation.

In recent years historians and other scholars have coined some striking phrases to describe Europe's plight: "the political collapse of Europe," "the un-making of Europe," "farewell to European history," "the passing of the European age," "the end of European history." [14] The tone of despair echoed from one of these phrases to another may well be called in question by the remarkable economic recovery and cultural resilience of Europe since 1945. Crane Brinton is to an extent justified in taking to task the prophets of doom and calling attention to the rising birth rate, the material prosperity, and the

13 See, for example, Robert E. Osgood, *Limited War: The Challenge to American Strategy* (Chicago, 1957), and John U. Nef, *War and Human Progress: An Essay on the Rise of Industrial Civilization* (Cambridge, Mass., 1950).

14 Hajo Holborn, *The Political Collapse of Europe* (New York, 1951); Oscar Halecki, *The Limits and Divisions of European History* (New York, 1950); Alfred Weber, *Farewell to European History or the Conquest of Nihilism* (New Haven, Conn., 1948); Eris Fischer, *The Passing of the European Age* (Cambridge, Mass., 1948); Geoffrey Barraclough, *History in a Changing World* (Norman, Okla., 1956).

intellectual activity in postwar Europe.[15] The end of European supremacy is not necessarily the end of Europe. The present argument, however, is not addressed to the question of the extent of cultural malaise in Europe nor to the validity of any of several cyclical theories of history. The point is simply one of relative power and influence, and no evidence so far presented disturbs the conclusion that an age of European preeminence in the world has come to a close. That age did not end overnight, nor does the explanation lie wholly in events of the last decade and a half, but awareness of the implications for history are only beginning to sink in.

Now that European power has dwindled or quite disappeared in Asia, Africa, and former insular dependencies, and now that Europe itself has become the theater for operations of non-European powers, their military bases, and power rivalries, the spell of an agelong European dominance begins to lift. It is difficult to realize how recently it was commonly assumed in informed circles that the world was the proper theater for European enterprises and adventures, that world leadership was a European prerogative, that trends and fashions in arts, ideas, and sciences were as a matter of course set in Europe, that European political hegemony and economic ascendancy were taken for granted, and that history of any consequence was a commodity stamped, "Made in Europe." The corollaries of these assumptions were that non-Europeans, apart from a few societies composed primarily of peoples of European stock, stood in perpetual tutelage to Europe, that non-European cultures were decadent, arrested, primi-

tive, or permanently inferior, and that progress was defined as successful imitation of the preferred European way of doing things.

The significance of all this for historiography lies in the fact that much of the history still read and believed and taught was written while these assumptions prevailed, and written by historians, non-European as well as European, who shared them. Three of the most productive and influential generations of historians in the whole history of Western culture, those between the Napoleonic Wars and the First World War, coincided in time with the crest of European ascendancy and presumption. The generation between the world wars of the twentieth century generally shared the same assumptions. The contribution they made to the enrichment of historical scholarship is invaluable and should be cherished. But in so far as it rests on a set of assumptions no longer tenable, their work would seem to stand in need of extensive revision and reinterpretation.

On the needs for reinterpretation of the history of Europe itself it might be the prudent thing for an American historian to rely on the judgment of European historians, several of whom have already expressed themselves on the subject. Geoffrey Barraclough, for example, believes that "a total revision of European history [is] imperative." In this connection he has written, "Ever since the end of the war [of 1939–1945] a change has come over our conceptions of modern history. We no longer feel that we stand four square in a continuous tradition, and the view of history we have inherited . . . seems to have little relevance to our current problems and our current needs." In his opinion the trouble is that "we are dealing with a conception of European history which is out of focus and there-

[15] Crane Brinton, *The Temper of Western Europe* (Cambridge, Mass., 1953).

fore misleading, because of the false emphasis and isolated prominence it gives to Western Europe, and which therefore needs revising not merely in its recent phases, but at every turn from the early middle ages onward." [16]

American historians will also have some reinterpreting to do, for in this as in so much of American cultural life, ideas were shaped by European examples and models. It should go without saying that American civilization is European derived. But the models of Europe-centered world history would seem to have restrained American historians from exploring the influence of their country upon European history and that of the world in general. There have been a few exceptions to the rule. One exception is R. R. Palmer, *The Age of the Democratic Revolution,* which demonstrates that an age traditionally called European shows the profound impact of the American Revolution on Europe. Another suggestive interpretation of the American influence on European history is Walter P. Webb, *The Great Frontier,* and yet another is Halvdan Koht, *The American Spirit in Europe.* Other neglected American themes of European history remain to be explored. The influence of European immigration on American history has received much attention. But the impact upon Europe itself of the emigration of 35,000,000 Europeans in the century between the Napoleonic Wars and the First World War remains to be acknowledged except in a few countries and has still to receive its just share of attention in the pages of European history. The importance of the West as a safety valve for American society has undoubtedly been exaggerated. But the significance of Amer-

ica as a safety valve for Europe and the effect of the closing of that valve after World War I remain to be fully assessed. Apart from the United States, other offshoots and overseas establishments of European powers, including those in South America, Australia, and the British Commonwealth countries, will inevitably discover that they have not been merely on the receiving end of the line of influence, but have had their own impact upon European and world history.

The same assumptions of Europocentric history have very largely shaped the interpretation of Asiatic, African, and other non-European history as well, for Europe successfully marketed its historiography abroad, along with its other cultural products, in remote and exotic climates. We may depend on it that the new opportunities for reinterpretation will not be lost upon New Delhi, Cairo, Tokyo, and Djakarta, to say nothing of Peiping and Moscow. Already an Indian historian, K. M. Panikkar, has defined the period of European preeminence in the Orient as "the Vasco Da Gama Epoch of Asian History." It began with the arrival of Da Gama at Calicut in 1498 and ended abruptly four and a half centuries later "with the withdrawal of British forces from India in 1947 and of the European navies from China in 1949." In the time dimensions of the Orient this could be regarded as only one of several episodes that have temporarily interrupted the flow of ancient civilizations. Relations between East and West continue and even increase in many ways, but, as Panikkar says, "the essential difference is that the basis of relationship has undergone a complete change . . . a revolutionary and qualitative change. . . ." The Indian historian concludes that "vitally important historical results may flow from

16 Barraclough, *History in a Changing World,* 9, 135, 178.

this new confrontation" between East and West.[17]

One of the historical results to flow from the confrontation between East and West should be a new and revised view of world history. The ethnocentric, or Europocentric, view that has been held for so long a time in the West can hardly be expected to survive the sweeping change in East-West relationships. The "new confrontation" of which the Hindu historian writes is another event of the present that necessitates many reinterpretations of the past.

Three fields for historical reinterpretation have been suggested: the first occasioned by the end of the age of free and effective security in America, the second by the end of an age of mass warfare, and the third by the end of the age of European hegemony. These subjects have been suggested to illustrate, not to exhaust, the list of possibilities for historical reinterpretation opened up since 1945. A complete list would not only be beyond the limits of this paper, but beyond the range of present vision. The need for reinterpretation is not always made immediately apparent by revolutionary events, while on the other hand such a need may easily be exaggerated by lack of sufficient perspective.

It may be noted that the ideological war between the Communist and the non-Communist worlds, which occupies so large a share of public attention at present, has not been mentioned. It could well be that the cold war and the triumphs that Russia and her allies have scored will upset more comfortable and traditional interpretations of history than the events we have listed

[17] K. M. Panikkar, *Asia and Western Dominance: A Survey of the Vasco Da Gama Epoch of Asian History, 1498–1945* (London, 1953), 11, 15.

above. It is even more probable, if we prove as myopic about our own times as historians have proved in the past, that we have overlooked or underestimated events that in future times will be accounted of far more historical significance than the noisier events we have noted. In such a situation the experienced historian will always take account of two powerful historical forces: the unforeseen and the unforeseeable. It may well turn out that new satellites for the earth will prove of more historical consequence than new satellites for earthly powers.

At least two objections to the proposal of reinterpreting history in the light of present events, however revolutionary, may be readily foreseen. The first is that the past is inviolable, that it is or should be unaffected by the present, and that it is the duty of the historian to guard its inviolability rather than to invade it with present preoccupations. But this would be to take an unhistorical view of historiography. Every major historical event has necessitated new views of the past and resulted in reinterpretations of history. This was surely true of the Reformation, of the discovery and exploration of the New World, of the Industrial Revolution, and of political upheavals such as the democratic and the Communist revolutions. These events did not leave the past inviolate, nor the traditional interpretations of it sacrosanct. There is no reason to believe that present and future revolutions will do so.

A second objection may be that if the revolutionary changes used as illustrations represent such a drastic and sharp break with the past, they render history irrelevant and useless to the needs and concerns of the present and future: that history is bypassed by events and reduced to antiquarianism. The answer to this objection is that if history is bypassed and rendered irrelevant and antiquarian, it will be due in large measure to the view that historians take of their own craft. Writing nearly half a century ago with regard to the disappearance of free land and its consequences in America, J. Franklin Jameson asked, "Can it be supposed that so great and so dramatic a transition . . . shall have no effect upon the questions which men ask concerning the past? Nothing can be more certain than that history must be prepared to respond to new demands. I do not think so ill of my profession as to suppose that American historians will not make gallant and intelligent attempts to meet the new requirements." [18]

The new demands and requirements to which Jameson urged historians to respond now come faster, more insistently, and in more momentous form than ever before. The historian, along with others, may be called upon soon to adjust his views to another age of discovery and exploration, one that transcends earthly limits. He is already confronted with a "population explosion" for which there is no precedent, not even a helpful analogy, and little but misleading counsel from classical theorists. In science and technology it is the age of the "break-through," when the curve of expansion suddenly becomes vertical on many fronts. Informed men of science speak of the possibility of tapping the ocean for unlimited food supplies, of curing the incurable diseases, of controlling the weather, and of developing limitless and virtually costless sources of power. Historical thought is involved as soon as men confront change with anachronistic notions of the past. Anachronism,

[18] J. Franklin Jameson, "The Future Uses of History" (1913), reprinted in *American Historical Review*, LXV (Oct. 1959), 69.

to repeat, is the special concern of the historian. If historians assume an intransigent attitude toward reinterpretation, they will deserve to be regarded as antiquarians and their history as irrelevant. The historian who can contemplate a single nuclear bomb that harbors more destructive energy and fury than mankind has managed to exert in all previous wars from the siege of Troy to the fall of Berlin and conclude that it has "no effect upon the questions which men ask concerning the past" would seem to be singularly deficient in historical imagination.

The present generation of historians has a special obligation and a unique opportunity. Every generation, of course, has a unique experience of history. "I had the advantage," wrote Goethe, "of being born in a time when the world was agitated by great movements, which have continued during my long life." But it is doubtful that any previous generation has witnessed quite the sweep and scope of change experienced by those who have a living memory of the two world wars of the twentieth century and the events that have followed. They carry with them into the new order a personal experience of the old. Americans among them will remember a time when security was assumed to be a natural right, free and unchallengeable. Among them also will be men of many nations who manned the ships and fought the battles of another age of warfare. And nearly all of this generation of historians will have been educated to believe that European culture was Civilization and that non-European races, if not natively inferior, were properly under perpetual tutelage. They will be the only generation of historians in history who will be able to interpret the old order to the new order with the advantage and authority derived from firsthand knowledge of the two ages and participation in both.

The historian sometimes forgets that he has professional problems in common with all storytellers. Of late he has tended to forget the most essential one of these—the problem of keeping his audience interested. So long as the story he had to tell contained no surprises, no unexpected turn of events, and lacked the elemental quality of suspense, the historian found his audience limited mainly to other historians, or captive students. While the newly dawned era adds new problems of its own to the historian's burden, it is lavish with its gifts of surprise and suspense for the use of the storyteller. If there are any readily recognizable characteristics of the new era, they are the fortuitous, the unpredictable, the adventitious, and the dynamic—all of them charged with surprise.

The new age bears another and more ominous gift for the historian, one that has not been conspicuous in historical writings since the works of the Christian fathers. This gift is the element of the catastrophic. The Church fathers, with their apocalyptic historiography, understood the dramatic advantage possessed by the storyteller who can keep his audience sitting on the edge of eternity. The modern secular historian, after submitting to a long cycle of historicism, has at last had this dramatic advantage restored. The restoration, to be sure, arrived under scientific rather than apocalyptic auspices. But the dramatic potentials were scarcely diminished by placing in human hands at one and the same time the Promethean fire as well as the divine prerogative of putting an end to the whole drama of human history.

Of one thing we may be sure. We come of an age that demands a great deal of historians. Of such a time Jacob Burckhardt once wrote, "The historical process is suddenly accelerated in terrifying fashion. Developments which otherwise take centuries seem to flit by like phantoms in months or weeks, and are fulfilled." [19] He could hardly have phrased a more apt description of our own time. It is doubtful that any age has manifested a greater thirst for historical meaning and historical interpretation and therefore made greater demands upon the historian. What is required is an answer to the questions about the past and its relation to the present and future that the accelerated process of history raises. If historians evade such questions, people will turn elsewhere for the answers, and modern historians will qualify for the definition that Tolstoi once formulated for academic historians of his own day. He called them deaf men replying to questions that nobody puts to them. If on the other hand they do address themselves seriously to the historical questions for which the new age demands answers, the period might justly come to be known in historiography as the age of reinterpretation.

[19] Jacob Burckhardt, *Force and Freedom* (New York, 1955), 238.

HISTORIOGRAPHICAL NOTE

If anything may be said to characterize the literature of the Cold War it is dissonance and discord. Studies of United States foreign policy since 1945 have reflected deep-seated antagonisms such as those that found expression while American troops fought in Korea, and later in Vietnam. Seldom have the events of any period aroused more passion, and seldom have historians had more difficulty in penetrating the arcanum of historical truth. Given the dimensions of the Cold War and the extent to which a concern for national security limits the amount of reliable information obtainable, it is not surprising that much of the writing on the years since Hiroshima and Nagasaki should be of a polemical nature. This is not to say that serious scholars have refused to examine the Cold War, but that those who have studied it have arrived at no generally accepted interpretation.

Early Cold War analysts were primarily interested in the confrontation of the two great powers that remained after World War II. And they devoted much effort to divining the thinking behind Soviet policy. Indeed, the early works on the Cold War may be placed in one of two categories depending on their general assessment of Soviet intentions.

On the one hand were observers who believed that the U.S.S.R. was dedicated to world domination and intended to exert unrelenting pressure until the West collapsed. This was a view advanced by books such as William C. Bullitt's *The Great Globe Itself* (New York, 1947) and James Burnham's *The Struggle for the World* (New York, 1947). Bullitt and Burnham believed that American efforts should be commensurate with a global challenge. The United States, they warned, must prepare for an ultimate showdown.

On the other hand were writers who conceived of the Soviet-American confrontation in more limited terms. George F. Kennan and Hans Morgenthau, for example, viewed the Russians as pursuing traditional policies, policies circumscribed by realistic considerations of power and national interest. Kennan, whose interpretation was summarized in *American Foreign Policy, 1900–1950* (Chicago, 1951), argued for the containment of Soviet expansionist tendencies. If Russian aggressiveness were limited, he suggested, the West could look forward to the development of pressures within Soviet society and a subsequent shift of emphasis from foreign affairs to domestic problems. When Soviet leadership was forced to come to grips with internal problems, the argument ran, it would necessarily meliorate its foreign policy. Kennan's suggestions were persuasive, so persuasive that containment of communism became American policy.

Containment, however, did not have the results Kennan predicted. It produced no unusual tensions within the Soviet Union, and it was at least partially responsible for the frustrations of limited war in Korea. Understandably, then, critics began to suggest that American policy was far too passive, even negative. It was a policy of reaction which left the initiative to the other side. Books presenting the case for a more positive, forward-looking program began to appear. Among the most important were James Burnham, *Containment or Liberation?* (New York, 1953); William Henry Chamberlain, *Beyond Containment* (Chicago, 1953); Thomas I. Cook and

Malcolm Moos, *Power Through Purpose* (Baltimore, 1954); Stefan T. Possony, *A Century of Conflict* (Chicago, 1953); and Robert Strausz-Hupe *et al.*, *Protracted Conflict: A Study of Communist Strategy* (New York, 1959). Such works, along with the insistent popular demands for a strategy of victory, had their influence during the Eisenhower-Dulles years. Cautious though he may actually have been in practice, Secretary of State Dulles at least employed positive and sometimes aggressive rhetoric. But aside from their influence, the works demanding a forward-looking strategy had something else in common: they assumed Soviet hostility to the West.

After John F. Kennedy entered the White House, and particularly after the Cuban missile crisis, those who reasoned from such a premise would seem to have been justified. But the missile crisis had results that few would have predicted in the fall of 1962. Instead of increasing tensions between the United States and the U.S.S.R., the Cuban confrontation had the opposite effect. At least, it seemed, the air had been cleared and East-West accommodation was now possible. But as the volume and tempo of war in Vietnam gradually increased, hopes for accommodation and negotiation began to fade.

Disappointment intensified and a strident new criticism swept over the country. In such books as David Horowitz's *Free World Colossus* (New York, 1965) that criticism raised fundamental questions about America's role throughout the entire period since 1945. Horowitz joined other critics —Denna F. Fleming, William L. Neumann, Stoughton Lynd, and perhaps most importantly, William Appleman Williams—in holding the United States partly responsible for international tensions. Another work, *Atomic Diplomacy: Hiroshima and Potsdam* (New York, 1965) by Gar Alperovitz, went so far as to suggest that by dropping the atomic bomb on Hiroshima the United States had initiated the Cold War. This was not a new idea (it had been suggested by British physicist P. M. S. Blackett as early as 1948), but as dissatisfaction over the Vietnamese conflict grew it took on a new relevance for Cold War revisionists. These kinds of criticism did not stay within the covers of scholars' books. They fed impassioned crowds of student demonstrators, both on campus and off, with new information and arguments. What we have called the "process of American history" became very tense and vital as the 1960's began to draw to a close. A generation of students and young scholars, many of them anxious to create a new present and future, began to search very self-consciously for a new past.